Lecture Notes in Computer Science 11616

More information about this series at http://www.springer.com/series/7411

Anna Tzanakaki · Manos Varvarigos ·
Raul Muñoz · Reza Nejabati ·
Noboru Yoshikane · Markos Anastasopoulos ·
Johann Marquez-Barja (Eds.)

Optical Network Design and Modeling

23rd IFIP WG 6.10 International Conference, ONDM 2019
Athens, Greece, May 13–16, 2019
Proceedings

 Springer

Editors
Anna Tzanakaki
National and Kapodistrian
University of Athens
Athens, Greece

Raul Muñoz
Parc Mediterrani de la Tecnologia
Barcelona, Spain

Noboru Yoshikane
KDDI Research
Fujimino, Japan

Johann Marquez-Barja 🆔
University of Antwerp - imec
Antwerp, Belgium

Manos Varvarigos
University of Patras
Patras, Greece

Reza Nejabati
Merchant Venturers Building
Bristol, UK

Markos Anastasopoulos
Merchant Venturers Building
Bristol, UK

ISSN 0302-9743   ISSN 1611-3349   (electronic)
Lecture Notes in Computer Science
ISBN 978-3-030-38084-7   ISBN 978-3-030-38085-4   (eBook)
https://doi.org/10.1007/978-3-030-38085-4

LNCS Sublibrary: SL5 – Computer Communication Networks and Telecommunications

This Springer imprint is published by the registered company Springer Nature Switzerland AG
The registered company address is: Gewerbestrasse 11, 6330 Cham, Switzerland

Preface

It was an honor and a pleasure to welcome everyone to ONDM 2019, the 23rd edition of the Optical Network Design and Modelling conference, which was held at the National and Kapodistrian University of Athens, Greece, May 13–16, 2019.

ONDM 2019 focused on cutting-edge research in established areas of optical networking as well as their adoption in support of a wide variety of new services and applications. This involved the most recent trends in networking, including 5G and beyond, big data and network data analytics, cloud/edge computing, autonomic networking, artificial intelligence assisted networks, secure and resilient networks, etc., that drive the need for increased capacity, efficiency, flexibility, and adaptability in the functions that the network can perform.

In this context new disaggregated optical network architectures were discussed, exploiting and integrating novel multidimensional photonic technology solutions, as well as adopting open hardware and software platforms relying on software defined networking (SDN) and network function virtualization (NFV) to allow support of new business models and opportunities.

Some of the thematic areas that were covered include:

- Novel and multidimensional optical network architectures
- Optical network control, management, and orchestration, including SDN and NFV solutions
- Slicing, virtualization, and multitenancy techniques for optical networks
- Optical networking supporting low latency and high bandwidth network function virtualization
- Optical and wireless network convergence, including radio-over-fiber access networks
- Optical networks in support of intra-/inter-data center connectivity and cloud/edge computing
- Artificial intelligence and data analytics techniques for optical networks
- Advances in optical network modeling and optimization
- Routing and spectrum assignment in fixed and flex-grid optical networks
- Novel optical node designs including disaggregation and open optical line systems
- Optical network availability, resilience, survivability, security, and privacy
- Optical networking in support of vertical industries
- Field trials and interoperability demonstrations of optical networks
- Techno-economic studies of optical networks with emphasis on 5G consideration

Some of the key take away messages of the conference include:

- The importance of network user increases, as armed with increasingly-capable smart devices drive network level specifications and design/operation choices
  - The concept of service is being expanded beyond the traditional end-user context to a variety of end-user and operational services that are ICT or vertical industry related

- This imposes the requirement for newer infrastructures, e.g., 5G, 6G and beyond consisting of (optical) communication networks, (edge and cloud) data centers, distributed network functions, etc., in order to become more agile and facilitate more application-centric services with improved user experience

- Infrastructures equipped with additional/newer resources supporting higher bandwidth and lower latency focusing only on the lower layers of the protocol stack are not sufficient anymore

  - Instead, novel, flexible, open, and scalable architectural approaches supporting technology convergence, not only across network domains but also across network and compute/storage domains, involving inter- and intra-Data Center connectivity, are becoming essential
  - Methods developing real-time network-, service-, and application-centric analytics, able to process huge volumes of data, adopting artificial intelligence and machine-learning methods are needed to offer improved network and network service performance as well as user-experience, in support of the vision of future IT infrastructures

- Significant experimentation activities in real-life test-beds (5G UK) have already provided proof of principle demonstrations of the use and potential of optical networking in support of the new 5G and beyond network paradigm to facilitate end-user services with emphasis in improved experience and quality of leaving
- Significant attention has been put towards resilience and security considerations in the context of optical networking and the role optical technologies can play to facilitate more resilient and secure future network infrastructures

ONDM 2019 was a single-track conference. The conference included two workshops, one industrial panel, and one summer school co-organized by the H2020 5G PPP project 5G-PICTURE and the Erasmus Mundus programme SMARTNET:

- Workshop I: Optical Networking an enabler for 5G Solutions, Trials and Demonstrators
- Workshop II: Optical Intra- and Inter- Data Center Networks
- Industry Panel: 5G in 2020 and beyond: reality check, rollout plans and path ahead

Attendance: 90 Attendees

May 2019

Anna Tzanakaki
Manos Varvarigos
Raul Muñoz
Reza Nejabati
Noboru Yoshikane
Markos Anastasopoulos
Johann Marquez-Barja

The original version of the book was revised: The affiliation of the volume editor Johann Marquez-Barja has been corrected. The correction to the book is available at https://doi.org/10.1007/978-3-030-38085-4_56

Organization

General Chair

Anna Tzanakaki   National and Kapodistrian University of Athens, Greece

General Co-chair

Manos Varvarigos   National Technical University of Athens, Greece

TPC Chairs

Raul Muñoz   CTTC, Spain
Reza Nejabati   University of Bristol, UK
Noboru Yoshikane   KDDI Research Inc., Japan

Local Organizing Committee

Hercules Avramopoulos   National Technical University of Athens, Greece
Dimitris Syvridis   National and Kapodistrian University of Athens, Greece

Publicity Chair

Markos Anastasopoulos   University of Bristol, UK

EDAS and Publication Chair

Johann M. Marquez-Barja   University of Antwerpen and imec, Belgium

Steering Committee

Lena Wosinska   KTH Royal Institute of Technology, Sweden
Piero Castoldi   SSSA, Italy
Pablo Pavón Mariño   UPCT, Spain
Tibor Cinkler   BME, Hungary
Marco Ruffini   Trinity College Dublin, Ireland
Anna Tzanakaki   National and Kapodistrian University of Athens, Greece

TPC Members

Slavisa Aleksic	Hochschule für Telekommunikation Leipzig, Germany
Markos Anastasopoulos	University of Bristol, UK
Bigomokero Bagula	University of the Western Cape, South Africa
Johan Bauwelinck	Ghent University and imec, Belgium
Andrea Bianco	Politecnico di Torino, Italy
Luiz Bonani	Universidade Federal do ABC, Brazil
Aparicio Carranza	New York City College of Technology, USA
Isabella Cerutti	Nokia Bell Labs, Italy
Jiajia Chen	KTH Royal Institute of Technology, Sweden
Kostas Christodoulopoulos	Nokia Bell Labs, Germany
Didier Colle	Ghent University and imec, Belgium
David Coudert	Université Côte d'Azur, Inria, CNRS, and I3S, France
Filippo Cugini	CNIT, Italy
Sandip Das	Trinity College Dublin, Ireland
Georgios Ellinas	University of Cyprus, Cyprus
Marija Furdek	KTH Royal Institute of Technology, Sweden
Maurice Gagnaire	Télécom Paris, France
Alessio Giorgetti	Scuola Superiore Sant'Anna, Italy
Philippe Gravey	Télécom Bretagne, France
Hiroaki Harai	National Institute of Information and Communications Technology, Japan
Hiroshi Hasegawa	Nagoya University, Japan
Yusuke Hirota	National Institute of Information and Communications Technology, Japan
Weisheng Hu	Shanghai Jiao Tong University, China
Brigitte Jaumard	Concordia University, Canada
Wojciech Kabacinski	Poznan University of Technology, Poland
Ezhan Karasan	Bilkent University, Turkey
Daniel Kilper	University of Arizona, USA
Ken-ichi Kitayama	The Graduate School for the Creation of New Photonics Industries, Japan
Nattapong Kitsuwan	The University of Electro-Communications, Japan
Panagiotis Kokkinos	National Technical University of Athens, Greece
Yao Li	University of Arizona, USA
Andrew Lord	British Telecom, UK
Guido Maier	Politecnico di Milano, Italy
Ricardo Martinez	Centre Tecnològic de Telecomunicacions de Catalunya, Spain
Barbara Martini	CNIT, Italy
Xavier Masip-Bruin	Universitat Politècnica de Catalunya, Spain
Francesco Matera	Fondazione Ugo Bordoni, Italy
Paolo Monti	KTH Royal Institute of Technology, Sweden
Francesco Musumeci	Politecnico di Milano, Italy
Antonio Napoli	Infinera, Germany

Contents

Poster Papers

Regular Papers

Hybrid Backup Resource Optimization for VNF Placement Over Optical Transport Networks

João Pedro[1,2]($\boxtimes$) (iD) and António Eira[1] (iD)

[1] Infinera Unipessoal Lda, Rua da Garagem 1, 2790-078 Carnaxide, Portugal
{JPedro,AEira}@Infinera.com
[2] Instituto de Telecomunicações, Instituto Superior Técnico, Avenida Rovisco Pais 1, 1049-001 Lisbon, Portugal

Abstract. The concept of edge computing is vital in the 5G ecosystem, as a means of introducing application awareness in the network and enabling constructs such as slicing to be effectively implemented. In this scope, an efficient infrastructure dimensioning requires visibility of both network and data-center resources. While this joint optimization is becoming increasingly common even at the optical layer, some aspects of the dimensioning remain siloed between the network/IT worlds. Survivability mechanisms are one such example, where protection for lightpaths and/or virtual network functions (VNFs) is typically provisioned independently, potentially incurring in resource overprovisioning. This paper investigates the merits of exploiting a hybrid strategy where backup resources are selectively distributed between the IT and optical layers in metro ring scenarios, according to specific service requirements such as latency and bandwidth. Critically, this analysis incorporates, through an integer linear programming (ILP) model, the effect of optical path performance on the cost efficiency of protection mechanisms, which is shown to greatly influence the optimal resource distribution in each deployment scenario.

Keywords: Routing and spectrum assignment · VNF placement · Network survivability

1 Introduction

The requirements of 5G services are transforming the way transport networks are architected. While capacity remains a key driver in their development, many emerging services relying e.g. on massive machine-to-machine type communications or crowdsourced video applications are introducing additional constraints with respect to service dynamicity, latency and availability. As a result, and in an effort to leverage existing central office assets and reduce bandwidth requirements towards the backbone, the computing resources required for these applications are more suitably co-located with metro aggregation nodes closer to end-users. These converged nodes mix data-center (DC) and virtualization capabilities with packet/optical transport network interfaces within the same physical location and switching infrastructure [1, 2].

© IFIP International Federation for Information Processing 2020
Published by Springer Nature Switzerland AG 2020
A. Tzanakaki et al. (Eds.): ONDM 2019, LNCS 11616, pp. 3–14, 2020.
https://doi.org/10.1007/978-3-030-38085-4_1

Within this scope, the traditional capacity planning of transport networks becomes entangled with the dimensioning of distributed mini data-center infrastructures. The placement of specific virtual network functions (VNFs) such as firewalling, video processing, etc. defines the logical topology required on the transport network, and thus its overall bandwidth requirements [3]. Therefore, consolidation of DC nodes and optimized placement of VNFs must take into account the specific requirements introduced on the optical transport side, in order to balance the cost effectiveness of converged central office/data-center architectures.

This joint IT/optical dimensioning is being increasingly explored in the context of edge computing, by extending traditional VNF placement and virtual network embedding (VNE) problems from packet networks to the optical circuit switching domain [4, 5]. The typical modeling of application-specific service requests involves defining a service chain, consisting of an ordered set of VNFs that must be traversed by a flow, with each hop between VNFs being characterized by a required bandwidth and allowable latency, and each VNF requiring a set amount of IT resources (e.g. instantiated virtual machines and/or storage space) [6].

A less explored aspect of this problem is how reliability is ensured at the different layers. Typically, backup resources are provisioned independently at the optical/IT layers, by provisioning protection lightpaths in the transport network and/or replicating VNFs at alternative DC locations for redundancy. Adding reliability on one layer independently of the other reduces complexity, but at the expense of resource overprovisioning. In [7], the authors present the comparative benefits of adding reliability at each layer, based on latency and bandwidth requirements, as well as the prevalent type of failures (optical link or in the DC). In [8], an approach considering protection at both layers simultaneously is introduced and shown to reduce the network and computing requirements.

In this paper, we focus on the specific constraints inherent to optical line-side protection, and how they influence the optimal resiliency strategy. We present an ILP model to select, given a set of service chains, the lowest cost solution leveraging a hybrid of backup lightpaths and VNFs. The trade-offs between transponder costs, IT requirements and latency performance are also exposed through this analysis, particularly for the common scenario of metro aggregation rings. In the remainder of the paper, Sect. 2 presents the network scenario and possible resiliency options, Sect. 3 details the optimization model used, and Sect. 4 discusses the results obtained through network simulations. Section 5 concludes the paper and points towards new research directions.

2 Network Scenario

The analysis in this work is focused on wavelength division multiplexing (WDM) metro rings, where each optical node may optionally be co-located with a DC possessing storage/compute resources. As Fig. 1 illustrates, service chains are deployed between a source and destination node by instantiating the set of required VNFs at one or more DCs. The logical topology established by the optical lightpaths over the WDM network must ensure that each set of VNFs in a chain can be traversed in the desired order. The placement of the VNFs across the network thus determines both the IT requirements at each DC, as well as the logical topology that supports it.

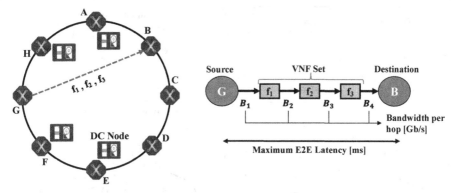

Fig. 1. Metro ring aggregation topology with co-located DCs and service chain characterization.

2.1 Survivability Mechanisms

Given the mission-critical nature of some 5G services, it is expected that reliability will be a key requirement in their deployment. Here, the focus is on guaranteeing that a chain can withstand any single optical link failure. In order to ensure this, it is possible to implement optical line-side protection, wherein a Y-cable splits the input signal to different directions, enabling the same transponder to be shared at the source/destination nodes of a lightpath. Alternatively, resilience against fiber link failures can be embedded in the application layer, by instantiating redundant VNFs at separate nodes and effectively creating a backup chain that is link-disjoint from the working one. Both options entail trade-offs with respect to the resource consumption (spectrum, transponders, storage/compute), and specific planning scenarios may favor one over the other. As such, combining both approaches in network dimensioning can potentially reduce the overall cost of providing reliable services. The following subsections detail the advantages and drawbacks of each single-layer technique, and showcases the motivation to consider a joint approach.

2.2 Hop Protection

Path protection is implemented by duplicating the signal at the source towards link-disjoint working and backup paths, while selecting the strongest signal at the receiver. This strategy overprovisions only the spectral resources needed on the backup path, since the transponders at the end-nodes are the same. In the context of a service chain, as Fig. 2(a) illustrates, every lightpath is protected by a backup. Hence, every VNF hop in a chain requiring optical connectivity is protected against a link failure. Note that sequential VNFs in a chain instantiated at a same node do not require WDM connectivity, and thus are not susceptible to fiber link failures.

One attribute of this survivability scheme is that the achievable rate of a lightpath may be different between the working/backup paths, according to the physical characteristics of each path (distance, number of spans). In a protection mechanism, the lowest common denominator between both paths must be used (i.e. the lowest bit-rate) since both paths are active at all times [9]. This is particularly critical in the case of ring topologies,

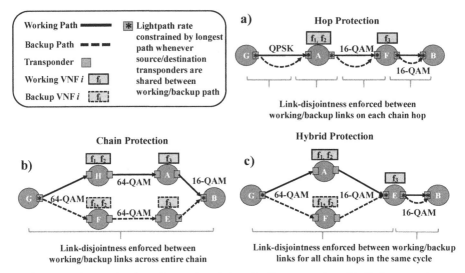

Fig. 2. Protection mechanisms for service chains: (a) Hop protection; (b) Chain protection; (c) Hybrid protection.

where the differences between working/backup paths are most extreme. The other issue affecting the performance of this scheme is end-to-end latency. For the whole chain, if a single link is used by multiple lightpaths on different VNF hops, then the backup path is triggered for each of them, further constraining the end-to-end latency budget.

2.3   Chain Protection

The main alternative to deploying protected lightpaths is to create an end-to-end alternative chain, replicating the required VNFs at different DCs, exemplified in Fig. 2(b). Ensuring survivability to link failures in this instance implies guaranteeing that the end-to-end (i.e. across the entire chain) working and backup links are disjoint, such that one chain is always available end-to-end. In a ring topology, such an approach has the benefit of ensuring the maximum latency is bounded by either the working or backup chain, regardless of which link may fail. Furthermore, the lightpaths are unprotected and hence can use the best transmission format unconstrained by servicing a protection path in simultaneous. As Fig. 2(b) shows, this may enable a higher average throughput in the deployed lightpaths. However, this strategy tends to be less efficient regarding resource provisioning. On the IT side, it requires additional storage/compute resources to duplicate all VNFs, although it provides further resilience against failures within the DCs. On the optical network side, creating an alternative chain through separate nodes may require additional transponders (if they are not already necessary for other chains).

2.4   Hybrid Protection

From the above descriptions, it is intuitive that there is a potential benefit in combining, for a single chain or a set of chains, both protection mechanisms selectively, in a way that minimizes resource overprovisioning. Figure 2(c) provides an example of this approach, where chain protection is used in the first two VNF hops, and hop protection (backup path protection) is used in the final chain hop. As the example in Fig. 2(c) shows, applying chain protection to only a subset of all VNF hops creates a cycle between two nodes, formed by two sets of lightpaths that must be entirely link-disjoint (i.e. a single link cannot break both sub-chains simultaneously).

3   Optimization Model

The optimal protection strategy, even for a single isolated chain, depends on the combination of the service bandwidth, possible DC placements, latency constraints, etc. As the examples in Fig. 2 illustrate, particular line-side protection setups can be detrimental to bandwidth efficiency, such that the best solution is either avoiding those configurations (working/backup lightpaths with accentuated performance differences) either through optimized placement of the VNFs, or by introducing VNF redundancy at specific portions of the chain. This highly multifactorial problem structure results in a complex optimization challenge, which must address a survivable VNE problem over an optical infrastructure (i.e. solving routing and spectrum assignment on top of the VNF placement), further considering the optical performance constraints of backup path protection.

Table 1. Parameters and sets.

$Src/Dst(p)$	Source/Destination node of path p
$p \in D$	Set of dummy paths between the same nodes
$B_{s,i}$	Required bandwidth [Gb/s] of the ith hop of chain s
M	Big-M value for constraint activation/de-activation
$ITcap_n$	Maximum IT resource capacity of node n
$IT_{s,i}$	Required IT resource units for the ith hop of chain s
$Linkcap$	Maximum number of channels per link
$maxLat_s$	Maximum allowable end-to-end latency for chain s [ms]
Lat_p	Propagation latency in path p [ms]
$maxIT$	Maximum number of DC nodes

As an exploratory approach to evaluate the potential benefits of combining chain and hop protection, we model the problem through an ILP formulation, which enables all of the interdependencies to be considered jointly, even if limited in computational complexity to small/medium sized networks. Particularly, as outlined in Sect. 2, metro aggregation rings are an interesting case study due to their relevance in the 5G/edge-computing landscape, as well as the optical performance differential that naturally arises between working/protection lightpaths in a ring topology. The model minimizes the transponder count for a set of service chains, imposing that both a working and a backup chain must be provisioned. The paths of the backup chain determine whether redundant

Table 2. Variables.

$x_{s,i,p}/y_{s,i,p} \in [0, 1]$	Binary variable equal to 1 if chain s uses working/backup path p on the ith hop
$w_{s,i,p} \in \mathbb{N}^0$	Number of transponders required to carry the traffic of chain s on path p for the ith hop
$b_{s,i,p}^{src}/b_{s,i,p}^{dst} \in \mathbb{N}^0$	Number of transponders required for protection at the source/destination node of path p for the ith hop of chain s
$z_{s,i,n} \in [0, 1]$	Binary variable equal to 1 if the working/backup paths on the ith hop of chain s converge at node n
$v_{n,f} \in \mathbb{N}^0$	Number of IT resources required for VNF f at node n
$c_n \in [0, 1]$	Binary variable equal to one if node n has a DC

VNFs are placed at alternative nodes, or if working lightpaths are simply path protected. As a simplifying assumption, only maximum number of channels per fiber restrictions are considered (no spectrum assignment). The model's parameters and variables are defined in Tables 1 and 2, respectively.

The ILP model can thus be formally defined as:

$$\min \sum_{s,i,p} 2w_{s,i,p} + b_{s,i,p}^{src} + b_{s,i,p}^{dst} \tag{1}$$

subject to:

$$\sum_p x_{s,i,p} = 1, \quad \forall s, i = 1 \tag{2}$$

$$\sum_p y_{s,i,p} = 1, \forall s, i = 1 \tag{3}$$

$$\sum_{p:n=Dst(p)} x_{s,i,p} = \sum_{p:n=Src(p)} x_{s,i+1,p}, \quad \forall s, i > 1, n \tag{4}$$

$$\sum_{p:n=Dst(p)} y_{s,i,p} = \sum_{p:n=Src(p)} y_{s,i+1,p}, \quad \forall s, i > 1, n \tag{5}$$

$$0 \leq \sum_{p:n=Dst(p)} x_{s,i,p} + \sum_{p:n=Dst(p)} y_{s,i,p} - 2z_{s,i,n} \leq 1, \forall s, i, n \tag{6}$$

$$\sum_{p \ni l} x_{s,q,p} + \sum_{\substack{m \in [k:i] \\ p \ni l}} y_{s,m,p} - M \sum_{n,m \in [k:i-1]} z_{s,m,n} \leq 1,$$
$$\forall s, l, i, k \in [1:i], q \in [k:i] \tag{7}$$

$$\sum_{p \ni l} y_{s,q,p} + \sum_{\substack{m \in [k:i] \\ p \ni l}} x_{s,m,p} - M \sum_{n,m \in [k:i-1]} z_{s,m,n} \leq 1,$$
$$\forall s, l, i, k \in [1:i], q \in [k:i] \tag{8}$$

$$w_{s,i,p} \geq \frac{x_{s,i,p} B_{s,i}}{Cap_p}, \quad \forall s, i, p \tag{9}$$

$$w_{s,i,p} \geq \frac{\sum_{p'} y_{s,i,p'} B_{s,i}}{Cap_{p'}} - M\left(1 - \sum_n z_{s,i-1,n} + \sum_{p' \neq p} x_{s,i,p'}\right), \quad \forall s, i, p \quad (10)$$

$$w_{s,i,p} \geq \sum_{p'} \frac{y_{s,i,p'} B_{s,i}}{Cap_{p'}} - M\left(1 - \sum_n z_{s,i,n} + \sum_{p' \neq p} x_{s,i,p'}\right), \quad \forall s, i, p \quad (11)$$

$$\sum_{p \in D} x_{s,i,p} + \sum_n z_{s,i,n} - \sum_{p \in D} y_{s,i,p} \leq 1, \quad \forall s, i \quad (12)$$

$$b_{s,i,p}^{src} \leq M\left(1 - \sum_n z_{s,i-1,n}\right), \quad \forall s, i, p \quad (13)$$

$$b_{s,i,p}^{src} \geq \frac{y_{s,i,p} B_{s,i}}{Cap_p} - M\left(1 - \left(\sum_n z_{s,i,n} - z_{s,i-1,n}\right)\right), \quad \forall s, i, p \quad (14)$$

$$b_{s,i,p}^{src} \geq \sum_{p'} \frac{x_{s,i,p'} B_{s,i}}{Cap_{p'}} - M\left(1 - \left(\sum_n z_{s,i,n} - z_{s,i-1,n}\right) + \sum_{p' \neq p} y_{s,i,p'}\right), \quad \forall s, i, p \quad (15)$$

$$b_{s,i,p}^{src} \geq \frac{y_{s,i,p} B_{s,i}}{Cap_p} - M\left(\sum_n z_{s,i,n} + z_{s,i-1,n}\right), \quad \forall s, i, p \quad (16)$$

$$b_{s,i,p}^{dst} \leq M\left(1 - \sum_n z_{s,i,n} + \sum_{p' \in D} x_{s,i,p'}\right), \quad \forall s, i, p \quad (17)$$

$$b_{s,i,p}^{dst} \geq \frac{y_{s,i,p} B_{s,i}}{Cap_p} - M\left(1 - \left(\sum_n z_{s,i-1,n} - z_{s,i,n}\right)\right), \quad \forall s, i, p \quad (18)$$

$$b_{s,i,p}^{dst} \geq \sum_{p'} \frac{x_{s,i,p'} B_{s,i}}{Cap_{p'}} - M\left(1 - \left(\sum_n z_{s,i-1,n} - z_{s,i,n}\right) + \sum_{p' \neq p} y_{s,i,p'}\right), \quad \forall s, i, p \quad (19)$$

$$b_{s,i,p}^{dst} \geq \frac{y_{s,i,p} B_{s,i}}{Cap_p} - M\left(\sum_n z_{s,i,n} + z_{s,i-1,n}\right), \quad \forall s, i, p \quad (20)$$

$$b_{s,i,p}^{dst} \geq \frac{y_{s,i,p} B_{s,i}}{Cap_p} - M\left(2 - \sum_n z_{s,i,n} - \sum_{p' \in D} x_{s,i,p'}\right), \quad \forall s, i, p \quad (21)$$

$$\sum_{\substack{(s,i) \in f \\ p:n=Dst(p)}} (x_{s,i,p} + y_{s,i,p}) IT_{s,i} - \sum_{(s,i) \in f} z_{s,i,n} IT_{s,i} \leq v_{n,f}, \quad \forall n, f \quad (22)$$

$$\sum_f v_{n,f} \leq c_n IT cap_n, \quad \forall n \quad (23)$$

$$\sum_{s,i,p \ni l} x_{s,i,p} + y_{s,i,p} \leq Linkcap_l, \quad \forall l \quad (24)$$

$$\sum_{i,p} x_{s,i,p} Lat_p \leq max Lat_s, \forall s \quad (25)$$

$$\sum_n c_n \leq max IT \quad (26)$$

The objective function (1) minimizes the total amount of transponders required for working and backup chains. Constraints (2–5) implement flow conservation for the first and subsequent hops in working and backup chains. Constraint (6) identifies if a cycle is closed when the working and backup paths of the same chain hop converge on the same node. Constraint (7) imposes that, for any sequence of hops forming a cycle, no link of the backup sub-chain may overlap with a link on the working one. Constraint (8) imposes the same condition, iterating instead over all working links. Constraints (9–12) enforce that the lightpath bit-rate on a given chain's hop is bound by the smallest rate achievable between the working/backup paths, whenever the source or destination nodes are shared between the paths (i.e. $z_{s,i-1,n}$ or $z_{s,i,n} = 1$). Constraints (13–16) impose that backup transponders are required on the source node of each hop, whenever the source node is not shared between the working/backup chains, or the lightpath bit-rates are different between them. Constraints (17–20) enforce the same restriction on the destination node of each VNF hop, requiring $b_{s,i,p}^{dst}$ backup transponders whenever a backup chain does not share the same destination node as the working one for the ith hop, or the working/backup lightpaths for that hop have different bit-rates. Constraint (21) covers the special case where the working lightpath is a dummy (i.e. sequential VNFs are instantiated at the same node), but a backup chain converges with the working one coming from a different node. Constraint (22) instantiates the required VNF capacity for each hop at the destination node of each hop's active lightpath. Constraint (23) limits the instantiated IT resources at node n to $ITcap_n$, provided n is an active DC node. Constraint (24) limits the number of lightpaths per link. Constraint (25) imposes that the sum of propagation latencies for each lightpath cannot exceed the end-to-end allowable latency of the chain. Finally, constraint (26) sets a hard limit on the number of nodes that may have co-located DCs.

The described model can decide, for each VNF hop, if protection should be implemented at the optical or application layer. The single-layer protection cases can be obtained by simple manipulation of the $z_{s,i,n}$ variables. For chain protection, all $z_{s,i,n}$ are forced to zero, except for the chain's last hop (the working/backup chains only converge at the destination node). In order to emulate the hop protection case, it must be imposed that every cycle must close at every VNF hop on a single node:

$$\sum_n z_{s,i,n} = 1, \quad \forall s, i \tag{27}$$

Latency restrictions are enforced end-to-end across an entire chain. This applies only to the working chain, since the actual end-to-end path of a complete chain in the event of a link failure depends on which specific link has failed. Thus, the latency performance of backup chains in each scenario is the object of study in the following Section.

The total number of variables in the ILP model is $5 * \left(|S| * |H| * \frac{N(N-1)}{2} * k \right) + |S| * |H| * |N| + N * |F| + |N|$, where $|S|$ is the number of service chain instances, $|H|$ is the (average) number of VNF hops per chain, $|N|$ is the number of nodes in the network, k is the number of candidate paths per node-pair, and $|F|$ is the number of VNFs in the scenario. Overall, the biggest complexity driver is the number of nodes, since the variable count evolves with $O(N^2)$ due to having to model all candidate paths between arbitrary node-pairs (for every chain hop). Note that, in the specific case of ring network topologies analyzed here, k always equals 2.

4   Results and Discussion

The three protection mechanisms outlined in Sect. 2 were comparatively evaluated with the ILP model. The network scenarios consisted of ring topologies with total lengths of 200 and 400 km. For each case, 5- and 10-node rings were considered, with evenly spaced spans. In order to enforce different levels of DC consolidation, $maxIT$ was set to 40% or 80% of the total node count. The transponders are assumed to be modulation format adaptive, operating on a 75 GHz grid with BPSK, QPSK, and 8/16/32/64-QAM (between 100 and 600 Gb/s bit-rates). For each format, the reach is obtained with a performance estimation approach detailed in [10]. The service chain profiles are taken from [11]. In each simulation run, 10 Tb/s of requested traffic (summing over all VNF hops of every chain) are generated uniformly between all nodes, and each network scenario is evaluated by averaging 10 independent runs.

Figure 3 illustrates the number of transponders required in each scenario for the three protection methods. Chain protection is considerably less efficient, requiring between 23% and 94% more transponders than hop protection. This strategy is particularly inefficient when rings are shorter and there are less available DC sites. The main reason behind this is that optical performance differences between two paths around a ring are less pronounced with both smaller rings and less nodes. Therefore, the fact that chain protection requires additional transponders for backup vastly outweighs having improved average lightpath bit-rates.

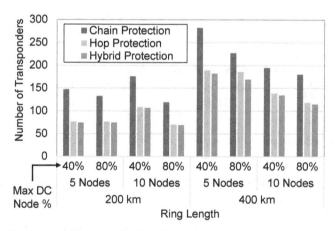

Fig. 3. Number of transponders per ring topology and protection mechanism.

Looking at the comparison between hop and hybrid protection, we find that the latter is able to improve the average transponder utilization in most scenarios. For smaller rings, this benefit is modest, standing at 3% on average for 200 km topologies. As outlined above, this is due to the unsuitability of chain protection mechanisms in these scenarios, which make hop protection the best strategy in the vast majority of chain hops. However, when considering 400 km rings, hybrid protection can save up to 9% transponders relative to hop protection. In these scenarios, protecting every lightpath has a toll on achievable throughput that makes mixing both baseline protection schemes more attractive in terms of cost efficiency.

Figure 4 shows the IT capacity requirements of each method for the same network scenarios. Naturally, chain protection requires the most resources, since it forcibly duplicates all VNFs at every node. Although it is clearly less resource efficient, it should be mentioned that it does provide an additional degree of resilience against failures within the DC. What is interesting to analyze is the comparative difference between hop and hybrid protection schemes. We find that, compared with Fig. 3, VNF capacity in the hybrid scheme is higher precisely in the cases where there was a higher benefit in saved transponders. This occurs because in such cases the model provisions a higher share of chain hops with VNF redundancy to reduce optical interfaces, at the expense of replicated VNFs. On the most extreme case (5-node ring with 400 km), the 9% saved transponders are obtained through an additional 24% IT resources provisioned.

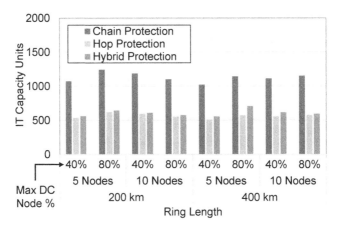

Fig. 4. IT resource unit requirements per ring topology and protection mechanism.

The final aspect to analyze is how each resiliency mechanism affects latency. The working chain's latency is straightforwardly given by the routing paths selected by the ILP model. For the backup chain calculation, we simulate a failure on every network link, and compute the worst-case end-to-end latency for each output of the ILP model. The results are shown in Fig. 5, which displays the average working/backup chain latency in each case.

The analysis reveals that using chain protection increases the working latency by an average of 20%. However, when fiber link failures occur, the backup latency is on average 5% smaller. For working chains, VNF replication requires a higher spread of functions across the available DCs, which implies a higher average number of physical hops per chain. However, a link failure automatically forces the hop protection case to route around the ring in the opposite direction, significantly degrading latency performance, particularly in longer rings with many nodes and few DCs (where VNFs are further apart).

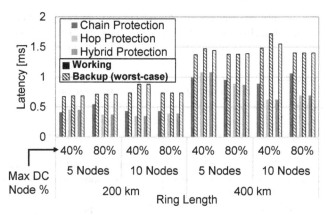

Fig. 5. Working chain latency and worst-case backup chain latency per ring topology and protection mechanism.

5 Conclusion and Future Work

This paper presented an ILP model to comparatively evaluate protection strategies for service chains based on provisioning backup resources exclusively at the optical layer, application layer, or both. The analysis showed that, although lightpath protection is the best option in terms of resource provisioning efficiency for the majority of VNF hops, in select cases combining this strategy with VNF replication can further reduce the overall solution cost. This is particularly true in scenario instances where there are significant optical performance differentials between working/backup paths, which can hinder overall throughput when working lightpath rates must be aligned by the backup ones. This is the case for reasonably large metro aggregation rings. The latency analysis concluded that VNF replication in ring topologies presents lower latencies in case of link failures, at the expense of additional IT resources.

Future expansions in order to further comprehend the potential of deploying such hybrid protection mechanisms should include the possibility of evaluating larger topologies, including meshed patterns. Additionally, the impact of client signal grooming on transponder utilization and end-to-end latency can also have a key effect on network efficiency. Realizing an optimization framework that can efficiently address all these joint factors is thus a challenging research prospect.

Acknowledgment. This work was partially supported by the H2020 Metro-Haul project, under grant agreement number 761727, and by FCT/MEC through national funds and when applicable co-funded by FEDER – PT2020 partnership agreement under the project UID/EEA/50008/2019.

References

1. Peterson, L., et al.: Central office re-architected as a data center. IEEE Commun. Mag. **54**(10), 96–101 (2016)

2. Yan, Y., Shu, Y., Saridis, G., Rofoee, B., Zervas, G., Simeonidou, D.: FPGA-based optical programmable switch and interface card for disaggregated OPS/OCS data centre networks. In: 41st European Conference on Optical Communication (ECOC), pp. 361–363. IEEE, Valencia (2015)
3. Li, F., Sun, W., Yue, S., Hu, W.: Trading storage for bandwidth – a simulation study of optical circuit switching with massive storage at network edge. In: 19th International Conference on Transparent Optical Networks (ICTON), paper We.D3.5. IEEE, Girona (2017)
4. Xia, M., Shirazipour, M., Zhang, Y., Green, H., Takacs, A.: Network function placement for NFV chaining in packet/optical datacenters. IEEE/OSA J. Lightwave Technol. **33**(8), 1565–1570 (2015)
5. Fang, W., Zeng, M., Liu, X., Lu, W., Zhu, Z.: Joint spectrum and IT resource allocation for efficient VNF service chaining in inter-datacenter elastic optical networks. IEEE Commun. Lett. **20**(8), 1539–1542 (2016)
6. Herrera, J., Botero, J.: Resource allocation in NFV: a comprehensive survey. IEEE Trans. Netw. Serv. Manage. **13**(3), 518–532 (2016)
7. Hmaity, A., Savi, M., Musumeci, F., Tornatore, M., Pattavina, A.: Virtual network function placement for resilient service chain provisioning. In: 8th International Workshop on Resilient Networks Design and Modeling (RNDM), pp. 245–252. IEEE, Halmstad (2016)
8. Kong, J., et al.: Guaranteed-availability network function virtualization with network protection and VNF replication. In: IEEE Global Communications Conference (GLOBECOM), pp. 1–6. IEEE, Singapore (2017)
9. Hai, D., Morvan, M., Gravey, P.: An efficient network-side path protection scheme in OFDM-based elastic optical networks. Int. J. Commun. Syst. **31**(1), paper e3410 (2017)
10. Eira, A., Costa, N., Pedro, J.: On the capacity and scalability of metro transport architectures for ubiquitous service delivery. In: 20th International Conference on Transparent Optical Networks (ICTON), paper Mo.D3.5. IEEE, Bucharest (2018)
11. Savi, M., Hmaity, A., Verticale, G., Höst, S., Tornatore, M.: To distribute or not to distribute? Impact of latency on virtual network function distribution at the edge of FMC networks. In: 18th International Conference on Transparent Optical Networks (ICTON), paper We.C3.4. IEEE, Trento (2016)

Software-Defined Reconfigurability, White Boxes, and Abstraction

Nicola Sambo$^{(\boxtimes)}$, Alessio Giorgetti, Andrea Sgambelluri, Piero Castoldi, and Luca Valcarenghi

Scuola Superiore Sant'Anna, Pisa, Italy
nicola.sambo@santannapisa.it

Abstract. Next generation networks – spanning from wide area networks to intra-datacenters – are expected to encompass devices and sub-devices from different vendors. Inter operability and vendor neutrality are now key topics for researchers and companies as a way to reduce costs avoiding to be tied to a single vendor. Also the management system is expected to be disaggregated from the hardware and possibly developed by a different company. An example is the *white box*, which disaggregates the software from the hardware and can be composed of modules from different vendors. Currently, NETCONF – based on YANG – is the protocol considered for the (re)configuration of white boxes. Discussions are being carried on to identify commonly agreed information models to guarantee vendor-neutral configuration and management of next generation networks.

In addition, emerging services (e.g., 5G) will impose the involvement of a variety of technologies (e.g., networks, datacenters) and resources (e.g., compute, storage, radio). Such heterogeneity will imply the cooperation of several business actors to bring services to the users. In such a scenario, the management of resources will require their abstraction in order to satisfy confidentiality as well as to increase scalability and, again, to provide information that is neutral with respect to the related vendor and technology.

In this paper, we propose to use NETCONF also for the exchange of resource information among different business actors considering the several network segments (wide area network, data centers, radio segment) involved in a 5G vertical. To this purpose, resource abstraction is proposed based on a YANG data model. An experiment will involve the (re)configuration of a wide area network composed of white boxes. Moreover, resource information (virtual links) will be exchanged through NETCONF with the objective of orchestrating resources.

Keywords: 5G · White box · Disaggregated networks · YANG · NETCONF

© IFIP International Federation for Information Processing 2020
Published by Springer Nature Switzerland AG 2020
A. Tzanakaki et al. (Eds.): ONDM 2019, LNCS 11616, pp. 15–25, 2020.
https://doi.org/10.1007/978-3-030-38085-4_2

1   Introduction

In the last years, a lot of interest within research and market has been directed to vendor-neutrality, inter-operability, and disaggregation of software from the hardware [1]. This movement started from network operators and service providers with the objective of removing the traditional vendor-lock-in of their networks. Indeed, up to now, multi-vendor-interoperability is not guaranteed, thus network upgrades must be performed by the same vendor. Similarly, the management system is tied to the network and typically proprietary of the vendor. These limitations impede the market. Inter-operability and vendor-neutral control and management permit operators and service providers to lower the costs avoiding to be tied to a single vendor and adopting the best of breed technologies. An example is the *white box* [2,3], a node disaggregating the hardware from the software (e.g., management systems) that can also be assembled by modules from different vendors. The control of white box is performed via the NETCONF protocol [4] supporting vendor-neutral YANG data models [5–8].

In addition, emerging services such as automotive, e-health, video streaming, documentation of mega events will be supported through the coordination of several heterogeneous technologies in different network segments. Datacenters, radio, and network technologies will be involved in the service delivery to the user requiring the cooperation of different business actors, each one administrating a network segment [9]. Such business actors will have to exchange their domain information (e.g., latency) so that services can be orchestrated. In such a scenario, the management of resources in play will require their abstraction (i.e., a simplification exchanging a reduced set of information) [10] in order to satisfy confidentiality as well as to increase scalability and provide information that is neutral with respect to the related vendor and technology. In particular, regarding resources, 5G services will exploit *network slice*: i.e., a set of virtualized functions, connectivity, compute, and storage resources [11]. The European Telecommunications Standards Institute (ETSI) is defining standard interfaces to enable domain managers (each belonging to the related company) in the exchange of their resource information (e.g., abstracted connectivity and compute resources) [12].

In this paper, we will first describe the NETCONF protocol (which operates in a client/server way) and its use for the (re)configuration of a white box acted by a Software Defined Networking (SDN) controller. Then, we will propose to exploit NETCONF also to manage abstracted domain information in a 5G scenario, leveraging the native characteristics of NETCONF in handling servers. An experiment will be presented showing the configurability of a wide area network (WAN) based on white boxes. The information exchanged between the different business actors will permit to set up resources satisfying the proper level of quality of service (in terms of latency). To this purpose, reconfiguration will be acted without exchanging information about the technology or detailed information of the network.

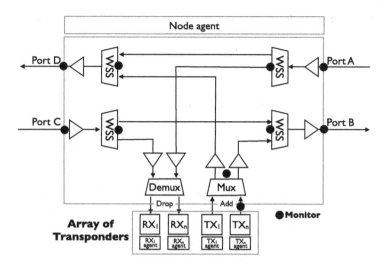

Fig. 1. White box

Table 1. Server describing configuration parameters of a cross connection

Parameter	Value
Input port	C
Output port	B
Central frequency	193.1
Width	37.5

2   NETCONF for White Box Configuration

A wide area network (WAN) based on flexible grid optical technology is assumed. In such a network scenario, white boxes (as the one shown in Fig. 1) assembled with several transponders, monitors, and filters (wavelength selective switches—WSSs) for switching and add/drop is considered as in [2]. The agent is the interface with the SDN controller. Regarding monitors, WSSs support the power monitor per channel, then other power monitors can be placed in the incoming and outgoing ports to measure the total channel power of the lines, as well as at the input and output of transponders. More advanced monitors (e.g., for filtering effects [2]) can be also assumed.

NETCONF, operating in a client server way, is responsible for the (re)-configuration of the white box. More specifically, NETCONF messages write or reports parameters' values stored into a server describing the configuration and the state of the white box. Such server reflects the information model describing the white box through a set of parameters. NETCONF messages contain fields associated to these parameters. In particular, *configuration* parameters are written to the proper configuration values via the NETCONF <edit-config> message. Table 1 shows an entry of the server related to a node cross-connection.

Table 2. Server describing configuration parameters of a transponder

Parameter	Value
net bit rate	100
baudrate	28
modulation format	pm-qpsk
FEC	7
launch power	0
central frequency	193.1

Table 3. State parameters of a transponder

Parameter	Value
pre-FEC BER	0.00213
osnr	16.4
cd	5133
pmd	5.19
B	33.2

In particular, the NETCONF <edit-config> message, sent from the SDN controller to the agent, writes the values of the proper parameters: input and output ports, and the frequency slot characterized by a central frequency (in THz) and a width (in GHz). Then, the agent is responsible to locally act, according to these entries, the cross connection configuration by properly configuring the WSSs. In the case of transponders, the <edit-config> message writes into the server the configuration parameters of a specific transponder (identified with an id). An example of configured values is reported in Table 2: net bit rate to 100 Gb/s achieved with polarization multiplexing quadrature phase shift keying (PM-QPSK) modulation format, 7% of forward error correction (FEC), and 28 Gbaud of symbol rate, at a central frequency of 193.1 THz with a launch power of 0 dBm.

Then, besides configuration parameters, even *state* parameters are included. They can only be read and are typically used to describe monitoring information. There are two ways to report monitoring information to an SDN controller. The SDN controller can send a <get> message to the agent requesting for the value of a specific parameter. The second way is asynchronous and based on a subscription and notification mechanism. The SDN controller, through the <create-subscription> message, asks to be notified when a state parameter exceeds a given value decided by the SDN controller. Table 3 shows parameters monitored by a transponder through the coherent receiver: pre-FEC bit error rate (pre-FEC BER), optical signal to noise ratio (OSNR), chromatic dispersion (CD), polarization mode dispersion (PMD), and signal bandwidth B. Then, other servers will be present for power monitors.

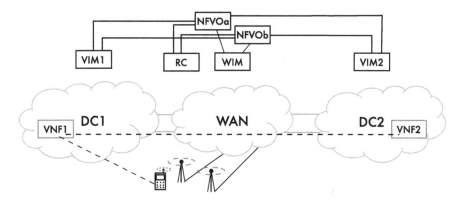

Fig. 2. Scenario involving multiple network technologies and domains

The next section describes how NETCONF messages can be used also for exchanging information about different network segments hiding the technology.

3   NETCONF for Slice Management

3.1   Scenario Description

The considered scenario is shown in Fig. 2. A user identified with a mobile phone exploits a service delivered by connecting the user to two virtual network functions (VNFs). This connection is enabled by virtual links involving the radio segment, the WAN, and data centers. VNFs are created using virtual storage and compute resources of datacenters. A Network Function Virtualization Orchestrator (NFVO), associated with a service provider, is responsible to orchestrate all the network, storage, and compute resources of each domain with the objective of satisfying quality of service (QoS). Several service providers exploits a network and each provider holds an NFVO (NFVO$_a$ and NFVO$_b$ in Fig. 2). Each domain can belong to a different business actor and is coordinated by a manager with the view of all the resources. In particular, the WAN Infrastructure Manager (WIM) [12] is responsible for the WAN, a Virtual Infrastructure Manager (VIM) [12] for a datacenter, and a Radio Controller (RC) for the radio. Each WIM, VIM, RC have the detailed view of their domain and can rely on an SDN controller for (re)configuring the domain.

3.2   Slice Management Through NETCONF

According to the slice definition, slice management implies the management of network, storage, compute, and radio resources. ETSI defined a set of interfaces to enable a consumer block (the NFVO) to *query* information about virtual network, storage, and compute resources to the VIM [12] to *reserve*, *allocate*, and *terminate* such resources. Moreover, an NFVO can also *subscribe* to *notifications*

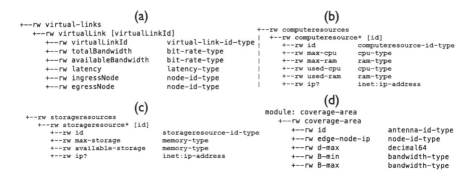

```
                        (a)                                           (b)
+--rw virtual-links                                  +--rw computeresources
   +--rw virtualLink [virtualLinkId]                    +--rw computeresource* [id]
      +--rw virtualLinkId        virtual-link-id-type      +--rw id        computeresource-id-type
      +--rw totalBandwidth       bit-rate-type             +--rw max-cpu   cpu-type
      +--rw availableBandwidth   bit-rate-type             +--rw max-ram   ram-type
      +--rw latency              latency-type              +--rw used-cpu  cpu-type
      +--rw ingressNode          node-id-type              +--rw used-ram  ram-type
      +--rw egressNode           node-id-type              +--rw ip        inet:ip-address
                                                                     (d)
                        (c)                           module: coverage-area
+--rw storageresources                                  +--rw coverage-area
   +--rw storageresource* [id]                              +--rw id         antenna-id-type
      +--rw id                   storageresource-id-type    +--rw edge-node-ip node-id-type
      +--rw max-storage          memory-type                +--rw d-max      decimal64
      +--rw available-storage    memory-type                +--rw B-min      bandwidth-type
      +--rw ip?                  inet:ip-address            +--rw B-max      bandwidth-type
```

Fig. 3. YANG data models for abstracted (a) virtual link, (b) compute, (c) storage resources, and (d) coverage area.

if the state of some resource changes and also if some performance parameter falls in a critical range. Network interfaces defined for the VIM are also considered between NFVO and WIM [13]. Based on the ETSI interfaces and operations, in this paper, we propose to use NETCONF to manage resource information about each domain, given the nature of this protocol in manipulating information stored into a server.

– <get> message: it can be used by the NFVO to query information about abstracted resources: virtual network topology (in the form of a list of virtual links), virtual compute and storage resources, radio coverage area
– <rpc-reply> message: upon query, this message can be used by a manager (e.g., WIM) to inform about abstracted resources. Figure 3 shows our own-developed YANG models describing the abstracted virtual link, compute, and storage resources and the radio coverage area. The virtual link is described with an identifier, with the IP addresses of ingress and egress nodes, an overall cumulated latency, and the total and available bandwidth. The whole path connecting the ingress and egress nodes, as well as the used technology, is hidden to NFVO (for scalability or confidentiality reasons), while WIM maintains the complete view of its WAN. Storage resources are mainly described by storage values (maximum and available), while compute resources by CPU and RAM. The radio coverage area is described by a maximum distance (d-max) covered by the antenna and by a maximum and minimum bandwidth that can be used for a service in this coverage area. The maximum bandwidth is computed in proximity of the antenna, while the minimum one is at d-max. These values depend on propagation models, in particular on the signal-to-interference-noise-ratio, sometimes translated into a parameter named Channel Quality Indicator (CQI) [14]
– <rpc> custom message: once the NFVO has decided for a specific resource (e.g., a virtual link characterized by the proper latency), this message is used to request a manager for the allocation of a specific resource. Then, the manager, as an example the WIM, handles the allocation by relying on an SDN

controller setting up (thus configuring white box in our case) a new lightpath between the ingress and egress pairs
- <create-subscription> message: an NFVO (e.g., $NFVO_a$ of Fig. 2) can request to a manger to be notified if a virtual resource changes (e.g., due to a service associated to $NFVO_b$ of Fig. 2) or if a monitored parameter falls in a critical range
- <notification> message: it is sent by the manager (e.g., a VIM) to NFVO if the event at the previous item occurs

Such use of the NETCONF protocol embraces the new trends of describing network elements and resources in a vendor-neutral way. Moreover, the abstraction models shown in Fig. 3 permit to describe all the resources in play also in a technology-neutral way. Indeed, regarding virtual link resources, NFVO is agnostic with respect to the technology that could be layer-3, optical, or any other. Thus, confidentiality reasons, vendor-neutrality, and also scalability are guaranteed.

4   Experimental Demonstration

The experiment is focused on the WAN and involves a WIM and a NFVO (for more details about an implementation related to the exchange of information from a VIM, the reader can refer to [15]). WIM relies on an ONOS SDN controller [16] for WAN (re)configuration. The data plane is emulated except a node, which is based on a Lumentum white box actually configured and reconfigured. Emulated devices are associated to NETCONF servers based on ConfD [17] storing the YANG parameters describing each device. The WAN topology is shown in Fig. 4. A service sensible to the latency is considered. NFVO requests an abstracted topology to WIM between the nodes with IP addresses 10.10.255.9 (the white box) and 10.10.255.6. At this stage, we forced the network to have just one route (shown in Fig. 4) between the two nodes. WIM replies with the message shown in Fig. 5 reporting the available virtual link (with identifier 20) characterized by a latency of 10.0 ms. NFVO evaluates such latency as critical but, given the presence of just this virtual link, NFVO selects it. Then, ONOS establishes the considered lightpath. Figure 6 shows the cross-connection information at the agent of the white box. Note that the XML content is based on a model proprietary of Lumentum, which describes the frequency slot with a start-frequency and a end-frequency instead of a central frequency and a width. Figure 6 also shows the input port 5101 and the output port 5202. Given that as policy NFVO prefers virtual links with shorter latency, NFVO periodically interrogates the WIM about the possibility to use another virtual link with shorter latency. At this stage we freed resources along an alternative route in the WAN. Consequently, WIM replies to NFVO with another available virtual link (with identifier 21). The related message is shown in Fig. 7 reporting the latency value of 8.5 ms and the same node pairs. Thus, NFVO can request to switch the service to the other virtual link exploiting a make-before-break approach. The new

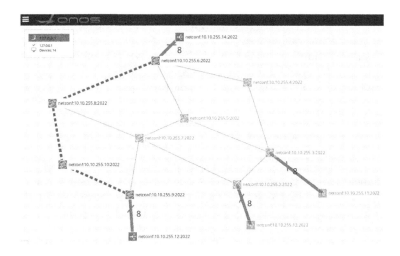

Fig. 4. WAN topology and lightpath associated to the first virtual link.

```
<virtualLink>
<virtualLinkId>20</virtualLinkId>
<totalBandwidth>100</totalBandwidth>
<availableBandwidth>100</availableBandwidth>
<latency>10.0</latency>
<ingressNode>10.10.255.9</ingressNode>
<egressNode>10.10.255.6</egressNode>
</virtualLink>
```

Fig. 5. <rpc-reply> sent by WIM to NFVO reporting the available virtual link.

route is shown in Fig. 8, while Fig. 9 shows the cross-connection information at the agent of the white box after reconfiguration. With respect to Figs. 6 and 9 shows a different output port (5201), which is the ones attached to the intermediate node 10.10.255.7. The make-before-break approach is implemented by the NFVO by requesting to WIM the allocation of a new virtual link and, once getting the acknowledgement, by terminating the old virtual link. Figure 10 shows the custom <rpc> including the identifier 21 to allocate the second virtual link, while Fig. 11 shows the custom <rpc> including the identifier 20 to terminate the second virtual link.

```
<start-freq>193675.00</start-freq>
<end-freq>193725.00</end-freq>
<attenuation>10.0</attenuation>
<blocked>false</blocked>
<power-target>0.00</power-target>
<power-target-tolerance>0.00</power-target-tolerance>
<input-port-reference>ne=1;chassis=1;card=1;port=5101
</input-port-reference>
<output-port-reference>ne=1;chassis=1;card=1;port=5202
</output-port-reference>
```

Fig. 6. Cross connection information at the agent of the destination edge associated to the first virtual link.

```
<virtualLink>
<virtualLinkId>21</virtualLinkId>
<totalBandwidth>100</totalBandwidth>
<availableBandwidth>100</availableBandwidth>
<latency>8.5</latency>
<ingressNode>10.10.255.9</ingressNode>
<egressNode>10.10.255.6</egressNode>
</virtualLink>
```

Fig. 7. <rpc-reply> sent by WIM to NFVO reporting the second virtual link.

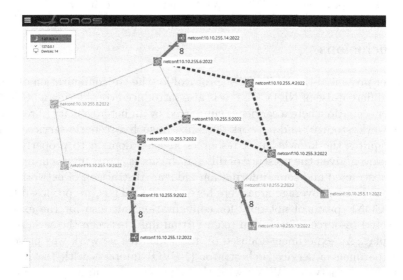

Fig. 8. WAN topology and lightpath associated to the second virtual link.

```
<start-freq>193675.00</start-freq>
<end-freq>193725.00</end-freq>
<attenuation>10.0</attenuation>
<blocked>false</blocked>
<power-target>0.00</power-target>
<power-target-tolerance>0.00</power-target-tolerance>
<input-port-reference>ne=1;chassis=1;card=1;port=5101
</input-port-reference>
<output-port-
reference>ne=1;chassis=1;card=1;port=5201
</output-port-reference>
```

Fig. 9. Cross connection information at the agent of the destination edge associated to the second virtual link.

```
<add-connection xmlns="http://sssup.it/wim">
<virtualLinkId>21</virtualLinkId>
<ingressNode>10.10.255.9</ingressNode>
<egressNode>10.10.255.6</egressNode>
</add-connection>
```

Fig. 10. <rpc> sent by NFVO to WIM to allocate the second virtual link.

```
<terminate-connection xmlns="http://sssup.it/wim">
<virtualLinkId>20</virtualLinkId>
<ingressNode>10.10.255.9</ingressNode>
<egressNode>10.10.255.6</egressNode>
</terminate-connection>
```

Fig. 11. <rpc> sent by NFVO to WIM to terminate the first virtual link.

5   Conclusions

This paper presented the NETCONF protocol for the (re)configuration of white boxes. A different use of NETCONF was also introduced considering a 5G/inter-datacenter scenario where a service is supported by an heterogeneity of resources (e.g., network, storage) and network domains. In such a scenario service orchestration requires the knowledge of resources at each domain to properly select them. However, given the presence of different business actors involved, resources must be abstracted and some information hidden. Abstraction of networks, datacenters, and radio coverage area were here provided. Thus, we proposed to use the NETCONF protocol not only for configuration but also for the exchange of abstracted resource information (e.g., virtual link) between the several managers in play. An experiment focused on the wide area network was presented. In the experiment a service orchestrator (NFVO) interacts with the manager of the wide area network (WIM) with the objective of obtaining a virtual link guaranteeing a proper latency value, thus the QoS. Future works will be focused on the information exchange between NFVO and the radio controller. Then, the objective is to provide an overall demo involving radio segment, wide area network, and datacenters.

Acknowledgement. This work was supported by the EC through the Horizon 2020 5G-TRANSFORMER project (grant agreement 761536).

References

1. Riccardi, E., Gunning, P., de Dios, O.G., Quagliotti, M., Lopez, V., Lord, A.: An operator view on the introduction of white boxes into optical networks. J. Lightwave Technol. **36**(15), 3062–3072 (2018)
2. Sambo, N., et al.: Experimental demonstration of a fully disaggregated and automated white box comprised of different types of transponders and monitors. J. Lightwave Technol. **37**(3), 824–830 (2018)
3. Velasco, L., et al.: Building autonomic optical whitebox-based networks. J. Lightwave Technol. **36**(15), 3097–3104 (2018)
4. Enns, R., Bjorklund, M., Schoenwaelder, J., Bierman, A.: IETF RFC 6241, June 2011
5. Bjorklund, M.: IETF RFC 6020
6. Dallaglio, M., Sambo, N., Cugini, F., Castoldi, P.: YANG models for vendor-neutral optical networks, reconfigurable through state machine. IEEE Commun. Mag. **55**(8), 170–178 (2017)
7. In http://www.openconfig.net
8. In http://www.openroadm.org
9. Iovanna, P., et al.: 5G mobile transport and computing platform for verticals. In: 2018 IEEE Wireless Communications and Networking Conference Workshops (WCNCW), pp. 266–271, April 2018
10. Fiorani, M., Rostami, A., Wosinska, L., Monti, P.: Abstraction models for optical 5G transport networks. IEEE/OSA J. Opt. Commun. Networking **8**(9), 656–665 (2016)
11. ETSI GR NFV-EVE 012 v3.1.1. ETSI standard (2017)
12. ETSI GS NFV-IFA 005 v2.1.1. ETSI standard (2016)
13. ETSI GS NFV-IFA 022 v3.1.1. ETSI standard (2018)
14. ETSI TS 136 213 V13.0.0. ETSI standard (2016)
15. Sgambelluri, A., et al.: Provisioning RAN as a service (RANaaS) connectivity in an optical metro network through NETCONF and YANG. In: 2018 European Conference on Optical Communication (ECOC), pp. 1–3, September 2018
16. In https://onosproject.org/
17. In http://www.confd.io/

Embedding Virtual Networks in Flexible Optical Networks with Sliceable Transponders

Juzi Zhao[1]([✉]) [iD] and Suresh Subramaniam[2] [iD]

[1] San Jose State University, San Jose, CA 95192, USA
juzi.zhao@sjsu.edu
[2] The George Washington University, Washington, DC 20052, USA
suresh@gwu.edu

Abstract. Emerging inter-datacenter applications involving data transferred, processed, and analyzed at multiple data centers, such as virtual machine migrations, real-time data backup, remote desktop, and
virtual data centers, can be modeled as virtual network requests that
share computing and spectrum resources of a common substrate physical
inter-datacenter network. Recent advances make flexible optical networks
an ideal candidate for meeting the dynamic and heterogeneous connection demands between datacenters. In this paper, we address the static
(offline) version of the virtual network embedding problem in flexible
optical networks equipped with sliceable bandwidth variable transponders (SBVTs). The objective is to minimize the total number of required
SBVTs in the network. An Integer Linear Programming (ILP) formulation is presented, lower bounds are derived, and four heuristics are
proposed and compared. Simulation results are presented to show the
effectiveness of the proposed approaches.

Keywords: Virtual networks · Flexible optical networks ·
Inter-datacenter networks · Embedding · Frequency slots · List
scheduling

1 Introduction

Flexible (or elastic) optical networks (FONs), with a fine-grained spectral spacing and variable channel center frequencies are promising for connecting geo-
distributed datacenters due to their capability to transfer large amounts of data
as well as efficiency and flexibility of utilizing spectrum resources [1,2].

Network virtualization breaks the network's rigidly fixed pattern by enabling
different virtual networks with various requirements to share the same substrate
physical network. Each virtual network (VN) request is a logical topology including a set of virtual nodes interconnected by virtual links. These requests require
not only communication resources on the optical links but also compute and storage resources at the physical nodes in the network. Emerging inter-datacenter
applications, such as virtual machine migration, database replication/backup,

© IFIP International Federation for Information Processing 2020
Published by Springer Nature Switzerland AG 2020
A. Tzanakaki et al. (Eds.): ONDM 2019, LNCS 11616, pp. 26–38, 2020.
https://doi.org/10.1007/978-3-030-38085-4_3

and virtual data centers, can be modeled as VN requests. The problem of allocating route(s) as well as appropriate spectrum, computing, and storage resources to a request or set of requests is commonly known as virtual network mapping/embedding problem (VNM/VNE), which is proved to be NP-hard [3].

There are several papers on VNE in FONs. The authors of [4] consider both static and dynamic cases, with the objective of maximizing spectrum slot utilization in static case and minimizing blocking ratio in dynamic case. Traffic grooming is taken into account in VNE problem in [5] over both WDM networks and FONs. In [6], an ILP formulation and heuristics to minimize the total spectrum slot usage are proposed for both transparent and opaque VNs. Two ILP formulations for VNE problem are presented in [7]. The authors of [8] take fragmentation-awareness and load-balancing features into account for the VNE, with an ILP formulation proposed. The authors of [9] propose relaxed ILP and heuristics for static version of VNE based on re-optimized VCAT framework. An ILP formulation to maximize the number of successful embeddings over transparent FONs considering transmission distance limits is proposed in [10]. The authors of [11] develop an ILP and a heuristic algorithm to minimize the total network cost considering impairment constraints and single link failures. The authors of [12] construct an auxiliary graph and utilize spectrum partitioning approaches to solve the cost-effective survivable VNE problem. Energy efficient VNE schemes are proposed for dynamic transparent VN requests in [13].

Sliceable Bandwidth Variable Transponders (SBVT, also called Multi-Flow Transponders) have been recently adopted in FONs. Multiple lightpaths with different destinations can be launched by a single SBVT, and thus transponder resources are effectively utilized. Many research directions in SBVT-enabled FONs have been explored. The authors of [14] propose dynamic routing, spectrum and transponder assignment schemes for two different types of SBVTs. The authors of [15] devise a dynamic distance-adaptive routing, spectrum, and modulation format assignment algorithm to optimize the utilization of spectrum and SBVTs. A model based on auxiliary graph is proposed in [16] to investigate the dynamic routing and spectrum assignment problem with traffic grooming.

In this paper, we consider the static version of VNE problem in FONs with SBVT allocation that has not been addressed before, to the best of our knowledge. A set of VN requests is given, where each request consists of a set of virtual nodes and the amount of computation resources required by virtual nodes, and bit rate required by virtual links connecting virtual nodes. The objective is to minimize the total number of required SBVTs for all requests. We present an ILP formulation, two lower bounds, and four heuristics based on List Scheduling and Tabu Search to embed the VN requests onto the physical optical inter-datacenter network, and assign VMs, frequency slots, and SBVTs to the requests.

2 Model and Problem Statement

The physical inter-datacenter network topology is $G_p(V_p, E_p)$, where V_p is the set of nodes (each is a data center associated with an optical switch), and E_p is the set of links. Each physical node has H virtual machines (VMs). Each SBVT at one physical node has C carriers. There are two fibers on each physical link with opposite directions, each has S frequency slots. The bandwidth of each frequency slot is 12.5 GHz. A number of frequency slots are allocated to each lightpath according to its spectrum requirement. The frequency slots allocated to each lightpath have to be contiguous (spectrum contiguity constraint), and the same band of frequency slots has to be allocated on each link traversed by the lightpath (spectrum continuity constraint). A guardband of G consecutive frequency slots has to be assigned between adjacent frequency slot bands allocated to different lightpaths if they share common physical links, in order to avoid interference [17]. K shortest distance paths between each pair of nodes are precomputed. One of M possible modulation formats is assigned to each lightpath. Each modulation format m has a maximum transmission reach R_m associated with it. A lightpath assigned modulation format m must has path distance less than R_m. Depending on the path length, each precomputed path has a highest modulation level that can be used. The physical network is considered as transparent, therefore, no spectrum converters exist in the network.

A VN request i can be represented as a graph $G_l^i(V_l^i, E_l^i)$, where V_l^i is the set of virtual nodes, and E_l^i is the set of virtual links. For clarity, we drop subscript l which indicates a virtual or logical topology. There is a bit rate requirement Λ_k^i for each virtual link $k^i \in E^i$ for bidirectional communication between the two end virtual nodes. Each virtual node j^i can be mapped to one physical node of a candidate physical node set (N_j^i), and requires h_j^i VMs. According to the candidate physical node sets of two end virtual nodes, virtual link k^i has a candidate path set P_k^i. Path $p \in P_k^i$ has a frequency slot requirement $b_k^i(p)$, based on the path's highest modulation format m^p and Λ_k^i, i.e., $b_k^i(p) = \lceil \Lambda_k^i/(s_p * 12.5) \rceil$, where s_p is spectrum efficiency of m^p in Gbps/GHz. In this paper, we assume two virtual nodes of the same VN request can be mapped to one physical node as long as the VM resources permit. In this case, there are no frequency slots nor SBVTs allocated to the virtual link connecting these two virtual nodes. (We note that the proposed approaches can be easily modified if this assumption does not hold, by adding an additional constraint that no two virtual nodes of the same request can be mapped to a single physical node.)

In this paper, we adopt the multi-laser sliceable bandwidth variable transponder (SBVT) model [14]. Each SBVT has C carriers. There is a dedicated tunable laser associated with each carrier, and the bandwidth of each carrier is U GHz. A single lightpath can be assigned 1 to C carriers based on its bandwidth requirement. If more than one carriers are assigned to a single lightpath, a 2 GHz guardband will be allocated between two carriers due to the center-frequency instability issue with lasers. Note that if multiple lightpaths are assigned the same SBVT at a particular node, then the bandwidths allocated to these lightpaths cannot have any overlap. This leads to the idea of extra links in the physical network as shown in Fig. 1 (only three SBVTs at node A are shown in the figure for illustration purpose). The original network has 9 links. The links between SBVTs and physical nodes can be treated as extra links. All lightpaths assigned SBVT a at node A will transverse extra link 10. Recall that for FONs, a single

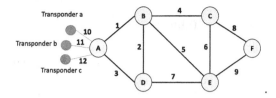

Fig. 1. Extra links introduced by transponders.

frequency slot on each link can be assigned to at most one lightpath (spectrum clash constraint). This constraint applies to both physical links and extra links.

In this paper, we consider static VNE problem where a set of requests are given *a priori*. Each virtual node in a request is mapped to a single physical node, with sufficient available VMs, selected from its candidate physical node set. Each virtual link is mapped to a physical path p, and a band of contiguous frequency slots is allocated to the virtual link based on its bit rate requirement. Two SBVTs on source and destination nodes, respectively, of path p have to be assigned to launch and terminate lightpath; and a corresponding number of carriers on the two assigned SBVTs are allocated to the virtual link. The objective is to minimize the total number of required SBVTs to map all requests.

3   Algorithms

In the following, we use pnode, vnode, plink, vlink, ppath, elink, and fslot to stand for physical node, virtual node, physical link, virtual link, physical path, extra physical link, and frequency slot, respectively. In addition, we use the letter i for virtual request index, j for vnode index, k for vlink index, n for pnode index, p for ppath index, and e for elink index.

3.1   ILP Formulation

There are several input parameters used in the ILP: a_{ijn} (binary), $a_{ijn} = 1$ if pnode n is in the candidate set (N_j^i) of pnodes to map to for vnode j in request i. h_j^i (integer), the number of VMs required by j in i. H_n (integer), the number of VMs on n. $S(p)$ (integer), source pnode of ppath p. $D(p)$ (integer), destination pnode of p. $S(k^i)$ (integer), source vnode of vlink k in request i. $D(k^i)$ (integer), destination vnode of k in i. $b_k^i(p)$ (integer), the number of fslots (including guardband) required by k in i if it is mapped to ppath p. $T(e)$ (integer), the SBVT with elink e. $B(e)$ (integer), the pnode with e. $c_k^i(p)$ (integer), the number of carriers required by k in i if it is mapped to p. η_{pl} (binary), $\eta_{pl} = 1$ if p transverses plink l. The variables in ILP formulation are shown in Table 1.

From Fig. 1, it can be seen that each elink is a SBVT, so minimizing total number of required SBVTs is minimizing the total number of used elinks.

$$\text{Objective: Minimize} \sum_e m_e$$

Table 1. Notations

Symbol	Meaning
x_{ijn}	$x_{ijn} = 1$ if vnode j in request i is mapped to pnode n
y_{ikp}	$y_{ikp} = 1$ if vlink k in i is mapped to ppath p, where p could be a dummy path with source pnode and destination pnode being a same pnode
u_{ikq}	$u_{ikq} = 1$ if k in i uses SBVT q on its source pnode
v_{ikq}	$v_{ikq} = 1$ if k in i uses SBVT q on its destination pnode
τ_{iks}	$\tau_{iks} = 1$ if the starting fslot for vlink k in i is fslot s
g_{iks}	$g_{iks} = 1$ if vlink k in request i uses fslot s
z_{ike}	$z_{ike} = 1$ if vlink k in request i uses elink e
ϕ_{ikls}	$\phi_{ikls} = 1$ if vlink k in request i uses fslot s on plink l
γ_{ikes}	$\gamma_{ikes} = 1$ if vlink k in request i uses fslot s on elink e
θ_{iknq}	the number of carriers required by k in i at SBVT q of n
m_e	$m_e = 1$ if elink e is used by some request

Constraints:

(1) $\sum_n x_{ijn} = 1$ for all i,j; (2) $\sum_n a_{ijn} x_{ijn} = 1$ for all i,j

(3) $\sum_{ij} h^i_j x_{ijn} \leq H_n$ for all n; (4) $\sum_p y_{ikp} S(p) = \sum n x_{iS(k^i)n}$ for all i,k

(5) $\sum_p y_{ikp} D(p) = \sum n x_{iD(k^i)n}$ for all i,k; (6) $\sum_p y_{ikp} = 1$ for all i,k

(7) $\tau_{iks_0} = g_{iks_0}$ for all i,k; (8) $\tau_{iks} \geq g_{iks} - g_{iks-1}$ for all i,k,s

(9) $\sum_s g_{iks} = \sum_p b^i_k(p) y_{ikp}$ for all i,k ; (10) $\sum_s \tau_{iks} \leq 1$ for all i,k

(11) $\sum_s g_{iks} \leq S \sum_s \tau_{iks}$ for all i,k; (12) $\sum_{ik} \theta_{iknq} \leq C$ for all n,q

(13) $\sum_q u_{ikq} = \sum_s \tau_{iks}$ for all i,k; (14) $\sum_q v_{ikq} = \sum_s \tau_{iks}$ for all i,k

(15) $z_{ike} \geq x_{iS(k^i)B(e)} + u_{ikT(e)} - 1$ for all i,k,e

(16) $z_{ike} \geq x_{iD(k^i)B(e)} + v_{ikT(e)} - 1$ for all i,k,e; (17) $m_e \geq z_{ike}$ for all i,k,e;

(18) $\phi_{ikls} \geq \sum_p y_{ikp} \eta_{pl} + g_{iks} - 1$ for all i,k,l,s

(19) $\gamma_{ikes} \geq z_{ike} + g_{iks} - 1$ for all i,k,e,s

(20) $\sum_{ik} \phi_{ikls} \leq 1$ for all l,s; (21) $\sum_{ik} \gamma_{ikes} \leq 1$ for all e,s

(22) $\theta_{iknq} \geq \sum_p c^i_k(p) y_{ikp} + C(x_{iS(k^i)n} - 1) + C(u_{ikq} - 1)$ for all i,k,n,q

(23) $\theta_{iknq} \geq \sum_p c^i_k(p) y_{ikp} + C(x_{iD(k^i)n} - 1) + C(v_{ikq} - 1)$ for all i,k,n,q

Constraints (1) and (2) ensure that each vnode is mapped to one of its candidate pnodes. Constraint (3) ensures that each pnode's VM capacity is not exceeded. Constraints (4) and (5) ensure that two end pnodes ($S(p)$ and $D(p)$) of ppath p assigned to vlink k must match the two pnodes assigned to two end vnodes ($S(k^i)$ and $D(k^i)$) of k. Constraint (6) ensures that each vlink is mapped to a ppath. Constraints (7) and (8) ensure spectrum contiguity constraint, where s_0 is the first fslot index. Constraint (9) ensures that the bit rate required by each vlink is satisfied. Note that if source pnode and destination pnode of p are the same pnode, then $b^i_k(p) = 0$, which makes $\sum_s g_{iks} = 0$ since no fslot is allocated. Constraints (10) and (11) ensure that each vlink has one starting fslot if its two end vnodes are not mapped to the same pnode ($\sum_s g_{iks} > 0$), where S is the number of fslots on each plink. Constraint (12) ensures that each SBVT's carrier capacity is not exceeded. Constraints (13) and (14) ensure that each vlink uses at most one SBVT each at source and destination pnodes. Note that a vlink does not need SBVTs if its two end vnodes are mapped to the same pnode. Constraints (15) and (16) ensure that if a vlink uses the corresponding pnode and SBVT with elink e, then the vlink uses e. Constraint (17) ensures that $m_e = 1$ if at least one vlink uses elink e. Constraint (18) ensures $\phi_{ikls} = 1$ if k uses plink l and fslot s. Constraint (19) ensures $\gamma_{ikes} = 1$ if k uses elink e and fslot s. Constraints (20) and (21) ensure that each fslot on each (extra) physical link can be assigned to at most one vlink. Constraints (22) and (23) ensure that the number of carriers of SBVT q on pnode n allocated to k (i.e., θ_{iknq}) depends on the number of required carriers (i.e., $\sum_p c_k^i(p) y_{ikp}$). If source vnode and destination vnode of k are not mapped to n (i.e., $x_{iS(k^i)n} = 0$ and $x_{iD(k^i)n} = 0$) or SBVT q is not assigned to k (i.e., $u_{ikq} = 0$ and $v_{ikq} = 0$), then θ_{iknq} can be set to 0. If there is a constraint that no two virtual vnodes of the same request can be mapped to a single pnode, then we need another constraint (24) $\sum_j x_{ijn} \leq 1$ for all i, n.

3.2 Lower Bounds

LB1. This bound is based on (1) each vlink's lightpath requires 0 or more carriers of SBVTs at the source and destination pnodes to which the end vnodes are mapped, (2) each SBVT has C carriers, and (3) there are S fslots on each plink.

For each vlink k of request i, according to the distance of each candidate ppath p_k^i in set P_k^i (in turn, the modulation format) and the bit rate requirement Λ_k^i, we can calculate the number of required fslots as $b_k^i(p)$ (including guardband) and the number of carriers $c_k^i(p)$ that need to be allocated to k of i if it is mapped to ppath p. ($b_k^i(p)$ and $c_k^i(p)$ are 0 if p is a dummy ppath with same end pnodes.) For vlink k of i, we can find the minimum number of carriers that have to be allocated as $\hat{c}_{ik} = \min_p c_k^i(p)$. $b_k^i(q)$ fslots will be allocated on every plink l along the ppath q_{ik} that achieves $\hat{c}_{ik}$.

For each plink l, there are several ppaths using fslots on it (according to the above minimum carrier allocation). Each ppath q_{ik} using l requires the minimum fslot $b_k^i(q)$. For each ppath q_{ik}, among all candidate ppaths for k, find the minimum number of required carriers g_{ikl} if plink l is *not* used by k. Let $v_q = g_{ikl} - \hat{c}_{ik}$ (i.e., if k does not use plink l, v_q more carriers have to be allocated). We now formulate a 0/1 knapsack problem (which can be solved easily) to obtain $LB1$. Let the capacity of knapsack be $S + G$ (G is guardband); there are several items with weight $b_k^i(q)$ and value v_q. The objective of 0/1 knapsack is to maximize total value of knapsack with weight constraint. Suppose the result is Z_l; this means that $y_l = \sum_q v_q - Z_l$ more carriers are required to satisfy all requests. Let $Y = \sum_{ik} \hat{c}_{ik} + \sum_l y_l$. Then $LB1 = \lceil Y/C \rceil$. The time complexity to compute $LB1$ is $O(IKV^2M + LIK(S + G))$, where I is number of requests, K is maximum number of vlinks per request, V is number of candidate pnodes per vnode, M is number of ppaths for each pair of pnodes, and L is number of plinks.

LB2. *LB2* is obtained by observing that (1) vlinks that share an end vnode must be allocated carriers at a single pnode (the pnode to which the end vnode is mapped) and (2) capacity constraint of each pnode (H VMs).

Consider a vnode j which has several candidate pnodes $n_1, n_2, n_3, \ldots$ There are several vlinks $k_1, k_2, k_3, \ldots$ that share j as one end vnode. If j is mapped to n_1, then some carriers of SBVTs at pnode n_1 will be allocated to $k_1, k_2, k_3, \ldots$ We can find the minimum number of required carriers for these vlinks if j is mapped to n_1 based on the candidate ppaths of $k_1, k_2, k_3, \ldots$ Denote $Q_j(n_1)$ as the value. Similarly, $Q_j(n_2), Q_j(n_3), \ldots$ can be calculated. Therefore, we can find the best pnode mapping for vnode j in terms of the number of required carriers $\bar{c}_j = \min(Q_j(n_1), Q_j(n_2), Q_j(n_3), \ldots)$.

For each pnode n, there are several vnodes j using VMs on it (according to the above allocation). Each vnode has a VM requirement h_j. For all vlinks with end vnode j, find the minimum number of required carriers g_{jn} for these vlinks if j is *not* mapped to n. Let $v_j = g_{jn} - \bar{c}_j$ (i.e., if j is not mapped to n, v_j more carriers have to be allocated). We again have a 0/1 knapsack problem for n. The capacity of the knapsack is H (the VM capacity), there are several items, with item j having weight h_j and value v_j. The objective is to maximize total value of knapsack with weight constraint. Suppose the result is Z_n, which means $y'_n = \sum_j v_j - Z_n$ more carriers are required to satisfy all requests. Let $Y' = \sum_j \bar{c}_j + \sum_n y'_n$. Then $LB2 = \lceil Y'/C \rceil$. The time complexity to compute $LB2$ is $O(IKV^2M + NIJH)$, where N is the number of pnodes, J is the maximum number of vnodes per request, and H is the number of VMs per pnode.

3.3 Proposed Heuristics

Although ILP can provide an optimal solution, it only works for small instances due to high time complexity. For larger instances, we propose two heuristics based on list scheduling, and then propose two improved meta-heuristics based on Tabu Search. Note that since VNE problem is NP-hard, the heuristics may occasionally fail to produce a result even though a valid mapping exists.

LL Heuristic. This heuristic first assigns a weight W_i to each request i based on its requirement, then requests are sorted by decreasing order of weights and mapped one by one (Steps 1 and 4 in Algorithm 1). Regarding a particular i under consideration, a weight ω_{ik} is assigned to each vlink k^i, and the vlinks are sorted by decreasing order of weights and are mapped following this order (Steps 4.a and 4.b). For vlink k^i being mapped, every possible candidate (as a combination of a ppath, a band of contiguous fslots and two SBVTs at source and destination pnodes respectively) is assigned a weight, and the combination with minimum weight is allocated to k^i (Steps 4.b(1)-4.b(3)).

Weight W_i is calculated as $W_i = \max\left(\frac{\hat{h}_i}{\bar{h}\mu}, \frac{\hat{\Lambda}_i}{\bar{\Lambda}\nu}\right)$, where $\hat{h}_i = \sum_j h_j^i$ is the total number of VMs required by i, $\hat{\Lambda}_i = \sum_k \Lambda_k^i$, is the total bit rate requirement of i, $\bar{h} = \sum_i \hat{h}_i$, $\bar{\Lambda} = \sum_i \hat{\Lambda}_i$, $\mu = \sum_{ij} f_j^i$ where f_j^i is the number of pnodes the

1 Step 1: Assign weight W_i to each VN request i; and sort the requests in decreasing order of weights
2 Step 2: TrivialRequestCheck()
3 Step 3: CheckOneCandidate()
4 Step 4: Schedule ordered unmapped requests one by one
5 **foreach** sorted request i **do**
6   Step 4.a: Assign weight ω_{ik} to each unmapped vlink k of i, and sort them in decreasing order of weights
7   Step 4.b: Schedule ordered unmapped vlinks of i one by one
8   **foreach** unmapped vlink k of request i **do**
9   **foreach** allocation-combination x (including candidate ppath p, fslot band f on p, SBVT $t_s(p)$ at source pnode of p, SBVT $t_d(p)$ at destination pnode of p) **do**
10   Step 4.b(1): Calculate Δ_x the weight of x
11   **end**
12   Step 4.b(2): Map vlink k to allocation-combination $\bar{x}$ that achieves $\min_x \Delta_x$
13   Step 4.b(3): CheckOneCandidate()
14   **end**
15 **end**

Algorithm 1. LL algorithm

vnode j can be mapped to, and $\nu = \sum_{ik} r_k^i$ where r_k^i is the number of candidate ppaths the vlink k can be mapped to. Decreasing order of request weights gives higher priority to resource-intensive requests.

Before mapping the requests, we check (in Step 2 *CheckTrivialRequests*) whether any request i can be mapped to a pnode n without affecting vnode mapping of other requests (i.e., all other vnodes can still be mapped to n if n is one of their candidate pnodes). It is best to map an entire request to a single pnode if possible since this mapping won't use any fslots nor SBVTs. There is another check made before mapping VN requests and after every vlink mapping (Steps 3 and 4.b(3)). There is a VM limit at every pnode and a fslot limit on each plink; the purpose of *CheckOneCandidate* is to share these limited resources fairly by first mapping vnodes and vlinks of all requests that have only one pnode and ppath to map to.

For a particular request i under consideration, each of its unmapped vlinks k is assigned a weight ω_{ik} (Step 4.a) as $\bar{b}_k^i/m_i^k$, where m_i^k is the number of possible candidate ppaths for k, and $\bar{b}_k^i$ is the current minimum number of required fslots for k among the m_i^k candidate ppaths. The vlinks of i are sorted in decreasing order of weights to first map vlinks requiring more fslots and having fewer candidate ppaths. Now we describe the vlink mapping steps (Steps 4.b(1)-4.b(3)). For each unmapped vlink k (with source vnode $s(k)$ and destination vnode $d(k)$) mapping, all of its currently available candidate x, as a combination of ppath p (with source pnode $s(p)$ and destination pnode $d(p)$), a band of fslots f on p, SBVT $t_s(p)$ at $s(p)$, and SBVT $t_d(p)$ at $d(p)$, will be assigned a weight $\Delta_x = h'_x + t'_x + b_k(p)/S + c_k(p)/C$, where $h'_x = \max(m_{s(k)}h_{s(k)}/H'_{s(p)}, m_{d(k)}h_{d(k)}/H'_{d(p)})$

if $s(p) \neq d(p)$, otherwise $h'_x = (m_{s(k)}h_{s(k)} + m_{d(k)}h_{d(k)})/H'_{s(p)}$, where $m_{s(k)} = 0$ ($m_{d(k)} = 0$) if $s(k)$ ($d(k)$) has already been mapped, otherwise they are set as 1; $h_{s(k)}$ ($h_{d(k)}$) is the number of required VMs for $s(k)$ ($d(k)$), and $H'_{s(p)}$ ($H'_{d(p)}$) is the number of currently available VMs at $s(p)$ ($d(p)$); t'_x is the number of newly allocated SBVTs (which have not been allocated so far) to k; $b_k(p)$ and $c_k(p)$ are the numbers of required fslots and required carriers, respectively, if k is mapped to p; S is the fslots capacity of each plink; and C is the number of carriers per SBVT. Vlink k is mapped to the candidate achieving the minimum value $\Delta = \min_x \Delta_x$. After that, VM, SBVTs (with carriers), and fslot resources are updated for the corresponding plinks and pnodes (allocated to vlink k and its end vnodes). At last, *CheckOneCandidate* function is called since the mapping of k might result in changes of other vnodes'/vlinks' available mapping candidates. This procedure is repeated until all vlinks of i are mapped. The time complexity of LL is $O(I^3 J^2 NK + V^2 MSI^3 K^3)$.

Note that if no two vnodes of the same request can be mapped to a single pnode, then there is no TrivialRequestCheck() function. Dummy paths (with the same end pnodes) will not be considered as candidate ppaths in all steps.

ALL Heuristic. ALL heuristic is similar to LL heuristic with the difference that LL first sorts VN requests, then does the vlink mapping for these requests one by one. In ALL heuristic, all vlinks of all requests are sorted by decreasing order of their weights ω_{ik} (defined in LL heuristic), and the vlinks are then mapped one by one. The time complexity of ALL is the same as LL.

Tabu Search. We utilize Tabu Search meta-heuristic to improve the LL and ALL heuristics performance, called LL-TS and ALL-TS, respectively. The main idea of Tabu search is to utilize a neighborhood search procedure to iteratively generate a better solution from one potential solution by exploring the neighborhood of current potential solution, until an attempt limit. In LL-TS algorithm (ALL-TS algorithm), the Tabu search method is utilized to iteratively generate different ordered sets of VN requests (virtual links), each order is treated as a Tabu Search solution. Given this order, the remaining steps in LL (ALL) are kept the same to find the number of required SBVTs. The initial request (vlink) order is the one used in LL (ALL). To create a new ordered set based on current order, two VN requests (vlinks) in current order are randomly selected and swapped. To improve performance, Θ different new ordered sets are created for each current order (according to different swaps). The new order that results in minimum number of required SBVTs will be used as current order for the next iteration. The procedure is repeated for Φ iterations. The larger the Θ and Φ values, the better the performance, but the longer simulation time. The time complexity is $O(\Theta \Phi I^3 J^2 NK + \Theta \Phi V^2 MSI^3 K^3)$.

4   Simulation Results

We present results for two network topologies, the small 6-node network, shown in Fig. 1 and Google data center network, shown in Fig. 2.

There are 3 modulation levels used in the simulations: DP-QPSK, DP-8QAM and DP-16QAM, and their corresponding transmission reach limits are 3000 km, 1000 km, and 650 km, respectively [15]. The spectrum efficiencies (in Gbps/GHz) of the three modulation formats are: 4, 6, and 8. The guardband is set as $G = 1$ frequency slot. The bandwidth of each carrier in SBVT is 25 GHz. There are 3 precomputed paths for each pair of physical nodes. Each virtual network request has either 3 or 4 virtual nodes (selected randomly). Each virtual node has randomly 1–3 physical node candidates. The probability that there is a virtual link between each pair of virtual nodes is set as 0.8 for small 6-node network and 0.6 for Google Network. The bit rate requirement for each virtual link is randomly set in the range 100–500 Gbps.

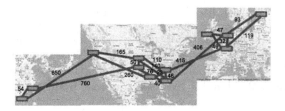

Fig. 2. Google Data Center Network with link distance in km.

4.1   Numerical Results for 6-Node Network

In this section, we compare the results of ILP, lower bounds, and four heuristics for small 6-node network topology. We assume that each physical node has 30 VMs and there are 30 frequency slots on each physical link. Each virtual node requires a random number between 1 and 5 VMs. The number of carriers per SBVT is set as $C = 5$. Let I denote the number of VN requests. The value of Θ is set as $I(I - 1)/2$ and the value of Φ is set as 500 for Tabu search algorithms. Sample results for 1 - 14 virtual network requests are shown in Table 2 (15 requests turn out to be infeasible due to node capacity), where LB is the minimum of $LB1$ and $LB2$; and *inf* means a feasible result was not found.

It can be seen that ALL algorithm outperforms LL algorithm, but both produce infeasible solutions for some cases. Tabu Search can improve heuristic results, suggesting that the order of requests (or virtual links) can affect performance especially for the cases that resources requirements are close to resources capacity (i.e., 13 and 14 request cases). The LB values are not far away from optimal ILP results.

Table 2. Number of required SBVTs in 6-node network

I	ILP	LB	LL	ALL	LL-TS	ALL-TS
5	6	4	6	6	6	6
6	8	6	8	8	8	8
7	9	7	11	9	9	9
8	10	8	14	12	11	10
9	10	8	18	14	12	10
10	10	8	20	14	12	12
11	12	10	inf	19	15	14
12	14	12	inf	21	18	16
13	16	13	inf	inf	20	20
14	18	14	inf	inf	22	22

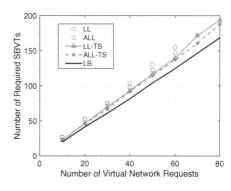

Fig. 3. Number of required SBVTs vs. number of requests.

4.2 Numerical Results for Google Network

For the larger Google network topology, we show the results for lower bounds, LL, ALL, LL-TS, and ALL-TS, as the average of 10 seeds simulation results. We assume that each physical node has 1000 VMs, and there are 320 frequency slots on each link (as optical C-band is 4000 GHz and each frequency slot is 12.5 GHz). The number of required VMs for each virtual node is randomly selected in {10, 20, 30, 40, 50}. The value of Θ is set as 20 and value of Φ is set as 25. Figure 3 shows the number of required SBVTs as a function of number of requests when there are 5 carriers per SBVT. Figure 4 shows number of required SBVTs for 50 requests versus number of carriers per SBVT. Figure 5 shows simulation results for mixed virtual links' bit rate requirements of 50 requests, where α percentage of virtual links have bit rate requirement in range 100–200 Gbps, $1-\alpha$ percentage of virtual links have bit rate requirement in range 400–500 Gbps (when there are

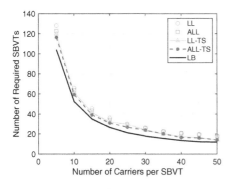

Fig. 4. Number of required SBVTs vs. number of carriers per SBVT.

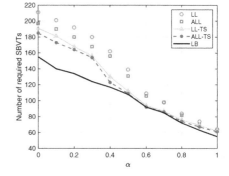

Fig. 5. Number of required SBVTs vs. parameter α.

5 carriers per SBVT). These results confirmed that performance of ALL is better than the performance of LL. Tabu Search produces feasible solutions when LL and ALL fail as shown in Fig. 3. The differences between Tabu Search and lower bound are on average 10%, 17%, and 11.2% in Figs. 3, 4, and 5 respectively.

5   Conclusions

A virtual network embedding problem is investigated in flexible optical inter-datacenter networks equipped with sliceable transponders. The objective is to minimize the total number of required sliceable transponders. We proposed an Integer Linear Programming formulation, two lower bounds, two heuristics based on list scheduling, and two meta-heuristics based on Tabu Search. Simulation results show that the Tabu Search variant of two proposed heuristics achieve quite good performance compared to the derived lower bounds.

Acknowledgment. This work was supported in part by NSF grants CNS-1813617 and CNS-1813772.

References

1. Tomkos, I., Azodolmolky, S., Sole-Pareta, J., Careglio, D., Palkopoulou, E.: A tutorial on the flexible optical networking paradigm: state of the art, trends, and research challenges. Proc. IEEE **102**(9), 1317–1337 (2014)
2. Jinno, M., et al.: Distance-adaptive spectrum resource allocation in spectrum-sliced elastic optical path network. IEEE Commun. Mag. **48**(8), 138–145 (2010)
3. Chowdhury, N.M.M.K., Rahman, M.R., Boutaba, R.: Virtual network embedding with coordinated node and link mapping. In: 28th Conference on Computer Communications (INFOCOM), pp. 783–791. IEEE, Rio de Janeiro (2009)
4. Zhao, J., Subramaniam, S., Brandt-Pearce, M.: Virtual topology mapping in elastic optical networks. In: International Conference on Communications (ICC), pp. 3904–3908. IEEE, Budapest (2013)
5. Zhang, S., Shi, L., Vadrevu, C.S.K., Mukherjee, B.: Network virtualization over WDM and flexible-grid optical networks. Opt. Switching Networking **10**(4), 291–300 (2013)
6. Gong, L., Zhu, Z.: Virtual optical network embedding (VONE) over elastic optical networks. J. Lightwave Technol. **32**(3), 450–460 (2014)
7. Wang, Y., McNulty, Z., Nguyen, H.: Network virtualization in spectrum sliced elastic optical path networks. J. Lightwave Technol. **35**(10), 1962–1970 (2017)
8. Madani, F.M., Mokhtari, S.: Fragmentation-aware load-balancing virtual optical network embedding (VONE) over elastic optical networks. In: The Sixth International Conference on Cloud Computing, GRIDs, and Virtualization, Nice, France, pp. 27–32 (2015)
9. Yu, C., Guo, L., Hou, W.: Novel elastic optical network embedding using re-optimized VCAT framework accompanied by hitless PPSM function. J. Lightwave Technol. **34**(22), 5199–5213 (2016)
10. Soto, P., Botero, J.F., Hesselbach, X.: Optimal occupancy mapping of virtual networks over elastic optical infrastructures. In: 19th International Conference on Transparent Optical Networks (ICTON), Girona, Spain, pp. 1–7 (2017)

11. Xie, W., et al.: Survivable virtual optical network mapping in flexible-grid optical networks. In: International Conference on Computing, Networking and Communications (ICNC), Honolulu, HI, USA, pp. 221–225 (2014)
12. Chen, B., Zhang, J., Xie, W., Jue, J., Zhao, Y., Shen, G.: Cost-effective survivable virtual optical network mapping in flexible bandwidth optical networks. J. Lightwave Technol. **34**(10), 2398–2412 (2016)
13. Zhu, M., Gao, P., Zhang, J., Zeng, X., Zhang, S.: Energy efficient dynamic virtual optical network embedding in sliceable-transponder-equipped EONs. In: IEEE Global Communications Conference, Singapore, pp. 1–6 (2017)
14. Dallaglio, M., Giorgetti, A., Sambo, N., Velasco, L., Castoldi, P.: Routing, spectrum, and transponder assignment in elastic optical networks. J. Lightwave Technol. **33**(22), 4648–4658 (2015)
15. Martinez, R., Casellas, R., Vilalta, R., Munoz, R.: GMPLS/PCE-controlled multiflow optical transponders in elastic optical networks. J. Opt. Commun. Networking **7**(11), B71–B80 (2015)
16. Zhang, J., et al.: Dynamic traffic grooming in sliceable bandwidth-variable transponder-enabled elastic optical networks. J. Lightwave Technol. **33**(1), 183–191 (2015)
17. Christodoulopoulos, K., Tomkos, I., Varvarigos, E.A.: Elastic bandwidth allocation in flexible OFDM-based optical networks. J. Lightwave Technol. **29**(9), 1354–1366 (2011)

Virtualized Controller Placement for Multi-domain Optical Transport Networks

Sabidur Rahman[1]($\boxtimes$), Tanjila Ahmed[1], Sifat Ferdousi[1], Partha Bhaumik[1],
Pulak Chowdhury[1], Massimo Tornatore[1,2], Goutam Das[3],
and Biswanath Mukherjee[1]

[1] University of California, Davis, USA
{krahman,tanahmed,sferdousi,pbhaumik,pchowdhury,bmukherjee}@ucdavis.edu
[2] Politecnico di Milano, Milan, Italy
massimo.tornatore@polimi.it
[3] Indian Institute of Technology, Kharagpur, India
gdas@gssst.iitkgp.ac.in

Abstract. Optical multi-domain transport networks are often controlled by a hierarchical distributed architecture of controllers. Optimal placement of these controllers is very important for their efficient management and control. Traditional SDN controller placement methods focus mostly on controller placement in datacenter networks. But the problem of virtualized controller placement for multi-domain transport networks needs to be solved in the context of geographically-distributed heterogeneous multi-domain networks. In this context, Edge Datacenters have enabled network operators to place virtualized controller instances closer to users, besides providing more candidate locations for controller placement. In this study, we propose a dynamic controller placement method for optical transport networks that considers the heterogeneity of optical controllers, resource limitations at edge hosting locations, latency requirements, and costs. Simulation studies considering practical scenarios show significant cost savings and delay reductions compared to standard placement approaches.

Keywords: SDN and optical controller · Optical transport network · Cost savings · Network virtualization · Edge computing

1 Introduction

Existing proposals for controller placement [1] have focused mostly on packet-switched Software-Defined Networks (SDNs) and they often ignore the complexity, heterogeneity, and vendor specificity of a transport-network control plane. Current technical solutions for transport-network control planes (e.g., Transport SDN, T-SDN) are designed for circuit-switched layer 0 (optical) and layer 1 (SONET/SDH and OTN). T-SDN supports multi-layer, multi-vendor, circuit-oriented networks

© IFIP International Federation for Information Processing 2020
Published by Springer Nature Switzerland AG 2020
A. Tzanakaki et al. (Eds.): ONDM 2019, LNCS 11616, pp. 39–50, 2020.
https://doi.org/10.1007/978-3-030-38085-4_4

that are different from packet-based SDN-controlled networks [2]. The control plane for optical transport networks employs a hierarchical distributed architecture [3] comprising heterogeneous (often vendor-specific) Optical Network (ON) Controllers (ONC) and SDN Controllers (SDNC).

Our study considers that T-SDN controllers can be deployed as virtualized controller instances (as in [5]). Virtualized controller placement has many benefits. First, manually deploying SDN and ON controllers in traditional 'hardware boxes' can take several days, compared to few minutes in case of virtualized instances (hosted on Virtual Machines (VMs), docker containers, etc.) in the cloud datecenter (DCs) or in computing nodes at edge datacenters (Edge-DCs) (such as Network Function Virtualization Infrastructure Points of Presence (NFVI-PoPs), metro datacenters (DCs), or Central Offices Re-architected as Datacenters (CORDs), etc.). Second, virtualized controllers can be easily recovered from failures or disasters using the backed-up/replicated virtual copy of the controllers. These instances can be easily moved from one location to another and can be redeployed [6] without significant down time. Third, operational cost savings for network operators and leasing cost savings for network leasers are other important motivations toward virtualization.

Prior studies exploring static [7,8], and dynamic [9] controller placement problems mostly focused on packet-based SDN controllers and DC networks [10,11]. But, as we discuss in Sect. 2, methods proposed in SDN and DC scenarios are often not applicable and not optimal for heterogeneous optical transport networks.

To the best of our knowledge, our study is the first to propose dynamic placement of controllers for heterogeneous, multi-domain transport networks comprising heterogeneous ON and SDN controllers, considering the complexity due to virtual instances hosted jointly on DCs and Edge (e.g. NFVi-PoPs), and inter-domain and intra-domain latency constraints. In addition, we observe that [2,4] both fixed-grid and flex-grid technologies might be required to co-exist (i.e., mixed-grid) with seamless interoperability (see Fig. 1). In this context, our proposed method can support the deployment of different controller types, by enforcing 'controller-type constraint' (e.g., flex-grid controllers for flex-grid domains, fixed-grid controllers for fixed-grid domains, etc.). In addition, we explore the technical details of the dynamic controller placement problem (e.g., latency requirements, resource limitations at Edge-DCs, controller capacity limitations, etc.), propose the Virtualized Controller Deployment Algorithm (VCDA), and report illustrative results comparing with prior studies.

This study is organized as follows. Section 2 reviews prior work on controller placement problems. Section 3 discusses the control-plane architecture. Section 4 provides a formal problem statement and describes the proposed solution method. Section 5 discussed numerical results on cost savings and delay minimization. Section 6 concludes the study.

2   Background and Related Work

In the context of SDN controllers, both static [7,8], and dynamic [9] placement problems have been explored. But most studies on SDN Controller Placement

Problems (CPPs), e.g., [7–9], consider placement of only controller 'middle-boxes', not virtualized instances. Ref. [15] considers recovery of SDN controllers in a disaster scenario. These early studies do not consider the additional complexities due to virtualization, delay constraints, hosting location constraints, etc.

Recently, control-plane architectures [12, 16] in T-SDN paradigm are proposed to accommodate multiple heterogeneous network domains and associated domain-specific ON controllers. But, as recent studies [2, 16] suggests, there is still no consensus on the design of the T-SDN control plane. Ref. [5] was among the first to propose a virtualized control plane architecture for transport networks, but not from placement perspective.

Recent studies [10, 11] on Elastic Control Placement (ECP) for SDN controllers discuss threshold-based methods to dynamically resize the ECPs. Ref. [10] focuses on DC networks managed through homogeneous SDN controllers, minimizing control-plane resizing delay. Refs. [10, 11] consider DC placement (of controller instances), which is practical for a DC network scenario. But, for a transport network with distributed heterogeneous domains, we also consider joint deployment in DCs and Edge-DCs. This introduces new constraints such as host location capacity, and inter-domain and intra-domain communication delays (which [10, 11] do not consider).

3   Control Plane Architecture

Figure 1 shows an example of a hierarchical control plane for heterogeneous transport networks. Domain-specific controllers are connected with 'parent controller(s)', which are connected to the 'application plane' (e.g., Transport Network Orchestrator (TNO), Operations Support Systems (OSS), etc.).

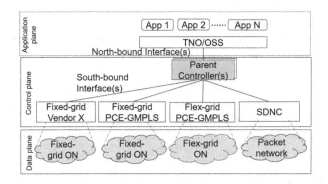

Fig. 1. Control-plane architecture for heterogeneous transport networks.

'Domain Controllers' are responsible for the communication between 'control plane' and 'data plane'. Different autonomous domains, depending on the underlying ONC/SDNC, use specific type of controllers and protocols to control the 'data plane' switches. Figure 1 shows three types of domains. This example architecture can be extended to support more variations of domain controllers and associated technologies.

4   Problem Statement and Solution Method

4.1   Problem Statement

The controller-placement problem is known to be NP-hard [1]. Traditional dynamic controller placement methods [9,10] focus on the 'switch-to-controller' mapping, ensuring that each switch (forwarding plane) is connected to at least one controller (control plane); incoming traffic flow requests originated inside a domain will be served by the same controller; and controller capacity limit is preserved. When a new traffic flow request arrives, the 'switch' depends on the controller for routing and path computation decisions.

The dynamic 'on-demand' controller deployment problem can be defined as follows: Given a topology, a set of controller hosting locations with limited capacity, arrival rate of traffic flows, a set of heterogeneous network domains, controller capacity, and constraints, deploy optimal number of controllers to satisfy all the domains, minimizing the leasing costs.

4.2   Input Parameters and Variables

- $G(V, E)$: Optical transport network topology where V is set of domains and E is set of links.
- M_v: set of controllers serving domain v.
- S_v: set of switches in domain v.
- T_v: domain-specific controller type.
- H_v: controller hosting location where $H_v \subseteq V$.
- χ_v^t: total compute capacity at v.
- χ_v^u: used compute capacity at v.
- ω_v^t: total memory capacity at v.
- ω_v^u: used compute capacity at v.
- T_v^μ: service capacity limit (i.e., maximum number of requests served per second) for controller type T_v.
- T_v^χ: compute resource requirement for controller-type T_v.
- T_v^ω: memory resource requirement for controller-type T_v.
- $\lambda(v)$: arrival rate of new traffic flows for a given domain (v), where r_v represents new arrival of flow routing request. S_r is the switch at which the request has arrived, and M_v gives the set of domain controllers the switch (S_r) is connected to.
- α: latency constraint (maximum allowed delay).
- C_T: variable containing total cost of running the controllers in all the domains (more details in Section IV.D).

4.3   Constraints

We consider the following constraints:

1. **Latency constraints**: Controllers must be placed within the allowed latency limit, i.e., switch-to-controller and controller-to-switch delay, including processing delay must not exceed the allowed delay limit:

$$D(s,h) + D_p + D(h,s) \leq \alpha; \forall s \epsilon S_v, \ \forall h \epsilon V \tag{1}$$

where function $D(x,y)$ represents transmission, propagation, and processing delay between points x and y, s is origin, h is controller hosting location, and D_p is processing delay at controller instances M_v.

2. **Controller type constraint**: To reflect heterogeneity, we enforce the following controller type constraints:

$$T_v == M_v^t; \ \forall v \epsilon V \tag{2}$$

where, the constraint enforces that all controller instances of v, (M_v^t) match the required controller type T_v.

3. **Controller capacity constraints**: Deployed controllers must have enough capacity to support domain switches:

$$\sum_{s \epsilon S_v} \lambda(s) \leq T_v^\mu * |M_v|; \ \forall v \epsilon V \tag{3}$$

4. **Controller host capacity limit**: Hosting location $(v.h)$ must have both compute and memory capacity:

$$\sum_{g \epsilon V} |M_g| * T_g^\chi \leq \chi_v^t; \ H_g == v; \forall v \epsilon V \tag{4}$$

$$\sum_{g \epsilon V} |M_g| * T_g^\omega \leq \omega_v^t; \ H_g == v; \forall v \epsilon V \tag{5}$$

4.4   Cost Models

Leasing Cost for Virtual Controller Instances. We consider that network operators lease capacity from DC operators. Virtual instance leasing cost C_C can be stated as:

$$C_C = \sum_{v \epsilon V} (|M_v| * \gamma * d) \tag{6}$$

where γ is per-unit compute per unit-time cost of leasing virtual instances and d is duration of operation.

Network Capacity Cost. Cost of network usage is often ignored in prior studies focusing on DC SDN scenarios. But the distributed nature of virtualized controller deployment for transport networks can add significant communication cost. First, switch-to-controller communication cost, C_N^S, is:

$$C_N^S = \left(\sum_{v \epsilon V} (B(S_v, M_v)) \right) * \pi \tag{7}$$

where B(x,y) gives bandwidth consumption between x and y, and π gives the per-GBps per unit-time bandwidth price.

Similarly, controller-to-controller (same domain) communication cost, C_N^M, is:

$$C_N^M = \sum_{v \in V} (B(M_v(i), M_v(j)); i \neq j)) * \pi \tag{8}$$

where $B(M_v(i), M_v(j)); i \neq j$ gives bandwidth consumption between controllers instances of the same domain.

Similarly, controller-to-controller (different domains) communication cost, C_N^P, is:

$$C_N^P = \sum_{p,q \in V} (B(M_p, M_p; p \neq q)) * \pi \tag{9}$$

In addition, controllers may require to be migrated from one hosting location to other. This live VM migration process adds to the network cost (C_N^V) as follows:

$$C_N^V = \sum_{v \in V} (B_{VM}(v)) * \pi \tag{10}$$

where $B_{VM}(.)$ is the bandwidth consumption due to migrations.

Hence, total network cost, C_N, is:

$$C_N = C_N^S + C_N^M + C_N^P + C_N^V \tag{11}$$

Delay Cost. We also consider the impact of controller delays on user experience (higher delay means unhappy user, leading to revenue penalty). This cost adds delay factor in decision making and encourages the algorithm to minimize delays. Similar to network cost, cost of switch-to-controller delay (C_U^S), controller-to-controller (same domain) communication delay (C_U^M), and controller-to-controller (different domains) delay (C_U^K) can be calculated by replacing B(x,y) with D(x,y) and π with σ in Eqs. (7), (8), and (9), respectively. Here, D(x,y) gives delay due to communication between sets x and y, and σ is cost (\$) associated to per unit-time delay. Also, our model considers cost due to processing delay at controllers, C_U^P.

Hence, total delay cost becomes:

$$C_U = C_U^S + C_U^M + C_U^K + C_U^P \tag{12}$$

Now, total cost is modeled as:

$$C_T = C_C + C_N + C_U \tag{13}$$

The objective of the proposed method is to minimize the cost of controller deployment:

$$Minimize(C_T) \tag{14}$$

4.5   Algorithm

We propose a polynomial-time heuristic, called Virtualized Controller Deployment Algorithm (VCDA), as a scalable solution for a heterogeneous optical transport network (see Algorithm 1). Since turning controllers on/off too often may make the network unstable, we introduce a decision epoch (e), a dynamic variable allowing network operators to tune the decision frequency. We also use two management entities: Network Management and Orchestration (NMO) and Distributed Cloud Management (DCM). NMO takes care of load balancing and assignment of switches and traffic with the controllers.

Algorithm 1. Virtualized Controller Deployment Algorithm (VCDA)

1: **Input:** $G(V, E), \lambda(v), \alpha, e$;
2: **for each** domain v **in** V **do**
3:   ▷ Calculate required number of controllers
4:        $c \leftarrow (count(r_v))/T_v^\mu$;
5:        **if** $|M_v| == c$ **then**
6:            Consolidate and load balance traffic flows among the M_vs using Eqns. (1-5);
7:   ▷ deploy more controllers
8:        **else if** $c > |M_v|$ **then**
9:            $h \leftarrow H_v$;
10:           $\delta \leftarrow c - M_v$;
11:   ▷ enough resources at h
12:           **if** $(\chi_h^t - \chi_h^u) > \delta * T_v^X$ & $(\omega_h^t - \omega_h^u) > \delta * T_v^\omega$ **then**
13:               Turn on additional δ controllers (T_v type) at location h;
14:               Load balance and re-route among the M_vs using Eqns. (1-5);
15:   ▷ not enough resources at h
16:           **else**
17:               $h' \leftarrow$ find optimum location to host c using Eqns. (1-5) and (6-14);
18:               Allocate c controllers (T_v type) at h' via **DCM**;
19:               Migrate all M_v instances to h' via **DCM**;
20:               Turn on δ additional controller instances via **DCM**;
21:               Load balance and re-route flows among the controller instances;
22:               Turn off M_v controllers at h via **DCM**;
23:           **end if**
24:   ▷ remove extra resources
25:        **else if** $c < |M_v|$ **then**
26:           $\delta \leftarrow c - M_v$;
27:           DCM finds optimum δ controllers to turn off;
28:           Reroute and load balance among the M_v using Eqns. (1-5);
29:           Turn off δ controllers;
30:        **end if**
31: **end for**
32: **if** e is expired **then**
33:     go to line 2;
34: **end if**

Our algorithm ensures that, for each domain, enough controllers are deployed to serve current load, observing the constraints. At a given load, if the controller capacity constraint holds, it means that we do not need additional controller instances (line 5). But, if the controller capacity constraint fails (line 9), the algorithm checks if the current hosting location (h) has enough compute and memory capacity to host the additional δ controllers (line 13). If yes, we turn on additional controllers and load balance the switches and traffic flows (line 14–17). If host location h does not have enough resources, the algorithm finds the next optimal location to host all the instances (line 20) following constraints as in Eqs. (1–5) and minimizing Eq. (14). In this step, we utilize the benefits of consolidation in computing. Placing controllers from the same domain closer to each other will reduce delay cost (Eq. (12)). We consider live VM migraion (line 24) to relocate the already-running controller instances to the new location with least interruption of services.

The algorithm turns off the extra controllers (line 32–37) to save operational cost. After each iteration, the algorithm waits for the epoch e to expire. The run-time complexity of VCDA depends on number of domains ($|V|$), maximum number of controllers ($max(|M_v|)$), maximum number of switches in a domain ($max(|S_v|)$), and number of host locations ($|H_v|$). The run-time complexity of VCDA can be expressed as $O(|V|*max(|M_v|)*max(|S_v|)+|V|*|H_v|*max(|M_v|)*max(|S_v|))$.

5   Illustrative Numerical Examples

We present illustrative results on a US-wide topology (see Fig. 2), with heterogeneous domains and Edge-DCs/DCs. Each network domain requires domain-specific controller(s), that are connected to other domains via backbone optical links. We consider two DC locations (2 and 13) and three Edge-DCs (6, 8, 10) to host controller instances. Capacities of DCs, racks, and servers vary significantly in practice. For Edge-DCs (6, 8, 10), we assume total compute capacity (χ_v^t) is 30 units and total memory capacity (ω_v^t) is 60 GB. For DCs, we consider 15000 compute and 30000 memory capacity (to represent virtually infinite capacity).

We observe that the size of the topology, number of domains, etc. have impact on the results from our study. Thus, we assume different domain scenarios using this topology: (a) for the results reported in Figs. 3 and 4, we assume that each of the nodes in topology is a domain. Hence, we have six individual fixed-grid domains (4, 5, 7, 9, 12), two packet-network domains (8 and 11), and six flex-grid domains (1, 2, 3, 10, 13, 14). and (b) Fig. 5 results consider larger six domains. Nodes 1, 2, and 3 create a flex-grid domain: 1-2-3. Similarly, the other domains are: 4-5-6-7 (fixed-grid), 8-11 (packet), 10-13-14 (flex-grid), 9 (fixed-grid), and 12 (fixed-grid).

Per census data, we have 47.6% of US population in Eastern time zone, 29.1% in Central, 6.7% in Mountain, and 16.6% in Pacific time zone. Our study uses this data to generate spatial variation of incoming load $\lambda(v)$. For example, full load ($\lambda = 1$) for the Eastern domains is 30,615 requests per seconds vs. 10,910

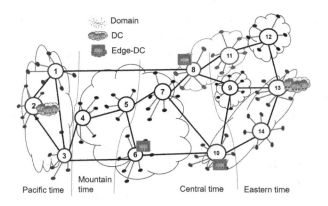

Fig. 2. Example optical network topology with controller host locations and heterogeneous domains (red denotes flex-grid, black denotes fixed-grid, and green denotes packet).

requests for Mountain domains. For illustrative examples, let $\alpha = 15$ ms, $T_v^\mu = 2500$ requests per second [9], per-controller instance compute requirement (T_v^χ) = 2 compute units [10], memory requirement $(T_v^\omega) = 4$ GB, $\gamma = \$0.01$ per unit per hour, $\sigma = \$0.0001$ per minute, and $\pi = \$70$ per GBps per month [14].

Figure 3 compares the normalized cost (Eq. (14)) among three different methods: (1) DC-Only method mimics controller placement methods which focus on dynamic placement of controllers inside DCs only; (2) Edge-Greedy method considering both DCs and Edge-DCs, but instead of consolidated VM placement considering delays, this method places VMs in a greedy way ignoring network cost (Eq. 7–11) and delay cost (Eq. 12) (similar to [9], evolved to host controllers at Edge); and (3) our proposed VCDA method considering consolidated VM placement, delay and capacity constraints (Eqs. (1–5)), and cost minimization (Eqs. (6–14)).

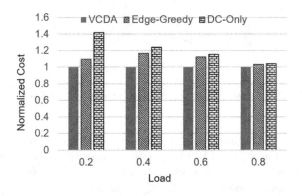

Fig. 3. Normalized cost versus load for topology scenario (a).

Figure 3 shows that our algorithm has lowest normalized cost among all three approaches. As expected, placing controllers only at DCs results in very high delays (see Fig. 4), causing higher delay cost. At lower load ($\lambda = 0.2$), Edge-Greedy placement saves cost compared to DC-Only (10% extra cost for Edge-Greedy vs. 41% extra cost for DC-Only), by placing the domain controllers closer to Edge. VCDA benefits more from Edge resources using consolidated placement and reducing inter-controller communication delays, resulting in cost saving. But, at higher load ($\lambda = 0.8$), VCDA saves less due to tighter capacity limits at Edge-DCs, as consolidated controllers need to move to DC locations, resulting in higher network and delay costs. Still, VCDA's cost savings is higher than the other two methods.

A major limitation of virtualized controller placement in transport networks is the additional delays. Edge-DCs helps to reduce those delays. But, as shown in Fig. 4, if the placement method is not aware of the delays (DC-Only) or takes a greedy placement approach (Edge-Greedy), the controllers will experience significant additional delays (resulting in higher delay cost). At lower load ($\lambda = 0.2$), DC-Only placement method places the controllers far from the domains, resulting in very high delays (60% extra delays). Even Edge-Greedy placement method (13.5% extra delays) reduces significant delays compared to DC-Only. But, as load increases ($\lambda = 0.6$), VCDA experiences higher delays as more controllers are now being placed at DCs (due to Edge-DC hosting capacity limit). Edge-Greedy also experience more delays at higher loads as, in addition to delays due to DC locations usage, more scattered controller instances lead to higher communication delays.

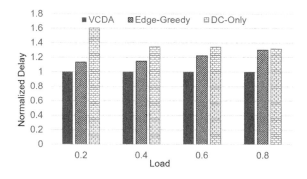

Fig. 4. Normalized delay versus load for topology scenario (a).

Figure 5 shows normalized cost for topology scenario (b) (only six domains, instead of 14). At lower load ($\lambda = 0.2$), cost savings is 30% compared to 'DC-Only'. VCDA looses some cost savings (compared to 41% for the same load in Fig. 3). This observation can be explained as follows. When node 10 was a separate domain, it's controllers were placed in the Edge-DC at 10. But, with the bigger domain 10-13-14, controllers for this domain are hosted in DC at

13, adding to the switch-to-controller network and delay cost. As load grows cost savings reduces and gets close to 'DC-Only' (0.358% cost savings at load $\lambda = 0.8$). This observation can be explained with the following example: for domain 4-5-6-7, initially at lower load, controllers were placed at Edge-DC at 6, but as load grew, requiring more resources for controllers, the controller instances were migrated to DC (reducing the cost gap).

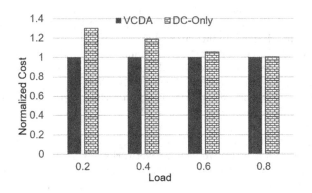

Fig. 5. Normalized cost versus load for topology scenario (b).

More Edge-DC and DC locations can significantly change the cost and delay. More Edge-DC locations will allow to save more cost and reduce delay even in higher loads ($\lambda = 0.8$). In our study, we consider two DC locations, in two corners of the topology, from these intuitions: (1) DC operators in USA tend to place DCs in more populated east coast and west coast regions; and (2) Placing DCs apart allows us to demonstrate the impact of Edge-DCs. But if we add more DCs or change the DC locations, that will impact the cost and delays as well.

6   Conclusion

Virtualized controller placement in multi-domain heterogeneous optical transport networks introduces new challenges for network management. Our proposed method for controller placement considers transport-network-specific properties and constraints such as heterogeneous optical controller types, resource limitations at edge-hosting locations, cost from additional delays, etc. Illustrative examples show that our proposed method saves cost and reduces delays significantly, compared to prior studies. Future studies should explore variation of compute/memory requirements, variation of Edge-DC capacities, variation of Edge-DC and DC locations, temporal variation of load, and more detailed cost models.

Acknowledgement. This work was supported by NSF Grant No. 1716945.

References

1. Wang, G., et al.: The controller placement problem in software defined networking: a survey. IEEE Netw. **31**(5), 21–7 (2017)
2. Alvizu, R., et al.: Comprehensive survey on T-SDN: Software-defined networking for transport networks. IEEE Commun. Surv. Tutorials **19**(4), 2232–2283 (2017)
3. Lopez, V., et al.: Control plane architectures for elastic optical networks. J. Opt. Commun. Netw. **10**(2), 241–249 (2018)
4. Ahmed, T., et al.: Dynamic routing and spectrum assignment in co-existing fixed/flex grid optical networks. In: Proceedings of IEEE Advanced Networks and Telecom Systems, Indore, India (2018)
5. Munoz, R., et al.: Integrated SDN/NFV management and orchestration architecture for dynamic deployment of virtual SDN control instances for virtual tenant networks. J. Opt. Commun. Netw. **7**(11), 60–70 (2017)
6. Rahman, S., et al.: Dynamic workload migration over optical backbone network to minimize data center electricity cost. IEEE Trans. Green Commun. Netw. **2**(2), 570–579 (2017)
7. Heller, B., et al.: The controller placement problem. In: Proceedings of 1st Workshop on Hot Topics in Software Defined Networks, pp. 7–12 (2012)
8. Yao, G., et al.: On the capacitated controller placement problem in software defined networks. IEEE Commun. Lett. **18**(8), 1339–1342 (2014)
9. Sallahi, A., et al.: Optimal model for the controller placement problem in software defined networks. IEEE Comms. Lett. **19**(1), 30–33 (2015)
10. Kim, W., et al.: T-DCORAL: a threshold-based dynamic controller resource allocation for elastic control plane in software-defined data center networks. IEEE Commun. Lett. **23**(2), 198–201 (2018)
11. Potluri , A., et al.: An efficient DHT-based elastic SDN controller. In: Proceedings of 9th International Conference on Communication Systems and Networks (COMSNETS), pp. 267–273 (2017)
12. Aguado, A., et al.: ABNO: A feasible SDN approach for multivendor IP and optical networks. IEEE/OSA J. Opt. Commun. Netw. **7**(2), A356–A362 (2015)
13. Rahman, S., et al.: Dynamic controller deployment for mixed-grid optical networks. In: Proceedings of Communications and Photonics Conference (ACP) (2018)
14. Rahman, S., et al.: Auto-scaling VNFs using machine learning to improve QoS and reduce cost. In: Proceedings of IEEE International Conference on Communications (May 2018)
15. Savas, S.S., et al.: Disaster-resilient control plane design and mapping in software-defined networks. In: Proceedings of 16th IEEE International Conference on High Performance Switching and Routing, pp. 1–6 (July 2015)
16. Lourenco, R.B., et al.: Robust hierarchical control plane for transport software-defined networks. Opt. Switching Netw. **30**, 10–22 (2018)

End-to-End Network Slicing in Support of Latency-Sensitive 5G Services

Rafael Montero$^{(\boxtimes)}$ ⓘ, Fernando Agraz ⓘ, Albert Pagès ⓘ, and Salvatore Spadaro ⓘ

Universitat Politècnica de Catalunya (UPC), Jordi Girona 1-3, 08034 Barcelona, Spain
`rafael.montero@tsc.upc.edu`

Abstract. Network slicing has been taking a major role in upcoming 5G network implementations. However, in order to provision and maintain end-to-end slices, the management and orchestration among different network segments is required. As a result, techniques and components have risen to fulfil these tasks. In this work, we present latency-aware slicing, which is enabled by the provisioning of network slices equipped with an end-to-end latency sensor. This sensor is added to the service chain, allowing for real time monitoring and eventually actuation upon latency requirements violations. Moreover, we introduce an architecture capable of handling the deployment of such sensors while also coordinating the provisioning of the slice across optically interconnected DCs. To experimentally demonstrate the deployment of a slice with latency sensing we set up a multi-segment testbed connecting client VMs. The presented results demonstrate the behavior of the latency sensor and how it enables latency optimization through path reconfiguration.

Keywords: 5G · Network Slicing · Slice Composition · Latency Sensor · Service Chaining · Optical networks

1 Introduction

The current trend towards enabling legacy network scenarios up to the 5G standards has become a challenge to network operators. Especially in the case where highly demanding service types such as enhanced mobile broadband (eMBB), ultra-reliable and low latency communications (URLLC), and massive machine-type communications (mMTC) arise with different requirements. Despite of this, the operators need to deploy these kinds of services over the same physical infrastructure, thus sharing the same network resources, but with the responsibility of maintaining a level of isolation between them, as well as guaranteeing a proper functionality according to their particular requirements.

In this regard, Network Slicing has come to help accommodate networks to this behavior. This technology entails that a physical network can be partitioned (i.e., sliced), to enable different services with different requirements to coexist using the same underlying network resources. A slice in turn, has to be able to allocate multiple services for a particular tenant. This way, a tenant is then able to deploy services/slices over an infrastructure that is shared with other tenants. To do this, a higher layer entity is

© IFIP International Federation for Information Processing 2020
Published by Springer Nature Switzerland AG 2020
A. Tzanakaki et al. (Eds.): ONDM 2019, LNCS 11616, pp. 51–61, 2020.
https://doi.org/10.1007/978-3-030-38085-4_5

required. Such entity takes charge of the slice management, as well as communicating the required configurations to each segment control entity to guarantee slice isolation. It is worth noting here that slice isolation can be either physical or virtual.

Another important aspect in 5G is the use of a virtualized approach for network function deployment, considering the introduction of Virtual Network Functions (VNFs). Such virtual functions are intended to provide specific functionalities according to service requirements. In this way, a service could be composed of multiple VNFs, which may be allocated in different physical segments of the infrastructure. Hence, some level of interconnection is required. The reachability between VNFs leads to the Service Chaining concept, which entails functions to be interconnected (i.e., chained) in a specific order to accomplish overall network service functionality.

Deploying a service composed by VNFs brings many other challenges. As noted before, such functions can be allocated in different network segments according to resource availability or functional requirements. Again, a high layer entity controlling slice provisioning is required to provide coordination between different segments and/or different technologies. To accomplish this, a new component (namely the NFV coordinator) is presented in this work to enable the communication between different network segments and components to provide multi-segment slices and their associated service chain.

Besides the deployment of a slice, it is also important to consider its maintenance over time according to specific client requirements. In this regard, latency appears as one of the most demanding requirements in the services defined in the 5G ecosystem. As a matter of fact, previous works have already considered it for slice provisioning [1]. However, real-time monitoring data becomes mandatory for any slice that has latency constraints. Gathering such monitoring data and further analyzing it, paves the way for management systems to react whenever latency levels reach non-desired points. The next step is to actuate according to the analyzed data. In this matter, it is possible to consider either acting reactively, preventively or predictively. In this work, we use a policy-based approach to perform preventive actions over the network (acting before service degradation), by putting emphasis on monitoring latency levels.

In light of the above, in this work we propose the use of a sensor (i.e., monitoring entity) in the form of a VNF to gather latency information from a running slice instance. The remainder of the paper is structured as follows, in Sect. 2 we present the architecture used, which evolves our previous work in [2]. Then, in Sect. 3, an in-depth analysis of the used latency sensing mechanism is given. Sect. 4 presents the experimental testbed that has been used for the functional validation, while Sect. 5 finally rounds up the main achievements of this work.

2 Provisioning and Maintenance of Network Slices in a Multi-segment Environment

As introduced in the previous section, a Network Slice (NS) may demand its provisioning over different segments of the underlying infrastructure. This entails that high level coordination of network components is required in order to fulfil slice deployment. Furthermore, slice maintenance is also a high priority, as it should be conformant with the demanding requirements established for 5G services. Therefore, both stages of the slice lifecycle must be handled by an architecture capable of providing such guarantees and functionality. In this paper we present an architecture for the deployment and maintenance of slices in a multi-segment scenario, considering as well a set of techniques and tools to achieve the discussed necessities.

The basics of the proposed architecture along with details regarding the behavior of each of its components are presented in the following subsection. Moreover, the newly implemented modules at the Management and Orchestration (MANO) and Software Defined Networking (SDN) control level are also introduced.

2.1 Architecture

Figure 1 depicts the overall architecture utilized in this work to enable multi-segment provisioning and maintenance of network services. As shown in the figure, the focus is on enabling optically interconnected Datacenter (DC) segments, in this case Multi-access Edge Computing (MEC) DC and Core DC, to allocate the required slice computational resources while considering as well their interconnection across the existent optical network segments (i.e., Metro/Access and Core). In terms of computational resources, a slice can be composed of several VNFs with different functionalities, which may also be chained in a specific order in spite of their physical location.

Accomplishing such performance requires involvement of different software components. At the lowest level, each network segment is exposed and configured though its own network control and management components (i.e., SDN Controller and/or Network Orchestrator). In the case of DC segments, which consider both computational and network resources, the controller allows configuring the DC network while the orchestrator is in charge of managing VNFs/Virtual Machines (VMs). On the other hand, optical network segments merely require network resources to be configured and exposed. In such case, only a SDN controller may be required. From a higher level point of view, the whole management of a compute plus network composed segment (e.g., DC) is seen as Virtual Infrastructure Management (VIM), while in the case of the optical network segments can be referred as Wide Area Network (WAN) Infrastructure Management (WIM).

Above the network segments, a MANO entity provides virtual network infrastructure as proposed by the ETSI in [3]. The Network Function Virtualization Orchestrator (NFVO) provides a set of blueprints for the NS and VNF creation. Hence, upon the request from an external client, the NFVO becomes in charge of orchestrating the whole lifecycle of the slice. The VIM Manager component in turn, allows registering each VIM so they become available for network slice deployment. Moreover, it is in charge of coordinating requests to each VIM coming from the NFVO. Additionally, the VNF Manager enables configuring VNFs at both slice provisioning and runtime stages.

To enable coordination between VIMs managed by the MANO entity and the WIMs in between, we introduce a new component named NFV Coordinator (NFV-C) which is responsible of handling slice requests coming directly from Operation Support Systems (OSS)/Business Support Systems (BSS) or the 5G Vertical. Furthermore, it is also in charge of providing guarantees to maintain NSs according to agreed Key Performance Indicators (KPI) and Service Level Agreements (SLA).

The Slice Manager (SM) at the NFV-C, uses the Slice Composition technique to trigger the deployment of the slice across VIMs and WIMs. A more in depth look at this technique is given in the next subsection. The Tunnel Manager (TM) and the Interface Manager (IM) in turn, are responsible for setting the interconnection between deployed VNFs. To accomplish this, an overlay tunnel is configured from source VIM to destination VIM where each VNF resides. The process starts by requesting the controllers at the edge VIMs to add interface and tunnel data to their databases, so this can be configured at the underlying Data Centre Network (DCN). The Inter-VIM Manager (IVM) module has been designed and added at the SDN Controller level to trigger these configurations upon the request from the NFV-C. Once the edge VIMs are configured, the controllers at the WIMs are also requested to set up required connectivity between VIMs. After setting up the tunnel, the VNFs are able to reach each other, completing the service chaining between them.

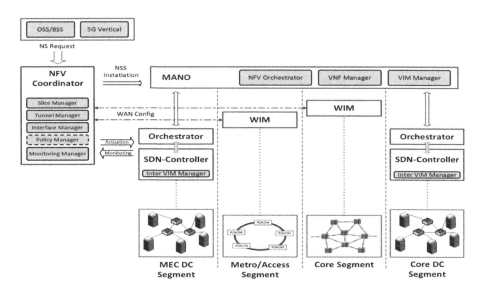

Fig. 1. Architecture for NS deployment and maintenance in optically interconnected DCs.

Regarding the maintenance of the slice, the Monitoring Manager (MM) gathers and processes data from the segments where the slice is deployed. Monitoring data can be retrieved at different levels, directly from the VNFs, from the SDN controller or from the network orchestrator. It is important to notice that monitoring of a particular slice should be focused only in parameters relevant to maintain the KPIs/SLAs agreed for the slice. By processing this information, the MM can act preventively in case service guarantees are compromised. The Policy Manager (PM) is the one responsible for executing the required configuration changes to maintain the proper slice functionality. These configurations are recognized as actuations and can also be executed over different levels, through the network orchestrator, at the SDN controller or directly at the data plane. A policy-based approach is used in this case, where the Policy Manager applies specific policies according to the received monitoring metrics.

2.2 Slice Composition

As introduced in the previous subsection, the SM uses a technique for provisioning NSs across multiple network segments. The method in particular, follows the Slice Composition concept (i.e., "slice-cum-slice") introduced by the 5G-PPP in [4]. It entails the construction of a slice from a set of individual slices. This means that a Network Slice Instance (NSI) can be instantiated by deploying a set of Network Slice Sub-Network Instances (NSSI) [5] and joining them together. Each NSSI represents configurations and resources deployed at one particular segment of the network. Following the architecture proposed in this work, upon the request for a NS, the SM decomposes it and asks the MANO entity for the required NSSI instantiation at specific VIMs according to resource and function availability. Moreover, it also contacts the TM and IM to trigger configuration at correspondent WIMs in between. After VNFs are instantiated and all configurations have been set across the segments, the NS becomes available for its utilization.

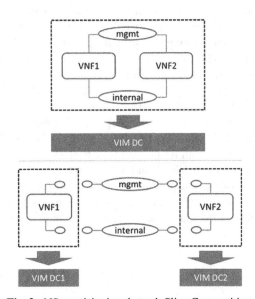

Fig. 2. NS provisioning through Slice Composition.

Figure 2 depicts an example of how a NS containing 2 VNFs, can be de-composed and instantiated in different DC segments, thereby using 2 NSSI to compose the original slice, when their provisioning requirement constrains demand them to be allocated in different segments. In this regard, enabling communication between VNFs needs to be considered, so a coordination entity in charge of this process is required. Using this approach, an end-to-end (E2E) NS can be deployed across different segments of the network by instantiating a set of NSSIs and configuring connectivity between them. That said, VNFs contained in this E2E NS are chained together in a specific order following the basis of service-chaining [6].

3   Latency Sensing and Actuations

Considering the demanding requirements given for 5G services, latency awareness becomes crucial for network slices operation and maintenance. Especially when agreed KPIs/SLAs include a maximum latency value for the proper service operation. This section covers the proposal made in this work to perform latency sensing inside a particular NS to enable real-time reconfiguration (i.e. actuation) when latency measurements reach an undesired level.

3.1   Sensing Mechanism

The mechanism presented for latency measurement is based on the presence of a latency sensor in the service chain associated to the provisioned end-to-end service. More specifically, this sensing entity, deployed as a VNF, analyses the TCP traffic passing through the service chain and estimates the latency based on the time delay computed between a TCP packet and the associated ACK. Figure 3 illustrates how the sensor VNF captures the packets exchanged by two end-points (VNFs as well in our case) and estimates the overall end-to-end latency introducing the minimum possible overhead. In this approach, Packet-LEFT arrival time (TPL) serves as a reference to calculate the round-trip time between the sensor and VNF2 (RTT-R). Therefore, after receiving and associating the ACK message for this particular packet, we use this PACKET-LEFT-ACK arrival time (TPLA) to the first part of the calculation. The operation will consider RTT-R = (TPLA – TPL). Similarly, we can also calculate the other way, the round-trip time connection between the sensor and VNF1 (RTT-L), by using RTT-L = (TPRA – TPR).

After having the results of both RTT-L and RTT-R, the next step will be to calculate the overall latency (L) between VNF1 and VNF2 with L = ((RTT-L + RTT-R)/2). The main responsibility of the sensor is taking samples of the traffic to perform these calculations during the slice lifetime and dumping the results to a local database so these become available via the management network to high layer clients (e.g., NFV Coordinator, Network Orchestrator).

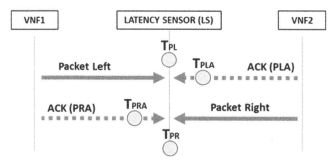

Fig. 3. Latency sensing mechanism.

3.2 Latency Sensor Provisioning

As introduced previously, the Latency Sensor (LS) considers having an entity deployed in the service chain associated to the slice. The approach entails that the LS VNF is provisioned during the NS provisioning stage. In this matter, the slice composition technique used in this work enables inserting the sensor in any of the de-composed NSSIs. As an example, if the NSSIs from Fig. 2 are considered, the LS can be deployed at the left NSSI as seen in Fig. 4.

The modified NSI will still consider the same VNF1 and VNF2 as originally, but in this case, the LS will be present as another VNF in between. The modified left NSSI will now contain VNF1 and LS connected via an internal network, besides their connection to the management network. Then, the LS will be the one to connect to VNF2 via the data network. In this sense, all work traffic flowing from VNF1 to VNF2 and back will pass through the LS, thus allowing it to capture samples of this traffic and execute its sensing mechanism.

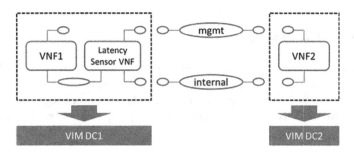

Fig. 4. Latency Sensor provisioning through Slice Composition.

3.3 Latency-Aware Path Selection Algorithm

In addition to the abovementioned LS, the introduced NFV-C is equipped with a latency-aware path selection algorithm to select the most appropriate end-to-end path across the involved segments to be compliant with latency requirements of deployed NS. More specifically, the TM executes such algorithm when it has to determine the route across the network segments interconnecting the DCs in which VNFs have been deployed.

In more details, the algorithm exploits the information gathered by multiple LSs. By extracting the measurements of the sensors deployed in each active NS, as well as the topological information exposed by network segment controllers, the algorithm correlates the route selection of previous deployed services with end-to-end measured latencies. Then, a graph representation of the multiple involved network segments and the estimated latency when crossing them following specific routes is constructed. With this, upon routing requests due to new service deployments or re-routing operations as consequence of actuations, the algorithm executes a simple shortest path mechanism, employing as weights of the constructed graph the estimated latencies, thus determining the sequence of segments and corresponding internal paths with the lowest latency.

3.4 Actuations Over Latency Monitoring

After deploying the sensor along with the slice, it starts collecting latency monitoring data from work traffic and saving it in its local database. The MM at the NFV-C then begins to gather this information straight from the LS through the management network and proceeds to analyze it. By processing such data and comparing it to the pre-established thresholds desired for latency levels, the MM can react preventively upon the possibility of violating agreed service guarantees.

The approach taken in this work considers policy-based configurations (i.e., actuations) to allow maintaining latency levels across a slice. In this matter, an information model [7] provided by the Simplified Use of Policy Abstractions (SUPA) working group initiative at the IETF allows representing different policies according to the case. Such policies are set following the ECA model (i.e., event-condition-action) to define the reason for triggering the policy (e.g. high latency), the threshold to be surpassed (e.g., greater than 1 ms) and the action to be executed (e.g., re-route slice traffic) to guarantee the maintenance of the slice according to agreed KPIs/SLAs.

4 Experimental Testing

In order to test the whole provisioning and runtime maintenance of a particular slice, an experimental multi-segment testbed (illustrated in Fig. 5) has been set up. Starting at the data plane, the testbed is composed of four emulated network segments: the MEC DC (left), the Metro/Access Network (middle), the Optical Core Network (middle) and

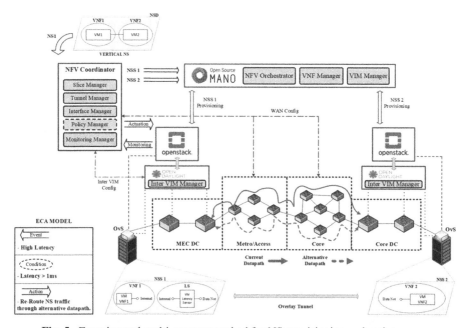

Fig. 5. Experimental multi-segment testbed for NS provisioning and maintenance.

the Core DC (right). Network resources at these particular segments are emulated using Mininet networking tool [8] to allow connecting computing resources from edge to edge. In the case of MEC and Core DCs, an Opendaylight (ODL) [9] SDN controller in its Carbon release provides control of both DC networks. Moreover, OpenStack [10] orchestrators at Queens release are also present at these segments to manage computing resources.

For our purposes, to allow for the configuration of optical resources at SDN controlled network segments, an extended version of ODL has been used, implementing extensions both at the southbound protocol and SDN applications levels [11]. The IM and TM components at the NFV-C in turn, upon request from the SM, configure the optical paths of the Metro/Access and Core networks, which provide the physical connectivity to the virtual IP tunnel that interconnects the service chain VNFs.

Above the segments control and orchestration, an instance of the Open Source MANO (OSM) [12] framework in its fourth release enables VIM registration and NSSI deployment over the OpenStack enabled segments. OSM has direct interface with the SM, which triggers NSSI requests to OSM at the slice provisioning stage. The NFV-C component (depicted in the upper left side of Fig. 5) contains the SM, IM, TM, PM and MM components previously discussed in Sect. 2.1. In practice, the interaction between these components and the open source frameworks deployed in the testbed may use different channels. In some cases, as the SM-OSM interaction, it runs through the OSM REST northbound interface (NBI). The IM-ODL connection on the other hand, uses ODL REST API and the remote procedure calls (RPC) defined at the IVM. Moreover, other interactions such as the one from TM-Mininet at the intermediate segments and the one from MM-VNFs are set through a series of scripts.

The slice provisioning stage begins upon the arrival of a network service request from the client (e.g., OSS/BSS, 5G Vertical), based on a Network Service Descriptor (NSD). In the realized tests, the NSD representing the virtual infrastructure is composed of two client VNFs (VNF1 and VNF2) and the latency sensor (LS) lying in between as part of the service chain. Then first, the SM decomposes the NSD into two NSSIs, as depicted in Fig. 2. The next step entails the request from SM to OSM for the deployment of NSSI-1 (VNF1 and LS) and NSSI-2 (VNF2) over OpenStack-LEFT and OpenStack-RIGHT VIMs respectively. While OSM contacts both VIMs for compute instantiation and IP network configuration, the TM configures the physical data path that connects the DC segments (i.e. the optical path crossing the Metro and Core segments) according to a simple path-selection routing algorithm, which considers latency as detailed in Sect. 3.3.

As soon as each DC VIM configures the local VNF network interface, it notifies the IM at the NFV-C, which triggers the cross-configuration of each interface at the other side DC VIM using RPCs defined by the IVM component. The main idea is that the Open Virtual Switch (OVS), which connects VNF1 and LS, is configured by ODL to flow traffic going to VNF2 through the established overlay tunnel over the Metro and Core network segments. This configuration is also set in the opposite way, allowing work traffic to flow over the data network, thus completing the VNF1-LS-VNF2 service chain. After triggering and executing slice configurations from SM, TM and IM via OSM, ODL and OpenStack, the NSI including all of its components becomes operative, thus concluding the provisioning stage. Figure 6 shows the OSM dashboard (a) with both NSSI-1 and NSSI-2 configured and running over the registered openstack-left and openstack-right VIMs. The OpenStack dashboard from the MEC DC (b) then shows configured VNF1 and LS, while the one from Core DC (c) shows VNF2. As seen in the figure, VNF1 connects to LS via an internal network, and then LS connects to VNF2 through an overlay IP tunnel configured over the data network. Finally, all VMs/VNFs also connect to the provider/management network for external access.

With the NSI up and running, the runtime stage, where MM and PM are the ones in charge of the slice maintenance, begins. In this case, the LS starts to capture samples of work traffic between VNF1-VNF2, computes the latency estimation, and dumps it to its local repository, which then accessed by the MM. After analyzing the data and upon the case of compromised latency levels, the MM contacts the PM to execute pre-established policy-based actuations following the ECA model. Actuations in this particular case, consider reaching the path-selection routing algorithm in order to re-route the physical data path associated to the virtual IP connection of the specific service. As said before, the path-selection algorithm uses overall latency information to compute a new data path fulfilling service latency requirements. Figure 5 illustrates the validation of the architecture. We saturate the current data path at the WAN segments by creating traffic congestion, in a way to surpass the permitted latency levels. In this way, the policies are activated and the overlay tunnel IP traffic is routed through an alternative data path. By means of this exercise it is possible to complete the flow for monitoring and policy-based actuations.

The results achieved using this testbed, prove the expected behavior for the whole architecture in both the provisioning and maintenance stages of the NSI. As for the future work, the NFV-C component still requires enhancement to accommodate its components to other functionalities. In this regard, the SM may also enable triggering NSSI deployment over different MANO entities according to the scenario. Furthermore, the MM and PM should be extended to provide slice maintenance according to other parameters, such as Bit Error Rate (BER), CPU usage, RAM usage, etc., as well as considering the implementation of cognitive-based predictive mechanisms. Finally, the TM to WIM interaction should also be furtherly enhanced.

Fig. 6. Open Source MANO (a) and OpenStack (b, c) dashboards with deployed NSI.

5 Conclusions

With the struggle to accommodate legacy network scenarios to the demanding requirements of modern networks and 5G services, there rises a need to have more up-to-date information regarding network operation. In this matter, we presented in this work a method to address latency sensing in multi-segment scenarios prepared for the deployment of network slices.

The architecture presented in this work allows coordinating VIM and WIM network segments for the provisioning and maintenance of network slices. A particular NFV-C component has also been introduced to work as the core part of this architecture, providing a common point for communication between the network client, the MANO entity and other network components/resources. Then, an experimental testbed has been used to demonstrate both the deployment of a NSI by means of the slice composition technique, while also considering its ongoing maintenance in terms of contracted latency levels. In this regard, experimental validation shows the correct NSI to NSSI-1 and NSSI-2 decomposition and instantiation over DC segments connected via an emulated WAN network. Moreover, it provides an example of latency monitoring and actuation, where upon the violation of a pre-established condition, a re-configuration of the routing path is triggered.

Acknowledgement. This work has been supported by the H2020 5GPPP SLICENET project (H2020-ICT-2016-2/761913) and the Spanish Government through project ALLIANCE-B (TEC2017-90034-C2-2-R) with FEDER contribution.

References

1. Moreno-Muro, F.J., et al.: Latency-aware optimization of service chain allocation with joint VNF instantiation and SDN metro network control. In: 2018 European Conference on Optical Communication (ECOC), Rome, Italy, pp. 1–3 (2018)
2. Montero, R., et al.: Supporting QoE/QoS-aware end-to-end network slicing in future 5G-enabled optical networks. In: PW 2019, San Francisco, United States, 2–7 February 2019 (2019)
3. ETSI GS NFV-MAN 001 V1.1.1, December 2014
4. 5G-PPP 5G Architecture White Paper, Version 2.0, December 2017
5. 3GPP TR 28.801. Study on management and orchestration of network slicing for next generation network, Version 15.1.0, January 2018
6. Herrera, G., Botero, J.F.: Resource allocation in NFV: a comprehensive survey. IEEE Trans. Netw. Serv. Manage. **13**(3), 518–532 (2016)
7. IETF draft-ietf-supa-generic-policy-info-model-03: Generic Policy Information Model for Simplified Use of Policy Abstractions (SUPA), May 30 2017
8. Mininet. https://mininet.org
9. OpenDaylight. https://www.opendaylight.org
10. OpenStack. https://www.openstack.org
11. Spadaro, S., et al.: Resource orchestration in SDN-based future optical data centres. In: 2016 International Conference on Optical Network Design and Modeling (ONDM), Cartagena, Spain, pp. 1–6 (2016)
12. Open Source MANO. https://osm.etsi.org

The Impact of the Optical Network on 5G – The Metro-Haul Project

Andrew Lord[1]($\boxtimes$), Albert Rafel[1], Michael Parker[2], and Adrian Farrel[3]

[1] Applied Research, British Telecommunications plc, Ipswich, UK
{andrew.lord,albert.2.rafel}@bt.com
[2] Lexden Technologies Ltd, Epsom, Surrey, UK
m.parker@lexdens.com
[3] Old Dog Consulting Ltd, Llangollen, UK
adrian@olddog.co.uk

Abstract. An overview of the current status of the EU Metro-Haul project and its impact on 5G End to End KPIs together with a summary of the use cases and demonstrations intended to illustrate the technology being developed.

Keywords: 5G · Optical networks · KPIs · SDN · Orchestration · Slicing

1 Introduction

Metro-Haul is an EU project in the 5G-PPP cluster that has been running since June 2017. It is focused on building the metro side of a future End-to-End (E2E) 5G network. The rationale behind the project is simple – we assume that an intelligent, dynamic and most importantly 5G-aware optical transport layer will assist far better in terms of performance and cost-effectiveness in the delivery and operation of 5G services, than a dumb and inevitably over-provisioned transport layer. Figure 1 [1], provides an overview of the Metro-Haul network architecture, showing how it acts as the intelligent interface between the 5G access (fixed & wireless) and photonic core of the overall telecommunications network.

In this paper, we focus on the major benefits that Metro-Haul technology brings to 5G, and we describe them in terms of so-called Golden Nuggets (GNs). Once these are highlighted, we go on to unpack Metro-Haul's contribution to the crucial 5G E2E Key Performance Indicators (KPIs) – indicators that are effectively our project's measure of the effectiveness of Metro-Haul technology. Note that this technology extends from the physical layer to control plane and monitoring layers – in other words, improving the underlying physical performance, introducing dynamic service level monitoring for individual slices and finally implementing a Software Defined Networking (SDN) based orchestration capability that can dynamically provision existing and new 5G slices on demand. The monitoring is handled by a key Monitoring and Data Analytics function developed within the project which is built into the overall SDN framework as well as capitalizing on recent AI developments for complex decision making/autonomous operation.

A. Tzanakaki et al. (Eds.): ONDM 2019, LNCS 11616, pp. 62–69, 2020.
https://doi.org/10.1007/978-3-030-38085-4_6

Finally, we look at the planned Metro-Haul demonstrations designed to illustrate our impact on the KPIs. Although Metro-Haul still has more than a year to run, with many of the demonstration-based results still to come, we already can see the very wide ranging and deep impact that the project will have on E2E 5G-sourced networks in the future.

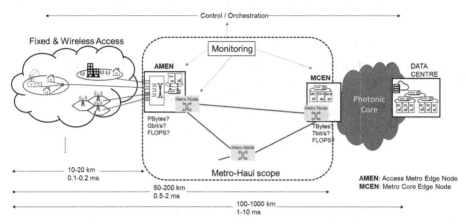

Fig. 1. Reference Metro-Haul network architecture

2 Metro-Haul Key Innovations (Golden Nuggets)

As an ambitious 5G research project, Metro-Haul distinguishes itself through a set of three key technical innovations. These have been referred to elsewhere as Golden Nuggets and can be understood to be the key "take home" messages offered by the project, representing its unique selling point (USP) amongst the other 5G projects being investigated around the world. These key technical innovations centre around the optical technologies that Metro-Haul is investigating to cater for the enhanced bandwidth and network operation requirements that the 5G use cases are expected to exploit. In addition, Metro-Haul is also investigating open, multi-layer disaggregation as a means to offer economies of scale, simplify network inventory, and offer enhanced network operational agility and flexibility. Finally, related to parallel developments in the artificial intelligence (AI) control of complex and adaptive systems, Metro-Haul is also testing technologies that offer real-time performance monitoring and analytics, and a network planning tool to assist in optimised investment and deployment of network resources. These key innovations are summarised as follows:

1. High capacity & flexible Metro optical network with edge computing

This provides for a dynamic data plane with an intelligent control plane involving multiple network segments and layers, spanning multiple geographical Data Centre (DC) locations, and addressing resource heterogeneity including, notably, the optical transport. Without these data and control plane architectures, network resources supporting future

5G services would require enormous over-provisioning of both optical transport capacity across metro and core networks, and edge Data-Centre resources such as compute and storage.

Aspects of this first Metro-Haul innovation are being demonstrated in Berlin (Germany) in a use case scenario consisting of real-time video surveillance and low-latency object tracking.

2. Open multi-layer disaggregated network

A systematic and unified approach based on model-driven development enables the SDN control of multilayer disaggregated and open transport networks, while allowing flexibility in deployment choices, extensibility for the integration of new technologies and agility in migration processes without vendor lock-in.

This particular aspect is being demonstrated in the city of Bristol (UK), featuring a crowd-sourced video broadcast use case scenario.

3. Real-time performance monitoring and analytics, and planning tool

A telemetry/monitoring framework that provides a global, real-time view of the E2E network performance. This new technology enables service configuration and reliable autonomous operation. It provides pro-active actions on early detection of issues. Machine-learning within the decision engine allows this new Metro-Haul technology to continually learn and improve as real network data is collected. It includes tools for state-of-the-art advanced planning, resource placement, and network re-optimization/re-configuration, enabling holistic optimization across heterogeneous resources.

Aspects of this third innovation are to be found in the Metro-Haul "portable" control plane demonstrator, where all software components from the project partners are integrated into a single platform.

3   Metro-Haul KPIs

5G is well recognised as a disruptive technology with wide impact on a broad set of vertical industries (automotive, health, media, public safety, energy, IoT, and Industry 4.0), social infrastructures (entertainment, education, leisure activities), as well as impacting on the more conventional telecom players (operators, manufacturers/vendors, and service providers etc.) associated with communications technology. Critical to ensuring the social, environmental, and techno-economic success of 5G (as indicated by an associated widespread take-up and seamless interoperability between different 5G technologies) are a successful suite of emerging 5G standardisations, as well as an objective means of benchmarking the developing 5G technologies. This latter aspect will be based on a set of Key Performance Indicators (KPIs) and Key Quality Indicators (KQIs) appropriate for both the physical (PHY) and service (i.e. QoS/QoE) levels.

Reaching a common understanding and consensus of the 5G KPIs is now a critical aspect of 5G research – especially with many groups and projects around the world working on competing or complementary visions. Initially, 5G was conceived as a radio access technology (RAT) providing an enhanced and upgraded technical solution to the earlier 3G and 4G mobile telephony and data technologies. However, as is always the case in technology evolution, convergence of disparate and independent technology areas also frequently provides an attractive opportunity to also improve end-user experience (e.g., via seamless and ubiquitous interconnectivity and new services) This convergence also achieves economies of scale on a unified platform (CapEx savings), improves overall efficiency of operation (OpEx savings), and enables new business models.

The Metro-Haul project is no exception to such a 5G trend – except that it is principally looking to understand 5G beyond the conventional RAT space, that is to say, to make the telecoms network that is closer to the core (i.e., the metro network) ready for the huge technical demands that new 5G services (i.e. eMBB, URLLC, mMTC use cases) will place on the overall network. Thus, Metro-Haul (as the name implies) is a metro-centric project.

Reflecting its metro-network emphasis, as well as its reliance on exploiting optical technologies to achieve the massive capacity increases with increased flexibility and efficiency of network operation, we have defined nine KPIs in the Metro-Haul project (Table 1) to assess the success of the Metro-Haul architecture to support vertical services enabled by 5G RAT technologies.

Table 1. Metro-Haul KPIs

KPI	Category	Target
1	Optical Point-to-Point connection set-up time	≤1 min
2	Metro-Haul E2E Point-to-Point connection set-up time	≤2 min
3	Set-up time of network service slice across Metro-Haul	≤1 h
4	Capacity of Metro-Haul controller	Control of 10–100 nodes (AMENs/MCENs, i.e., Open Disaggregated ROADMs)
5	Fault/degradation detection time	To be defined
6	Capacity of Metro-Haul infrastructure	100x more 5G capacity supported over the same optical fibre infrastructure
7	New optical components/systems	To be defined
8	CapEx reduction	To be defined
9	Energy consumption	To be defined

We now discuss the Metro-Haul KPIs in greater detail, describing how the KPIs are defined, their context and use case application, and how they are to be measured. It is worth noting that aspects of these KPIs (e.g. targets, or how to be measured) is still work on progress and hence have yet to be completely defined.

KPI#1. Optical Point-to-Point connection set-up time (control plane across optical transport layer)

This KPI is the configuration time in the Optical Layer to set up or reconfigure services handling 5G applications enabled by the SDN-based management framework. The new optical nodes use disaggregated solutions. This KPI is composed of the following elements:

– Control plane latency and optical node reconfiguration delay.
– Time required to instantiate a network connection through the optical layer.

This KPI will be measured using traces from the SDN controller, and time stamps and protocol analysers. The target is under one minute.

KPI#2. Metro-Haul E2E Point-to-Point connection set-up time
This KPI is the connection set-up time between two Virtual Network Function (VNF) elements as part of a service slice, using the SDN-based management framework. It includes Packet over an Optical Point-to-Point Connection.

This KPI is composed of the following elements:

– The VNFs, which are already available in the Virtual Machines (VMs)
– Control plane latency and device reconfiguration latency
– Time required to instantiate a network service
– Time required to create and install all required flow entries

The target time for this KPI is under two minutes.

KPI#3. Set-up time of network service slice across Metro-Haul
This KPI is the time to set up a network slice as a set of interconnected VNFs, and the target is under one hour.

KPI#4. Capacity of Metro-Haul Controller
This KPI is the maximum number of Netconf devices that a single SDN optical controller can support. The target is the control of 10–100 nodes (AMENs/MCENs, i.e., Open Disaggregated ROADMs).

KPI#5. Fault/degradation detection time
This KPI is the time between the instant a fault/degradation actually happens (e.g., some threshold is violated or an unexpected trend is confirmed) until it is detected. The target for this KPI is still to be defined.

KPI#6. Capacity of Metro-Haul infrastructure
This KPI is measured as the number of service instances that can be supported. This capacity combines the optical connections and AMEN capacities (throughput, storage, and computing). The specific services that are used to assess the capacity and the specific services configuration are still to be defined.

KPI#7. New Optical Components/Systems
This KPI relates to the new components being defined in the Metro-Haul and are still to be defined.

KPI#8. CapEx Reduction
This KPI relates to the relative cost reduction with respect to baseline network cost to support a predefined set of vertical services. The baseline network costs represent the costs of supporting the vertical services using current technologies and will be defined during the course of the project using techno-economic modelling comparisons.. The target is still to be defined.

KPI#9. Energy Consumption

This KPI is the reduction of energy consumption achieved using new node technologies (e.g., PIC, filterless technology) and the dynamic service infrastructure (set-up/tear-down of services) relative to the energy use made by technologies that make the Baseline Metro Network (based on current network technologies). The target for this KPI will be defined during the project.

4 Use Case Scenarios

Having defined the Metro-Haul KPIs and the key technical innovations being investigated within the project, we now describe some of the important 5G use cases and scenarios for which we expect these 5G innovations to be particularly of advantage. The use case scenarios also provide an opportunity to measure, calibrate, and verify the Metro-Haul performance in a realistic 5G networking context by examining the performance of the technologies against the project KPIs.

The Metro-Haul project is focusing on three demonstration testbeds. These will exercise the key use case scenarios and will provide valuable test and measurement information with respect to the emerging Metro-Haul 5G optical technologies and network architecture solutions.

1. Crowdsourced Video Broadcasts

The Crowdsource Video Broadcast demonstration testbed will be hosted at the University of Bristol. The setup demonstrates the ability to provision low-latency compute resources and connectivity at the AMEN locations.

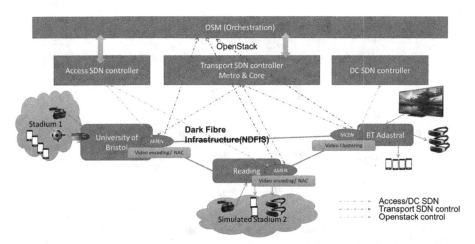

Fig. 2. Crowd-sourced video broadcast demonstration network

The overall architecture of the crowd sourced video broadcast demo is shown in Fig. 2. It consists of 2 AMEN as aggregators and 1 MCEN node for core network access. The nodes are placed in active node locations of the UK National Dark Fibre Infrastructure so that the demonstration can run over this network.

The Bristol-based AMEN node has connection to the stadium and will aggregate crowd-sourced video stream traffic to client connections to transponder client ports. The site will also host compute nodes needed for VNFs and software components. The Reading node will use an emulator to generate similar high bandwidth video streams of the order of multiple 100G. Multiple wavelengths from AMEN node will congregate at MCEN node which will connect to the crowdsource video app software hosted in a cloud. Both the BT Adastral and Bristol Labs have the capability to host MCEN and AMEN nodes, with BT Adastral site hosting the MCEN.

The use case follows the partial disaggregated optical network scenario. Here, the Optical Line System (OLS) is managed as a single black box supporting different mux/transponders. This OLS "black box" transport system, is open to support Optical Channels from external Terminal Points (TPs) as client signals, whose characteristics are specified by the Single Wavelength Interfaces (SWI). An OLS North Bound Interface (OLS-NBI) API is needed to configure and report events from the OLS. This OLS-NBI should be standard to help in the process of vertical integration with the Open WDM Transport Controller of the whole WDM system.

2. Real-time Low-Latency Object Tracking

The Real-time Low-Latency Object Tracking demonstration testbed will be hosted in Berlin. This demonstration will show the ability to provision low-latency compute resources and connectivity at the AMEN locations. Utilizing these resources, real-time object tracking is performed by automatic control of PTZ cameras based on analysis of video streams from fixed and mobile cameras as well as from thermal cameras.

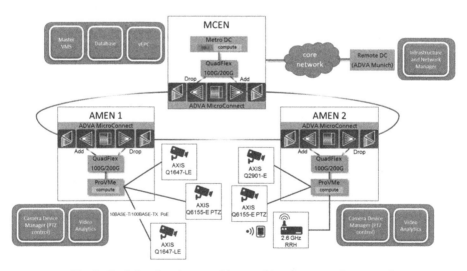

Fig. 3. Real-time low-latency object tracking demonstration network

The network constructed in support of this demonstration is shown in Fig. 3. It is a metro-ring with three semi-filterless nodes (one MCEN and two AMENs) based on coherent transponders, filterless add/drop paths and wavelength blockers in the express path of the nodes. At the edge of the network are compute units integrated with AMENs and with locally attached IP cameras and Remote Radio Heads (RRH). The RRH is driven by a BBU located in the MCEN's metro data centre, where the Core Node or EPC (Evolved Packet Core) is also located. Note that for practical reasons 4G technology will be used for this demo.

3. Remote Participation Demonstration

While the first two demonstrations require hardware to be physically located at the test sites, the remote participation demonstration is designed to facilitate inclusion of equipment that is not sited at the central demonstration site, and in particular is intended to allow testing of software components that can be hosted on computer equipment that is interconnected over the Internet.

This environment is known as the Metro-Haul "portable" control plane demonstrator, where all software components from the project partners are integrated into a single platform.

The SDN architecture of the demonstration is based on the concept of hierarchical orchestration, serving data connectivity to an OSM-based NVF-O. The parent controller acts as the single entry-point for systems to request network resources, with two Metro-Haul nodes interconnected via the optical networks, with NFVI at each node to support VNFs according to the placement constraints. In addition, monitoring and data analytics are demonstrated in a testbed in Barcelona with monitoring probes incorporated in a Madrid-based testbed.

5 Conclusions

The paper has presented a snap shot of the current state of development of the EU Metro-Haul project. This project has identified key benefits of designing and operating a fully orchestrated E2E solution for 5G, including the optical transport layer as well as compute and storage functions. These key benefits have associated KPIs which provide a mechanism to quantify the benefit. Finally the paper has presented some of the demonstrations designed to prove Metro-Haul technology. The remaining, crucial techno-economic aspect will develop models designed to calculate performance, CAPEX and OPEX benefits – and this will be the topic of further work.

Acknowledgment. The research leading to this paper has received funding from the European Commission for the H2020-ICT-2016-2 METRO-HAUL project (G.A. 761727). The authors would like to acknowledge the support of the partners of the Metro-Haul project.

More information about the Metro-Haul project can be found on the project's web site https:// metro-haul.eu/.

Reference

1. Metro-Haul deliverable D2.2: Functional Architecture Specifications and Functional Definition, October 2018. https://metro-haul.eu/deliverables/

Availability-Guaranteed Slice Provisioning in Wireless-Optical Broadband Access Networks Supporting Mobile Edge Computing

Ke Chen[1], Gangxiang Shen[1(✉)], Shuiping Jie[2], Boping Jiang[2], and Sanjay K. Bose[3]

[1] Soochow University, Suzhou, People's Republic of China
shengx@suda.edu.cn
[2] Zhongtian Broadband Technology, Rudong, People's Republic of China
[3] Indian Institute of Technology Guwahati, Guwahati, India

Abstract. A wireless-optical broadband access network (WOBAN) shows promise as potential 5G access infrastructure. Since network slicing allows efficient sharing of physical network resources, we consider the provisioning of availability-guaranteed slices in a WOBAN supporting mobile edge computing (MEC). A new definition for the availability of a slice is proposed accounting for a slice that functions only partially because of the failure of a fiber link, a microwave link, a base station (BS) node, and/or an optical line terminal (OLT). An integer linear programming (ILP) model and a simple but effective heuristic algorithm that balances the network traffic load and maximizes the slice availability are developed to maximally provision availability-guaranteed slices. Simulation results show the efficiency of the proposed approaches.

Keywords: WOBAN · MEC · Slice provisioning · Availability guarantee

1 Introduction

5G access networks carry various applications that require ultra-fast data transfer and flexible device support. WOBAN [1, 2] shows promise as potential 5G access infrastructure. To efficiently share physical resources in such a system, it would be desirable to implement network slicing [3, 4] to support diverse applications [5], with each slice flexibly running a specific application. Although there have been studies on how to efficiently provision slices in a 5G access network [6], how to guarantee the availability of each provisioned slice is still not well investigated. A guaranteed availability is critical for a service provider to meet its service level agreement (SLA) when provisioning slices to its users [7–9]. Therefore, it is vital to address this issue for slice provisioning in a WOBAN.

Our earlier work in [10] reported on a preliminary study maximizing the availability-weighted slice capacity for a sliceable WOBAN, in which, however, the availability of each provisioned slice is not guaranteed. From the SLA point of view, it is more practical to consider slice provisioning with a guaranteed availability for each slice. Therefore,

© IFIP International Federation for Information Processing 2020
Published by Springer Nature Switzerland AG 2020
A. Tzanakaki et al. (Eds.): ONDM 2019, LNCS 11616, pp. 70–81, 2020.
https://doi.org/10.1007/978-3-030-38085-4_7

this study focuses on the problem of provisioning availability-guaranteed slices in a sliceable WOBAN. To formulate the slice availability, four failure scenarios, including the failures of a fiber link, a microwave link, a BS node, and an OLT, are considered. A new definition of availability is made for a slice that functions only partially. To maximize the number of slices provisioned with guaranteed availability, we formulate the problem into an ILP model and develop a simple but effective heuristic algorithm. Simulation results show the efficiency of the proposed approaches.

2   Sliceable WOBAN Supporting MEC

Figure 1 shows a typical WOBAN example, which contains two passive optical networks (PONs) [11, 12] and one wireless mesh network (WMN) [13, 14]. Each PON is composed of an OLT and several ONU-BSs, each of which consists of an optical network unit (ONU) and a wireless BS. In the WMN, the ONU-BSs and BSs are connected via microwave links and each BS provides wireless access for local users. Unlike a conventional WOBAN, which merely provides communication capacity for users, here we also consider the computing/storage (C/S) capacity, measured in units of virtual machines (VMs), available at each BS node to support the MEC function [15–17] that is critical for the 5G access network [18].

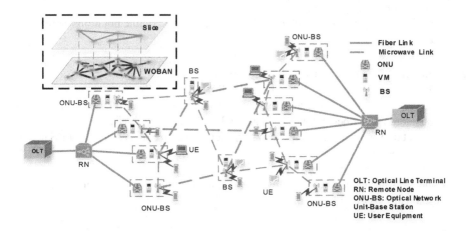

Fig. 1. Example of a sliceable WOBAN [10].

A sliceable WOBAN is a WOBAN that can be divided into multiple slices with each provisioning services for different applications. A slice is considered as an independent network consisting of multiple virtual nodes and virtual links. Figure 1 also shows the example of a slice, in which virtual nodes are connected via virtual links and are assigned with C/S capacities for supporting MEC. Each virtual node is embedded in a physical node and each virtual link is mapped onto a physical path traversing multiple physical links.

3   Maximizing Number of Slices Provisioned with Guaranteed Availability

Based on a sliceable WOBAN introduced in the previous section, our problem is to maximize the number of slices provisioned with guaranteed availability subject to limited communication and C/S capacities. For this, we first define a new availability measure for a WOBAN slice. This is followed by an ILP model and heuristic algorithms that maximize the number of slices provisioned.

3.1   Definition of Slice Availability

The availability of a system is generally defined as $A = MTTF/(MTTF + MTTR)$, where *MTTF* is the mean time to failure and *MTTR* is the mean time to repair of the system [7]. If a system consists of multiple (n) components and the failure of any component would cause the failure of the system, then its *MTTF* and *MTTR* can be derived as $MTTF = 1/\sum_{i=1}^{n} \lambda_i$ and $MTTR = \sum_{i=1}^{n} (\lambda_i \cdot MTTR_i)/\sum_{i=1}^{n} \lambda_i$, where λ_i and $MTTR_i$ are the respective mean failure rate and *MTTR* of the ith system component. Note that the above equation holds when the probability of a single component failure is much higher than that of a two-component simultaneous failure. This condition is true in most cases since in general $p_1 \gg p_1 \cdot p_2$ where p_i is the failure probability of a component and is typically very small.

To calculate the availability of a WOBAN slice, we first define notations as follows.
Sets:

P The set of OLTs each of which corresponds to a PON.
N The set of BS nodes which can be ONU-BSs or pure BSs.
L The set of fiber links. Each optical distributed network (ODN) of a PON is considered as a fiber link between an OLT and multiple ONUs.
M The set of microwave links in the WMN each of which connects a pair of BS nodes.
S The set of slices.
V^s The set of virtual links in slice s.
K_v^s The set of the candidate paths in the physical topology that are eligible to establishing virtual link v of slice s.

Parameters:

B_v^s The capacity required by virtual link v in slice s.
$\theta_{v,k}^{s,x}$ This takes the value of 1 if the kth path for establishing virtual link v in slice s passes BS node x; 0, otherwise.
$\sigma_{v,k}^{s,p}$ This takes the value of 1 if the kth: path for establishing virtual link v in slice s passes OLT p; 0, otherwise.
$\alpha_{v,k}^{s,l}$ This takes the value of 1 if the kth path for establishing virtual link v in slice s passes fiber link l; 0, otherwise.

$\mu_{v,k}^{s,m}$ This takes the value of 1 if the kth path for establishing virtual link v in slice s passes microwave link m; 0, otherwise.

$MTTF_{v,k}^s$ The *MTTF* of the kth path that can be used for establishing virtual link v in slice s.

$MTTR_{v,k}^s$ The *MTTR* of the kth path for establishing virtual link v in slice s.

Variables:

$\beta_{v,k}^s$ A binary variable that equals 1 if virtual link v in slice s is mapped onto (or established via) its kth eligible path; 0, otherwise

A_s The estimated availability of slice s

Based on the above notations, we can calculate $MTTF_{v,k}^s$ for each virtual link in a slice, which can be seen as a serial system consisting of multiple components, i.e., the physical links and nodes traversed by the virtual link. This is derived as

$$MTTF_{v,k}^s = \frac{1}{\sum_{i=1}^n \lambda_i}$$

$$= \frac{1}{\sum_{l \in L} \lambda_1 + \sum_{m \in M} \lambda_2 + \sum_{x \in N} \lambda_3 + \sum_{p \in P} \lambda_4} \quad \forall s \in S, v \in V^s, k \in K_v^s \tag{1}$$

where $\lambda_1 = \alpha_{v,k}^{s,l} \cdot \lambda_l \cdot d_l$, $\lambda_2 = \mu_{v,k}^{s,m} \cdot \lambda_m \cdot d_m$, $\lambda_3 = \theta_{v,k}^{s,x} \cdot \lambda_x$ and $\lambda_4 = \sigma_{v,k}^{s,p} \cdot \lambda_p$. Specifically, d_l and d_m are the physical distances of a fiber link and a microwave link in units of km, λ_l and λ_m are the failure rates (in FIT per km) of the fiber link and the microwave link, and λ_x and λ_p are the failure rates (in FIT) of a BS node and an OLT node. Here we assume that a pure BS and an ONU-BS have the same failure rate and require the same repair time. Similarly, we can calculate $MTTR_{v,k}^s$ for each slice virtual link by (2).

$$MTTR_{v,k}^s = \frac{\sum_{i=1}^n \lambda_i \cdot MTTR_i}{\sum_{i=1}^n \lambda_i}$$

$$= \frac{\varphi_1 + \varphi_2 + \varphi_3 + \varphi_4}{\sum_{l \in L} \lambda_1 + \sum_{m \in M} \lambda_2 + \sum_{x \in N} \lambda_3 + \sum_{p \in P} \lambda_4} \quad \forall s \in S, v \in V^s, k \in K_v^s \tag{2}$$

where $\varphi_1 = \sum_{l \in L} (\lambda_1 \cdot MTTR_l)$, $\varphi_2 = \sum_{m \in M} (\lambda_2 \cdot MTTR_m)$, $\varphi_3 = \sum_{x \in N} (\lambda_3 \cdot MTTR_x)$, and $\varphi_4 = \sum_{p \in P} (\lambda_4 \cdot MTTR_p)$. λ_1, λ_2, λ_3, and λ_4 have the same definitions as in (1), and $MTTR_l$, $MTTR_m$, $MTTR_x$, and $MTTR_p$ are the MTTRs of a fiber link, a microwave link, a BS node, and an OLT, respectively. Therefore, (2) calculates the average repair time of a virtual link.

It is important to note that in a network slice consisting of multiple virtual links, a single network failure would not cause all the virtual links to fail as a partial set of virtual links may still be functioning. This implies that when calculating the availability of a slice, we should not simply consider a *zero-one* situation, but consider the capacities of the virtual links that still functions when a network failure is being repaired. This led us to define a new availability, specifically for a partially functioning system, given as

$$A_s = \frac{C^s_{normal} + C^s_{partial}}{C^s_{total}} \quad \forall s \in S \tag{3}$$

Here C^s_{total} is the time-weighted total capacity provisioned by a slice, C^s_{normal} is the time-weighted total capacity provisioned by the slice during the period that the slice does not incur a failure, and $C^s_{partial}$ is the time-weighted total capacity provisioned by a partially functioning slice when a network failure is being repaired. The three terms are derived as follows.

$$C^s_{normal} = \sum_{v \in V^s, k \in K^s_v} \left(\beta^s_{v,k} \cdot MTTF^s_{v,k} \right) \cdot B^s_v \ \forall s \in S \tag{4}$$

$$C^s_{total} = \sum_{v \in V^s, k \in K^s_v} \left(\beta^s_{v,k} \cdot \left(MTTF^s_{v,k} + MTTR^s_{v,k} \right) \right) \cdot B^s_v \ \forall s \in S \tag{5}$$

In (4), $\beta^s_{v,k} \cdot MTTF^s_{v,k}$ is the $MTTF$ of virtual link v if its candidate path k is used for establishing the virtual link. Thus, (4) finds the total time-weighted capacity provisioned by the slice in the period that the slice does not incur a failure. In (5), $\beta^s_{v,k} \cdot \left(MTTF^s_{v,k} + MTTR^s_{v,k} \right)$ is the sum of the $MTTF$ and the $MTTR$ of virtual link v if its candidate path k is used for establishing the virtual link. Therefore, (5) finds the total time-weighted capacity provisioned by slice s.

To derive $C^s_{partial}$, we need to consider the different network failure scenarios, including the failures of a fiber link, a microwave link, a BS node, and an OLT. We first define the total time-weighted capacity provided by a partially functioning slice when one of the four network failure scenarios occurred and the failure is being repaired as follows.

$$B^{s,l}_{partial} = \sum_{v \in V^s, k \in K^s_v} \left(\beta^s_{v,k} \cdot MTTR_l \cdot B^s_v \cdot \left(1 - \alpha^{s,l}_{v,k} \right) \right) \forall s \in S, l \in L \tag{6}$$

$$B^{s,x}_{partial} = \sum_{v \in V^s, k \in K^s_v} \left(\beta^s_{v,k} \cdot MTTR_x \cdot B^s_v \cdot \left(1 - \theta^{s,x}_{v,k} \right) \right) \forall s \in S, x \in N \tag{7}$$

$$B^{s,p}_{partial} = \sum_{v \in V^s, k \in K^s_v} \left(\beta^s_{v,k} \cdot MTTR_p \cdot B^s_v \cdot \left(1 - \sigma^{s,p}_{v,k} \right) \right) \forall s \in S, p \in P \tag{8}$$

$$B^{s,m}_{partial} = \sum_{v \in V^s, k \in K^s_v} \left(\beta^s_{v,k} \cdot MTTR_m \cdot B^s_v \cdot \left(1 - \mu^{s,m}_{v,k} \right) \right) \forall s \in S, m \in M \tag{9}$$

Here $B^{s,l}_{partial}$ is the total remaining capacity of slice s weighted by the mean time to repair the failure of fiber link l that affects the slice. $B^{s,x}_{partial}$ is similar to $B^{s,l}_{partial}$ for the failure of a BS node, $B^{s,p}_{partial}$ is for the failure of an OLT, and $B^{s,m}_{partial}$ is for the failure of a microwave link. Then, we can derive $C^s_{partial}$ as

$$C^s_{partial} = \sum_{l \in L} \frac{\lambda_l \cdot d_l \cdot B^{s,l}_{partial}}{W} + \sum_{m \in M} \frac{\lambda_m \cdot d_m \cdot B^{s,m}_{partial}}{W}$$
$$+ \sum_{x \in N} \frac{\lambda_x \cdot B^{s,x}_{partial}}{W} + \sum_{p \in P} \frac{\lambda_p \cdot B^{s,p}_{partial}}{W} \quad \forall s \in S \tag{10}$$

where $W = \sum_{l \in L} (\lambda_l \cdot d_l) + \sum_{m \in M} (\lambda_m \cdot d_m) + \sum_{x \in N} \lambda_x + \sum_{p \in P} \lambda_p$ denotes the mean failure rate of a WOBAN.

Because (3) is nonlinear, we convert it to linear for subsequent ILP modeling. For this, we define a new variable $\varepsilon_{v,k}^s$ to replace the nonlinear term $\beta_{v,k}^s \cdot A_s$ and convert (3) to (11)–(15) as follows.

$$\sum_{v \in V^s, k \in K_v^s} \left(\varepsilon_{v,k}^s \cdot \left(MTTF_{v,k}^s + MTTR_{v,k}^s \right) \right) \cdot B_v^s = C_{normal}^s + C_{partial}^s \quad \forall s \in S$$
(11)

$$\varepsilon_{v,k}^s \le \beta_{v,k}^s \quad \forall s \in S, v \in V^s, k \in K_v^s$$
(12)

$$\varepsilon_{v,k}^s \le A_s \quad \forall s \in S, v \in V^s, k \in K_v^s$$
(13)

$$\varepsilon_{v,k}^s \ge A_s - \left(1 - \beta_{v,k}^s \right) \quad \forall s \in S, v \in V^s, k \in K_v^s$$
(14)

$$\varepsilon_{v,k}^s \ge 0 \quad \forall s \in S, v \in V^s, k \in K_v^s$$
(15)

3.2 ILP Model

We develop an ILP model to maximize the number of slices provisioned with guaranteed availability. In addition to the terms defined earlier, the additional sets, parameters, and variables of the ILP model are defined as follows.

Sets:

I^s The set of virtual nodes in slice s.

Parameters:

CS_i^s The C/S capacity required by virtual node i in slice s in units of VMs (for supporting MEC).

B_{max} The maximum transmission capacity of a PON (i.e. the maximum transmission capacity of its OLT).

T_m The maximum transmission capacity of microwave link m.

C_x The total C/S capacity deployed at physical node x.

$\gamma_{i,x}^s$ This takes the value of 1 if virtual node i in slice s is mapped onto physical node x which means that this slice has local users served by the current physical node; 0, otherwise.

Variables:

δ_s A binary variable that equals 1 if slice s is successfully provisioned; 0, otherwise.

The objective and the constraints of the model are as follows.
Objective: maximize $\sum_{s \in S} \delta_s$

Subject to:

$$\sum_{s\in S, v\in V^s, k\in K_v^s} \beta_{v,k}^s \cdot \sigma_{v,k}^{s,p} \cdot B_v^s \leq B_{max} \ \forall p \in P \tag{16}$$

$$\sum_{s\in S, v\in V^s, k\in K_v^s} \beta_{v,k}^s \cdot \mu_{v,k}^{s,m} \cdot B_v^s \leq T_m \ \forall m \in M \tag{17}$$

$$\sum_{k\in K_v^s} \beta_{v,k}^s = \delta_s \ \forall s \in S, v \in V^s \tag{18}$$

$$\sum_{s\in S} \left(\delta_s \cdot \sum_{i\in I^s} \gamma_{i,x}^s \cdot CS_i^s\right) \leq C_x \ \forall x \in N \tag{19}$$

$$A_s \geq 0.99999 \ \forall s \in S \tag{20}$$

The objective is to maximize the number of slices provisioned with guaranteed availability. In addition to (11)–(15), we also have constraints (16)–(20). Constraint (16) ensures that the sum capacity of all the slice virtual links that share a common PON should not exceed the maximum transmission capacity of the PON. Constraint (17) ensures that the sum capacity of all the slice virtual links that traverse a common microwave link should not exceed its maximum transmission capacity. Constraint (18) means that a slice is fully provisioned only if all of its virtual links are established. Constraint (19) ensures that the sum C/S capacity required by all the slice nodes should not exceed the C/S capacity at each physical node. Constraint (20) ensures the availability of each slice.

3.3 Heuristic Algorithms

We have developed two heuristics for the above slice provisioning problem which are expected to be computationally easier than the optimization described earlier. Specifically, we consider two types of link metrics when searching for a path for establishing a slice virtual link. The first metric is based on the length of each physical link, referred to as Heu_length. Note that the physical length of a link essentially corresponds to the unavailability of the link since they hold a linear relationship. The second metric considers the load of each physical link in addition to its unavailability, referred to as Heu_load. The steps of these two algorithms are the same except for the metrics adopted, which include the steps of virtual node mapping and virtual link mapping.

Specifically, in the Heu_load algorithm, the metric for the shortest path route searching is defined as follows.

$$c_l = u_l \cdot U_l \tag{21}$$

Here as shown in Fig. 2, u_l is the capacity utilization or load on link l, which is defined as the ratio of the capacity used to the total capacity of the link. U_l is the unavailability of link l, which jointly considers the availability of the source node of the link and the availability of the link itself and is defined as

$$U_l = 1 - A_s \cdot A_l \tag{22}$$

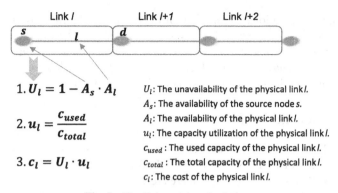

Fig. 2. The link metric calculation.

where, as shown in Fig. 2, A_s is the availability of the source node of the link and A_l is the availability of the link itself. For a path traversing k links, we have the following approximation when the unavailability of each link is very small.

$$U_p \approx U_1 + U_2 + \cdots + U_k \tag{23}$$

where U_k is the unavailability of the kth link, calculated by (22). Therefore, using (21) as a metric to search for the shortest route is essentially to minimize the unavailability of a found route, weighted by the traffic load on each of the traversed links. As such, the found route can simultaneously balance its traffic load and maximize its availability, thereby achieving efficient provisioning performance.

Based on the above route-searching metric, we next present the detail of the Heu_load algorithm.

Algorithm	Heu_Load
Step 1	For a slice request s, map its virtual nodes onto corresponding physical nodes, and judge whether the remaining C/S capacity of each mapped physical node is sufficient to satisfy the demand of the virtual node. If not, fail to provision the slice and stop; otherwise, move to the next step.
Step 2	For each virtual link in s, try to employ the shortest path algorithm to establish the virtual link along physical links with sufficient remaining capacity. The algorithm uses the metric in (21) as the cost of each physical link l for shortest path searching.
Step 3	Repeat Step 2 until either all the virtual links in slice s are established or any one of the virtual links cannot be established due to the lack of link capacity. For the former, move to the next step; for the latter, fail to provision the slice and stop.
Step 4	Compute the availability of slice s; if its availability is no less than 0.99999, the slice is provisioned successfully; otherwise, fail to provision the slice and stop.

The overall computational complexity of the proposed algorithm is at the level of $O\left(\|\boldsymbol{V}^s\| \cdot (\|\boldsymbol{N}\| + \|\boldsymbol{P}\|)^2\right)$, where $\| \cdot \|$ finds the size of the set. Although straightforward, the algorithm is efficient to *jointly consider both the capacity utilization and the unavailability of each physical link*, which can balance the traffic load of the system and maximize the availability of each provisioned slice simultaneously.

4 Simulations and Performance Analyses

We use Figs. 1 and 3 as our test networks for the following performance evaluation. Figure 1 consists of two PONs with 10 ONU-BSs, and 2 BSs function as relay to connect the two PONs, between which there are 22 microwave links. Figure 2 contains 66 ONU-BSs and 9 BSs, placed on a real geographic information system (GIS) map. These ONU-BSs and BSs are shown to be clustered into 5 PONs. Note that for the sake of clarity, we only draw representative links in Fig. 2.

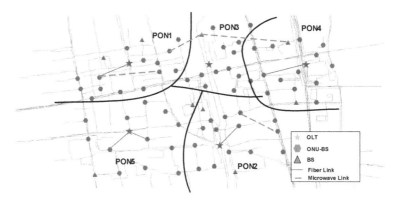

Fig. 3. Test network 2 in a GIS map [10].

The system parameters for the simulations are as follows. We set λ_l, λ_m, λ_x, and λ_p to be 200 FIT/km, 2000 FIT/km, 20 FIT, and 2 FIT, respectively. We also set the MTTRs of a fiber link, a microwave link, a BS node, and an OLT to be 6, 3, 2, and 1 h, respectively. For each slice, different numbers N of virtual nodes (ranging from 4 to half of the total number of physical nodes) and virtual links (ranging from N to $1.5 \times N$) are randomly generated, and each virtual link in a slice requests for a random bandwidth within the range of [50, 100] Mb/s. The maximum transmission capacity of each PON is assumed to be 10 Gb/s. The maximum transmission distance of a microwave link is 20 km, and its actual transmission capacity depends on its distance. Specifically, for a distance shorter than 10 km, the transmission capacity is assumed to be 3 Gb/s. For a distance (d) between 10–20 km, the transmission capacity is estimated as $3.6 - 0.06 \times d$ Gb/s. The number of microwave links established from/to each physical node is at the most 4. The C/S capacity at each physical node is limited to 100 VMs and each slice node needs 4 VMs. Based on these parameters, we ran simulations to show the following results.

Figure 4 shows the results of the small network. Specifically, Fig. 4(a) shows the number of availability-guaranteed slices provisioned. With an increasing number of slices requested, the maximum number of slices provisioned increases accordingly, but is eventually saturated when the number of slices requested exceeds a certain threshold. This is because of the limited communication and C/S resources in a physical system. Whenever the physical resources are exhausted, no more slices can be provisioned. In addition, the Heu_load algorithm can provision more slices than that of the Heu_length algorithm. The Heu_load algorithm performs closer to the ILP model. When the number of slices requested is small, they perform similarly and only when the number of slices requested becomes larger that they perform differently. This is because of the extra load-balancing effort by the Heu_load algorithm. The Heu_length algorithm uses the route that has the maximum availability to establish a virtual link, which however ignores the impact of unbalanced load in a network, leading to the blocking of many slices due to insufficient capacity. In contrast, the Heu_load algorithm can balance both the aspects, and therefore demonstrates more efficiency in availability-guaranteed slice provisioning.

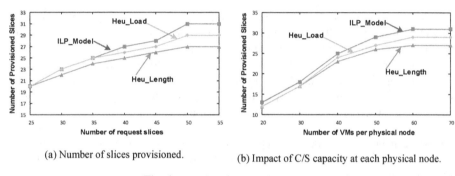

(a) Number of slices provisioned.   (b) Impact of C/S capacity at each physical node.

Fig. 4. Results of the small network.

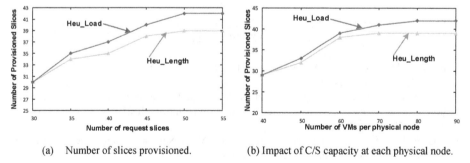

(a)   Number of slices provisioned.   (b) Impact of C/S capacity at each physical node.

Fig. 5. Results of the larger network.

Figure 4(b) shows how the C/S capacity at each physical node affects the number of slices provisioned when there are 50 slices to be provisioned in the small network. With an increasing C/S capacity at each physical node, the maximum number of slices provisioned increases, and reaches a saturation level when the C/S capacity exceeds a threshold. This is because, before the threshold, the availability of VMs is more critical in limiting the success of slice provisioning, whereas after the threshold, with sufficient VMs, the link capacity of the system starts to play a more critical role. Again, in Fig. 4(b), we observe that the Heu_load algorithm is efficient to perform closer to the ILP model and outperforms the Heu_length algorithm.

Similar results were obtained for the larger test network shown in Fig. 5. Here due to the computational intractability, we do not provide the result of the ILP model, but show the results of the two heuristic algorithms. We can see that the Heu_load algorithm is more efficient to outperform the Heu_length algorithm to provision more availability-guaranteed slices. This is again attributed to the load-balancing effort made by the Heu_load algorithm.

5 Conclusion

We maximize the number of availability-guaranteed slices provisioned in a sliceable WOBAN that supports MEC. By considering different failure scenarios, a new definition of availability is made for a slice that functions only partially. We formulate the slice provisioning problem using an ILP model, and also develop two heuristic algorithms based on different link cost metrics. Simulation studies show the efficiency of the proposed heuristic algorithm that jointly considers capacity utilization and unavailability of a physical link when provisioning availability-guaranteed slices.

Acknowledgement. This work was supported by National Natural Science Foundation of China (NSFC) (61671313) and the Project of Suzhou Key Laboratory of "Advanced Optical Communication Networks".

References

1. Shen, G., Tucker, R.S., Chae, C.: Fixed mobile convergence architectures for broadband access: integration of EPON and WiMAX. IEEE Commun. Mag. **45**(8), 44–50 (2007)
2. Chowdhury, P., Mukherjee, B., Sarkar, S., Kramer, G., Dixit, S.: Hybrid wireless-optical broadband access network (WONAN): prototype development and research challenges. IEEE Netw. **23**(3), 41–48 (2009)
3. Afolabi, I., Taleb, T., Samdanis, K., Ksentini, A., Flinck, H.: Network slicing and softwarization: a survey on principles, enabling technologies, and solutions. IEEE Commun. Surv. Tutor. **20**(3), 2429–2453 (2018)
4. Foukas, X., Patounas, G., Elmokashfi, A., Marina, M.K.: Network slicing in 5G: survey and challenges. IEEE Commun. Mag. **55**(5), 94–100 (2017)
5. Samdanis, K., Costa-Perez, X., Sciancalepore, V.: From network sharing to multi-tenancy: the 5G network slice broker. IEEE Commun. Mag. **54**(7), 32–39 (2016)
6. Gong, X., Guo, L., Shen, G., Tian, G.: Virtual network embedding for collaborative edge computing in optical-wireless networks. IEEE/OSA J. Lightwave Technol. **35**(18), 3980–3990 (2017)
7. Clouqueur, M., Grover, W.D.: Availability analysis of span restorable mesh networks. IEEE J. Sel. Areas Commun. **20**(4), 810–821 (2002)

8. Kiese, M., Georgieva, E., Schupke, D., Mukherjee, B., Eberspacher, J.: Availability evaluation of hybrid wireless optical broadband access networks. In: 2009 IEEE International Conference on Communications (ICC), Dresden, pp. 1–6 (2009)
9. Shao, X., Yeo, Y., Ngoh, L., Cheng, X., Rong, W., Zhou, L.: Availability-aware routing for large-scale hybrid wireless-optical broadband access network. In: 2010 Conference on Optical Fiber Communication (OFC/NFOEC), Collocated National Fiber Optic Engineers Conference, San Diego, CA, pp. 1–3 (2010)
10. Chen, K., Guo, C., Li, L., Bose, S.K., Shen, G.: Maximizing availability-weighted slice capacity for sliceable wireless-optical broadband access networks. In: 2018 Optical Fiber Communications Conference and Exposition (OFC), San Diego, CA, pp. 1–3 (2018)
11. McGarry, M.P., Reisslein, M., Maier, M.: WDM Ethernet passive optical networks. IEEE Commun. Mag. **44**(2), 15–22 (2006)
12. Kramer, G., Pesavento, G.: Ethernet passive optical network (EPON): building a next-generation optical access network. IEEE Commun. Mag. **40**(2), 66–73 (2002)
13. Akyildiz, I.F., Wang, X.: A survey on wireless mesh networks. IEEE Commun. Mag. **43**(9), S23–S30 (2005)
14. Chen, H., Li, L., Li, Y., Zhang, Y., Bose, S.K., Shen, G.: Hybrid fiber and microwave restoration for enhancing availability of fiber-wireless integrated networks. In: 2016 Asia Communications and Photonics Conference (ACP), Wuhan, China, pp. 1–3 (2016)
15. Zhang, K., et al.: Energy-efficient offloading for mobile edge computing in 5G heterogeneous networks. IEEE Access **4**, 5896–5907 (2016)
16. Abbas, N., Zhang, Y., Taherkordi, A., Skeie, T.: Mobile edge computing: a survey. IEEE Internet Things J. **5**(1), 450–465 (2017)
17. Mao, Y., You, C., Zhang, J., Huang, K., Letaief, K.: A survey on mobile edge computing: the communication perspective. IEEE Commun. Surv. Tutor. **19**(4), 2322–2358 (2017)
18. Rimal, B.P., Van, D.P., Maier, M.: Mobile edge computing empowered fiber-wireless access networks in the 5G era. IEEE Commun. Mag. **55**(2), 192–200 (2017)

DU/CU Placement for C-RAN over Optical Metro-Aggregation Networks

Hao Yu[1,2] , Francesco Musumeci[2], Jiawei Zhang[1], Yuming Xiao[1],
Massimo Tornatore[1], and Yuefeng Ji[2(✉)]

[1] Beijing University of Posts and Telecommunications, Beijing, China
{yuhao92,zjw,yumingxiao,jyf}@bupt.edu.cn
[2] Politecnico Di Milano, Milan, Italy
{francesco.musumeci,massimo.tornatore}@polimi.it

Abstract. To meet emerging mobile traffic requirements, Centralized
Radio Access Network (C-RAN) has been proposed to split the base station (BS) into two functional entities: the baseband units (BBU) and the
remote radio heads (RRH). In C-RAN, by centralizing BBUs into BBU
pools and leaving the RRHs in the cell sites, significant cost and energy
savings and improved radio coordination can be achieved. However, C-
RAN requires a costly high-capacity and low-latency access/aggregation
network to support fronthaul traffic (i.e., digitized baseband signal).
Hence, more recently, a new C-RAN architecture has been proposed (i.e.,
by 3GPP, IEEE 1914 WG), that defines three baseband function entities (or "splits"): central unit (CU), distributed unit (DU) and remote
unit (RU). These three entities are expected to be interconnected by two
external interfaces, called F1 and Fx. By transforming the RAN into a
3-layer (CU-DU-RU) architecture, more flexible deployment of the baseband functions can be achieved that better adapts to the heterogeneous
characteristics of incoming 5G service requirements. It is also expected
that, by properly placing CUs and DUs in the metro/aggregation network, higher benefits in terms of cost and power consumption can be
achieved with respect to the previous 2-layer (BBU-RRH) architecture.
In this paper, we investigate the optimal CU/DU placement problem in
a 3-layer RAN architecture and formalize it by integer linear programming. We evaluate the benefits of the 3-layer architecture compared to
the 2-layer architecture, showing that the consolidation degree of baseband processing depends heavily on fronthaul traffic latency, transport
network capacity and processing capacity.

Keywords: C-RAN · Functional splits · Fronthaul · Baseband
processing deployment · Wavelength division multiplexing · 5G

1 Introduction

Ever-increasing mobile-traffic demand requires operators to deploy more base
stations and to keep updating their radio access network (RAN). In the future,

© IFIP International Federation for Information Processing 2020
Published by Springer Nature Switzerland AG 2020
A. Tzanakaki et al. (Eds.): ONDM 2019, LNCS 11616, pp. 82–93, 2020.
https://doi.org/10.1007/978-3-030-38085-4_8

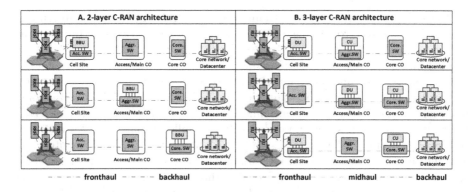

Fig. 1. Illustration of 2-layer and 3-layer C-RAN architecture

5G RAN is set to provide an even larger variety of services with widely varying requirements on bandwidth and latency. Therefore, future RAN design is expected to satisfy the very stringent constraints in terms of tolerable latency and required data rate [1], e.g., end-to-end latency requirements below 1 ms, more than $250\,\mathrm{Gb/s/km^2}$ in dense-urban areas and device density in the order of thousands per $\mathrm{km^2}$ [2]. Overall, a very large amount of baseband processing resources and network resources will be required to be deployed in the RAN.

In 4-th generation LTE networks, Distributed Radio Access Network (D-RAN) is the dominant RAN paradigm, where the Base Station (BS) comprises two modules: Remote Radio Head (RRH) for transmission and reception of radio signals, frequency up/down conversion and power amplification, and Baseband Unit (BBU) to perform digital processing of baseband signal. The BBU and RRH were traditionally co-located in the same housing facility, so the maintenance and investment costs of networks increase linearly with the number of BSs, which leads to a not scalable solution. An alternative RAN architecture, called Centralized Radio Access Network (C-RAN), has been proposed as a scalable solution in terms of both power and cost efficiency. In C-RAN, the BBUs are centralized into larger housing facilities, called BBU pools, which are connected with the RRHs through a high-capacity and low-latency "fronthaul" network [3]. Optical metro/aggregation networks based on wavelength division multiplexing (WDM) are considered as a promising candidate for transport network of RAN. Besides performing traffic aggregation and switching (SW), the central offices (COs) at different hierarchical stages of the metro network can be also equipped with processing resources to process baseband signal. The procedure of moving BBUs from cell sites to COs is called BBU hotelling, as shown in Fig. 1(left). From cell site to access/main CO, to core CO, the fewer COs need to be used as BBU hotels, and the more "consolidation" is achieved through BBU hotelling. As the motivations of BBU hotelling are to allow operators to save costly installation and maintenance of processing facilities inside COs, centralizing more BBU into COs in higher stages of networks can increase these benefits.

However, due to the high fronthaul cost of C-RAN [4], RAN architecture is further evolving towards decentralizing part of baseband processing functions at the network edge, in order to decrease the fronthaul bandwidth. BBU is now divided into two parts: Distributed Unit (DU) and Central Unit (CU). The DU contains some real-time baseband processing functions, i.e., Hybrid Automatic Repeat Request (HARQ) processing, radio coordination, while CU contains some non real-time baseband processing functions. Original RRH with part of PHY-layer functions comprises Remote Unit (RU). It follows that the RAN architecture evolves from a 2-layer (BBU-RRH) to 3-layer (CU-DU-RU) architecture. Through flexible distribution of CUs and DUs in the metro transport network, service requirements can be satisfied according to different DU/CU hotelling schemes. As shown in the right side of Fig. 1, the RU replaces the RRH at the cell sites, and DUs/CUs can be placed at any locations starting from the cell sites up to the COs at the different stages of the metro network. Compared with 2-layer RAN architecture, a new network segment is introduced, called midhaul, which connects DU and CU. In this paper, we re-consider the DU/CU placement problem in the 3-layer RAN architecture by minimizing the number of active COs for CU/DU hotelling. We also provide a mathematical model for this placement problem, and we apply this model over a limited, yet realistic network scenario. This model allows us to show the interplay between DU/CU placement and front/mid/back-haul, and to investigate the relation between the consolidation of baseband processing functions and the processing/bandwidth capacity constraints, as well as service latency. For the metro transport solutions, we consider OTN (more specifically, we assume a version of OTN optimized for mobile transport, called M3C-OTN, aiming at Mobile optimized, Multi-service and Metro Cloud OTN solution for the 5G scenario) and overlay, in line with the assumptions used in [8].

The remainder of this paper is organized as follows. Section 2 introduces the related works. Section 3 introduces functional split based 3-layer RAN architecture. Section 4 illustrates joint DU/CU placement problem in the metro networks. Section 5 shows the illustrative numerical results. Section 6 concludes the work.

2   Related Works

The problem of baseband functions placement and traffic routing has been investigated in recent years. In traditional C-RAN architecture, authors in [5] propose the energy-efficient virtual base station (vBS) formation problem, where they combine the virtual passive optical network (vPON) with vBS to form a virtual RAN (vRAN) and minimize the number of active digital units (DUs) in the DU pool and the number of wavelengths in the PON at the same time. In [6], a "BBU aggregation" problem is proposed to minimize the number of the active BBUs for energy saving. BBU aggregation is modeled as an evolved 2D bin-packing problem and two heuristics to solve this problem are proposed. Authors in [7] motivate energy-efficient BBU aggregation problem in an AWGR-based passive WDM network. They introduce the AWGR decomposition into the

BBU aggregation to help reduce the cost of the tunable transceivers and BBUs. The problem of BBU placement over a metro/aggregation network was first proposed in [8], where the relation between latency and the consolidation of BBUs is discussed under the OTN and overlay cases separately. In addition to BBU placement problem, BBU pool allocation and selection problem for C-RAN is also proposed in [9], the authors investigated how to deploy BBU pool among the optical network nodes and how to choose BBU pool to host the BBU of each traffic request with the objective of maximizing traffic acceptance ratio and minimizing network resource usage.

For baseband function placement in a functional spilt RAN architecture, Ref. [10] proposes a graph-based framework for flexible baseband function splitting and placement problem, and determines how to split the baseband function chain for each cell to maximize the utilization of processing resources under the constraint of latency and processing capacity using genetic algorithm. In [11], the authors propose a fully flexible functional split RAN architecture and define a new baseband entity, called flexible unit (FU). Based on this, they motivate a minimal number of active central office problem through the energy-efficient placement of FUs.

In summary, most existing works consider baseband function placement in the 2-layer RAN, while there are no works providing the analysis of the CU and DU placement problem in 3-layer C-RAN based on the 3GPP standard functional split options and the relation between the consolidation of CU/DU and constraints of latency, network capacity, as the one provided in this paper.

3 Functional Split Based 3-Layer C-RAN Architecture

According to 3GPP [12] and other standardization bodies, the 5G RAN architecture has been defined as a 3-layer architecture consisting of a CU, a DU, and a RU. Accordingly, the network between cell sites and mobile core is also divided into three segments: fronthaul, midhaul and backhaul. To address the strict bandwidth and latency requirements in 5G-RAN, 3GPP has proposed multiple functional spilt options, typically listed from option 1 to option 8, as shown in Fig. 2. In this paper we consider that the baseband processing entities (CU, DU and RU) are connected via two interfaces, F1 and Fx, as the split at Option 2 (interface F1) and Option 7 (interface Fx) have been selected by ITU [14] as the standard split options. According to [13], different baseband functions have various characteristics in terms of bandwidth requirement and processing complexity. The bandwidth, processing and latency requirement of CU, DU and RU can be summarized as follows.

Transport Bandwidth: In the cell level, the F1 interface scales and dynamically varies with the air interface traffic load, so midhaul bandwidth scales with traffic load as backhaul and requires only slightly more bandwidth than backhaul. The fronthaul bandwidth at Fx also varies with the air interface traffic load but requires higher rates (typically by up to an order of magnitude compared to backhaul). In the user level, the bandwidth requirement of a user is related to the resource blocks (RB) occupied by this user in the carrier spectrum.

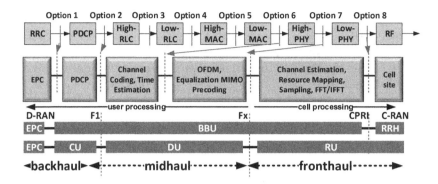

Fig. 2. Example of function split options

Processing Complexity: The processing complexity of baseband functions can be measured in Giga Operation Per Second (GOPS) [19]. The processing complexity of channel estimation, resource (de)mapping, FFT/IFFT is related to carrier bandwidth and number of antennas (called cell-processing functions), whereas the processing complexity of MAC/RLC/PDCP layer and the other functions in the PHY layer are related also to the traffic load besides carrier bandwidth and number of antennas (called user-processing functions). According to 3GPP [12], for option 2, RRC and PDCP are in the CU, while RLC, MAC, part of physical layer are in the DU. For the option 7 OFDM and MIMO precoding reside in the DU, FFT, resource mapping and RF resides in RU. So the processing complexities of DU and CU are all user load dependent. The details for the calculation of bandwidth requirement between CU, DU, RU and processing complexity of each entity used in this paper can be found in [13].

Transport Latency: Transport latency requirements for backhaul and midhaul links are determined by service latency requirements, i.e. around 10 ms for eMBB, about 1 ms for URLLC and ranging from 1 ms to several 10 ms for mMTC [16]. For the fronthaul links at Option 7, the latencies are determined by the requirements of the RAN technology. To satisfy the HARQ processing latency requirement, a total round-trip latency budget of $RTT_{BBU-RRH} = 3$ ms is available between a BBU and its corresponding RRH. It means that the NACK/ACK should be transported on the fronthaul link within hundreds of microseconds [15]. As we know the HARQ processing function is located in the low-MAC layer and MAC layer is in the DU, so latency requirement between DU and RU should be the same as HARQ processing latency requirement. According to [17], the reference values of the latency in different parts of networks are given as follows:

– Signal processing latency: The BBU completes the processing and send ACK/NACK usually within 2.75 ms. In the 3-layer architecture, no matter where the DU and CU are placed, the total processing can be seen as a fixed value.

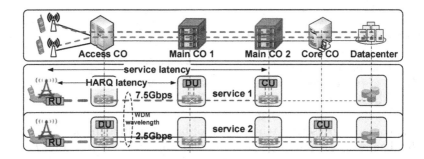

Fig. 3. Illustration of possible baseband function placement

- Signal propagation latency: For HARQ processing, propagation latency is related to the distance between RU and DU, and for the whole service, the propagation latency is related to the distance between the server and the RU (we ignore wireless transmission latency).
- Switching latency: We assume an active solution for the fronthaul, for OTN encapsulation, the latency is about 40 μs, for the non-OTN encapsulation, the latency is about few μsec.
- Encapsulation (like CPRI) processing latency: Before the CU or DU transmit or receive the data, the data must be encapsulated or de-encapsulated with CPRI protocol. This procedure will cost around 10 μs.

4   Joint DU/CU Placement in Metro Networks

4.1   Problem Statement

The DU/CU placement problem over metro/aggregation networks can be stated as follows. Given network topology, number of wavelengths per link and their line-rate capacity, set of traffic requests, maximum fronthaul latency (HARQ latency) and service latency, decide the placement of DUs and CUs in different COs that maximizes the consolidation of the baseband processing functions (i.e., minimizes the number of CO housing processing) under latency and capacity constraints.

The placement of CU/DU is not only restricted by the processing capacity and network capacity, but also subjected to the RAN latency and service latency constraints. Figure 3 shows an example of CU/DU placement with two service requests from different cell sites. For service 1, the DU and CU are placed in main COs for a higher consolidation, whereas for service 2, restricted by the bandwidth capacity, the DU of service 2 must be placed in the access CO. Next, we will show the mathematic model of the DU/CU placement problem.

4.2 Model

(1) **Given sets and parameters**
  V: set of COs
  S: set of service requests
  N: set of processing elements: RU, DU, CU, server
  C_p^i: processing capacity of COs i(GOPS)
  C_w: bandwidth of wavelength (Gbps)
  G_n: computing resource requirement of baseband function n
  B_n: bandwidth requirement between baseband function n and $n+1$
  $T^{i,j}$: transport latency between CO i and j
  T_{oe}: latency for switching and encapsulation
  T_{HARQ}: latency requirement for HARQ processing
  T_s: latency requirement for service request
  $K_{s,i}$: service s accessed into CO i
  Max: a large positive value

(2) **Decision Variables**
  $Y_i^{s,n}$: 1, if the function n of service s is located in CO i, otherwise 0
  $X_{s,n}^{i,j,w}$: 1, if the function n and $n+1$ of service s is located in the CO i,j separately using wavelength w
  D_i: 1, if the baseband processing functions (either CU or DU) are placed in CO i, otherwise 0
  $H_{s,r}$: 1, if the service s is processed in the CO r

(3) **Objective**
  Minimize the number of active COs:

$$\min\{\sum_{i \in V} D_i\} \tag{1}$$

(4) **Constraints**
  Routing:

$$Y_i^{s,n} = \begin{cases} K_{s,i}, & if\ n = 1 \\ 1, & if\ i = dest, n = N \end{cases} ,\forall s \in S, i \in V, N \in N \tag{2}$$

$$\sum_{n \in N, i \in V, w \in W} X_{s,n}^{i,k,w} - \sum_{n \in N, j \in V, w \in W} X_{s,n}^{k,j,w}$$
$$= \begin{cases} -1, if\ K_{s,k} = 1 \\ 1, if\ k = 1 \quad \forall s \in S, k \in V, l \in L \\ 0,\ otherwise \end{cases} \tag{3}$$

Baseband function placement:

$$Y_r^{s,k} \leqslant \sum_{j \in V, w \in W, k \leqslant l \leqslant N-1} X_{s,n}^{i,j,w} \cdot M^{r,j} \leqslant Y_i^{s,k},$$
$$\forall s \in S, k \in N, r \in V, K_{s,r} = 1 \tag{4}$$

$$2Y_r^{s,k} \leqslant \sum_{i \in V, w \in W, 0 \leqslant l \leqslant k-1} X_{s,l}^{i,r,w} \cdot M^{i,r}$$
$$+ \sum_{j \in V, w \in W, k \leqslant h \leqslant N-1} X_{s,h}^{r,j,w} \cdot M^{r,j} \leqslant Y_r^{s,k} + 1, \tag{5}$$
$$\forall s \in S, k \in N, r \in V, K_{s,r} \neq 1$$

$$D_i \leqslant \sum_{s \in S, n \in N} Y_i^{s,n} \leqslant Max \cdot D_i, \ \forall i \in V \tag{6}$$

$$\sum_{i \in V} Y_i^{s,n} = 1, \forall s \in S, n \in N \tag{7}$$

$$H_{s,r} \leqslant \sum_{n \in N} Y_r^{s,n} \leqslant Max \cdot H_{s,r}, \forall s \in S, r \in V \tag{8}$$

Capacity:

$$\sum_{s \in S, n \in N} G_n \cdot Y_i^{s,n} \leqslant C_p^i, \forall i \in V \tag{9}$$

$$\sum_{s \in S, n \in N} B_n \cdot X_{s,n}^{i,j,w} \leqslant C_w, \forall i, j \in V, i \neq j, w \in W \tag{10}$$

Latency:

$$\sum_{i,j \in V, w \in W} T^{i,j} \cdot X_{s,0}^{i,j,w} \leqslant T_{HARQ}, \forall s \in S \tag{11}$$

$$\sum_{i,j \in V, n \in N, w \in W} X_{s,n}^{i,j,w} \cdot T^{i,j} + \sum_{r \in V} H_{s,r} \cdot T_{oe} \leqslant T_s, \tag{12}$$
$$\forall s \in S$$

Additional bandwidth capacity constraint for overlay network:

$$\sum_{s \in S, n \in N} X_{s,n}^{i,j,w} \leqslant 1, \forall i, j \in V, w \in W \tag{13}$$

Equations (2), (3) enable the routing of requests over the lightpaths, the source/ destination of a request is given and the baseband functions are flexibly placed in the intermediate nodes. Equations (4) and (5) restricts the services starting from the source node of a request and the links between the intermediate nodes. Equation (6) indicate that if the CO i is active. Equation (7) ensures that one baseband processing entity must be located in only one CO. Equation (8) indicates that if the service is processed in the CO r. Equations (9 and 10) is the capacity constraints of processing and bandwidth. Equation (11) ensures that the placement of DU is restricted by the HARQ processing latency. Equation (12) is for the service latency. Equation (13) is the additional bandwidth constraint for the overlay solution.

Table 1. No. users of the considered geotypes

	Dense urban	Urban	Suburban
Total area of 32 sites $[km^2]$	8	22	160
Total number of users	2.4×10^4	2.2×10^4	8×10^4

5   Illustrative Numerical Results

5.1   Evaluation Settings

We consider a 15-node WDM metro/aggregation network topology as shown in Fig. 4, under three different geographical type areas (geotypes) - Dense urban, Urban, and Sub-urban - with 32 cell sites distributed in that area. The total area of cell sites for different geotypes and the total number of users in the corresponding area are shown in Table 1 [18]. For the cell site, we assume a radio configuration with 20 MHz, 2×2 MIMO antenna, 64QAM modulation scheme and full system load, and the reference value for processing complexity [19] of different baseband entities and bandwidth requirements [13] of different network segments for the mentioned radio configuration is shown in Table 2. We assume that the resource blocks of a cell are uniformly allocated to all users, that are normally distributed in the whole area, so the processing complexity and bandwidth requirement is equally divided by all the users associated with the same cell site. For the transport network, the COs in different stages are equipped with different levels of baseband processing and switching capacity. COs are organized in a ring topology and are connected via bidirectional monofiber links, carrying W wavelengths at 10 Gb/s. For the latency constraint, according to [17], maximum HARQ latency (RU-DU) is set to be 246 µs and maximum service latency is set to be 1000 µs. When below 246 µs, the HARQ latency requirement and service latency requirement are equal, and when above 246 µs, the HARQ latency is fixed at 246 µs. We define a performance metric R, called consolidation factor, which is used to evaluate multiplexing gain of function in our simulation. $R = N_{co}/N_{cs}$, N_{co} is the numbers of active COs and cell sites, N_{cs} is the number of cell sites. R=1 indicates no consolidation, that is all the baseband functions are located in the cell sites, whereas $1/N_{cs}$ indicates the highest consolidation degree.

Table 2. The value of processing complexity (GOPS) and bandwidth requirement (Gbps) with radio configuration of 20 MHz, 2×2 MIMO, 64QAM (Downlink)

Baseband entities	Value	Network segment	Value
RU	48.1	Fronthaul	0.97
DU	9.1	Midhaul	0.299
RU	18.7	Backhaul	0.299

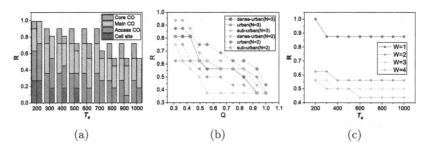

Fig. 4. (a) R value for increasing T_s, and different RAN architectures (2-layer vs 3-layer, Q = 75%); (b) R values for increasing Q under different geotypes (overlay case; latency = 800 μs); (c) R values for the increasing W (OTN case; Q = 50%)

5.2   Evaluation Results

Figure 4(a) shows the relationship between R and service latency requirement T_s, for the 2-layer and 3-layer RAN architecture (left and right bars, respectively), when considering overlay transport technology, urban geotype case and actual processing capacity set to be 75 % of maximum processing capacity. The value of R represented as the sum of four contributions, corresponding to consolidation degree in each stage of the network. With the increase of T_s, CUs and DUs can be consolidated in fewer COs to minimize the number of active COs, due to the fact that less stringent latency requirement allows the services to route along a longer path and end up in the COs of higher stages. For example, when the $T_s \geq$ 600 μs, there is no baseband function located in the cell sites (red color). We can also find that R value of 3-layer RAN architecture is less than the one of 2-layer RAN architecture, because flexible functional split divides the traditional BBU into multiple parts which can be deployed into COs more flexibly.

Figure 4(b) shows R as a function of $Q = \text{GOPS}_a/\text{GOPS}_m$ for the different geotypes and RAN architectures when considering $T_s = 800$ μs and overlay case. $\text{GOPS}_a/\text{GOPS}_m$ is the total actual processing capacity of all the COs divided by the maximum processing capacity in the networks. We can observe that higher consolidation is obtained when Q is increasing, especially for the suburban case. Because with the increasing processing capacity of COs, the DU and CU can be finally placed in the main or core COs when the latency requirement is relatively relaxed. For example, when Q goes near to 1, the value of R reaches the lowest level among almost all the scenarios. Note also that, due to the lower number of requests in the suburban area, the DUs/CUs are more easily deployed in the COs of higher stage. From this result, we can also find that 3-layer architecture benefits more in terms of consolidation that 2-layer architecture because of the flexibility in placement.

Figure 4(c) shows the relationship between R and network capacity in terms of number of wavelengths W. We can find that the relation between R and latency depends on the bandwidth constraint. When the number of wave-lengths is limited, no matter how loose the maximum latency requirement is, consolidation factor R will not decrease when it arrives at a critical point. This can be explained since when if enough wavelengths are provided, the provision of baseband functions can be more flexible; whereas if the bandwidth between different COs is limited, the location of baseband functions tends to be closer to the cell sites.

6   Conclusion

In this work, we have modeled an optimized DU/CU placement problem for C-RAN deployment over a WDM metro/aggregation network and formalized it into an ILP model. Compared to the original 2-layer RAN architecture, we proved that the 3-layer RAN architecture has higher consolidation of baseband functions thanks to the increased placement flexibility. We also observed that: (1) looser latency constraint leads to a high degree consolidation of baseband functions; (2) the processing capacity of COs also influences the consolidation of baseband functions; (3) adopting overlay transport solution can lead to a higher baseband function consolidation. In this work, the functional split options between RU, DU and CU are fixed. In the future, we will investigate the DU/CU placement problem when the functional split options is flexible, so the relation between flexible DU/CU placement and flexible functional split option needs to be jointly evaluated. Also, the heuristics for this problem will be proposed for the realistic scenario with larger network topology. Moreover, compared to the static DU/CU placement, dynamic DU/CU allocation problem according to real-time service requests from mobile users is worthy to be investigated.

Acknowledgment. This work was supported by the National Nature Science Foundation of China Projects (No. 61871051, 61771073), the Nature Science Foundation of Beijing project (No. 4192039), the fund of State Key Laboratory of Advanced Optical Communication Systems and Networks, China, No. 2019GZKF5, and China Scholarship Council Foundation.

References

1. Hossain, E., Hasan, M.: 5G cellular: key enabling technologies and research challenges. IEEE Instrum. Meas. Mag. **18**(3), 11–21 (2015)
2. 5G White Paper: Next generation Mobile Network (NGMN) Alliance. White paper, February 2015. https://www.ngmn.org
3. Pizzinat, A., Chanclou, P., Saliou, F., Diallo, T.: Things you should know about fronthaul. IEEE/OSA J. Light. Technol. **33**(5), 1077–1083 (2015)
4. Zhang, J., Xiao, Y., Song, D., Bai, L., Ji, Y.: Joint wavelength, antenna, and radio resource block allocation for massive MIMO enabled beamforming in a TWDM-PON based fronthaul. IEEE/OSA J. Light. Technol. https://doi.org/10.1109/JLT.2019.2894152
5. Wang, X., et al.: Energy-efficient virtual base station formation in optical-access-enabled cloud-RAN. IEEE J. Sel. Areas Commun. **34**(5), 1130–1139 (2016)

6. Zhang, J., Ji, Y., Xu, X., Li, H., Zhao, Y., Zhang, J.: Energy efficient baseband unit aggregation in cloud radio and optical access networks. IEEE/OSA J. Opt. Commun. Netw. **8**, 893–901 (2016)

7. Yu, H., Zhang, J., Ji, Y., Tornatore, M.: Energy-efficient dynamic lightpath adjustment in a decomposed AWGR-based passive WDM fronthaul. IEEE/OSA J. Opt. Commun. Netw. **10**(9), 749–759 (2018)

8. Musumeci, F., Bellanzon, C., Carapellese, N., Tornatore, M., Pattavina, A., Gosselin, S.: Optimal BBU placement for 5G C-RAN deployment over WDM aggregation networks. IEEE/OSA J. Lightwave Technol. **34**, 1963–1970 (2016)

9. Li, Y., et al.: Joint optimization of BBU pool allocation and selection for C-RAN networks. In: 2018 Optical Fiber Communications Conference and Exposition (OFC), San Diego, CA, pp. 1–3 (2018)

10. Liu, J., Zhou, S., Gong, J., Niu, Z., Xu, S.: Graph-based framework for flexible baseband function splitting and placement in C-RAN. In: 2015 IEEE International Conference on Communications (ICC), London, pp. 1958–1963 (2015)

11. Xiao, Y., Zhang, J., Ji, Y.: Energy efficient placement of baseband functions and mobile edge computing in 5G networks. In: Asia Communications and Photonics Conference (ACP), pp. 1–3, October 2018

12. 3GPP TR 38.801 V14.0.0 (2017–03): Radio access architecture and interfaces (Release 14)

13. Small Cell Forum: Functional splits and use cases for small cell virtualization, January 2016

14. G.sup.5GP: 5G Wireless Fronthaul Requirements in a PON Context, ITU-T (expected to be released by October 2018)

15. 3GPP TS-36.213 (Physical layer procedures) (2015). http://www.3gpp.org

16. Nokia: White Paper "5G new radio network". Document code SR1803023634EN, April

17. Netmanias: Fronthaul Size: Calculation of maximum distance between RRH (at cell site) and BBU (at CO). Tech-Blog

18. Deliverable 3.3: Analysis of Transport Network Architectures for Structural Convergence: COnvergence of fixed and Mobile BrOadband access/aggregation networks- COMBO Project, Technical report, July 2015. https://www.ict-combo.eu

19. Debaillie, B., Desset, C., Louagie, F.: A flexible and future-proof power model for cellular base stations. In: 2015 IEEE 81st Vehicular Technology Conference (VTC Spring), Glasgow, pp. 1–7 (2015)

Adaptive Function Chaining for Efficient Design of 5G Xhaul

Bahare M. Khorsandi[1(✉)], Didier Colle[2], Wouter Tavernier[2], and Carla Raffaelli[1]

[1] DEI, University of Bologna, Bologna, Italy
bahare.masood@unibo.it
[2] IMEC, Ghent University, Ghent, Belgium

Abstract. Next generation fronthaul interface has been recently proposed to support different functional splits in 5G access networks. Each split option is characterized by different requirements in terms of latency and bandwidth. The mapping of different functional splits on the nodes of 5G access network introduces several degrees of freedom in relation to the variation of the traffic during the day. This paper proposes a novel function location algorithm, which adopts dynamic function chaining in relation to the evolution of the traffic estimate. The obtained results show remarkable improvement in terms of bandwidth saving and multiplexing gain with respect to conventional C-RAN fronthaul and suggest design criteria for the emerging 5G access network.

Keywords: 5G · Xhaul · NGFI · C-RAN · Function chain · Location algorithm · Multiplexing gain

1 Introduction

Today's networks continue to face rapidly growing traffic demands while supporting an increasingly wide range of services and applications. Future 5G is expected to provide end users with unbeatable user experience in terms of data rate, ultra-low latency, and unlimited access. In addition to enhanced Mobile Broadband (eMBB) service, 5G will exceed 4G systems with better support of two other kinds of applications: ultra Reliable Low Latency Communications (uRLLC) and massive Machine Type Communication (mMTC). These types of applications highly rely on optical networks. 4G radio access network with baseband processing at every access points may not scale well for the high capacity and a large number of demands which are expected in 5G networks [1].

Cloud/Centralized Radio Access Networks (C-RAN) have been proposed as a scalable solution by separating the radio components, namely Remote Radio Unit (RRU) from the BaseBand Unit (BBU), in order to gain the efficiency and flexibility of centralization and cloud computing for radio networks. C-RAN has demonstrated its advantages on network deployment speed-up, cost saving

A. Tzanakaki et al. (Eds.): ONDM 2019, LNCS 11616, pp. 94–107, 2020.
https://doi.org/10.1007/978-3-030-38085-4_9

and power efficiency. Introduction of shared processing resources and commodity hardware used in the C-RAN architecture provide various benefits, such as low energy consumption, statistical multiplexing gain, and Coordinated Multi-Point (CoMP) transmission/reception.

In the 5G era, C-RAN is evolving by itself with additional features such as Software-Defined Networks (SDN), Network Function Virtualization (NFV) and new fronthaul solutions. In particular, NFV coupled with SDN control and management capabilities add extreme flexibility in service configuration and allow full exploitation of new methodologies that make service provisioning to shift from static hardware to dynamically reconfigurable virtual machines [2].

Despite C-RAN appealing design aspects, one key obstacle in its adoption is the excessive capacity requirements on the fronthaul links to provide BBU and RRU connections. Shifting all baseband processing to the remote BBU hotel implies the adoption of a high number of optical channels with strict latency constraints. To relax the excessive fronthaul requirements, the concept of C-RAN is being revisited, and more flexible distribution of baseband functionalities between the RRU and BBU hotel is considered. Rather than offloading all baseband processing to a single entity like the BBU hotel, it is possible to divide it into several blocks throughout the network which leads to significant reduction of the bandwidth needed on the transport links [3]. This concept is known as "functional split" and was firstly introduced in the new architecture design for the 5G access network named "xhaul" or "crosshaul" [4]. Next Generation Fronthaul Interface (NGFI) is defined as the fronthaul interface between BBU and RRU for the next generation of radio network infrastructure. NGFI redefines the baseband processing split through the positioning of baseband processing stack components between BBU and RRU. The basic idea of NGFI is to design a fronthaul interface with traffic-dependent and antenna-independent data rate. Traffic-dependent feature means that the data rate is dynamically changing with the real network traffic, i.e., as the traffic increases, the fronthaul data rate increases too and vice versa. In this way, the fronthaul transport capacity can be efficiently shared by actual traffic. The antenna-independent feature decouples the number of antennas and dedicated interfaces from the actual fronthaul traffic, by applying statistical multiplexing. In other words, the impact of the number of antennas is reduced and multiple antenna systems can be efficiently supported by fronthaul transport networks. Design methodologies to apply functional split in the 5G network in order to exploit this potential still need investigation. In particular, the bandwidth available on the fronthaul links should be efficiently used and dynamically allocated to service slices [5].

In this work, a methodology is proposed to implement an adaptive function chain, based on the dynamic 24-hour behavior of the antennas connected to a 5G access area. The aim is to achieve efficiently use of the bandwidth of the involved fronthaul segments. The effectiveness of the approach is shown in comparison with conventional C-RAN by evaluating the bandwidth multiplexing gain and taking into account the effect of different constraints, namely distance and processing units.

The paper is organized as follows. In Sect. 2 previous and related works are introduced. Section 3 describes the architecture and the methodology used in this work. The numerical results are reported in Sect. 4 and finally Sect. 5 draws the conclusions.

2   Related Work

One of the motivations of xhaul network is its ability to split different functions and executes them in separate entities. Functional splits determine the number of functions which stay locally and the number of baseband functions which are centralized in the relatively well-connected locations in the network. There is a vast number of works already done in the literature which study different functional splits.

The concept of NGFI (xhaul) was proposed for the first time in 2014 to meet the ambitious targets of 5G demands [4]. They specifically introduced a two-level NGFI architecture and defined in details the effect of different functional splits in their proposal. Main reasons to introduce NGFI for 5G deployment are the greatly reduced data rate, the independence of the number of antennas, the possibility to apply statistical multiplexing on fronthaul links. In [6], the authors proposed a dynamic PHY split strategy as well as using the edge data centers in order to distribute processing throughout the network so, as a result, optical transport requirements are reduced about 45 %. The heuristic algorithm considers only the split for PHY level and drops requests not finding a suitable connection to the data center. In a similar line of research, authors of [7] designed an adaptive strategy for placement of processing units in WDM-based aggregation network in case of dynamic traffic. Their results show striking a balance between processing unit consolidation and traffic blocking probability. Eliminating the blocking probability in such a system with sensitive requirements is one of our main goals in this paper.

The concept of "soft failure" has been investigated in [8]. The authors consider a soft failure as the degradation resulting in bit error rate over acceptable thresholds. In their performance evaluations, they investigated only two options, conventional C-RAN and split in PHY layer (options 8 and 7a respectively according to 3GPP terminology [9]). They run the system by option 7a and in case of distortion, the splits automatically scale up to option 8. Their proposal supported by the experimental evaluation clearly shows the ability of fast recovery of optical layer even when rerouting is not possible.

Transition from C-RAN to the new proposed architecture is a major issue which has to be addressed carefully. In [10] the authors proposed a framework for current C-RAN that can support both a flexible functional split and fronthaul transport protocol over Ethernet. Their results are obtained by OpenAirInterface (OAI), a software implementation of LTE/LTE-A systems, under two functional splits and different deployment scenarios.

The authors of [11] proposed similar architecture under the name "Flexible RAN" in which baseband processing distributed within the access network.

They investigated the trade-off between radio performance maximization and transport capacity minimization. They introduced two methods of distributions (fully and partially) and applied them on a ring and tree-like topology. Based on their results the full distribution of processing units can achieve better performance in terms of utilization of transport resources.

3   Architecture and Methodology

The methodology presented here is referred to the 5G network architecture as defined by 3GPP [9]. This architecture consists of two parts: radio access network and core network. The radio access network is expected to be based on concepts like xhaul which differs from current implementation in many ways. First, it extends between the user and the base station, which is called "gNodeB" (gNB). The gNB consists of three logical entities: Central Unit (CU), Distributed Unit (DU) and Remote Unit (RU). One gNB could contain one CU and multiple DUs and several RUs. In this sense, a gNB is a kind of mini-C-RAN. Each split option comes with different requirements such as latency, bandwidth, and usage of Processing Units (PU).

Figure 1 shows a 5G logical network architecture as divided into 3 parts. Fronthaul is the network segment from RU till the corresponding DU. The distance of these two entities can not be more than 20 km due to the delay sensitive functionalities which will be executed in DU. Normally the bandwidth in this segment is the highest because of the low layers splits. The network segment between DU and responsible CU, where upper layer BBU functionalities are performed, is called midhaul. Several DUs can reside in this part of the network which are connected to the same CU. The distance in this segment is more relaxed (80–100 km), compared to the fronthaul, due to more relaxed delay requirements of upper layers splits. The third part is the backhaul which is extended between gNB and the core network.

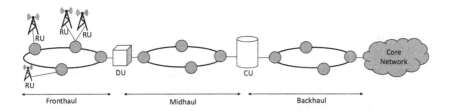

Fig. 1. Scheme of the xhaul network.

As far as the latency we assumed that the reference access network has a diameter less than 20 km, which ensures the latency constraint for the most demanding option 8, that is 250 microseconds. In addition, we need to assign the PUs to each functionality allocated in a node. The baseband functions can be executed on the General Purpose Processor (GPP) x86 architecture [12]. Based on [12] one Intel x86 CPU core with the 2.07 GHz frequency is considered suitable to meet the processing delay requirements. There are several splits options with specific requirements can be applied and investigated. Table 1 shows the three different functional splits chosen in this work and their requirements. Based on [13], each functional split is assigned a fraction of the total processing unit needed for whole functionality.

Table 1. Functional splits requirements

Layers	Split option	Bandwidth [Gbps]	PU units
L1	Opt.8	2.4	0.5 PU
L2	Opt.6	0.152	0.3 PU
L3	Opt.2	0.151	0.2 PU

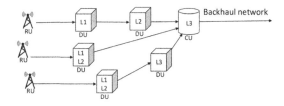

Fig. 2. Sample xhaul function chain configurations considered in the algorithm.

In relation to the adoption of different functional split options, in this paper, the classic residential-industrial traffic over 24 h has been considered but the approach presented here can be adapted to any other variation of the traffic. The possibility to dynamically assigning different functions to different entities

Table 2. Notation used in the algorithm

N	Set of nodes in the network $|N| = n$
d_i	Nodal degree of node $i \in N$
$S_{DU,i}$	Set of active DUs under the hop and processing units constraint for node $i \in N$
S_A	Set of active nodes in the network
DU_i	DU in the location of node $i \in N$
P_i	Total processing units of the DU in node $i \in N$
$P_{i,1}$	Number of PUs for $L1$ in node $i \in N$
$P_{i,2}$	Number of PUs for $L2$ in node $i \in N$
$P_{i,3}$	Number of PUs for $L3$ in node $i \in N$
A_i	Number of active antennas at node $i \in N$
$Path_{ij}$	The shortest path between nodes i and $j \in N$

and nodes in the access network is studied according to the traffic profile. As it can be seen in Fig. 2 this approach assumes that function splits are not statically assigned but instead, depending on the traffic demand and availability of the PUs, dynamic chaining of the function is configured based on the xhaul to efficiently allocate network resources. In order to make this function chaining feasible there are a few constraints that need to be taken into consideration:

– Latency: Among all the options for splitting, PHY and MAC layers are the most delay sensitive. The main reason is due to the Hybrid Automatic Repeat Request (HARQ) which is controlled by lower layer MAC and executed in the PHY layer. Splitting the PHY and MAC layers lead to stricter requirements over latency. In this work, we evaluated the latency parameters as a function of distance in terms of hops.
– Bandwidth: As we mentioned several times one of the major benefits of functional splits in the xhaul network, is the bandwidth usage reduction. Since NGFI is traffic dependent, in case of low traffic extra bandwidth can be used for other purposes. By implementing the functional chain, there is the possibility for executing the bandwidth hungry functions in the local or the closest DU. As a result, the outgoing low bandwidth signal can be routed throughout the network to be executed on another DU or in the CU.
– Processing units (PU): in the previous generation of the access network, all functionalities were executed in either data center or BBU hotels with high amount of resources. Xhaul, on the other hand, is introducing the possibility to perform some processing in DUs with a limited amount of processing resources (namely the number of PUs). In CUs, instead of unlimited processing resources are still considered, as in previous configurations. As a consequence, the proper dimensioning of the PUs in DUs is an important aspect of optimization.

The heuristic algorithm presented here aims at locating baseband functionalities in the access network as a reconfigurable function chain, by efficiently adapting to traffic generated by active antennas, in relation to distance (hop) and PU constraints. The problem to solve is formally defined as follows (Table 2):

– **Given** the physical network with interconnected nodes supporting antennas, the number and placement of CUs, the number of PUs in DUs and the daily traffic profile.
– **Find** the minimum number of active DUs according to delay (hops) and PU constraints in order to adapt to the daily traffic profile while dynamically reconfiguring the xhaul function chain.

Algorithm 1. Function chain

```
1  Initialization: S_{DU,i}, S_A ← ∅
2  while (N ≠ ∅) do
3  │   find node i ∈ N s.t. d_i is maximum
4  │   create S_{DU,i}
5  │   if (S_{DU,i} ← ∅) then
6  │   │   S_A ← DU_i
7  │   │   P_i = P_i − A_i * Σ^3_{x=1} P_{i,x}
8  │   else
9  │   │   for each node j ∈ S_{DU,i} do
10 │   │   │   if (P_j ≥ A_i * Σ^3_{x=1} P_{i,x}) then
11 │   │   │   │   P_j = P_j − A_i * Σ^3_{x=1} P_{i,x}
12 │   │   │   │   update bandwidth in Path_{ij}
13 │   │   │   else if (P_j ≥ A_i * Σ^2_{x=1} P_{i,x}) then
14 │   │   │   │   P_j = P_j − A_i * Σ^2_{x=1} P_{i,x}
15 │   │   │   │   update bandwidth in Path_{ij}
16 │   │   │   │   if (∃ z ∈ [S_{DU,i} − j] s.t. P_z ≥ [P_{i,3}] * Ai) then
17 │   │   │   │   │   P_z = P_z − [P_{i,3}] * A_i
18 │   │   │   │   │   update bandwidth in Path_{jz}
19 │   │   │   │   else
20 │   │   │   │   │   find closest CU
21 │   │   │   │   │   P_{CU} = P_{CU} − P_{i,3} * A_i
22 │   │   │   │   │   update bandwidth in Path_{jCU}
23 │   │   │   else if (P_j ≥ P_{i,1} * A_i) then
24 │   │   │   │   P_j = P_j − P_{i,1} * A_i
25 │   │   │   │   update bandwidth in Path_{ij}
26 │   │   │   │   if (∃z ∈ [S_{DU,i} − j] s.t. P_z ≥ A_i * Σ^3_{x=2} P_{i,x}) then
27 │   │   │   │   │   P_z = P_z − A_i * Σ^3_{x=2} P_{i,x}
28 │   │   │   │   │   update bandwidth in Path_{jz}
29 │   │   │   │   else
30 │   │   │   │   │   find closest CU
31 │   │   │   │   │   P_{CU} = P_{CU} − A_i * Σ^3_{x=2} P_{i,x}
32 │   │   │   │   │   update bandwidth in Path_{jCU}
33 │   │   │   else
34 │   │   │   │   S_A ← DU_i
35 │   │   │   │   P_i = P_i − A_i * Σ^3_{x=1} P_{i,x}
36 │   remove node i from N
```

The algorithm is executed sequentially in all the nodes of the network. Each node has the possibility to execute the baseband functionalities but they are all assumed to be de-activated before starting the algorithm. The algorithm stops after the last node in the network executes the algorithm (the condition in line 2). It is also assumed that the dimensioning of the PUs has been precomputed and all DUs have a certain amount of available PUs.

The algorithm starts in line 3 in the node $i \in N$ with the highest nodal degree. The effect of the starting point in the assignment algorithm has been already studied [14]. Depending on different constraints (maximum distance and available PUs) the set $S_{DU,i}$ is created in line 4. This set is composed of all the possible DU candidates under the requirement constraints. If node i is the first node that executes the algorithm or, the constraints are so tight that there is no possible DU candidate, then the set $S_{DU,i}$ turns out empty. Lines 5 to 7 investigate this situation. If node i cannot find any DU, then it activates the DU in its own location and the active DU_i will be added to the set S_A in line 6. This set contains all active DUs in the network. In line 7 node i uses the available PUs in DU_i. Since DU_i is just opened, it has enough PUs to executes all the layers (line 7). On the other hand, if there are some possible DU candidates exist, a decision has to be made regarding the assignment (line 8). The decision making logic is based on finding the DU with the highest available PUs in order to execute all the layers and prevent routing and assigning the bandwidth throughput of the network. In line 9 each DU in the set $S_{DU,i}$ namely DU in node j is checked for the availability of the PUs. If DU in node j has enough PUs that can execute all the layers (line 10) then node i will be connected to the DU in node j and related PUs will be assigned to it (line 11). For assigning the bandwidth, the algorithm finds the shortest path between nodes i and j which has been precomputed and allocates the required bandwidth to all the links associated to the $Path_{ij}$ (line 12). Lines 13 to 23 consider the situation when the chosen DU has only enough PUs to executes layer 1 and 2 (line 13). In that case, node i will be connected to DU in node j and uses the available PUs for layer 1 and 2 (lines 13–14). Upon the connection to DU in the node j, all the links in the $Path_{ij}$ also get the required bandwidth (line 15). For the execution of layer 3, the algorithm first searches for all the possible DUs namely $z \in S_{DU,i}$ under the required constraints (line 16). If such DU exists then node i uses its PUs for executing layer 3 functions (line 17). The required bandwidth also will be assigned to all the links in the shortest path between nodes j and z (line 18). Otherwise, the shortest path towards all predefined CUs will be computed and the closest one will be identified (line 20) so that the rest of the functions will be routed and executed in that CU (lines 21–22). In line 23 the last possible scenario will be tested. If the available DU only has enough PUs for the execution of layer 1, then node i will be connected to DU in node j and executes layer 1 functions (line 24). The bandwidth in the shortest path between nodes i and j also will be updated in line 25. For the rest of the functions again the algorithm looks for all the possible DUs in the set $S_{DU,i}$ (line 26). If such DU exists, in line 27, the assignment for layer 2 and 3 is presented and the related bandwidth will be updated accordingly (line 28). Otherwise, the algorithm connects node j to the closest CU (based on the shortest path) and uses the available PUs for executing layer 2 and 3 (lines 30–31). The related bandwidth will be updated accordingly in line 32. If none of the above conditions hold, then node i activates the DU in its location and the new DU will be added to the set S_A in line 34. Upon the assignment, all the layers will be executed in the newly opened DU in line 35. In line 36, node i will be removed from the set N and the algorithm passes the control to the next highest nodal degree node in the network. The worst case complexity of the algorithm is $\mathcal{O}(N^3)$. It is calculated by considering the maximum number of iterations for all the loops in the algorithm.

4   Numerical Results

To show the effectiveness of the algorithm, a set of results is here presented organized into two parts. Firstly, the algorithm is applied with no limitation on PUs to evaluate the effect of distance constraints, expressed in hops. In the second part, the effect of the combination of the two constraints, namely the maximum distance and the PUs available in the nodes is outlined. In all the cases considered the benchmark is the conventional C-RAN, designed based on the location algorithms previously developed [15].

Figure 3 shows the reference network for evaluations, consisting of 38 nodes and 48 high capacity transport links. Three CUs are considered to serve the network where data centers are located. The figure also is shown two simple examples of the decision logic of the algorithm. The connection between RUs and CUs for service purposes can happen through a chain of intermediate DUs. All the nodes in the network including the one hosting CUs can produce traffic and need to be assigned to proper entities for processing.

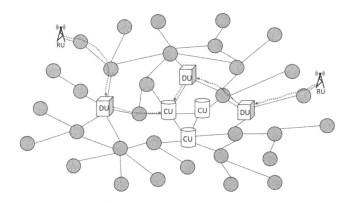

Fig. 3. Reference access network for evaluations.

The main motivation of the algorithm is to adopt the proper amount of network resources to the traffic pattern evolution, assumed in Fig. 4 as the number of active antennas per node over 24 h of the day [1]. The pattern presents low traffic in the early hours of the day, a peak in the middle and then decreases while reaching the end of the day. In this paper, we assumed the same amount of traffic at each hour for all the nodes in the network. This value is the highest amount of traffic predicted on each specific hour of a day.

The total number of the PUs is calculated based on the average of this pattern, in relation to the requirements of each functional layers and then averaged on the number of nodes in the network. The aim of the algorithm is to find suitable chaining of the functions throughout the network while using the available resources and avoiding any blocking of requests.

Figure 5 shows the comparison of C-RAN and xhaul in terms of activated nodes, namely BBU hotels, DUs and CUs respectively, varying the distance constraints. It is assumed the latency constraint is not violated for both architectures due to the diameter of 20 km of the use case in terms of hops. For this comparison, the xhaul network does not have any limitation over the available PUs in DUs which is the same situation in the C-RAN architecture. As a consequence, the variation of the traffic during the day does not affect the number

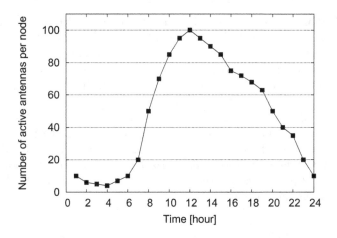

Fig. 4. Evolution of the number of active antennas per node during the 24 h.

of active DUs in the network. In all distance constraints, the two approaches achieve close results. In C-RAN the number of active BBU hotels decreases as the constraint on distant relaxes. This is also true for the xhaul except in the cases that algorithm due to the physical network topology cannot find a better solution even by relaxing the distance (hops 3 and 4). In the xhaul, the trend also shows the contribution of DUs and CUs. When distance constraint is strict (1 hop) the algorithm relies also on CUs for execution of functions. In the very relax distance constraints (5 and 6 hops) the dependencies on CUs is completely eliminated due to the fact that the algorithm prioritizes using DUs over CUs. In the 6 hops constraint, C-RAN and xhaul have the same requirement of activating only 1 node that corresponds to full centralization.

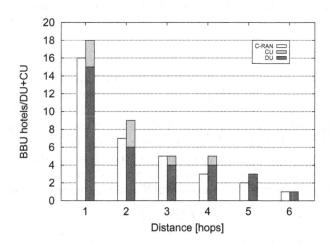

Fig. 5. Comparison of the total number of active nodes (BBU hotels, DUs and CUs) as a function of the distance constraint for C-RAN and xhaul with no limitation on the PU.

Figure 6 reports the evaluation of the required bandwidth in the same conditions of Fig. 5, showing the real advantage of the xhaul architecture. This figure compares the total assigned bandwidth in the network as a function of the distance constraint, again for C-RAN and xhaul, with no limitation on the PUs. By relaxing the distance constraint, the total bandwidth usage increases in all scenarios, which represents the well-known cost of centralization. Even though the PUs are assumed to be infinite, the variation of the traffic during the day sensibly affects the bandwidth in xhaul. Instead, being C-RAN at a constant bit rate, the variation of the traffic does not affect the assigned bandwidth. In particular, xhaul adapts to the traffic variations and in both the low (6 a.m.) and the peak (12 p.m.) traffic situations there are effective bandwidth savings in adopting the xhaul approach.

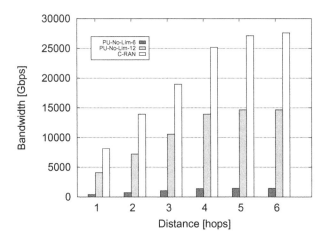

Fig. 6. Comparison of the total bandwidth as a function of the distance constraint for C-RAN and xhaul with no limitation on the PU in two different traffic situations (i.e. at 6 a.m. and 12 p.m. from Fig. 4).

This is also shown in Fig. 7 by plotting the multiplexing gain in terms of bandwidth indicated by G in Eq. 1. It is defined as the difference between the total amount of used bandwidth in C-RAN (BW_c) and xhaul (BW_x) scenarios divided by the value for the C-RAN. This value shows the statistical saving in the usage of bandwidth in xhaul compares to the C-RAN. The multiplexing gain results almost independent of the distance constraint and much higher for xhaul then for C-RAN. This means that with xhaul the access network is able to allocate more services with respect to C-RAN, given a set of transport resources.

$$G = \frac{BW_c - BW_x}{BW_c} \quad (1)$$

Figures 8 and 9 show the results for the xhaul architecture when both limitations over distance and available PUs have been applied, in the low (6 a.m.)

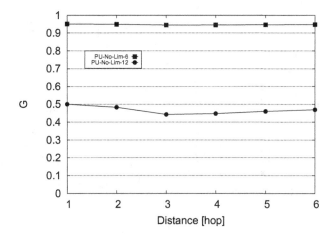

Fig. 7. Comparison of the xhaul multiplexing gain with respect to the C-RAN with no limitation on the processing units in low (6 a.m.) and peak (12 p.m.) traffic hours.

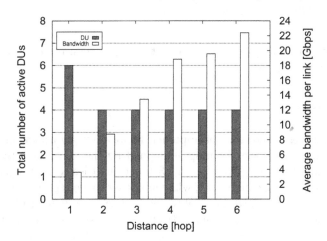

Fig. 8. Comparison of the average bandwidth per link and total active DUs as a function of the distance constraints for xhaul with the limitation on both processing units and hops in the low traffic (6 a.m.).

and the peak (12 p.m.) traffic situations, respectively. The figures are showing the comparison of the total number of active DUs and bandwidth per link as a function of different distance constraints. The dimensioning of the PUs in the nodes is based on the average traffic and on the processing required for each layer. As the distance constraint is relaxed, the constraint on PUs leads to a higher number of active nodes with respect to the ideal case. As far as the bandwidth, even with the same number of active DUs, having longer path means also more bandwidth needed. These figures both suggest designing the network to

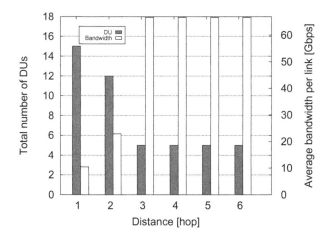

Fig. 9. Comparison of the average bandwidth per link and total active DUs as a function of the distance constraints for xhaul with the limitation on both processing units and hops in the high traffic (12 p.m.).

have a distance around 2 or 3 hops so that both aspects, number of nodes and bandwidth, can be optimized.

5   Conclusions

This paper has described a novel approach to location algorithm in 5G access network, based on function chaining as defined by the xhaul architecture. The algorithm is able to assign L1, L2 and L3 functionalities to nodes according to distance and processing constraints, while adapting to aggregate traffic variation during the day. Results have been obtained in terms of nodes to be activated, bandwidth and multiplexing gain on transport links, showing the benefits of the xhaul approach with respect to conventional C-RAN fronthaul, especially in terms of bandwidth saving. The multiplexing gain with respect to dedicated channels as in C-RAN shows the margin for dynamic bandwidth allocation to other service slices. The effectiveness of this design can be also shown in terms of centralization gain and can be further extended to support reliability in relation to specific use cases.

References

1. Larsen, L.M.P., et al.: A survey of the functional splits proposed for 5G mobile crosshaul networks. IEEE Commun. Surv. Tutor. **21**, 146–172 (2018)
2. Askari, L., et al.: Virtual-network-function placement for dynamic service chaining in metro-area networks. In: Proceedings of IEEE ONDM, pp. 136–141 (2018)
3. Small Cell Virtualization: Functional Splits and Use Cases, Small Cell Forum release 7.0 (2016)

4. Chih-Lin, I., et al.: RAN revolution with NGFI (xHaul) for 5G. IEEE/OSA JLT **36**(2), 541–550 (2018)
5. Raza, M.R., et al.: Dynamic slising approach for multi-tenant 5G transport networks. IEEE/OSA JOCN **10**(1), A77–A90 (2018)
6. Yu, J., et al.: Midhaul transmission using edge data centers with split PHY processing and wavelength reassignment for 5G wireless networks. In: Proceedings of IEEE ONDM (2018)
7. Musumeci, F., et al.: Dynamic placement of baseband processing in 5G WDM-based aggregation networks. In: Proceedings of OSA OFC, p. M2G-4 (2017)
8. Kondepu, K., et al.: Orchestrating lightpath adaptation and flexible functional split to recover virtualized RAN connectivity. In: Proceedings of OSA OFC (2018)
9. 3GPP: Study on new radio access technology; radio access architecture and interfaces, 3GPP TR 38.801, vol. 2.0.0 (2017)
10. Chang, C.Y., et al.: FlexCRAN: a flexible functional split framework over ethernet fronthaul in Cloud-RAN. In: Proceedings of IEEE ICC (2017)
11. Li, Y., et al.: Flexible RAN: a radio access network concept with flexible functional splits and a programmable optical transport. In: Proceedings of IEEE ECOC (2017)
12. Nikaein, N.: Processing radio access network functions in the cloud: critical issues and modeling. In: Proceedings of ACM (2015)
13. Harutyunyan, D., et al.: Flex5G: flexible functional split in 5G networks. IEEE Trans. Netw. Serv. Manage. **15**(3), 961–975 (2018)
14. Khorsandi, B.M., et al.: BBU location algorithms for survivable 5G C-RAN over WDM. Comput. Netw. **144**, 53–63 (2018)
15. Khorsandi, B.M., et al.: Centralized vs. distributed algorithms for resilient 5G access networks. Photon. Netw. Commun. (2019). https://doi.org/10.1007/s11107-018-00819-7

Dynamic Softwarised RAN Function Placement in Optical Data Centre Networks

Nikolaos Gkatzios[1]([✉]) [iD], Markos Anastasopoulos[2] [iD], Anna Tzanakaki[1,2], and Dimitra Simeonidou[2] [iD]

[1] National and Kapodistrian University of Athens, Athens, Greece
ngkatzio@phys.uoa.gr
[2] HPN Group, University of Bristol, Bristol, UK

Abstract. The ability to assign functions that comprise the BBU processing in centralized softwarised Radio Access Networks into different servers the, have been proven to be beneficial, in terms of energy efficiency. This paper proposes a heuristic suitable for BBU functions allocation and evaluates the impact of dynamic resource management in these environments facilitated through Virtual Machine (VM) live migration. The benefits associated with VM migration are quantified through a series of experiments. Our results show notable improvement in terms of resource and energy efficiency.

Keywords: RAN · BBU · Heuristic · Compute disaggregation · VM migration

1 Introduction

The increased bandwidth, connectivity and mobility requirements associated with 5G have led to the densification of wireless access technologies and the introduction of very stringent requirements in the Radio Access Networks (RANs). In these dense environments distributed RAN solutions, where Base Band Units (BBUs) and radio units (RUs) are co-located, suffer several limitations including increased capital and operational expenditures as well as CO_2 footprint. To increase infrastructure efficiency and address these challenges Cloud Radio Access Networks (C-RANs) have been proposed. In C-RAN, a centralized approach is adopted according to which distributed Remote Radio Heads (RRHs) are connected to a BBU pool located at the Central Unit (CU). The CU can be hosted in Data Centres (DCs) comprising General Purpose Processors (GPPs) that can be shared efficiently across a set of RRHs. However, although this centralized architecture is more efficient compared to the distributed approach it imposes the need of a high bandwidth transport network to support interconnection of the RRHs with the CU known as fronthaul (FH) [1]. The interface between RUs and CU is standardized through the Common Public Radio Interface (CPRI).

When adopting the centralized architectural model proposed by C-RAN it is very important to identify the optimal allocation of functions comprising the BBU function chain to the appropriate servers hosted by the CU. The concept of compute resource

© IFIP International Federation for Information Processing 2020
Published by Springer Nature Switzerland AG 2020
A. Tzanakaki et al. (Eds.): ONDM 2019, LNCS 11616, pp. 108–117, 2020.
https://doi.org/10.1007/978-3-030-38085-4_10

disaggregation approach [2] allows individual allocation of these processing functions, associated with a specific FH service, to different servers depending on the nature and volume of their processing requirements.

In addition, dynamic access and efficient sharing of compute resource for BBU type of processing, through the adoption of Cloud Computing, takes advantage of the notion of virtualisation that has become key technology for DC resource management. In this context, virtualisation can assist in improving performance and reliability as well as operational costs reduction. Virtual Machine (VM) migration is one of the features provided through virtualization. Migration of operating system instances across different servers is a crucial tool, which is used to achieve different performance goals.

To quantify the benefits of live VM migration in a 5G environment employing centralized BBU processing, a heuristic that is able to assign different functions composing the BBU chain to an appropriate set of servers at the CU, was developed. A set of experiments where the developed heuristic was called to allocate the incoming FH traffic to suitable DC resources for the required processing were conducted. Each experiment assumed different initial DC loading conditions referring not only to the absolute processing load, but also to the load distribution to different servers within the DC. Our results show that when we are able to redistribute the load of the compute resources within the DC, considerable benefits can be achieved, in terms of resource as well as energy efficiency and therefore operational cost reduction.

2 Problem Statement

A generic 5G C-RAN is considered, where compute resources located at the CU support the processing requirements of a group of RRHs. The compute resources at the CU comprise a set General Purpose Processors (GPPs). These servers are arranged in a simple tree topology shown in Fig. 1. The required compute capacity to support FH service provisioning, is supplied by these servers. These employ an implementation of softwarised BBU processing that executes the baseband signal processing to support the operation of RRHs. The requirements, in terms of compute resources, for the baseband processing of an RU, can be estimated as the sum of all compute elements performing the BBU functions. These functions include: Single Carrier - Frequency Division Multiple Access (SC-FDMA) Demodulation, Subcarrier Demapping, Frequency Domain Equalizer, Transform Decoding, Constellation Demapping, Descrambling, Rate Matching and Turbo Decoding. It should be noted, that as shown in Fig. 1, these functions need to be performed in a specific order.

The main objectives of this work are:

- to identify, in real time, optimal allocation of the BBU functions to the DC servers in order to minimize the total power consumption at the DC, while, at the same time, complying with the stringent delay constrains imposed by the CPRI protocol.
- to investigate the benefits, in terms of power consumption, which arise from the live migration of VMs in a DC.

To achieve the first objective, we are taking into consideration the processing requirements, in terms of Instructions, for each baseband processing function [2]. Then, a heuristic algorithm, with low computation complexity, is developed that tries to match the BBU Service Chain functions to the best suited servers, in terms of power consumption, inside a DC.

For the second objective the first step is to quantify the benefits of live VM migration. The services that are already running at the DC are utilising a percentage of the total available resources. We will refer to these resources as initial DC load. The VMs that correspond to already existing services can either remain allocated to the original set of servers or can be reallocated to a set of different servers with the aim to improve a specific metric in our case utilisation. Utilisation here is defined as the ratio of the servers that are switched-on compared to the total number of servers available in the DC. A set of experiments that aim to allocate DC resources is conducted adopting this heuristic assuming different initial loading conditions and load distributions across the set of servers that are being used.

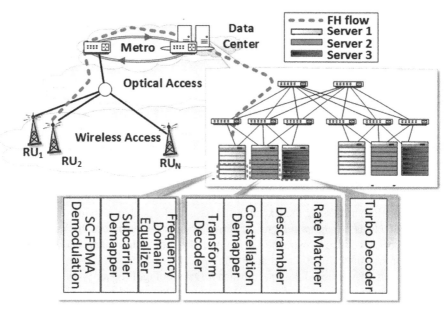

Fig. 1. Centralized processing of softwarised-RAN functions on a data centre hosting different type of servers

3   Framework

3.1   Heuristic Design

As shown in our previous work [2], a multi-stage Integer Linear Programming (ILP) model can be effectively used to identify the optimal placement of BBU functions within the DC, but it suffers high computational complexity thus making it unsuitable for real time system deployments. To address this issue, a heuristic algorithm with low computational complexity is proposed that tries to identify the optimal compute resources required to support the most energy efficient processing of the BBU Service Chain within the DC.

The analysis of the LTE uplink application, provided by the WiBench suite [3], showed that different construction elements of the BBU chain have different requirements in terms of processing. From the 8 different functions, Turbo Decoder was proven to be the one with the dominant contribution to the total BBU service chain instruction requirements, as shown in Figs. 2 and 3.

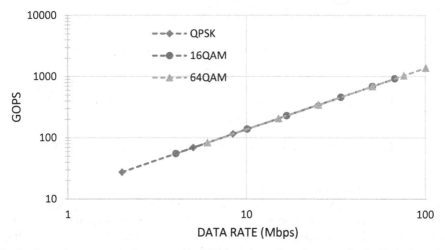

Fig. 2. Operations per second, measured in GOPS, under various data rates for the Turbo Decoder

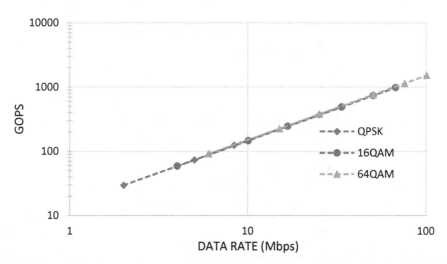

Fig. 3. Operations per second, measured in GOPS, under various data rates for the total BBU Service Chain

Taking this information into consideration, in order to limit the complexity of the heuristic, we divide the 8 different BBU processing functions into two sub-sets of functions (1st and 2nd) sub-set, as shown in Fig. 4. To satisfy the requirements of the BBU Service Chain, the order of these processing functions is always maintained within and across the 2 different sets of functions defined. The first sub-set includes the SC-FDMA, Sub-carrier Demapper, Frequency Domain Equalizer, Transform Decoder and Constellation Demapper functions, while the second sub-set comprises Descramble, Rate Matcher and Turbo Decoder functions. As shown in [4], the proposed grouping policy has been selected as it requires a relatively small amount of network resources for the interconnection of the first (1st) with the second (2nd) sub-set of functions while the computational requirements of the 2nd sub-set is still very high.

Fig. 4. Reduction of complexity through grouping of BBU functions into 2 sets

The main objective of the proposed heuristic is to allocate an input BBU service chain to the most energy efficient servers that have sufficient capacity to process it. The input service can be split and allocated to a set of servers, in case that splitting the service across servers is a more energy efficient option. A more detailed description regarding the server allocation process is provided in Fig. 5.

> **for each** RU:
>> **if** a server that is already used can process it in time:
>>> *assign* it to that server
>>> *update* that server's capacity
>> **else:**
>>> *assign* it to the most efficient server type (search between types 1-3) which can process it
>>> *update* that server's capacity
>>> **if** only the least energy efficient server type (type 4) can process it:
>>>> *check* the thresholds to decide if and which split option should be enabled
>>>> **if** split is enabled:
>>>>> *create* the 2 sets of functions
>>>>> *find* the closest appropriate servers (*Dijkstra*)
>>>>> *assign* the sets to the appropriate servers
>>>>> *update* the servers' capacity
>>>> **else:**
>>>>> *assign* it to a least energy efficient server (type 4)
>>>>> *update* the server's capacity

Fig. 5. The Heuristic developed for BBU assignment problem

In our analysis, we were aiming at always serving the input traffic, independent of the volume of incoming data to be processed, satisfying at the same time, the time constraints associated with the service. Therefore, we are considering the ratio of the number of instructions required for the 2nd sub-set of functions to be performed, over the number of instructions of the 1st sub-set of functions.

The scenario considered assumes the DC topology illustrated in Fig. 6. This topology includes 6 racks. Figure 6a depicts the interconnection of the Top-of-the-Rack (ToR) switches. Each rack incorporates 48 servers, as shown in Fig. 6b. The connectivity between the racks is assumed to be provided by an optical switching solution described in [5]. For the numerical calculations, four different server types were randomly placed within each rack. The technical specifications of the servers assumed are provided in Table 1. These servers can be classified according to their performance in terms of energy efficiency, with type 1 server being the most energy efficient, while type 4 the least energy efficient server.

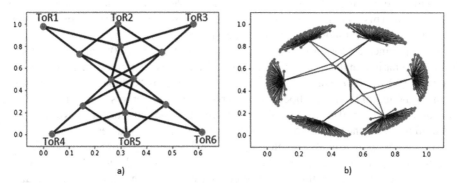

Fig. 6. The DC topology used for the experiments. In (a) is presented the interconnection of the ToRs in the DC and in (b) is displayed the total intra-DC network, including the servers under each ToR

Considering this assumption, we calculate the ratios of the capacity of the larger type of server (type 4 server, least energy efficient) over the capacities of the rest of the servers (type 1, type 2 and type 3). Based on these ratios and the time constraints associated with the LTE upload service (in total <1 ms per sub-frame), we define a set of thresholds that can be used to identify whether an incoming service chain (including a set of functions) can be split between the larger server type and any other of the smaller available type of servers.

For the specific functional split and the set of servers considered in this study, the numerical values of the thresholds we have identified are: (a) 68% of type 4 server processing capacity if the 1st sub-set of functions is allocated to server type 1, (b) 69% of type 4 server processing capacity if the 1st sub-set of functions is allocated to server type 2 and (c) 70% of type 4 server processing capacity if the 1st sub-set of functions is allocated to server type 3. It should be noted that in our calculations additional processing margins of the order of 2% have been allowed.

Table 1. Technical specifications of the servers used in the numerical evaluations

Computer/Device	Servers	Chips	Cores	Threads	GOPS	Power (Watt)	GOPS/Watt	Idle (Watt)
SuperMicro X11DPi-N(T) SMC X11	2x Intel Xeon Platinum 8160	2	48	96	1071.37	360	2.976	53.4
SuperMicro X11DPG-QT	2x Intel Xeon Gold 6140	2	36	72	888.52	336	2.644	52.4
SuperMicro X10Dai SMC X10	2x Intel Xeon E5-2683 v4	2	32	64	700.94	288	2.434	81
Sugon I908-G20	8x Intel Xeon E7-8860 v3	8	128	256	2510.56	1344	1.868	269

3.2 Numerical Results

To quantify the benefits of the VM migration, the simple DC network topology of Fig. 6 is considered. This comprises 6 racks, each one composed of 48 servers. Four different types of servers were randomly placed inside each rack.

We experimented for various initial DC loads (10%, 15%, 20% and 25%), for 2 different scenarios. In the first scenario, the initial load was distributed on a low number of servers (80 servers). This scenario will be referred to as "compact". In the second scenario, the initial load was allocated to a large number of servers (180 servers). This scenario will be referred to as "spread". In both scenarios the heuristic that was developed was used to assign the incoming traffic to the remaining DC resources.

Through our experiments we calculated the total power consumption of the DC, the average CPU utilisation of the switched-on servers, as well as the total DC utilisation. The total DC utilisation is defined as the percentage of the switched-on servers compared to the total number of DC servers. All the experiments showed that the scenario with the "compact" initial load had much better utilisation of the DC resources and much lower power consumption than the "spread" scenario.

Figure 7 presents the benefits, in terms of power consumption, in the case where live VM migration is applied. It also shows that by migrating the initial DC load, a great reduction of the number of switched-on servers can be achieved. In Fig. 8 we observe that the average CPU utilisation of the switched-on servers is much higher in case of the "compact" scenario compared to the "spread" scenario. It can be also noted that the CPU utilisation reaches a maximum value introduced due to live VM migration. In order to migrate a VM in real time, some of its resources have to be used to support the migration. To address this requirement, a threshold of 75% of CPU usage was adopted, as proposed by [6].

The difference in the power consumption of the schemes under evaluation observed in Fig. 7, is due to the minimization of the power achieved when setting servers to the idle state. The idle state consumes less power but none the less it still adds a fair amount to the total power consumption. In the "spread" scenario most of the switched-on servers had low CPU utilization, which means that they spend a considerable amount of time idle. On the other hand, in the "compact" scenario the number of switched-on servers

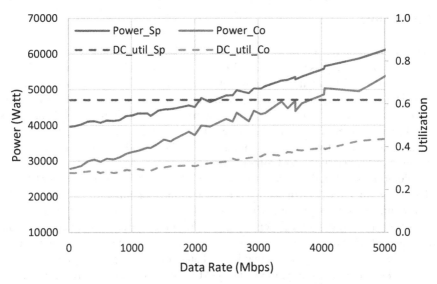

Fig. 7. Power consumption and DC utilisation for 15% initial DC load for various data rates. Dotted lines correspond to the DC's utilisation while solid lines to the power consumption. Red corresponds to the "spread" scenario while blue to the "compact" (Color figure online)

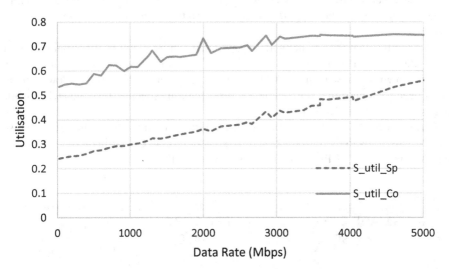

Fig. 8. Switched-on servers' utilisation for 15% initial DC load for various data rates. The red dotted line corresponds to the "spread" scenario while the blue solid line to the "compact" (Color figure online)

were significantly reduced, which led to the high CPU utilisation of these servers and the reduction of their time spent in the idle state.

4 Discussion

Although VM migration comes with great benefits for the DCs, it also contains the risk of service disruption and as such Service Level Agreement (SLA) violations [6–10]. In order to migrate a VM, one must contemplate the total time during which the services, supported by this VM, would be unavailable and try to maintain this below an acceptable threshold. A second aspect to consider is the total migration time in which both machines are synchronizing their states and therefore reliability might be affected. Finally, one must ensure that the active services running on the DC would not be disrupted due to the resources allocated to the VM migration.

The duration between the initiation of the live VM migration and the moment during which the original VM can be discarded is defined as the total migration time and can be divided in three phases as shown in Fig. 9. The first phase referred to as "image-copy" phase, is the phase where all the memory pages from the source VM are copied to the destination VM. During this process, a number of memory pages may change. At the pre-copy phase, the memory pages that have changed are re-copied. At the stop-copy phase, also known as downtime, the source VM is suspended and the remaining dirty pages are transferred to the destination VM which spins up.

The total migration time is vastly affected by the volume of the VM and the network capacity, since migration involves the transfer of the entire VM volume from one physical server to another. While this transfer takes place, the rest of the services already running at the DC will have to be supported without disruption, thus maintaining the relevant resources.

This implies that the DC network capacity that can be used for migration purposes is only the one remaining unused by the rest of the running services. In addition, for scenarios in which more than one VMs need to migrate in a short-time window, there is a clear need for identifying suitable migration scheduling schemes to avoid DC network congestion situations [10, 11].

Furthermore, the additional CPU overhead during migration may cause service disruption. This leads to the introduction of a threshold to the CPU utilization, in order to be able to manage the CPU overhead caused by migration.

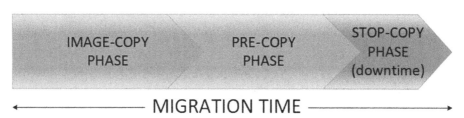

Fig. 9. Live VM migration phases

The main element that affects the downtime is the dirty page rate. The rate at which the memory of the source VM is being written, during the migration process, is called dirty page rate, measured in pages per second, or dirty rate, measured in MBps and in the case in which the dirty rate is similar with the transfer rate, the result is the increase of the downtime.

5   Conclusions

This paper focused firstly on the design of a heuristic, which assigns the BBU functions to the DC servers in order to minimize the total power consumption at the DC and secondly on the investigation of the benefits of VM migration inside a DC. Experimental results have shown significant power savings and substantial reduction of the total DC resources utilisation, in a heterogeneous DC, when live VM migration is applied. A discussion on how live migration can be performed in these environments is also provided.

Acknowledgements. This work has been financially supported by the EU Horizon 2020 project 5G-PICTURE under grant agreement No 762057 and the EU Horizon 2020 project IN2DREAMS under grant agreement No 777596.

References

1. Tzanakaki, A., et al.: Wireless-optical network convergence: enabling the 5G architecture to support operational and end-user services. IEEE Commun. Mag. **55**(10), 184–192 (2017)
2. Gkatzios, N., Anastasopoulos, M., Tzanakaki, A., Simeonidou, D.: Compute resource disaggregation: an enabler for efficient 5G RAN softwarisation. In: 2018 European Conference on Networks and Communications (EuCNC), Ljubljana, Slovenia, pp. 1–5 (2018)
3. Zheng, Q., et al.: WiBench: an open source kernel suite for benchmarking wireless systems. In: 2013 IEEE International Symposium Workload Characterization (IISWC), Portland, OR, pp. 123–132 (2013)
4. Tzanakaki, A., Anastasopoulos, M., Simeonidou, D.: Converged access/metro infrastructures for 5G services. In: Optical Fiber Communication Conference, OSA Technical Digest (online). Optical Society of America (2018). paper M
5. Perelló, J., et al.: All-optical packet/circuit switching-based data center network for enhanced scalability, latency, and throughput. IEEE Netw. **27**(6), 14–22 (2013)
6. Wood, T., Shenoy, P., Venkataramani, A., Yousif, M.: Black-box and gray-box strategies for virtual machine migration. In: Proceedings of the 4th USENIX Conference on Networked Systems Design & Implementation (NSDI 2007), p. 17. USENIX Association, Berkeley (2007)
7. Clark, C., et al.: Live migration of virtual machines. In: Proceedings of the 2nd Conference on Symposium on Networked Systems Design & Implementation - Volume 2 (NSDI 2005), vol. 2, pp. 273–286. USENIX Association, Berkeley (2005)
8. Voorsluys, W., Broberg, J., Venugopal, S., Buyya, R.: Cost of virtual machine live migration in clouds: a performance evaluation. In: Jaatun, M.G., Zhao, G., Rong, C. (eds.) CloudCom 2009. LNCS, vol. 5931, pp. 254–265. Springer, Heidelberg (2009). https://doi.org/10.1007/978-3-642-10665-1_23
9. Verma, A., Ahuja, P., Neogi, A.: pMapper: power and migration cost aware application placement in virtualized systems. In: Issarny, V., Schantz, R. (eds.) Middleware 2008. LNCS, vol. 5346, pp. 243–264. Springer, Heidelberg (2008). https://doi.org/10.1007/978-3-540-89856-6_13
10. Bari, M.F., Zhani, M.F., Zhang, Q., Ahmed, R., Boutaba, R.: CQNCR: optimal VM migration planning in cloud data centers. In: 2014 IFIP Networking Conference, Trondheim, pp. 1–9 (2014)
11. Stage, A., Setzer, T.: Network-aware migration control and scheduling of differentiated virtual machine workloads. In: Proceedings of the 2009 ICSE Workshop on Software Engineering Challenges of Cloud Computing (CLOUD 2009), pp. 9–14. IEEE Computer Society, Washington, D.C. (2009)

Techno-Economic Aspects of 5G Transport Network Deployments

I. Mesogiti[1]([✉]) [ID], E. Theodoropoulou[1], G. Lyberopoulos[1], F. Setaki[1], K. Filis[1], A. Di Giglio[2], A. Percelsi[2], and Anna Tzanakaki[3]

[1] COSMOTE Mobile Telecommunications S.A., Athens, Greece
{imesogiti,etheodorop,glimperop,fsetaki,cfilis}@cosmote.gr
[2] Telecom Italia, Turin, Italy
{andrea.digiglio,alessandro.percelsi}@telecomitalia.it
[3] University of Bristol, Bristol, UK
anna.tzanakaki@bristol.ac.uk

Abstract. 5G networks will comprise multiple, versatile infrastructures at finest granularity consisting of multiple disaggregated pools of network, compute and storage resources. To support the 5G network architectures and satisfy the access network demanding performance requirements, transport networks consisting of various converging technologies shall provide mechanisms to support deployment flexibility and scalability. The deployment of the complementary or alternative transport network technologies in real network deployments shall take into account various factors such as area specifics, technologies' deployment feasibility, traffic/usage forecasts considering long-term services roadmaps and certainly, the implicated costs. Thus, transport network planning and dimensioning shall be tightly accompanied by the techno-economic analysis of the various deployment alternatives. This paper provides insights on the techno-economic aspects of 5G transport network technologies and its applicability on the architectural concepts of 5G-XHaul and 5G-PICTURE 5G-PPP projects.

Keywords: 5G · Transport network · Wireless-optical convergence · Techno-economic · Fronthaul · Backhaul

1 Introduction

5G access network deployments will pose stringent requirements to the transport network, to support high capacity Macro Sites (MS), dense layers of high capacity Small Cells (SCs), as well as versatile Distributed and Cloud-based Radio Access Networks (C-RAN/Cloud RAN), D-RAN (Distributed-RAN), DA-RAN (Dis-Aggregated-RAN) [2]) setups in coexistence with the traditional architectures. To support the 5G networks/services' requirements, the transport network shall be equipped with mechanisms to support flexible and scalable access network deployments, to converge fronthaul (FH) and backhaul (BH) traffic of various functional splits (FS) over a single infrastructure consisting of various wireless and optical technologies [3, 4].

A. Tzanakaki et al. (Eds.): ONDM 2019, LNCS 11616, pp. 118–129, 2020.
https://doi.org/10.1007/978-3-030-38085-4_11

A number of research projects addresses the development of next generation transport network technologies while all major infrastructure vendors focus on enhancing their products to meet the 5G access network requirements. In this context, the 5G-XHaul project [1] has proposed a converged optical-wireless network solution capable of delivering BH and FH connectivity for versatile 5G access network deployments. Leveraging on this, the 5G-PICTURE project [2] aims at delivering a paradigm shift, from D- and C-RAN to the DA-RAN approach, by "disaggregating" hardware and software components across wireless, optical and compute/storage domains. To support this approach, 5G-PICTURE focuses on advanced optical and wireless transport network technologies.

However, the actual deployment of the complementary or alternative transport network technologies meeting the 5G requirements is not a straightforward task. In practice, lots of factors shall be taken into account, such as reuse of legacy networks/infrastructures, area specifics, deployment feasibility, long-term services delivery roadmaps, traffic forecasts and, last but not least, the implicated costs. This paper proposes a methodology for the techno-economic evaluation of large-scale transport network deployments aiming at indicating cost optimal network deployment solutions while various technological aspects and critical related parameters can be investigated. The methodology is based on a fully parameterized expandable techno-economic analysis tool that can reflect the architectural concepts of 5G-XHaul and 5G-PICTURE by modeling the network segments under study which are then cost for a desired time period and a specific geographical area. Initial results from the applicability of the tool in the 5G-XHaul project confirm the capabilities and its usage potential.

The paper is organized as follows: Starting from the 5G networks physical architecture overview, the 5G-XHaul and 5G-PICTURE transport network technologies are identified in the various network segments, while access network aspects are touched upon. In the next section, a methodology for 5G transport network cost analysis is described, based on a techno-economic tool which performs network modeling and dimensioning –based on practical rules and deployment aspects- and allows for cost assessment of various deployment scenarios. A number of transport network deployment alternative scenarios are identified and evaluated from a techno-economic perspective. Finally, potential enhancements of the techno-economic tool are presented before conclusions are drawn.

2   5G Network Physical Architecture Overview

The common set of principles underpinning the 5G network architectures, as proposed by SDOs (Standards Developing Organizations) [4–7], 5G-PPP projects (e.g., [1, 2]), infrastructure vendors and mobile operators roadmaps, consider 5G networks comprising multiple network and compute infrastructure setups [7], at finest granularity, including multiple disaggregated pools of network, compute and storage resources as proposed by the 5G-PICTURE project [2]. The baseline of the physical architecture of these resources has been introduced in [3], and in more detail in [8] and [15] – further elaborated in Fig. 1.

More specifically, the 5G data-plane architecture considers an integrated optical and wireless network topology and infrastructure to support jointly backhauling of SCs/MSs,

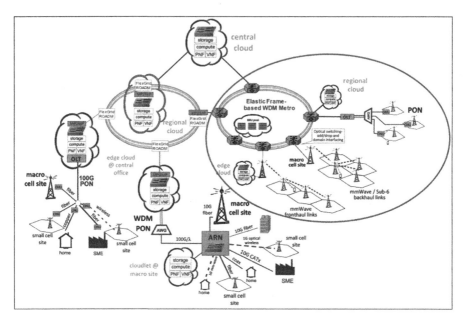

Fig. 1. Physical architecture - converged fixed-mobile 5G network

fronthauling of various FSs (as defined in [7]) of Remote Radio Heads (RRHs) as well as fixed network access. The wireless domain comprises a dense layer of SCs to serve the high traffic demand which is complemented by a MS layer for maximizing coverage. Due to the high capacity requirements, MSs can be considered as predominantly attached to the optical transport network. SCs can be wirelessly backhauled to MSs using a combination of wireless technologies (mmWave and Sub-6). Alternatively, SCs can be directly connected to a central office (CO), using either optical or wireless network technologies.

Compute resources are present at various physical and logical locations of the network for hosting network services and/or applications. These are indicated as edge (close to the location of or collocated with a MS), regional (at COs), or central clouds (at core network), where Virtual Base Band Units (vBBUs) considered as "network services" are hosted.

The access transport links are aggregated using optical network technologies and the traffic is forwarded to the backbone optical transport network. A dynamic and flexible/elastic frame or time-based optical network solution is considered for aggregation and transport core network segments.

2.1   5G-XHaul and 5G-PICTURE Transport Network Technologies

Considering the 5G-XHaul and 5G-PICTURE transport network technologies the identified deployment options are:

- mmWave transceivers for last mile transport BH and/or FH links providing 3.5 Gbps average data rates per link, taking into account the link capacity achieved in 5G-XHaul [12]; depending highly on the spectrum (frequency, bandwidth), the distance between the two nodes and the radio environment.
- Sub-6 transceivers for last mile transport BH links providing 500 Mbps average data rates per link as achieved in 5G-XHaul [13].
- Point-to-Point optical or WDM-PON connections (ONUs/OLTs) for last mile transport BH/FH links providing data rates of 10 Gbps (for the 10 G interfaces) and 25 Gbps (for the 25 G interfaces) and 40 Gb/s for aggregating transport network interfaces [14].
- Ethernet type connections (denoted as Flex-E in [17, 18]) aggregating various Ethernet PHY (cable, optical, wireless, etc.) and MAC interfaces into a high speed Optical Ethernet trunk reaching 100GE or 400GE in the future [17, 18]. This technology can be considered as a substitute of WDM-PON, complementary to Optical Ethernet G.698.4-based for aggregating wireless transport links, or even complementary to TSON (Time-Shared Optical Network) components at transport core segment with the future 400GE release.
- Optical Ethernet (G.698.4-based) type connections at aggregation transport network segment; aggregating 10x10GE (Gigabit-Ethernet) optical links to an optical 100GE channel link [16–18]. This can be considered as a substitute of WDM-PON or another aggregation layer.
- TSON edge nodes, aggregating 4 × 10 Gbps Optical Ethernet interfaces in the context of 5G-XHaul [19], especially for optical backbone transport segments. The TSON

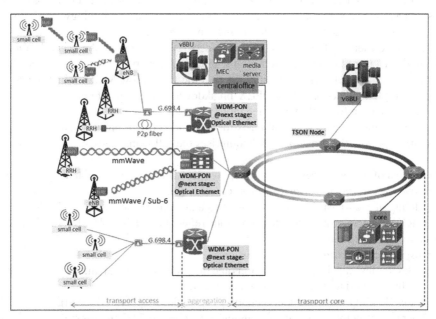

Fig. 2. 5G-XHaul and 5G-PICTURE technologies applicability

release developed in 5G-PICTURE, incremental aggregation of up to 12×10 Gbps interfaces to 100 Gbps optical Ethernet while allowing for 100 Gbps pass-through traffic can be considered.

It is obvious that these technologies can be deployed alternatively or complementarily at different network segments (last-mile transport, aggregation, backbone), as depicted in Fig. 2.

3   Methodology for Techno-Economic Analysis

3.1   Techno-Economic Tool Description

In the context of 5G-XHaul [19], a fully parameterized tool has been developed, to be further expanded in 5G-PICTURE, mainly to support cost analysis and cost efficient deployment of 5G-XHaul solution (FH/BH/BB transport networks) in a selected area, for a desired timeframe, by running various scenarios of: coverage area and traffic, usage of various optical/wireless network technologies (i.e. WDM-PON, mmWave, Sub-6), FS for FH/BH and various MIMO schemes. In addition, the tool can assist in performing comparative analysis and concluding on technologies' utilization and deployments by flexibly modifying the input.

The innovation of the tool lies in the modeling of the 5G transport network technologies and architectural/deployment options, as defined in the 5G-PPP general architecture and refined in the 5G-XHaul and 5G-PICTURE physical network architectures, based on rules and assumptions resembling usage/operation conditions (technology restrictions, loading factors, fiber deployment, etc.) in the most realistic way.

The usage methodology of the tool includes: (i) definition of the scenario under evaluation, (ii) introduction of assumptions, input parameters and network dimensioning rules based on network modeling, and (iii) the Cash Flow Model which leads to automatically calculated CAPEX/OPEX breakdown, using separate cost models and pricing information for each type of technology/equipment.

More specifically, on an annual basis for a specific area of interest and a definable deployment period, the usage of a tool comprises the following steps:

- Definition of various access network deployment scenarios; either manually or based on coverage, traffic, services and resources utilization;
- Modeling of the transport network segments and technological options (BH/FH, FS, MIMO in relevant grades of adoption), thus reflecting the 5G-XHaul/5G-PICTURE architectural concepts;
- Transport network dimensioning, considering:
  - technologies' capabilities/restrictions and their inherent, default dimensioning rules - tightly related to their incremental cost models,
  - nodes' loading factors (either technology-specific or operator defined),
  - fiber infrastructure deployments ranging from Greenfield scenarios (implying costs for digging, trenching, permits, personnel costs, etc.) to Brownfield scenarios (assuming existing fiber infrastructure owned or provided/leased by a 3rd party).

- CAPEX/OPEX breakdown, taking into account:
  - equipment costs based on cost models specific to each type of equipment and pricing (considering purchase, installation, maintenance/service costs, and estimated annual prices erosion or escalation). Since the cost models are technology- and vendor- specific and adhere to specific commercialization policies, they have been made modifiable and expandable to adapt to other technology implementations and commercial offerings as well. Indicative cost models are the following:

    for wireless links: the cost of the link equals the cost of the set(s) of transceivers required calculated by the BH/FH traffic to be served divided by the average datarates achieved per technology, adjusted accordingly to the number of hops (for the multi-hop cases). Once the maximum link datarates are reached, the incremental cost equals to the cost of the additional set(s) of transceivers required for serving any additional traffic.

    for WDM-PON links: the cost model takes into account (1) the initial cost of an OLT and the initial number of provided interfaces, (2) OLT's incremental cost based on the additional interfaces to be provided at second stage, as well as (3) the cost of the ONUs. Both the number of OLTs and the provided interfaces are related to the OLT loading factor decided by the network operator. Similar is the cost model in the case of the Optical Ethernet technologies' equipment.

  - fiber deployment specific costs; for the Greenfield scenario (that is, there is no previously deployed infrastructure) not only the necessary hardware has been taken into account but also aspects such as digging and trenching, permits, necessary personnel etc., and the costs are calculated on the basis of average fiber deployment cost per Km (country/area-specific parameter), while for the Brownfield scenario as a percentage of the Greenfield deployment cost, accounting for the extra mile that an existing deployment needs to be extended to reach a certain number of SC sites.
  - labor costs for network deployment, operations and maintenance,

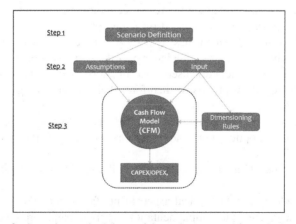

Fig. 3. Stepwise methodology of the techno-economic analysis tool

– other financial figures of extra costs such as Weighted Average Cost of Capital (WACC) and Tax Deduction (% of Equipment Cost).

3.2 Network Modeling, Dimensioning and Deployment Aspects as Input to the Tool

Access Network Deployment Dimensioning. The 5G access network deployment for a specific geographical area (dense urban, urban, suburban, rural) refers to the locations of MSs/RRHs, SCs, fixed network nodes serving corporate users and aggregating traffic from residential users and the dimensioning, according to broadly and well-established access network planning principles:

- Targeted coverage (for the calculation of MSs) and capacity (for the calculation of MSs and SCs);
- Actual and forecasted traffic patterns and services, especially with regard to the maximum traffic requirements (based on the concurrent services mix) for the 5G mobile and fixed access network. Leveraging on ITU's IMT-2020 and 3GPPs' 5G services' and verticals' identification, forecasted patterns and services for 5G networks have been studied in [9–11];
- Existing aggregation sites of mobile network and fixed access nodes (e.g., corporate users, COs).

5G Transport Network Deployment Modeling. The 5G transport network deployment shall be based on the access network requirements and technologies, taking also into account the following practical rules:

- The MSs that are fronthauled (Remote Radio Head, RRH) have no associated SCs, while the vBBUs preferably reside at edge or regional cloud (i.e., at COs' locations).
- SCs will be mainly backhauled with wireless technologies or optical links: the traffic of the former is eventually transported over the optical aggregation and backbone network by hops of backhauled SCs (usually not more than two to satisfy latency requirements), while the traffic of the latter over the optical aggregation network.
- For the corporate fixed network users, one or more optical network components (ONUs) are deployed on premises; therefore, their dimensioning is based on the number of users.
- The residential users' traffic is summed at first level at ONUs (residing at centralized locations) and then at optical aggregation network; thus, dimensioning is based on the aggregated traffic.
- Aggregation and backbone transport network will reuse (part of) existing COs.

However, besides the technological aspects (interfaces, performance, etc.), in real network deployments the actual implementation highly depends on the cost, provided that the quality of services offered is guaranteed.

4   5G Transport Network Deployments' Techno-Economic Evaluation (Scenarios and Results)

Considering the 5G-XHaul technologies (BH/FH/BB), a number of transport network deployment scenarios for a specific dense area in Barcelona have been assessed with the tool in terms cost. Preliminary cost information has been used since some of these technologies are at pre-commercial product Technology Readiness Level (TRL), while the pricing information accuracy varies depending on the development and commercial maturity of the technologies.

The evaluated transport network deployment scenarios (depicted in Fig. 3) consider optical and wireless deployments, ranging from purely optical (Greenfield, and Brownfield of various legacy fiber network penetration) to hybrid ones (with varying level of MSs/SCs deployment) to purely wireless, combined with converged BH/FH scenarios with varying level of BH/FH adoption from BH only to FH only, assuming either SISO or MIMO schemes.

These scenarios have led to a set of results and conclusions regarding the cost efficient utilization of the 5G technologies especially in large scale deployments. Some of them are not straightforward, while others refer to technologies not commercialized yet. The tool can assist in defining the factors that influence significantly the transport network deployment cost and in making the best decision on selecting 1. wireless vs. optical techs, 2. alternative FSs (for BH/FH), 3. MIMO configurations; as well as investigating possible relationship between these options. Indicatively:

- From the techno-economic point of view there are marginal differences among the various hybrid optical-wireless transport network deployment options, irrespectively of the degree to which each type of technology is utilized (Fig. 4).
- The cost raises significantly -almost doubles- in case of a pure wireless Brownfield deployment due to the increased usage of the wireless equipment cost (high cost vs. low capacity and cost of optical equipment). Therefore, in the area under study, deployment shall be based primarily on optical technologies especially for the MSs BH/FH, complemented with wireless links (where fiber is not in place) along with a mix of optical and wireless links for SCs backhauling. In practice, we can consider the 2nd hybrid solution as the most viable deployment.
- For a converged scenario (i.e. Hybrid 2), the selection of BH or FH highly depends on the actual FS option for FH, but it seems that there are marginal differences between the various FH/BH deployment options, when leaving aside CPRI as a choice, and considering that all FH traffic is transmitted over optical connections due to the significant capacity vs. cost advantage they exhibit in all scenarios.
- Provided the current price estimations of optical interface and Sub-6 transceiver components, in extreme deployment scenarios, a FH-only deployment over optical links can be even more cost efficient than a BH-only using a significant number of Sub-6 links. At the same time the capacity vs. cost for mmWave is higher than that for optical links which implies that FH traffic over optical links can cost marginally the same as if backhauled over mmWave, depending on the air-interface overhead. For SISO links, the cost in all converged scenarios options is almost the same (Figs. 5 and 6).

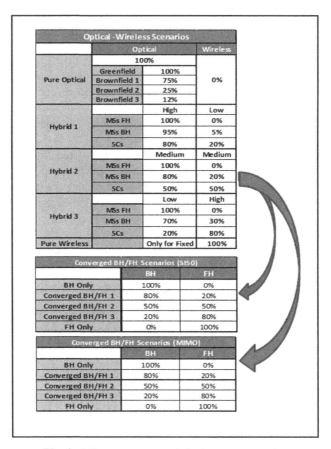

Fig. 4. 5G transport network deployment scenarios

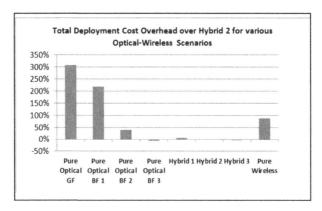

Fig. 5. Comparative cost for various optical-wireless transport network deployment scenarios

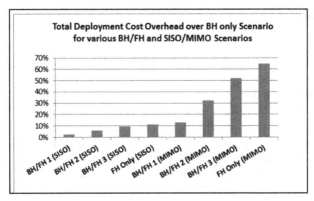

Fig. 6. Comparative cost for various BH/FH and SISO/MIMO transport network deployment scenarios

- Considering the effect of MIMO schemes at the access network, when using 4 × 4 MIMO for interference cancellation the total cost escalates with greater steps for FH compared to SISO, leading to more than 60% of additional cost for FH-only deployment compared to BH only. Therefore, MSs operating with higher order MIMO schemes for interference cancellation shall be backhauled.
- OPEX is a very small fraction of total cost compared to CAPEX. To sum up, the main factors that affect the total cost are: the trenching/civil works/etc. for the optical network, the usage of Sub-6 network equipment, the usage of MIMO schemes for FH, a BH-only deployment of numerous Sub-6 links.

5   Potential Future Expansions of the Tool

Although the tool has been developed for the needs of a specific 5G-PPP project, it could be tailored to "assess" more technological and architectural concepts, and provide insights on the relative cost efficiency and the investment viability of alternative deployments. Indicatively, the tool could incorporate:

- Additional deployment options, such as the placement of vBBU pools, the adoption of edge-computing, cloud-computing for specific services' hosting, other wireless/optical technologies, etc.
- Business aspects, such as licensing, and/or revenues coming from 5G transport service offerings, and additional financial calculations (e.g., RoI, NPV, IRR, Profitability Index).

   The tool can be also used in the opposite manner, that is, for a given investment provide the deployment options to support the maximum possible traffic in a certain area. In the mid-term, the tool is planned to accommodate the architectural evolution of 5G-PICTURE, while the business factors still remain out of the 5G-PPP projects scope.

6 Conclusions

In this paper, a methodology framework for the techno-economic analysis of the prominent, highly converged, 5G transport networks is presented. A fully parameterized techno-economic tool, developed for the needs of the 5G-XHaul and 5G-PICTURE 5G-PPP projects enables the cost evaluation of various transport network technologies and deployment options, by modeling, dimensioning and costing while taking into account a plethora of critical technology-related parameters. Initial results from the applicability of the tool in indicative (5G-XHaul) deployment scenarios provide interesting conclusions on the potential utilization of 5G technologies achieving higher cost efficiency. Flexible by nature, the tool can be further expanded to include additional technologies, more complex deployment options as well as business factors, to enable the investigation of cost efficient high performance 5G network solutions' deployments as well as deeper understanding and familiarization with the yet unknown 5G ecosystem.

Acknowledgments. The research leading to these results has received funding from the European Union's Framework Programme Horizon 2020 under grant agreements (1) No. 671551 and project name "5G-XHaul: Dynamically Reconfigurable Optical-Wireless Backhaul/Fronthaul with Cognitive Control Plane for Small Cells and Cloud-RANs" and (2) N° 762057 and project name "5G-PICTURE: "5G Programmable Infrastructure Converging disaggregated neTwork and compUte REsources".

References

1. 5G-PPP Project 5G-XHaul. http://www.5g-xhaul-project.eu/
2. 5G-PPP Project 5G-PICTURE. http://www.5g-picture-project.eu/index.html
3. 5G-PPP View on 5G Architecture, Version 1.0 (2015). https://5g-ppp.eu/wp-content/uploads/2014/02/5G-PPP-5G-Architecture-WP-For-public-consultation.pdf
4. 5G-PPP View on 5G Architecture, Version 2.0 (2017). https://5g-ppp.eu/wp-content/uploads/2018/01/5G-PPP-5G-Architecture-White-Paper-Jan-2018-v2.0.pdf
5. 3GPP TS 22.261 V16.1.0 (2017-09) 3rd Generation Partnership Project; Technical Specification Group Services and System Aspects; Service requirements for the 5G system, Stage 1 (R16)
6. 3GPP, TS 28.530 V15.3.0 (2019-12) 3rd Generation Partnership Project; Technical Specification Group Services and System Aspects; Management and orchestration; Concepts, use cases and requirements, (R15)
7. 3GPP TS 23.501 V16.0.0 (2019-03), 3rd Generation Partnership Project; Technical Specification Group Services and System Aspects; System Architecture for the 5G System; Stage 2 (R16)
8. 5G-XHaul Project, Deliverable D2.2. System Architecture Definition, July 2016
9. Lyberopoulos, G., Theodoropoulou, E., Mesogiti, I., et. al.: Fiber-wireless Fronthaul/Backhaul network architectures for 5G. In: Proceedings of the Computer Aided Modeling and Design of Communication Links and Networks (CAMAD), IEEE 20th International Workshop, Barcelona, Spain, 17–19 September 2018 (2018)
10. Goodarzi, M., Maletic, N., Sark, V., Camps Mur, D., et al.: 5G-XHAUL, Deliverable D3.3. D3.3 5G-XHaul algorithms and services Design and Evaluation, June 2018
11. 5G-PICTURE, Deliverable D2.2. System architecture and preliminary evaluations, May 2018

12. Legg, P., Kalokidou, V., Pelham, T.: 5G-XHAUL, Deliverable D4.7. Test results from field trial, real time algorithms in BWT DP1 platform, December 2016
13. Villegas, E.G., Demirkol, I., Camps, D.: 5G-XHAUL, Deliverable D4.11. Wireless backhauling using Sub-6 GHz systems, December 2016
14. Zou, J., Eiselt, M.: 5G-XHAUL, Deliverable D4.2. Optical Fronthauling Solution, October 2017
15. Tzanakaki, A., et al.: 5G infrastructures supporting end-user and operational services: the 5G-XHaul architectural perspective. In: IEEE ICC 2016, Workshop on 5G Architecture, Kuala Lumpur, Malaysia, May 2016
16. Zou, J., et al.: Field-trial evaluation of low-latency and timing-accurate 100G Ethernet aggregator for converged mobile X-haul. In: ECOC 2018, Rome, Italy (2018)
17. 5G-PICTURE Deliverable D4.1. State of the art and initial function design, February 2018
18. 5G-PICTURE Deliverable D4.2. Complete design and initial evaluation of developed functions, November 2018
19. G-XHaul D6.4. 5G-XHaul Techno-economic Study, July 2018

RHODA Topology Configuration Using Bayesian Optimization

Maotong Xu[1] , Min Tian[1](✉) , Eytan Modiano[2] ,
and Suresh Subramaniam[1]

[1] George Washington University, Washington, DC 20052, USA
{htfy8927,mtian39,suresh}@gwu.edu
[2] Massachusetts Institute of Technology, Cambridge, MA 02139, USA
modiano@mit.edu

Abstract. The rapid growth of data center traffic requires data center networks (DCNs) to be scalable, energy-efficient, and provide low latencies. Optical Wavelength Division Multiplexing (WDM) is a promising technique to build data centers comprising millions of servers. In [24], a WDM-based Reconfigurable Hierarchical Optical DCN Architecture (RHODA) was presented, which can accommodate up to 10+ million of servers and a variety of traffic patterns. RHODA also saves tremendous amounts of power and cost through its extensive use of passive optical devices, and minimal use of power-hungry and costly devices. RHODA achieves high throughput through reconfigurable clustering of racks of servers. In this paper, we focus on the design of the cluster topology (also called inter-cluster network). Given the pair-wise cluster traffic, our objective for the cluster topology is to minimize the average hop length. In [24], a simple variant of the Hungarian algorithm that maximizes the one-hop or direct traffic among clusters was used. In this paper, we leverage the Bayesian Optimization (BO) framework and propose a fast algorithm to minimize the average number of hops in the inter-cluster network of RHODA. To the best of our knowledge, this is the first paper that employs BO to optimize optical DCN performance. We present our design decisions and modifications to BO based on the network constraints. Results show that BO can achieve optimal or near-optimal results, and outperforms a well-known regular topology (Gemnet) and the Hungarian-based method by up to 13% and 58%, respectively.

Keywords: Bayesian Optimization · Data center networks · Inter-cluster network · RHODA

1 Introduction

Data center (DC) traffic has experienced dramatic growth, increasing at an annual rate of 31%, and will reach 3.3 ZB per year [22]. To store and process huge amounts

Supported by NSF award CNS-1618487 and CNS-1617091.

© IFIP International Federation for Information Processing 2020
Published by Springer Nature Switzerland AG 2020
A. Tzanakaki et al. (Eds.): ONDM 2019, LNCS 11616, pp. 130–141, 2020.
https://doi.org/10.1007/978-3-030-38085-4_12

of data, DCs will consist of millions of servers. For example, Microsoft owns over one million servers and a single DC alone contains over 250,000 servers [23]. On the other hand, interactive applications, e.g., web searches and social media, require low network latency. For example, the acceptable latency range for stock exchange transactions is 5–100 ms [20]. Traffic within a DC is usually not uniformly distributed. For instance, measurements on a 1500-server Microsoft production DC network (DCN) reveal that only a few ToRs (Top-of-the-Rack, used as an alternative for rack) are hot and most of a ToR's traffic goes to a few other ToRs [11]. Finally, power consumption of data centers will reach 140 billion kilowatt-hours annually by 2020, and it will cost \$13 billion annually [16].

Conventional electrical DCNs (e.g., FatTree [1], Bcube [8], VL2 [7] and Flattened Butterfly [5]) are built using a multi-layer approach, with a large number of switches at the bottom level to connect with servers/racks and a few high-end switches located at the upper layers to aggregate and distribute the traffic. Those networks rely heavily on high-cost and power-hungry electrical switches, and operators are facing limited scalability, high latency and low energy efficiency problems.

Optical Wavelength Division Multiplexing (WDM) is a promising technology for meeting the traffic demand of data centers. It can support hundreds of wavelengths per fiber and 100 Gbps transmission rate per wavelength. Moreover, large-scale optical switches consume less power per bit/s, making the network architecture scalable and energy-efficient. RHODA [24] is a WDM-based reconfigurable hierarchical optical DCN architecture. The architecture can scale up to 10+ million servers and support various traffic patterns. RHODA achieves high throughput through reconfigurable clustering of racks of servers. Racks with large amounts of mutual traffic can be grouped into clusters, and a high-bandwidth intra-cluster network connects racks within a cluster. The clusters are connected through an inter-cluster network which is also reconfigurable based on the traffic demands among clusters. The inter-cluster network uses wavelength selective switches (WSSs) and optical space switches to achieve topology reconfigurability. The resulting inter-cluster network topology is degree-constrained because of port count limitation of WSSs. RHODA saves large amount of power and cost by extensively using passive devices (couplers, Arrayed Waveguide Grating Routers (AWGRs), and mux/demuxes), and minimally using power-hungry and expensive devices (e.g., WSSs).

Once clusters are defined and the intra- and inter-cluster topologies have been established, flows are routed within and between clusters over those topologies, possibly using multiple hops, where each hop corresponds to one optical transmission and reception. As packets have to be converted from optical to electrical to optical form for each hop, and queued up for transmission at intermediate nodes (ToRs), the network latency is largely determined by the number of hops. The focus of this paper is on the design of the inter-cluster network topology to minimize the average number of hops (weighted by traffic demands). In [24], the inter-cluster topology is constructed using a Hungarian-based method [12]. The method first builds a circle/ring among clusters to first make the inter-cluster topology connected, and then the Hungarian algorithm is iteratively used to find a perfect bipartite matching to maximize the total traffic over the directly connected clusters (i.e., single-hop traffic). General regular topologies, e.g., Hypercube [6] and Gemnet [10], are attractive for uniform traffic, but they do not minimize the average hop distance for skewed traffic. In this paper, we propose an algorithm for inter-cluster topology design based on Bayesian Optimization (BO), and demonstrate that it produces optimal or near-optimal results very quickly.

Bayesian optimization (BO) [14] is a powerful tool to find optimal or near-optimal solutions for black-box problems, i.e., it is suitable in situations where a closed-form expression for the objective function is unknown. BO first uses a statistical model, e.g., Gaussian Process, to fit the objective function. Then, a pre-defined acquisition function is used to locate the next point to sample. The acquisition function can trade off between exploration and exploitation. This means that BO does not get stuck in local optima and can often find the global optimal solution.

In this paper, we use BO to find an inter-cluster topology for RHODA to minimize the average traffic-weighted hop distance. We describe our design decisions – the choice of prior model, acquisition function and optimizing algorithm. Further, we describe several modifications to BO based on topology constraints. Finally, we compare BO with the optimal solution obtained through solving an integer-linear program (ILP), and with the hop distances in the Gemnet topology and using Hungarian-based method. Our results show that BO can achieve optimal or near-optimal results, and outperforms Gemnet and Hungarian-based method by up to 13% and 58%, respectively.

The rest of this paper is organized as follows: Sect. 2 briefly describes the RHODA architecture. Section 3 presents the ILP model and our design decisions and modifications of BO based on network requirements. Section 4 presents performance evaluation results, and Sect. 5 concludes the paper.

2   RHODA Architecture

In this section, we briefly describe the RHODA architecture. The reader is referred to [24] for more design details of RHODA.

As Fig. 1 illustrates, RHODA is a DCN architecture consisting of N servers grouped into M racks, so that there are $m = N/M$ servers per rack. Each rack has a ToR switch used for both electronic switching of the packets within a rack and for communication with other racks. Each ToR connects to all of the m servers within the rack. For communication to and from other ToRs, each ToR has $T^{intra} + T^{inter}$ tunable transceivers (TRXs). RHODA consists of five parts, namely, cluster membership network (CMN), intra- and inter- signals demultiplexing part, intra-cluster network, inter-cluster network, and intra- and inter- signals multiplexing part.

RHODA lets cluster membership be reconfigurable. This is achieved by the CMN using a set of k/α $V \times V$ cluster configuration switches (CCS), where

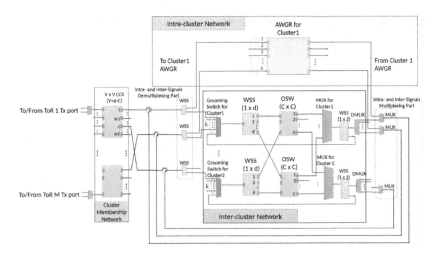

Fig. 1. The RHODA architecture. M: number of racks; k: number of racks per cluster; d: egress degree of a cluster; C: number of clusters.

$V = \alpha \cdot C$ and α is a positive integer parameter that is chosen as a trade-off between the cost and complexity of the CMN and the reconfiguration flexibility.

Since most of the heavy communication in a data center is carried over small subsets of ToRs [17] (and these ToRs would ideally be configured to the same cluster), RHODA equips each cluster with a $k \times k$ AWGR to support large amounts of intra-cluster traffic. In the inter-cluster network, each cluster can be considered as the smallest communication element. Flows from racks are merged (using optical-to-electrical-to-optical conversion) by grooming switches (GSs) to reduce the number of wavelengths needed. The communication graph between clusters (i.e., the cluster topology) is then determined by C $1 \times d$ WSSs and d $C \times C$ optical space switches (OSWs). In particular, each cluster can send signals to up to d other clusters. Demultiplexers (DMUXs) split signals carried by different wavelengths. A signal carried on wavelength w is forwarded to the $\lceil \frac{w}{k} \rceil$th port of the DMUX.

3   Topology Configuration Algorithm

Our objective is to minimize the traffic-weighted average number of hops in the inter-cluster network of RHODA. We first present an ILP formulation, and then present the BO framework adapted to solve our topology design problem.

3.1   ILP Formulation

The network has a set of nodes (which are the clusters) $\mathcal{C}$, and a traffic matrix T. The number of nodes/clusters, $C = |\mathcal{C}|$. Each node has both an in-degree and out-degree constraint of d. The following ILP constructs the degree-constrained and directed topology, and minimizes the traffic-weighted average hop distance over all node-pairs, assuming that multi-hop traffic is routed over the shortest path in the topology.

$$\min \frac{\sum_{i,j \in C} T_{ij} \cdot H_{ij}}{\sum_{i,j \in C} T_{ij}} \tag{1}$$

$$\text{s.t.} \qquad L_{ij} \in \{0,1\}, \quad \forall i,j \in C \tag{2}$$

$$\sum_{j \in C, j \neq i} L_{ij} \leq d, \quad \forall i \in C \tag{3}$$

$$\sum_{j \in C, j \neq i} L_{ji} \leq d, \quad \forall i \in C \tag{4}$$

$$L_{ii} = 0, \quad \forall i \in C \tag{5}$$

$$H_{ii} = 0, \quad \forall i \in C \tag{6}$$

$$0 < H_{ij} < C, \quad \forall i,j \in C, i \neq j \tag{7}$$

$$H_{ij} = 1, \quad for \ L_{ij} = 1, \\ \forall i,j \in C, i \neq j \tag{8}$$

$$H_{ij} = \min(H_{ik} + \\ ((L_{kj} - 1) * (-a)) + 1)), \quad for \ L_{ij} \neq 1, \\ \forall i,j,k \in C, \\ i \neq j, j \neq k, i \neq k \tag{9}$$

In the above formulation, the decision variables are the L_{ij}'s, where $L_{ij} = 1$ implies the establishment of a link between node i and j, and no link is established if $L_{ij} = 0$. H_{ij} represents the number of hops on the shortest path from i to j. In this ILP formulation, (1) is our objective, to optimize the traffic-weighted average number of hops. Inequalities (3) and (4) ensure that the in-degree and out-degree of each node is not more than D. The values of H_{ij}'s are determined by (6), (7), and (8). If a link from node i to j exists, H_{ij} is 1; on the other hand, if there is no link from i to j, H_{ij} is defined as the minimum value of $H_{ik} + ((L_{kj} - 1) * (-a) + 1)$, where a is defined as a large positive integer, so that if L_{kj} does not exist, $H_{ik} + ((L_{kj} - 1) \cdot (-a) + 1)$ will be an integer far larger than $C - 1$.

3.2   Bayesian Optimization

The ILP is too time-consuming for large instances (e.g., when there are more than 10 clusters and the degree is 4 or higher) and cannot be used in an online setting where the traffic dynamically changes and the topology needs to be configured quickly so that packets are not blocked for extended periods while the configuration takes place. We therefore seek a fast heuristic algorithm to minimize average hop distance. In [24], the topology is constructed by adapting the well-known Hungarian assignment method [12] for finding the maximum-weight

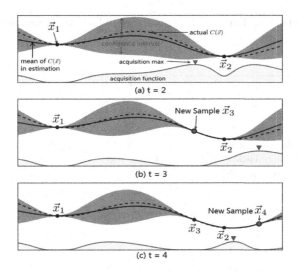

Fig. 2. An example of BO's working process [2].

matching in a bipartite graph. Once a circle is formed among the clusters to ensure that the topology is connected, our approach in [12] iteratively applied the Hungarian algorithm until the degree constraint is violated. The resulting topology, however, may turn out to have a large *average* hop-distance. Grid Search and Random Search [3] can be used for our problem, but time consumption would be too large.

In this paper, we turn to a widely used framework to solve optimization problems, namely, Bayesian optimization (BO). For instance, it is useful for solving the following problem (shown in one dimension here):

$$\min_{x \in A} f(x),$$

where structure/concavity of objective function $f(x)$ is unknown but can be observed through evaluations. Further, BO aims to minimize the number of evaluations to save optimization cost/time.

Figure 2 shows an example of running BO on a 1D problem. The blue area is an area in which the objective function is expected to lie in with, say, 95% probability. The optimization starts with two points, i.e., x_1 and x_2. At each iteration, BO decides that the next point is sampled at the argmax of a predefined acquisition function. As shown in Fig. 2, x_3 and x_4 are sampled in the next two iterations.

BO consists of two essential components, i.e., a statistical model for modeling the objective function, and an acquisition function for deciding the next point to sample. First, BO evaluates the objective function based on multiple randomly chosen initial points (e.g., 5). Then, BO iteratively uses all available data to update the posterior probability on the objective function, use the current posterior probability to compute the acquisition function, and argmax the acquisition function to find the next point at which to evaluate the objective function. The pseudocode is shown in Algorithm 1.

Algorithm 1. Bayesian Optimization Algorithm

1: Use a statistical model to model the objective function f
2: **while** Stopping condition is not satisfied **do**
3:    Update the posterior probability distribution
4:    Calculate the acquisition function using posterior distribution
5:    Argmax the acquisition function to locate next point
6:    Evaluate f with sample point
7:    Update dataset
8: **end while**

To leverage BO to find a good topology in our problem, we need to make several design decisions and modifications based on our requirements.

Choice of Prior Model. We choose Gaussian Process as the statistical model for modeling the objective function. The Gaussian Process has desirable features, e.g., it is non-parametric and the model is approximately Gaussian (central limit theorem).

Random Point. We provide several random "points" for BO's first step. In our case, we provide several adjacency matrices (representing random degree-constrained topologies) as input to evaluate $f(x)$. We generate such a random matrix as follows. First build a circle among nodes to guarantee that all nodes are connected. We then randomly assign $d - 1$ 1s (edges) on each row of the adjacency matrix. Then, we iterate over all columns and rows of the adjacency matrix in random order and adjust the entries to guarantee that each node has no more than d ingress/egress edges. The pseudocode is shown in Algorithm 2.

Acquisition Function. There are three main acquisition functions used in BO, i.e., Probability of Improvement (PI) [13], Expected Improvement (EI) [4], and GP Upper Confidence Bound (GP-UCB) [21]. PI can get stuck in local optima and under-explored globally [19], and GP-UCB needs extra effort to tune its own parameter. So, in this paper, we use EI as the acquisition function.

Optimization Algorithm. As shown in Line 5 of Algorithm 1, BO finds the argmax of the acquisition function to locate the next sample point. In our case, BO inputs a random point (i.e., adjacency matrix) for an optimizing algorithm (Opt-Alg), e.g., Limited-memory Broyden-Fletcher-Goldfarb-Shanno algorithm (L-BFGS) [15]. Then, L-BFGS uses the random point as an initial point and obtains derivatives of the acquisition function to identify the direction of steepest

Algorithm 2. Random points Algorithm

1: Input: C, d
2: Output: Adjacency Matrix (AM)
3: Build a circle among clusters
4: **for** r in range(C) **do**
5:    Randomly assign $d - 1$ elements to 1 in r^{th} row
6: **end for**
7: Find a random permutation of list range($1, C$) called (L_{col})
8: **for** c in L_{col} **do**
9:    $n\_edge = 0$
10:    Find a random permutation of list range($1, C$) called (L_{row})
11:    **for** r in L_{row} **do**
12:       **if** $AM[r, c] == 1$ **then**
13:          **if** $n\_edge \le d - 1$ **then**
14:             $n\_edge += 1$
15:          **else**
16:             $AM[r, c] = 0$
17:          **end if**
18:       **end if**
19:    **end for**
20: **end for**

descent. However, the result (a matrix) from L-BFGS might not satisfy our topology degree constraints.

We use two steps to make the result from L-BFGS be a valid (i.e., connected and degree-constrained) topology. First, we build a circle among clusters. Then, we sort the elements of the result matrix from L-BFGS in descending order and build edges between nodes one by one without violating degree constraints. The pseudocode is shown in Algorithm 3.

Algorithm 3. Conversion Algorithm

Input: Result/Matrix from L-BFGS (RM)
Output: Adjacency matrix (AM)
Build a circle among nodes in AM
Sort elements of RM in descending order (L_{sort})
for e in L_{sort} **do**
   if Egress degree of c_i and ingress degree of c_j
   are both less than d **then**
      Build an edge from c_i to c_j
   end if
end for

Stopping Condition. BO needs a stopping condition, e.g., based on time and/or iterations, and the best solution achieved in that period is taken as the

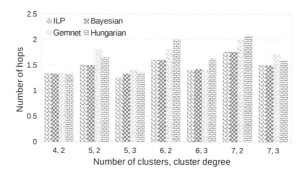

Fig. 3. Performance comparisons of Bayesian-based, Gemnet and Hungarian algorithms in cluster network.

final result. The more iterations, the better the final result, but as we seek a solution quickly, we use a stopping condition of ϵ sec, e.g., 1 sec. After ϵ sec, BO outputs the best achievable topology.

4   Evaluation

In this section, we conduct simulation results to compare the BO-based method with ILP, Hungarian-based method (HG), and Gemnet [10], in terms of the average number of hops. The ILP gives the optimal value, but it can only be obtained for small topologies in reasonable time. Gemnet provides a general method to build a topology with several desirable properties such as small average hop distance, diameter, etc. As opposed to ShuffleNet [9] and de Bruijn graph [18], Gemnet has no restriction on the number of nodes in its topology, and typically achieves smaller hop distances. Gemnet(M, K) arranges clusters in a cylinder of K columns and M clusters per column.

4.1   Cluster Topology

We first compare BO with ILP, Gemnet, and HG in terms of the average number of hops of the cluster topologies they produce. Flows are sent from each cluster to other clusters (uniform traffic), and the flow rate equals 1 Gbps. Figure 3 shows in terms of average number of hops, BO can achieve optimal results in some cases, and ILP outperforms BO by no more than 6% in the considered cases. Also, BO outperforms Gemnet and HG by up to 21% and 15%, respectively.

Then, we compare BO with Gemnet and HG with different traffic patterns in large networks and show comparison results in Fig. 4. Figure 4(a) shows comparison results with different number of clusters under uniform traffic. Results show BO outperforms Gemnet and HG by up to 21% and 58%, respectively. Clearly, HG is not a good choice to configure topology under uniform traffic. The reason is that HG aims to find a matching to maximize single-hop traffic, and under uniform traffic, HG might perform the same as a random topology.

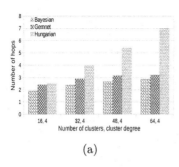
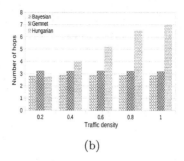

(a)   (b)

Fig. 4. Comparisons of Bayesian-based, Gemnet and Hungarian algorithms in cluster networks: (a) Comparison with different number of clusters and cluster degrees. (b) Comparison with different traffic densities.

Figure 4(b) shows comparison results under different traffic densities in a network of 64 clusters with a cluster degree equal to 4. We define traffic density as the probability of a flow existing between clusters. The flow rate is randomly chosen between 1 and 100 Gbps. Results show BO outperforms Gemnet and HG by up to 13% and 58%, respectively. Also, results show that HG outperforms Gemnet in a network with low traffic density. Under low traffic density, building direct links between clusters with large traffic benefits more in terms of the average number of hops.

4.2   RHODA

We now evaluate the various algorithms based on how the generated inter-cluster topologies perform in the entire RHODA architecture. Recall that the overall hop distance in RHODA is based on both the intra- and inter-cluster hop distances, and we have only tried to optimize the inter-cluster topology in this paper. We assume the following numbers for the DCN: the number of clusters is 64, and each cluster has 64 racks ($k = 64$). The number of wavelengths on a fiber is 128, the bandwidth of a wavelength is 100 Gbps, and both T^{intra} and T^{inter} are equal to 2 (i.e., a total of 4 transceivers per rack). The degree of WSS is 4 (i.e., $d = 4$). We consider three traffic patterns, i.e., uniform, low density traffic (LT), and high density traffic (HT). We set the rack flow rate to be $1/k^2$ Gbps (the total flow rate from a cluster to another cluster equals 1 Gbps). Under uniform traffic pattern, a rack sends a flow to each of the other racks. Under LT and HT, the probability that a cluster sends flows to another cluster is 0.2 and 0.8, respectively. Given cluster c_i sends flows to cluster c_j, each rack in c_i sends a flow to each rack in c_j.

In Fig. 5, we show comparison results of BO, Gemnet, and HG in RHODA with different metrics, i.e., the average number of hops, the average switch load, and the maximum switch load. Results show that RHODA outperforms Gemnet by up to 11%, 11%, and 77% in terms of average hop distance, average switch load, and maximum switch load, respectively. Also, RHODA outperforms HG by

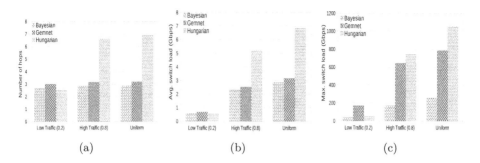

Fig. 5. Comparisons of Bayesian-based, Gemnet and Hungarian algorithms in RHODA: (a) Comparison in terms of number of hops. (b) Comparison in terms of average switch load. (c) Comparison in terms of maximum switch load.

up to 58%, 58%, and 77% in terms of average hop distance, average switch load, and maximum switch load, respectively. Thus, the topology configured by BO not only achieves small hop distances, but also balances the traffic well among switches.

5   Conclusion

A reconfigurable hierarchical optical DCN architecture (RHODA) was introduced in an earlier paper. RHODA groups racks into clusters and enables both clusters and the inter-cluster topology to be configurable. In this paper, we focus on optimizing the inter-cluster topology in terms of the weighted hop distance, and present an approach based on Bayesian Optimization (BO). We compare BO with ILP, Gemnet, and the Hungarian-based method. Results show that BO can achieve optimal or near-optimal results within a small amount of time, and it outperforms Gemnet and Hungarian-based method by up to 13% and 58%, respectively.

References

1. Al-Fares, M., Loukissas, A., Vahdat, A.: A scalable, commodity data center network architecture. ACM SIGCOMM Comput. Commun. Rev. **38**, 63–74 (2008)
2. Alipourfard, O., Liu, H.H., Chen, J., Venkataraman, S., Yu, M., Zhang, M.: CherryPick: adaptively unearthing the best cloud configurations for big data analytics. In: NSDI, vol. 2 (2017). 4–2
3. Bergstra, J., Bengio, Y.: Random search for hyper-parameter optimization. J. Mach. Learn. Res. **13**, 281–305 (2012)
4. Brochu, E., Cora, V.M., De Freitas, N.: A tutorial on Bayesian optimization of expensive cost functions, with application to active user modeling and hierarchical reinforcement learning. arXiv preprint arXiv:1012.2599 (2010)
5. Csernai, M., Ciucu, F., Braun, R.P., Gulyás, A.: Towards 48-fold cabling complexity reduction in large flattened butterfly networks. In: 2015 IEEE Conference on Computer Communications (INFOCOM), pp. 109–117. IEEE (2015)

6. Dally, W.J., Towles, B.P.: Principles and Practices of Interconnection Networks. Elsevier, San Francisco (2004)
7. Greenberg, A., et al.: VL2: a scalable and flexible data center network. ACM SIGCOMM Comput. Commun. Rev. **39**, 51–62 (2009)
8. Guo, C., et al.: BCube: a high performance, server-centric network architecture for modular data centers. ACM SIGCOMM Comput. Commun. Rev. **39**(4), 63–74 (2009)
9. Hluchyj, M.G., Karol, M.J.: Shuffle net: an application of generalized perfect shuffles to multihop lightwave networks. J. Lightwave Technol. **9**(10), 1386–1397 (1991)
10. Iness, J., Banerjee, S., Mukherjee, B.: GEMNET: a generalized, shuffle-exchange-based, regular, scalable, modular, multihop, WDM lightwave network. IEEE/ACM Trans. Network. (TON) **3**(4), 470–476 (1995)
11. Kandula, S., Padhye, J., Bahl, P.: Flyways to de-congest data center networks (2009)
12. Kuhn, H.W.: The hungarian method for the assignment problem. Naval Res. Logistics Q. **2**(1–2), 83–97 (1955)
13. Kushner, H.J.: A new method of locating the maximum point of an arbitrary multipeak curve in the presence of noise. J. Basic Eng. **86**(1), 97–106 (1964)
14. Mockus, J.: Bayesian heuristic approach to global optimization and examples. J. Global Optim. **22**(1–4), 191–203 (2002)
15. Mokhtari, A., Ribeiro, A.: Global convergence of online limited memory BFGS. J. Mach. Learn. Res. **16**(1), 3151–3181 (2015)
16. Delforge, P.: (2015). http://www.nrdc.org/energy/data-center-efficiency-assessment.asp
17. Roy, A., Zeng, H., Bagga, J., Porter, G., Snoeren, A.C.: Inside the social network's (datacenter) network. ACM SIGCOMM Comput. Commun. Rev. **45**, 123–137 (2015)
18. Sivarajan, K., Ramaswami, R.: Multihop lightwave networks based on De Bruijn graphs. In: The Conference on Computer Communications. Tenth Annual Joint Comference of the IEEE Computer and Communications Societies Proceedings, IEEE INFCOM 1991, pp. 1001–1011. IEEE (1991)
19. Snoek, J., Larochelle, H., Adams, R.P.: Practical Bayesian optimization of machine learning algorithms. In: Advances in Neural Information Processing Systems, pp. 2951–2959 (2012)
20. Some interesting bits about latency. https://www.citycloud.com/city-cloud/some-interesting-bits-about-latency
21. Srinivas, N., Krause, A., Kakade, S.M., Seeger, M.: Gaussian process optimization in the bandit setting: no regret and experimental design. arXiv preprint arXiv:0912.3995 (2009)
22. Wang, L., et al.: Scheduling with machine-learning-based flow detection for packet-switched optical data center networks. J. Opt. Commun. Netw. **10**(4), 365–375 (2018)
23. Who Has the Most Web Servers. http://www.datacenterknowledge.com/archives/2009/05/14/whos-got-the-most-web-servers
24. Xu, M., Diakonikolas, J., Modiano, E., Subramaniam, S.: A hierarchical WDM-based scalable data center network architecture. In: 2019 IEEE International Conference on Communications (ICC), IEEE (2019). arXiv preprint arXiv:190106450

Dynamic Abstraction of Optical Networks with Machine Learning Technologies

Shuangyi Yan[1]([✉]) [iD], Zhengguang Gao[1,2], Rui Wang[1], Alex Mavromatis[1],
Reza Nejabati[1], and Dimitra Simeonidou[1]

[1] High Performance Networks Group, University of Bristol, Bristol, UK
Shuangyi.Yan@bristol.ac.uk
[2] State Key Lab of Information Photonics and Optical Communications, BUPT,
Beijing, China

Abstract. The emerging 5G network will bring a huge amount of network traffic with big variations to optical transport networks. Software-defined optical networks and network function virtualization contribute to the vision for future programmable, disaggregated, and dynamic optical networks. Future optical networks will be more dynamic in network functions and network services, with high-frequency network reconfigurations. Optical connections will last shorter than that of the static optical networks. It's straightforward that Programmable optical hardware will require a reduced link margin to improve the hardware utilization. To configure network dynamically, real-time network abstractions are required for both current links and available-for-deploy links. The former abstraction guarantees the established links not be interfered by the newly established link while the latter abstraction provides information for intelligent network planning. In this talk, we use machine-learning technologies to process the collected monitoring data in a field-trial testbed to abstract performances of multiple optical channels. Based on the abstract information, a new channel can be established with maximum performance and minimized interference on the current signals. We demonstrated the dynamic network abstraction over a 563.4-km field-trial testbed for 8 dynamic optical channels with 32 Gbaud Nyquist PM-16QAM signals. The work can be further extended to support complex optical networks.

Keywords: Machine learning · Network abstraction · Low-margin networks

1 Introduction

Optical networks have becoming the essential infrastructure for the future fifth generation (5G) networks. 5G transport networks, including fronthaul, middle-haul and backhaul networks, rely on optical network infrastructure [19]. Optical

This work is supported by the UK EPSRC through the TOUCAN project (EP/L020009/1) and the INSIGHT project (EP/L026155/2), the EU-H2020 Metro-Haul project (761727).

© IFIP International Federation for Information Processing 2020
Published by Springer Nature Switzerland AG 2020
A. Tzanakaki et al. (Eds.): ONDM 2019, LNCS 11616, pp. 142–153, 2020.
https://doi.org/10.1007/978-3-030-38085-4_13

and wireless converged network architecture was proposed to support operational network and end-user services [20]. In addition, the emerging 5G applications, such as augmented reality applications, require more interactions with computing resource that located either in the cloud or in the edge. Compared to the previous mobile networks, an increased proportion of mobile traffic will be sent to metro and core networks. The successful deployments of 5G networks require lot of innovations to be made in optical networks. In 5G networks, a peak data rate up to 20 Gbit/s is provided for per user [12], which is comparable to optical channel capacities in optical networks providing 100G Ethernet standard still dominates the market [6]. Therefore, dynamic network traffic with big variations in 5G networks need to be supported by a flexible and dynamic optical network.

On the other side, optical networks are continuously evolving to be more flexible and dynamic. Software-defined optical networks (SDN) decouple the control plane and data plane, allowing the independent developments of both technologies [3]. Network function virtualization (NFV) brings flexibility of network functions to be configured, migrated or terminated in optical networks. End-to-end network service orchestration can deploy network services over multiple network domains [1, 22]. In the perspective of optical hardware, hardware-programmable network functions have been developed to deliver node functions in an on-demand way [14].

In dynamic optical networks, network services or connections will serve in a short time and high-frequency network re-configurations will be expected in optical networks. From the perspective of network operators or network controllers, it is straightforward that optical networks should be planned at short timescales rather than the end of life (EoL) of network facilities. Network margins part of which were reserved for aging can be eliminated by considering the service life period [17].

Dynamic optical networks with reduced network margins raise many challenges for network operations. One of the key challenges is that network controllers need up-to-date information about dynamic networks to dynamic configure optical networks with a reduced margin. Network abstraction that abstracts information of network states assists network controllers to deploy services according to the current network states. In addition, the abstract process needs to evaluate the impact of the new established services or links on the previous services or links. The latter abstraction function guarantees the established links not be interfered by the newly established link. In margin-reduced networks, the dynamic abstraction becomes more critical. Due to the fast-frequency network re-configurations, the dynamic abstraction need to be continually updated after each reconfiguration with a fast response time.

In optical networks, one of the key information regarding per link is the link impairment, which is affected by operation parameters of network facility and network configurations. Static network abstraction can be achieved by testing link performance in advance [4]. However, the static network abstraction neglects the dynamics in network payloads and other physical parameters. In margin-reduced dynamic optical networks, it is of vital importance to abstract optical

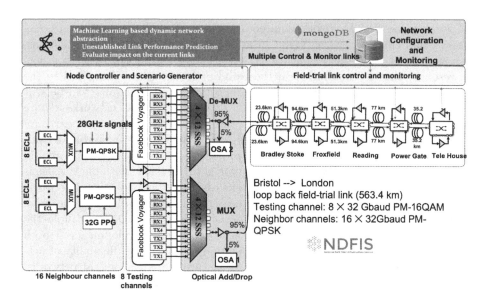

Fig. 1. Field-trial demonstration over a 560-km link between Bristol and London.

network impairments dynamically. Therefore, time-consuming link optimization can be eliminated to support high-frequency network reconfigurations.

In this paper, we explored machine-learning technologies to process the collected optical performance monitoring data and operation data of the key equipment in a field-trial testbed to dynamically abstract qualities of transmission (QoTs) of multiple optical channels. For the first time, we developed machine-learning (ML) based dynamic network abstraction using Random forest regression. The developed ML-based dynamic network abstraction is able to predict the transmission quality, i.e., BERs of the un-established optical channels and to evaluate the impact on the previously established channels. The ML-based predictor can predict the link performance up to 8 channels simultaneously. The evaluation of the current link is essential for a low-margin network. In the demonstration, a field-trial link between Bristol and London is setup with 24 optical channels transmitting over 564 km. A network-scale cloud network configuration and monitoring database (CMDB) is implemented over the field-trial link based on [15], with extensions to include parameters of EDFA pump lasers, such as pump laser current and temperature. The central 8-channel signals, generated by eight real-time PM-16QAM transponders, are configured dynamically with real-time BER (Bit Error Rate) measurements. Random forest regression based network abstraction algorithm is developed to abstract all the eight channels by the transmission performance. With 4324 training data sets, the developed network abstraction algorithm can predict the performance of the un-established channels based on the current network states. The algorithm can also evaluate the impacts on the previous established channels. The experimental results show the developed network abstraction algorithm could abstract network performance with a high precision. The dynamic network abstraction can assist network controller to deploy new services based on link performance while minimize the disturbance on current services. The work will be one of the potential enabling technologies for a reliable margin-reduced network.

2   Literature Review of Network Abstraction with Machine Learning Technologies

To abstract optical network impairments, multiple technologies have been explored. Gaussian-noise (GN) model has been developed extensively to provide a relatively simple and sufficiently-reliable tool for performance predictions [9,10]. Considering the complexity in dynamic optical networks, the complex calculation in GN-model prohibits its deployment in practical networks for network planning. Some simplified analytical models have been developed to reduce the complexity in [2,11]. Such analytical models could be used for general analysis to support network design. Nokia bell labs also reported a similar system design tool to facilitate the design of the terrestrial transmission systems with high-order modulation formats and coherent detection technologies [7]. In [5], an open source QoT estimator was developed with the capability to predict performance with an accuracy of ±0.75 db. This kind of analytical models can't provide precision predictions to reflect the impairments, especially the dynamic impairments in optical networks. Therefore, these tools were mainly used at the network design phase. In margin-reduced networks, more precise QoT estimation with a short computation time is required. The QoT prediction needs to be done for each operation.

Thanks to the advance of machine learning technologies, many researchers started to explore network dynamics in optical networks with advanced machine learning technologies. Artificial neural network based QoT prediction algorithms have been developed to predict the performance of the un-established optical channels [8,13,15]. Most of the previous works use network configurations, such as modulation formats, link distance, fiber parameters, to predict the QoT of the unestablished channels. In such case, the QoT-prediction actually neglects the dynamics in optical devices, especially the active devices, whose operation parameters affect the transmission performance significantly. The developed QoT prediction algorithm worked well in the collected data in a short time. However, failure to handle dynamics in optical device will lead to inaccuracy of QoT estimations in long term. In [15,16,21], we built a cloud network configuration and optical performance monitoring database to collect the physical parameters over the whole network. ANN-based QoT prediction was developed to predict a single channel. Combining with network configurations, the developed ANN-based QoT prediction algorithm is able to handle the dynamics in optical networks, which could be reflected in the operation parameters in optical devices. In this paper, we further developed the concept to dynamic optical network with multiple channels.

3   Field-Trial Demonstration of Dynamic Network Abstraction

Figure 1 shows experimental setup of the field-trial testbed. Total 24-channel optical signals are generated with three sets of transmitters in our lab. Eight external cavity lasers (ECLs) are combined together and then modulated with a dual-polarization IQ modulator to generate 8 × 28 Gbaud PM-QPSK signals. The IQ modulator is driven by four 28 Gbaud electrical signals, which are generated by a high-performance FPGA. In a similar way, another eight ECLs are modulated by another IQ modulator driven by a 32 Gbaud pulse pattern generator (PPG), to generate 32 Gbaud PM-QPSK signals. Another 8-channel real-time Nyquist PM-16QAM signals are generated by two Facebook Voyager transponders, which also provide BER measurements of per channels. The total 24 channel optical signals are multiplexed together by a 4 × 20 Wavelength Selective Switches (WSSs). After auto equalization, the combined 24-channel signal is launched to the 563.4-km fiber link between Bristol and London. The optical spectrum of the 24-channel optical signal is shown in Fig. 2. In this paper, the developed dynamic network abstraction will focus on the dynamic channels as indicated in Fig. 2. The node controller and scenario generator controls the three transmitter sets and WSSs. It can generate any combination with different channel slot "on". By configuring the three transmitter sets, various network scenarios with different channel distribution can be configured.

The used link which is part of the national dark fiber infrastructure (NDFIS) includes five intermediate nodes. Each intermediate node includes EDFA, DCM and a Polatis fiber switch to allow remote reconfiguration and monitoring of the fibers and amplifiers. The fiber switch monitors the launch power of each span. The operation parameters of the EDFAs are sent back to the cloud monitoring database. The launch power for each span was estimated using incoherent GN model. After transmission over the field-trial link, the signals are demultiplexed by another 4 × 20 WSS. Then the BER measurements will be carried out for each channel. The BER measurements of the 8-channel PM-16QAM signals are also collected and sent to the cloud monitoring database.

3.1   Cloud Monitoring Database

To dynamic configure a margin-reduced network, network controller requires up-to-date network state information. In addition to the dynamic network payloads (spectrum allocations), operation states of the key infrastructure in the link can provide in-depth information to abstract link impairments. The EDFAs in the link contribute to the most OSNR penalties. On the other hand, optical powers play a significant role for nonlinear effects, which limit the maximum transmission distance. Thus, a cloud monitoring database (CMDB) is implemented to collect network configuration information, operation information of key infrastructure, and the quality of transmission per links. The database creates the relationship between network configurations and the corresponding transmission performance. The design of the cloud monitoring database enables reusing

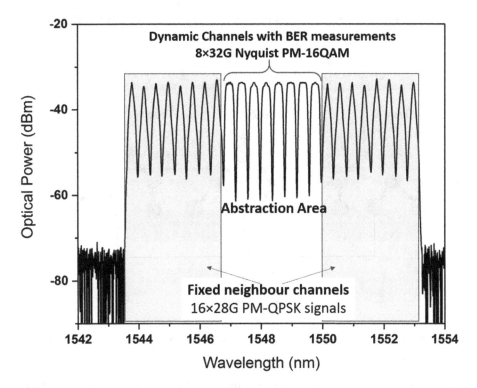

Fig. 2. Optical spectrum of the 24-channel optical signal. The dynamic abstraction focuses on the 8×32 Gbaud PM-16QAM signals.

of the local monitoring data. The separation of database from the SDN controller allows the possibility to deploy high-performance computing resource to analysis collected data and implement powerful machine-learning algorithms to serve the SDN controller as a network abstraction service.

The proposed CMDB is implemented over the field-trial testbed as shown in Fig. 1. The CMDB collects network configuration information from the SDN controller, such as channel configurations, wavelength, modulations, link lengths. The optical link monitoring information in the CMDB includes optical launch power monitored at each span, operation parameters of all EDFAs, and optical spectrum information at the transmitters and receivers. Regarding EDFAs, the CMDB collects operation information from each EDFA, include temperature and bias of the pump laser, optical power of the input and output ports, and the noise figure.

3.2 Machine Learning Based Network Abstraction

Considering that the data contains a lot of features, Random Forest Regression is chosen as a Machine Learning algorithm to predict link performance and evaluate the impact on the current channels. Random Forest is one of the most

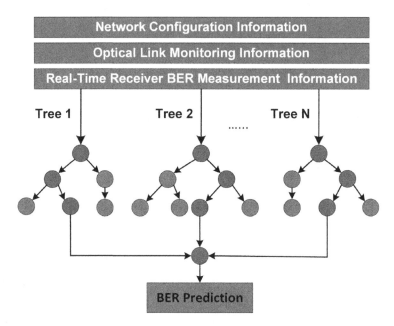

Fig. 3. Structure of BER prediction algorithm based on random forest regression.

effective ensemble learning algorithms, which includes N random decision Trees. Its final prediction result is combined from a set of base models, which improve its performance compared with a single model [18]. Furthermore, it handles thousands of features efficiently and runs on big data bases. Figure 3 shows the structure of BER prediction algorithm based on monitoring data from the CMDB. Monitoring data include three parts: network configuration information, optical link monitoring information and the BER measurements from the 8-channel real-time transponders. In order to improve the accuracy of prediction, the interrelationship of established channels is characterized by One-Hot coding.

In order to generalize the network state, the node controller and scenario generator as shown in Fig. 1 configures the transmitter sets to generate different scenarios of the 8 dynamic channels. We collected 4324 data to train the model. Each data include information about the transmitters, optical links, and receiver-side BER measurements.

3.3 Results of Dynamic Network Abstraction

To verify proposed network abstraction algorithm, one scenario with only channel 2 "on" is considered. To deploy new link, the network abstraction algorithm will predict the BER performance of all the available channel slots and evaluate the corresponding impact on the Channel 2. Figure 4 shows the comparison of the predicted and actual BERs for un-established channel when only channel 2 is established. The developed network abstraction algorithm predicted the BER of

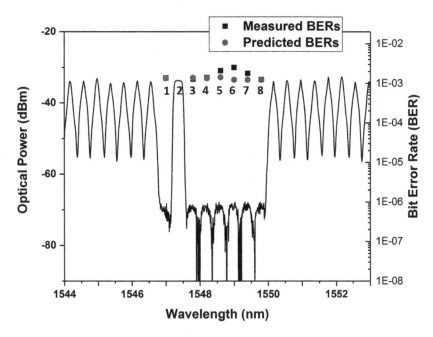

Fig. 4. Predicted BERs vs. Real BERs for all the available channel slots in the choosed scenario.

all the available channels (Channel 1, 3, 4, 5, 6, 7, 8). As show in the Fig. 4, the implemented network abstraction algorithm predicted the link BERs of the unestablished channel with a high precision. The maximum error occurs at Channel 5. The different performances for channel 5 and other channels contribute to the difference. The predicted performance for all the available channel slots can help network controller to deploy optical links intelligently. In the future work, the transmitter performance will be also included in the prediction model.

In the margin-reduced dynamic network, another challenge is to ensure the established channels not to be disturbed by the new deploy channels. Therefore, in the phase of network planning, the proposed network abstraction algorithm can evaluate the impact of the establishing links on the current channels. The evaluation will prohibit the failure of current channels. In the same scenario, the network abstraction algorithm predicts BERs of the channel 2 when the new established channel is deployed in the available channel slots, such as Channel 1, 3, 4, 5, 6, 7, 8. Figure 5 shows the comparison of predicted BERs and the actual BER for existed channel 2 when channel 1, 3, 4, 5, 6, 7, 8 is switched on respectively. We can see the prediction is very accurate, and the performance of existed optical path almost remains unchanged as the experiment platform is very stable. By adding another channel, the impact on the current channel is very limited.

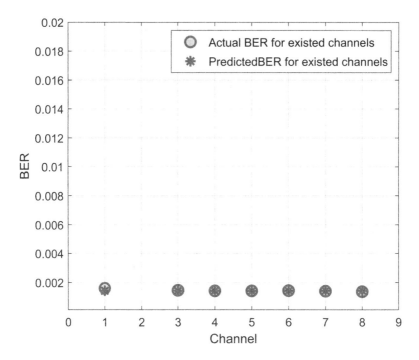

Fig. 5. Evaluation of the impacts on the current link by choosing different wavelength slots to establish a new link. The channel number is the choosed wavelength slot. The corresponding BER is the predicted BER performance of the previous link when the new link is established.

3.4 Scalabilities of the Cloud Monitoring Database and Machine-Learning Based QoT Predictor

In this paper, we extended the previous work to dynamically abstract the QoTs of multiple channels. The experimental demonstration shows the ML-based QoT prediction can help the SDN controller plan the network efficiently, i.e., to maximize the link capacity by reducing link margins with precise QoT predictions and minimize the interference on the current established channels. The QoT prediction relies on the collected massive network operation data from both the SDN controller and the optical performance monitoring. In current demonstration, the OSNR penalties of the multiple paths connected several optical nodes can be predicted with the implemented cloud monitoring database. To deploy the ML-based QoT predictor in the future optical networks, scalabilities of both cloud monitoring database and the ML-based QoT predictor need to be considered.

Regarding the cloud monitoring database, i.e., NCMDB, each physical transmitter is used with the event time together to generate the record ID. All the other information is linked to the record ID. In such approach, the whole network activities can be recorded and linked to each transmitter. Therefore, the scale of the NCMDB depends on the deployed transmitters in the link. Especially in core networks, there are limited numbers of nodes and links. The NCMDB can be easily scaled up to store more network information. The centralized monitoring data hub collects the monitoring information through dedicated links. The dedicated link could provide enough bandwidth to allow the NCMDB to collect raw data. Therefore, the data can be re-used by multiple network analytic applications. The network analytic applications that run on top of the NCMDB also provides an interface for the SDN controller to access the processed monitoring information. Therefore, the developed network abstraction application is deployed as a service. In such way, the centralized network information hub simplifies the work-flow of SDN controller to use the monitoring information. The design of the NCMDB provides good scalability for future big networks.

As far as the scalability of the ML-based QoT prediction technique is concerned, an increase in network size will definitely result in an increase in the number of links parameters (e.g. the number of operation parameters of EDFAs) which are used by our ML model for OSNR monitoring. This implies that the computational resources/time required for the training of ML will also increase significantly in this case. However, we would like to emphasize that the training procedure of ML model is conducted completely offline and prior to actual deployment in an SDN. Once the parameters of an ML are optimized offline, the actual OSNR monitoring process in SDNs employing trained ML model involves few simple matrix multiplications. Therefore, we believe that the computational complexity and processing time will keep at a low level and possible provide real-time network abstractions.

4   Conclusion

In this paper, random forest regression based network impairment abstraction algorithm is developed to analyze the implemented cloud monitoring and configuration database (CMDB). The network abstraction algorithm predicts the performance of all the available channel slots and also evaluate the impact on the current links when any available slot is selected to deploy new links. We demonstrated the network impairment abstraction up to 8-channels over a 564-km field-trial link. The implemented algorithm could predict the channel performance with a high precision to support margin-reduced optical network. The dynamic network abstraction could be integrated with the SDN controller to achieve low-margin dynamic optical networks. The introduced CMDB and the network analytic applications open new possibilities for future dynamic optical networks.

References

1. Bonafiglia, R., Castellano, G., Cerrato, I., Risso, F.: End-to-end service orchestration across SDN and cloud computing domains. In: 2017 IEEE Conference on Network Softwarization (NetSoft), pp. 1–6 (2017). https://doi.org/10.1109/NETSOFT.2017.8004234

2. Bosco, G., Poggiolini, P., Carena, A., Curri, V., Forghieri, F.: Analytical results on channel capacity in uncompensated optical links with coherent detection **19**(26), B440–B451 (2011). https://doi.org/10.1364/OE.19.00B440. http://www.opticsexpress.org/abstract.cfm?URI=oe-19-26-B440

3. Channegowda, M., Nejabati, R., Simeonidou, D.: Software-defined optical networks technology and infrastructure: enabling software-defined optical network operations [Invited]. J. Opt. Commun. Network. **5**(10), A274–A282. https://doi.org/10.1364/JOCN.5.00A274. 00120

4. Ives, D.J., et al.: A comparison of impairment abstractions by multiple users of an installed fiber infrastructure. In: Optical Fiber Communication Conference (OFC 2019), San Diego, CA, paper M4J.4, p. M4J.4 (2019)

5. Filer, M., Cantono, M., Ferrari, A., Grammel, G., Galimberti, G., Curri, V.: Multivendor experimental validation of an open source QoT estimator for optical networks **36**(15), 3073–3082. https://doi.org/10.1109/JLT.2018.2818406

6. Houtsma, V., van Veen, D., Harstead, E.: Recent progress on standardization of next-generation 25, 50, and 100G EPON. J. Lightwave Technol. **35**(6), 1228–1234. https://doi.org/10.1109/JLT.2016.2637825

7. Lavigne, B., et al.: System design tool for high bit rate terrestrial transmission systems with coherent detection **18**(3), 251–266. https://doi.org/10.1002/bltj.21637

8. Mo, W., et al.: ANN-based transfer learning for QoT prediction in real-time mixed line-rate systems. In: Optical Fiber Communication Conference, Paper W4F.3, W4F.3. Optical Society of America (2018). https://doi.org/10.1364/OFC.2018.W4F.3. https://www.osapublishing.org/abstract.cfm?uri=OFC-2018-W4F.3

9. Poggiolini, P.: The GN model of non-linear propagation in uncompensated coherent optical systems **30**(24), 3857–3879. https://doi.org/10.1109/JLT.2012.2217729

10. Poggiolini, P., Bosco, G., Carena, A., Curri, V., Jiang, Y., Forghieri, F.: The GN-model of fiber non-linear propagation and its applications **32**(4), 694–721. https://doi.org/10.1109/JLT.2013.2295208

11. Poggiolini, P., Carena, A., Curri, V., Bosco, G., Forghieri, F.: Analytical modeling of nonlinear propagation in uncompensated optical transmission links **23**(11), 742–744 (2011). https://doi.org/10.1109/LPT.2011.2131125

12. El Hattachi, R., Erfanian, J.: NGMN 5G Initiative White Paper

13. Rottondi, C., Barletta, L., Giusti, A., Tornatore, M.: Machine-learning method for quality of transmission prediction of unestablished lightpaths **10**(2), A286–A297. https://doi.org/10.1364/JOCN.10.00A286

14. Shuangyi, Y., Emilio, H.S., Yanni, O., Reza, N., Dimitra, S.: Hardware-programmable optical networks (Invited) **59**(10). https://doi.org/10.1007/s11432-016-0358-0

15. Yan, S., et al.: Field trial of machine-learning-assisted and SDN-based optical network planning with network-scale monitoring database. In: ECOC 2017, TH.PDP.B4, ECOC Proceeding (2017)

16. Yan, S., Nejabati, R., Simeonidou, D.: Data-driven network analytics and network optimisation in SDN-based programmable optical networks. In: ONDM 2018, pp. 234–238 (2018)

17. Soumplis, P., Christodoulopoulos, K., Quagliotti, M., Pagano, A., Varvarigos, E.: Network planning with actual margins. J. Lightwave Technol. **35**(23), 5105–5120. https://doi.org/10.1109/JLT.2017.2743461

18. Ho, T.K.: The random subspace method for constructing decision forests. IEEE Trans. Pattern Anal. Mach. Intell. **20**(8), 832–844. https://doi.org/10.1109/34.709601

19. Tzanakaki, A., Anastasopoulos, M.P., Simeonidou, D.: Optical networking inter-connecting disaggregated compute resources: an enabler of the 5G vision. In: 2017 International Conference on Optical Network Design and Modeling (ONDM), pp. 1–6. https://doi.org/10.23919/ONDM.2017.7958550

20. Tzanakaki, A., et al.: Wireless-optical network convergence: enabling the 5G architecture to support operational and end-user services. IEEE Commun. Mag. **55**(10), 184–192. https://doi.org/10.1109/MCOM.2017.1600643. http://ieeexplore.ieee.org/document/8000808/

21. Yan, S., et al.: Field trial of machine-learning-assisted and SDN-based optical network management. In: Optical Fiber Communication Conference (OFC) 2019, Paper M2E.1, M2E.1. Optical Society of America (2019). https://doi.org/10.1364/OFC.2019.M2E.1. https://www.osapublishing.org/abstract.cfm?uri=OFC-2019-M2E.1

22. Yoshida, Y., et al.: SDN-based network orchestration of variable-capacity optical packet switching network over programmable flexi-grid elastic optical path network **33**(3), 609–617. https://doi.org/10.1109/JLT.2014.2351852. 00000

Novel P-Cycle Selection Algorithms for Elastic Optical Networks

Rujia Zou$^{(\boxtimes)}$ (ID) and Suresh Subramaniam (ID)

The George Washington University, Washington, DC 20052, USA
{rjzou,suresh}@gwu.edu

Abstract. Elastic optical networks (EONs) promise to provide high spectrum utilization efficiency due to flexibility in resource allocation. Survivability is regarded as an important aspect of EONs. P-cycle protection is very attractive for EONs due to fast restoration and high protection efficiency. P-cycles have been extensively studied for conventional fixed-grid WDM networks; however, p-cycle design and selection for EONs has received much less attention. In this paper, we consider the design and selection of p-cycles for EONs with distance-dependent modulation. We propose two novel link-based p-cycle evaluation methods: individual p-cycle selection and p-cycle set selection for EONs. Based on these methods, two p-cycle design algorithms, namely, Traffic Independent P-cycle Selection (TIPS) and Traffic-Oriented P-cycle Selection (TOPS), are proposed to find the best set of p-cycles that is able to provide 100% failure-dependent protection against single link failures. We evaluate our algorithms using both static and dynamic traffic models. Simulation results indicate that the proposed algorithms have better performance than commonly used baseline algorithms.

Keywords: Computational geometry · Graph theory · Hamilton cycles

1 Introduction

With the dramatic growth of network traffic, elastic optical networks (EONs) have arisen as an efficient solution due to their flexibility in resource allocation and spectrum assignment [6]. The resource in EONs is assigned as frequency slot (FS) instead of wavelength. Therefore, the routing and wavelength assignment problem in Wavelength Division Multiplexing (WDM) optical networks has evolved into the Routing and Spectrum Assignment (RSA) problem with spectrum continuity and spectrum contiguity in EONs [1].

Survivability is regarded as an important aspect for optical networks, and many methods have been developed for protection [4,10,12,13]. Among these methods, p-cycle protection is considered to be particularly promising due to fast restoration and high protection efficiency. The key feature of p-cycle protection is that the backup capacity is pre-connected by ring-like structures. Compared with ring protection, p-cycle is able to support the protection of both

© IFIP International Federation for Information Processing 2020
Published by Springer Nature Switzerland AG 2020
A. Tzanakaki et al. (Eds.): ONDM 2019, LNCS 11616, pp. 154–167, 2020.
https://doi.org/10.1007/978-3-030-38085-4_14

on-cycle link and straddling link, which leads to huge advantages in protection efficiency. An attractive feature of failure-independent p-cycles is that the protection switches can be pre-configured, leading to very fast switchover times in the event of a failure. P-cycles can also be designed to provide failure-dependent link protection, i.e., the p-cycles may share some links; in this case too, all protection switches, except the switches at the forking points of two shared cycles, can be pre-configured before the failure. There exists some research on link-based p-cycle protection in EONs. In [7], a heuristic link-based p-cycle protection algorithm with spectrum sharing and defragmentation is investigated. Several dynamic p-cycle protection algorithms with spectrum planning are discussed in [5]. A service availability-oriented p-cycle algorithm for dynamic EONs is studied in [2]. A failure-independent path protection p-cycle approach in EONs is designed with modulation format consideration in [3]. Nevertheless, p-cycle selection and p-cycle set evaluation for EONs are still under-explored.

In this work, we study link-based p-cycle protection in EONs and aim to provide 100% failure-dependent protection against any single link failure. We design two novel p-cycle evaluation methods for EONs based on two cost metrics: individual p-cycle cost and p-cycle set cost. Both of these methods consider the physical distance and usable modulation level. Then, two heuristic algorithms are proposed to generate p-cycles: Traffic-Independent P-cycle Selection (TIPS) and Traffic-Oriented P-cycle Selection (TOPS). The contributions of our work can be summarized as follows:

- We propose a novel pair of p-cycle cost metrics, i.e., individual p-cycle cost and p-cycle set cost, and corresponding p-cycle evaluation methods, to select p-cycles that can provide 100% failure-dependent protection in EONs. To the best of our knowledge, this is the first paper that considers both individual p-cycle and set of p-cycles evaluation in EONs.
- We propose two heuristic algorithms to select p-cycles with and without traffic information.
- Simulation results show the effectiveness of our metrics and algorithms for both static and dynamic traffic.

2   Motivation and Problem Statement

2.1   Motivation

In p-cycle protection, different sets of p-cycles may lead to different performance of protection. Therefore, p-cycle selection is the core part of the protection scheme. There are many papers that have studied p-cycle evaluation and selection. In [8], a mixed integer linear programming model is formulated to minimize the total power consumption for p-cycle protection. However, this work does not allow for spectrum sharing between protection cycles if the corresponding working paths have no common link. In [14,15], all the candidate cycles in a network are ranked using a metric called A Priori Efficiency (AE). The set of p-cycles that is used for protection is determined by using different limited numbers of top-ranked candidate cycles for ILP designs, but AE was not designed specifically for EONs.

A load-balance-aware p-cycle protection heuristic algorithm and an ILP formulation are proposed in [16]. An individual p-cycle is evaluated with traffic load balance, but physical distance and modulation format are not considered. In [9], a distance-adaptive p-cycle protection algorithm without candidate cycle enumeration in mixed-line-rate optical networks is proposed, and an individual p-cycle is evaluated with transponder cost and spare capacity cost. However, the p-cycle evaluation and spectrum assignment are designed without frequency slot consideration.

None of the above papers consider optical signal modulation format and length of the p-cycle. For instance, since the modulation format is determined by the physical distance of p-cycle, large cycles have to be assigned a lower level modulation format for protection while small cycles can be assigned higher level modulation to achieve better spectrum efficiency. The length of p-cycle also influences the protection efficiency. A large p-cycle implies more FSs are needed to protect from a single link failure, but the protection capacity can be shared among many links. A small p-cycle requires fewer FSs for each failure, but small p-cycles have a lower probability of having straddling links, leading to a lower efficiency. Besides these conventional trade-offs, distance-dependent modulation in EONs requires that the physical length of p-cycles also be considered in the evaluation and selection of a p-cycle.

2.2 Problem Statement

For example, given a network, consider two sets of p-cycles that can provide 100% protection: one consists of several small cycles, and the other is a large Hamiltonian cycle. The performance of these two sets of p-cycles (e.g., amount of protection bandwidth needed) will be different of course. Further, in the small p-cycle case, choosing the best individual p-cycles one by one until the network is fully protected does not mean that the entire set of cycles is collectively a good set of p-cycles, as bandwidth sharing among p-cycles may not be high in this case. Metrics and evaluation methods for a set of p-cycles that collectively protect every link in the network and which considers the above factors are therefore needed.

3   P-Cycle Evaluation

In this and the next section, we present our methods to generate an efficient set of p-cycles for 100% protection. Our first approach is applicable when the p-cycles are designed without a priori knowledge of the traffic requests, for instance, in a dynamic traffic scenario. When the set of lightpath requests is known a priori, as in typical provisioning problems, it is possible to use this information to design a set of p-cycles that is tailor-made for this set of lightpaths. We call these the Traffic-Independent P-Cycle Selection and the Traffic-Oriented P-Cycle Selection methods, respectively. For each of the design methods, we propose cost metrics to evaluate a single p-cycle as well as a set of p-cycles in this section.

3.1   Traffic-Independent P-Cycle Selection (TIPS)

Here, we aim to design a set of p-cycles that provide 100% protection when the traffic is not known ahead of time. We first propose the individual and set cost metrics here and the p-cycle selection algorithms are presented in the next section.

Individual Cycle Protection Cost. In order to evaluate the efficiency and cost of cycles with different modulation formats, the novel metric Individual Cost for TIPS (IC_{TIPS}) is proposed. It is given by:

$$IC_{TIPS} = \frac{M \times L}{S} \times A \qquad (1)$$

where M is the modulation index, L is the number of links on the p-cycle, and S is the number of links that can be protected by the p-cycle. A is the average protection distance (in hops). A is calculated by finding the number of hops on the p-cycle for each potential failed link, and then calculating the average number of hops. The rationale for this cost is as follows. A higher level modulation has lower value of M indicating that fewer slots are needed for a given data rate. Here, since we do not know the working paths, M is determined by the physical length of the p-cycle. For BPSK, QPSK, and 8QAM, the corresponding spectrum efficiencies are 1, 2, and 3 bits/s/Hz; therefore we choose the corresponding M as 1, 0.5, and 0.34, respectively [5]. The modulation index represents the required spectrum resource normalized by that for the lowest modulation level, to support the same transmission bandwidth as its corresponding protection cycle.

The ratio L/S is a measure of the protection bandwidth needed per protected link of the p-cycle – since every on-cycle link is allocated protection bandwidth but straddling links are not. A is designed to capture the risk of unshareable protection due to load imbalance. If the working capacity on a link is higher than on other links, a p-cycle with larger A implies a larger number of backup FSs for an individual link failure.

We need to emphasize that Individual Cost (IC) is a metric for an individual p-cycle that is based purely on the network topology. A p-cycle with a lower IC is expected to be more efficient than a p-cycle with a higher IC.

Cycle Set Protection Cost. As p-cycles may overlap with each other, and since a link is only protected by one p-cycle, adding the ICs of the p-cycles in a set of p-cycles may not be an effective cost metric for a *set* of p-cycles. The evaluation of a set of p-cycles is based on p-cycle Set protection Cost (SC). Since overlap between p-cycles in a set is possible, we assume that every link is protected by the lowest IC p-cycle from the selected set that can provide protection to this link. If a link can be protected by multiple p-cycles that have the same lowest IC, which is unlikely to happen, the link will be assigned to one of them at random. The SC is calculated as follows:

$$SC_{TIPS} = \sum_{p \in \mathbf{P}} M_p \times A_p \times N_p \qquad (2)$$

where **P** is the set of candidate p-cycles that provides full protection for the network, p is an individual p-cycle in the set, M_p is the modulation index of p, and A_p is the average protection distance of p in hops, and N_p is the number of links protected by p. As before, smaller M and A indicate that fewer protection FSs are required. N_p is a measure of the possibility of unshareable protection and load imbalance. The more links that are protected by the p-cycle, the higher the risk of load imbalance. We need to emphasize that not all the links that can be protected by a p-cycle are in fact protected by this p-cycle due to the overlapping of p-cycles. A p-cycle set with a lower SC is expected to a better set of cycles and is encouraged to be used for protection.

3.2   Traffic Oriented P-Cycle Selection (TOPS)

Individual Cycle Protection Cost. In TOPS, the p-cycle evaluation and selection are based on the given traffic. Given a set of lightpath requests with data rate in Gbps, we first route all the lightpath requests without any spectrum assignment using Dijkstra's shortest path algorithm with physical distance. We use the total data rate on each link when evaluating the p-cycles. The IC and SC for TOPS are calculated as follows:

$$IC_{TOPS} = M \times D_{\max} \times L^2 \tag{3}$$

where M is the modulation index (same as in $TIPS$), $D_{\max}$ is the maximum data rate over all the links that can be protected by this cycle, and L is the length of the cycle in hops. M, $D_{\max}$ and L are used to measure the consumption of backup FSs in full protection sharing scenario. We use another factor of L here to capture the risk of unshareable protection FSs. If the backup FSs of a link cannot be shared with other links, the backup capacity is increased, and a larger L indicates more backup extra FSs.

Cycle Set Protection Cost. In TOPS, the cycle set evaluation is also based on data rate. The SC is calculated as follows:

$$SC_{TOPS} = \sum_{p \in \mathbf{P}} M_p \times D_{p,\max} \times L_p \times N_p \tag{4}$$

where **P** is the set of p-cycles that provides full protection, $D_{p,\max}$ is the maximum data rate over all the links that are protected by p-cycle p, L_p is the length of p in hops, and N_p is the number of links that are assigned to be protected by p. Smaller M, $D_{\max}$, and L indicate fewer backup FSs required, while larger N indicates higher unshareable consumption and lower possibility for a full sharing scenario. The p-cycle set that has a lower SC_{TOPS} is considered to be better.

4   Static P-Cycle Set Generation and RSA

4.1   Cycle Generation

In this subsection, we describe the algorithm for finding a set of p-cycles based on IC and SC. This algorithm is used in both TIPS and TOPS, and the pseudocode is shown in Algorithm 1.

Algorithm 1. Finding a set of p-cycles

Require: Network topology
Ensure: A candidate set of p-cycles
1: **while** the network is not fully protected **do**
2:     Randomly select an unprotected link l
3:     Use Dijkstra's algorithm with physical distance to find a shortest path sp between the two ends of the link
4:     Merge l and sp as a p-cycle p and initialize the candidate p-cycle as p
5:     Calculate IC for p as p_{IC}
6:     Initialize $IC_{\min}$ as p_{IC}
7:     **while** EXPAND_P-CYCLE(p) $\neq NULL$ **do**
8:         $p' = $ EXPAND_P-CYCLE(p)
9:         Calculate the IC of p' as p'_{IC}
10:        **if** $p'_{IC} < IC_{\min}$ **then**
11:            Update the candidate p-cycle to p'
12:            Update $IC_{\min}$ to p'_{IC}
13:        **end if**
14:        $p = p'$
15:     **end while**
16:     Add the candidate p-cycle to p-Cycle set P
17:     Mark links that can be protected by candidate cycle as *protected*.
18: **end while**

We start by randomly finding a link l in the network. Then we find a shortest path sp between two ends of this link. Let the selected link l and the path sp be combined to form a basic p-cycle p. Calculate the IC for this p-cycle and mark this p-cycle as a candidate p-cycle.

Continue to expand the p-cycle unless the p-cycle cannot be expanded further. The pseudocode of expanding p-cycle is shown in Algorithm 2. For each expanding step, assume that the p-cycle after expanding is p'. Calculate the IC of p'. If the IC of p' is lower than $IC_{\min}$, update the candidate p-cycle to p' and update $IC_{\min}$ to p'_{IC}. After the expansion phase is over, put the candidate p-cycle into the p-cycle set and mark the links that can be protected by this p-cycle as *protected*. If the network is not fully protected, randomly select a link that is not protected and add another candidate p-cycle into the cycle set again and continue. After all the links in the network are marked as protected, we have a set of p-cycles that can be used to protect the network.

The above procedure produces a "good" p-cycle set since we used IC to expand the p-cycles, but the p-cycle set is also somewhat random because since the starting link and expansion phase for each p-cycle are based on randomly selected links. We generate a large number of such p-cycle sets (by using different random links as starting link for each p-cycle and while expanding). Then, we choose the best p-cycle set among these as the set with the lowest SC. Later, we will compare the performance of such a p-cycle set (simply called *Best*) with some baseline algorithms for selecting p-cycle sets.

Algorithm 2. EXPAND_P-CYCLE

Require: p-cycle p
Ensure: Larger p-cycle p'
 1: Randomly select an on-cycle link l on cycle p
 2: Mark two ends of l as a, b
 3: Remove all the links on p from the network
 4: Use Dijkstra's algorithm with physical distance to find the shortest route R in physical distance between a and b
 5: **if** R does not exist **then**
 6:     **goto** line 1
 7: **end if**
 8: Merge R and p as the new cycle p'

4.2 Routing and Spectrum Assignment

This section focuses on routing and spectrum assignment for the working paths and p-cycle protection. This process is separated into two steps: p-cycle selection and spectrum assignment. Both TIPS and TOPS use this RSA algorithm.

In TIPS, the Best p-cycle set can be found purely based on topology. In TOPS, the working paths are first routed without spectrum assignment by using Dijkstra's shortest path algorithm and the maximum data rate on links is recorded. Then the IC and SC for TOPS are used to find the Best p-cycle set.

In the spectrum assignment step, first we use Dijkstra's shortest path algorithm to find a route for the working path. Then we fail the links on this working path one by one. For each failed link, we select the p-cycle with minimum IC to protect this link. The total physical distance of the protection path can be calculated by adding up the length of the working path (excluding the failed link) and the length of the protection path on the protection cycle for the failed link. Note that we use the shorter of the two cycle paths for protecting straddling links. The highest modulation index that is acceptable for this total length is then recorded, and the minimum of these modulation indexes (over all failed links) is then chosen as the modulation index for this lightpath. The lowest modulation index ensures that the distance constraint is satisfied no matter which link fails. After the modulation format is selected, the spectrum assignment is completed by using the first fit method if slots are available. Otherwise, the request is blocked.

We adapt the above approaches for dynamic traffic as follows. Since the lightpath requests are not known in advance in this case, we use TIPS here. Therefore, a set of p-cycles based on IC and SC are selected at the beginning, and when a new lightpath request arrives, only RSA is performed and a modulation index is selected as described above. If FSs are not available for the request, the request is blocked.

5   Simulation Results

In this section, simulation results are presented to demonstrate the effectiveness of our proposed p-cycle design methods under both static and dynamic traffic. The network topologies used for simulations are the COST239 network and the pan-European network. The COST239 network consists of 11 nodes and 26 links (shown in Fig. 1), while the pan-European network consists of 28 nodes and 44 links (shown in Fig. 2). The physical distance in km is shown adjacent to the links. On each link in the network, a pair of working fibers in opposite directions are used for working path, and a pair of protection fibers in opposite directions are used for protection. In static traffic model, a set of unidirectional traffic requests is to be assigned a working path and protection path in the network. The source and destination nodes for each connection request are uniformly randomly selected from the nodes of the network. We assume three different types of demands with rate 40/100/400 Gbps. The data rate is generated from the following distribution: 40 Gbps, 100 Gbps, and 400 Gbps with probability 0.2, 0.5, and 0.3, respectively. The number of required FSs for a lightpath is determined by its data rate and modulation format. Table 1 shows the number of FSs corresponding to different data rates under different modulation formats [13]. The performances are evaluated in terms of spectrum usage per link (the total number of used FSs for both working and protection on all links divided by number of links in the network). Moreover, in order to evaluate the spectrum

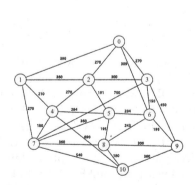

Fig. 1. 11-node COST239 network.

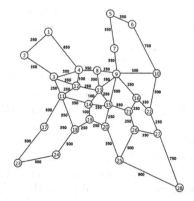

Fig. 2. 28-node pan-European network.

usage without blocking, we assume that there are an unlimited number of FSs on each fiber.

In dynamic traffic model, the lightpath requests arrive to the network according to a Poisson process with different arrival rates. Each request has a mean duration time of 1 (arbitrary time unit) with exponential distribution. The distribution of data rate of requests is the same as before. The highest FS available on each fiber is assumed to be 352. We use the demand blocking ratio of dynamic traffic requests to indicate the performance of p-cycle selection and protection. For each simulation, the results of 1 million dynamic requests are computed.

For each modulation format, the physical distance limitations are shown in Table 2 [13]. The modulation index in p-cycle evaluation and selection are also determined by this limitation. In our tests, we assume that there is no physical distance limitation for BPSK in order to guarantee that all the requests can be established in the static case. We also present the bandwidth blocking ratio if the distance limit for BPSK is set to 4000 km.

Table 1. Number of required FSs for various data rates and modulations [13].

Modulation	Date rate		
	40	100	400
8QAM	2	3	11
QPSK	3	5	17
BPSK	4	9	33

Table 2. Physical distance limitation for different modulations [13].

Modulation	Transparent reach
8QAM	1000 km
QPSK	2000 km
BPSK	>2000 km

For p-cycle selection, the Best p-cycle set is found in advance by generating a large number of ($\approx$ 3000) p-cycle sets and selecting the one with the lowest SC, which is SC_{TIPS} for TIPS and SC_{TOPS} for TOPS. While the p-cycle sets in TIPS are based only on topology, the sets are also based on the traffic and data rate in TOPS, as explained earlier. We compare the Best p-cycle set selection algorithm with the following three baseline algorithms for p-cycle set selection: namely, random cycle set (Random), top individual p-cycle set (TopIC), Hamiltonian cycle [11],[1] and top A Priori Efficiency p-cycle set (TopAE). A Priori Efficiency (AE, $AE = \sum_{i \in E} \chi_{ij} / \left(\sum_{k \in E} \delta_{kj} \times C_k \right)$, where χ_{ij} refers to the number

---

[1] Both the topologies in this paper have a Hamiltonian cycle.

of paths can be provided by the cycle j if link i fails; the possible values are 0, 1 for on-cycle link and 2 for straddling link; δ_{kj} is a binary parameter that equals 1 if link i is on cycle j and 0 otherwise; C_k is the cost of link k and which is assumed 1 in this work) was proposed as a single p-cycle evaluation for WDM networks without modulation and spectrum sharing consideration [14,15]. For Random, TopIC, and TopAE, the set $\mathcal{C}$ of all candidate cycles is first generated offline in advance using a depth-first-search algorithm. In Random, a random p-cycle set is formed by randomly selecting cycles from $\mathcal{C}$ one by one until the network is fully protected. In TopIC and TopAE, the cycles in $\mathcal{C}$ are sorted based on IC or AE, respectively, in non-decreasing order, and the TopIC p-cycle set and TopAE p-cycle set are formed by selecting cycles in this order until the network is fully protected. In both cases, only cycles that protect at least one as-yet unprotected link will be added to the p-cycle set.

5.1   Performance Analysis

Figures 3 and 4 show the results for spectrum usage (i.e., number of FSs used per link) in COST239 and pan-European network respectively. We make several observations from the results. First, we compare the Best cycle set with Hamiltonian cycle and Random cycle set. There is an improvement of more than about 40% in spectrum usage in COST239 network, while the improvement is more than about 20% in pan-European network. The Best cycle set has a better performance because we select cycles with lower individual cost and cycle set cost.

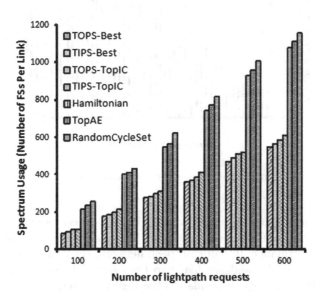

Fig. 3. Spectrum usage in COST239.

Compared with TopAE, the Best and TopIC p-cycle sets have much better performance, which shows the need for an improved p-cycle evaluation method which takes modulation and cycle size into account in EONs. Moreover, the results show that the cycle set consisting of the top individual cycles is not the best cycle set. This demonstrates the effectiveness of cycle set evaluation. Since we take load balance risk into account when the IC is measured, the TopIC cycle sets have a good performance as well. Moreover, for the Best cycle set, the performance of TOPS is better than TIPS, because TOPS also takes into account traffic and data rate. Suppose we assume that there is a 4000 km physical distance limitation for BPSK. In COST239, the bandwidth blocking ratio for all the proposed algorithms and baseline algorithms are lower than 0.5%. In pan-European network, the bandwidth blocking ratio for TOPS-Best, TOPS-TopIC, TIPS-Best, and TIPS-TopIC are lower than 1%, whereas it is 94% and 91% for the Hamiltonian cycle and random cycle sets, respectively, due to the large network size. Therefore with physical distance limitation, large cycles are even more vulnerable to failure and blocking.

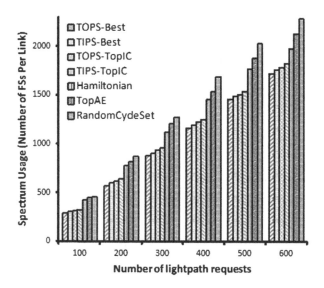

Fig. 4. Spectrum usage in pan-European.

Figures 5 and 6 show the result of blocking ratio under dynamic traffic for the COST239 and Pan-European networks. We can see that the Best cycle set has the best performance. In pan-European network, the p-cycles in TopIC tend to be small-sized cycles and are likely to be assigned high modulation index, therefore the blocking ratio is similar to the Best cycle set.

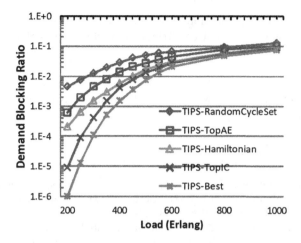

Fig. 5. Demand blocking ratio in COST239.

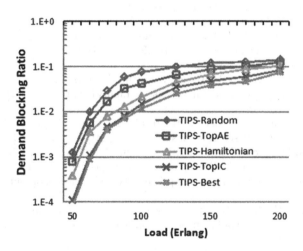

Fig. 6. Demand blocking ratio in pan-European.

6   Conclusion

P-cycles are attractive for protection in optical networks because of their fast switching. In this work, we propose metrics to evaluate the cost of an individual p-cycle as well as a set of p-cycles, and use these metrics to generate a set of p-cycles that can provide 100% protection against single-link failures in EONs. Unlike previous work, our costs and cycle generation and selection algorithms consider factors such as path length, modulation index, and shareability of links. We proposed algorithms to select p-cycles both in the absence of traffic knowledge (Traffic-Independent P-cycle Selection, TIPS) and with traffic knowledge

(Traffic-Oriented P-cycle Selection, TOPS). From extensive simulation results, we observed that the performances of the proposed selection algorithms are significantly better than baseline algorithms in terms of required spectrum and blocking ratio.

Acknowledgment. This work was supported in part by NSF grants CNS-1818858 and CNS-1813617.

References

1. Cai, A., Guo, J., Lin, R., Shen, G., Zukerman, M.: Multicast routing and distance-adaptive spectrum allocation in elastic optical networks with shared protection. J. Lightwave Technol. **34**(17), 4076–4088 (2016)
2. Chen, X., Ji, F., Zhu, Z.: Service availability oriented p-cycle protection design in elastic optical networks. IEEE/OSA J. Opt. Commun. Networking **6**(10), 901–910 (2014)
3. Chen, X., Zhu, S., Jiang, L., Zhu, Z.: On spectrum efficient failure-independent path protection p-cycle design in elastic optical networks. J. Lightwave Technol. **33**(17), 3719–3729 (2015)
4. Eshoul, A.E., Mouftah, H.T.: Survivability approaches using p-cycles in WDM mesh networks under static traffic. IEEE/ACM Trans. Network. (TON) **17**(2), 671–683 (2009)
5. Ji, F., Chen, X., Lu, W., Rodrigues, J.J., Zhu, Z.: Dynamic p-cycle protection in spectrum-sliced elastic optical networks. J. Lightwave Technol. **32**(6), 1190–1199 (2014)
6. Jinno, M., Takara, H., Kozicki, B., Tsukishima, Y., Sone, Y., Matsuoka, S.: Spectrum-efficient and scalable elastic optical path network: architecture, benefits, and enabling technologies. IEEE Commun. Mag. **47**(11), 66–73 (2009)
7. Ju, M., Zhou, F., Xiao, S., Wu, H.: Leveraging spectrum sharing and defragmentation to p-cycle design in elastic optical networks. IEEE Commun. Lett. **21**(3), 508–511 (2017)
8. Ju, M., Zhou, F., Xiao, S., Zhu, Z.: Power-efficient protection with directed p-cycles for asymmetric traffic in elastic optical networks. J. Lightwave Technol. **34**(17), 4053–4065 (2016)
9. Ju, M., Zhou, F., Zhu, Z., Xiao, S.: Distance-adaptive, low capex cost p-cycle design without candidate cycle enumeration in mixed-line-rate optical networks. J. Lightwave Technol. **34**(11), 2663–2676 (2016)
10. Oliveira, H.M., da Fonseca, N.L.: Algorithm for FIPP p-cycle path protection in flexgrid networks. In: 2014 IEEE Global Communications Conference, pp. 1278–1283. IEEE (2014)
11. Schupke, D.A.: On Hamiltonian cycles as optimal p-cycles. IEEE Commun. Lett. **9**(4), 360–362 (2005)
12. Shen, G., Guo, H., Bose, S.K.: Survivable elastic optical networks: survey and perspective. Photon Netw. Commun. **31**(1), 71–87 (2016)
13. Wang, C., Shen, G., Bose, S.K.: Distance adaptive dynamic routing and spectrum allocation in elastic optical networks with shared backup path protection. J. Lightwave Technol. **33**(14), 2955–2964 (2015)
14. Wei, Y., Xu, K., Jiang, Y., Zhao, H., Shen, G.: Otimal design for p-cycle-rotected elastic otical networks. Photon Netw. Commun. **29**(3), 257–268 (2015)

15. Wei, Y., Xu, K., Zhao, H., Shen, G.: Applying p-cycle technique to elastic optical networks. In: 2014 International Conference on Optical Network Design and Modeling, pp. 1–6. IEEE (2014)
16. Wu, J., Liu, Y., Yu, C., Wu, Y.: Survivable routing and spectrum allocation algorithm based on p-cycle protection in elastic optical networks. Optik-Int. J. Light Electron Opt. **125**(16), 4446–4451 (2014)

How to Survive Targeted Fiber Cuts: A Game Theoretic Approach for Resilient SDON Control Plane Design

Jing Zhu[1], Marija Furdek[2], Carlos Natalino[2], Lena Wosinska[2], and Zuqing Zhu[1($\boxtimes$)]

[1] University of Science and Technology of China, Hefei 230027, Anhui, China
zqzhu@ieee.org
[2] Chalmers University of Technology, 412 96 Gothenburg, Sweden
furdek@chalmers.se

Abstract. Software-defined optical networking (SDON) paradigm enables programmable, adaptive and application-aware backbone networks via centralized network control and management. Aside from the manifold advantages, the control plane (CP) of an SDON is exposed to diverse security threats. As the CP usually shares the underlying optical infrastructure with the data plane (DP), an attacker can launch physical-layer attacks to cause severe disruption of the CP.

This paper studies the problem of resilient CP design under targeted fiber cut attacks, whose effectiveness depends on both the CP designer's and the attacker's strategies. Therefore, we model the problem as a non-cooperative game between the designer and the attacker, where the designer tries to set up the CP to minimize the attack effectiveness, while the attacker aims at maximizing the effectiveness by cutting the most critical links. We define the game strategies and utility functions, conduct theoretical analysis to obtain the Nash Equilibrium (NE) as the solution of the game. Extensive simulations confirm the effectiveness of our proposal in improving the CP resilience to targeted fiber cuts.

Keywords: Software-defined optical networks · Control plane resilience · Targeted fiber cuts · Non-cooperative game

1 Introduction

As the underlying infrastructure of backbone networks, optical networks support diverse vital network services and require efficient network control and management (NC&M) [11]. The widely accepted software-defined networking (SDN) paradigm decouples the network control and the data planes (CP and DP) [12].

This work was supported by the NSFC projects 61871357 and 61701472, CAS key project (QYZDY-SSW-JSC003), and NGBWMCN key project (2017ZX03001019-004). M. Furdek, C. Natalino, and L. Wosinska are supported in part by the COST Action 15127 RECODIS.

A. Tzanakaki et al. (Eds.): ONDM 2019, LNCS 11616, pp. 168–180, 2020.
https://doi.org/10.1007/978-3-030-38085-4_15

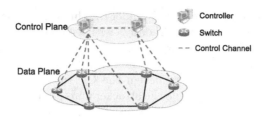

Fig. 1. The data and the control plane of an SDON.

In SDN, NC&M is carried out by logically centralized controller(s) in the CP, while the DP devices only need to execute packet forwarding/data transmission tasks. The controller(s) collect the status of DP devices to maintain a global view of the network, and then intelligently instruct the devices to perform corresponding tasks [10]. By implementing SDN in optical networks, software-defined optical networks (SDONs) have the programmability and application-awareness that allow operators to flexibly customize networks and significantly expedite the launch of new services [20,25,26].

One of the essential problems in SDON planning is the design of the CP. As shown in Fig. 1, the CP of an SDON is generally composed of one or more controllers, each of which controls a subset of optical devices (e.g., optical transponders and switches) via signalling in control channels. As the traffic in each fiber link can reach Tb/s or even Pb/s, the CP should be well-designed to meet the requirements of low communication latency and high reliability [3]. To this end, previous studies investigated the disruptions due to random failures (e.g., random link cuts), and proposed several CP design schemes [1,4,5,7,9,13,21–23]. Nevertheless, they overlooked the threats from deliberate attacks disrupting the underlying network infrastructure.

Although logically decoupled, the CP and the DP of a backbone SDON typically share the same fiber infrastructure, which is vulnerable to various physical-layer attacks [19]. Targeted fiber cuts can result in severe disruption of the CP by interrupting communication among CP elements or increasing latency to an unacceptable level. Existing CP design schemes that protect from random failures do not guarantee robustness to targeted cuts. Unlike random cuts which are usually accidental, targeted cuts can be launched with embedded intelligence to boost the efficiency of the attack and aggravate its effects. A common attacker's strategy would be to sever the fiber links which are most critical for network operation. As existing CP design schemes usually use the shortest paths to route the control channels, they may concentrate on links with high betweenness centrality [17], which can be easily identified by attackers as possible targets. Therefore, preparing for the attackers' likely strategies of targeting links when disrupting the CP is paramount for resilient CP design. Hence, the problem can be viewed as a game between two rational entities (i.e., the CP designer and the attacker). To solve it, a game theoretic approach is needed, which, to the best of our knowledge, has not yet been applied for CP design.

In this paper, we consider an SDON under the threat from targeted fiber cuts, and address the problem of robust CP design with a game theoretic approach. We model the problem as a non-cooperative game between the CP designer and the attacker, and define the game strategies and the utility functions for both players. In the game, the designer tries to design the CP such that the damage from targeted fiber cuts is minimal, while the attacker aims at cutting the most critical links to maximize CP disruption. To solve the game, we conduct theoretical analysis to obtain the Nash Equilibrium (NE), which is widely accepted as the solution of a game [16]. Simulation results confirm that under the guidance of the NE, the designer can mitigate the damage from attacks. This verifies the effectiveness of our proposal in increasing resilience of the CP under targeted fiber cuts.

The rest of the paper is organized as follows. Section 2 reviews the related work. The CP design problem as a non-cooperative game is described in Sect. 3. In Sect. 4, we analyze the NE to solve the game. Simulations are performed and the results are discussed in Sect. 5. Finally, Sect. 6 concludes the paper.

2   Related Work

Extensive efforts have been carried out to improve the performances and availability of the CP. The basic CP design problem of deciding how many controllers to deploy and where to place them has been formulated in [3]. In [1,4,5,7,9,13,21–23], the authors studied resilient CP design under various failure scenarios, which can be classified into controller failures, switch failures and link failures. To address controller failures, researchers have considered managing each switch by multiple controllers [1,7,9,13,23]. In [9], the authors applied Byzantine fault tolerant mechanism and studied the assignment of controllers to switches. CP design algorithms with various primary-backup models for controllers have been investigated in [1,23]. In [13], both Byzantine fault tolerant mechanism and primary-backup model were used when addressing controller-switch mapping. To address switch failures, tree-like CP design that maximizes single-node failure survivability was proposed in [21]. Assuming both switches and links can fail, the work in [22] proposed a controller placement scheme aimed at minimizing the connectivity loss between controllers and switches, while the study in [5] compared different controller placement schemes in terms of CP connectivity. For similar assumptions, the authors of [4] introduced a Pareto-optimal framework for CP design to balance communication latency and resiliency. Nevertheless, none of these studies considered failures caused by deliberate physical-layer attacks.

A relatively straightforward method of attacking the optical infrastructure is disabling the fibers or optical nodes [19]. The impact of such attacks on the DP has been investigated in [8,15,18]. The study in [8] evaluated the robustness of large-scale network topologies under targeted attacks. In [18], the authors identified the critical nodes/links in a topology, whose removals would minimize the network connectivity. The work in [15] studied how targeted fiber cuts affect the robustness of fiber-based content delivery networks. Given the CP, our previous work [24] evaluated the CP robustness under targeted fiber cuts. These investigations suggested that the intelligence of attackers in selecting targets plays an important role, and this motivates us to leverage game theory for CP design. Game theory is a powerful mathematical tool to analyze the competition and cooperation among rational decision-makers, and has been used to solve the problems of network topology design in [2,14]. In [14], a multi-player game was formulated to assist each node with neighbor selection in order to optimize link establishment price, path delay and proneness to congestion. A dynamic game for network topology design was modeled in [2], where the designer and attacker add and remove links so as to maximize their utilities in terms of considered network properties (e.g., connectivity) and operational costs.

3 Game Model for Control Plane Design

We consider a backbone SDON, whose optical infrastructure carries the mutually disjoint control and data plane. The physical topology is modeled as an undirected graph $G(V, E)$, where V and E represent the sets of nodes and undirected fiber links, respectively. Each node $v \in V$ hosts an optical switch and/or a network controller. The subset of nodes that host controllers is denoted by U, where the number of controllers $|U|$ is given *a priori*. Each edge $e \in E$ denotes a fiber link that can carry data and/or control channels (i.e., in-band control). The set of links that carry control channels is denoted by L. Consequently, U and L constitute the CP topology $G^c(U, L)$. Each controller manages a cluster of switches, while, for simplicity, we assume that each switch is under control of a single controller[1]. As an attacker can launch fiber link cut attacks aimed at disrupting the CP property (e.g., connectivity and communication latency) to the largest extent, a designer needs to design a resilient CP by carefully determining the sets U and L. In general, fiber cuts can disrupt the communication between switches and controllers, among the switches, and among the controllers. Here, we focus only on the communication between switches and controllers. The problem of designing a resilient CP can be viewed as a two-player non-cooperative game between the designer and the attacker as shown in Fig. 2. In the game, the players' strategies and utility functions are as follows.

The finite strategy space of the designer is denoted as $S^d = \{s_1^d, s_2^d, \cdots\}$, where s_i^d refers to a specific CP design strategy of determining U and L. An example strategy s_i^d is to minimize $|L|$, as proposed in [6]. By implementing a strategy s_i^d, the designer obtains a CP solution at the cost D_i, which relates to $|L|$ and can be expressed as:

$$D_i = f_1(|L|). \tag{1}$$

Here, $f_1(\cdot)$ is assumed to be a linear increasing function of $|L|$, as a higher number of links included in the CP would increase both its capital and operational expenses [6]. Meanwhile, the attacker aims at maximizing CP disruption

---

[1] In more sophisticated scenarios, an optical switch can be assigned to multiple controllers to improve CP resiliency.

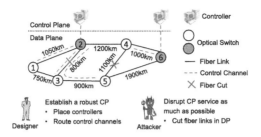

Fig. 2. An example of a non-cooperative game between the network designer and the attacker.

by deliberately cutting n critical links, whose set is denoted as E_c ($|E_c| = n$). The finite strategy space of the attacker is denoted as $S^a = \{s_1^a, s_2^a, \cdots\}$. An example strategy s_j^a is to select links whose removal minimizes the connectivity of $G^c(U, L)$, i.e., maximizes the number of disconnected controller-switch pairs. Each s_j^a corresponds to a cost A_{ij}, which is also related to the designer's strategy s_i^d. For instance, in the simple SDON example shown in Fig. 2 for $|U| = 2$, the designer has established a CP by placing two controllers at nodes 2 and 6, and routing the control channels over the paths marked by the dashed lines. In this case, assuming $n = 1$, the attacker is likely to cut link 2–3.

The cost A_{ij} relates to both n and the geographical distribution of the links in E_c, and can be written as:

$$A_{ij} = f_2(n, \sum_{e_1, e_2 \in E_c} x_{e_1, e_2}), \tag{2}$$

where x_{e_1, e_2} is a boolean variable with value equal to 1 if two links e_1 and e_2 do not share any end-nodes and 0 otherwise. $f_2(\cdot)$ is a linear increasing function of n and x_{e_1, e_2} which ensures that cutting more, and non-adjacent links is more costly. Once the designer and the attacker select s_i^d and s_j^a to take their actions, the SDON is left with a CP affected by n fiber cuts. The CP's property in terms of controller-switch connectivity and communication latency can be described by:

$$P_{ij} = f_3(c(n), l(n)). \tag{3}$$

In Eq. (3), $c(n)$ and $l(n)$ are two CP metrics defined in [24], i.e., the average CP connectivity and the average CP transmission distance after n link cuts, respectively. $f_3(\cdot)$ is a linear function of $c(n)$ and $l(n)$, which decreases with $c(n)$ and increases with $l(n)$. Upon an attack, the attacker obtains a gain of P_{ij} while the designer suffers a loss of P_{ij}. Based on D_i, A_{ij} and P_{ij}, the utility functions F_{ij}^d and F_{ij}^a of the designer and the attacker, respectively, can be calculated as:

$$F_{ij}^d = -\alpha \cdot P_{ij} - D_i, \qquad F_{ij}^a = \beta \cdot P_{ij} - A_{ij}. \tag{4}$$

where α and β are constant coefficients. In the game, both players are rational in choosing strategies to benefit themselves unilaterally, i.e., to maximize their own expected utilities.

Table 1. Game in strategic form

	s_1^a	s_2^a	$\cdots$
s_1^d	$(F_{11}^d \ , \ F_{11}^a)$	$(F_{12}^d \ , \ F_{12}^a)$	$\cdots$
s_2^d	$(F_{21}^d \ , \ F_{21}^a)$	$(F_{22}^d \ , \ F_{22}^a)$	$\cdots$
$\cdots$	$\cdots$	$\cdots$	$\cdots$

Table 1 shows the game in strategic form. For example, when the two players act with strategy profile (s_2^d, s_1^a), their utilities would be F_{21}^d and F_{21}^a, respectively. Assuming that s_2^d creates the CP solution shown in Fig. 2 and s_1^a cuts links 2–3 and 4–5, all nodes can still connect to their own controllers, but nodes 3 and 5 have to use longer paths for control channels, resulting in $c(2) = 1$ and $l(2) = 1458$ km. Therefore, we obtain $F_{21}^d = -\alpha \cdot f_3(1, 1458) - f_1(4)$ and $F_{21}^a = \beta \cdot f_3(1, 1458) - f_2(2, 1)$.

4   Nash Equilibrium for Control Plane Design

In the described game, each player tries to find their own best response to their opponent's strategy. Therefore, to obtain the design scheme that leads to a resilient CP, we need to find the strategy profile in which neither the designer nor the attacker can increase their utilities by unilaterally adjusting their own strategies, which is essentially the Nash equilibrium (NE) [16]. In an NE, the designer's strategy is precisely the solution of the CP design problem. As each player in the game has a finite strategy space, the game admits at least one mixed-strategy NE [16]. To obtain it, we formulate the game as optimization problems of the two players, and analyze their best response functions to derive the general form of the NE. Then, we adapt the formulations of the optimization problems to obtain the NE with a simplex-based method.

Notations and Variables:

- Φ^d/Φ^a: the utility matrix of the designer/attacker.
- ϕ^d/ϕ^a: variable, the expected utility of the designer/attacker.
- $\mathbf{y}^d$: variables, the vector of probability distribution $(y_1^d, y_2^d, \cdots)^T$ to indicate how the designer selects strategies[2], (e.g., y_1^d is the probability that the designer selects strategy s_1^d).
- $\mathbf{y}^a$: variables, the vector of probability distribution $(y_1^a, y_2^a, \cdots)^T$ to indicate how the attacker selects strategies, (e.g., y_1^a is the probability that the attacker selects strategy s_1^a).
- $\mathbf{y}_*^d/\mathbf{y}_*^a$: variables, the best response function of the designer/attacker.
- $\mathbf{z}^d/\mathbf{z}^a$: auxiliary variables, the vector with the form similar to $\mathbf{y}^d/\mathbf{y}^a$.

For the designer, we can formulate the game as the following optimization problem.

---

[2] The superscript T in $(y_1^d, y_2^d, \cdots)^T$ represents the transposition operator.

Objective:

$$Maximize \quad \phi^d = (\mathbf{y}^d)^T \cdot \Phi^d \cdot \mathbf{y}^a. \tag{5}$$

Constraints:

$$\begin{cases} \mathbf{y}^d \geq \mathbf{0}, \quad \mathbf{1}^T \cdot \mathbf{y}^d = 1, \\ \Phi^d \cdot \mathbf{y}^a \leq \mathbf{1} \cdot \phi^d. \end{cases} \tag{6}$$

The designer tries to maximize the objective function in (5) under the constraints in (6). The first two equations in (6) are the nonnegativity and regularity constraints for the probability distribution vector of strategy selection, while the third one ensures that the designer cannot increase their utility by changing the strategy.

Analogously, for the attacker, the game can be formulated as the following optimization problem.

Objective:

$$Maximize \quad \phi^a = (\mathbf{y}^d)^T \cdot \Phi^a \cdot \mathbf{y}^a. \tag{7}$$

Constraints:

$$\begin{cases} \mathbf{y}^a \geq \mathbf{0}, \quad \mathbf{1}^T \cdot \mathbf{y}^a = 1, \\ (\Phi^a)^T \cdot \mathbf{y}^d \leq \mathbf{1} \cdot \phi^a. \end{cases} \tag{8}$$

Equations (7)–(8) express the attacker's objective function and constraints, respectively.

Using the above formulations, the best response functions of both players can be expressed as:

$$\mathbf{y}_*^d(\mathbf{y}^a) = \arg \max_{\mathbf{y}^d} \left(\phi^d \right), \tag{9}$$

$$\mathbf{y}_*^a(\mathbf{y}^d) = \arg \max_{\mathbf{y}^a} \left(\phi^a \right). \tag{10}$$

Specifically, given that the attacker selects strategies with $\mathbf{y}^a$, the designer uses (9) to obtain the best response $\mathbf{y}_*^d$. Similarly, the attacker leverages (10) to get their best response $\mathbf{y}_*^a$ to designer strategy $\mathbf{y}^d$. Hence, by definition, the NE can be derived as $(\mathbf{y}_*^d, \mathbf{y}_*^a)$, where $\mathbf{y}_*^d$ provides the solution of the CP design problem. In order to find $(\mathbf{y}_*^d, \mathbf{y}_*^a)$, we first adapt the above formulations of optimization problems by introducing $\mathbf{z}^d = \frac{\mathbf{y}^d}{\phi^a}$ and $\mathbf{z}^a = \frac{\mathbf{y}^a}{\phi^d}$.

The designer's optimization problem can be expressed as:

Objective:

$$Maximize \quad \phi^d = \frac{1}{\mathbf{1}^T \cdot \mathbf{z}^a}. \tag{11}$$

Constraints:

$$\begin{cases} \mathbf{z}^a \leq \mathbf{0}, \\ \varPhi^d \cdot \mathbf{z}^a \geq 1. \end{cases} \tag{12}$$

The attacker's optimization problem is adapted as:
Objective:

$$Maximize \quad \phi^a = \frac{1}{1^T \cdot \mathbf{z}^d}. \tag{13}$$

Constraints:

$$\begin{cases} \mathbf{z}^d \geq \mathbf{0}, \\ (\varPhi^a)^T \cdot \mathbf{z}^d \leq 1. \end{cases} \tag{14}$$

By applying the simplex-based Lemke-Howson algorithm in [16], we solve the problems in (11)–(14) in a coordinated way for $\mathbf{z}^d$ and $\mathbf{z}^a$. Hence, the NE $(\mathbf{y}^d_*, \mathbf{y}^a_*)$ can be obtained as $(\mathbf{z}^d \cdot \frac{1}{1^T \mathbf{z}^d}, \mathbf{z}^a \cdot \frac{1}{1^T \mathbf{z}^a})$, where $\mathbf{y}^d_* = \mathbf{z}^d \cdot \frac{1}{1^T \mathbf{z}^d}$ provides the solution of the CP design problem. The complexity of the algorithm is at most $O(M \cdot N)$, where M and N are the respective numbers of vertices of the polytopes defined by (12) and (14).

5   Simulation Results

In order to validate the proposed game theoretic approach for resilient CP design, we perform simulations on the SprintNET shown in Fig. 3 [24]. In the game, we assume that the designer has two strategies and the attacker has three strategies. The designer's strategies are:

- s^d_1: the algorithm from [24], which places controllers at nodes with the highest degree,
- s^d_2: the genetic algorithm from [6], which adopts the placement scheme that aims at minimizing the number of control links.

In both strategies, the shortest physical paths are used for control channels. The attacker's strategy is always to cut n links deemed most critical, i.e., whose cutting maximizes P_{ij}. However, the link criticality assessment is based on three different assumptions:

- s^a_1: the physical topology only (no CP considerations),
- s^a_2: the CP realized according to strategy s^d_1,
- s^a_3: the CP realized according to strategy s^d_2.

The coefficients α and β in the utility functions are set to ensure $P_{ij} \gg D_i/A_{ij}$, so that the attacker has the incentive to launch attacks and the designer to defend against them.

We first set the number of controllers and link cuts to $|U| = 2$ and $n = 2$, respectively. The resulting controller placement for the designer's strategies s^d_1

Table 2. Game in strategic form with $n = 2$

	s_1^a	s_2^a	s_3^a
s_1^d	(−84.1, 71.1)	(−92.8, 77.8)	(−83.1, 70.1)
s_2^d	(−102.6, 88.6)	(−95.6, 79.6)	(−116.5, 102.5)

and s_2^d, as well as the results of link cuts under the attacker's strategies s_1^a, s_2^a and s_3^a, are depicted in Fig. 3. For example, when the attacker adopts s_2^a, links 7–8 and 10–11 are cut, as the links deemed most critical under the assumption of strategy s_1^d applied for CP design. Based on this, Table 2 elaborates on the utilities of the two players under different strategy profiles, whose rationality can be analyzed as follows. As can be seen in the table, the designer always has higher utility when the attacker's utility is lower, regardless of the adopted strategies. For instance, if the designer's strategy is fixed to s_1^d, the attacker gains the maximum utility when it selects strategy s_2^a. This is because in s_2^a, the attacker detects the most critical links based on the CP implementation determined by s_1^d, which verifies that the attacker can maximize utility under the correct assumption of the designer's strategy. Under this strategy profile, i.e., (s_1^d, s_2^a), the designer has the minimum utility of −92.8, which represents the largest loss on the CP resilience. Compared to the other two strategy profiles (i.e., (s_1^d, s_1^a) and (s_1^d, s_3^a)), the utility of the attacker for (s_1^d, s_1^a) is higher than that for (s_1^d, s_3^a). This bears an important implication for the attacker – if the information about the CP implementation is not available, launching attacks based on criticality of links evaluated for the physical topology may be more favorable than that based on a CP implementation guess. Observations similar to above hold for the designer's strategy s_2^d as well.

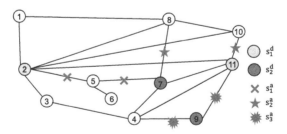

Fig. 3. SprintNET topology.

If the attacker's strategy is fixed, e.g., to s_2^a, the designer's utility under strategy s_2^d is lower than under s_1^d. This may seem counterintuitive as s_2^a is based precisely on the correct assumption of the CP implemented using s_1^d, yet s_1^d yields higher robustness than s_2^d. However, as indicated by the utilities for the other two attacker's strategy profiles, the CP implemented with s_2^d is

Table 3. NEs of games with different n

n	$\mathbf{y}_*^d$	$\mathbf{y}_*^a$
1	(0.493, 0.507)	(1.0, 0.0, 0.0)
2	(0.746, 0.254)	(0.0, 0.0, 1.0)
3	(0.625, 0.375)	(0.0, 0.0, 1.0)
4	(0.670, 0.330)	(0.0, 0.0, 1.0)
5	(0.563, 0.437)	(0.0, 0.0, 1.0)

Table 4. Game in strategic form with $n = 1$

	s_1^a	s_2^a	s_3^a
s_1^d	(−81.2, 69.2)	(−86.5, 74.5)	(−78.4, 66.4)
s_2^d	(−93.5, 80.5)	(−88.4, 75.4)	(−94.4, 81.4)

more vulnerable than that implemented with s_1^d. If the designer chooses s_2^d, link cuts can be more damaging even when the attacker bases the link criticality assessment on the wrong assumption of the CP design strategy. Consequently, by analyzing the game, the designer tends to prioritize s_1^d for a more resilient CP, which is reflected in the resulting NE.

By solving the game in Table 2, we obtain an NE $(\mathbf{y}_*^d, \mathbf{y}_*^a)$ as $((0.746, 0.254)^T,$ $(0.0, 0.0, 1.0)^T)$, where the designer selects strategy s_1^d with the probability of 0.746 and strategy s_2^d with the probability of 0.254, while the attacker uses strategy s_3^a in all cases. Namely, in the NE, when the attacker uses s_3^a for their own benefit, the designer defends by selecting s_2^d with a comparatively lower probability. Hence, by following the NE, the designer can avoid large damages to the CP.

We assess the game when the number of fiber cuts n changes within $[1, 5]$. The NEs of the games are listed in Table 3. For example, when $n = 1$, the game is shown in Table 4, whose rationality can be analyzed similarly as the one in Table 2. In this game, the NE suggests that the designer should select s_1^d and s_2^d with probabilities of 0.493 and 0.507, respectively, to defend against the attack performed with s_1^a. When n changes from 2 to 5, the probability of selecting s_1^d by the designer is always higher than s_2^d, while the attacker would never use s_2^a otherwise the designer would suffer from the largest CP robustness loss, which violates the NE.

To gain insight into the CP solutions resulting from the NEs, we use two metrics to measure their properties in terms of the expected average CP connectivity $\bar{c}(n)$ and the expected average CP transmission distance $\bar{l}(n)$. These are calculated as:

$$\bar{c}(n) = (\mathbf{y}_*^d)^T \cdot \mathbf{C} \cdot \mathbf{y}_*^a, \qquad \bar{l}(n) = (\mathbf{y}_*^d)^T \cdot \mathbf{L} \cdot \mathbf{y}_*^a, . \tag{15}$$

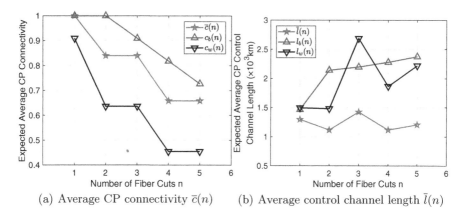

(a) Average CP connectivity $\bar{c}(n)$ (b) Average control channel length $\bar{l}(n)$

Fig. 4. The expected average CP connectivity and control channel length for different number of cut links.

where both **C** and **L** are $|S^d| \times |S^a|$ matrices, each element of **C** is the average CP connectivity $c(n)$ and each element of **L** is the average control channel transmission distance $l(n)$ under the corresponding pure strategy profile. The pure strategy profile refers to the one in which both players select one strategy from their own strategy space deterministically. Figures 4(a) and (b) show the respective results of $\bar{c}(n)$ and $\bar{l}(n)$ under the NE. For comparison, we also provide the results under the best and the worst scenarios resulting from the pure strategy profiles, denoted with $c_b(n)$ and $c_w(n)$, respectively. Naturally, in Fig. 4(a), the average CP connectivity $\bar{c}(n)$ exhibits a downward trend when n increases.

As shown in Fig. 4(a), $\bar{c}(n)$ is higher than $c_w(n)$, while Fig. 4(b) shows the advantage of $\bar{l}(n)$ over $l_w(n)$. This verifies that, guided by the NEs, the designer can mitigate the effectiveness of attacks, and thus improve the CP robustness. However, $\bar{c}(n)$ cannot reach $c_b(n)$, which is inevitable for the existence of an intelligent attacker. Note that, in Fig. 4(b), the (expected) average transmission distance of control channels can increase or decrease with n. The reason for the increase is that the control channels have to traverse longer paths, while the decrease occurs when the connectivity between some switch-controller pairs is lost and, thus, the control channels disappear.

6   Conclusion

This paper considered an SDON under the threat from targeted fiber cut attacks and studied the problem of resilient CP design. To solve it, we proposed a game theoretic approach where the problem was modeled as a non-cooperative game between the CP designer and the attacker, and defined the game strategies and the utility functions for both players. In the game, the goal of the designer was to minimize the CP connectivity and latency degradation caused by targeted fiber cuts, while the attacker aimed at maximizing the CP disruption by cutting the most critical links. Theoretical analysis were conducted to obtain the Nash Equilibrium (NE) as the solution. Extensive simulation results suggested that following the NE enabled the designer to avoid the worst-case scenario where the CP suffers the largest losses, which confirmed the effectiveness of the proposed game-theoretic approach in improving the CP resilience to targeted fiber cuts.

References

1. Chen, X., et al.: Leveraging master-slave openflow controller arrangement to improve control plane resiliency in SD-EONs. Opt. Express **23**, 7550–7558 (2015)
2. Ciftcioglu, E., et al.: Topology design games and dynamics in adversarial environments. IEEE J. Sel. Areas Commun. **35**, 628–642 (2017)
3. Heller, B., et al.: The controller placement problem. In: Proceedings of HotSDN 2012, pp. 7–12 (2012)
4. Hock, D., et al.: Pareto-optimal resilient controller placement in SDN-based core networks. In: Proceedings of ITC 2013, pp. 1–9 (2013)
5. Hu, Y., et al.: On reliability-optimized controller placement for software-defined networks. China Commun. **11**, 38–54 (2014)
6. Hu, Y., et al.: The energy-aware controller placement problem in software defined networks. IEEE Commun. Lett. **21**, 741–744 (2017)
7. Huang, H., et al.: Realizing highly-available, scalable and protocol-independent vSDN slicing with a distributed network hypervisor system. IEEE Access **6**, 13513–13522 (2018)
8. Iyer, S., et al.: Attack robustness and centrality of complex networks. PLoS ONE **8**, 1–17 (2013)
9. Li, H., et al.: Byzantine-resilient secure software-defined networks with multiple controllers in cloud. IEEE Trans. Cloud Comput. **2**, 436–447 (2014)
10. Li, S., et al.: Protocol oblivious forwarding (POF): software-defined networking with enhanced programmability. IEEE Netw. **31**, 58–66 (2017)
11. Lu, P., et al.: Highly-efficient data migration and backup for big data applications in elastic optical inter-datacenter networks. IEEE Netw. **29**, 36–42 (2015)
12. McKeown, N., et al.: OpenFlow: enabling innovation in campus networks. Comput. Commun. Rev. **38**, 69–74 (2008)
13. Mohan, P., et al.: Primary-backup controller mapping for Byzantine fault tolerance in software defined networks. In: Proceedings of GLOBECOM 2017, pp. 1–7 (2017)
14. Nahir, A., et al.: Topology design of communication networks: a game-theoretic perspective. IEEE/ACM Trans. Netw. **22**, 405–414 (2014)
15. Natalino, C., et al.: Content accessibility in optical cloud networks under targeted link cuts. In: Proceedings of ONDM 2017, pp. 1–6 (2017)
16. Nisan, N.: Algorithmic Game Theory. Cambridge University Press, Cambridge (2007)
17. Rueda, D., et al.: Robustness comparison of 15 real telecommunication networks: structural and centrality measurements. J. Netw. Syst. Manage. **25**, 269–289 (2017)
18. Shen, Y., et al.: On the discovery of critical links and nodes for assessing network vulnerability. IEEE/ACM Trans. Netw. **21**, 963–973 (2013)
19. Skorin-Kapov, N., et al.: Physical-layer security in evolving optical networks. IEEE Commun. Mag. **54**, 110–117 (2016)
20. Thyagaturu, A., et al.: Software defined optical networks (SDONs): a comprehensive survey. IEEE Commun. Surv. Tutorials **18**, 2738–2786 (2016)

180 J. Zhu et al.

21. Yang, Z., et al.: An efficient algorithm for constructing controller trees in SDN. In: Proceedings of GLOBECOM 2017, pp. 1–6 (2017)
22. Zhang, Y., et al.: On resilience of split-architecture networks. In: Proceedings of GLOBECOM 2011, pp. 1–6 (2011)
23. Zhao, B., et al.: Survivable control plane establishment with live control service backup and migration in SD-EONs. J. Opt. Commun. Netw. **8**, 371–381 (2016)
24. Zhu, J., et al.: Control plane robustness in software-defined optical networks under targeted fiber cuts. In: Proceedings of ONDM 2018, pp. 118–123 (2018)
25. Zhu, Z., et al.: Demonstration of cooperative resource allocation in an openflow-controlled multidomain and multinational SD-EON testbed. J. Lightw. Technol. **33**, 1508–1514 (2015)
26. Zhu, Z., et al.: Build to tenants' requirements: on-demand application-driven vSD-EON slicing. J. Opt. Commun. Netw. **10**, A206–A215 (2018)

Joint Fronthaul Optimization and SDN Controller Placement in Dynamic 5G Networks

Victoria-Maria Alevizaki[1](✉) ⓘ, Markos Anastasopoulos[2] ⓘ, Anna Tzanakaki[1,2], and Dimitra Simeonidou[2] ⓘ

[1] Department of Physics, National and Kapodistrian University of Athens, Athens, Greece
vikalevizaki@phys.uoa.gr
[2] Department of Electrical and Electronic Engineering, University of Bristol, Bristol, UK

Abstract. To address the limitations of current Radio Access Networks (RANs), centralized-RANs adopting the concept of flexible splits of the BBU functions between Radio Units (RUs) and the central unit (CU) have been proposed. This concept can be implemented combining both the Mobile Edge Computing model and relatively large-scale centralized Data Centers. This architecture requires high bandwidth/low latency optical transport networks interconnecting RUs and compute resources adopting SDN control. This paper proposes a novel mathematical model based on Evolutionary Game Theory that allows to dynamically identify the optimal split option with the objective to unilaterally minimize the infrastructure operational costs in terms of power consumption. Optimal placement of the SDN controllers is determined by a heuristic algorithm in such a way that guarantees the stability of the whole system.

Keywords: Cloud · C-RAN · Evolutionary Game Theory · Functional splits · MEC · Replicator Equation · SDN

1 Introduction

The immense increase of network-connected devices and internet users, services and applications, creates huge bandwidth, mobility and speed demands, that cannot be fulfilled by existing technologies, mainly due to capital and operational costs [1]. Thus, a transition from current closed, static and unagile networks to open infrastructures that focus on flexible and optimized service delivery is needed. However, to achieve this, multiple requirements (data rate, latency, energy efficiency, bandwidth and network capacity etc.) have to be met, as different applications may require different network capabilities, features and performance.

In order to address the growth of traffic, network densification seems to be a promising solution. The main idea is to create very dense cells (Ultra Dense Networks - UDNs) by installing a large number of antennas with reduced range, achieving high bandwidth, and short delays [2]. Of course, this results in increased network capacity through the densification of the infrastructure. Although, we can solve the issue of increased traffic in data transmission by applying the classical technique of network densification, the

A. Tzanakaki et al. (Eds.): ONDM 2019, LNCS 11616, pp. 181–192, 2020.
https://doi.org/10.1007/978-3-030-38085-4_16

economical and environmental impact of the investment in such an infrastructure should be taken into consideration. Beyond the increase in the associated capital expenditure significant increase in the overall energy consumption of the infrastructure is expected as additional base stations required to support the dense antenna deployment would be also needed. This will have a direct impact not only in the CO_2 footprint of these solutions but also in the infrastructure operating costs directly associated with the energy consumption of the infrastructure.

Cloud Radio Access Networks (C-RANs) propose to overcome these limitations, by decoupling the BaseBand Units (BBUs) from the Base Stations (BSs) and place them in the Cloud, thus achieving a centralized manner of signal processing and management. The connection of the RU, and the Central Unit (CU), where the baseband processing is performed, is supported through an optical transport network. The combination of Cloud Computing with the centralized RAN architecture is ideal for planning shared network radio access, handling interference between nearby cells, and quickly and easily upgrading the network. Nevertheless, C-RAN suffers several limitations, the most important of which is the need for high capacity transport links to support fronthaul (FH) services, i.e. high bandwidth and very low latency connectivity between the RU and the CU [1]. Existing backhaul (BH) solutions are unable to offer the required capacity for the converged FH/BH transport network of future communication environments. In this manner, along with the adoption of advanced wireless and optical technologies (e.g. ub-6 GHz and 60 GHz bands, Wavelength Division Multiplexing (WDM) optical networks [1]), the concept of baseband processing split that allows some functions of the 5G protocol stack to be processed at the RUs, while the remaining ones to be processed at the CU has been proposed [1]. Flexible Functional Splits (FFS) specified by both 3GPPP and eCPRI [10] can relax FH requirements in terms of transport network specifications, but they may be both economically and environmentally inefficient. This is due to that, this architecture still requires the presence of computation and storage components at each RU in order to process the subset of BBU functions that will be dynamically decided to be performed locally at the RUs at different time instances.

To address this architectural inefficiency, Mobile Edge Computing (MEC) can be combined with the notion of flexible functional splits for making the system as cost and energy efficient as possible. In such a system, a set of low or medium processing power servers is placed in the wireless access domain or close to the edge of the network [3]. The processing capabilities that are required for the adoption of the FFS approach, can be removed from each RU and be placed in the MEC to which they are connected. Hence, the FFS technique can be addressed by adopting an architecture able to assign BBU processing functions dynamically between MEC servers and large-scale DCs placed at the optical access and metro domains that are hosting general purpose servers.

In general, 5G aims at incorporating many technologies, under the same infrastructure (FH/BH network). Efficient management and operation of such a heterogeneous infrastructure can be achieved applying novel network designs that are aligned with the Software Defined Networking (SDN) open reference architecture [4]. SDN refers to the migration of the control level out of the switches and its placement externally in a logical entity called a controller. The controller is in charge of populating the forwarding table of the switch. The communication between the two entities is carried out through a secure channel. This centralized structure makes the controller able to perform network management functions, while allowing easy modification of the network behavior through the centralized control layer. However, in such infrastructures the end to end latency is augmented. Considering that latency is critical to many network applications, a subject of current research is the size of the SDN network (controller placement problem) in order to be able to cope with the timing requirements of network services and applications [5, 6].

In this paper, we propose a next generation network solution that includes: (a) the concept of FFS between a set of servers that can offer a range of processing capabilities and can be geographically distributed across the network infrastructure, (b) the employment of the MEC architecture in the form of specific purpose low processing power servers embedded in the wireless access network (also known as cloudlets) and (c) a FH/BH transport network with SDN control, connecting the MEC domains with medium to large-scale DCs hosting general purpose servers placed at the optical access and metro domains. In this environment, the controller placement problem is investigated, under the scope of the stability of the whole system. To address this issue, we propose a novel mathematical model based on Evolutionary Game Theory (EGT) that allows network operators to dynamically adjust their FH split options with the objective to minimize their total operational expenditures. The stability of the proposed scheme depends on network latency, thus a metric for sizing the SDN FH/BH network is proposed.

The rest of the paper is organized as follows. After a brief overview of EGT in Sect. 2 the problem under consideration is analyzed in Sect. 3. Then, its application to the proposed network model is presented in Sect. 4, where the optimal split is identified applying EGT and the controller placement problem is addressed. Finally, conclusions are drawn in Sect. 5.

2 Evolutionary Game Theory: Basic Concepts

Evolutionary Game Theory (EGT) studies the interactions of non-cooperative players that play repeatedly strategic games [7]. Contrary to classic Game Theory that examines the behavior of rational players, EGT focuses on how the strategies can "survive" through evolution and how they help the players who choose them to "strengthen" and better meet their needs.

Evolutionary processes are described by three main components: the population, the game and the dynamical model that describe the processes. The most common dynamics is called the Replicator Equation (RE) and can be expressed as:

$$\dot{x}_i(t) = x_i(t)\big(F_i(\boldsymbol{x}(t)) - \overline{F}(\boldsymbol{x}(t))\big), \ i \in S \tag{1}$$

where S is the set of strategies that are available to the population, $\boldsymbol{x}(t) = [x_1(t) \ x_2(t) \ \dots \ x_i(t) \ \dots]^T$ is the population state at time t with $x_i(t)$ symbolizing the proportion of the population that uses strategy i at time t, and $F_i(\boldsymbol{x}(t))$, $\overline{F}(\boldsymbol{x}(t))$ are the expected payoff of strategy i and the mean payoff respectively [7]. According to this equation the percentage growth rate $\dot{x}_i/x_i$ of the strategies that are currently used is equal to the excess of the current payoff versus the average population's payoff. This means that strategies employed at present will be spread or eliminated depending on whether their payoff is better or worse than the average.

In the above, the interaction between individuals is assumed to be instant and their results immediate. However, this is not the case in most realistic scenarios. In communication networks especially, the impact of an action may be belated, due to network latency. Thus, it is more realistic to consider a system where the strategies evolve considering the payoff values perceived in a past moment. The adjusted RE is given below [8, 9]:

$$\dot{x}(t) = x_i(t) \cdot \left(f_i(x(t-\tau)) - \sum_{i \in S} x_j(t) \cdot f_j(x(t-\tau)) \right) \qquad (2)$$

3   Application to 5G Networks

We consider the 5G network topology shown in Fig. 1. In this scenario, the RUs are installed, managed and operated by coexisting Mobile Network Operators (MNOs). The RUs share a set of computational resources that are located both at the edge of the access network (in a MEC server) and at the metro/core network (in the Cloud). The interconnection between the MEC server and the central cloud servers is carried out by an SDN- controlled optical FH/BH transport network.

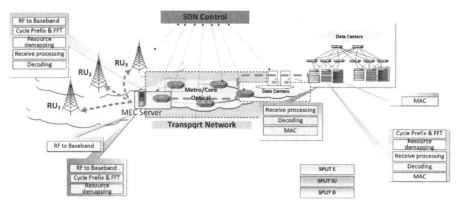

Fig. 1. Network architecture. In the MEC, a decision about which functions should be processed locally is made for each RU. The remaining set of functions for each RU are transferred through a common network infrastructure with centralized control to a DC for further processing.

The MNOs can decide where to perform the processing of the low layer functions of the LTE protocol stack. According to the eCPRI specification, three possible functional splits can be identified [10]. In split E (split 1 for simplicity) MEC is responsible for the RF processing of the received signals and the Cloud performs the entire baseband processing. In split IU (split 2), MEC handles the per cell processing (RF processing, cyclic prefix (CP) elimination, frequency domain transformation (FFT) and resource demapping), while the remaining functions are performed at the Cloud (Equalization,

IDFT, QAM, multi-antenna processing, Forward Error Correction (FEC), higher level operations (MAC, RLC, PDCP). Finally, in split D (split 3) the entire lower layer function chain is performed at the MEC server, and the higher lever functions in the Cloud. One can conclude that as the split is placed lower in the 5G protocol stack, the required transport capacity increases [11].

Each RU periodically selects one of the three possible functional splits with probability x_i, $i = 1, .., 3$. The decisions are sent to the SDN controller, who is responsible for the application of the policies. We consider the scenario in which all the necessary resources are available. When the policies have been applied, the payoffs are calculated and the RUs are reviewing their split option strategy. Specifically, if a better (lower) payoff is observed; then the probability of an RU to select the specific split option increases (decreases). The new policies are sent to the controller and the same procedure is repeated. The time between each repetition is referred to as revision time. To address this scenario, EGT can provide a suitable optimization framework that can be used to support energy-aware FH service provisioning over a common infrastructure.

Denote as $x(t) = [x_1(t)\ x_2(t)\ x_3(t)]^T$ the state vector of the RU, where $x_i(t)$ refers to the RU's probability of choosing split i. If the RU revises its strategy with a time rate $r_i(x)$, the change of the proportion of the probabilities is described by the following dynamical equation:

$$\dot{x}_i(t) = \sum\nolimits_{j \in S} x_j(t) r_j(x(t)) p_j^i(x(t)) - \sum\nolimits_{j \in S} x_i(t) r_i(x(t)) p_i^j(x(t)) \qquad (3)$$

where S is the set of strategies that consists of the three possible splits and $p_i^j(x)$ is the rule of change in the probability of choosing split i when the RU changes from split i to split j and can be expressed as:

$$p_i^j(x(t)) = \begin{cases} x_j(t)(u(j, t) - u(i, t)) & j \neq i \\ 1 - \sum\nolimits_{j \neq i} x_j(t)(u(j, t) - u(i, t)) & otherwise \end{cases} \qquad (4)$$

with $u(i, t)$ symbolizing the payoff of split i at time t. Constituting Eqs. (4) to (3) and making the assumption that all time rates are constantly equal to one ($r_i(x) \equiv 1$), the following differential equation comes up:

$$\dot{x}_i(t) = x_i(t) \left[u(i, t) - \sum\nolimits_{j \in S} x_j(t) u(j, t) \right] \qquad (5)$$

which satisfies the replicator dynamics model introduced in Sect. 2.

3.1 Payoff Function

The objective of the MNOs is to minimize their own service power consumption requirements and, hence, the service operational costs. Thus, the payoff function per operator is formed by summing up the power consumption of the network and compute elements required to support FH services. Table 1 summarizes the network and processing demands of each functional split.

Table 1. Network and processing demands of each functional split

Split	Network rate	Processing functions	
		Local	Remote
1 (E)	$R_1 = N_o \cdot f_s \cdot N_Q \cdot N_R$	RF	FFT, RE Demapping, Rx Processing, DEC, MAC
2 (I_U)	$R_2 = N_{sc} \cdot T_s^{-1} \cdot 2 \cdot N_Q \cdot N_R \cdot \eta$	RF, FFT, RE Demapping	Rx Processing, DEC, MAC
3 (D)	$R_3 = N_{sc} \cdot T_s^{-1} \cdot \eta \cdot S$	RF, FFT, RE Demapping, Rx Processing, DEC	MAC

For this problem setting, the payoff of an RU operated by an MNO that chooses split i against another RU operated by a different MNO who chooses split j is described by the payoff matrix A, with elements:

$$a_{ij} = -\left(P_{PROCESSING_{ij}} + P_{NET_{ij}}\right) + b, \quad i, j \in S \tag{6}$$

where $P_{PROCESSING}$ and $P_{NET_{ij}}$ refer to the total compute and network energy consumption respectively, when split i competes with split j and b is a positive constant that guarantees the robustness of the system. Technical parameters like the oversampling factor (N_o), the sampling frequency (f_s), the quantization bits per I/Q (N_Q), the number of receiving antennas (N_R), the number of subcarriers used (N_{sc}), the percentage of used resource elements (η), and the spectral efficiency (S) affect the required capacity and the power consumption of each processing function [11, 12].

Due to the nature of the SDN transport network, the payoff values are provided to the MNOs through the SDN controller. It is evident, that this kind of procedure indicates that the strategies will evolve based on information related to a past moment. This will be reflected to the expected payoff of the strategies.

Network delay is mainly composed of propagation, serialization, switching/routing and queuing delay. Although propagation and switching/routing delays are constant, the rest are highly affected by the network traffic. Due to this, we expect that network delay is a random variable that is characterized by a probability density function. Specifically, if the payoff is received not instantly, but after a random delay τ, with probability distribution $P(t)$ the expected payoff of an RU using strategy i as well as the average payoff are determined by [13]:

$$u(i, t) = \int_0^\infty P(\tau)(Ax(t - \tau))_i \quad \& \quad \bar{u} = \sum_{j \in S} x_j(t)u(j, t) \tag{7}$$

3.2 Stability Analysis

Substituting Eqs. (7) in (5) we get a nonlinear system of differential equations. Since this system cannot be easily solved by analytical methods it is important to examine its qualitative behavior without actually solving it. We concentrate on finding the stability of a solution exploiting the Lyapunov stability theorem. This method is based on the expansion of the right part of the dynamical system as a Taylor series about an equilibrium point x^0. If the initial condition $x(0) = x_0$ is close enough to x^0, then x will be a small perturbation for some time interval extending from zero. Thus, it is acceptable to neglect the higher-order terms, and approximate the nonlinear system by the linear system [9]:

$$\dot{x}(t) = J_o x(t) + J_1 x(t - \tau) \tag{8}$$

where $J_o \in \mathbb{R}^{2x2}$ and $J_1 \in \mathbb{R}^{2x2}$ are respectively, the Jacobian matrix, and the delayed Jacobian matrix evaluated at equilibrium at x^0.

The stability of the system requires that all roots of its characteristic equation have a negative real part. The characteristic equation can be expressed as:

$$\det(I\lambda - J_o - J_1 Q) = 0 \Rightarrow \lambda^2 + D\lambda + E\lambda Q + FQ^2 + GQ + H = 0 \tag{9}$$

where $\lambda \in \mathbb{C}$, I is the NxN identity matrix, $Q = \int_0^\infty P(\tau)e^{-\lambda\tau}$ corresponds to the Laplace transform of the delayed term in Eq. (8) and the parameters depend on the Jacobian matrices' elements.

The system admits to seven equilibrium points: three corner points, one interior and three corner side points. The linearization about each of the three corner critical points produces an ordinary differential equation that is independent of the delayed variables as in the non-delayed three strategies game.

At the interior critical point all the payoffs are equal. The differential system that emerges depends only on the delayed variables, thus one should anticipate that the distributed delay will affect its stability. The characteristic equation is formed as:

$$u^2 + E \cdot u + F = 0, \quad u = \frac{\lambda}{Q} \tag{10}$$

The last three critical points are equilibriums where only two of the three strategies survive (corner side points). Their characteristic equation can be written as:

$$(\lambda - l_1) \cdot (\lambda - l_2 Q) = 0 \tag{11}$$

where the parameters l_1 and l_2 depend on the corner side equilibrium point.

As we can conclude from the above, our analysis can be restricted for finding the solution of the equation:

$$\lambda - C \int_0^\infty P(\tau)e^{-\lambda\tau} = 0 \tag{12}$$

The above equation is the characteristic equation of the linear differential equation:

$$\dot{x}(t) = C \int_0^\infty x(t - \tau)f(t)d\tau \tag{13}$$

Thus, the conclusions derived for the stability of Eq. (13) can be expanded to our case. From [14] we derive the following necessary and sufficient condition for the asymptotic stability of the equilibriums:

Proposition: If $C < 0$ and the expected value (E) of the delay's probability density satisfies the condition:

$$E(\tau) < \frac{\pi}{\gamma \cdot |C|} \qquad (14)$$

where $\gamma = 2$ when the pdf is symmetrical, or else $\gamma = \sup\{\gamma \,|\, \cos w = 1 - \frac{\gamma w}{\pi},\ w > 0\}$, then the equilibrium point is stable (the proof can be found in [14]). Last but not least, as far as the variance of the distribution is concerned, the stability of the system increases as the variance grows [14].

3.3 SDN Controller Placement

As it was mentioned earlier, the SDN controller is responsible for collecting and providing to the MNOs of the RUs the required information from all controlled devices. The maximum delay corresponds to the delay of the most distant node to the controller path plus the delay of the controller-MEC path. Thus, assuming that each controlled device may host a MEC, the stability of the system is achieved only when the round-trip time (RRT) of the controller's path to the most remote device is less than the limit imposed by Eq. (14). Based on this limit, we propose a heuristic algorithm that tries to identify the minimum number and associated position of SDN controllers with the aim to guarantee the stability of the 5G infrastructure. This is performed with low computational complexity.

At first, the heuristic algorithm finds the maximum network radius, that is the number of hops of the longest end-to-end path. Then, for each node it calculates the maximum RRT to all the other nodes inside the network radius. If the result of all nodes is a number higher than the limit imposed in Eq. (14), the network radius is reduced by one, and the same procedure is repeated, until a case is found where the RRT from a node to all other nodes within the network radius meets the condition of Eq. (14). The nodes that meet this requirement, are marked as possible controller candidates. From this set, the algorithm chooses as the first controller the one that is connected to the largest number of devices within the network radius. These devices and the first controller are removed from the network, and the whole procedure is repeated for the downscaled network. The algorithm ends when the downscaled network has no network nodes.

4 Results and Discussion

In order to see the effectiveness of our model we considered the system described in Fig. 1 with the system parameters shown in Table 2. The cost ratio (remote/central processing) was assumed to be equal to two. Furthermore, the relationship of the transport network's energy consumption with the required capacity for the support of the FH services was assumed to be nonlinear, since the non-linear model is best to describe the technology advancements in terms of energy efficiency of network devices [12, 15].

The stability analysis of system (5) indicates that the equilibrium point in such a scenario is $x_1^* = 0.2957$, $x_2^* = 0.7043$, $x_3^* = 0$. This means that in the non-delayed system the optimal split choice is split 2. However, as it was stated previously the SDN

Table 2. Parameters of the system configuration

Symbol	Quantity	Value
B	Bandwidth	20 MHz
Ant	Number of the rx antennas	2
M	Modulation	6 bits/symbol
R	Coding rate	1/2
dt	Time-domain duty-cycling	100%
f_s	Sampling frequency	30.72 MHz
N_o	Oversampling factor	2
N_{sc}	Number of used subcarriers	1200
T_s	Symbol duration	66.6 μs
N_Q	Quantization bits per I/Q	10
S	Spectral efficiency	3 bit/cu
η	Assumed RB utilization	70%

transport network introduces additional delay to the system. This delay can be divided to two main components, namely the processing delay of the SDN controller and the transport delay.

The SDN controller chosen for the implementation is the Opendaylight controller (ODL), that is a scalable controller infrastructure that supports SDN implementations in modern heterogeneous networks of different vendors [16]. For measuring the processing delay of the ODL controller, we developed an application that communicates externally with the controller. For evaluations, a linear network topology with Out of Band control plane was emulated in Mininet, a tool that can emulate and perform the functions of network devices in a single physical host or virtual machine (VM) [17]. Both Mininet and Opendaylight controller were implemented on the same machine (Intel® Core™ i5-7400U CPU @ 3.00 GHZ (4 cores)) to overcome the Ethernet interface speed limitations. 7.7 GiB of memory was available. The system was running Ubuntu 16.04 LTS-64 bit. The application implements at first step a mechanism for collecting data on the network topology and at second step a mechanism for sending echo messages to all switches simultaneously, and measuring the maximum time elapsed for receiving a reply. The time response of ODL is measured by averaging the results of a hundred number of tests, in order to achieve higher accuracy. The results showed an exponential relation between the controller's processing delay and the network devices.

As far as the transport delay is concerned, we used monthly delay measurements extracted from GRNET [18], in order to find the dependence of the end to end transport delay on the end to end hops. Our analysis concluded that this relationship can be well approximated with a linear function. Furthermore, the best pdf that fitted the end to end delay was the generalized t-student distribution [19].

Taking these into consideration, we expect that the total induced SDN network's delay will be a random variable that is characterized by the generalized t-student distribution, with expected value that depends on the size of the transport network and the hops between two network nodes. Thus, the upper delay limit for our example is given by Eq. (14) as: $E_{max} = 1.6449$ time units.

The assumed FH/BH transport network's topology for our example is depicted in Fig. 2. The figure also shows the possible controller placements after implementing the heuristic algorithm described in the previous section. In order to test the validity of the heuristic, we investigate the evolution of strategies in two cases: (1) when the controller is placed in one of the proposed locations by the heuristic, (2) when the controller is placed in the location identified by the average propagation latency optimization technique described in [5]. Figure 3 illustrates the evolution of split option selection probability under the proposed EGT based approach and the average latency minimization scheme described above. As can be seen in the former case (Fig. 3a) after few sampling periods the scheme converges to a mixed solution where all antennas operate under a single split option mode that will be either split 1 or split 2. However, in the second case, the placement of the SDN controller at a node that does not satisfy the stability threshold imposed by Eq. (14) leading to an unstable operational mode for the 5G network. The reason behind this is that the increased control plane delay in this case introduces inaccurate information of the network status at the controller. Therefore, decision making is performed with outdated information that leads to an oscillation around the optimal operating point preventing it from converging to a stable solution.

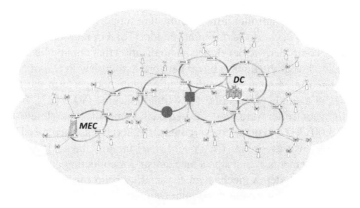

Fig. 2. Assumed FH/BH transport network for the system described in Fig. 1. The red circle represents the position of the SDN controller, after the implementation of the heuristic algorithm described in Sect. 3.3. The red square represents the optimal position estimated according to the average propagation latency-case described in [5]. (Color figure online)

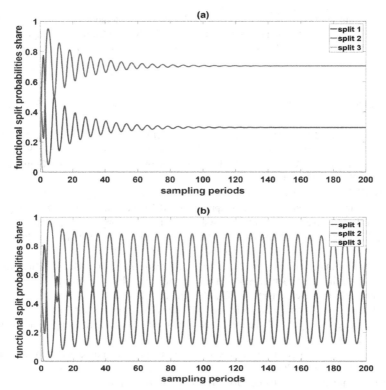

Fig. 3. Evolution of the probabilities of the three split options, with the parameters described in Table 2, when: (a) the controller is placed in the proposed location (red circle in Fig. 2) by the heuristic, (b) the controller is placed in the proposed location (red square in Fig. 2) of the average propagation latency-case described in [5]. (Color figure online)

5   Conclusion

To address the limitations of current RANs, centralized-RANs adopting the concept of flexible splits of the BBU functions between RUs and the CU have been proposed. To achieve further efficiency gains in terms of cost and energy consumption we proposed the implementation of this architectural model exploiting compute resources, required for the BBU function processing, located both at the MEC and relatively large-scale centralized DCs. This architecture adopts high bandwidth/low latency SDN controlled optical transport networks. In this scenario, and with the aim to dynamically identify the optimal split option that minimize infrastructure operational costs in terms of power consumption we have proposed a novel mathematical model based on EGT. In addition, optimal placement of the transport network SDN controllers is determined by a heuristic algorithm with the objective to guarantee the stability of the whole system.

Acknowledgment. This research is co-financed by Greece and the European Union (European Social Fund- ESF) through the Operational Programme «Human Resources Development, Education and Lifelong Learning» in the context of the project "Strengthening Human Resources

Research Potential via Doctorate Research" (MIS-5000432), implemented by the State Scholarships Foundation (IKY)», the EU Horizon 2020 project 5G-PICTURE under grant agreement No. 762057 and the EU Horizon 2020 project IN2DREAMS under grand agreement No. 777596.

References

1. Tzanakaki, A., et al.: Wireless-optical network convergence: enabling the 5G architecture to support operational and end-user services. IEEE Commun. Mag. **55**(10), 184–192 (2017)
2. Kamel, M., Hamouda, W., Youssef, A.: Ultra-dense networks: a survey. IEEE Commun. Surv. Tutorials **18**(4), 2522–2545 (2016)
3. Liu, H., Eldarrat, F., Alqahtani, H., Reznik, A., de Foy, X., Zhang, Y.: Mobile edge cloud system: architectures, challenges, and approaches. IEEE Syst. J. **12**(3), 2495–2508 (2018)
4. Software-Defined Networking. https://www.opennetworking.org/sdn-definition/
5. Heller, B., Sherwood, R., McKeown, N.: The controller placement problem. In: Proceedings of Hot Topics in Software Defined Networking (HotSDN) (2012)
6. Hock, D., Hartmann, M., Gebert, S., Jarschel, M., Zinner, T., Tran-Gia, P.: Pareto-optimal resilient controller placement in SDN-based core networks. In: Proceedings of the 2013 25th International Teletraffic Congress (ITC), Shanghai, pp. 1–9 (2013)
7. Weibull, J.W.: Evolutionary Game Theory. MIT Press, Cambridge (1997)
8. Yi, T., Zuwang, W.: Eject of Time Delay and Evolutionarily Stable Strategy. Academic Press Limited (1997)
9. Obando, G., et.al.: Replicator dynamics under perturbations and time delays. Math. Control Signals Syst. **28**(3), 20 (2016)
10. eCPRI Specification V1.1, 10 January 2018. http://www.cpri.info/
11. Wübben, D., et.al.: Benefits and impact of cloud computing on 5G signal processing. IEEE Sig. Process. Mag. **31**(6), 35–44 (2014)
12. Desset, C., et.al.: Flexible power modeling of LTE base stations. In: IEEE Wireless Communications and Networking Conference (WCNC), Shanghai, China, April 2012
13. Ben-Khalifa, N., El-Azouzi, R., Hayel, Y.: Random time delays in evolutionary game dynamics. In: 2015 54th IEEE Conference on Decision and Control (CDC), Osaka, pp. 3840–3845 (2015)
14. Bernard, S., et al.: Sufficient conditions for stability of linear differential equations with distributed delay. Discrete Continuous Dyn. Syst. -Series B **1**(2), 233–256 (2001)
15. Baliga, J., Ayre, R., Hinton, K., Sorin, W.V., Tucker, R.S.: Energy consumption in optical IP networks. J. Lightwave Technol. **27**(13), 2391–2403 (2009)
16. Platform Overview. https://www.opendaylight.org
17. Mininet Overview. http://mininet.org/overview/
18. https://grnet.gr/infrastructure/network-and-topology/
19. Student's t-distribution. https://en.wikipedia.org/wiki/Student%27s_t-distribution

3-Stage Hierarchical Quality of Service for Multi-tenant Passive Optical Networks

Frank Slyne[1]([✉]), Bruno Cornaglia[2], Marco Boselli[2], and Marco Ruffini[1]

[1] Connect Research Center, Trinity College, Dublin, Ireland
fslyne@tcd.ie
[2] Vodafone Group Technology, Turin, Italy

Abstract. Passive Optical Networks (PONs) are an economically efficient means of providing high bandwidth services to end users because end-points can share the cost and the benefit of fibre optic connection. There is a growing interest in the use of PONs as a bearer for services such as Long Term Evolution (LTE), however work remains to be done to ensure stable, low latency and low packet loss for full duplex Transmission. In this paper we are mostly concerned with the characteristics of the downstream channel so as to further the case for PON sharing. We review typical downstream schedulers used in the industry and propose a three-stage downstream scheduler that assures quality of service, accurately, across Virtual Network Operators (VNOs) in multi-tenant PONs environment. We benchmark our scheduler against other algorithms, obtaining almost ideal scheduling performance.

Keywords: Quality of service · Two rate three color marker · Scheduler · Policer · Passive Optical Networks · Virtualization · Slicing

1 Introduction

Up until recently, residential broadband has been the dominant service delivered over PONs. However, because PONs are an economically efficient means of providing high capacity bandwidth across wide rural and urban geographical areas [1], they are becoming increasingly attractive for the delivery of non-retail services such as LTE [2], where dedicated fibre capacity would not be economically feasible. PON sharing across multiple VNOs is also becoming increasingly important, in order to foster competition without replicating costly hardware infrastructure. Thus, in a multi-tenant scenario each VNO should have the ability to assign its portion of assured and best effort traffic to its customers, without affecting or being affected by other VNOs. Given that LTE, when implemented as Cloud Radio Access Networks (C-RAN) has a low tolerance to excessive packet jitter and latency, the VNO needs granular slicing and resource control in order to share PON infrastructure with non-critical services such as residential broadband.

Achieving separation between VNOs in a PON environment is complicated by the fact that upstream and downstream transmissions function in different manners. Unfortunately, granular resource control is only defined for upstream traffic in the PON standards, with downstream left to the devices of operators and whatever capabilities their

© IFIP International Federation for Information Processing 2020
Published by Springer Nature Switzerland AG 2020
A. Tzanakaki et al. (Eds.): ONDM 2019, LNCS 11616, pp. 193–203, 2020.
https://doi.org/10.1007/978-3-030-38085-4_17

vendor supplied equipment provide. By its nature, upstream transmission in a PON is a TDM channel where there is an inherent control over how much and when each Traffic Container (TCont) of each Optical Network Terminations (ONT) can transmit, down to the granularity of each 32-bit word [3]. In this context a TCont can be thought of as a dedicated queue at the ONT to which a specific class of service can be assigned. The scheduling of the upstream transmission is regulated by the Dynamic Bandwidth Allocation (DBA) mechanism [4], which allocates capacity to the ONTs located at the end user side [5]. One solution to provide full control to the VNOs over their upstream capacity allocation, by virtualizing and slicing the DBA mechanism, was recently proposed in [6], prototyped in [7] and standardized in [8].

Of most pertinence in this paper, is the downstream channel of the PON which functions in the manner of a statistically multiplexed packetized channel or shared bus. The packetization of data followed by statistical multiplexing through a shared transmission channel is an essential means of increasing the utilization of the channel, when compared to time or frequency division multiplexing means over the same channel. This technological trend is similar to how synchronous SDH and cell-based ATM networks in the core and metro networks are being replaced by multi-gigabit Ethernet [9] networks running over Dense Wave Division Multiplexing (DWDM) fiber [10], at times over an Optical Transmission Network (OTN) sublayer [11]. However, a drawback for real-time services that use a statistical multiplexed channel is the lack of a guarantee over the data information rate, packet loss and latency, which go together to define QoS. As central office infrastructure is moving towards virtualization and slicing [12], the ability to provide assurance over QoS is becoming increasingly important to provide slice independence across multiple tenants, as though they were being served by dedicated infrastructure. This is typically achieved through appropriate queue management, to separate traffic with different QoS requirements and policing the rate of incoming traffic. However, such methodology is not defined in PON standards, where decisions on how to implement downstream QoS are left to vendors and operators. Typically, the options vary between over-dimensioning capacity on each PON, executing vendor specific scheduling and policing, or shaping traffic prior to entering the Optical Line Termination (OLT) [2].

In this paper, we first review the current practices used by operators for the scheduling of downstream traffic in a PON, typically divided into one-stage and the two-stage scheduler architectures. We will show that while these methods can be effective in single-operator scenarios, they fail to provide the necessary support for VNOs sharing the same infrastructure. We thus propose a novel three-stage scheduler that includes a QoS stage for providing additional separation between VNOs. In order to make the case for the scheduler, we build the architecture for the one-, two- and three- stage schedulers in a simulator, which are then exercised using a common set of scenarios. The performance of the three simulators are then compared using typical metrics such as packet loss. Throughout the experiment, we are careful to distinguish between the packet handling capabilities for both High Priority (HP) and Low Priority (LP) traffic. Examples of HP traffic includes Signal data and traffic related to services that deteriorate significantly due to packet loss, such as Voice over IP (VoIP) [13]. Examples of LP traffic includes streaming Video and raw data, both of which can be buffered and replayed in the event of packet loss.

2 Downstream Scheduling

Typically, downstream PON QoS is implemented through queue management functions defined by Internet Engineering Task Force (IETF) Request For Comment (RFC)s. These functions include Strict Priority (SP), Weighted Round Robin (WRR), Weighted Fair Queuing (WFQ) and two rate three color marker (trTCM) which operate on network packet flows and which we distinguish as follows. A SP queue function has N input ports (numbered from 0 to N-1) and 1 output port. It will serve packets from port 0, if they are present, ahead of a lower priority (1 to N-1) port. Likewise, a SP queue will serve packets from port 1, if they are present, ahead of a lower priority (2 to N-1) port. While a SP can guarantee packets from higher priority ports to be delivered to the output port, there is no rate-limiting function that prevents the output port from being overloaded by lower priority packets. A WRR queue function has N input ports (numbered from 0 to N-1) and 1 output port. Packets are served from the input ports according to a weighted distribution function, typically denoted by φ (phi), and averaged over a unit of time. The downside of the WRR queue function is that it only distinguishes between packet counts and not packet sizes. A small number of very large packets served to low weighted port can skew the queue output in its favor. This is rectified in the WFQ. The weighted distribution function φ (phi) is defined in a similar way to that of the WRR queue function, except that it operates according to bytes offered to each port, as opposed to packets. The trTCM is an example of a Policer that can implement rate-limiting functionality. trTCM accepts flows of data on typically a single physical input port, which are then sent to a single output port. These flows can be passed through (logically tagged Green), dropped (Red) or remarked and passed (Yellow) depending on predefined data rate rules. Examples of the specific operation of the trTCM are given below. The mechanism by which these queue management functions can be composed into typical downstream QoS schedulers are shown in Fig. 1. Firstly, we see a single-stage QoS mechanism in Fig. 1(a), where QoS is only implemented at the ONT level, with WRR scheduling traffic within the same priority class, and SP operating across the classes to provide, for example, strict higher priority to voice and signaling with respect to video and other data types. Secondly, Fig. 1(b) shows an alternative two stages vendor solution. The first stage operates at the ONT level and is composed of 4 queues, a SP scheduler and trTCM policer. The SP scheduler handles traffic in the decreasing priority of signaling, voice and the weighted fair queuing balancing of video and data. The SP assigns a color to the traffic based on the source. Both signaling and voice are HP and thus marked as green. Video and data are instead LP and marked as yellow. Because the color of the traffic is already configured by SP, trTCM is configured in color-blind mode, according to RFC 4115 [14], and passes the colored traffic directly to the egress Committed Information Rate (CIR) and Excess Information Rate (EIR) ports respectively. A weighed fair queuing is applied at the ONT level between video and data, while strict priority is assigned to voice and signaling. trTCM policers enforce proportionality between CIR and EIR by marking the packets according to RFC2698 (trTCM) color definition [15].

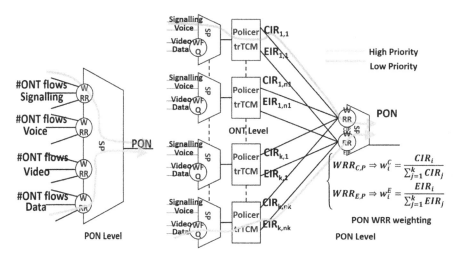

Fig. 1. Architecture of single-stage (a) and two-stage (b) reference schedulers (Color figure online)

Packets that are marked as red are dropped, green packets are passed through, yellow packets are remarked packets that may be dropped at a later stage or passed if there is sufficient available capacity. At the OLT port level, a weighted round robin mechanism is applied to schedule packets across all ONTs, respecting aggregate levels of CIR and EIR. The second stage is the PON port module, composed of two WRR queues operating on the CIR and EIR queues. The weighting of the WRR queues is based on the total service profile, CIR and EIR respectively, that each ONT should carry as a proportion of the total capacity allowed in the PON port. For example, the weighting given to the packets from the ith ONT

$$w_i^c = \frac{CIR_i}{\sum_{j=1}^{k} CIR_j}, \ w_i^e = \frac{EIR_i}{\sum_{j=1}^{k} EIR_j}$$

Where w_i^c and w_i^e are the fractions of configured CIR and EIR for that ONT over the total CIR and EIR respectively for all (k) ONTs. The total weightings for each WWR then sums to 1.

$$\sum_{i=1}^{k} w_i^c = 1, \sum_{i=1}^{k} w_i^e = 1$$

It should be noticed that QoS scheduling becomes especially important in multi-tenant scenarios, where different VNOs can have different QoS contracts with their own customers and with the infrastructure provider. However, current scheduling mechanisms such as those described above, do not take into consideration the existence of multiple VNOs, and thus there is no QoS differentiation at the VNO level. In this paper we attempt to tackle this issue by proposing a novel three-stage scheduler that adds VNO-oriented scheduling layer and by comparing its performance improvement against the baseline mechanisms shown in Fig. 1.

Finally, we can define the behavior of the ideal scheduler, against which current and proposed architectures can be compared. To do this, we calculate X_i^{HP} and X_i^{LP} the expected HP and LP traffic egressing from the PON related to the ith ONT, given offered traffic Z_i^{HP} and Z_i^{LP}. The high priority traffic marked as green should not exceeded the CIR allocated to that ONT. In the event, that HP traffic exceeds the CIR, the excess is recolored as yellow.

$$G_i^{HP} = min\left(Z_i^{HP}, CIR_i\right), \quad Y_i^{HP} = Z_i^{HP} - G_i^{HP}$$

Any excess CIR may be used to allow LP traffic to be colored as green. The excess LP traffic is marked yellow.

$$G_i^{LP} = CIR_i - G_i^{HP}, \quad Y_i^{LP} = Z_i^{LP} - G_i^{LP}$$

The expected HP traffic egressing from the PON related to the ith ONT is a sum of HP traffic marked as green and HP traffic marked as yellow contending for the total EIR EIRT. w_i^c and w_i^e are as defined above.

$$X_i^{HP} = G_i^{HP} + w_i^c . EIR_T . \frac{Y_i^{HP}}{Y_i^{HP} + Y_i^{LP}}$$

Similarly, the expected LP traffic egressing from the PON related to the ith ONT is a sum of LP traffic marked as green and LP traffic marked as yellow contending for the total EIR EIR_T.

$$X_i^{LP} = G_i^{LP} + w_i^e . EIR_T . \frac{Y_i^{LP}}{Y_i^{LP} + Y_i^{LP}}$$

In the next section we explain the architecture of our proposed three-stage QoS scheduler and the implementation of the simulation environment. This allows us to compare the results of our scheduler with the one-stage and two-stage schedulers described above, showing the advantages brought by our three-stage design for multi-tenant operations.

3   Three-Stage Scheduler Description and Architecture

The architecture of our Hierarchical three-stage scheduler is shown in Fig. 2, and uses the same array of functions (SP, WRR, WFQ and trTCM) as the one- and two- stage schedulers. We note that in recent years the IETF has developed algorithms and techniques for Queue management and schedulers, such as Controlled Delay (CoDel) and Active Queue Management (AQM) respectively that deal with anomalous treatment of TCP/IP transport flows due to excess buffering of packets. This anomalous behavior is a result of a phenomenon known as Bufferbloat [16], that is, the use of excessively large buffers in routers, switches and modems, that disrupt how normal functioning of TCP/IP flow control mechanism. IETF has combined CoDel and AQM into a single RFC (8290) known as Flow Queue CoDel Packet Scheduler and Active Queue Management Algorithm (FQ-CoDel) [17]. With respect to the reference two-stage scheduler shown

Fig. 1(b), we have added a further WRR followed by a trTCM function that operate at the individual VNO level. The scope of this additional stage is to further partition the overall capacity, so that any excess capacity from a VNO is preferentially re-distributed across the ONTs belonging to the same VNO. Hierarchical Scheduler is located as a single functional block at the head end of the PON, that is at the OLT. It functions at 3 levels, that is, at the level of the ONT, at the level of the Operator and at the level of the PON, where WRR, SP and WFQ assure proportionality between contracted bandwidths. Downstream from the ONT and Operator schedulers, trTCM policers enforce proportionality between CIR and EIR by marking the packets according to RFC2698 (trTCM) color definition [15]. Packets that are marked as Red are dropped, Green Packets are passed through, Yellow packets are remarked packets that may be dropped at a later stage or passed if there is enough bandwidth. In an ideal scenario, but not implemented here, a feedback path from the PON functional block, similar to Call Admission Control (CAC), directs specific ONTs to block new flow requests, where the CIR is higher than a specific percentage (typically 50%) of the total capacity of the PON or indeed should the CIR of an operator exceed a specific threshold agreed with the PON infrastructure provider.

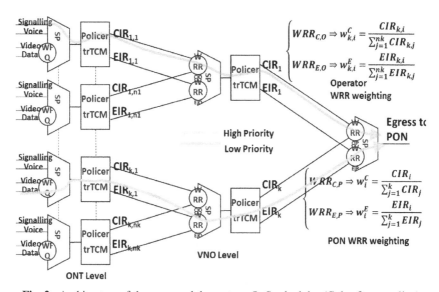

Fig. 2. Architecture of the proposed three-stage QoS scheduler (Color figure online)

4   Simulator

In order to compare the QoS performance improvement of the three-stage scheduler in PON multi-tenant scenarios we have developed a QoS discrete event simulator based on the Python SimPy [18] package. We use several fundamental QoS modules (trTCM, WRR, WFQ and SP) to construct the downstream PON schedulers operating in the

OLT. The trTCM object class marks packets with the three colors: green, yellow and red, depending both on any original marking and on the CIR and the EIR parameters. It should be noticed that the decision on whether incoming data is above or below the CIR and EIR thresholds is computed based on average values across a given burst data size. In the simulation we used burst sizes values for the CIR and the EIR typically configured in Cisco and Juniper routers of 64 Kbytes and 128 Kbytes, respectively. The WRR module accepts packets from several inputs streams and assures fairness based upon a predefined distribution based on number of packets in the input buffer for each stream. WFQ behaves similarly to WRR but uses number of bytes in the input buffer for each stream as a means of determining the fairness. Finally, SP selects packets from different queues in ascending order of priority and being strict it will only select packets from a lower priority queue once the higher priority ones are empty.

The ONT module is made up of 4 queues each with a buffer size of 128 Kbytes, a SP scheduler and trTCM policer. The SP scheduler handles traffic in the decreasing priority of signaling, voice and the weighted fair queuing balancing of video and data. The SP assigns a color to the traffic based on the source. Both signaling and voice are HP and thus marked as green. Video and data are instead LP and marked as yellow. Because the color of the traffic is already configured by SP, trTCM is configured in colorblind mode, according to RFC 4115 [14], and passes the colored traffic to the egress CIR and EIR ports respectively. This is constructed similarly to the ONT QoS module, however there is a pair (that is for both CIR and EIR) of WRR schedulers for each VNO, whose weightings are calculated based on the total capacity assigned to the specific VNO. Thereafter a trTCM policer colors the aggregate traffic from the SP scheduler as passed (green), remarked (yellow) or dropped (red). The PON port QoS module is composed of two WRR queues whose weighting are based on the aggregate service profiles, CIR and EIR respectively, that each other operator carries. The PON QoS module does not have a policer, but instead must aggregate both CIR and EIR onto the common downstream physical link. To assess the performance of the Hierarchical QoS (H-QoS), we also emulate one and two stage QoS architectures. The one stage architecture is composed of just the PON module from the three-stage architecture, which has been extended to have 4 WRR queues, terminating the Signaling, Voice, Video and Data links. The weighting of the WRR queues is based on the total service profile CIR and EIR respectively that each other ONT carries as a proportion of the total for the PON.

The two-stage architecture Fig. 1(b) is composed of the ONT and PON modules from the three-stage architecture Fig. 2, omitting the Operator QoS modules. The ONTs connect directly to the PON. The weighting of the PON WRR queues is based on the total service profile CIR and EIR respectively that each other ONT carries as a proportion of the total for the PON.

5 Simulation Scenarios and Results

In our simulation, we assume that there are 2 VNOs which share a common PON downstream capacity of 2.488 Gbps [3], of which 1.760 Gigabits per second (Gbps) is allocated to CIR. We define a service profile as a fixed mix of committed and excess information rates that may be assigned by any VNO to one of its ONTs. We denote this mix as a tuple (CIR, EIR). In our simulations, we define two service profiles, Profile-1 (10,100) and Profile2 (100,1000), measured in Megabits per second (Mbps). In order to gauge the ability of the QoS mechanisms described to schedule capacity appropriately across VNOs we introduce an imbalance between their user base. Operator A has 24 ONTs, of which half are Profile-1 and half are Profile-2.

Operator B has 4 ONTs with Profile-1 and 4 with Profile-2. The net result is that Operator A carries three quarters of the total traffic and Operator B carries one quarter. We are especially interested in what happens to bandwidth which is offered to an ONT that is either in excess or in deficit of its service profile's CIR and EIR, which we call the Nominal information rates. For this purpose, traffic offered at each ONT is transmitted at either +20% or −20% of the nominal CIR or EIR for the configured service profile. For instance, ONTs with service profile Profile-1 may be offered (8, 80), (8, 120), (12, 80) or (12, 120) Mbps. Finally, in addition to providing a comparison between our three-stage QoS mechanism and the two other baseline algorithms described in Sect. 1, we also provide the output of an ideal scheduler as described previously, under the same conditions, that is, whose output is computed mathematically rather than simulated. This allows use to assess the three QoS architectures against an ideal scheduler.

The results of our simulations are reported in Fig. 3 showing the throughput of the different schedulers for HP and LP traffic. The x axis represents the different ONTs, which are identified by the triplet (x:y:z), where x identifies the VNO (A or B), y is the (CIR/EIR) profile (i.e., Profile-1 or Profile-2, as described in the previous section) and z is the ONT identifier. To simplify the plot, we only show the results for a subset of ONTs, which is representative of the performance provided by the three schedulers. In the Fig. 4(a) plot, we see that both the proposed three-stage (in orange), the baseline two-stage (in gray) and the baseline one-stage (in yellow) algorithms follow the ideal output (shown in blue) quite closely. This is to be expected since the purpose of CIR is to strictly cap the capacity at the agreed levels, which can be easily enforced already at the ONT level.

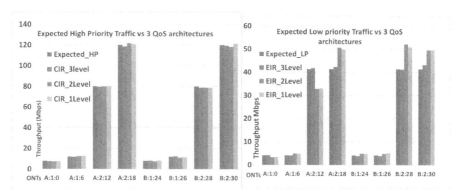

Fig. 3. Comparison of (a) High Priority (HP) and (b) Low Priority (LP) traffic (Color figure online)

As we see in Fig. 3, where the three-stage mechanism provides considerable improvements over the two-stage and the one-stage is in the handling of LP traffic. Since the EIR traffic is only scheduled if there is spare capacity, our additional VNO-level QoS can reassign such capacity appropriately within each VNO.

The three-stage algorithm provides a much closer output to the ideal scheduler both across ONTs and across VNOs, showing a maximum deviation of ±5%, compared to the two-stage scheme that deviates between ±25%. This accuracy is highly desirable in a multi-tenant Fixed Access Network Sharing (FANS) scenario [19], where each VNO pays the infrastructure provider for assuring a given level of aggregate CIR and EIR. The one-stage shows a ±26% deviation, however this on the basis that video, and data share the same WRR queue. If this were the not case, then the video queue would always be served at the expense of the data (least priority) queue in this scenario. Figure 4 shows the capacity variance for HP traffic (top graph) and for LP traffic (bottom graph) with respect to the ideal case for the three different scheduling algorithms (labeled three-stage, two-stage and one-stage).

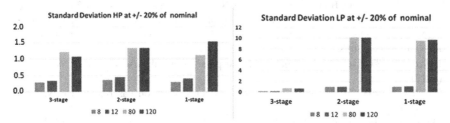

Fig. 4. Variance of (a) HP data and (b) LP data against expected ideal behavior (Color figure online)

The different bars group the results for all ONTs that offer, respectively, 8, 12, 80 and 120 Mb/s of HP traffic (the first two rates are for ONTs in Profile-1 with a 10 Mb/s CIR and the second two rates for ONTs in Profile-2 with 100 Mb/s of CIR). We see that the proposed three-stage architecture provides the lowest variance for all traffic levels, especially for the allocation of capacity to LP traffic. Finally, the one-stage architecture performs poorest with a deviation from the desired output between +80% and +200%.

6 Conclusions

In this paper, we have presented a three-stage scheduling architecture that can implemented at the head-end of the PON or the OLT. This has several benefits. Firstly, the OLT has full knowledge of the traffic that is being offered to the PON and provides real-time insight to network planners as to how the network is complying with contracted QoS metrics. Indeed, the three-stage scheduler is in the best position to react to changing network demands. Secondly, while the data-path of the three-stage scheduler may be implemented in high-speed Application Specific Integrated Circuit (ASIC), the parameters of the WRR, WFQ and trTCM can be dynamically tuned at the discretion of a centralized Software Defined Network (SDN) control plane or orchestrator. Thirdly, the centralization of the scheduler simplifies the functionality of the ONT, allowing for easier functional upgrades, and virtualization of the PON.

We have assumed that the CIR for each operator is equal to the sum of the CIR of all its' customers. However, in our future work, we will analyze where the CIR is less than the sum of the CIR of all its customers (over-subscription) as well as greater than the sum of the CIR of all its customers (under-subscription).

Acknowledgement. Financial support from Science Foundation Ireland (SFI) grants 14/IA/2527 (OSHARE) and 13/RC/2077 (CONNECT) is gratefully acknowledged.

References

1. Ruffini, M., Payne, D.B., Doyle, L.: Protection strategies for long-reach PON. In: 36th European Conference and Exhibition on Optical Communication, 19 September 2010, pp. 1–3. IEEE (2010)
2. Alvarez, P., Slyne, F., Bluemm, C., Marquez-Barja, J.M., DaSilva, L.A., Ruffini, M.: Experimental demonstration of SDN-controlled variable-rate Fronthaul for converged LTE-over-PON. In: 2018 Optical Fiber Communications Conference and Exposition (OFC), pp. 1–3. IEEE, 11 March 2018
3. I. Rec "G. 987. 6-2012," 10-Gigabit-capable passive optical network (XG-PON) systems (2012)
4. "G. 983. 1-1998," Broadband optical access systems based on Passive Optical Networks (PON) (1998)
5. Skubic, B., Chen, J., Ahmed, J., Wosinska, L., Mukherjee, B.: A comparison of dynamic bandwidth allocation for EPON, GPON, and next-generation TDM PON. IEEE Commun. Mag. **47**(3), S40–S48 (2009)
6. Elrasad, A., Afraz, N., Ruffini, M.: Virtual dynamic bandwidth allocation enabling true PON multi-tenancy. In: Optical Fiber Communication Conference, pp. M3I–3. Optical Society of America, 19 March 2017
7. Slyne, F., Giller, R., Singh, J., Ruffini, M.: Experimental demonstration of DPDK optimized VNF implementation of virtual DBA in a multi-tenant PON. In: 2018 European Conference on Optical Communication (ECOC), 23 September 2018, pp. 1–3. IEEE (2018)
8. Broadband Forum, BBF technical report tr-402, functional model for PON abstraction interface. In: Optical Fiber Communication Conference. Broadband Forum (2018)
9. Winzer, P.J.: Beyond 100G ethernet. IEEE Commun. Mag. **48**(7), 26–30 (2010)
10. Anderson, J., Traverso, M.: Optical transceivers for 100 gigabit ethernet and its transport [100 gigabit ethernet transport]. IEEE Commun. Mag. **48**(3), S35–S40 (2010)
11. Roese, J., Braun, R.P., Tomizawa, M., Ishida, O.: Optical transport network evolving with 100 gigabit ethernet evolving with 100 gigabit ethernet [100 gigabit ethernet transport]. IEEE Commun. Mag. **48**(3), S28–S34 (2010)
12. Ruffini, M., Slyne, F.: Moving the network to the cloud: the cloud central office revolution and its implications for the optical layer. J. Lightwave Technol. **37**(7), 1706–1716 (2019)
13. Collins, D.: Carrier Grade Voice Over IP. McGraw-Hill, New York (2003)
14. Aboul-Magd, O., Rabie, S.: A differentiated service two-rate, three-color marker with efficient handling of in-profile traffic (2005)
15. Heinanen, J., Guérin, R.: A single rate three color marker (1999)
16. Gettys, J.: Bufferbloat: dark buffers in the internet. IEEE Internet Comput. **19**(3), 96 (2011)

17. Hoeiland-Joergensen, T., McKenney, P., Taht, D., Gettys, J., Dumazet, E.: The Flow Queue CoDel Packet Scheduler and Active Queue Management Algorithm (2018)
18. Matloff, N.: Introduction to discrete-event simulation and the simpy language. Davis, CA. Dept of Computer Science. University of California at Davis, pp. 1–33, 02 August 2009. Accessed Aug 2008
19. Cornaglia, B., Young, G., Marchetta, A.: Fixed access network sharing. Opt. Fiber Technol. **1**(26), 2–11 (2015)

Machine Learning Assisted Optical Network Resource Scheduling in Data Center Networks

Hongxiang Guo$^{(\boxtimes)}$, Cen Wang, Yinan Tang, Yong Zhu, Jian Wu, and Yong Zuo

Beijing University of Posts and Telecommunications, Beijing 100876, China
hxguo@bupt.edu.cn

Abstract. Parallel computing allows us to process incredible amounts of data in a timely manner by distributing the workload across multiple nodes and executing computation simultaneously. However, the performance of this parallelism usually suffers from network bottleneck. In optical switching enabled data center networks (DCNs), to satisfy the complex and time-varying bandwidth demands from the parallel computing, it is critical to fully exploit the flexibility of optical networks and meanwhile reasonably schedule the optical resources. Considering that the traffic flows generated by different applications in DCNs usually exhibit different statistical or correlative features, it is promising to schedule the optical resources with the assistance of machine learning. In this paper, we introduce a framework called intelligent optical resources scheduling system, and discuss how this framework can assist resource scheduling based on machine learning approaches. We also present our recent simulation results to verify the performance of the framework.

Keywords: Machine learning · Optical switching · Data center network · Parallel computing

1 Introduction

In the age of big data, various large-scale parallel computing frameworks (e.g. Hadoop and Spark) have been widely applied in commercial data centers. Due to the diverse network patterns and the huge traffic volume caused by the parallel computing jobs, the traditional electrical data center networks (DCNs) are currently hard to satisfy their networking demands. In contrast, optical switching enabled DCNs possess advantages of high bandwidth, low latency and multi-dimensional (e.g., space/time/wavelength) switching capability and thus have been regarded as a potential solution for the next generation DCNs.

Supported by the National Natural Science Foundation of China (NSFC) under Grant No. 61331008 and No. 61471054.

A. Tzanakaki et al. (Eds.): ONDM 2019, LNCS 11616, pp. 204–210, 2020.
https://doi.org/10.1007/978-3-030-38085-4_18

However, it is still a challenge to effectively schedule the optical network resources to meet the requirement of parallel computing. On one hand, because multiple parallel computing jobs may usually coexist in DCNs, it is hard to individually allocate optimal optical resources for each job. On the other hand, the background applications (e.g. virtual machine migration and data backups) will inevitably appear in DCNs and generate large background flows to compete the network resources with the running parallel computing jobs, leading to a significant slowdown of computing process. As a result, it is difficult to directly adapt the optical resources to the network traffic demands of parallel computing jobs.

Recent advances in machine learning (ML) have achieved remarkable performance in dealing with a variety of pattern recognition and classification problems. In DCNs, the statistical property of the traffic generated by different applications (i.e. background applications and parallel computing applications) shows significant difference. For instance, the parallel computing jobs usually generate socalled Coflows [1], which consist of many parallel flows with a common performance goal (e.g., a common completion deadline). Thus, the ML approach seems highly suitable to act as a traffic pattern recognizer and assist the optical resource scheduling process. Indeed, once the runtime network traffic patterns are accurately recognized before the optical resource scheduling, the multi-dimensional switching capability of optical switching enabled DCNs is expected to be exploited more effectively, and accordingly the upper-layer parallel computing can also be accelerated.

In this paper, we make a discussion on ML assisted optical network resource scheduling in DCNs. We introduce a framework named Intelligent Optical Resources Scheduling System (IORSS), which relies on ML techniques to classify the mixed traffic flows, recognize the traffic patterns of concurrently running parallel computing jobs, and then assist the optical switching enabled DCNs to appropriately scheduling its multi-dimensional network resources. We simply review our recent research works and shed light on the feasibility of our IORSS. We also verify the outstanding performance of IORSS through simulations.

2   Intelligent Optical Resource Scheduling System

The overview and the workflow of IORSS are shown in Fig. 1. The aim of IORSS is to recognize the traffic pattern by examining the collected traffic statistics, and then guide the DCN to reasonably allocate the optical resources for parallel computing jobs. To this end, a flow classification module is necessary to firstly distinguish and extract the network traffic generated by parallel computing applications. In other words, the original mixed traffic matrix R is divided into two parts, a background traffic matrix B and a mixed Coflow matrix C. Obviously, $R = B + C$, and the matrix B is relatively sparse as it is not likely that the large volume of background traffic arises throughout the whole DCN. As for the matrix C, it may contain several concurrent Coflows that are needed to be further decomposed, namely $C = \sum_{k=1}^{m} A^{(k)}$, in which m denotes the total number of Coflows and $A^{(k)}$ represents the traffic matrix of kth Coflow. Therefore, a

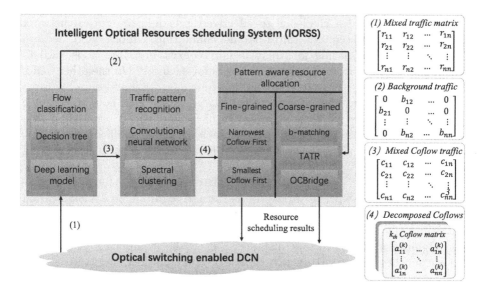

Fig. 1. Intelligent optical resource scheduling system (IORSS) for optical switching enabled data center network. The figure also presents several example algorithms about how to realize each module in IORSS.

traffic pattern recognition module is utilized to analyze and recognize the traffic pattern of each individual parallel computing application. Finally, according to the recognized traffic pattern, an optical resources allocation model is required to adapt the optical resources to the running parallel computing applications as well as background flows.

2.1 Flow Classification Module

In DCNs, because the network traffic demands of different applications are usually mixed together, the flow classification module needs to identify the type of each flow according to the collected traffic statistics, and then classify it into different groups (i.e., whether or not the flow is generated by parallel computing jobs). The commonly used statistics may include the flow level information such as five-tuple, and the packet level statistics such as time stamp, average packet size and packet size variation.

Currently, machine learning algorithms have shown outstanding performance in solving the classification problem. Similarly, given the sufficient amount of related network statistics, we may anticipate a well-trained machine learning model (e.g., deep learning model) can provide an accurate mapping from the input statistics to the flow type. One example is our previously proposed decision tree model [2], which is capable of identifying the type of flow according to the packet size variation.

2.2   Traffic Pattern Recognition Module

Different from the point-to-point flows produced by background applications, the "all-to-all" network traffic in parallel computing is actually much more complicated. As for the resource scheduling in the case of multiple computing jobs, several heuristic approaches such as Narrowest-Coflow-First [3] and Smallest-Coflow-First [3] have proven their superiority, but the priori knowledge of the traffic pattern (e.g. which flows belong to the same computing job) is necessarily required. However, because the networking demands generated by concurrent computing jobs are also mixed up, the individual traffic pattern of the mixed flows are hard to be recognized and separated, leading to the difficulty in directly allocating optical resources for the mixed traffic of parallel computing jobs. Fortunately, the traffic flows of each job are usually clustered and show a potential correlation, which provides an opportunity to discover the traffic pattern by using ML techniques.

To obtain the traffic pattern, after extracting the statistics of the flows generated by parallel computing jobs, an intuitive way is to directly feed these flow statistics into a fullyconnected deep learning model and find a mapping which outputs the traffic pattern. Nevertheless, because the basic neural network cannot effectively deal with the input with 2D pattern (i.e., matrix), it is not suitable to recognize the traffic pattern of a specific computing job from mixed flows. Besides, the huge amount of flow statistics in DCN will definitely cause many difficulties in training a large scale fully-connected learning model. In our recent research [4], we provided an alternative solution, which applies a convolutional neural network (CNN) to learn the number of parallel computing jobs running concurrently in DCNs, and then uses a spectral clustering method to obtain the set of worker nodes within each parallel computing job. By this way, the traffic pattern can be clearly figured out to guide the optical resource allocation process.

2.3   Optical Resource Allocation Module

Considering the traffic characteristics in data centers, it is beneficial to construct an optical switching enabled DCN by combining the coarse-grained optical circuit switching (OCS) and the fine-grained time-slotted optical switching. For the OCS resource allocation, the main principle is to offload the heavy stable network traffic in DCNs. According to the background flows classified by the flow classification module, the OCS reconfiguration strategies, such as b-matching [5], traffic adaptive topology reconstruction (TATR) [6] and OCBridge [7], can be simply employed. For the fine-grained optical resources, after obtaining the traffic pattern learnt by the traffic pattern recognition module, a simple but effective heuristic algorithm such as Smallest-Coflow-First [3] can be applied as the principle of allocating the time-slotted optical network resources.

3   Performance Evaluation

In order to verify the feasibility and evaluate the performance of IORSS, we conducted a simulation on the OpenScale [8], which is a small-world topology based optical DCN architecture. Moreover, to validate the applicability of IORSS to different optical switching enabled DCN architectures, we further extended our IORSS into a Fat tree DCN architecture with OCS capability.

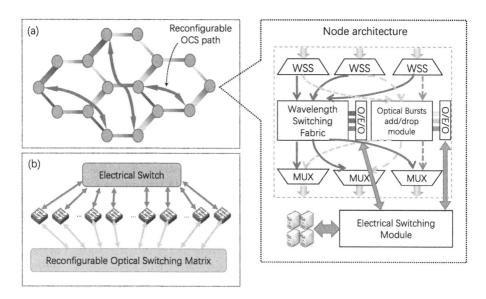

Fig. 2. (a) OpenScale architecture and (b) Fat tree architecture with OCS capability.

3.1   DCN Architectures and IORSS Implementation

The architecture as well as the node design of OpenScale is depicted in Fig. 2(a). In OpenScale, several hexagon rings are organized into a regular lattice structure. The nodes in each ring operate in a time-slotted switching manner to provide logical full-mesh connections among the adjacent nodes. Each node also has wavelength switching capability, so it can build a number of OCS paths to connect remote nodes directly. In summary, OpenScale is a typical optical DCN architecture which relies on both coarse-grained and fine-grained optical resources allocation. In our simulation, the OpenScale architecture consisted of 216 nodes. Each node was capable of building one OCS connection, and the bandwidth of each OCS path was set as 10 Gbps. We simplified the time-slotted switching in each ring as a time-slot based static allocation process. More specifically, each node was statically allocated 1 Gbps to communicate with other nodes within the same ring.

The Fat tree architecture is depicted in Fig. 2(b), where all nodes are connected with a high-radix electrical switch as well as a reconfigurable optical switching matrix. In the simulation, there were also 216 nodes included in the Fat tree architecture. The bandwidth of optical link and electrical link were set to 10 Gbps and 1 Gbps, respectively. Similar with the OpenScale, each node also had the capability to build one OCS connection to communicate with another node.

Regarding the implementation of IORSS, a decision tree based method [2] was deployed as the flow classification module, in order to extract Coflows [1] (i.e. all the correlated flows generated by parallel computing jobs) from the mixed traffic. For the traffic pattern recognition module, we used the method proposed in [4]. Finally, we employed TATR [6] as the coarse-grained OCS resources scheduling algorithm. We deployed Smallest-Coflow-First (SCF) algorithm [3] to guide the fined-grained time-slotted resources, which means the bandwidth of time-slotted optical resources were firstly assigned to the smaller Coflows.

3.2   Simulation Setup and Results Analysis

In our simulation, the raw traffic requests were generated by mixing background flows and the traffic flows of multiple (from 1 to 6) Coflows. The size of background flows followed a uniform distribution from 10^5 Mbytes to 10^7 Mbytes, while the total size of each Coflow followed a uniform distribution from 1 Mbytes to 10^5 Mbytes. We randomly generated 200 groups of raw traffic requests and recorded the average Coflow completion time (CCT) under the ML assisted resource scheduling of IORSS. We compared the CCT result with the baseline scheduling method which randomly built OCS connections among the nodes and applied the round-robin algorithm to schedule the time-slotted optical resources.

As shown in Fig. 3(a), it can be found that when multiple Coflows coexisted in DCNs, our IORSS could provide an effective resource allocation in both OpenScale and Fat tree architectures. With the increasing number of concurrent Coflows, the performance promotion became more significant. According to the results shown in Fig. 3(b), we can find that with the help of SCF, the smaller

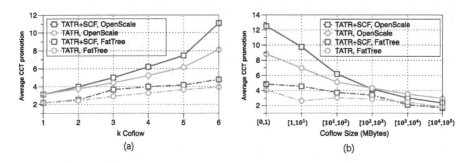

Fig. 3. Simulation results. The promotion ratio is defined by dividing the absolute CCT value under the IORSS by the CCT of baseline scheduling method.

Coflows had a better CCT promotion. As a result, the average CCT could be effectively reduced, and accordingly the parallel computing jobs were expected to be accelerated.

4   Conclusion

Parallel computing has become one of the most popular applications in modern DCs. To fully take the advantage of optical switching enabled DCN architectures, a machine learning assisted intelligent optical resources scheduling system (IORSS) is introduced and discussed in this paper, and its applicability to different DCN architectures has also been successfully verified by simulations. We believe our IORSS can drive the optical switching enabled DCN architectures to more effectively scheduling their optical network resources, and improve the performance of the upper layer parallel computing applications.

References

1. Chowdhury, M., Stoica, I.: Coflow: a networking abstraction for cluster applications. In: Proceedings of the 11th ACM Workshop on Hot Topics in Networks, pp. 31–36, Washington (2012)
2. Wang, C., Cao, H., Yang, S., Guo, J., Guo, H., Wu, J.: Decision tree classification based mix-flows scheduling in optical switched DCNs. In: Proceedings on Optical Fiber Communication Conference, San Diego, paper W1C.4 (2018)
3. Chowdhury, M., Zhong, Y., Stoica, I.: Efficient coflow scheduling with varys. In: Proceedings of the 2014 ACM Conference on SIGCOMM, pp. 443–454, Chicago (2014)
4. Wang, C., Guo, H., Gao, X., Chen, Y., Tang, Y., Wu, J.: Efficient topology reconstruction via machine learning based traffic patterns recognition in optically interconnected computing system. IEEE Access **7**, 28548–28558 (2016)
5. Yang, T., Zhang, D., Guo, H., Wu, J.: Topology reconstruction strategy with the optical switching based small world data center network. In: 21st OptoElectronics and Communications Conference, Niigata, paper WA2-108 (2016)
6. Zhang, D., Yang, T., Guo, H., Wu, J.: Enabling traffic optimized topology reconstruction with the optical switching based small world data center network. In: 41st European Conference on Optical Communication, Valencia, pp. 6–11 (2015)
7. Tang, Y., et al.: Effectively reconfigure the optical circuit switching layer topology in data center network by OCBridge. J. Lightwave Technol. **37**(3), 897–908 (2019)
8. Zhang, D., Guo, H., Yang, T., Wu, J.: Optical switching based small-world data center network. Comput. Commun. **103**, 153–164 (2017)

Machine Learning Assisted Quality of Transmission Estimation and Planning with Reduced Margins

Konstantinos Christodoulopoulos[1]([✉]), Ippokratis Sartzetakis[2], Polizois Soumplis[2], and Emmanouel (Manos) Varvarigos[2]

[1] Nokia Bell Labs, Stuttgart, Germany
konstantinos.1.christodoulopoulos@nokia-bell-labs.com
[2] School of Electrical and Computer Engineering, National Technical University of Athens, Athens, Greece

Abstract. In optical transport networks, the Quality of Transmission (QoT) using a physical layer model (PLM) is estimated before establishing new or reconfiguring established optical connections. Traditionally, high margins are added to account for the model's inaccuracy and the uncertainty in the current and evolving physical layer conditions, targeting uninterrupted operation for several years, until the end-of-life (EOL). Reducing the margins increases network efficiency but requires accurate QoT estimation. We present two machine learning (ML) assisted QoT estimators that leverage monitoring data of existing connections to understand the actual physical layer conditions and achieve high estimation accuracy. We then quantify the benefits of planning/upgrading a network over multiple periods with accurate QoT estimation as opposed to planning with EOL margins.

Keywords: Overprovisioning · Static network planning · End-of-life margins · Physical layer impairments · Monitoring · Cross-layer optimization · Incremental multi-period planning · Marginless

1 Introduction

Coherent transmission and Elastic Optical Networks (EONs) deployed today promise higher spectral efficiency, increased capacity, and reduced network costs [1]. However, optical networks are traditionally planned to be operated statically; planning relies on abundant margins [2, 3] to ensure that all connections/lightpaths have acceptable Quality of Transmission (QoT) until the end of life (EoL). Lowering the margins and increasing efficiency reduces network costs, motivating various research directions [4]. Refs. [5, 6] studied the planning of an EON over multiple periods to harvest the evolution of margins over time. Certain connection parameters are adjusted at a given time granularity (e.g., 1–2 years) and new equipment is added, when actually needed, according to current traffic and physical layer conditions. Therefore, instead of overprovisioning to reach EoL, the network is operated with just in time provisioning, increasing the efficiency, postponing or avoiding equipment purchase, and reducing the network costs. An EON can

© IFIP International Federation for Information Processing 2020
Published by Springer Nature Switzerland AG 2020
A. Tzanakaki et al. (Eds.): ONDM 2019, LNCS 11616, pp. 211–222, 2020.
https://doi.org/10.1007/978-3-030-38085-4_19

be operated even more dynamically, by adapting the transmission parameters at shorter timeframes. Refs. [7, 8] and other works consider the dynamic spectrum/capacity adaptation according to traffic demands. The efficient management of failures also pertains to dynamic network operation. [9] studies the dynamic adaptation of the connections' parameters to current physical layer conditions (e.g., in case of QoT degradation). The dynamic operation of a marginless network is experimentally demonstrated in [10].

Considering the above, an accurate QoT estimator is the key component for (i) reducing the margins during planning/upgrades, and (ii) realizing a more dynamic operation of the network. Figure 1a shows how a QoT estimation tool (or Qtool) is used by an optimization (planning or dynamic) algorithm. The Qtool consists of a physical layer model (PLM), which is analytical or semi-analytical and makes certain assumptions to estimate with certain accuracy the QoT (e.g. SNR, BER) of new or reconfigured connections. The Qtool takes as input the parameters of the established connections (in case of an operating network), and also certain physical layer parameters, such as spans, fibers, amplifiers and node parameters, etc. The values of the physical layer input parameters are not accurately known, due to lack or limited accuracy of measuring equipment, outdated measurements, etc. To cover the model and input parameter inaccuracies, the design margin is used (2 dB in SNR as a references [2, 3]). Moreover, traditional network planning targets for new connections to have acceptable QoT at EOL, e.g. after 10–15 years. Modeling equipment ageing, increase of interference, reparations of fiber cuts, etc. contributes to the system margin (3 dB in SNR as a references [2, 3]). A great deal of recent research effort was directed towards the application of Machine Learning (ML) in various areas of optical networking both at the physical and network layers [11]. ML has also been applied to improve the accuracy of QoT estimation and reduce the design and system margins [12–17] (Fig. 1b).

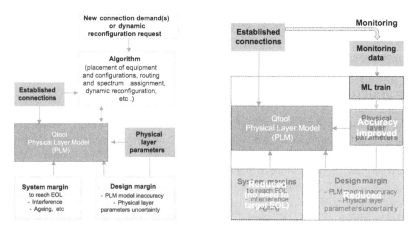

Fig. 1. (a) QoT estimation tool (Qtool) used by an algorithm to reconfigure or establish lightpaths, its inputs, and design and system margins, (b) Machine learning assisted QoT estimation to reduce the margins.

In this paper, which outlines [19] and [6, 20] we start by presenting two ML assisted QoT estimators. We then evaluate the accuracy of the estimators under various scenarios and observe quite low estimation error with relatively low information (few established lightpaths). We then quantify the cost savings that can be obtained by accurate QoT estimation in a multiperiod planning network scenario. To do so we interface the ML assisted QoT estimator with the incremental algorithm of [6, 20] and use that to (accurately) estimate the QoT of new and existing lightpaths and provision/reconfigure them with reduced margins.

2   Quality of Transmission (QoT) Estimation

We assume an EON with Reconfigurable Optical Add/Drop Multiplexers (ROADMs) connected through uncompensated fiber links. Each link consists of a number of fiber spans that terminate at an EDFA that compensates the span loss. We assume that there are no spectrum converters and thus a lightpath is allocated the same spectrum throughout its path. For long connections, regenerators are placed. The set of established lightpaths and their attributes (e.g., modulation format, baudrate) is denoted by P which will also be referred to as the *state* of the network at a given time. We also assume that we can obtain monitoring information from the coherent receivers. Coherent receivers deployed today are packed with DSP capabilities, so they can function as Optical Performance Monitors (OPMs) [4]. So we assume that an OPM (receiver) monitors the lightpath's SNR with certain accuracy. We use this information to improve the QoT estimation accuracy and reduce the margins of new or reconfigured lightpaths.

In particular, we denote by $Q^*(P)$ the *vector* that contains the SNR values of all established lightpaths $p \in P$. The mapping $Q^*(P)$ is nonlinear and unknown to us. For the set of established lightpaths P we denote by $Y(P)$ the vector of their monitored SNR values. The monitoring error consists of a systematic and a random error. The systematic error can be reduced through proper calibration, while the random error can be reduced by averaging measurements over time (at a shorter timescale than a natural change of the monitored value would occur). As monitoring errors are small and can be reduced, we ignore them here for simplicity. So, we will assume we monitor the true SNR for the paths ($Y(P) = Q^*(P)$ for $p \in P$).

We consider the case where a new lightpath $w \notin P$ is about to be established, and we want to estimate (i) the QoT of that new lightpath w, and (ii) how QoT of existing lightpaths $p \in P$ will be affected by the establishment of w. Stated formally, we are given the measurements $Y(P) = Q^*(P)$ of QoT metrics at the current network state P. Our objective is to *estimate* the new QoT metrics $Q^*(P \cup \{w\})$ after the new lightpath $w \notin P$ is established. Note that $Q^*(P \cup \{w\})$ contains the (new) QoT metrics of existing lightpaths $p \in P$, which in general will be affected by the establishment of w. Also note that the above problem definition can be extended to include the establishment of a set or the reconfiguration of a single or a set of lightpaths.

3   Machine Learning Assisted QoT Estimation

In QoT estimation, our goal is to identify a parametric function $\widetilde{Q}(r, P)$ that approximates well the actual QoT of the connections $Q^*(P)$. Here r is a set of parameters of the model. The parametric function $\widetilde{Q}(r, P)$ does not have to be a closed form expression; it can also be the output of a simulation. What is important is that (i) $\widetilde{Q}(r, P)$ approximates $Q^*(P)$ relatively well and that (ii) given the set r, it is relatively easy computationally to obtain $\widetilde{Q}(r, P)$ for the given state P. The following two subsections describe two approximating architectures, corresponding to different parametric function choices, the first based on a physical layer model (PLM) and the second based on a machine learning (ML) model and features extraction (Fig. 2).

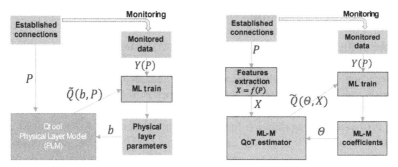

Fig. 2. Flowcharts of (a) machine learning physical layer model (ML-PLM) and (b) machine learning model (ML-M) QoT estimators.

3.1 Machine Learning Physical Layer Model (ML-PLM)

The first approach considers a physical layer model (PLM) as the approximating architecture. In this case, $\widetilde{Q}(r, P)$ takes as input r the PLM input parameters, denoted by b, which can include: per span length, fiber attenuation, dispersion and nonlinear coefficients, the noise figure of each EDFA, its gain, etc. So, following the above we denote the PLM model with $\widetilde{Q}(b, P)$. In this paper, we will use the GN model [18] as the PLM, but the method is generic and applicable to other PLMs. The assumption is that the initial parameter values are close to the actual ones but not close enough to provide accurate QoT estimation. They could be based on datasheets or even field measurements that however cannot be taken continuously and with high accuracy, so they would be partially outdated/inaccurate. The objective of the machine-learning (ML)-PLM is to use monitoring information from the established lightpaths $Y(P)$ to train and learn the physical layer parameters and thus improve the accuracy of future QoT estimations. The model also uses the set of lightpaths' parameters included in the network state P, which can be: the route, central frequency, baudrate, modulation format, launch power, etc. The parameters in P are assumed to be perfectly known, as opposed to the parameters in b. Regarding the learning algorithm, if we have closed forms for the partial derivatives $\partial \widetilde{Q}/\partial b_j$ with respect to all physical layer parameters b_j of b, we could use gradient decent to obtain better estimates of b as in [16]. Here we assume a generic case where $\widetilde{Q}(b, P)$ is unknown. Assuming that QoT depends non-linearly on some input parameter, we use a nonlinear method to fit the model.

3.2 Machine Learning Model (ML-M)

The second investigated approach uses a Machine Learning Model (ML-M) and features extraction. Features extraction maps the state P into a matrix $X = f(P)$, called the *features matrix*. The mapping function f is chosen to summarize in a heuristic way the important characteristics of P with respect to QoT estimation. The main idea is that through the change of variables from P to $X = f(P)$, the unknown mapping $Q^*(P)$ of the true QoT is approximated well by the function $\tilde{Q}(\Theta, X) = \tilde{Q}(\Theta, f(P))$, where Θ are the ML-M parameters (coefficients). The type of coefficients Θ depends on the particular model (linear regression, neural network-NN, Support Vector Machine-SVM, etc.). The ML-M $\tilde{Q}(\Theta, X)$ is trained with an appropriate regression algorithm, using, as in previous section, training data $(P, Y(P))$. After implementing and testing several such models, we observed that the choice of features is of utmost importance for the estimation accuracy, at least considering medium size networks (10–20 nodes). So, in the following we present the formulation that achieved the best performance.

We follow a link-level feature formulation to account for network heterogeneity. So, in our ML estimation model we consider each lightpath's link attributes separately. Thus, the model distinguishes, for example, two lightpaths that have similar lengths but cross different links and possibly exhibit different QoT due to heterogeneities of link attributes. We do not consider span level features since a lightpath will always cross all spans of a link. We organize the feature matrix X so that each row corresponds to one lightpath $p \in P$, while the columns represent (link, impairment) features. We defined three sets of link-impairment features corresponding to the major impairment classes affecting the QoT. More specifically, we define A as a $|P| \times |L|$ link-level feature matrix designed to account for the ASE noise. Element A_{pl}, corresponding to lightpath p and link l, is set equal to 1 if it contains link l, and is set to zero, otherwise. We also define the link-level feature matrix S to account for Self-Channel Interference (SCI) noise [18]. Element S_{pl} is set equal to the inverse of the square of the lightpath's baudrate if lightpath p contains link l, and is set to zero, otherwise. Finally, we define a link-level feature matrix W to account for the interference of neighboring lightpaths (cross channel interference-XCI [18]). The elements of this matrix are derived from an equation that involves the baudrate of the lightpath under consideration, and for each of its neighboring lightpaths the spectrum distance and its baudrate, following Eq. (40) of [18]. We also consider an additional feature, the bias term (denoted by BT). Bias can account for the monitoring error in $Y(P)$, impairments not modeled, etc. We concatenate all the link-level feature matrices and the bias into one feature matrix $X = f(P)$:

$$X = [BT \ A \ S \ W]_{|P|x(3|L|+1)}$$

Focusing on a lightpath p, its features are designed to represent its noise contributing parameters (considering the major types of impairments, both linear and non-linear) per link. Assuming $x_{p,j}$ is the jth feature of lightpath p, the noise contribution of the related impairment/link is approximated well with a linear function, i.e. $n_j(x_{p,j}, \Theta) = x_{p,j} \cdot \theta_j$, where θ_j is the related impairment-link coefficient. We assume that the noise of the different types of impairments is additive on a link level and over the path, following the assumptions of the GN model [18]. In other words, the total noise accumulated over lightpath p is given by $\sum_j n_j(x_{p,j}, \Theta)$. This assumption makes possible the correlation of the noise contributions at impairment and link levels. Based on these assumptions we estimate the total noise of the lightpaths by

$$\widetilde{N}(\Theta, X) = X \cdot \Theta.$$

From that we obtain the SNR of the lightpaths by

$$\widetilde{Q}(\Theta, X) = \frac{B_N \cdot l_p}{B_r \cdot \widetilde{N}(\Theta, X)}$$

where B_N is the noise bandwidth, l_p is the launch power, and B_r is the baudrate of the lightpaths. Then we use the SNR measurements $Y(P)$ and a linear regression/gradient descent algorithm to learn Θ.

Note that we derived a linear model to approximate $\widetilde{Q}$. However, we performed a non-linear transformation f of the input P, carefully designed so that the subsequent fitting would be well approximated using a linear model. The above described ML-M concept is quite generic. We can define different features X, and model more complicated features – noise functions n_j with other ML models, such as NN or SVM, and train them with appropriate algorithms. Another possibility, under the linear feature – noise functions assumption, is to use a constrained least squares solver, where we can add constraints that exploit certain expected QoT relationships. For example, a link that is 200 km longer is highly unlikely to contribute lower noise. The additional constraints help the model to provide better estimations especially in cases with low amount of information (lightpaths).

4   Machine Learning Assisted QoT Estimation

We evaluated the proposed machine learning QoT estimators through simulations. We considered the DT topology with 12 nodes and 40 bidirectional links. We assumed 4 traffic loads of 100, 200, 300 and 400 total connections with uniformly chosen source-destinations and random baudrates from the set $\{32, 43, 56\}$ Gbaud. Regarding the physical layer, we assumed a span length of 80 km, EDFA noise figure 5 dB and SSMF with mean attenuation coefficient 0.23 dB/km, mean dispersion coefficient 16.7 ps/nm/km, and mean nonlinear coefficient 1.3 1/W/km. We set the launch power at 0 dbm. The actual (unknown) values of the fiber coefficients for each span were drawn from uniform distributions ranging by 0%, 10% or 20% around the above means, thus defining 3 uncertainty scenarios. The GN model was used as the ground truth with these values. For the ML-PLM case, the b vector consisted of the attenuation, dispersion, and nonlinear coefficients, initiated with their mean values. So, the case with 0% variation implies that the ML-PLM estimator has accurate knowledge of the physical layer parameters. The training of ML-PLM was done with nonlinear regression and in particular the Levenberg-Marquardt algorithm. For ML-M, we tried various models and we finally used the features described in Sect. 3.2 and the constrained least square solver that provided the best results.

For each traffic load and physical layer parameters uncertainty setting we executed 500 iterations with random traffic and span parameters. For each instance we used 85%

of the lightpaths for training and 15% for testing. We excluded from the testing set the lightpaths that include links for which we have no QoT information (links that no lightpath from the training set cross). The training goal was to minimize the MSE but the max overestimation is also a very useful metric because it defines the design margin. This has to be used to be on the safe side, so that we never overestimate the QoT and establish a lightpath with unacceptable QoT.

Figure 3a shows the MSE and Fig. 3b the max overestimation error. For both estimators the MSE decreases as the number of lightpaths increases. The ML-M has consistent performance for all the uncertainty scenarios (0% to 20% variations) since it does not assume any previous knowledge. On the other hand, ML-PLM's performance is affected by the magnitude of the uncertainty, since the ground truth values deviate from the model's initial values. The ML-PLM is more accurate than ML-M in all cases except for the case with high uncertainty ($>10\%$) and few connections (100) where the ML-M achieved lower max overestimation. This is expected since the ML-PLM is a good approximation of the actual physical layer, in the sense that the ground truth function $Q^*(P)$ was taken to be the GN model, which is also the ML-PLM function $\widetilde{Q}(b, P)$. So, ML-PLM only needs to fit the parameters b that are uncertain and starts from good (mean) values. The ML-PLM's max overestimation was around 0.05 dB for more than 200 lightpaths while ML-M's max overestimation was 0.2 dB. The training time was in the order of seconds for the ML-M/linear regression and minutes for the ML-PLM/nonlinear regression. Once trained, estimations are quite fast (<0.1 s). So, the estimators can be used even in dynamic (re)configuration cases. We also obtained results for other ML estimators with end-to-end features as opposed to the link-level features. As expected, end-to-end features resulted in larger MSE and max overestimation for the high uncertainty cases, since in those cases the network is non-homogeneous and end-to-end features do not cover that. Detailed results are presented in [19].

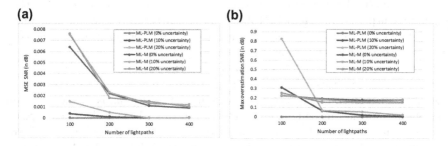

Fig. 3. (a) MSE and (b) maximum overestimation for 0%, 10% and 20% uncertainty.

5 Planning with Reduced Margins - Algorithm

In Sect. 3 we presented two ML QoT estimators that were shown in Sect. 4 to achieve good accuracy and a low design margin. To quantify the benefits of an accurate QoT estimator we use/interface that to an incremental planning algorithm [21, 22] and in particular to the incremental planning algorithm of [6, 20]. This incremental planning algorithm is involved before a planned network upgrade or even at the initial period (greenfield). So, the algorithm starts from a given network state P, with a set of deployed equipment, e.g. transponders/regenerators, established lightpaths with known transmission parameters, routes and spectrum, or even from an empty network. The algorithm takes as input a new set of demands and the available equipment at that time, e.g. available transponders, their capabilities and costs. To serve the demands, it interfaces with a QoT Estimator (see Fig. 1a) to account for the physical layer behavior.

If the network is planned with high margins, which is the traditional approach, then the QoT Estimator uses a high design margin and EOL system margin (to target acceptable QoT after e.g. 10–15 years). So, the efficiency is low, more transponders/regenerators are placed, but lightpaths are ensured to be uninterrupted, to have acceptable QoT, until EOL. Instead, if we leverage an accurate QoT estimator we can use an appropriate algorithm to plan the network with reduced margins. In the first period, we will serve the new demands with a high design margin (no feedback/no establish connections to monitor, train and refine the QoT estimator), and with a reduced system margin to reach the next upgrade period (several months - few years, but lower than EOL). Then at an intermediate period, we train the QoT estimator, and we reduce the design margin. So, at each period the incremental planning algorithm performs two tasks: (i) checks the remaining margins of previously established connections and reconfigures/adds transponders or regenerators to restore those that run out of margins (will have unacceptable QoT performance before the next or a targeted period), (ii) serves the new demands by placing transponders/regenerators. In both cases it chooses the configuration of the transponders/regenerators, and decides the routes, and spectrum allocation, by interacting with the QoT estimator to check the physical layer performance.

In more detail, the algorithm starts in phase 1 by freeing resources for removed connections (not demanded anymore). This equipment can be repurposed, reused at its current position (for free) or moved (with a penalty) to serve some other demand. Then the algorithm in phase 2 fixes the established connections that are running out of margins. The algorithm decides how to reconfigure and/or add new transponders/regenerators so that they have enough margins to reach the next or certain periods ahead. The algorithm's objective is to minimize the added cost, and as a secondary objective (controlled through a weight) to avoid extensive reconfigurations. For example, when adding a regenerator, the used path is broken into two segments and the same spectrum is allocated at both segments, avoiding any reconfiguration to other lightpaths. Then the algorithm in phase 3 serves the new demands by adding adequate transponders/regenerators and choosing the routes and spectrum. Since, adding new lightpaths (phases 2 and 3) increases interference, the algorithm rechecks with the QoT estimator the QoT all lightpaths. The algorithm repeats phase 2 considering all previous and new lightpaths. Since the algorithm in phase 2 might add new lightpaths to restore some problematic, interference can increase again, and the algorithm repeats phase 2 until QoT is acceptable for all lightpaths.

The incremental algorithm is a heuristic. It processes the previously established lightpaths and serves new demands one by one, in some particular order. Since the performance depends on that order, we can use simulated annealing or some other meta-heuristic to search among orderings and find better solutions. Note that the execution time is not a major concern, since calculations are supposed to be offline, to decide the changes for the next upgrade. In any case planning is NP-hard. Jointly planning and accounting for the physical layer (also called impairment-aware or cross-layer) requires the integration of the planning algorithm and the Qtool. Some optimal formulations for DWDM [23] and EON [24] have appeared, where the resource allocation formulation is extended to include (simplified) impairment/Qtool constraints. Such simplifications would require a higher design margin. In this paper we consider the Qtool as an external optimization module; such separation could result in some loss of optimality. Nevertheless, the Qtool can be more complicated and accurate, and we can use techniques such as ML to reduce and regulate the related margins, which in the end could yield better performance than a joint algorithm.

6 Planning with Reduced Margins – Case Study

To quantify the benefits of the developed accurate QoT estimators and the incremental planning algorithm with low margins we dimensioned a network over multiple periods and calculated the capital expenditure (CAPEX) at each period. We compare that with planning with EOL margins. The network topology we studied was the 12 node DT network topology as in Sect. 4. We planned the network over 11 periods (initial/brownfield and 10 incremental/greenfield periods); one period would roughly correspond to one year. The initial traffic (period τ_0) consisted of 200 connections with uniformly chosen source-destination pairs and uniformly demanded traffic between 100 to 200 Gbps. So, the initial traffic was 30 Tbps and it was increased by 20% each period by creating new demands in the same way. We assumed two types of elastic transponders (ET): (i) 32 Gbaud, modulating with DP-QPSK, or DP-8QAM, or DP-16QAM, supporting capacities of 100, 150, and 200 Gbps, respectively, and (ii) 64 Gbaud, modulating from DP-QPSK to DP-32QAM, supporting capacities of 200 up to 500 Gbps, respectively. The first ET of 32 Gbaud was assumed to be available at the initial period τ_0 with price equal to 1 cost unit (CU) and the second ET of 64 Gbaud was assumed available at period τ_5 with price again 1 CU (at that period). The ET prices were assumed to fall by 10% per period (so when the second ET is introduced the price of the first was 0.59 CU).

We again used the GN model to model the physical layer. In the first period τ_0 we initialized the model with heterogeneous span parameters with 10% uncertainty, similar to Sect. 4. We executed 10 problem instances with different traffic and span parameters and averaged the results. To model the ageing of the network we considered the increase of fiber attenuation (e.g. due to cuts), ageing of ETs, EDFAs, and nodes (OXC). The interference was modeled according to the network load. Table 1 shows the increase of the model parameters per period. Note that the increase was uniform for all spans, but since we started with heterogeneous and uncertain conditions, they remained heterogeneous and unknown for all subsequent periods.

When planning the network with EOL margins, the Qtool uses a system margin based on the parameters of Table 1 assuming 10 periods (~3 dB), and full network load (each link with 60×32 Gbaud connections). The design margin was set to 2 dB (1 dB

Table 1. Parameters to model the network evolution over time.

Physical layer parameters evolution		Increase per period
Ageing	Transponder margin (dB)	0.05
	Attenuation (dB/km)	0.0015
	EDFA noise figure (dB)	0.1
	OXC loss (dB)	0.3
	Interference	According to load

for the model inaccuracy and 1 dB for the input parameters inaccuracy). When planning the network with reduced margins, we used the ML-M estimator (Sect. 3.2). The system margin was based on the parameters of Table 1 assuming 2 periods (~0.6 dB). Then we assumed that at each period we monitor and obtained the SNR values, $Y(P)$, for the established connections (the monitored parameters were calculated by the GN model, with the random created initial parameters and ageing according to the period and Table 1 – unknown to the used QoT estimator). We used the monitored SNR values to train the ML-M and obtain the coefficients for that period, and also the max overestimation error. The design margin was set equal to 1 dB for the model inaccuracy, plus the maximum between 0.2 dB (the design margin of the extensive simulations in Sect. 4) and the max overestimation in the training for that period. Note that we chose the system margin for the next 2 periods and a design margin greater than 1.2 dB to be conservative. In total when we plan the network with reduced margins we harvest ~3 dB when compared to EOL planning.

Figure 4a presents the total cost of the deployed elastic transponders (ET) per period for the two provisioning approaches. As expected, reducing the margins yields lower

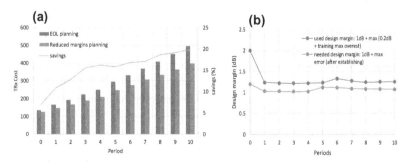

Fig. 4. (a) Total cost (in cost units) and savings of elastic transponders (ET) per period when planning with accurate QoT estimation/reduced margins and with high margins, (b) Used and needed design margin.

costs. Reducing the system margins postpones the purchase of ET and we obtain savings from the 10% depreciation. Reducing the design margin avoids the purchase of equipment. Figure 4a also presents the relative savings, found to be about 20% at the end of the examined periods. Note that the savings would reduce at later periods if we only assumed a single type of ET for all periods. The introduction of the higher rate transponder boosts the savings after period τ_5. Figure 4b shows the design margin used and the actual maximum estimation error. In all simulations (10 instances $\times$ 11 periods) we never observed a QoT problem, all lightpaths had adequate QoT when reaching the next period. The closest we got to margins limit was at period τ_5, where the new ET (thus a new baudrate) was introduced, and some parameters were not learned accurately enough with only the first ET (32 Gbaud).

A factor not included in the above evaluation is the time value of money; money saved at intermediate periods can be invested (or loans can be avoided) resulting in extra savings. Additional savings can be also obtained by power optimization [6].

7 Conclusions

Estimating the Quality of Transmission (QoT) is typically performed before establishing new or re-configuring existing connections using a physical layer model (PLM). Traditional planning uses high margins to account for inaccuracies and to target connections with acceptable QoT after several years (EOL). Reducing the margins increases network efficiency but requires accurate QoT estimation. We presented two machine learning (ML) assisted QoT Estimators that leverage monitoring information of existing connections to understand the actual physical conditions and achieve good estimation accuracy. We then quantified the benefits of planning/upgrading a network with accurate QoT estimation. We interfaced the developed accurate ML QoT estimator with an incremental planning algorithm that handles the reduction of margins. We compared the multi-period planning of the network with accurate QoT estimation/reduced margins to planning with EOL margins, and observed savings that reach 20% at the end of the examined periods.

Acknowledgment. I. Sartzetakis was supported by IKY Greek State PhD scholarship co-funded by the European Social Fund and the Greek State.

References

1. López, V., Velasco, L. (eds.): Elastic Optical Networks. ON. Springer, Cham (2016). https://doi.org/10.1007/978-3-319-30174-7
2. Pointurier, Y.: Design of low-margin optical networks. JOCN **9**(1), A9–A17 (2017)
3. Auge, J.L.: Can we use flexible transponders to reduce margins? In: OFC (2013)
4. Christodoulopoulos, K., et. al.: ORCHESTRA-optical performance monitoring enabling flexible networking. In: ICTON (2015)
5. Pesic, J., Zami, T., Ramantanis, P., Bigo, S.: Faster return of investment in WDM networks when elastic transponders dynamically fit ageing of link margins. In: OFC (2016)

6. Soumplis, P., Christodoulopoulos, K., Quagliotti, M., Pagano, A., Varvarigos, E.: Network planning with actual margins. JLT **35**(23), 5105–5120 (2017)
7. Christodoulopoulos, K., Tomkos, I., Varvarigos, E.: Time-varying spectrum allocation policies and blocking analysis in flexible optical networks. IEEE J. Sel. Areas Commun. **31**(1), 13–25 (2013)
8. Rafique, D., Velasco, L.: Machine learning for network automation: overview, architecture, and applications. JOCN **10**(10), D126–D143 (2018)
9. Sartzetakis, I., Christodoulopoulos, K., Varvarigos, E.: Cross-layer adaptive elastic optical networks. JOCN **10**(2), A154–A164 (2018)
10. Delezoide, C., et al.: Marginless operation of optical networks. JLT **37**(7), 1698–1705 (2019)
11. Musumeci, F., et al.: An overview on application of machine learning techniques in optical networks. arXiv:1803.07976, December 2018
12. Samadi, P., Amar, D., Lepers, C., Lourdiane, M., Bergman, K.: Quality of transmission prediction with machine learning for dynamic operation of optical WDM networks. In: ECOC (2017)
13. Barletta, L., Giusti, A., Rottondi, C., Tornatore, M.: QoT estimation for unestablished lighpaths using machine learning. In: OFC (2017)
14. Aladin, S., Tremblay, C.: Cognitive tool for estimating the QoT of new lightpaths. In: OFC (2018)
15. Morais, R.M., Pedro, J.: Machine learning models for estimating quality of transmission in DWDM networks. JOCN **10**(10), D84–D99 (2018)
16. Seve, E., Pesic, J., Delezoide, C., Bigo, S., Pointurier, Y.: Learning process for reducing uncertainties on network parameters and design margins. JOCN **10**(2), A298–A306 (2018)
17. Bouda, M., et al.: Accurate prediction of quality of transmission based on a dynamically configurable optical impairment model. JOCN **10**(1), A102–A109 (2018)
18. Poggiolini, P.: The GN model of non-linear propagation in uncompensated coherent optical systems. JLT **30**(24), 3857–3879 (2012)
19. Sartzetakis, I., Christodoulopoulos, K., Varvarigos, E.: Accurate quality of transmission estimation with machine learning. JOCN **11**(3), 14–150 (2019)
20. Soumplis, P., Christodoulopoulos, K., Quagliotti, M., Pagano, A., Varvarigos, E.: Multi-period planning with actual physical and traffic conditions. JOCN **10**(1), A144–A153 (2018)
21. Meusburger, C., Schupke, D.A., Lord, A.: Optimizing the migration of channels with higher bitrates. JLT **28**(4), 608–615 (2010)
22. Eira, A., Pedro, J., Pires, J.: Optimal multi-period provisioning of fixed and flex-rate modular line interfaces in DWDM networks. JOCN **7**(4), 223–234 (2015)
23. Christodoulopoulos, K., Manousakis, K., Varvarigos, E.: Offline routing and wavelength assignment in transparent WDM networks. IEEE/ACM Trans. Networking **18**(5), 1557–1570 (2010)
24. Yan, L., Agrell, E., Dharmaweera, M.N., Wymeersch, H.: Joint assignment of power, routing, and spectrum in static flexible-grid networks. JLT **35**(10), 1674–1766 (2017)

Network Programmability
and Automation in Optical Networks

Ricard Vilalta$^{(\boxtimes)}$ ⓘ, Ramon Casellas ⓘ, Ricardo Martínez ⓘ,
and Raul Muñoz ⓘ

Centre Tecnològic de Telecomunicacions de Catalunya (CTTC/CERCA),
Castelldefels, Spain
ricard.vilalta@cttc.es

Abstract. During last years, novel protocols and data models are arising to control and monitor optical network equipment. These protocols enable network programmability and automation by fulfilling the vision introduced by Software Defined Networking (SDN).

This paper offers an overview and hands-on experience on programming the necessary tools to control and monitor the network equipment. These tools introduce the necessary network programmability that will enable its automation, following current Zero-Touch service control and management. Data modelling languages are firstly explored. Later, protocols for control and monitoring are presented. Moreover, common standards data models are discussed. Finally, an evaluation of the different presented protocols and data models is provided, which includes recommendations for their selection and deployment.

Keywords: Data models · Protocols · Optical networking

1 Introduction

To understand properly the evolution of control, management, and orchestration of Optical Networks, the authors in [1] suggest that the main trigger for this network evolution is the need for an automated networks, which is able to auto-configure, auto-deploy and auto-heal.

In order to fulfil this view, novel market trends can be easily identified. Basically, three main drivers are foreseen: novel kinds of business consumer and end consumers, and a new kind of a service provider. New business consumer request private and public clouds, in order to provide them with the necessary elastic compute and storage. End consumers are currently living in the cloud, consuming cloud applications such as streaming downloads, thus, driving new network loads. Novel Service Providers are proposing novel services such as software as a service (SaaS), IaaS, PaaS, Multi-tenancy, elatric compute and storage. In view of these trends, it can be concluded that a novel programmable and automated network is required.

© IFIP International Federation for Information Processing 2020
Published by Springer Nature Switzerland AG 2020
A. Tzanakaki et al. (Eds.): ONDM 2019, LNCS 11616, pp. 223–234, 2020.
https://doi.org/10.1007/978-3-030-38085-4_20

This network programmability brings new innovations in optical transports. It opens the door for new service models. Moreover, it also bring in service differentiation through new applications. Network programmability also allows simplified architectures that provide both integrated E2E/Multi-layer service creation, as well as, automatic reaction on errors or changes. Moreover, it also provides some financial benefits, such as both efficient service setup (OPEX), and fast return of investment (ROI) utilization (CAPEX).

This paper proposes novel control and monitoring mechanisms for network programmability. It is important to keep in mind that there are some metrics of success. On one hand, the industry adoption of these mechanisms will determine their success. On the other hand, multi-vendor interoperability will also be important for their success.

This paper is structured as follows. Firstly presents an overview of available data modelling languages: YANG and Protocol Buffers data modeling languages. Later, protocols for control and monitoring are exposed, including NETCONF, RESTconf and gRPC protocols. Later, several data models defined in Standards Defining Organizations (SDO) are presented. These include ONF Transport API, IETF ACTN, OpenROADM and OpenConfig. Finally, presented data modelling languages, protocols and data models are compared and discussed in order to provide guidance of deployment of network programmability.

2 Data Modeling Languages for Network Programmability and Automation

It has been currently detailed the need for better management frameworks and protocols for optical network control and management. Some examples of management tasks are definition of routing policies, configuration of routing peers, which are performed by the operator and can be automated. The configuration management can be properly modelled using a unified information and data modelling language to describe network element or system capabilities, attributes, operations and notifications.

In general, an information model describes the device capabilities, in terms of operations and configurable parameters, using high level abstractions without specific details on aspects such as a particular syntax or encoding. On the other hand, a data model determines the structure, syntax and semantics of the data that is externally visible.

2.1 YANG Language

YANG is a data modeling language, initially conceived to model configuration and state data for network devices Models define the device configurations & notifications, capture semantic details and are easy to understand [2].

During last years, adoption of YANG as a data modelling language across standard defining organizations (SDO) and open source software (OSS) projects has been notable. IETF, ETSI, ONF, MEF, 3GPP, among others have adopted this data modelling language in order to provide standard data models.

A Yang model includes a header, imports and include statements, type definitions, configurations and operational data declarations as well as actions (remote procedure calls - RPC) and notifications. Configuration and operational data are structured into data trees (datastores), using containers and lists. Conditionals can be used to the support of optional features. An important ability of the language is the capacity to extend and constrain existing models (by inheritance/augmentation), resulting in a hierarchy of models, which might derive from abstracted models to more detailed and specific ones.

If a connection service YANG model is described, typically the module connection imports topology YANG file. The data tree consists of a list named connection that includes connection grouping elements. Each connection grouping includes several connection leaves (e.g., connectionId, source-node, target-node). Each leaf is determined by its type (e.g., string, uint32, leafref - a reference to another leaf of the data tree).

YANG data modelling language has open source tools which help the validation and the ease of programmability with the related models. The most significant is pyang [3], which is an extensible YANG validator. Pyang provides a framework for plugins that can convert YANG modules to other formats. Some examples of the possible outputs are UML diagrams, or tree diagrams, and encoded messages in XML or JSON. Pyangbind is one of the extension plugins [4] that generates a Python class hierarchy from a YANG data model. The resulting classes can be directly interacted with in Python.

2.2   Protocol Buffers

Protocol buffers (also known as protobuf) are a flexible, efficient, automated mechanism for serializing structured data in a byte-oriented protocol becoming smaller, faster, and simpler [5].

Protobufs, similarly to YANG, include an open source software tool-chain that allows special generated source code to easily write and read the structured data to and from a variety of data streams and using a variety of languages.

As you can see, the message format is simple – each message type has one or more uniquely numbered fields, and each field has a name and a value type, where value types can be numbers, booleans, strings, or other protocol buffer message types, allowing to structure data hierarchically. Optional fields can be specified, as well as required fields or repeated fields.

You specify how you want the information you're serializing to be structured by defining protocol buffer message types in .proto files. Each protocol buffer message is a small logical record of information, containing a series of name-value pairs.

3 Protocols for Network Programmability and Automation

Once the most significant data modelling languages have been presented, it is turn to specify which protocols are suitable to use the necessary models for handling optical network elements and services. YANG data models can be properly configured using NETCONF and RESTconf protocols, while Protocol Buffers are related with gRPC protocol. Each subsection includes some examples of usage in state of the art and from the authors detailing the usage of the proposed protocols.

3.1 NETCONF

NETCONF is a protocol based on the exchange of XML-encoded RPC messages over a secure (commonly Secure Shell, SSH) connection [6]. It offers primitives to view and manipulate data, providing a suitable encoding as defined by the data-model. As it use YANG models, data is arranged into one or multiple configuration datastores and provides the set of rules by which multiple clients may access and modify a datastore within a NETCONF server.

Figure 1 shows the NETCONF layering. Over a secure transport layer, a message layer for RPC messages or notifications is included. On top, an operations layer determines the type of operation (e.g., <get-config>, <edit-config>) and finally, configuration or notification data is included in the content layer.

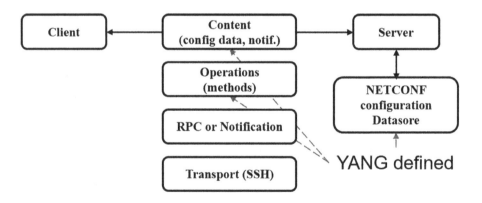

Fig. 1. Netconf protocol stack

One of the most early and significant contributions to the usage of NETCONF in optical network is [7]. This paper proposes a YANG model to describe a sliceable transponder to be deployed in an elastic optical network with variable rate, code, modulation formats, and monitoring capabilities. Two use cases are introduced by this paper: transponder configuration and notification upon BER threshold exceed. It is significant to observe the messaging of NETCONF, which includes edit-config, subscription, and notification messages.

The authors have also presented several papers with special focus on using YANG/NETCONF to enable the SDN control of Sliceable multidimensional (Spectral and Spatial) Transceivers (S-SST) [8,9]. The presented data model encompassed a list of slices. Each slice is composed of a slice ID, a list of optical-channels and a list of optical-signal parameters (associated to the optical-channels). The paper showed the used sequence of NETCONF messages employed for provisioning one slice and requesting the BER.

3.2 RESTconf

In order to offer an ease of use protocol, based on HTTP, in order to properly modify and configurate the YANG datastores. Representational State Transfer (REST) is an architectural style that defines a set of constraints to be used for creating Web services. RESTful Web services allow their clients to access and manipulate textual (JSON/XML) representations of Web resources by using a uniform and predefined set of stateless operations.

With this in mind, RESTCONF was defined as a REST-like protocol that provides a HTTP-based API to access the data, modeled by YANG [10]. The REST-like operations are used to access the hierarchical data within a datastore. The information modeled in YANG is structured in the following tree:

- /restconf/data: "Data (configuration/operational) accessible from the client"
- /restconf/modules: "Set of YANG models supported by the RESTCONF server"
- /restconf/operations: "Set of operations (YANG-defined RPCs) supported by the server"
- /restconf/streams: "Set of notifications supported by the server"

One of the first models of network services using YANG and connection establishment using RESTconf protocol was presented in as an experimental demonstration of distributed cloud and heterogeneous network orchestration with a common Transport API for E2E services with QoS [11]. The proposed Transport API would evolve in future ONF Transport API, which is later described in next section.

Other uses of RESTconf protocol have been demonstrated, with special focus on experimental validation of a converged metro architecture for transparent mobile front-/back-haul traffic delivery using SDN-enabled sliceable bitrate variable transceivers [12].

Moreover, a programmable SDN-enabled S-BVT based on hybrid electro-optical MCM [13] has been presented. On it, the programmable parameters of the SDN-enabled S-BVT were identified enabling the control plane to configure the transceiver according to the network requirements. The reconfiguration time of the S-BVT was up to 90 s, due to the use of offline DSP.

3.3 gRPC

gRPC Remote Procedure Calls [14] is a cloud native high performance, general purpose, RPC framework open sourced by Google. It uses HTTP/2 as a transport protocol and uses protocol buffers encodings for transported messages.

This protocol has an open source tool chain that allows the generation of efficient client libraries. As it is based on HTTP/2 transport protocol and uses byte-oriented encoding, it introduces low latency. It is highly scalable and it is a good fit for distributed systems.

It has been presented to be used for high performance in optical telemetry streaming [15]. It was demonstrated that streaming telemetry capabilities for optical networks could be implemented as modular software service, allowing very high frequencies of all critical optical performance metrics.

4 Standards of Network Programmability and Automation

In the previous sections, data modelling languages and protocols have been presented. During last years, the usage of them has been a significant revolution in the control and management of optical networks and devices. In order to provide adoption, operators and vendors have joint standard defining organizations or other kinds of multi-lateral agreements in order to solidify specific data models to provide inter-vendor compatibility.

ONF Transport API and IETF TEAS models have been proposed as valid control and management solutions for optical networks. Besides, OpenROADM and Openconfig are focused to the control and management of network elements, with special focus on disaggregated optical networks.

4.1 ONF Transport API

In Transport Networks, where network-control function and behavior are well-understood and established, standardizing application programmer's interfaces (APIs) to the network control functions becomes important. ONF has proposed the set of functional requirements and information model for the Transport API (T-API) [16].

The T-API abstracts the main services for an SDN controller: (1) Network Topology, (2) Connectivity Requests, (3) Path Computation, (4) Network Virtualization, and (5) Notification.

Network Topology functionality requires, at a minimum, that the interface exports the context, which is the scope of control, interaction and naming that a particular T-API provider (SDN controller) or client application has with respect to the information exchanged over the interface. The context describes the Service Interface Points, which refer to the customer-facing aspects of the Node Edge Points functions, and the Network Topology. The SDN controller provides information about the links and nodes in the domain (complete or abstracted, depending on the configured shared context). It is clear that the more information is shared, the less abstracted the network appears.

The Connectivity Service represents an "intent-like" request for connectivity between two or more Service Interface Points. Instead, a connection is the provisioned potential for forwarding (circuit/packet) between two or more Node Edge Points of a Node. However, there are other Connectivity Constraints that can be requested, such as: excluding or including nodes/links for traffic engineering, defining the protection level, defining its bandwidth or defining its disjointness from another connection.

ONF Transport API was first demonstrated in [17], as a solution for SDN in carriers networks. A first implementation of topology and connectivity services was provided, alongside a discuss of the clear benefits of providing an standard interface for multi-vendor inter-operability.

The authors have proposed several extensions to ONF T-API to support multiple novel technologies, such as Space Division Multiplexing. [18] demonstrated an experimental NFV MANO Framework for the Control of SDM/WDM-Enabled Fronthaul and Packet-Based Transport Networks by Extending the TAPI.

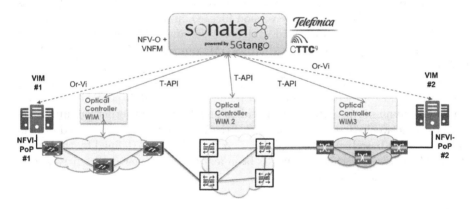

Fig. 2. Interconnection of multiple NFV infrastructure points of presence using ONF T-API

Figure 2 shows the interoperbility demonstration and the usage of Transport API extensions for the Interconnection of Multiple NFV Infrastructure Points of Presence [19].

Finally, Transport API has also been demonstrated as a valid solution of hierarchical control and management of optical networks [20].

4.2 IETF ACTN

IETF has proposed the Abstraction and Control of TE Networks (ACTN) as a framework with multiple data models that has been demonstrated as a feasible and scalable solution for multi-domain, multi-technology transport network scenarios to provide E2E network services. In the proposed architecture, the Multi-Domain Service Coordinator (MDSC) offers a Transport NBI in order to retrieve network topology [21] and establish tunnel connectivity [22].

The authors extended this framework in order to allow the control and management of Flexible Ethernet (FelxE) over OTN networks using RESTconf protocol [23]. In this work, extensions were proposed to enable that specific FlexE capabilities are supported within the YANG data models currently being defined within the context of IETF TEAS working group: topology5 and tunnel6, which define a Transport NBI.

The demonstration in [24] presented Cross Stratum Orchestration (CSO) as a feasible solution for NFV points of presence interconnection. The demo architecture and the interfaces/APIs were aligned with IETF ACTN.

4.3   OpenROADM

The Open ROADM Multi-Source Agreement (MSA) defines interoperability vendor-neutral specifications for Reconfigurable Optical Add/Drop Multiplexers (ROADM) [25]. Included are the ROADM switch as well as transponders and pluggable optics. Specifications consist of both Optical interoperability as well as YANG data models. First version focuses on Metro fixed-grid Networks. Second version includes Flex-grid and Long distance networks. Current third version includes support of Layer 0 (ROADM components) and Layer 1 (OTN: Lambda, ODU).

One of the first OpenROADM demonstrations was presented by [26]. This demo shows how a hierarchical control plane of ONOS SDN controllers orchestrates the dynamic provisioning of end-to-end Carrier Ethernet circuits on a composite network. This demo integrates the control of a disaggregated optical metro network based on NETCONF and on YANG models defined by the Open-ROADM project. For this, ONOS has been featured with new device drivers and with a suitable northbound application.

4.4   Openconfig and gNMI

OpenConfig is led by network operators who share the goal of more dynamic, programmable infrastructure by adopting software-defined networking principles [27].

In the next sections, the proposed data models are discussed, as well as the gRPC Network Management Interface(gNMI).

Data Models. OpenConfig focuses on compiling a consistent set of vendor-neutral YANG data models. These data models cover a variety of network elements, from routers to optical switches. The set of models provided for optical-transport provide a configuration and state model for terminal optical devices within a DWDM system, including both client- and line-side parameters.

gNMI. gNMI is part of Openconfig and it is a standardized protocol defined in protocol buffers to deal with YANG-based data models and to interact using a specific Network Management Interface [28]. The main operations are detailed:

- SetRequest: is sent from a client to the server to update values in the data tree.
- SetResponse: is the response to a SetRequest, sent from the server to the client.
- GetRequest: is sent when a client initiates a Get RPC. It is used to specify the set of data elements for which the server should return a snapshot of data.
- GetResponse: is used by the server to respond to a GetRequest from a client.
- Subscription: Subscription is a single request to subscribe to a certain path that is specified and interpreted as the elements of the data tree that the client is subscribing to. The mode determines how the server should trigger updates to be sent.

Although the specification claims that the data can be either enconded in JSON or in Protobuf, open source implementations currently only use JSON, which does not benefit from a byte-oriented protocol.

5   Evaluation

This section provides a basic summary of the presented data models, protocols and standards that have been detailed during this invited paper. The objective of this section is to provide a quick guide in order to select the most suitable solution for the inclusion of control and management mechanism in optical use cases and scenarios. Each of the proposed solutions has been demonstrated its validity and necessity, but it is true that each solution provides some specificities that make it more adequate for certain scenarios and use cases.

Detailed examples for each of the proposed solutions can be found in the repository [29].

5.1   Data Modelling Languages

In Table 1, YANG and Protocol Buffers are compared. The key fundamental differences are the protocols that can be combined, its usage focus and the encoding types.

Table 1. Data modelling languages

Data models	YANG	Protocol buffers
Protocol	NETCONF, RESTconf, gNMI	gRPC
Focus	Model of config and state data	Structured serialization
Encoding	JSON, XML	Byte-oriented

5.2   Protocols

NETCONF, RESTconf and gRPC are compared in Table 2. These protocols can be compared using the transport layer behind, the different data encoding formats, their own auto-discovery mechanisms, their efficiency and protocol delay.

If we consider transport mechanisms, NETCONF uses SSH, while RESTconf introduces HTTP (adding slight protocol delay and reducing effiency), and gRPC introduces HTTP/2 to overcome the HTTP limitations in terms of efficiency and protocol delay. Auto-discovery is a significant feature in NETCONF and RESTconf that is not introduced in gRPC, being necessary the previous knowledge of common protocol buffers between the client and the server.

Table 2. Protocols

Protocols	NETCONF	RESTconf	gRPC
Transport	SSH	HTTP	HTTP/2
Encoding	XML	XML/JSON	byte
Autodiscovery	yes	yes	no
Efficiency	low	low	high
Protocol delay	slow	slow	fast

5.3   Standards

Table 3 summarizes the presented standards for control and management of optical networks. They can be compared depending on the data modelling language of use (basically YANG), the complexity of data model (based on the length of the proposed data trees), and the standardization defining organization that has validated the data models.

Table 3. Standards

Standards	T-API	IETF TEAS	OpenROADM	OpenConfig	gNMI
Focus	Transport SDN Controller NBI	Transport SDN Controller NBI	Disaggregated ROADM	Router and line card config	Operations and notifications of network elements
Data Model	YANG	YANG	YANG	YANG	Protobuf
Complexity	low	high	high	high	low
SDO	ONF, OIF	IETF	MSA	–	–

6   Conclusions

This paper has justified the need for data models and protocols in order to control and monitor optical networks and elements. The authors have reviewed the current state of the art with significant contributions to each of the proposed solutions. Finally, a comparison of the proposed solutions is provided in order to better adapt them to the necessary optical use cases and scenarios.

Acknowledgments. Research partly funded by EC H2020 5GPPP 5GTANGO (H2020-ICT-2016-2 761493) and Spanish MINECO project AURORAS (RTI2018-099178-B-I00).

References

1. Casellas, R., Martínez, R., Vilalta, R., Muñoz, R.: Control, management, and orchestration of optical networks: evolution, trends, and challenges. J. Lightwave Technol. **36**(7), 1390–1402 (2018)
2. Bjorklund, M.: Yang-a data modeling language for the network configuration protocol (netconf). Technical report (2010)
3. Pyang. https://github.com/mbj4668/pyang/. Accessed 14 Feb 2019
4. Pyangbind. https://github.com/robshakir/pyangbind. Accessed 14 Feb 2019
5. Buffers, P.: Google's data interchange format (2011)
6. Enns, R., Bjorklund, M., Schoenwaelder, J., Bierman, A.: Network configuration protocol (netconf). Technical report (2011)
7. Dallaglio, M., Sambo, N., Akhtar, J., Cugini, F., Castoldi, P.: Yang model and netconf protocol for control and management of elastic optical networks. In: Optical Fiber Communications Conference and Exhibition (OFC), pp. 1–3. IEEE (2016)
8. Muñoz, R., et al.: SDN control of sliceable multidimensional (spectral and spatial) transceivers with yang/netconf. J. Opt. Commun. Networking **11**(2), A123–A133 (2019)
9. Muñoz, R., et al.: SDN control and monitoring system for soft-failure detection and optical restoration of spectral/spatial superchannels. In: 2018 European Conference on Optical Communication (ECOC), pp. 1–3. IEEE (2018)
10. Bierman, A., Bjorklund, M., Watsen, K.: Restconf protocol. Technical report (2017)
11. de Lerma, A.M.L., et al.: First experimental demonstration of distributed cloud and heterogeneous network orchestration with a common transport API for E2E services with QoS. In: Optical Fiber Communication Conference, pp. Th1A–2. Optical Society of America (2016)
12. Fabrega, J.M., et al.: Experimental validation of a converged metro architecture for transparent mobile front-/back-haul traffic delivery using SDN-enabled sliceable bitrate variable transceivers. J. Lightwave Technol. **36**(7), 1429–1434 (2018)
13. Nadal, L., et al.: Programmable SDN-enabled S-BVT based on hybrid electro-optical MCM. IEEE/OSA J. Opt. Commun. Networking **10**(6), 593–602 (2018)
14. grpc. https://grpc.io/. Accessed 14 Feb 2019
15. Sadasivarao, A., et al.: High performance streaming telemetry in optical transport networks. In: Optical Fiber Communication Conference, pp. Tu3D-3. Optical Society of America (2018)
16. Sethuraman, K., et al.: Functional requirements for transport API. v. 0.16, ONF (2016)

17. Lopez, V., et al.: Transport API: a solution for SDN in carriers networks. In: Proceedings of 42nd European Conference on Optical Communication, ECOC 2016, pp. 1–3. VDE (2016)
18. Vilalta, R., et al.: Experimental demonstration of the BlueSPACE's NFV MANO framework for the control of SDM/WDM-enabled fronthaul and packet-based transport networks by extending the TAPI. In: 2018 European Conference on Optical Communication (ECOC), pp. 1–3. IEEE (2018)
19. Vilalta, R., de Lerma, A.M.L., López, V., et al.: Transport API extensions for the interconnection of multiple NFV infrastructure points of presence. In: Optical Fiber Communication Conference. Optical Society of America (2019)
20. Mayoral, A., Vilalta, R., Muñoz, R., Casellas, R., Martínez, R., López, V.: Cascading of tenant SDN and cloud controllers for 5G network slicing using transport API and Openstack API. In: Optical Fiber Communications Conference and Exhibition (OFC), pp. 1–3. IEEE (2017)
21. Liu, X., Bryskin, I., Beeram, V., Saad, T., Shah, H., De Dios, O.G.: Yang data model for TE topologies. draft-ietf-teas-yang-TE-topo, work in progress (2016)
22. Xhang, X., et al.: A yang data model for traffic engineering tunnels and interfaces. draft-ietf-teas-yangte, work in progress
23. Vilalta, R., et al.: Network slicing using dynamic flex ethernet over transport networks. In: 2017 European Conference on Optical Communication (ECOC), pp. 1–3. IEEE (2017)
24. Vilalta, R., et al.: Towards IP & transport network transformation using standardized transport northbound interfaces. In: 2018 Optical Fiber Communications Conference and Exposition (OFC), pp. 1–3. IEEE (2018)
25. MSA, O.R.: Open ROADM overview (2016)
26. Morro, R., et al.: Automated end to end carrier ethernet provisioning over a disaggregated WDM metro network with a hierarchical SDN control and monitoring platform. In: 2018 European Conference on Optical Communication (ECOC), pp. 1–3. IEEE (2018)
27. Shaikh, A., Hofmeister, T., Dangui, V., Vusirikala, V.: Vendor-neutral network representations for transport SDN. In: Optical Fiber Communication Conference, pp. Th4G-3. Optical Society of America (2016)
28. Shakir, R., et al.: gRPC network management interface (GNMI). draft-openconfig-rtgwg-gnmi-spec-01, work in progress
29. Ofc2019 short course 472 - hands-on: controlling and monitoring optical network equipment with netconf/yang. Accessed 14 Feb 2019

Fragmentation Metrics in Spectrally-Spatially Flexible Optical Networks

Piotr Lechowicz[1]([✉]), Massimo Tornatore[2], Adam Włodarczyk[1],
and Krzysztof Walkowiak[1]

[1] Department of Systems and Computer Networks, Wrocław University of Science
and Technology, Wrocław, Poland
piotr.lechowicz@pwr.edu.pl
[2] Department of Electronics, Information, and Bioengineering, Politecnico di Milano,
Milan, Italy

Abstract. Spectrally-spatially flexible optical networks (SS-FONs) are
proposed as a solution for future traffic requirements in optical backbone
networks. As SS-FONs operate within flex-grid, the provisioning of lightpaths spanning multiple frequency slots results in spectrum fragmentation, especially in presence of dynamic traffic. Fragmentation, in turn,
may lead to blocking of dynamic requests due to the lack of sufficiently-
large free spectral windows. In this paper, to reach a better understanding of fragmentation in SS-FON, we extend several metrics used
in (single-core) elastic optical networks to measure the fragmentation in
SS-FONs. Next, we apply these metrics to a dynamic-routing algorithm
with the goal of minimizing bandwidth blocking. Finally, we analyze the
impact of spatial continuity constraint (SCC) on the network fragmentation. Simulations run on two representative network topologies show
that the root mean square factor metric yields the best performance in
terms of blocking when compared to other analyzed metrics.

Keywords: Spectrally-spatially flexible optical networks · Network
fragmentation · Network optimization · Routing · Space · Spectrum
allocation

1 Introduction

According to various statistics, network traffic has been growing in last two
decades 30% to 60% per year, depending on the nature and penetration of services offered by network operators. Since there is no indication that this growth
trend will cease anytime soon, in near future we will face a 'capacity crunch' consisting in incremental exhaustion of available capacity in optical transport networks [17,18]. One possible solution is space division multiplexing (SDM) - a new
optical transmission approach designed to scale the capacity of wavelength division multiplexing (WDM) network and flex-grid elastic optical network (EON)

© IFIP International Federation for Information Processing 2020
Published by Springer Nature Switzerland AG 2020
A. Tzanakaki et al. (Eds.): ONDM 2019, LNCS 11616, pp. 235–247, 2020.
https://doi.org/10.1007/978-3-030-38085-4_21

technologies. SDM enables parallel transmissions of a number of co-propagating spatial modes (fibers, cores, or modes) in appropriately designed optical fibers. The concept of spectrally-spatially flexible optical networks (SS-FONs) combines SDM and EONs technologies, and offers several advantages such as substantial increase in transmission capacity, extended flexibility in resource management due to the introduction of spatial domain (spatial modes), and potential cost savings due to the possibility of resource sharing and the use of integrated devices [6,8,11,12].

One of the potential drawbacks of the flex-grid is the fact that provisioning of lightpaths satisfying continuity and contiguity constraints and using multiple relatively-small (e.g., 12.5-GHz) frequency slices instead of a fixed larger channel spacing (e.g., 50 GHz) introduces spectrum fragmentation, especially in dynamic traffic context. The key negative consequence of high fragmentation is that dynamic requests can be blocked due to lack of sufficient spectral resources to provision the requests. Therefore, properly addressing the fragmentation problem can allow network operator to allocate more requests in the network. One possible way to mitigate spectrum fragmentation consists in performing periodic or on-demand spectrum defragmentation. However, defragmentation entails complex operational procedure to avoid traffic interruptions, and several studies have instead suggested to to limit fragmentation by performing fragmentation-aware routing, spatial mode, and spectrum allocation (RSSA) [1,2,14].

Several research problems related to fragmentation in EONs have been already investigated (see survey papers [1,2]). However, only few papers have so far focused on fragmentation in SDM optical networks. In [3], a core classification method is proposed for multi-core fibers (MCFs), where each fiber core is dedicated to realize requests of certain size. A similar approach is presented in [15], where prioritized areas in the frequency domain are used, instead of dedicated spatial mode resources. In [7], a fragmentation-aware routing algorithm with congestion avoidance is proposed. In [20], a crosstalk-aware defragmentation method is described, which uses 'spectrum compactness' metric to trigger and control the defragmentation process. In [14], some of the connections are established using advanced reservation, i.e., these requests can tolerate a certain delay before setup. To the best of our knowledge, even though in the context of EONs several fragmentation metrics have been studied (as external fragmentation, Shannon entropy, access blocking probability [1,2], and root mean square factor [19], just to name few), there is a lack of investigation on the definition of fragmentation metrics in SS-FONs. Note that in SS-FONs the additional spatial dimension triggers new challenges, since each lightpath can be allocated on various spatial modes. A key issue here is the *space continuity constraint (SCC)*. In particular, if we assume a precise indexing of spatial modes, the same in each network link, the SCC implies that a unique spatial mode shall be assigned to all the channels along a lightpaths. The SCC is enforced by some switching architectures, allowing for devices complexity and cost reduction, at the expense of limited resource allocation flexibility [8,10]. Since the SCC imposes to assign the same spatial mode index along the whole end-to-end routing path, the RSSA problem becomes more challenging and it may significantly increase requests blocking.

The main contribution of this paper is threefold. First, we formulate several fragmentation metrics that can be used in SS-FONs. To this end, we adapt fragmentation metrics proposed for EONs to SS-FONs. Second, we discuss simulation results showing performance of the proposed fragmentation metrics applied in dynamic routing in terms of the bandwidth blocking probability. Finally, we investigate the impact of SCC on the spectrum fragmentation in SS-FONs. To the best of our knowledge, this is the first paper that proposes and analyzes various fragmentation metrics in SS-FONs.

The rest of the paper is organized as follows. In Sect. 2, we present the considered network model. Section 3 discusses our proposed fragmentation metrics. Finally, in Sect. 4 numerical results are presented, and Sect. 5 concludes this work.

2 Network Model

The SS-FON is modeled as directed graph $G(V, E)$ where V is the set of network nodes and E is the set of physical links that interconnects them. Each link $e \in E$ comprises a set of spatial modes $K(e)$, where each spatial mode may refer to fiber in a bundle, core in MCF or mode in multi-mode fiber, without loss of generality. Each spatial mode provides B THz of available spectrum, divided into FS small frequency slots (slices). By grouping several adjacent slices, a spectral super-channel (SCh) can be formed and used to provision the request. As in [9], the network is equipped with coherent transceivers that use digital signal processing for distortion compensation and operate at fixed baud-rate of 37.5 GBaud. Each transceiver occupies 3 optical carriers of 12.5 GHz width. Table 1 presents supported bit-rates and transmission reaches for various MFs for single transceiver [5,9]. If the requested bit-rate exceeds supported maximum capacity of a transceiver, the signal can be transmitted using several adjacent transceivers creating a SCh. Each SCh is separated from the adjacent one with 12.5 GHz-wide guardband. Request realization using single SChs allows for spectrum savings, as only one guardband is required. The highest considered request bit-rate is equal to 1 Tbps, thus possible SChs granularities are equal to $3n + 1$, where $n \in \{1, \ldots, 20\}$ [16].

For the sake of simplicity, we do not consider inter-core crosstalk (IC-XT) physical layer impairments, however the applied model can be easily modified to include them, e.g., through an application of worst-case IC-XT estimation [16].

Table 1. Transmission reach and supported bit-rate for MFs.

	BPSK	QPSK	8-QAM	16-QAM
Transmission reach [km]	6300	3500	1200	600
Bit-rate [Gbps]	50	100	150	200

3 Fragmentation Metrics and Fragmentation-Aware Dynamic RSSA Algorithm

We consider several metrics adapted from EONs to determine the link fragmentation in SS-FONs, namely, *external fragmentation* (EF), *Shannon entropy* (SE), *access blocking probability* (ABP) [2], *root of sum of squares* (RSS), *root mean square factor* (RMSF) [19]. Let F_e^m denote a fragmentation of link $e \in E$, calculated according to some metric m defined further. The fragmentation of whole network using metric m (denoted as F_m) is calculated as the average value of link fragmentation F_e^m among all links $e \in E$ as presented in Eq. (1).

$$F_m = \frac{\sum_{e \in E} F_e^m}{|E|} \qquad (1)$$

It should be stressed that the link fragmentation metrics developed in the context of EONs cannot be directly applied in SS-FONs due to the introduction of the additional spatial dimension. Thus, below we modify the EON link fragmentation metrics in order to address multiple spatial modes. The general idea is to construct the SS-FON metric as the average of the corresponding EON metric calculated for each spatial mode separately.

3.1 Notation

Let introduce notation used to define fragmentation metrics. As described in Sect. 2, each link $e \in E$ consists of $K(e)$ spatial modes. Each spatial mode $k \in K(e)$ contains S slots. Set $\Gamma(e, k)$ denotes blocks of available contiguous slots on spatial mode $k \in K(e)$ on link $e \in E$, and for each block $\gamma_{ek} \in \Gamma(e, k)$ we define $|\gamma_{ek}|$ as its size in slices. The highest allocated slice on the spatial mode $k \in K(e)$ on link $e \in E$ is represented by s_{ek}^{max}. Set G denotes types of granularities used by transceivers, i.e., what are the possible sizes of spectral SChs supported by the transceiver [2] assuming guardbands. According to applied network model, the set G contains values equal to $3n + 1$, where $n \in \{1, \dots, 20\}$. Next, $\lfloor a/b \rfloor$ is the integer division of a/b.

3.2 Fragmentation Metrics

The first considered metric is EF, originated in computer memory management (Eq. (2)). EF depends on the ratio of largest free contiguous fragment of memory to the total free memory on each core. As the main drawback, the EF metric does not reflect changes in smaller free portions of spectrum until the size of the largest free block is not changing. In consequence, when comparing two fragmented links, the result obtained by this metric is not always meaningful, as it does not prevent from fragmenting smaller portions of spectrum than the largest free block [1,2].

$$F_e^{EF} = 1 - \frac{1}{|K(e)|} \cdot \sum_{k \in K(e)} \frac{\max_{\gamma_{ek} \in \Gamma(e,k)} |\gamma_{ek}|}{\sum_{\gamma_{ek} \in \Gamma(e,k)} |\gamma_{ek}|} \tag{2}$$

The SE in information theory is the amount of information available in the message. Equation (3) presents adaptation for fragmentation in SS-FONs. In contrast to EF, SE takes into the account sizes and amount of smaller portions of free spectrum blocks, which makes it more meaningful to compare two links [1,2,4,13].

$$F_e^{SE} = \frac{1}{|K(e)|} \cdot \sum_{k \in K(e)} \sum_{\gamma_{ek} \in \Gamma(e,k)} \frac{|\gamma_{ek}|}{S} \cdot \ln \frac{S}{|\gamma_{ek}|} \tag{3}$$

The ABP metric is formulated based on the available granularities of the transceivers (Eq. (4)). More specifically, it depends on the ratio between the sum of possible channels created with transceivers operating at various granularities in every free spectrum fragment, to the number of possible channels created with various transceivers granularities assuming that all slots are contiguous. Comparing to other metrics, ABP is aware of the possible sizes of SChs that can be created in the network [1,2].

$$F_e^{ABP} = 1 - \frac{1}{|K(e)|} \cdot \sum_{k \in K(e)} \frac{\sum_{\gamma_{ek} \in \Gamma(e,k)} \sum_{g \in G} \lfloor |\gamma_{ek}|/g \rfloor}{\sum_{g \in G} \lfloor \left(\sum_{\gamma_{ek} \in \Gamma(e,k)} |\gamma_{ek}| \right)/g \rfloor} \tag{4}$$

Another possible metric is RSS, presented in Eq. (5). It depends on the sum of square roots of sum of sizes of all free segments on each spatial mode. As SE, this metric can reflect the changes in smaller free segments of the spectrum.

$$F_e^{RSS} = 1 - \frac{1}{|K(e)|} \cdot \sum_{k \in K(e)} \frac{\sqrt{\sum_{\gamma_{ek} \in \Gamma(e,k)} (|\gamma_{ek}|^2)}}{\sum_{\gamma_{ek} \in \Gamma(e,k)} |\gamma_{ek}|} \tag{5}$$

The RMSF is defined in Eq. (6) as a function of the highest allocated slice on each core S_{ek}^{max}, number of free spectrum segments $|\Gamma(e,k)|$ and their sizes $\gamma_{ek} \in \Gamma(e,k)$. The metric increases, when (i) a higher slot is allocated in each spatial mode; (ii) there are more free contiguous segments on spatial modes, i.e., available slices are divided into a larger set of free segments; (iii) the size of large free segments decreases at the cost of increase of smaller segments size [19].

$$F_e^{RMSF} = \frac{1}{|K(e)|} \cdot \sum_{k \in K(e)} \frac{s_{ek}^{max} \cdot |\Gamma(e,k)|}{\sqrt{\frac{\sum_{\gamma_{ek} \in \Gamma(e,k)} |\gamma_{ek}|^2}{|\Gamma(e,k)|}}} \tag{6}$$

Note that for metrics EF, ABP and RSS, in order to avoid the division by 0 when there are no available free segments on a spatial mode, the value inside the

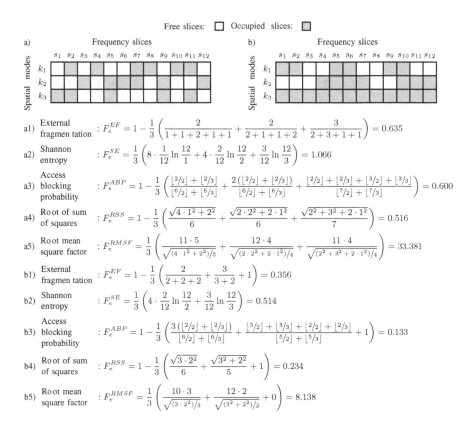

Fig. 1. Example of fragmentation metrics calculations.

sum is replaced with 1. Contrarily, in RMSF in such case, the value is replaced with 0. Moreover, for all metrics except se and RMSF, values vary within $\langle 0, 1\rangle$ range, while for SE and RMSF within $\langle 0, +\infty)$.

In Fig. 1, we present an example of metrics calculation for two different links. The gray squares indicate slices utilized by lightpaths, while white squares are free slices. The operator $\lfloor a/b \rfloor$ denotes the integer division a/b. In the example, the available granularities of transceiver are $G = \{2, 3\}$, therefore, free segments of size 1 are ignored in the F_e^{ABP} equations.

3.3   Fragmentation-Aware Dynamic RSSA Algorithm

In this work, we consider a dynamic routing, i.e., requests arrive dynamically to the network and for each request a lightpath is selected, otherwise the request is rejected. For this purpose, we propose a fragmentation minimizing k-shortest path (FM-kSP) heuristic, where the objective is to minimize the amount of rejected traffic. For each request, FM-kSP selects one path out of k-shortest paths, in order to realize the lightpath aiming for the minimum increase of the network fragmentation F_m, considering one of link fragmentation F_e^m definitions. In more detail, when a new request arrives to the network, the algorithm investigates all precomputed candidate shortest routing paths. For each path, the lowest possible SCh is found, i.e., a SCh with the lowest ending slice index forming a candidate lightpath. Note, the selection of SCh respects the network constraints, i.e., SCC, continuity and contiguity constraints. For each obtained lightpath, the variation in terms of overall network fragmentation ΔF is calculated as follows:

$$\Delta F_m = \frac{\sum_{e \in E} F_e^{m'} - F_e^m}{|E|}, \tag{7}$$

where $F_e^{m'}$ is the fragmentation measure of link e when the new lightpath is allocated, and F_e^m is the link fragmentation in current state of network. To calculate F_e^m and $F_e^{m'}$, one of the introduced above metrics is used. Next, the lightpath with the lowest fragmentation difference ΔF_m is selected, and request is realized on that lightpath. Note that if the difference is negative, the network fragmentation has improved. If there is no lightpath satisfying all constraints, the request is blocked.

4   Numerical Experiments

In this section, we evaluate the performance of proposed allocation strategies based on the fragmentation metrics under dynamic traffic requests in SS-FON. We study two network topologies: (i) European network (Euro28) - 28 nodes, 82 links and average link length of 625 km; (ii) United States network (US26) - 26 nodes, 84 links and average link length of 755 km (see Fig. 2). The considered SS-FON operates with a flexible grid of 12.5 GHz slices and each network link comprises 7 spatial modes. Each spatial mode provides 4 THz bandwidth divided into 320 slices, each of 12.5 GHz width.

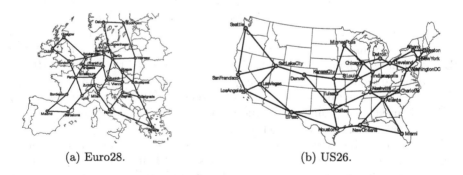

(a) Euro28.   (b) US26.

Fig. 2. Network topologies.

In this study, dynamic traffic requests arrive following a Poisson process with an average arrival rate of $\lambda = 10$ requests per unit time. The lifetime of each request follows a negative exponential distribution with an average of $1/\mu$. Therefore, the traffic load is λ/μ normalized traffic units (NTUs). The requested bit-rate of each request is selected randomly within 50 Gbps to 1 Tbps range, with 50 Gbps granularity. Therefore, traffic of 100 NTUs refers to around 52.5 Tb/s of overall traffic load. We investigate two types of requests distributions: (i) traffic A - the source and destination nodes are selected with uniform distribution; (ii) traffic B - the source and destination nodes are selected proportionally to the distance (in kilometers) between them, i.e., the nodes which are located more closely to each other are more often selected to realize the request. For each analyzed value of traffic load expressed in NTUs, one set with 60 000 requests is processed, however, first 10 000 requests are excluded from the analysis to enable the network to achieve a steady state. For each request, the number of candidate routing (shortest) paths is 10. Additionally, we consider two scenarios, with SCC and with SCC relaxed (denoted as no SCC).

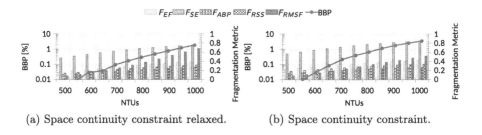

(a) Space continuity constraint relaxed.   (b) Space continuity constraint.

Fig. 3. BBP and value of fragmentation metrics as a function of NTUs for FF heuristic, Euro28 network topology, traffic A.

The main performance metric is *bandwidth blocking probability (BBP)*, defined as the sum of bit-rates of rejected requests, over the sum of bit-rates of all requests offered to the network. As an additional performance metric, the *accepted traffic* for 1% threshold of BBP is used. In more detail, for each scenario the maximum value of traffic load expressed in NTUs is selected, for which the BBP is not larger than 1%, which is a commonly accepted threshold for BBP.

To allocate requests, the FM-kSP algorithm is used (see Sect. 3.3) considering all presented fragmentation metrics. As a reference, first-fit k-shortest path (FF) method is used, which allocates requests on the first possible SCh, processing candidate paths in increasing order of lengths in km.

The first experiment presents relation between values of various fragmentation metrics and BBP as a function of NTUs for FF methods, fragmentation metrics are evaluated afterwards traffic allocation. Figure 3 presents results for traffic A, with and without SCC. The offered traffic load varies from 500 to 1 000 NTUs with 50 NTUs granularity. As the values of RMSF (Eq. 6) can be higher than 1, they are normalized to fit the range of other metrics, i.e., from $\langle 0, 1 \rangle$. Thus, these results are divided by 600. The first observation is that

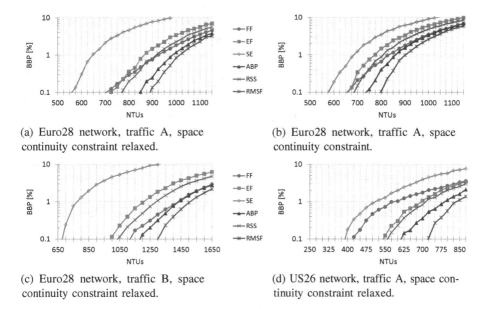

(a) Euro28 network, traffic A, space continuity constraint relaxed.

(b) Euro28 network, traffic A, space continuity constraint.

(c) Euro28 network, traffic B, space continuity constraint relaxed.

(d) US26 network, traffic A, space continuity constraint relaxed.

Fig. 4. BBP for FM-kSP heuristic using various fragmentation minimizing strategies and FF method as a function of NTUs.

BBP increases exponentially (linear growth on logarithmic axis) with the linear increase of NTUs offered to the network. Furthermore, the value of fragmentation metrics also increases, suggesting that for higher values of NTUs, the network is more fragmented, and explaining the rapid increase of BBP. When SCC is assumed, the BBP is 120.5 % higher in average between 600 and 1 000 NTUs. Note, most of the fragmentation metrics are higher, i.e., 19.4%, 14.8%, 10.3%, and 16.6% for EF, SE, ABP and RSS, respectively. Surprisingly, the RMSF is 10.7% lower assuming SCC. Similar trends were obtained for traffic B and for US26 network topology and are not reported.

In the next experiment, performance of proposed FM-kSP algorithm using various fragmentation metrics is compared in terms of BBP. Figure 4 presents BBP for various algorithms as a function of NTUs. In the following results, the names of metrics correspond to the FM-kSP algorithm utilizing that metric, exceptd FF which denotes the reference first fit k-shortest path algorithm. The first observation is that the RMSF algorithm provides the lowest BBP for most values of NTUs. For instance, for 1 000 NTUs the RMSF allows to decrease BBP by 28.8% and 53.8% in regard to the second best strategy, ABP, and the reference one, FF, respectively, for traffic A and SCC relaxed (Fig. 4a). On average RMSF, allows accepting 5.9 % and 8.8% more NTUs for 1% BBP threshold, in reference to ABP and FF, respectively. Further, SCC relaxation allows allocating larger NTUs achieving the same BBP, e.g., 11.1% of gain considering 1% of BBP and the RMSF strategy in Euro28 network (compare Figs. 4a and b). Next, requests following traffic B provide lower BBP when compared to traffic A, e.g., with a difference of 50.0% for BBP of 1% for RMSF (compare Figs. 4a and c). Finally, the US26 network can accommodate smaller overall traffic with the same performance than Euro28 network. For BBP of 1% and RMSF, the difference between allocated NTUs is equal to 21.2% (compare Figs. 4a and d). Comparing RMSF to other metrics, the conclusions are as follows: (i) as all other metrics, it is aware of the number of free segments; (ii) as all other metrics except EF, it is aware of the size of free segments; (iii) contrarily to other metrics, it is aware of the highest allocated slice on each spatial mode. The last property might be the main factor determining the best performance of the RMSF metric. In context of EONs, RMSF outperforms two other metrics, namely, spectrum compactness and utilization entropy [19]. However, to the best of our knowledge, RMSF has not been compared to metrics proposed in this paper. Moreover, as EON is a special case of SS-FON assuming one spatial mode, the difference in performance of proposed metrics should be valid also for EON.

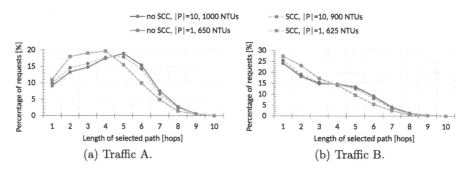

(a) Traffic A.   (b) Traffic B.

Fig. 5. Percentage of requests as a function of selected path length for Euro28 network, 1% threshold of BBP, RMSF strategy.

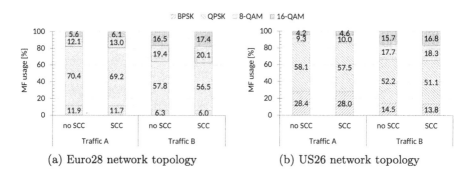

(a) Euro28 network topology   (b) US26 network topology

Fig. 6. MFs percentage usage for 1% BBP threshold as a function of traffic profile and SCC presence for RMSF strategy.

Next, we provide a detailed analysis of performance differences between considered scenarios for the RMSF metric, which - as shown above - provides the best results in terms of BPP. Figure 5 presents percentage of served requests as a function of length of selected routing path in hops for Euro28 network for accepted traffic for 1% threshold of BBP. The results are presented for two numbers of available candidate paths, i.e., $|P| = \{1, 10\}$. Figure 5a presents results for traffic A with SCC and with SCC relaxed, while Fig. 5b for traffic B. Additionally, the corresponding values of traffic in NTUs are reported. Note, the lines for SCC and SCC relaxed for $|P| = 1$ are almost overlapping. Firstly, it is easy to notice that in traffic A the most often selected paths contains 5 hops ($|P| = 10$), while in traffic B the corresponding value is 1 hop, which is strictly related to the source-destination nodes selection probability distribution in each traffic type. Secondly, increasing the number of candidate routing paths, results with selection of longer routing paths, and in consequence, it is possible to accommodate higher amount of NTUs. Additionally, for $|P| = 10$, the accepted traffic is higher for SCC relaxed when compared to SCC non-relaxed. This is because, algorithm in the SCC scenario tends to select longer paths more often. Moreover, relaxation of SCC facilitates allocation of requests even in a fragmented network, since it is possible to freely switch lightpaths among the spatial modes. Contrarily, when $|P| = 1$, there is no significant difference between SCC and SCC relaxed case. Finally, the higher values of traffic can be accepted in traffic B comparing to traffic A, as the distances between source-destination nodes in traffic B are more often shorter. Requests with shorter distances are easier to realize, especially in highly fragmented network, as the continuity constraint is more challenging on path involving higher amount of links.

The last Fig. 6 presents percentage of MFs usage for the RMSF strategy for 1% BBP threshold. For both network topologies, more efficient MFs are more often selected comparing traffic B to traffic A because average length of shortest path for requests is lower in traffic B. Moreover, when SCC is present, higher amount of more efficient MFs is selected,but achieving least amount of accepted traffic for 1% BBP threshold. When SCC is relaxed, increased flexibility allows to allocate additional traffic using longer paths. Finally, in US26 less efficient MFs are more often selected, regardless of traffic profile or SCC. The reason for this is that US26 network has higher average link length when compared to Euro28 network.

5   Concluding Remarks

In this work, we have focused on the performance of dynamic allocation algorithm applying various fragmentation metrics used to provision dynamic traffic in SS-FONs. According to results of simulations, the RMSF metric allows to decrease BBP and in consequence allows to accept around 8.8% more traffic (NTUs) assuming 1% threshold of BBP, when compared to the reference method. Additionally, the relaxation of space continuity constraint allows to allocate 11.1% more traffic comparing to the case without relaxation. Finally, the traffic profile (i.e., source-destination node selection probability distribution) and the number of available candidate paths have a significant impact on BBP. In the future work, we plan to develop defragmentation methods in SS-FONs based on proposed fragmentation metrics.

Acknowledgments. The work of P. Lechowicz was supported National Science Centre, Poland under Grant 2015/19/B/ST7/02490. The work of A. Włodarczyk and K. Walkowiak was supported by National Science Centre, Poland under Grant 2017/27/B/ST7/00888.

References

1. Amar, D., Le Rouzic, E., Brochier, N., Auge, J.L., Lepers, C., Perrot, N.: Spectrum fragmentation issue in flexible optical networks: analysis and good practices. Photonic Netw. Commun. **29**(3), 230–243 (2015)
2. Chatterjee, B.C., Ba, S., Oki, E.: Fragmentation problems and management approaches in elastic optical networks: a survey. IEEE Commun. Surv. Tut. **20**(1), 183–210 (2018)
3. Fujii, S., Hirota, Y., Tode, H., Murakami, K.: On-demand spectrum and core allocation for reducing crosstalk in multicore fibers in elastic optical networks. IEEE/OSA J. Opt. Commun. Netw. **6**(12), 1059–1071 (2014)
4. Horota, A., et al.: Routing and spectrum assignment algorithm with most fragmented path first in elastic optical networks. In: 7th IEEE Latin-American Conference on Communications (LATINCOM), pp. 1–6 (2015)
5. Khodashenas, P.S., et al.: Comparison of spectral and spatial super-channel allocation schemes for SDM networks. J. Light. Technol. **34**(11), 2710–2716 (2016)
6. Klinkowski, M., Lechowicz, P., Walkowiak, K.: Survey of resource allocation schemes and algorithms in spectrally-spatially flexible optical networking. Opt. Switch. Netw. **27**, 58–78 (2018)
7. Liu, L., et al.: 3D elastic optical networks in temporal, spectral, and spatial domains with fragmentation-aware RSSMA algorithms. In: The European Conference on Optical Communication (ECOC), pp. 1–3 (2014)
8. Marom, D.M., Blau, M.: Switching solutions for WDM-SDM optical networks. IEEE Comm. Mag. **53**(2), 60–68 (2015)
9. Rottondi, C., Tornatore, M., Gavioli, G.: Optical ring metro networks with flexible grid and distance-adaptive optical coherent transceivers. Bell Labs Technol. J. **18**(3), 95–110 (2013)
10. Rumipamba-Zambrano, R., et al.: Space continuity constraint in dynamic flex-grid/SDM optical core networks: an evaluation with spatial and spectral super-channels. Comput. Commun. **126**, 38–49 (2018)
11. Saridis, G.M., Alexandropoulos, D., Zervas, G., Simeonidou, D.: Survey and evaluation of space division multiplexing: from technologies to optical networks. IEEE Commun. Surv. Tut. **17**(4), 2136–2156 (2015)
12. Shariati, B., et al.: Realizing spectrally-spatially flexible optical networks. IEEE Photon. Soc. Newsl. **31**(6), 4–9 (2017)
13. Shen, J., Chen, J., Sun, Y.: Fragmentation aware routing and spectrum assignment algorithm for elastic optical networks. In: TENCON 2015–2015 IEEE Region 10 Conference, pp. 1–4 (2015)

14. Sugihara, S., et al.: Dynamic resource allocation for immediate and advance reservation in space-division-multiplexing-based elastic optical networks. IEEE/OSA J. Opt. Commun. Netw. **9**(3), 183–197 (2017)
15. Tode, H., Hirota, Y.: Routing, spectrum, and core and/or mode assignment on space-division multiplexing optical networks [invited]. IEEE/OSA J. Opt. Commun. Netw. **9**(1), A99–A113 (2017)
16. Walkowiak, K., et al.: Dynamic routing in spectrally spatially flexible optical networks with back-to-back regeneration. IEEE/OSA J. Opt. Commun. Netw. **10**(5), 523–534 (2018)
17. Winzer, P.J.: Optical networking beyond WDM. IEEE Photonics J. **4**(2), 647–651 (2012)
18. Winzer, P.J.: Spatial multiplexing in fiber optics: the 10x scaling of metro/core capacities. Bell Labs Technol. J. **19**, 22–30 (2014)
19. Ye, Z., Patel, A.N., Ji, P.N., Qiao, C.: Root mean square (RMS) factor for assessing spectral fragmentation in flexible grid optical networks. In: 2014 OptoElectronics and Communication Conference and Australian Conference on Optical Fibre Technology, pp. 357–358 (2014)
20. Zhao, Y., et al.: Crosstalk-aware spectrum defragmentation based on spectrum compactness in space division multiplexing enabled elastic optical networks with multicore fiber. IEEE Access **6**, 15346–15355 (2018). https://doi.org/10.1109/ACCESS.2018.2795102

Intrinsically Resilient Optical Backbones: An Efficient Ring-Based Interconnection Paradigm

Marcia H. M. Paiva[1](✉) (ID), Gilles Caporossi[2], Moises R. N. Ribeiro[1] (ID),
and Marcelo E. V. Segatto[1] (ID)

[1] Universidade Federal do Espírito Santo, Vitória, Brazil
marcia.paiva@ufes.br, {moises,segatto}@ele.ufes.br
[2] GERAD and HEC Montréal, Montréal, Canada
gilles.caporossi@hec.ca

Abstract. Physical topologies are evolving from elementary survivable rings into complex mesh networks. Nevertheless, no topology model is known to provide an economic, systematic, and flexible interconnection paradigm for ensuring that those meshes bear resilience features. This paper argues that intrinsic resilience can be brought by twin graph topologies, as they satisfy equal length disjoint path property with minimal number of physical links. An exhaustive investigation is performed across twin graph families composing networks from 4 to 17 nodes, whereas diverse real-world topologies and ring networks are used as benchmarks. First, we illustrate the growing process, and discuss the topology diversity of twin graphs. We analyze the impact of single cable cuts between neighbouring nodes, then we stress topologies with 2, 3, and 4 simultaneous cable cuts. Improved resiliency is seen for neighbor nodes and also reduction of cut sets able to disconnect the twin topologies in comparison with real-world networks. Finally, we present as a use case the redesign of CESNET into a resilient network.

Keywords: Network physical topology design · Optical backbone networks · Resilience · Twin graphs

1 Introduction

The provisioning of uninterrupted connectivity services is an indispensable feature of optical backbones. Considerable amounts of tangible and intangible losses, i.e., legal and reputation damages, can result from mere cable cuts as high aggregates of traffic are nowadays transported over a fiber strand [1]. Therefore,

This work was partially supported by FAPES, CAPES, and CNPq (Brazil), and NSERC (Canada). It is also part of the FUTEBOL project, which has received funding from the European Union's Horizon 2020 (grant no. 688941), as well from the Brazilian Ministry of Science, Technology and Innovation (MCTI) through RNP and CTIC.

© IFIP International Federation for Information Processing 2020
Published by Springer Nature Switzerland AG 2020
A. Tzanakaki et al. (Eds.): ONDM 2019, LNCS 11616, pp. 248–260, 2020.
https://doi.org/10.1007/978-3-030-38085-4_22

in order to properly serve new demands from an information-dependent society, networks must be designed using architectures not only with intrinsic abilities to survive, but they also must be resilient in face of a reasonable set of fault events.

Survivability is defined in [2,3] as the ability of networks to fulfill their mission in a timely manner in the presence of attacks, failures or accidents. Raising the bar for network architects, resilience is defined in [4] as the capability of a network to minimize link or node failures effects, by assuming the sustainability of the provided services. For instance, a 16-node ring network survives to any single node or link failure, but this network is not resilient. When any link fails in this network, the distance between the corresponding neighbor nodes increases from 1 to 15 hops, and a 2-hop path must be replaced by a 14-hop path after any node failure. Therefore, considerable side effects can be felt on higher network layers and, as a result, implications to the service delivered to end users.

Modern optical backbones encompass complex multilayer mechanisms. Wavelength division multiplexing (WDM) transparently provides end-to-end interconnects over the physical topology. The coarse bandwidth granularity and rigid spectrum allocation of WDM have motivated recent developments in elastic networks and flexible transmission technologies. They aim at better grooming and transmitting heterogeneous traffic demands [5]. Indeed, these new spectral and bit-rate manageable solutions provide extra degrees of freedom (i.e., elastic and tuneable transponders) in accommodating extra demands arising from restoring impacted traffic demands, over sub and super-wavelength services, for improving the overall network resilience [6].

Nevertheless, re-grooming, re-routing or just switching traffic demands around faulty elements, with the least impact on both working and protected/restored demands, still is a huge challenge for backbone network architects. The intrinsic complexity of this multilayer problem turns exact optimization approaches unlikely to be solved in polynomial time. But there is a fundamental aspect that has been overlooked when trying to improve network resiliency. Regardless of the overlay grooming and transmission technologies, the outcomes of traffic engineering optimization tools will always be constrained by the connectivity diversity of the underlay graph at physical layer.

Nowadays, survivability is a necessary but not a sufficient condition. It is no longer acceptable to design networks for just providing means of service continuity. For instance, there is the challenge for designing optical backbones for supporting the emerging services from the 5th Generation (5G) mobile communications network. The Ultra-reliable and low-latency communications (URLLC) assume that there will be latency-bound and highly dependable underlayer connectivity across distributed datacenters [7]. Thus, optical backbones, operating under either normal or faulty conditions, should meet stringent requirements far beyond mere survivability metrics.

Unfortunately, the topological design of backbones is a complex task in its own right; and that is why the literature already addresses them using heuristic, rule-of-thumb based, and demographic methods, e.g., [8–10]. Lately, graph theory has joined forces in this front. By abstracting physical aspects and demand parameters, graph theory focus simply on identifying potentially good templates for network topologies, rather than chasing them in extremely large multidimensional search spaces from multi-parameter models. Previous works already investigated Harary graphs tacking survivability in optical backbones [11], twin graphs in datacenter networks [12], and graph invariant optimization for optical backhaul networks [13].

The contribution of this paper is to propose to the network community an interconnection paradigm that is able to systematically tackle resiliency (and survivability as a consequence) when designing or evolving backbone networks. Grounded on graph theory, our solution exploits a particular 2-geodetically connected (2-GC) graph family called twin graphs. A key point is that such graphs are already optimal in providing 2-GC with the least number of links. They can also be adapted over the classical ring-based legacy solutions, which were originally designed only having survivability in mind. Thus, backbones designed under this new paradigm can gracefully evolve networks from survivable rings into intrinsically resilient meshes.

The remainder of the paper is organized as follows. Section 2 discusses the evolution of backbone networks toward resilient and affordable architectures in face of growing demands from dependable services. We then present in Sect. 3 a formal definition of twin graphs, and a constructive method to generate them [14]. In order to demonstrate the practical relevance of twin graphs, we perform comparisons with a set of real-world backbone topologies (and rings) with the same number of nodes in Sect. 4. Finally, Sect. 5 brings a use case for direct comparison of a geographically mapped twin topology with a real-world topology. Section 6 presents our concluding remarks and future works.

2 Why Rings Are No Longer Good Enough for Our Networks?

Survivability in ring topologies is due to their 2-connectivity property, whereas resilience refers to 2-geodetically connectivity that rings are unable to provide. The difference is that any 2-geodetically connected topology intrinsically provides at least two node disjoint (working and backup) paths of minimal length (i.e., geodesics) connecting each node pair of the network, whereas a 2-connected topology provides at least two node disjoint paths connecting each node pair of the network, no matter their lengths. Thus, besides the survivability assured by the simple existence of backup paths, backbone networks should ensure the existence of backup paths not much longer than the working ones in order to provide service resilience either through protection or restoration strategies. Protection refers to techniques in which backup paths are defined prior to the occurrence of any failure, whereas in restoration techniques the backup paths are only defined when failures occur.

On the other hand, ring topology is a prototype traditionally used to address the survivability issue with the least number of extra links. The transition from survivable to resilient topologies should take this legacy architecture into account and upgrade it as inexpensively as possible. Service providers cannot afford to abundantly deploy spare resources for protecting network elements in face of their ever diminishing revenues.

2.1 Evolving Rings into Meshes

Ring topologies have scalability limitation. Big rings, i.e., many nodes spread across large geographical areas, are not economically nor technically viable. For instance, SONET/SDH and Resilient Ethernet Protocol limit their rings to 16 nodes [15]. Currently, interconnected rings is still believed to be the appropriate architectural arrangement for larger networks. Hierarchical structures composing collector and core rings can be built [1]. But note that a single node failure can isolate parts of the network. Therefore, the dual-homed ring is the most appropriate approach to follow when building interconnected rings, in spite of its higher deployment cost. Standardization bodies also support the multi-ring/ladder network prototype as a way of building a mesh through interconnected rings, e.g., [15]. Note that such an arrangement also makes network topologies to gradually depart from the simple and cost effective ring-based approach, demanding also more complex and less effective protection schemes [16].

As a result, network architects are already arguing against a rigid (dual-homed) ring hierarchy and advocating for a flexible mesh hierarchy [17]. Note that there is still an evident inclination in those modern proposals of following classic rules of thumb, such as building meshes with concentric and interconnected rings [1], to ensure survivability. There are initiatives such as the use of bounded rings in [18], which provides an integer linear program model to design such a topology; and some heuristic algorithms are also presented in [19–21]. Unfortunately, so far no systematic and scalable topology model has been proposed to grow survivable ring networks into resilient meshes.

2.2 How Can Graph Theory Help?

We argue in this paper that the principle of network resilience has been neglected at network topology design phase. Usually resilience has been left to be resolved by protection and restoration techniques, after a survivable network topology has been put in place.

It is usually assumed that survivability and resiliency are different instances of the network design problem; or at least a far too complicated problem to be solved at once. Not only inefficient solutions are being proposed for protecting traffic, but also complex and slow mechanisms for traffic restoration can be the result of an underlying constrained physical topology. Note that a consistent study of graph properties can address resiliency (and survivability as a consequence) and also unlock features to be used by overlay networks embedded in this physical topology.

But to be practical, this topology design coming from graph theory must prove to be geographically viable. Network architects should be also able to expand their network in a pay-as-you grow style, without being constrained by modular, "exotic", or inflexible node interconnection architectures. It is also highly desirable that these graphs could resemble (or be compatible) with legacy solutions, such as multi-ring topologies. This may ease its adaptation to existing operator's control and management frameworks.

3   Background: Twin Graphs

Twin graphs are particular 2-connected graphs that have at least 2 node-disjoint geodesics between every two non-adjacent nodes, and require for that the minimum number of links [22]. In graph theory literature, they are called minimum-size 2-geodetically-connected graphs. Each twin graph has order $n \geq 4$ nodes and size $m = 2n - 4$ links [22].

Twin graphs are recursively defined as follows [22]: (i) the cycle of order 4 (C_4) is a twin graph; (ii) if G is a twin graph of order n and (u, v) is a twin pair in G (i.e., a pair of nodes that have the same node neighbors), then the addition of a new node v' by using two new links uv' and vv' produces a twin graph G' of order $n + 1$. Thus, in order to grow a twin graph G, only two steps are needed:

1. Identify a twin pair (u, v) in G;
2. Build G', where $V(G') = V(G) \cup \{v'\}$ and $E(G') = E(G) \cup \{uv', vv'\}$.

Notice that this scaling up process can also be used to add to a twin graph more than one node at the time. Indeed, one can add a new node in each of the twin pairs of interest in order to build larger twin graphs. Moreover, there are other graph operations, such as the merging process proposed in [14], that can be used to build larger twin graphs.

When recursively generating a twin graph from the C_4, whenever a node is added, it creates new cycles of order 4, thus all nodes and links of each twin graph belong to cycles of order 4 (see Fig. 1 in Sect. 4).

In summary, twin graphs can be easily generated by a recursive method, which consists of adding nodes by means of twin pairs. One can always grow a twin graph by adding a node to a twin pair, and in general it can be done in several ways, since twin pairs are not unique [22].

4   Results

In this Section practical issues are objectively investigated before suggesting twin topologies to network architects. Although it is not an exhaustive list of practical points to be considered, we expect to provide preliminary and yet solid results supporting twin graphs as a reference model for optical backbone topological design. Cable cuts caused by construction work is the more frequent disruption to optical backbones [23]. Therefore, this paper only focus on link failure analysis when testing resiliency and survivability.

4.1   Scalability and Flexibility

To illustrate the twin topologies scalability discussed in Sect. 3, Fig. 1 presents the growing process (from n to $n + 1$) for all (non-isomorphic) twin topologies from 4 up to 7 nodes. Let $\mathbb{H}_n$ denote a twin topology on n nodes. Starting from the $C_4 = \mathbb{H}_4$ (first row, first column), by adding an extra node, only one twin topology $\mathbb{H}_5$ can be built (second row, first column). Now starting from the $\mathbb{H}_5$ (first row, second column), two different twin topologies $\mathbb{H}_6^1$ and $\mathbb{H}_6^2$ can be built (second row, second column). They, in turn, can generate only two different twin topologies $\mathbb{H}_7^1$ and $\mathbb{H}_7^2$ (second row, third column) on 7 nodes. Finally, starting from $\mathbb{H}_7^1$ and $\mathbb{H}_7^2$ (first row, fourth column), one can generate four different twin topologies on 8 nodes (second row, fourth column).

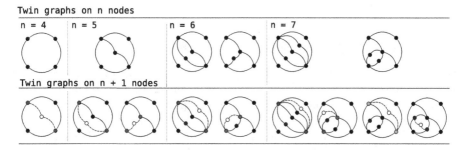

Fig. 1. Growing twin topologies from the C_4. Blank nodes and dashed lines represent all possible (non-isomorphic) ways for growing twin topologies of order $4 \leq n \leq 7$ (on the top) by means of twin pairs, which are highlighted in colors, in order to build new twin topologies of order $n + 1$ (on the bottom). (Color figure online)

4.2   Topology Diversity

An optical backbone is a complex physical system and a graph is merely a very simplified abstraction meant just to represent node adjacency. Physical distance, link capacity and other aspects are not represented. Perhaps a given graph is not feasible due to geographical obstacles, so topology diversity provides designers options to pick and choose from a set of equivalent and yet different solutions. The importance of topology diversity and graph weighting will be latter illustrated in an use case.

Expanding results previously illustrated in Fig. 1 beyond $n = 7$, Table 1 brings the number of twin topologies with $n \leq 17$ nodes. As expected, the number of twin topologies increases with n, since all twin topologies of order $n + 1$ can be generated from a twin topology of order n.

For each n there is a twin topology of diameter 2, namely, the complete bipartite graph $K_{2,n-2}$ [22]. This particular instance is also known as dual hub

Table 1. Number of twin topologies with $n \leq 17$ nodes.

n	4	5	6	7	8	9	10	11	12	13	14	15	16	17
#	1	1	2	2	4	5	9	13	23	35	63	102	182	310

architecture [24]. Besides this, for each $n \leq 17$, we have found at least one twin topology for each diameter in the range from 2 to $\lfloor n/2 \rfloor$.

Another important feature of twin topologies is that, given the network order, the number of possible topologies is bounded. For instance, for $n = 17$ there are 310 twin topologies to be investigated. This diversity also helps solving the physical topology design problem by finding topologies with a good trade-off between diameter and maximum degree depending on the specificity interconnect problems, e.g., [12].

4.3   Neighbor Nodes Resiliency to Link Failures

Every twin topology survives single link failures, as well as every 2-connected topology. However, a cut between neighbouring nodes in any topology always comes with a negative impact on routing. In this particular case, a working path of length one would necessarily be replaced by a longer backup path. We propose the *link removal impact*, denoted as Δ_h, to measure the extent of that impact on routing, by summing up the differences in length of backup and working paths for each pair of nodes. More formally, the link removal impact is written as:

$$\Delta_h = \sum_{u=1}^{n-1} \sum_{v=u+1}^{n} (h_{uv}^b - h_{uv}^w), \tag{1}$$

where h_{uv}^b and h_{uv}^w are, respectively, the length of the backup and working paths, in number of hops, from node u to node v.

Results of the link removal impact can be seen in Fig. 2 for all twin topologies with $4 \leq n \leq 17$ nodes, rings with up to 20 nodes, and real-world optical backbone topologies (reported on [25]) of order up to 20. It is noteworthy the fact that in Fig. 2 all twin topologies with a given number of nodes have the same link removal impact. Moreover, compared to the rings and the real-world networks under study, the twin topologies present the lowest link removal impact. Thus, among these sets of networks, the twin topologies are the most resilient regarding cuts between neighbouring nodes.

It is important, however, to remind that any pair of non-adjacent nodes in a twin graph will have at least one backup path exactly with the same number of hops as the working path since twins are 2-GC topologies. So the removal of links, other than neighboring ones, in twin nodes has absolutely no impact on routing in terms of hop count.

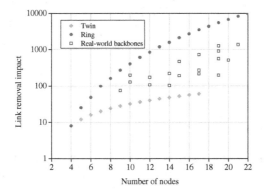

Fig. 2. Impact of all possible cuts between neigbouring nodes, for twin graphs with up to 17 nodes, rings with up to 20 nodes, and real-world optical backbone topologies (reported on [25]) of order up to 20.

4.4   Suvivability to Multiple Link Failures

Any twin topology will survive a single failure but its 2-GC feature can not guarantee that it will survive multiple failures. Following the procedure described in [11], we computed the relative number of link cut sets of sizes 2, 3 and 4 for the three sets of topologies. That procedure allow us to analyze twin topologies stressed with multiple failures.

The number of link cut sets of size i, denoted as S_i, gives the number of ways a network becomes disconnected after removing i links. When normalizing S_i with respect to the total number of sets of i links, we get the relative number of cut sets of size i, which is denoted as $S_i(\%)$. We can formally present it as:

$$S_i\ (\%) = \frac{S_i}{\binom{m}{i}} 100, \tag{2}$$

where $\binom{m}{i}$ it the combination of m links taken i at a time without repetition.

Figure 3 shows $S_i\ (\%)$ for $i = 2$, 3 and 4. For instance, when $S_2\ (\%) = 25\%$ it means that a quarter of all possible simultaneous failures in two links will disconnect the network. Thus, the higher this number, the more likely is the network to be disconnected.

Results in Fig. 3 show, as expected, that ring topologies become disconnected after removing 2 or more links. The larger is the cut set, the better twin-graph families perform in comparison to the group of real-world topologies. There is a clear and consistent trend: A lower probability of disconnecting the network when larger cut sets are considered for twin graph topologies in comparison to real-world topologies. This is highlighted by $S_4\ (\%)$ in Fig. 3(c) when $n \geq 9$. Results for real-world networks is highly topology depended and therefore are scattered in contrast with twin topologies outcomes clustered in a narrow range despite their topology diversity seen in Table 1. This result shows that the

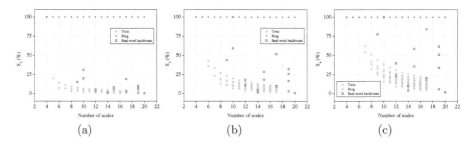

Fig. 3. Relative number of cut sets of sizes (a) 2, (b) 3, and (c) 4 versus the number of nodes, for ring topologies, twin topologies, and real-world backbone topologies.

overall vulnerability to simultaneous failure events can be significantly reduced by designing physical topologies with twin topologies.

4.5   Number of Additional Links to Provide Intrinsic Resilience

We must test if twin topologies produce networks that would be compatible with current optical backbone networks. For that, we present in Fig. 4 the number of links versus the number of nodes for all twin topologies, rings and real-world backbones under study. Evidently, the ring topology provides the lower bound and it can be seen that twin topologies in general require few more links than real-world optical backbones.

The literature shows that real-world optical backbones typically have average degree (that is twice the number of links over the number of nodes) ranging from 2 to 4 [26]. For twin graphs, the average degree $\overline{d}$ is given by:

$$\overline{d} = \frac{2m}{n} = \frac{4n - 8}{n} = 4 - \frac{8}{n}.$$ (3)

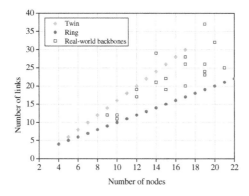

Fig. 4. Number of links required by twin graphs with up to 17 nodes, rings up to 20 nodes, and real-world optical backbone topologies (reported on [25]) of order up to 20.

Thus, it is noteworthy to see that the average node degree is bounded to the interval $2 \leq \overline{d} < 4$ for twin topologies of any order. In other words, the number of links of twin and real-world topologies with n nodes is between n and $2n$.

We can conclude that, for a given n node topology, we can provide intrinsic resiliency with almost the same number of links used by real-world topologies. Thus, all the aforementioned advantages of twin topologies may come at a very reasonable cost.

5   Use Case: A Resilient CESNET Redesign

In order to illustrate how our paradigm can be used in practice, we have chosen to redesign the 12-node CESNET network shown in Fig. 5(a) to improve its resilience. Out of the set of real-world networks, this is the one with the closest average degree to a twin graph.

For mapping nodes from a twin topology to cities in their geographical positions, we have exhaustively analyzed twin topologies with 12 nodes looking for the minimal total fiber length. The result of CESNET redesigned as a twin expending the least accumulated fiber length is shown in Fig. 5(b). It is noteworthy that 11 out of 19 links of the original network remain unchanged (solid lines) in its Twin version.

Note that in this paper, we have initially chosen to consider only unweighted links because we focus on topological features of twin graphs. However, there is no constraint in considering, *a posteriori*, links weighted by geographical distances between nodes to optimally map a twin graph to geographical positions. Note that one may also use link capacities or any other link weighting parameter.

The total fiber length of the original CESNET topology and the corresponding twin topology are about 1842 km, and 2137 km, respectively. This 16% increase is somewhat expected since the original CESNET topology has 19 links, whereas any twin topology with 12 nodes has 20 links. Nevertheless, the benefits for resilience is clear as the link removal impact, Δ_h, which is originally at 106, reduces to 40 (62% smaller) for our twin-graph-based redesign. In addition, a significant improvement is achieved on the survivability to multiple link failures, measured by the relative number of cut sets of sizes 2, 3, and 4 shown in Table 2. For instance, 23.3% of all possible simultaneous failures in four links will disconnect the original CESNET topology, compared to only 15.3% for its twin version shown in Fig. 5(b).

Table 2. Comparison of resilience and survivability for topologies shown in Fig. 5.

	Δ_h	$S_2(\%)$	$S_3(\%)$	$S_4(\%)$
Twin version	40	2.1	7.0	15.3
CESNET	106	3.5	11.2	23.3

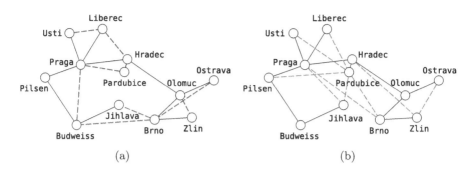

Fig. 5. (a) The original CESNET topology; (b) A twin topology labelled according to CESNET nodes in order to minimize the total fiber length. Solid lines represent links that exist in both network versions. Dashed lines represent removed links in (a) and added links in (b), respectively.

6   Concluding Remarks

We proposed the twin topology as a new reference model to design (or redesign) physical topologies for next generation optical backbone networks. Twin graphs have an average degree in agreement with the average degree of real-world optical backbone topologies. Besides its intrinsic resilience given by their 2-GC, we found out improved survivability to multiple failures, fine granularity for scalability, and topology diversity for better matching graphs to the real problem.

We noticed also that the twin graph on n nodes minimizing the diameter, i.e, the complete bipartite graph $K_{2,n-2}$, corresponds to the solution presented by [24] to the problem of designing physical topologies that ensure logical rings of size $n-2$ can be embedded in a survivable manner. Since solutions of this problem must have at least $2n-4$ links ([24], Theorem 2.5), it is interesting to investigate which twin graphs on n nodes also satisfy it.

Twin topologies solve, for $\kappa = 4$, the problem stated in [18], i.e., the problem of finding a 2-connected network such that each link belongs to a cycle of length at most κ. For future work, it is interesting to investigate topologies based on cycles of different order (e.g., $3, 5$, and 6) in the context of the design of optical backbone networks.

The implications for this new topology design on WDM systems are yet to be investigated. An exhaustive analysis over all 7-node networks have shown that throughput and blocking ratio strongly depends on physical interconnection topology [27]. These results suggest that wavelength requirements will be also affected by physical interconnection topology. It is expected that intrinsic 2-GC features of twin topologies can facilitate wavelength routing and therefore reduce wavelength counting. Future work will also involve the impact of our underlay twin topology on the multi-layer resilience mechanisms considering elastic and flexible optical transmission technologies.

References

1. Wu, T.-H.: Fiber Network Service Survivability. Artech House Inc., Norwood (1992)
2. Al-Kuwaiti, M.H., Kyriakopoulos, N., Hussein, S.: Towards a standardized terminology for network performance. IEEE Trans. Reliab. **57**(2), 267–271 (2008)
3. Kerivin, H., Ridha Mahjoub, A.: Design of survivable networks: a survey. Networks **46**(1), 1–21 (2005)
4. Ramirez, W., Masip-Bruin, X., Marin-Tordera, E., Sanchez-Lopez, S.: Managing resilience in carrier grade networks: survey, open issues and trends. Comput. Commun. **61**, 1–16 (2015)
5. Papanikolaou, P., Christodoulopoulos, K., Varvarigos, E.: Joint multi-layer survivability techniques for IP-over-elastic-optical-networks. IEEE/OSA J. Opt. Commun. Networking (2017)
6. Miladić-Tešić, S., Marković, G., Radojičić, V.: Traffic grooming technique for elastic optical networks: a survey. Optik **176**, 464–475 (2019)
7. Liberato, A., et al.: RDNA: residue-defined networking architecture enabling ultra-reliable low-latency datacenters. IEEE Trans. Netw. Serv. Manage. **15**(4), 1473–1487 (2018)
8. Kamiyama, N., Satoh, D.: Network topology design using analytic hierarchy process. In: 2008 IEEE International Conference on Communications, pp. 2048–2054, May 2008
9. Baroni, S., Bayvel, P.: Wavelength requirements in arbitrarily connected wavelength-routed optical networks. J. Lightw. Technol. **15**(2), 242–251 (1997)
10. Grey, M., Theil, M., Rossberg, M., Schaefer, G.: Towards a model for global-scale backbone networks. In: 2015 IEEE International Conference on Communications (ICC), pp. 6086–6091, June 2015
11. Pavan, C., de Lima, L.S., Paiva, M.H.M., Segatto, M.E.V.: How reliable are the real-world optical transport networks? IEEE/OSA J. Opt. Commun. Networking **7**(6), 578–585 (2015)
12. Vassoler, G.L., Paiva, M.H.M., Ribeiro, M.R.N., Segatto, M.E.V.: Twin datacenter interconnection topology. IEEE Micro **34**(5), 8–17 (2014)
13. Frascolla, V., et al.: Optimizing C-RAN backhaul topologies: a resilience-oriented approach using graph invariants. Appl. Sci. **9**(1), 136 (2019)
14. Chang, J.-M., Ho, C.-W., Hsu, C.-C., Wang, Y.-L.: The characterizations of hinge-free networks. In: Proceedings of the International Computer Symposium on Algorithms, Taiwan, pp. 105–112 (1996)
15. ITU 2015: Ethernet ring protection switching. Technical Report Recommendation ITU-T G.8032/Y.1344, August 2015
16. Resendo, L.C., Ribeiro, M.R.N., Pires, J.J.O.: Optimal multilayer grooming-oriented design for inter-ring traffic protection in DNI multiring WDM networks. J. Opt. Netw. **7**(6), 533–549 (2008)
17. Alexander, S.: Intelligent infrastructure provides new broadband opportunities. Slides from Ciena CTO Steve Alexander's presentation at the CommDay Melbourne Congress event, October 11–12, 2011 in Melbourne, Australia. http://www.slideshare.net/CienaCorp/intelligent-infrastructure-provides-new-broadband-opportunities
18. Fortz, B., Labbé, M.: Two-connected networks with rings of bounded cardinality. Comput. Optim. Appl. **27**(2), 123–148 (2004)

19. Fortz, B., Labbé, M.: A tabu search heuristic for the design of two-connected networks with bounded rings. Technical report IAG Working Papers 74–02, Université Catholique de Louvain (2002)
20. Ventresca, M., Ombuki, B.M.: A genetic algorithm for the design of minimum-cost two-connected networks with bounded rings. Int. J. Comput. Intell. Appl. **05**(02), 267–281 (2005)
21. Foxwell, E.B., Ombuki-Berman, B.: Particle swarm optimisation for the design of two-connected networks with bounded rings. Int. J. High Perform. Syst. Archit. **1**(4), 220–230 (2008)
22. Farley, A.M., Proskurowski, A.: Minimum self-repairing graphs. Graphs Comb. **13**(4), 345–351 (1997)
23. Farhan Habib, M., Tornatore, M., Dikbiyik, F., Mukherjee, B.: Disaster survivability in optical communication networks. Comput. Commun. **36**(6), 630–644 (2013)
24. Narula-Tam, A., Modiano, E., Brzezinski, A.: Physical topology design for survivable routing of logical rings in WDM-based networks. IEEE J. Sel. Areas Commun. **22**(8), 1525–1538 (2004)
25. Morais, R.M., Pavan, C., Ferreira da Rocha, J.R., Pinto, A.N.: Estimating extra capacity for dedicated protection in mesh optical transport networks. In: 16th European Conference on Networks and Optical Communications and Conference on Optical Cabling and Infrastructure (NOC/OC), pp. 165–168. IEEE, July 2011
26. Pavan, C., Morais, R.M., Ferreira da Rocha, J.R., Pinto, A.N.: Generating realistic optical transport network topologies. IEEE/OSA J. Opt. Commun. Networking **2**(1), 80–90 (2010)
27. Tessinari, R.S., et al.: On the impact of the physical topology on the optical network performance. In: 2018 IEEE British and Irish Conference on Optics and Photonics (BICOP), pp. 1–4, December 2018

Experimental Evaluation of Dynamic Resource Orchestration in Multi-layer (Packet over Flexi-Grid Optical) Networks

Silvia Fichera[1(✉)], Barbara Martini[2], Ricardo Martínez[3], Ramon Casellas[3], Ricard Vilalta[3], Raul Muñoz[3], and Piero Castoldi[1]

[1] Scuola Superiore Sant'Anna, Pisa, Italy
barbara.martini@cnit.it, {s.fichera,castoldi}@santannapisa.it
[2] CNIT, Pisa, Italy
[3] Centre Tecnòlogic de Telecomunicacions de Catalunya (CTTC/CERCA), Barcelona, Spain
{rmartinez,rcasellas,rvilalta,rmunoz}@cttc.es

Abstract. In future 5G infrastructures, network services will be deployed through sets of Virtual Network Functions (VNFs) leveraging the advantages of both Software Defined Networking (SDN) and Network Function Virtualization (NFV). A network service is composed of an ordered sequence of VNFs, i.e., VNF Forwarding Graph (VNFFG), deployed across distributed data centers (DCs). Herein, we present a Cloud/Network Orchestrator which dynamically processes and accommodates VNFFG requests over a pool of DCs interconnected by a multi-layer (packet/flexi-grid optical) transport network infrastructure. We propose two different cloud and network resource allocation algorithms aiming at: (i) minimizing the distance between the selected DCs, and (ii) minimizing the load (i.e., consumed cloud resources) of the chosen DCs. Both algorithms run on a Cloud/Network Orchestrator and are experimentally validated and benchmarked on the CTTC ADRENALINE testbed.

Keywords: Resource orchestration · SDN · NFV

1 Introduction

5G networks are being designed to leverage the inherited benefits brought by both softwarized networks and virtualization techniques (e.g., SDN and NFV). In this context, end-to-end 5G network services will be composed of an ordered set of interconnected network functions deployed in the cloud and running on

This work is partially funded by the EU H2020 5G TRANSFORMER project (761536) and the Spanish AURORAS project (RTI2018-099178).

© IFIP International Federation for Information Processing 2020
Published by Springer Nature Switzerland AG 2020
A. Tzanakaki et al. (Eds.): ONDM 2019, LNCS 11616, pp. 261–273, 2020.
https://doi.org/10.1007/978-3-030-38085-4_23

commercial-off-the-shelf servers as virtual machines (i.e., VNFs). ETSI NFV defined an architectural framework for the coordinated VNF MANagement and Orchestration (NFV MANO framework [1]) also across different hypervisors and computing resources deployed in remote cloud infrastructures (i.e., DCs) [2]. The resulting logical VNF topology accommodating a given end-to-end network service is defined as VNF Forwarding Graph (VNFFG) [3]. To this end, it is needed that the VNFs placed in remote DCs and their interconnections ensure QoS demands in terms of availability, bandwidth, latency also considering the current load of both cloud and network resources [4]. This entails in particular to properly select the network resources to provide DC interconnections, especially in the context of heterogeneous (packet and flexi-grid optical) transport infrastructures (i.e., Multi-Layer Network - MLN).

In this paper we present a cloud and network resource orchestration system and discuss the implications when dynamically serving VNFFG requests on top of the considered MLN. The orchestration of cloud and network resources is performed by an allocation engine (referred to as *Allocator*) complementing the ETSI NFV Orchestrator (NFVO) in the dynamic selection of the DCs and respective interconnections underpinning the VNFFG over a distributed DC infrastructure interconnected by a MLN [5]. Every DC is physically attached to packet switch nodes (e.g., MPLS), named as packet Gateways (Gws). Such Gws are equipped with sliceable bandwidth variable transceivers (SBVTs) providing the interconnection among them over a flexi-grid optical infrastructure. Upon receiving a new VNFFG request, the *Allocator* computes the cloud and networking resources and interacts with specialized controllers to yield the programmability and instantiation of such resources. In particular, for the networking resources the *Allocator* relies on a Transport SDN Controller (T-SDN) [6] enabling the resource computation and configuration of the underlying MLN infrastructure. In the adopted MLN scenario, it is worth outlining that opportunistic traffic *grooming* decisions are fostered to attain efficient use of network resources in terms of packet ports, SBVTs' transceivers and the optical spectrum.

In light of the above scenario, two on-line resource orchestration algorithms are proposed for selecting virtual resources: *(i)* compute resources at cloud DCs hosting VNFs and, *(ii)* network links enabling the VNF connectivity across the MLN. The key objective is to not only effectively deploy and satisfy VNFFG requirements but also accomplishing efficient use of the overall resources to favour serving subsequent VNFFG requests. This objective is generically integrated into the problem of embedding a virtual network onto a physical cloud and transport infrastructure which is referred to as Virtual Network Embedding (VNE) [7]. The VNE problem can be decomposed into two sub-problems: *virtual node mapping* and *virtual link mapping*. The ordering and criteria to execute them do impact on the attained resource utilization and, thereby on the resulting network service performance [8]. A number of VNE mechanisms have been proposed in the last years to optimally map virtual networks over a substrate infrastructure and guarantee end-to-end network services' requirements [18]. In a nutshell, these mechanisms address the optimal accommodation of virtual network demands from different perspectives, ranging from ensuring end-to-end QoS [9,10], economical targets [11], addressing survivability and energy-efficiency [12–14], etc. Concerning flexi-grid optical networks, in [16], the problem of the interconnecting myriad of DCs by virtual networks on top of an elastic optical network has been tackled. Moreover, in [15], a combined orchestration process for both cloud and network resources to interconnect multiple DCs over a packet and optical transport infrastructure has been proposed. As far as our knowledge, all these approaches focus on optimizing the resource consumption and do not consider the impact of the network delay which is becoming an important requirement when deploying network services across distributed DCs [17]. Moreover, the proposed solutions have been barely evaluated over experimental testbeds thus overlooking on the actual feasibility and efficiency of the algorithms in a real network deployment scenario.

In this paper the VNE problem is addressed by the two proposed resource orchestration algorithms which are experimentally evaluated within the CTTC ADRENALINE testbed [6] using a myriad of figures of merit. More specifically, the following metrics inspired by the VNE problems [18] are considered: the *path length* metric and the *stress level*. With the first metric, the targeted and stringent QoS requirement in terms of end-to-end latency can be effectively represented and quantified. In general, the larger is the connection path, the higher the experienced delay is. Thus, the first resource orchestration algorithm leads to select cloud DC resources which do minimize the resulting network delay when providing DC inter-connectivity. The (*stress level*) metric allows reflecting the DC occupancy. The second resource orchestration algorithm uses such a metric to prioritize a load balancing strategy for selecting the DCs hosting the required VNFs.

2   Resource Orchestration Set-Up in a MLN Infrastructure

The considered cloud/network resource orchestrator system governing a pool of distributed DCs interconnected by a MLN is depicted in Fig. 1. This constitutes the set-up (reproduced into the CTTC ADRENALINE testbed) used for realizing the experimental evaluation [5]. As mentioned the connectivity between a pair of DCs is done interconnecting respective packet Gws through a flexi-grid optical network. In this MLN scenario, *grooming* decisions are exploited to leverage the best of both packet and optical switching technologies: (*i*) statistical multiplexing (i.e., mutiple packet traffic flows being transported over the same optical connection), and (*ii*) huge transport capacity provided by optical transmission. The MLN is controlled by a T-SDN based on a PCE Central Controller (PCECC) [6]. Consequently, for an incoming network service requiring a packet connection between a pair of DCs hosting two VNFs, the T-SDN Controller triggers a constrained shortest path computation (CSPF) algorithm taking into account technological constraints and required service and performance objectives. To this end, the algorithm uses as inputs: (*i*) the updated state of the network resources (i.e., packet ports utilization, optical spectrum availability, SBVT usage, etc.), *(ii)* the network service requirements such as demanded bandwidth and maximum tolerated latency. It is worth outlining that eventual flex-grid optical connections deployed between a pair of packet nodes (Gws) are derived on the so-called virtual packet link (VL). These VLs inherit attributes (e.g., available bandwidth, accumulated delay, etc.) from their underlying (optical) connections [6], and its spare available bandwidth can be considered by subsequent CSPF computations to accommodate new packet connections demands exploiting the targeted grooming opportunities.

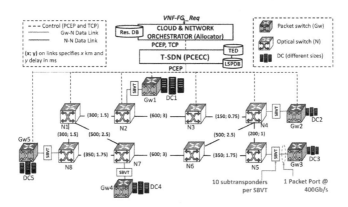

Fig. 1. Resource orchestration on top of a MLN set-up

The functions (i.e., network resource computation and MLN programmability) made by the T-SDN controller are coordinated by the cloud/network orchestrator (i.e., the *Allocator*). Specifically, the *Allocator* is the frontend for processing incoming VNFFG requests, checking DCs' resource availability, deciding for the proper selection of both cloud and network resources based on their load and availability, and finally allocating selected resources (assisted by the T-SDN controller as for network links). In other words, the *Allocator* is able to perform not only cloud/DC selection but also inter-DC path computations based on retrieved abstracted network information passed by the T-SDN controller. For the latter, the *Allocator* and the T-SDN Controller communicate among themselves using two APIs: (i) standard Path Computation Element Protocol (PCEP) [22] for requesting path computation and/or instantiating feasible paths derived from the abstracted topology; (ii) a proprietary TCP API for retrieving the abstract network information. To do the above, the *Allocator* relies on two repositories: *Cloud database* storing the DC cloud resource status and the *Traffic Engineering Database* (TED) storing the abstracted network topology (i.e., VLs between connected DCs)[1]. Recall that VLs are dynamically set up through the establishment of low-data rate packet connections over coarse flexi-grid optical bandwidth connections. Based on the repositories' information, the *Allocator* runs a particular on-line orchestration algorithm to properly select the (cloud and network) resources to address the VNFFG requirements while meeting specified goals, e.g., minimize the latency and balancing the DC resources load. A detailed description of the two proposed orchestration algorithms is provided in the following section.

3   On-Line Resource Orchestration Algorithms

Without lack of generality, we assume that a VNFFG request is composed of interconnected VNFs deployed at two different DCs. The required VNFs are deployed over a set of virtual machines (VMs) supporting the demanded capabilities and capacities specified in the network service request. Therefore, for every VNFFG request (*req*), cloud resources are allocated into two DCs (i.e., *srcDC* and *dstDC*). Every *req* (Fig. 2) specifies the number of VMs along with their computing requirements (i.e., CPU, RAM and Storage) per DC (*srcDC* and *dstDC*) as well as the inter-DC networking requirements: bandwidth (in Bytes/s) and maximum tolerated latency (in ms). The details of the proposed resource orchestration algorithms are discussed in the following:

VNFFG dynamic request generation	
Description	srcDC and number of VMs to allocate with IT (CPU.RAM and Storage) and Network (Bw and Latency) demand
Num reqs	1000; **Poisson** (mean interarrival time: 25s); **Exponential** duration (Holding Time. HT) varied from 200.250.300 and 350s
Num VMs per DC in a req	Uniformely distributed [1.5]
Resources per VM	Uniformely distributed: CPU [1.4]cores. RAM [1.6]GB. Storage [4.10.20.40]GB
Network Resources per Packet_LSP₁	**Bandwidth** unoformely distributes: 10. 40 and 100 Gb/s; **Latency**: uniformely distributed [6.12]ms

Fig. 2. VNFFG req generation details

– *Minimum Distance* (MD): given the specified *srcDc* in the *req*, it selects the *dstDC* out of a candidate set of DCs resulting the closest in terms of distance (km) provided that: (i) it has sufficient available cloud resources to serve the *req* and, (ii) the inter-DC bandwidth requirement is fulfilled. By doing so, MD allows minimizing the experienced network delay due to the connectivity

---

[1] The MANO functions and the NFVO are not explicitly shown in the set-up, since their functions that are relevant in this work, i.e., VNFFG request processing and WIM function, are realized by the *Allocator*, that is particularly focused on the dynamic network resource selection and allocation process. Similarly, the DC infrastructure and the VIM functions have not been actually deployed yet emulated.

between both *srcDC* and *dstDC* leading to better deal with the *req*'s latency upper limit.

– *Less Loaded DC* (LLDC): given the *srcDC* in the *req*, LLDC chooses the *dstDC* out of a candidate set of DCs having the larger amount of available cloud resources (i.e., less loaded DC) provided that: (i) it has sufficient available cloud resources to serve the *req*; (ii) the inter-DC bandwidth requirement is fulfilled, and (iii) the maximum required tolerated latency is not exceeded.

Figure 3 shows the control workflows (i.e., interactions between the *Allocator* and the T-SDN Controller) required for MD and LLDC algorithms when serving a VNFFG request. Regardless of the algorithm, upon receiving a *req*, the *Allocator* verifies whether the *srcDc* has enough available computing resources. Additionally, it seeks for a subset of candidate *dstDCs* able to address the cloud resource demands using either MD or LLDC. If either conditions fails *req* is refused.

Focusing in the MD approach, in Fig. 3(a), the *Allocator* sends to the T-SDN Controller a PCEP Path Computation Request (PCReq) message to compute a path from the *srcDC*'s Gw to all the possible *dstDCs*' Gws. The PCReq message carries the Gws endpoints and the requested bandwidth (Bw). For each PCReq message, the T-SDN Controller triggers a K-CSPF algorithm (described in [5]) to satisfy both Bw and latency constraints. The K-CSPF algorithm aims at finding a feasible MLN path attaining the most efficient use of the network resources (i.e., packet ports, optical spectrum, S-BVT devices, etc.). If a path is found, the T-SDN Controller sends a PCEP Path Computation Reply (PCRep) message to the *Allocator* with the path (i.e., nodes, links, frequency slot, modulation format, SBVTs subtransponders) along with a metric value reflecting the actual distance (in km) between the Gw's endpoints. This metric then allows the *Allocator* selecting the *dstDC* with the lowest distance (in km). Afterwards, the *Allocator* addresses the allocation of the selected *dstDC* cloud and network resources over the pre-computed inter-DC path.

In the LLDC approach, in Fig. 3(b), for each candidate *dstDC*, the *Allocator* computes the percentage of available cloud resources as a ratio between the amount of unused cloud resources over the sum of the whole deployed resources. Next, the *Allocator* selects the DC having the highest ratio, i.e., less loaded DC. Once the *dstDC* is chosen, the *Allocator* retrieves via the T-SDN controller the abstracted network view. Using the set of gathered VLs, the *Allocator* runs a shortest path route computation to connect both *srcDC* and *dstDC* Gws. The goal is to reuse as much as possible the spare available bandwidth of the existing VLs exploiting the benefits of grooming strategies. If this succeeds, the *Allocator* sends a PCEP PCInitiate message to the T-SDN controller with the computed route (i.e., set of VLs carried into Explicit Route Object, ERO) to perform the network programmability. Otherwise, the *Allocator* cannot find a feasible route (e.g., the set of VLs does not provide connectivity between the *srcDC* and *dstDC* Gws), and delegates to T-SDN controller the path computation over the MLN to provided the targeted DC connectivity.

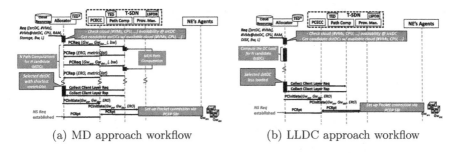

(a) MD approach workflow   (b) LLDC approach workflow

Fig. 3. Cloud/Network orchestrator - T-SDN controller workflows

In both resource orchestation strategies, if the DC connectivity succeeds, a PCEP Path Computation Report (PCRpt) message is sent back to the *Allocator*. Conversely, a Path Computation Error (PCErr) is sent to the *Allocator* informing that no connectivity between the selected *srcDC* and *dstDC* Gws is found, and thus the network service request is blocked.

4   Experimental Performance Evaluation

The performance evaluation of the proposed resource orchestration algorithms is conducted within the CTTC ADRENALINE testbed rolling out the cloud/network orchestrator and MLN infrastructure shown in Fig. 1.

The cloud infrastructure is made up of 5 (emulated) DCs of different size (i.e., supporting different amount of cloud resources) which are connected to their corresponding 5 Gw nodes (i.e., MPLS switches). In particular, we consider 2 small DCs (40 CPU Cores, 160 GB of RAM and 7 TB of Storage) connected to both Gw2 and Gw3, 2 medium DCs (80 CPU cores, 320 GB of RAM and 10TB of Storage) connected to Gw4 and Gw5 and 1 large DC (500 CPU cores, 2400 GB of RAM and 135 TB of Storage) connected to Gw1. Each Gw node has a single packet port (operating at 400 Gb/s) connected to the optical flexi-grid network via an SBVT with 10 subtransponders. Each subtransponder can use 3 different modulation formats (MFs), i.e., DP-16QAM, DP-8QAM and DP-QPSK, enabling 3 different bit rates, i.e., 200, 150 and 100 Gb/s, for maximum distances, i.e., 650, 1000 and 3000 km, respectively. Optical links support 128 Nominal Central Frequencies spaced 6.25 GHz. Optical fiber distances in Fig. 1 are necessary for determining the MF when executing the K-CSPF computation as well as the accumulated path delay for checking the *req* latency restriction. Specific details of the *req* generation including the amount of demanded cloud resources and bandwidth and latency needs are described in Fig. 2. In a nutshell, each experimental data point is realized with 1000 requests following a Poisson process VNFFG request whose mean inter-arrival time is set to 25 s, and the duration (holding time, HT) is exponentially modeled varying its mean to 200, 250, 300, and 350 s. This provides different offered traffic loads (expressed in Er): 8, 10, 12, and 14. The requirements of each VNFFG requests are generated as

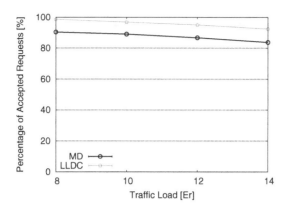

Fig. 4. Percentage of accepted requests vs. Traffic Load (Er)

follows: the number of VMs per DC is uniformly distributed between [1, 5]; the IT resources (i.e., CPU, RAM and disk) are randomly chosen in the ranges of [1, 4] cores, [1, 6] GB and [4, 10, 20, 40] GB, respectively; the demanded bandwidth is randomly selected among [10, 40, 100] Gb/s; and the latency (l) is in the range of [6, 12] ms.

Figure 4 shows the percentage of the accepted *reqs* versus the offered traffic load in Erlangs (Er) when applying either MD or LLDC. We observe that higher rate of accepted *reqs* are attained by LLDC. This means that LLDC objective fostering to prioritize selected *dstDC* being less loaded leads to attain a more efficient use of all DC resources which in turn increases the chances to serve future network services. To consolidate this statement, it is thoroughly explored the reason why a *req* could be blocked. In Fig. 5 we show the two main causes of requests rejection: lack of cloud resources at the DCs as well as the lack of network resources entailing the unavailability to satisfy the latency and/or bandwidth requirements imposed by each VNFFG request. In other words, for those VNFFG requests that cannot be accommodated, it is depicted the number of rejected requests per traffic load related to either of the above blocking causes. Figure 5(a) shows that most of the blocked requests are due to the cloud resource unavailability in the MD case. This is because the selection of the *dstDC* is exclusively done by minimizing the distance with the *dstDC*. That is, no strategy providing efficient compute resource utilization among all DCs is applied leading to exhaust resources at specific DCs. On the other hand, Fig. 5(b) shows that at lowest traffic load, the rejection due to the network unavailability is similar for both MD and LLDC. At a traffic load of 12 Er, the LLDC experiences more blocked requests caused by the network unavailability. Here the reason is the opposite with respect to the previous case wherein as traffic load grows the LLDC finds more problems to satisfy network requirements especially the latency requirement.

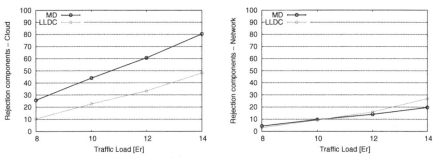

(a) Rejection due to Cloud unavailability (b) Rejection due to the Network availability

Fig. 5. Request rejection analysis

In Fig. 6 the propagation delay experienced by data from *srcDC* and *dstDC* using the two resource orchestration approaches is depicted. As expected, MD lowers the obtained delay since it performs cloud and network resource computation aiming at minimizing the inter-DC path distance between both *srcDC* and *dstDC*. Consequently, MD always performs accomplishing the lowest propagation delay. Conversely, LLDC approach attains an accumulated propagation delay almost doubling the one achieved by the MD algorithm. As said, LLDC targets a better optimization of the DC resources whilst the distance between DCs (i.e., resulting propagation delay) is not minimized. Observe that as the traffic load is increased, LLDC propagation delay is smoothly decreased. Indeed, as network service requests are increased, resources are more used and making more difficult to dealt with the network constraints. Aligned to the above, it becomes more complicated to satisfy the latency requirement for the incoming requests as shown in Fig. 5(b). Therefore, in LLDC, at high traffic load, successfully established services tend to be deployed in shortest inter-DC paths, which entail shortest propagation delay.

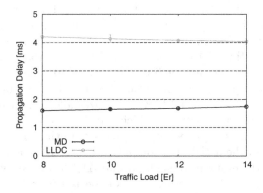

Fig. 6. Propagation delay vs. Traffic Load (Er)

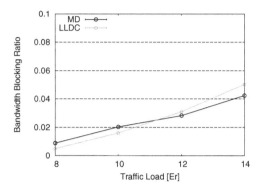

Fig. 7. Bandwidth Blocking Ratio vs. Traffic Load (Er).

Figure 7 plots the obtained Bandwidth Blocking Ratio (BBR). BBR provides the ratio between the amount of bandwidth being blocked and the total bandwidth being requested for all the received *reqs*. This figure of merit becomes relevant to show how well the K-CSPF algorithm performs when computing paths over the MLN infrastructure targeting grooming opportunities. In other words, exploiting grooming decisions leads to accomplish better use of the network resources which in turn does make lowering the BBR. That said, from the results one may realize that the resource orchestration algorithm applied in the *Allocator* when selecting *dstDc* has notable impact on the obtained BBR. In this regard, observe that as traffic load is increased MD performs better (i.e., lower BBR) when compared to LLDC. The reason behind that is as traffic load grows, network resources tend to be more occupied. This complicates the K-CSPF to find feasible MLN paths (when needed) satisfying the set of imposed technological constraints such as spectrum continuity and contiguity. Consequently, adopting a resource orchestration strategy which minimizes the distance between *srcDC* and *dstDC* leads to use, in general, less network resources. Consequently, MD selection facilitates the K-CSPF algorithm to deal with those mentioned technological constraints.

In Fig. 8 the amount of CPU being allocated for each DC size is shown for the two approaches. MD tends to allocate more VNFs in the small and medium DCs. In Fig. 8(a) the MD approach occupies almost the 60% of the CPU available in the small DCs when HT = 14 Er whereas the LLDC approach reaches the 50%. This behaviour is also seen for medium DC (Fig. 8(b)). However, this trend is reversed for large DC (Fig. 8(c)) where the MD and LLDC occupy 10% and 20% of the CPU, respectively. In fact LLDC prioritizes allocating cloud resources in DC having more available resources, which uses to be the larger DCs.

Finally, in Fig. 9 it is depicted the average set-up time, i.e., the overall time required to: (i) select the *dstDC*, (ii) compute the inter-DC connectivity, and (iii) allocate the network resources of such an inter-DC connectivity (either reusing VLs or allocating new MLN resources). As expected from the above discussed workflows, MD approach requires longer time to set up the network services

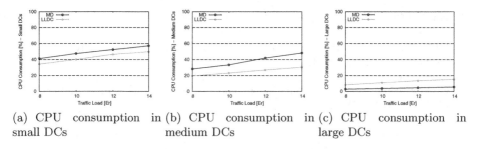

(a) CPU consumption in small DCs

(b) CPU consumption in medium DCs

(c) CPU consumption in large DCs

Fig. 8. CPU consumption in different DC sizes

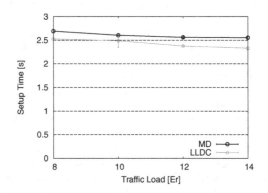

Fig. 9. Setup time vs. Traffic Load (Er)

mainly due to the amount of control interactions between the *Allocator* and the T-SDN Controller to derive the shortest distance for each candidate *dstDC*.

5   Conclusions

In this paper, we compared two on-line cloud and network resource orchestration algorithms (MD and LLDC) to dynamically accommodate network services (expressed as VNFFGs) within distributed remote DCs being inter-connected through a MLN infrastructure. The performance evaluation of both algorithms has been done experimentally within the CTTC ADRENALINE testbed using a myriad of figures of merit such as the acceptance ratio, the BBR, the consumed CPU resource per DC size, etc. using different traffic loads associated to the amount of generated VNFFG requests. The MD algorithm aims at minimizing the inter-DC connectivity distance between the selected DCs to lower the resulting end-to-end latency. On the other hand, LLDC is devised to attain a more efficient use of the compute resources throughout all the DCs. In light of the obtained results, one can state that LLDC algorithm does improve the network service request acceptance thanks to the beneficial effect of balancing the compute resource load at the expenses of increasing the end-to-end latency.

References

1. ETSI: Network Functions Virtualisation (NFV); Management and Orchestration. Group Specification (2014)
2. ETSI: Network Functions Virtualisation (NFV) Release 3; Management and Orchestration; Report on Management and Connectivity for Multi-Site Services. ETSI GR NFV-IFA 022 V3.1.1 (2018)
3. ETSI: Network Functions Virtualisation (NFV); Management and Orchestration; Or-Vi reference point - Interface and Information Model Specification. ETSI GS NFV-IFA 005 V2.1.1 (2016)
4. Martini, B., Paganelli, F.: A service-oriented approach for dynamic chaining of virtual network functions over multi-provider software-defined networks. Future Internet 8(2), 24 (2016)
5. Fichera, S., et al.: Experimental evaluation of orchestrating inter-DC quality enabled VNFFG services in packet/flexi-grid optical networks. In: proceedings of ECOC, September 2018
6. Martínez, R., et al.: Experimental evaluation of a PCE transport SDN controller for dynamic grooming in packet over flexi-grid optical networks. In: Proceedings of ECOC, September 2017
7. Haider, A. et al.: Challenges in resource allocation in network virtualization. In: 20th ITC Specialist Seminar, vol. 18 (2009)
8. Gharbaoui, M., et al.: Cloud and network orchestration in SDN data centers: design principles and performance evaluation. Comput. Netw. 108, 279–295 (2016)
9. Trinh, T., et al.: Quality of service using careful overbooking for optimal virtual network resource allocation. In: The 8th Electrical Engineering/Electronics, Computer, Telecommunications and Information Technology (ECTI) Association of Thailand - Conference, pp. 296–299 (2011)
10. Zhang, X., et al.: An overlay mapping model for achieving enhanced QoS and resilience performance. In: 3rd International Congress on Ultra Modern Telecommunications and Control Systems and Workshops (ICUMT), Budapest (2011)
11. Rahman, M.R., Aib, I., Boutaba, R.: Survivable virtual network embedding. In: Crovella, M., Feeney, L.M., Rubenstein, D., Raghavan, S.V. (eds.) NETWORKING 2010. LNCS, vol. 6091, pp. 40–52. Springer, Heidelberg (2010). https://doi.org/10.1007/978-3-642-12963-6_4
12. Shamsi, J., Brockmeyer, M.: Efficient and dependable overlay networks. In: IEEE International Symposium on Parallel and Distributed Processing (2008)
13. Botero, J.F., et al.: Energy efficient virtual network embedding. IEEE Commun. Lett. 16(5), 756–759 (2012)
14. Sun, G., et al.: The framework and algorithms for the survivable mapping of virtual network onto a substrate network. In: 2011 IETE Technical Review (2011)
15. Kong, B., et al.: Demonstration of application-driven network slicing and orchestration in optical/packet domains: on-demand vDC expansion for Hadoop MapReduce optimization. Opt. Express 26, 14066–14085 (2018)
16. Zhu, Z., et al.: Build to tenants' requirements: on-demand application-driven vSD-EON slicing. IEEE/OSA J. Opt. Commun. Networking 10(2), A206–A215 (2018)
17. Martini, B., et al.: Latency-aware composition of virtual functions in 5G. In: Proceedings of the 1st IEEE Conference Network Softwarization (NetSoft), April 2015
18. Fischer, A., et al.: Virtual network embedding: a survey. IEEE Commun. Surv. Tutorials 15, 1888–1906 (2013)
19. https://cloudify.co/

20. https://openbaton.github.io/
21. https://osm.etsi.org/
22. Vasseur, J.P., et al.: Path computation element (PCE) communication protocol (PCEP). In: IETF RFC 5440, March 2018

Optics for Disaggregating Data Centers and Disintegrating Computing

Nikos Terzenidis[1,2], Miltiadis Moralis-Pegios[1,2], Stelios Pitris[1,2],
Charoula Mitsolidou[1,2], George Mourgias-Alexandris[1,2], Apostolis Tsakyridis[1,2],
Christos Vagionas[1,2], Konstantinos Vyrsokinos[3], Theoni Alexoudi[1,2],
and Nikos Pleros[1,2(✉)]

[1] Department of Informatics, Aristotle University of Thessaloniki, Thessaloniki, Greece
npleros@csd.auth.gr
[2] Center for Interdisciplinary Research and Innovation, Balkan Center, Thessaloniki, Greece
[3] Department of Physics, Aristotle University of Thessaloniki, Thessaloniki, Greece

Abstract. We present a review of photonic Network-on-Chip (pNoC) architectures and experimental demonstrations, concluding to the main obstacles that still impede the materialization of these concepts. We also propose the employment of optics in chip-to-chip (C2C) computing architectures rather than on-chip layouts towards reaping their benefits while avoiding technology limitations on the way to many-core set-ups. We identify multisocket boards as the most prominent application area and present recent advances in optically enabled multisocket boards, revealing successful 40 Gb/s transceiver and routing capabilities via integrated photonics. These results indicate the potential to bring energy consumption down by more than 60% compared to current QuickPath Interconnect (QPI) protocol, while turning multisocket architectures into a single-hop low-latency setup for even more than 4 interconnected sockets, which form currently the electronic baseline.

Keywords: Computing architectures · Disintegrated computing ·
Network-on-Chip · Silicon photonics

1 Introduction

Workload parallelism and inter-core cooperation are forcing computing to rely at a constantly growing degree on data movement. That led to an upgraded role for the on-chip and off-chip communication infrastructures that support low-power and high-bandwidth interconnect technologies. This came almost simultaneously with the revolutionary advances triggered in the field of optical interconnects [1] and silicon photonics [2]. The last 20 years, optical interconnects were transformed to a mature technology for rack-to-rack [3] and board-to-board communications [4], supporting also the emerging concepts of disaggregated computing [5] and leaf-spine Data Center architectures [6]. However, the on-chip and chip-to-chip photonic technologies are still far away

© IFIP International Federation for Information Processing 2020
Published by Springer Nature Switzerland AG 2020
A. Tzanakaki et al. (Eds.): ONDM 2019, LNCS 11616, pp. 274–285, 2020.
https://doi.org/10.1007/978-3-030-38085-4_24

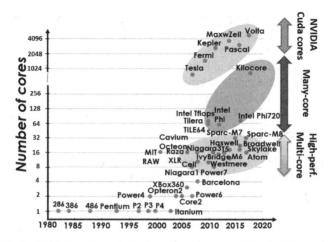

Fig. 1. Evolution from single- to many-core computing architectures.

from commercialization, despite the fact that various photonic Network-on-Chip (NoC) architectural concepts have already proposed [7].

In parallel, computing has also experienced some radical advances by turning from simple dual- and quad-core layouts into a highly heterogeneous environment both at chip- and system-level. As shown in Fig. 1, General-Purpose Graphic Processing Units (GP-GPUs) [8] can host more than 4000 CUDA cores on the same die, offering, however, only a 2 Gflop per core processing power. Processing power per core increases in manycore architectures, where up to 1000 cores can be employed [9]. However, when high-performance cores are required as in the case of Chip Multiprocessor (CMP) configurations [10] only a number of up to 32 cores can fit on the same die. The ideal scenario towards boosting processing power would of course imply a die that employs as many cores as a GPU does, but with core capabilities similar to the high-performance cores available in CMPs.

The number of high-performance cores performing as a single computational entity can scale to higher values only through multi-socket designs with 4 or maximum 8 interconnected sockets. The most recent top-class Intel Xeon 8-socket board yields a total number of up to 224 cores [11], requiring, of course, the use of high-bandwidth off-chip inter-socket interconnects. Going one step beyond the multisocket scheme, disintegration of processor dies has been coined in the recent years as a way to form macrochips that will synergize a high amount of high-performance cores, usually exploiting optical inter-die links [12]. This versatile environment at chip-scale suggests a diverse set of requirements that has to be met by optics, depending on the application. However, it creates also a new opportunity to rethink the role of optics in on- and off-chip computing, building upon the proven capabilities of optical hardware towards strengthening the compute architecture/technology co-design perspective.

In this paper, we attempt to investigate the new perspectives for optics in computing, reviewing the high-priority challenges faced currently by the computing industry and evaluating the credentials of state-of-the-art photonics to address them successfully. We provide a review of the work on photonic NoCs, highlighting the bottlenecks towards their materialization. Building on the state-of-art pNoC implementations [13–33], we conclude to a solid case for employing integrated photonics in inter-chip multisocket and disintegrated layouts rather than in Network-on-Chip (NoC) implementations, proposing at the same time a flat-topology chip-to-chip multisocket interconnect technology. We demonstrate experimental results for 40 Gb/s multi-socket boards (MSBs) operation, showing the potential to scale to >8-socket designs boosting the number of directly interconnected high-performance cores. Combined with the Hipoλaos Optical Packet Switch (OPS) that has been recently shown to support sub-μsec latencies [34], an optically-enabled rack-scale 256-socket disaggregated setting using a number of 32 interconnected optical 8-socket MSBs, could be implemented, forming in this way a powerful disaggregated rack-scale computing scheme.

The paper is organized as follows: Section 2 outlines the main challenges faced today in the computing landscape, providing also an overview of the research on pNoC architectures, concluding to their main limitations. Section 3 argues for the employment of optics in MSBs and provides experimental results on a 40 Gb/s flat-topology 8-node chip-to-chip (C2C) layout, using O-band integrated photonic transceiver and routing circuitry. Finally, Section 4 concludes the paper.

2   Overview of the PNoC Architectures

In order to define and refine the role of optics in the current computing landscape, it is critical to identify the main challenges currently experienced by the computing industry along the complete hierarchy from on-chip through multi-socket chip-to-chip computational modules. Figure 2 provides an illustrative overview of the main bandwidth, latency and energy needs for different on-chip and off-chip interconnect layers and data transfer operations in a 20×20 mm^2 processor chip fabricated by a 28 nm Integrated Circuit (IC) CMOS technology.

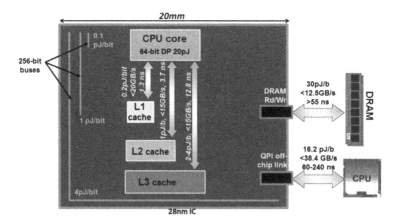

Fig. 2. Energy, bandwidth and latency requirements at different on-chip and off-chip communication needs. The size of every cache memory is bigger for larger capacity caches and their distance from the core is higher as the cache hierarchy increases.

A digital processing operation performed by the core consumes only 20 pJ/bit, but sending data across the chip requires 0.1 pJ/bit for a 1 mm long electrical link, 1 pJ/bit for a 10 mm link and goes up to 4 pJ/bit for a link length of 40 mm. When going off-chip in order to access DRAM, a high amount of 30 pJ/bit is consumed, while a chip-to-chip interconnect link like QPI requires 16.2 pJ/bit. Accessing L1 cache requires 0.2 pJ/bit, while L2 and L3 access requires 1 and 2–4 pJ/bit, respectively. Memory bandwidth reduces with increasing memory hierarchy, with L1 memory bandwidth approaching 20 GB/s and gradually decreasing when going to L2 and L3 access until an upper limit of 12.5 GB/s in the case of DRAM access. Latency follows the inverse path, starting from a high >55 nsec value when fetching from DRAM and gradually reducing with increased memory hierarchy, with L1 access latency being around 1.3 nsec. Having this overview, the main challenges today are formed around:

(i)   Interconnect energy consumption: A modern CPU consumes around 1.7 nJ per floating-point operation [35, 36], being 85x higher than the 20 pJ per floating point required for reaching the Exascale milestone within the gross 20 MW power envelope. Current architectures rely to a large degree on data movement, with electronic interconnects forming the main energy consuming factor in both on- and off-die setups [36]. With the energy of a reasonable standard-cell-based, double-precision fused-multiply add (DFMA) being only ~20 pJ, it clearly reveals that fetching operands is much more energy-consuming than computing on them [35, 36].

(ii) Memory bandwidth at an affordable energy envelope: The turn of computing into strongly heterogeneous and parallel settings have transformed memory throughput into a key factor for increasing processing power [35], with the most efficient way for improvement still being the use of wider memory buses and hierarchical caching. However, the highest memory bandwidth per core in modern multicore processors can hardly reach 20 GB/s [37], with L1 cache latency values still being >1 nsec.

(iii) Die area physical constraints: The need to avoid the latency and energy burden of DRAM access has enforced a rich on-chip L1, L2 and L3 cache hierarchy that typically occupies >40% of the chip real-estate [38], suggesting that almost half of the die area is devoted to memory and interconnects instead of processing functions.

(iv) Cache coherency-induced multi- and broadcasting traffic patterns: The need for cache coherency at intra-chip multi- and manycore setups, as well as at inter-chip multisocket systems, yields communication patterns with strong multi- and broad-cast characteristics, that have to be satisfied at a low- latency low-energy profile by the interconnect and network-on-chip infrastructure. Multibus ring topologies form a widely adopted multicast-enabling NoC architecture in current modern multi-core processors [39], but still the cache coherency control messages may often account for more than 30% of the total available bandwidth, which may reach even 65% in multisocket settings [40].

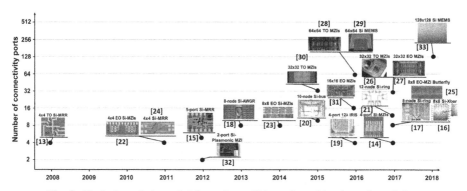

Fig. 3. Evolution of photonic Network-on-Chip and on-chip photonic switches.

The first attempts to exploit photonics for overcoming the on-chip bandwidth, energy and latency bottlenecks mainly inspired by the rapidly growing field of silicon photonics [2]. A number of breakthrough computing architectures relying on pNoC were demonstrated, proposing and utilizing novel silicon photonic transceiver and switching schemes. The pioneering work on photonic Torus [7] was followed by performance and energy advances in pNoC-enabled many-core designs, addressing even cache-coherency needs [41]. All this shaped a promising roadmap for the many-core computing architectures [7, 42–47]. At the same time, it revealed the requirements to be met by silicon photonics towards materializing their on-chip employment in practical NoC layouts: transceiver line-rates between 1–40 Gb/s and optoelectronic conversion energies between a few tens to a few hundreds of fJ/bit were considered in the vast majority of pNoC schemes [7, 42–47]. Driven by these efforts, photonic integration technology achieved the performance metrics required by pNoC architectures with silicon photonic modulators and SiGe Photo-diodes (PDs) operating at data rates up to 56 Gb/s exhibiting an energy efficiency less than a few tens of fJ/bit [48].

Figure 3 summirizes the most important pNoC and on-chip switches up to now [13–33]. Silicon switches have witnessed a remarkable progress yielding high-port connectivity arrangements with a variety of underlying physical mechanisms like the thermo-optic (TO), electro-optic (EO) and opto-mechanical effects [49], allowing for 32×32 EO Mach-Zehnder Interferometric (MZI)-based layouts [27], 64×64 TO MZI designs [28] and up to 128×128 Microelectromechanical switches (MEMS) [33].

All these demonstrations indicate that integrated photonics can now indeed offer the line-rate, energy, footprint and connectivity credentials required by pNoC-enabled manycore computing architectures. However, the realization of a manycore machine that employs a pNoC layer seems to be still an elusive target, with the main reason being easily revealed when inspecting the non-performance-related co-integration and integration level details of a pNoC-enabled computational setting. Manycore architectures necessitate the on-die integration of a few thousands of photonic structures [7], residing either on 3D integration schemes [50] or on monolithically co-integrated electronic and photonic structures, with transistors and optics being almost at the same layer [51]. However, 3D integration has still not managed to fulfil the great expectations that were raised and is still struggling to overcome a number of significant challenges [52]. On the other hand, monolithic integration has recently accomplished some staggering achievements reporting on real workload execution over an opto-electronic die with optical core-memory interconnection [51]. Nevertheless, this technology has still a long-way to go until reaching the complexity and functionality level required by a many-core pNoC design.

With almost the complete Photonic Integrated Circuit (PIC) technology toolkit being today available as discrete photonic chips, computing can reap the benefits of optics by employing photonics for off-die communication in (i) multisocket and (ii) disintegrated layouts. Both schemes can yield a high number of directly interconnected high-performance cores, unleashing solutions that cannot be met by electronics. At the same time, this approach is fully inline with the 2.5D integration scheme that employs discrete photonic and electronic chips on the same silicon interposer and has made tremendous progress in the recent years [53]. To this end, the employment of off-die communications via discrete photonic chips can form a viable near-term roadmap for the exploitation of photons in computational settings.

3   Optics for Multi-socket Boards

MSB systems rely currently on electrically interconnected sockets and can be classified in two categories:

(i)   "glueless" configurations, where point-to-point (P2P) interconnects like Intel's QPI [54] can offer high-speed, low-latency, any-to-any C2C communication for a number of 4 or 8 sockets. A 4-socket setup can yield a cache-coherent layout with directly interconnected sockets and latency values that range between 60–240 nsec. Scaling to 8-socket designs can only be met through dual-hop links, degrading latency performance but still comprising a very powerful cache-coherent computational setting: Intel's Xeon E7-8800 v4 was the first processor supporting 8-socket configurations and was by that time advertized as being suitable to "dominate the world" [55]. Figure 4(a) depicts a 4-socket (4S) and 8-socket (8S) layout, respectively, along with their respective interconnects. A typical interconnect like Intel's QPI operates at a 9.6 Gb/s line-rate and consumes 16.2 pJ/bit, while the total bandwidth communicated by every socket towards all three possible directions is 38.4 GB/s, i.e. 307.2 Gb/s [56].

(ii) "glued" configurations, where scaling beyond 8-socket layouts is accomplished by exploiting active switch-based setups, such as PCI-Express switches, in order to interconnect multiple 4- or 8-socket QPI "islands" [56].

With latency and bandwidth comprising the main performance criteria in releasing powerful MSB configurations, "glueless" layouts offer a clear latency-advantage over the "glued" counterparts avoiding by default the use of any intermediate switch. Photonics can have a critical role in transforming "glued" into "glueless" architectures even when the number of interconnected sockets is higher than 8, enabling single-hop configurations, with Fig. 4(b) illustrating how the basic flat-topology can be accomplished for the case of an 8-Socket layout. This has been initially conceived and proposed by

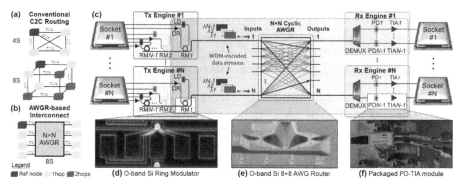

Fig. 4. (a) C2C routing in current electronic 4S and 8S MSBs, (b) Flat-topology 8S layout using AWGR-based routing, (c) proposed N × N AWGR-based optical C2C interconnect for MSB connectivity. Photonic integrated circuits employed as the basic building blocks in the 40 Gb/s experimental demonstration: (d) Ring Modulator, (e) 8 × 8 cyclic-frequency AWGR and (f) PD-TIA module. (blue-highlighted areas: part of the architecture demonstrated experimentally, white-highlighted areas: basic building blocks used for the demonstration).

UC Davis in their pioneering work on Flat-Topology computing architectures [57] via Arrayed Waveguide Grating Router (AWGR) interconnects, utilizing low-latency, non-blocking and all-to-all optical connectivity credentials enabled by their cyclic-routing wavelength properties. UC Davis demonstrated via gem5 simulations the significant execution time and energy savings accomplished over the electronic baseline [57], revealing also additional benefits when employing bit- parallel transmission and flexible bandwidth-allocation techniques. Experimental demonstrations of AWGR-based interconnection for compute node architectures were, however, constrained so far in the C-band regime, limiting their compatibility with electro-optic Printed Circuit Board (PCB) technology that typically offers a low waveguide loss figure at the O-band [58]. As such, AWGR-based experimental compute node interconnect findings were reported so far only in pNoC architectural approaches, using a rather small line-rate operation of 0.3 Gb/s [18].

The European H2020 project ICT-STREAMS is currently attempting to deploy the necessary silicon photonic and electro-optical PCB technology toolkit for realizing the AWGR-based MSB interconnect benefits in the O-band and at data rates up to 50 Gb/s [59]. It aims to exploit wavelength division multiplexing (WDM) Silicon photonics transceiver technology at the chip edge as the socket interface and a board-pluggable O-band silicon-based AWGR as the passive routing element, as shown in a generic N-socket architecture depicted in Fig. 4(c). Each socket is electrically connected to a WDM-enabled Tx optical engine equipped with N-1 laser diodes (LD), each one operating at a different wavelength. Every LD feeds a different Ring Modulator (RM) to imprint the electrical data sent from the socket to each one of the N-1 wavelengths, so that the Tx engine comprises finally N-1 RMs along with their respective RM drivers (DR). All RMs are implemented on the same optical bus to produce the WDM-encoded data stream of each socket. The data generated by each socket enters the input port of the AWGR and is forwarded to the respective destination output that is dictated by the carrier wavelength and the cyclic-frequency routing properties of the AWGR [57]. In this way, every socket can forward data to any of the remaining 7 sockets by simply modulating its electrical data onto a different wavelength via the respective RM, allowing direct single-hop communication between all sockets through passive routing. At every Rx engine, the incoming WDM-encoded data stream gets demultiplexed with a 1:(N-1) optical demultiplexer (DEMUX), so that every wavelength is received by a PD. Each PD is connected to a transimpedance amplifier (TIA) that provides the socket with the respective electrical signaling.

The AWGR-based interconnect scheme requires a higher number of transceivers compared to any intermediate switch solution, but this is exactly the feature that allows to combine WDM with AWGR's cyclic frequency characteristics towards enabling single-hop communication and retaining the lowest possible latency. Utilizing an 8 × 8 AWGR, the optically-enabled MSB can allow single-hop all-to-all interconnection between 8 sockets, while scaling the AWGR to 16 × 16 layouts can yield single-hop communication even between 16 sockets, effectively turning current "glued" into "glueless" designs. The ICT-STREAMS on-board MSB aims to incorporate 50 GHz single-mode O-band electro-optical PCBs [60], relying on the adiabatic coupling approach between silicon and polymer waveguides [61] for low-loss interfacing of the Silicon-Photonics (Si-Pho) transceiver and AWGR chips with the EO-PCB.

Next, the first 40 Gb/s experimental results of demonstration with the fiber-interconnected integrated photonic building blocks is presented, extending the recently presented operation of the 8-socket architecture at 25 Gb/s [62]. The main integrated transmitter, receiver and routing building blocks that were used, comprise three discrete chips, i.e. a Si-based RM [48], a Si-based 8 × 8 AWGR routing platform [63] and a co-packaged PD-TIA [64], which are depicted in Fig. 4(d), (e) and (f), respectively. The silicon O-band carrier-depletion micro-ring modulator is an all-pass ring resonator fabricated on imec's active platform with demonstrated 50 Gb/s modulation capabilities [48]. The RM can be combined with a recently developed low-power driver [65], leading to an energy efficiency of 1 pJ/bit at 40 Gb/s. For the routing platform, the demonstration relied on an O-band integrated silicon photonic 8 × 8 AWGR device [63] with 10 nm-channel spacing, a maximum channel loss non-uniformity of 3.5 dB and a channel crosstalk of 11 dB. Finally, the Rx engine employed a co-packaged uni-traveling InGaAs-InP PIN photodiode (PD) connected with a low-power TIA implemented in 0.13 μm SiGe BiCMOS [64]. The PD-TIA energy efficiency for operation at 40 Gb/s is 3.95 pJ/bit.

The energy efficiency of the proposed 40 Gb/s chip-to-chip (C2C) photonic link is estimated at 5.95 pJ/bit, assuming a 10% wall-plug efficiency for the external laser. This indicates that the proposed architecture has the credentials to lead to 63.3% reduction in energy compared to the 16.2 pJ/bit link energy efficiency of Intel QPI [56]. Figure 5 (a)–(h) show the eye diagrams of the signal at the 8 outputs of the AWGR coressponding to the 8 routing scenarios for all possible input-output port combination, indicating clear eye openings and successful routing at 40 Gb/s with ER values of 4.38 ± 0.31 dB and AM values of 2.3 ± 0.3 dB, respectively. The RM was electrically driven with a peak-to-peak voltage of 2.6 Vpp, while the applied reverse DC bias voltage was −2.5 V. The optical power of the CW signal injected at the RM input was 8 dBm, with the modulated data signal obtained at the RM output having an average optical power level of −6.3 dBm.

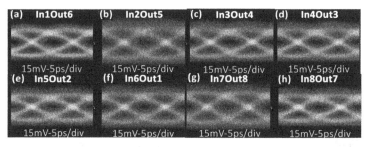

Fig. 5. Eye diagrams (a)–(h) after routing via the respective In#iOut#j I/O ports of the AWGR.

Going a step further, the proposed optically-enabled MSBs can be beneficially employed in rack-scale disaggregated systems when equipped with an additional transceiver lane for dealing with the off-board traffic and are combined with the recently demonstrated Hipoλaos high-port switch architecture [34]. Recently in [66], it was shown that rack-scale disaggregation among a 256-node system can be successfully accomplished for a variety of communication patterns with an ultra-low mean latency value of <335 nsec for 10 Gb/s data rates. The disaggregated architecture are expected to improve drastically when scaling Hipoλaos data-rates to 40 Gb/s, making this compatible with the 40 Gb/s silicon photonic transmitter reported in this paper.

4 Conclusion

We reviewed the pNoC-enabled manycore architectures proposed over the last decade. After analyzing the co-integration aspects as the main limitation for the realization of pNoC-based computing, we have defined a new role for photonics in the landscape of computing related to off-die communication. We discussed how optics can yield single-hop low-latency multisocket boards for even more than 4 interconnected sockets, demonstrating experimental results for 40 Gb/s C2C interconnection in a 8-node setup via integrated photonic transmitter and routing circuits. Combining 8-socket optical boards with a Hipoλaos optical packet switch shown in [34], photonics can yield a powerful 256-node compute disaggregated system with latency below the sub-μs threshold considered for memory disaggregation environments.

Acknowledgment. This work is supported by the H2020 projects ICT-STREAMS (688172) and L3MATRIX (688544).

References

1. Bergman, K.: Photonic networks for intra-chip, inter-chip, and box-to-box interconnects in high performance computing. In: European Conference on Optical Communication (ECOC), Cannes, France (2006)
2. Lipson, M.: Guiding, modulating, and emitting light on Silicon-challenges and opportunities. J. Lightw. Techn. **23**(12), 4222–4238 (2005)

3. Intel SiP 100G PSM4 Optical Tx. https://www.intel.com/content/www/us/en/architecture-and-technology/silicon-photonics/optical-transceiver-100g-psm4-qsfp28-brief.html. Accessed 12 Apr 2019

4. Luxtera 2x100G-PSM4 OptoPHY Product Family. http://www.luxtera.com/embedded-optics/. Accessed 12 Apr 2019

5. Zervas, N.G., Yuan, H., Saljoghei, A., Chen, Q., Mishra, V.: Optically disaggregated data centers with minimal remote memory latency: technologies, architectures, and resource allocation. J. Opt. Commun. Netw. **10**(2), A270–A285 (2018)

6. Bielski, M., et al.: dReDBox: materializing a full-stack rack-scale system prototype of a next-generation disaggregated datacenter. In: 2018 Design, Automation & Test Conference & Exhibition (DATE) (2018)

7. Shacham, A., Bergman, K., Carloni, L.: Photonic networks-on-chip for future generations of chip multiprocessors. Trans. Comput. **57**(9), 1246–1260 (2008)

8. Kider, J., NVIDIA Fermi architecture. http://www.seas.upenn.edu/~cis565/Lectures2011/Lecture16_Fermi.pdf. Accessed 12 Apr 2019

9. Bohnenstiehl, B., et al.: KiloCore: a 32-nm 1000-Processor computational array. IEEE J. Solid State Circ. **52**(4), 891–902 (2017)

10. Intel Xeon Platinum 8180 Processor. https://ark.intel.com/products/120496. Accessed 12 Apr 2019

11. Supermicro Super Server 7089P-TR4T. www.supermicro.com/products/system/7U/7089/SYS-7089P-TR4T.cfm. Accessed 12 Apr 2019

12. Raj, K., et al.: "Macrochip" computer systems enabled by silicon photonic interconnects. In: Optoelectronic Interconnects and Component Integration IX (2010)

13. Sherwood-Droz, N., et al.: Optical 4 × 4 hitless silicon router for optical networks-on-chip (NoC). Opt. Express **16**(20), 15915 (2008)

14. Jia, H., et al.: Four-port optical switch for fat-tree photonic network-on-chip. J. Lightw. Technol. **35**(15), 3237–3241 (2017)

15. Yang, L., et. al.: Optical routers with ultra-low power consumption for photonic networks-on-chip. In: Proceedings Conference on Lasers and Electro-Optics (CLEO), San Jose, CA (2012)

16. Fan, G., Orobtchouk, R., Han, B., Li, Y., Li, H.: 8 × 8 wavelength router of optical network on chip. Opt. Express **25**(20), 23677 (2017)

17. Zhang, C., Zhang, S., Peters, J., Bowers, J.: 8 × 8 × 40 Gbps fully integrated silicon photonic network on chip. Optica **3**(7), 785 (2016)

18. Yu, R., et al.: A scalable silicon photonic chip-scale optical switch for high performance computing systems. Opt. Express **21**(26), 32655 (2013)

19. Testa, F., et al.: Design and implementation of an integrated reconfigurable silicon photonics switch matrix in IRIS project. J. Sel. Topics Quant. Electr. **22**(6), 155–168 (2016)

20. Dong, P., et al.: Reconfigurable 100 Gb/s silicon photonic network-on-chip. In: Proceedings of Optical Fiber Communication Conference (OFC) (2014)

21. Gambini, F., et al.: Experimental demonstration of a 24-port packaged multi-microring network-on-chip in silicon photonic platform. Opt. Express **25**(18), 22004 (2017)

22. Yang, M., et al.: Non-Blocking 4 × 4 electro-optic silicon switch for on-chip photonic networks. Opt. Express **19**(1), 47 (2010)

23. Lee, B., et al.: Monolithic silicon integration of scaled photonic switch fabrics, CMOS logic, and device driver circuits. J. Lightw. Technol. **32**(4), 743–751 (2014)

24. Hu, T., et al.: Wavelength-selective 4 × 4 nonblocking silicon optical router for networks-on-chip. Opt. Lett. **36**(23), 4710 (2011)

25. Dupuis, N., et al.: Nanosecond-scale Mach-Zehnder-based CMOS photonic switch fabrics. J. Lightw. Technol. **35**, 1 (2016)

26. Dumais, P., et al.: Silicon photonic switch subsystem with 900 monolithically integrated calibration photodiodes and 64-fiber package. J. Lightw. Technol. **36**(2), 233–238 (2018)
27. Qiao, L., Tang, W., Chu, T.: 32 × 32 silicon electro-optic switch with built-in monitors and balanced-status units. Sci. Rep. **7**(1), 1 (2017)
28. Qiao, L., Tang, W., Chu, T.: Ultra-large-scale silicon optical switches. In: Proceedings 2016 IEEE International Conference on Group IV Photonics (GFP), Shanghai (2016)
29. Seok, T.J.: 64 × 64 Low-loss and broadband digital silicon photonic MEMS switches. In: Proceedings European Conference on Optical Communication (ECOC), Valencia (2015)
30. Tanizawa, K., et al.: Ultra-compact 32 × 32 strictly-non-blocking Si-wire optical switch with fan-out LGA interposer. Opt. Express **23**(13), 17599 (2015)
31. Lu, L., et al.: 16 × 16 non-blocking silicon optical switch based on electro-optic Mach-Zehnder interferometers. Opt. Express **24**(9), 9295 (2016)
32. Papaioannou, S., et al.: Active plasmonics in WDM traffic switching applications. Sci. Rep. **2**(1), 652 (2012)
33. Kwon, K., et al.: 128 × 128 silicon photonic MEMS switch with scalable row/column addressing. In: Proceedings Conference on Lasers and Electro-Optics (2018)
34. Terzenidis, N., Moralis-Pegios, M., Mourgias-Alexandris, G., Vyrsokinos, K., Pleros, N.: High-port low-latency optical switch architecture with optical feed-forward buffering for 256-node disaggregated data centers. Opt. Express **26**, 8756–8766 (2018)
35. Parker, S.: The evolution of GPU accelerated computing. In: Proceedings Extreme Scale Computing, IL, USA, 29 July 2013
36. Dally, B.: Challenges for future computing systems. In: Proceedings HiPEAC 2015, Amsterdam, NL (2015)
37. Saini, S., et al.: Performance evaluation of the intel sandy bridge based NASA pleiades using scientific and engineering applications. NAS Technical Report: NAS-2015-05
38. Borkar, S., Chien, A.A.: The future of microprocessors. Commun. ACM **54**(5), 67–77 (2011)
39. Kumashikar, M., Bendi, S., Nimmagadda, S., Deka, A., Agarwal, A.: 14 nm broadwell Xeon® processor family: design methodologies and optimizations. In: Proceedings 2017 IEEE Asian Solid-State Circuits Conference (A-SSCC) (2017)
40. Bull, S.A.S.: An efficient server architecture for the virtualization of business-critical applications. White paper 2012. https://docuri.com/download/bullion-efficient-server-architecture-for-virtualization_59c1dc51f581710b28689168_pdf. Accessed 12 Apr 2019
41. Kurian, G., et al.: ATAC. In: International Conference on Parallel Architectures and Compilation techniques - PACT 2010 (2010)
42. Chen, C., Joshi, A.: Runtime management of laser power in silicon-photonic multibus NoC architecture. J. Sel. Top. Quant. Electr. **19**(2), 3700713–3700713 (2013)
43. Li, Z., Qouneh, A., Joshi, M., Zhang, W., Fu, X., Li, T.: Aurora: a cross-layer solution for thermally resilient photonic network-on-chip. Trans. VLSI Syst. **23**(1), 170–183 (2015)
44. Bahirat, S., Pasricha, S.: METEOR. ACM Trans. Embed. Comput. Syst. **13**(3), 1–33 (2014)
45. Wang, X., Gu, H., Yang, Y., Wang, K., Hao, Q.: RPNoC: a ring-based packet-switched optical network-on-chip. Photonics Technol. Lett. **27**(4), 423–426 (2015)
46. Gu, H., Chen, K., Yang, Y., Chen, Z., Zhang, B.: MRONoC: a low latency and energy efficient on chip optical interconnect architecture. Photonics J. **9**(1), 1–12 (2017)
47. Werner, S., Navaridas, J., Luján, M.: Efficient sharing of optical resources in low-power optical networks-on-chip. J. Opt. Commun. Netw. **9**(5), 364–374 (2017)
48. Pantouvaki, M., et al.: Active components for 50 Gb/s NRZ-OOK optical interconnects in a silicon photonics platform. J. Lightw. Technolo. **35**(4), 631–638 (2017)
49. Lee, B.: Silicon photonic switching: technology and architecture. In: 2017 European Conference on Optical Communication (2017)
50. Yoo, S.J.B., Guan, B., Scott, R.: Heterogeneous 2D/3D photonic integrated microsystems. Microsyst. Nanoeng. **2**(1), 16030 (2016)

51. Sun, C., et al.: Single-chip microprocessor that communicates directly using light. Nature **528**(7583), 534–538 (2015)
52. Li, C., et al.: Chip scale 12-channel 10 Gb/s optical transmitter and receiver subassemblies based on wet etched silicon interposer. J. Lightw. Technol. **35**(15), 3229–3236 (2017)
53. Zhang, X., et al.: Heterogeneous 25D integration on through silicon interposer. Appl. Phys. Rev. **2**(2), 021308 (2015)
54. Intel: An Introduction to the Intel QuickPath Interconnect. https://www.intel.com/content/www/us/en/io/quickpath-technology/quick-path-interconnect-introduction-paper.html. Accessed 12 Apr 2019
55. Intel: Intel® Xeon® Processor E7-8800/4800/2800 Families. https://www.intel.com/content/www/us/en/processors/xeon/xeon-e7-8800-4800-2800-families-vol-2-datasheet.html. Accessed 12 Apr 2019
56. Maddox, R., Singh, G., Safranek, R.: Weaving High Performance Multiprocessor Fabric. Intel Press, Hillsboro (2009)
57. Grani, P., Proietti, R., Cheung, S., Yoo, S.J.B.: Flat-topology high-throughput compute node with AWGR-based optical-interconnects. J. Lightw. Technol. **34**(12), 2959–2968 (2016)
58. Sugama, A., Kawaguchi, K., Nishizawa, M., Muranaka, H., Arakawa, Y.: Development of high-density single-mode polymer waveguides with low crosstalk for chip-to-chip optical interconnection. Opt. Express **21**(20), 24231 (2013)
59. Kanellos, G.T., Pleros, N.: WDM mid-board optics for chip-to-chip wavelength routing interconnects in the H2020 ICT-STREAMS. In: SPIE, February 2017
60. Lamprecht, T., et al.: EOCB-platform for integrated photonic chips direct-on-board assembly within Tb/s applications. In: Proceedings 68th Electronic Components and Technology Conference (ECTE), pp. 854–858 (2018)
61. Dangel, R., et al.: Polymer waveguides enabling scalable low-loss adiabatic optical coupling for silicon photonics. J. Sel. Top. Quant. Electr. **24**(4), 1–11 (2018)
62. Moralis-Pegios, M., et al: Chip-to-chip interconnect for 8-socket direct connectivity using 25 Gb/s O-band integrated transceiver and routing circuits. In: ECOC, Rome, Italy (2018)
63. Pitris, S., et al.: Silicon photonic 8 × 8 cyclic arrayed waveguide grating router for O-band on-chip communication. Opt. Express **26**(5), 6276–6284 (2018)
64. Moeneclaey, B., et al.: A 40-Gb/s transimpedance amplifier for optical links. IEEE Photonics Technol. Lett. **27**(13), 1375–1378 (2015)
65. Ramon, H., et al.: Low-power 56 Gb/s NRZ microring modulator driver in 28 nm FDSOI CMOS. IEEE Photonics Technol. Lett. **30**(5), 467–470 (2018)
66. Terzenidis, N., et al.: Dual-layer locality-aware optical interconnection architecture for latency-critical resource disaggregation environments. In: International Conference on Optical Network Design and Modeling (ONDM), May 2019

Simplifying Optical DCN Fabrics with Blocking Space Switching and Wavelength-Constrained WDM

Konstantinos Kontodimas[1][(✉)], Kostas Christodoulopoulos[2],
and Emmanouel Varvarigos[1]

[1] School of Electrical & Computer Engineering, National Technical University of Athens,
Athens, Greece
vmanos@central.ntua.gr
[2] Nokia Bell Labs, Stuttgart, Germany

Abstract. The introduction of all-optical switching in data center interconnection networks (DCN) is key to addressing some of the shortcomings of state-of-the-art electronic switched solutions. Limitations in the port count, reconfiguration speed and cost of optical switches, however, require novel optical switching and DCN designs. We present the concept of a simplified DCN fabric that relies on a lean optical switch design of limited but scalable functionality that offers high reconfiguration speeds, real-time scheduling, efficient control and low equipment cost. To achieve these objectives, the proposed architecture relaxes the usual non-blocking switching requirements but opts for switching modules that are constrained in terms of the achievable space and wavelength input-output configurations. We analytically compare the functionality and complexity of the simplified fabric with those of a non-blocking switch. We evaluate the throughput performance of the simplified DCN fabric and compare it to that of other fabrics with a different level of functionality and centralized control.

Keywords: Time-wavelength-space division multiplexing · Blocking design · Slotted and synchronous operation · Dynamic resource allocation, scheduling · Matrix decomposition

1 Introduction

The widespread availability of cloud applications to billions of users and the emergence of software-, platform- and infrastructure-as-a-service models rely on Data Centers (DCs). As traffic within a DC (east-west) is higher than incoming/outgoing (south-north) traffic [1], DC interconnection networks (DCN) play a crucial role to the overall DC performance. State-of-the-art DCNs are based on electronic switches connected in Fat-Tree topologies using optical fibers, with electro-opto-electrical transformation at each hop [2]. However, Fat-Trees tend to underutilize resources, require a large number of cables and switches, suffer from poor scalability and upgradability and exhibit high energy consumption [3].

© IFIP International Federation for Information Processing 2020
Published by Springer Nature Switzerland AG 2020
A. Tzanakaki et al. (Eds.): ONDM 2019, LNCS 11616, pp. 286–298, 2020.
https://doi.org/10.1007/978-3-030-38085-4_25

The introduction of optical switching in DCN is key to resolving these shortcomings. Many recent works proposed hybrid electrical/optical switched DCN [4–13]. However, optical switches have high reconfiguration times, posing barriers in their applicability in DCNs.

The first barrier in using all-optical DCN comes from the cost and reconfiguration speed of (full) crossbar optical switches. The trade-off between the radix and reconfiguration speed is not adequate for large scale DCNs, and the switches are expensive.

The second barrier comes from the need to compute schedules to allocate the optical resources which is infeasible to perform optimally or even sub-optimally in real-time. NEPHELE [12] studied a distributed crossbar optical network fabric using WSSs interconnected in several wavelength-division multiplexing (WDM) fiber rings. This is promising, as reconfiguration speed is improved, but the architecture is still not scalable as creating long rings (which essentially replace the optical crossbars) induces losses and makes synchronization harder.

The third barrier comes from the control plane. Typically, centralized control is assumed in hybrid electrical/optical DCNs, following the SDN paradigm [6, 10, 12], where a central controller/scheduler collects monitored traffic and reconfigures the optical switches accordingly. Such closed-loop operation is inefficient, since the control plane induces high latency, requires tight synchronization of the optical switches with each other and with the scheduler, and has difficulties in following the DC traffic which is rather dynamic with time [3]. In [14], Patronas et al. showed that centralized scheduling calculations can be accelerated, but the signaling overhead identifying flows, monitoring, communicating configurations to the optical switches) remains hard to scale.

In this paper we investigate approaches for overcoming these shortcomings by departing from prior optical DCN architectures in the following ways:

(a) By designing custom lean but constrained (in their space- wavelength-time switching capabilities) optical switches, we call them SLIM, that use a small fixed set of switching states [15], supporting much fewer than the $(nW)!$ input-output configurations/mappings that are possible for fabrics that operate as distributed crossbars of n radix and W wavelengths. The custom switches use hard-wired interconnection mappings and the number of their internal switching components may vary. Because of their simplified internal design, they could render a great increase in terms of ports-speed capabilities. Moreover, the cost of these optical switches is expected to be substantially lower. The drawback is of course the limited (blocking) functionality of these SLIM switches, which has to be overcome through intelligent design of the scheduling architecture of the overall DCN.

(b) By reducing the level of centralized control with the development of appropriate algorithms to allocate the resources sub- but near-optimally and in real time. As the switches support only a few input-output matchings, scheduling complexity decreases. The freedom of non-blocking switches is not really needed and (b) it cannot be exploited in real-time because of the need to choose among too many configurations.

Deterministic round robin scheduling (RRS) is a scheduling policy that statically rotates though all source-destination assignments. For n radix, this policy supports $O(n)$ input-output matchings and is sufficient to serve well uniform traffic patterns and it doesn't require centralized control. However, traffic in DC is not generally uniform. For non-uniform traffic, we investigate the scheduling approach of an adaptive Birkhoff von Neumann decomposition method (referred to as A-BvN) that produces the schedules by taking into account the traffic demands. In terms of signaling and scheduling complexity, the level of centralized control required by A-BvN is lower than the case of full crossbar decomposition, since the complexity depends on the number of supported input-output matchings. In what follows we distinguish a DCN fabric/architecture as either non-blocking or blocking, depending on whether it can implement any one-to-one input-output configuration/permutation or it supports a reduced set of input-output matchings.

2   A Lean Non-crossbar Switch Design

2.1   Shift Shuffle

First of all, we define the *shift shuffle*. A k-shift shuffle $SS_k(n)$ is a static interconnection mapping between n input and n output ports, according to the function $SS_k(n) : i \rightarrow (i + k - 2) \bmod n + 1$, for $1 \leq i \leq n$ and $k \geq 1$. In particular, the mapping is a k-shift cyclic permutation.

2.2   The Selector and De-Selector Element

In [15] the authors proposed a switch design using a monolithic gang-switched module as its elementary building block. The gang-switched module is implemented with MEMS beam-steering micromirrors. In our work, we call a slightly modified version of this module as *Selector Element*. A Selector Element $SE(n, m)$ has n space inputs and $n \cdot m$ space outputs and can be set in one of m states. For state i, with $i = 1, 2, \ldots, m$, input signal j, is forwarded to output $(i - 1) \cdot n + j$. Conversely, we define a complementary module called *De-Selector Element*. A De-Selector Element $DSE(n, m)$ has $n \cdot m$ space inputs, n space outputs and can be set in one between m states. For state i with $1 \leq i \leq m$, input signal j with $1 \leq j \leq n \cdot m$ is forwarded to output $(i - 1) \cdot n + j \bmod m$. Since the implementation of (De-)Selector Elements is MEMS-based, the number of states is the number of tilting positions (i.e. m), which affects the reconfiguration speed. Note that each input of an $SE(n, m)$ (or $DSE(n, m)$) may carry W wavelengths, with all wavelengths of a (space) input carried to the same (space) output.

2.3   The SLIM Switch as a Concept

The concept of SLIM switch is based on the idea of *active* Selector Elements and *fixed* (hard-wired) k-shift shuffles. We differentiate from the work proposed by the authors of [15] by allowing WDM multiplexing and a variable number of Selector Elements, which can be considered as a generalization of the switch design of [15]. The number of Selector Elements is configurable, defining the *complexity* of the SLIM switch. A SLIM switch is defined by the tuple (M, C) and is a two-stage switch, consisting of $SE(M, M)$ modules in the input stage and $DSE(M, C)$ modules in the output stage, with C being the number of (D)SE modules of a stage (both input and output stages have the same number of (D)SEs). In other words, $N = M \cdot C$ is the total number of fiber (space) inputs to the switch, which are divided in C groups, each of M fibers, and each group forms the inputs of a $SE(M, M)$ module of stage. Each of the N outputs of the input stage are connected to all the inputs of the output stage through a fixed/hard-wired interconnection pattern.

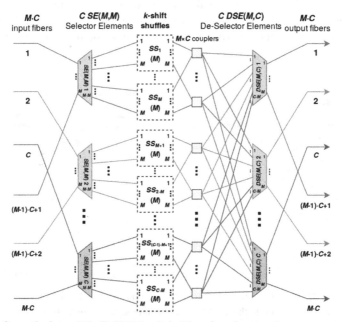

Fig. 1. The figure depicts a (M, C) SLIM switch. There is an input and an output stage: the input stage consists of C $SE(M, M)$ and the outputs stage consists of $DSE(M, C)$. There are M k-shift shuffles $SS_k(M)$ for $1 \leq k \leq M \cdot C$. The $M \cdot C$ input fibers are evenly distributed between the C SEs. Each SE of the first stage forwards M fibers to one between the $\cdot C$ $SS_k(M)$, according to its state. The fibers are then combined according to the figure and broadcasted to all DSEs.

Each of the N outputs of the input stage are connected to $M \times C$ couplers through a fixed/hard-wired $(M^2 \cdot C) \times (M^2 \cdot C)$ [i.e., $(N \cdot M) \times (N \cdot M)$] interconnection pattern. Then the couplers are connected to the inputs of the output stage through a $(M \cdot C^2) \times (M \cdot C^2)$ [i.e., $(N \cdot C) \times (N \cdot C)$] interconnection pattern, as shown in general in Fig. 1. Each group k of M consecutive outputs of the SEs implements a distinct k-shift shuffle $SS_k(M)$. The fibers that are shuffled together are distributed between M couplers. Since only one group output of an SE contains active fibers, there are no conflicts in the couplers. Then, each coupler broadcasts its active signal to all DSEs. Depending on their states, the DSEs select to forward the signals originating by a particular SE.

3 A DCN Architecture with Non-crossbar Switches

3.1 The Architecture Specifications

The DCN model combines Electronic Packet Switching (EPS) and Optical Circuit Switching (OCS). The DCN architecture (Fig. 2) is organized in *racks/ToRs, PODs* and *SLIM switches*. Each rack hosts a ToR (top-of-rack) switch which is responsible for intra-rack and inter-rack communication of that particular rack. The ToR switch supports (a) EPS for intra-rack and (b) OCS for inter-rack communication using *tunable transmitters*.

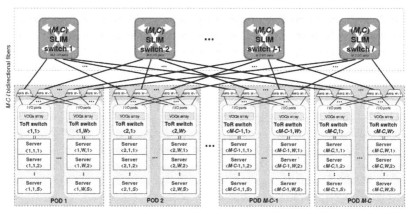

Fig. 2. There are $M \cdot C$ PODs, W racks/ToRs in each POD and W used wavelengths. The parameters M and C, also characterize the SLIM switches and they determine the number of switching patterns which are supported by the fabric. S is the number of servers/racks, I is the number of SLIM switches. Each server is identified by a $\langle p, w, s \rangle$ and each ToR/rack by a $\langle p, w \rangle$, where the p is the index of the POD, w is the index of a rack inside a POD and s is the index of a server inside a rack, with $1 \leq p \leq M \cdot C$, $1 \leq w \leq W$ and $1 \leq s \leq S$. The ToRs use I ports directed to the SLIM switches. All links imply bidirectional fibers. The servers in the same rack communicate with each other through EPS.

The racks are grouped in PODs (points of delivery). The racks in the same POD communicate with the racks of only one other POD, at the same time. The network carries WDM signal with wavelengths equal to the number of racks per POD. Each ToR listens to a wavelength, mitigating the conflicts among racks of the same POD. The tunable transmitters use the wavelength of the destination ToR. The ToRs belonging to the same POD (de)multiplex signals with arrayed waveguide gratings (AWGs). There are fibers for all switch-POD pair. A ToR switch dedicates an incoming and an outgoing port to a particular switch.

The racks communicate in a slotted manner, resembling the operation of a large TDMA switch with the ports of the ToRs being their input/output ports. The network maintains the timeslot component of TDMA, with the difference that slots are not statically assigned to circuits (ToR-to-ToR communications) but dynamically by a central scheduler according to traffic requirements. Deploying multiple SLIM switches extends the capacity. We generalize the timeslots to *generalized slots*.

Resource allocation is performed in *periods* of a number of timeslots; this enables important savings through the aggregation and suppression of control information and also helps absorb traffic peaks, reducing the dynamicity of resource allocation.

The parameters of a blocking DCN architecture are M, W, C, S, I and T. W is the number of racks/ToRs per POD, the number of wavelengths that the SLIM switch is able to carry, as long as the number of inputs (outputs) of the AWG (de)multiplexers. S is the number of servers per rack, I is the number of SLIM switches as long as the number of incoming/outgoing ports of the OCS interfaces of the ToR switches and their corresponding tunable transmitters. The number of PODs of the DCN is defined by the product $M \cdot C$. The factors M and C define the configuration of the SLIM switches. Finally, T is the number of timeslots of a period for which the scheduling decisions are made. Therefore, the number of racks/ToRs (size of the network) is $M \cdot W \cdot C$ racks, or equivalently $M \cdot W \cdot C \cdot S$ servers.

DCN's control is handled through a SDN-enabled *control plane*. The period is divided to three phases: *monitoring*, *scheduling* and *reconfiguration*. During monitoring phase, the control plane reads the traffic demands from the ToRs. Then, a batch scheduling is performed in order to decide which source-destination rack pairs take place at each generalized slot. In the last phase, the control plane disseminates the schedule to the switches. The ToRs use Virtual Output Queues (VOQs) in order to mitigate head-of-line blocking (HOL). The number of VOQs in each ToR switch is $M \cdot W \cdot C$. Using a SDN-enabled control plane also allows application-aware scheduling. Such option would further reduce the control cycle inefficiencies by eliminating the monitoring overhead altogether.

3.2 A Blocking DCN Fabric

The number of supported switching patterns by a switching fabric defines its *functionality*. In order to express a supported switching pattern by a blocking DCN fabric during a particular timeslot, we use matrix notation from linear algebra. In particular, it is expressed through a (M, W, C) *permutation matrix* (PM), defined as a $M \cdot W \cdot C \times M \cdot W \cdot C$ matrix $\mathbf{P} = \begin{bmatrix} p_{ij} \end{bmatrix}$ with $1 \leq i, j \leq M \cdot W \cdot C$ and $p_{ij} \in \{0, 1\}$ that can be partitioned into $(M \cdot C)^2$ $W \times W$ submatrices (blocks) $\mathbf{P}_{rc}$, with $1 \leq r, c \leq M \cdot C$. r and c denote the indices of row and column partitions. A (M, W, C) PM satisfies the following constraints:

- C_1: Each row can have at most one entry set to '1'.
- C_2: Each column can have at most one entry set to '1'.
- C_3: If a submatrix is non-zero $\mathbf{P}_{rc}$, for $1 \leq r, c \leq M \cdot C$, a row partition $r' = (r + k \cdot C - 1) \bmod (M \cdot C) + 1$ can only have one non-zero submatrix in position $c' = (c + k \cdot C - 1) \bmod (M \cdot C) + 1$, for $1 \leq k \leq M$.
- C_4: If a submatrix $\mathbf{P}_{rc}$ is non-zero, for $1 \leq r, c \leq M \cdot C$, a column partition $c' = (c + k \cdot C - 1) \bmod (M \cdot C) + 1$ can only have one non-zero submatrix in position $r' = (r + k \cdot C - 1) \bmod (M \cdot C) + 1$, for $1 \leq k \leq M$.

- C_5: A submatrix $\mathbf{P}_{rc}$, for $1 \leq r, c \leq M \cdot C$, can have non-zero entries only in one diagonal between its main diagonal and the ones parallel to the main diagonal.
- A (M, W, C) PM generalizes the definition of permutation matrix. C_1 and C_2 are describe that a single source ToR can only be connected to at most one destination ToR vice versa. For C_3, C_4 and C_5 let us consider the following expressions. For $1 \leq r, c, r', c' \leq M \cdot C$:

$$r' = (r + k \cdot C - 1) \mod (M \cdot C) + 1 \tag{1}$$

$$c' = (c + l \cdot C - 1) \mod (M \cdot C) + 1 \tag{2}$$

Figure 3 in the next page, shows submatrix dependencies. C_5 forces the usage of only W cyclic matching between the ToRs of a given pair of PODs. This constraint doesn't reduce equipment of the DCN, but it reduces the scheduling complexity and the reconfiguration message overhead. There are various similar formal definitions regarding the distinction between a non-blocking and a blocking switching fabric. In our case, it is determined by whether there exist any switching patterns satisfying the trivial constraints C_1 and C_2 that cannot happen, or not.

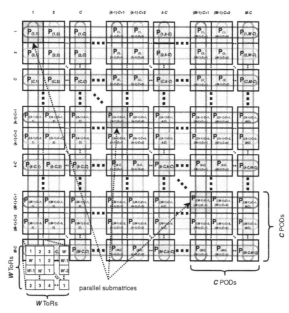

Fig. 3. The figure depicts a (M, W, C) permutation matrix, in submatrix level. The numbers index the row and column partitions of the matrix. Given a particular submatrix, all submatrices that belong to row (column) partitions that share the same color with the row (column) partitions of the former are *row-dependent* (*column-dependent*) to the former. The highlighted submatrices are examples of *parallel* submatrices. The inner entries submatrix $\mathbf{P}_{(M \cdot C, 1)}$ with the same number show which ones can mutually have non-zero entries.

For a network with size $M \cdot W \cdot C$ a non-blocking fabric supports all $(M \cdot W \cdot C)!$ switching patterns, deriving from all permutations of size $M \cdot W \cdot C$, while a blocking fabric supports less. The limited functionality of fabric applies when $W > 1$ or $M > 1$.

Theorem 1: A (M, C) SLIM switch carrying W wavelengths supports $C! \cdot \left(M \cdot W^M\right)^C$ switching patterns.

The proof is omitted due to space limitations.

4   Blocking VS Non-blocking Complexity

4.1   Control Message Complexity Comparison

The control message complexity is a factor that burdens the efficiency of a closed-loop non-blocking DCN. In a blocking fabric, at each period of T timeslots, the whole traffic matrix is required by the control plane, as in the case of I large crossbar switches of size $M \cdot W \cdot C$. Therefore, the monitoring complexity is $\Theta\left((M \cdot W \cdot C)^2\right)$. However, the complexity of the control messages for the reconfiguration phase is reduced. The non-blocking fabric induces a complexity of $O(T \cdot I \cdot M \cdot W \cdot C)$ due to the fact that each one of the source ToRs has to be informed for their scheduled destination ToR, for all non-zero generalized slots of a period which are upper-bounded by $T \cdot I$. On the other hand, the complexity for the messages in a blocking DCN is reduced to $O(T \cdot I \cdot M \cdot C)$. This is due to C_5 constraint, described in Sect. 3.2, which dictates only cyclic assignments of wavelengths to the ToRs that belong to the same POD. Therefore the wavelength assignment can be sufficiently described just by a scalar with a value ranging between 1 and W.

4.2   Scheduling Complexity Comparison

In this section we investigate the scheduling complexity. Let's use the notation of the *traffic matrices*. A traffic matrix $\mathbf{D} = \left[d_{ij}\right]$ is a $M \cdot C \cdot W \times M \cdot C \cdot W$ matrix, where each entry d_{ij} is the total number of *cells* that need to be transmitted from ToR switch i to ToR switch j. As cells, we define the normalized demands in bandwidth, with the respect to the capacity provided by a generalized slot. A traffic matrix can be partitioned into $(M \cdot C)^2$ $W \times W$ submatrices $\mathbf{D}_{r,c}$ for $1 \leq r, c \leq M \cdot C$. A traffic matrix is transferred to the control plane at each period consisting of T timeslots, describing the accumulated traffic of that period.

We define the *critical sum* h of the traffic matrix $\mathbf{D}$ as $h \triangleq \max\left\{\sum_{i'=1}^{M \cdot C \cdot W} d_{i'j}, \sum_{j'=1}^{M \cdot C \cdot W} d_{ij'}\right\}, \forall i, j$ where $1 \leq i, j \leq M \cdot C \cdot W$. According to a well-known theorem (shown in [17], p. 57), in order to decompose a traffic matrix $\mathbf{D}$ with critical sum h into a sum of permutation matrices, a scheduler would need to iteratively execute a maximum cardinality matching algorithm for h times. In a non-blocking fabric, the optimal scheduling would be handled through a Birkhoff von Neumann (BvN) decomposition algorithm. We refer to the BvN decomposition algorithm that is applied to a non-blocking fabric as EXACT [18]. Such decomposition gives a sequence of permutations of maximum cardinality, while the constraints described in Sect. 3.2 hold. Using the Hopcroft-Karp [16] algorithm, the complexity of finding a maximum matching for a dense matrix is $O((M \cdot W \cdot C)^{5/2})$. We consider a traffic matrix as *admissible* if its critical sum is $h \leq T \cdot I$. The traffic described by an admissible traffic matrix can be served with the capacity of $T \cdot I$ generalized slots of a period. For an admissible traffic matrix, the number of steps is upper-bounded by $T \cdot I$. Therefore, the worst-case complexity is $O(T \cdot I \cdot (M \cdot W \cdot C)^{5/2})$.

In the case of a blocking DCN fabric that uses (M, C) SLIM switches with W wavelengths, the scheduling is reduced to a decomposition of an admissible traffic matrix into a sum of (M, W, C) PMs which follow the fabric's blocking constraints. The decomposition algorithm A-BvN is a generalization of a regular BvN decomposition algorithm.

Algorithm 1 Decomposition algorithm A-BvN

Step 1) *Inputs*. Inputs are the traffic matrix $\mathbf{D} = [\mathbf{D}_{rc}] = [d_{ij}]$ with $1 \leq r, c \leq M \cdot C$ and $1 \leq i, j \leq M \cdot W \cdot C$ and the scalars M, W, C, T and I.

Step 2) *Definitions*. Define the matrices $\mathbf{A} = [a_{ij}] \in \mathbb{N}^{M \cdot C \times M \cdot C}$, $\mathbf{Q} = [q_{ij}] \in \mathbb{N}^{C \times M \cdot C}$, $\mathbf{Z} = [z_{ij}] \in \mathbb{N}^{C \times C}$, $\mathbf{Y} = [y_{ij}] \in \mathbb{N}^{C \times C}$, $\mathbf{S} = [s_{ij}] \in \mathbb{N}^{T \cdot I \times M \cdot W \cdot C}$, $\mathbf{X} = [x_{rcw}] \in \mathbb{N}^{M \cdot C \times M \cdot C \times W}$ and $\mathbf{e} = [e_i] \in \mathbb{N}^C$.

Step 3) *Init*. Set schedule matrix to zero $\mathbf{S} \leftarrow [0]^{T \cdot I \times M \cdot W \cdot C}$ and slot $t \leftarrow 0$.

Step 4) *Find maximum cardinality diagonals*. For each $r \in [1, M \cdot C]$, $c \in [1, M \cdot C]$ and $w \in [1, W]$: compute the cardinality of non-zero entries of the diagonal w, which is determined by the column index of the diagonal's first row entry, of the submatrix $\mathbf{D}_{rc}$; store the computed cardinality to x_{rcw} and save index w of the maximum diagonal to a_{rc}.

Step 5) *Compute sums of parallel matrices*. For each $r' \in [1, C]$, $c \in [1, M \cdot C]$: sum x_{rcw} with $r = (r' + k \cdot C - 1) \bmod (M \cdot C) + 1$ and $w = a_{rc}$ for all $k \in [1, M]$; store the sum to $q_{r'c}$.

Step 6) *Find maximum between column-dependent matrices*. For each $r \in [1, C]$ and $c \in [1, C]$: find $c_{\max}$ such that $q_{rc_{\max}} \geq q_{rc'}$ with $c' = (c + k \cdot C - 1) \bmod (M \cdot C) + 1$ for all $k \in [1, M]$ and set $z_{rc} \leftarrow c_{\max}$ and $y_{rc} \leftarrow q_{rc_{\max}}$.

Step 7) *Schedule*. Set $t \leftarrow t + 1$.

Step 8) *Run MWM*. Consider the square matrix $\mathbf{Y}$ as a weighted bipartite graph, where y_{ij} is the weight of the edge (i, j). Run a Maximum Weighted Matching (MWM) algorithm with the square matrix $\mathbf{Y}$ as input. The output is a vector $\mathbf{e}$ with e_r, $1 \leq r \leq C$ having the column index c with the maximum value.

Step 9) *Loop over submatrices*. For each $r' \in [1, C]$ and $k \in [1, M]$: set $c \leftarrow z_{r'c'}$, $r \leftarrow (r' + k \cdot C - 1) \bmod (M \cdot C) + 1$ and $l \leftarrow 0$ with $c' = e_{r'}$:

  Step 9a. Update the schedule. For each $i' \in [1, W]$ set $i \leftarrow (r - 1) \cdot W + i'$ and $j \leftarrow (c - 1) \cdot W + j'$ with $j' = (i' + a_{rc} - 2) \bmod W + 1$; if $d_{ij} > 0$ then set $s_{ti} \leftarrow j$ and $l \leftarrow l + 1$, which is the count of covered non-zeros.

  Step 9b. *Update maximum diagonal*. Set $x_{rcw} \leftarrow x_{rcw} - l$ with $w = a_{rc}$. Find the new maximum diagonal among the already computed cardinalities $x_{rcw'}$ for all $w' \in [1, W]$ and store the diagonal index to a_{rc}.

  Step 9c. *Update subsidiary matrices*. Set $q_{r'c} \leftarrow q_{r'c} - l + x_{rcw}$ with $w = a_{rc}$.

  Step 9d. *Update maximum between column-dependent matrices*. Find $c_{\max}$ such that $q_{r'c_{\max}} \geq q_{r'c''}$ with $c'' = (c' + k \cdot C - 1) \bmod (M \cdot C) + 1$ for all $k \in [1, M]$ and set $z_{r'c'} \leftarrow c_{\max}$ and $y_{r'c'} \leftarrow q_{r'c_{\max}}$.

Step 10) *Loop*. If there exist i, j s.t. $d_{ij} > 0$ and $t < T$, then go to Step 7.

Step 11) *Finish*. Return the schedule $\mathbf{S}$.

Theorem 2: The worst case complexity of A-BvN is $O(T \cdot I \cdot (M \cdot W \cdot C)^2)$.

The proof is omitted due to space limitations.

4.3 Reconfiguration Speed Comparison

The reconfiguration speed depends on the number states of the SEs. All SEs have to tilt between all shift shuffles. For a DCN fabric based on (M, C) SLIM switches all C SEs need to tilt between $M \cdot C$ shift shuffles. The reduction of reconfiguration delay is derived from the decrease of the $M \cdot W \cdot C$ positions of a non-blocking fabric to $M \cdot C$, which is achieved through WDM. Thus, a (M, C) SLIM switch induces an increase in reconfiguration speed with the trade-off of limited switching flexibility. However, since the SEs don't tilt between consecutive shift shuffles, this reconfiguration speed applies to the worst case scenario. Therefore, the reconfiguration speed, in terms of asymptotic complexity, is $O(M \cdot C)$, which is lower than $O(M \cdot W \cdot C)$ of the case of a non-blocking fabric.

4.4 Cost Comparison

Another factor of inefficiency of the non-blocking fabric is the cost of its optical SEs. We compare the cost between the case of deploying a non-blocking DCN architecture and the case of deploying a DCN architecture based on SLIM the switch; the comparison takes place with respect to the number of (a) SEs used in each case and (b) the number of tunable transmitters. We consider the network parameters to be equal between the two DCNs. A MEMS-based non-blocking fabric consisting of I crossbar $M \cdot W \cdot C \times M \cdot W \cdot C$ switches would require $I \cdot M \cdot W \cdot C = \Theta(I \cdot M \cdot W \cdot C)$ MEMS in total. A blocking DCN fabric with I (M, C) SLIM switches requires a total number of $I \cdot C = \Theta(I \cdot C)$. However the blocking fabric uses WDM that requires the deployment of tunable transmitters at each ToR switch. The number of tunable transmitters deployed at each ToR is I, equal to the overall number of SLIM switches. Therefore, there is an additional cost for the deployment of $I \cdot M \cdot W \cdot C$ tunable transmitters for all $M \cdot W \cdot C$ ToRs. A non-blocking fabric, with features similar to the architecture we propose, wouldn't require the deployment of tunable transmitters in the ToR switches. However, for large radix the scenario of such a network is infeasible anyway, due to the rest of inefficiency factors.

Table 1. A summary of the complexity comparison.

	Non-blocking	Blocking
Reconfiguration Control	$O(T \cdot I \cdot M \cdot W \cdot C)$	$O(T \cdot I \cdot M \cdot C)$
Cost in MEMS	$\Theta(I \cdot M \cdot W \cdot C)$	$\Theta(I \cdot C)$
Cost in tunable Tx	–	$\Theta(I \cdot M \cdot W \cdot C)$
Reconfiguration speed	$O(M \cdot W \cdot C)$	$O(M \cdot C)$
Algorithm Complexity	$O(T \cdot I \cdot \left(M \cdot W \cdot C\right)^{5/2})$	$O\left(T \cdot I \cdot (M \cdot W \cdot C)^2\right)$

5 Simulation Results

In this section, we present a set of simulation results, comparing the achievable through-put between three architecture scenarios with their corresponding algorithms. The first scenario applies to a blocking DCN fabric with a decentralized control plane (abbrev. as *decentralized scenario*). Since this architecture is traffic-agnostic, there is no need to implement a larger set than the trivial $M \cdot W \cdot C$ cyclic switching patterns. The second scenario applies to a blocking DCN fabric that deploys a centralized control plane (abbrev. as *semi-centralized scenario*). In fact, the semi-centralized scenario simulates the operation of a SLIM switch-enabled fabric. The last scenario applies to a fully non-blocking (crossbar-like) DCN fabric that deploys a centralized control plane (abbrev. as *centralized scenario*).

The scheduling policies that apply to each of the scenarios are RRS, A-BvN (Algo-rithm 1 of Sect. 4.2) and EXACT, for the decentralized, semi-centralized and centralized scenarios, respectively.

The flow-level simulation framework was implemented in Python 2.7. The network configuration parameters are $M \cdot C = W = T = I = 12$. The traffic is synthetic, generating at each cycle an admissible traffic matrix (according to the load ρ). The results are sampled for the load levels of $\rho = 10\%, 50\%$ and 90%. The level of load dynamicity is fixed to 1%, while the level of flow dynamicity is 0.1%. We also classify the traffic in two distinct flow densities, by randomly selecting a non-conflicting pattern of $M \cdot C$ hotspots of the size of PODs. The flows belonging to a hotspot have 100% density while the rest of the flows are characterized by 8% density. This configuration generates a spatially non-uniform and slowly changing traffic pattern that is suitable for exhibiting the adaptability of the semi-centralized fabric, depending on its complexity. The distinction in two levels of flow density is quite realistic, since the DCN traffic is naturally classified into intra-POD and intra-POD.

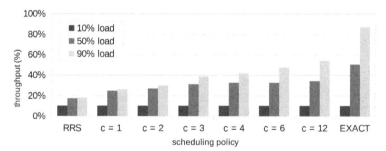

Fig. 4. The achieved throughput. RRS is used in the decentralized scenario while EXACT in the centralized. The semi-centralized scenarios in-between run A-BvN with complexities $C = 1, 2, 3, 4, 6, 12$.

It is clear by Fig. 4 that the decentralized scenario (RRS) is highly affected by the level of uniformity of the traffic pattern reaching a level of throughput of just 18%. The exact opposite is the case of the centralized scenario (EXACT) which reaches a maximum throughput of 87% for $\rho = 90\%$. The centralized scenario running EXACT is completely unaffected from the anomalies of the traffic as soon as the traffic matrix is admissible. However, the centralized scenario is not a sustainable option due to the inefficiencies presented in the previous sections. The in-between cases apply to semi-centralized cases under A-BvN. These cases achieve an adaptive level of throughput, namely 26% for $C = 1$, 30% for $C = 2$, 39% for $C = 3$, 42% for $C = 4$ and 47% for $C = 6$ and 54% for $C = 12$ (Table 1).

6 Conclusion

We presented a concept design of a blocking optical DCN fabric that copes with various inefficiencies of the operation of a fully non-blocking DCN architecture. The inefficiencies are caused due to high control overhead, high reconfiguration time in high radix and high deployment cost. This is achieved by utilizing the deployment of a blocking optical switch which supports a reduced set of hard-wired interconnection mappings and WDM. We analytically compared the complexity between the case of a blocking and a non-blocking fabric. The simplification causes reduced functionality which affects the throughput. We presented a flow-level evaluation, through simulations, that compares the achieved throughput between non-blocking and blocking fabric designs that deploy decentralized, semi-centralized and fully centralized control. The results show that for admissible synthetic traffic with long-term flows and a high degree of locality, the semi-centralized control has an advantage of at least 45% in comparison to the decentralized control. The throughput increases by utilizing a larger number of SEs. The difference between a blocking and the non-blocking architecture is not so high, considering the benefits of the reduced complexity.

Acknowledgment. This research is co-financed by Greece and the European Union (European Social Fund-ESF) through the Operational Programme «Human Resources Development, Education and Lifelong Learning» in the context of the project "Strengthening Human Resources Research Potential via Doctorate Research" (MIS-5000432), implemented by the State Scholarships Foundation (IKY).

References

1. Cisco Global Cloud Index: Forecast and Methodology, 2014–2019
2. Al-Fares, M., Loukissas, A., Vahdat, A.: A scalable, commodity data center network architecture. ACM SIGCOMM **38**(4), 63–74 (2008)
3. Roy, A., Zeng, H., Bagga, J., Porter, G., Snoeren, A.: Inside the social network's (Datacenter) network. ACM SIGCOMM **45**(4), 123–137 (2015)
4. Farrington, N., et al.: Helios: a hybrid electrical/optical switch architecture for modular data centers. ACM SIGCOMM **41**(4), 339–350 (2010)
5. Wang, G., et al.: c-through: part-time optics in data centers. ACM SIGCOMM **41**, 327–338 (2010)
6. Christodoulopoulos, K., Lugones, D., Katrinis, K., Ruffini, M., O'Mahony, D.: Performance evaluation of a hybrid optical/electrical interconnect. IEEE/OSA J. Lightw. Technol. **7**(3), 193–204 (2015)

7. Ben-Itzhak, Y., et al.: "C-share: optical circuits sharing for software-defined data-centers. arXiv preprint arXiv:1609.04521 (2016)
8. Singla, A., et al.: Proteus: a topology malleable data center network. ACM SIGCOMM Workshop on Hot Topics in Networks (2010)
9. Peng, S., et al.: Multi-tenant software-defined hybrid optical switched data centre. IEEE/OSA J. Lightw. Technol. **33**(15), 3224–3233 (2015)
10. Saridis, G., et al.: LIGHTNESS: a function-virtualizable software defined data center network with all-optical circuit/packet switching. IEEE/OSA J. Lightw. Technol. **34**(7), 1618–1627 (2016)
11. Porter, G., et al.: Integrating microsecond circuit switching into the data center. ACM SIGCOMM **43**, 447–458 (2013)
12. Bakopoulos, P., et al.: NEPHELE: an end-to-end scalable and dynamically reconfigurable optical architecture for application-aware SDN cloud datacenters. IEEE Commun. Mag. **56**(2), 178–188 (2018)
13. Calabretta, N., Miao, W.: Optical switching in data centers: architectures based on optical packet/burst switching. In: Testa, F., Pavesi, L. (eds.) Optical Switching in Next Generation Data Centers, pp. 45–69. Springer, Cham (2018). https://doi.org/10.1007/978-3-319-61052-8_3
14. Patronas, I., Gkatzios, N., Kitsakis, V., Christodoulopoulos, K., Varvarigos, E., Reisis, D.: Scheduler Accelerator for TDMA Data Centers", Parallel, Distributed, and Network-Based Processing (2018)
15. Mellette, W.M., et al.: A scalable, partially configurable optical switch for data center networks. IEEE/OSA JLT **35**(2), 136–144 (2017)
16. Hopcroft, J.E., Karp, R.M.: An n^5/2 algorithm for maximum matchings in bipartite graphs. SIAM J. Comput. **2**(4), 225–231 (1973)
17. Ryser, H.J.: Combinatorial Mathematics (No. 14) Mathematical Association of America; distributed by Wiley New York (1963)
18. Inukai, T.: An efficient SS/TDMA time slot assignment algorithm. IEEE Trans. Commun. **27**(10), 1449–1455 (1979)

Dual-Layer Locality-Aware Optical Interconnection Architecture for Latency-Critical Resource Disaggregation Environments

Nikos Terzenidis[1][(✉)] , Miltiadis Moralis-Pegios[1] , Theoni Alexoudi[1] ,
Stelios Pitris[1] , Konstantinos Vyrsokinos[2], and Nikos Pleros[1]

[1] Department of Informatics, Aristotle University of Thessaloniki, Thessaloniki, Greece
nterzeni@csd.auth.gr
[2] Department of Physics, Aristotle University of Thessaloniki, Thessaloniki, Greece

Abstract. Significant research efforts, both industrial and academic, have been committed in the direction of Rack-scale computing through resource disaggregation, that aims to increase resource utilization at a reduced energy and cost envelope. However, the realization of resource disaggregation necessitates an underlying network infrastructure that can compete with a challenging set of requirements including low-latency performance and high-port count connectivity, as well as high data-rate operation. At the same time, it is crucial for the interconnection architecture to be able to accommodate efficient delivery of traffic with different locality characteristics. We propose a dual-layer locality-aware optical interconnection architecture for disaggregated Data Centers by combining the STREAMS silicon-based on-board communication paradigm with the disaggregation-oriented Hipoλaos high-port count switch. Simulation evaluation of a 256-node disaggregated system, comprising 32 optically-interconnected 8-socket boards, revealed up to 100% throughput and mean, p99 latencies not higher than 335 nsec and 610 nsec, respectively, when a 50:50 ratio between on- and off-board traffic is employed. Evaluation of the same layout with 75:25 on-/off-board traffic yields even lower mean and p99 latency at 210 ns and 553 ns, respectively.

Keywords: Silicon-photonics · Optical switch · Interconnection architecture · Disaggregated data center · Traffic locality

1 Introduction

The ever-increasing energy consumption of Data Centers (DCs), projected to rise to 3% of the global electricity demand by 2020 [1], along with the huge waste of resources, that is observed in traditional DCs and may reach up to 50% [2–3], have forced DC operators to invest in solutions that will considerably improve energy efficiency. In this context, resource disaggregation in computing and network architectures is under heavy research [4–6], as a groundbreaking innovation that could amortize the energy and cost

© IFIP International Federation for Information Processing 2020
Published by Springer Nature Switzerland AG 2020
A. Tzanakaki et al. (Eds.): ONDM 2019, LNCS 11616, pp. 299–309, 2020.
https://doi.org/10.1007/978-3-030-38085-4_26

impact caused by the vast diversity in resource demand of emerging DC workloads [7]. This architectural shift breaks the tight co-integration of CPU, memory and storage resources from a single server board, towards disaggregated systems with multiple resources organized in trays and synergized via the DC network. The first promising results of a full-fledged CPU-memory disaggregated prototype, from the EU-funded project dRedBox, suggest an important decrease in Total Cost of Ownership (TCO) [6], while the deployment of partially-disaggregated servers in Intel's DCs contributed to an impressive power usage effectiveness (PuE) rating of 1.06 [8].

However, resource disaggregation, by breaking apart the critical CPU-to-memory path, introduces a challenging set of requirements in the underlying network infrastructure [9], that has to support low latency and high throughput communication, while providing connectivity to an increased number of nodes. At the same time, it is crucial for the interconnection architecture to be able to accommodate efficient unicast and multicast traffic delivery with different locality characteristics. To this end, recent studies [10–12] have indicated heavy traffic exchange within the boundaries of a Rack, that can be observed through a variety of emerging DC workloads, while a number of applications span their communication capacity through the entire network hierarchy [10], requiring all-to-all connectivity. The transition to a disaggregation paradigm endorses this type of mixed communication profile and effectively narrows down the locality pattern to board-level, where for example computing resources are synergized in homogeneous pools exhibiting highly localized traffic, while requiring also connectivity with the memory or storage pools located in other trays of the system.

During the first demonstrations of disaggregated systems [6] optical circuit switches (OCS) have been employed to provide rack-level connectivity between resource bricks residing in different trays, due to their high-radix, scaling to hundreds of ports, along with their datarate-transparent operation. However, currently available OCS solutions based either on 3D Micro Electromechanical Systems (MEMS) [13–14] or piezoelectric beam steering technology [15] come at the cost of ms switching time values, that effectively limit their employment as slow reconfigurable backplanes [16]. To this end, we have recently demonstrated the Hipoλaos optical packet switch (OPS) architecture [17–21], that provides low-latency connectivity between a high number of ports, while at the same time enabling dynamic switching operation with packet granularity. Moreover, Hipoλaos OPS offers up-to 95% throughput for unicast traffic when interconnecting 1024 nodes located in 32 different trays [19], enabling this way efficient communication through the whole Rack hierarchy.

Moving on to the next DC hierarchy layer, the tray, electrical switching solutions have been employed in the first disaggregated prototypes to provide on-board connectivity, following the established paradigm of interconnection architectures for multi-socket boards (MSB), that are currently dominated by electrical point-to-point (P2P) links. While P2P interconnects, like Intel QPI [22] and AMD Infinity fabric, can definitely offer low latency and high bandwidth communication, their scalability is typically limited to 4 endpoints, before requiring extra latency-inducing hops or active switch-based solutions like Oracle Bixby [23] or PCIe switches. Recent advances on board-compatible optical interfaces highlight the significant throughput and delay improvements that can be released through optically-interconnected blade technologies [24], paving the way for their employment in high-density MSB scenarios. To this end, we have demonstrated, in the context of STREAMS project [25], a Silicon-photonics-based interconnection scheme for up to 40 Gb/s chip-to-chip communication [26] using an integrated Ring-Modulator (RM) transmitter (Tx) [36], an 8×8 Arrayed Waveguide Grating Router (AWGR)-based routing circuitry and a co-packaged InP-based photodiode (PD) and Transimpedance Amplifier (TIA) receiver (Rx). The STREAMS architecture is able to provide high-bandwidth communication to 8 on-board nodes, while the AWGR-based routing ensures ultra-low latency and efficient multicast/broadcast traffic delivery encompassing the requirements of coherency-induced multi- and broad- casting traffic patterns.

In this paper we combine the STREAMS silicon-based on-board interconnection architecture with the disaggregation-oriented Hipoλaos high-port count switch, in a dual-layer locality-aware Rack interconnection scheme that efficiently accommodates the need for transparent on-board local traffic forwarding in a disaggregated environment with hundreds of nodes. We evaluate via an Omnet++ simulation analysis, this novel rack configuration with 256 disaggregated nodes using a number of 32 optically-inter- connected 8-socket MSBs. This 256-socket setup can take advantage of traffic localization techniques towards low-latency workload execution, forming a powerful disaggregated rack-scale computing scheme with mean and p99 latencies not higher than 335 nsec and 610 nsec, respectively, when a 50:50 ratio between on- and off-board traffic is employed. Finally, evaluation of the same system with 75:25 on-:off-board traffic yields even lower mean and p99 latency at 210 ns and 553 ns, respectively.

2   Hipoλaos and STREAMS Optical Interconnects

2.1   Hipoλaos Rack-Level Optical Switch Architecture

Hipoλaos (High port λ routed all optical switch) manages to combine low latency and high-throughput performance into high-port count configurations, through a hybrid scheme exploiting Spanke switching and wavelength routing. The Hipoλaos switch differentiates from alternative OPS layouts by incorporating the multi-lambda routing capabilities of AWGRs, along with careful optimizations in the different stages of the Spanke architecture, that can be classified into four main categories/features:

(i)   Distributed control: The Hipoλaos architecture overcomes the scalability limitations of Spanke designs, towards high-port count layouts, by distributing the control and switching functions in small clusters, named as Planes. Moreover, this distributed nature of the architecture minimizes the computational time associated with forwarding and scheduling, contributing this way to lower total latency of the switch fabric.

(ii)   Feed-forward buffering: The adoption of small-scale optical buffering [27] enables the realization of high-throughput performance while at the same time reducing latency by avoiding optoelectronic buffering and the associated Optical/Electrical/Optical conversions.

(iii)   Advanced Wavelength Conversion schemes: Wavelength converters (WC) on the different stages of the Spanke layout utilize the differentially biasing scheme [28], that has been shown to operate successfully with up to 40 Gb/s NRZ signals, fulfilling the requirement for high datarates.

(iv) Multi-wavelength routing: The architecture utilizes the cyclic routing properties of AWGRs in order to extend the switch radix through a collision-less WDM routing mechanism, that ensures non-blocking forwarding of the different packets to the desired destination node. Moreover, it enables the realization of multicast functionality building upon the proven efficiency of AWGR devices in multicast operations [29].

Figure 1(b) depicts a schematic illustration of the Hipoλaos OPS architecture, configured in a N2 × N2 layout, interconnecting #N Rack trays with #N computing nodes in every tray. The switch is organized in #N Planes that are interconnected to #N AWGR devices. On the ingress path, every node communicates with a specific Plane over a different fiber link, while the Plane's role is to aggregate traffic from #N input ports and forward it via a BS scheme, with every 1:N splitting node corresponding to the 1:N switches employed in the Spanke architecture, as depicted in Fig. 1(a). The N:1 switches at the outputs of the Spanke design are modified to incorporate an Optical Delay-Line Bank (DLB), forming this way an optical contention resolution stage comprising #N DLBs. Packets leaving the contention resolution stage are finally delivered to the destination node after passing through a wavelength routing stage comprising tunable WCs and cyclic routing AWGRs.

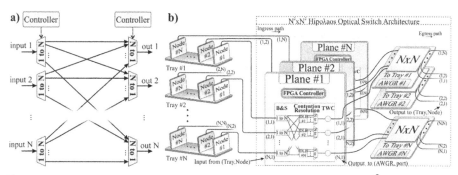

Fig. 1. (a) N×N Spanke switch architecture, (b) Schematic illustration of a N^2-node DC, organized in #N Rack-Trays with #N nodes per tray and interconnected via a N2 × N2 ToR Hipoλaos switch

The feasibility of the Hipoλaos architecture has been validated through a prototype experimental evaluation following the design principles of the 256-port layout [17], while its network performance characteristics have been evaluated through a variety of unicast traffic scenarios [18] revealing a high throughput value of >85%, for up to 100% loads, along with 605 nsec latency, even for 2 packet-size optical buffers. An actual photo of the experimental prototype is depicted in the right inset of Fig. 3. A scalability analysis of the Hipoλaos architecture, considering also the main limiting factors, has been presented in [18], concluding to an attainable port-count of at least 1024-ports, with the experimental evaluation in unicast and multicast operational mode presented in [19].

2.2 STREAMS Silicon-Photonics Board-Level Interconnect

The European H2020 project ICT-STREAMS is currently attempting to deploy the necessary silicon photonic and electro-optical PCB technology toolkit for realizing the AWGR-based MSB interconnect benefits in the O-band and at data rates up to 50 Gb/s [25, 30]. It aims to exploit wavelength division multiplexing (WDM) Silicon photonics transceiver technology at the chip edge as the socket interface and a board-pluggable O-band silicon-based AWGR as the passive routing element, as shown in a generic N-socket architecture depicted in Fig. 2. Each socket is electrically connected to a WDM-enabled Tx optical engine equipped with N-1 laser diodes (LD), each one operating at a different wavelength. Every LD feeds a different Ring Modulator (RM) to imprint the electrical data sent from the socket to each one of the N-1 wavelengths, so that the Tx engine comprises finally N-1 RMs along with their respective RM drivers (DR). All RMs are implemented on the same optical bus to produce the WDM-encoded data stream of each socket. The data stream generated by each socket enters the input port of the AWGR and is forwarded to the respective destination output that is dictated by the carrier wavelength and the cyclic-frequency routing properties of the AWGR [31]. In this way, every socket can forward data to any of the remaining 7 sockets by simply modulating its electrical data onto a different wavelength via the respective RM, allowing direct single-hop communication between all sockets through passive wavelength-routing. At every Rx engine, the incoming WDM-encoded data stream gets demultiplexed with a 1:(N-1) optical demultiplexer (DEMUX), so that every wavelength is received by a distinct PD. Each PD is connected to a transimpedance amplifier (TIA) that provides the socket with the respective electrical signaling.

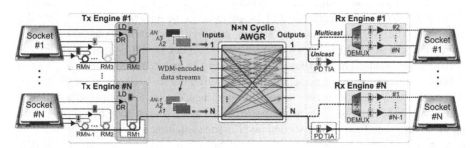

Fig. 2. STREAMS optical N × N AWGR-based interconnection concept for MSB connectivity exploiting WDM-enabled Tx/Rx engines.

This flat-topology AWGR-based interconnect scheme requires a higher number of transceivers compared to any intermediate switch solution, but this is exactly the feature that allows to combine WDM with AWGR's cyclic frequency characteristics towards enabling single-hop communication and retaining the lowest possible latency. Link capacity can be increased in this case by residing on channel bonding through bit-parallel schemes, as already reported in [32], by using AWGR designs for waveband instead of single wavelength routing. Utilizing an 8 × 8 AWGR, the optically-enabled MSB can allow single-hop all-to-all interconnection between 8 sockets, while scaling the AWGR to 16×16 layouts can yield single-hop communication even between 16 sockets, effectively turning current "glued" into "glueless" designs. The ICT-STREAMS on-board MSB aims to incorporate 50 GHz single-mode O-band electro-optical PCBs [33], relying on the adiabatic coupling approach between silicon and polymer waveguides [34] for low-loss interfacing of the Silicon-Photonics transceiver and AWGR chips with the EO-PCB.

The first 40 Gb/s experimental demonstration of the fiber-interconnected integrated photonic building blocks when performing in the AWGR-based 8-socket MSB architecture, presenting the 40 Gb/s experimental results have been reported in [26]. The energy efficiency of the proposed 40 Gb/s C2C photonic link is estimated at 24 pJ/bit, but can dramatically go down to 5.95 pJ/bit when transferring the demonstrated fiber-pigtailed layout into an on-board assembled configuration and assuming a 10% wall-plug efficiency for the external laser. This indicates that the on-board version has the credentials to lead to 63.3% reduction in energy compared to the 16.2 pJ/bit link energy efficiency of Intel QPI [35].

3   Dual-Layer Locality-Aware Optical Interconnection Architecture

Figure 3 presents a schematic illustration of a 256-node DC system comprising 32 optically-enabled STREAMS boards, with every board incorporating 8 network nodes. Every node in the proposed dual-layer network hierarchy is connected via different optical links to an on-board 8×8 AWGR, serving as the intra-board routing infrastructure, as well as to a Hipoλaos-based 256 port switch, providing inter-board all-to-all connectivity. The internal node architecture is depicted in the left inset of Fig. 3, where a CPU, for example, can communicate with any of the remaining 7 nodes of the board by utilizing links #1 to #7 that effectively forward data via the underlying silicon photonics Tx engine. The WDM-encoded data stream, comprising seven lambdas, is forwarded to the on-board AWGR device where every wavelength channel is finally delivered to a different end node. This first layer of switching can ensure maximum throughput of on-board traffic, being in agreement with the requirement for transparent localized traffic forwarding, while the latency associated with header processing and scheduling is eliminated, since the routing decision is performed in the source node by simply selecting the appropriate link(s). The second layer in the switching topology can be accessed through link #8, that forwards inter-board traffic, via a fixed-wavelength optical data stream, to the Hipoλaos switch. The internal architecture of the 256-port Hipoλaos layout, that has been described in detail in [17], comprises 16 switch Planes with every Plane aggregating traffic from 16 nodes. Due to the mismatch between the number of nodes per board and the number of ports per Plane, the input port allocation per switch plane is performed so that Node#i, $1 \leq i \leq 8$, from the odd-numbered boards#j, $j = 1,3,$ ..,31, connects to the input#k, $k = (j + 1)/2$, of Plane#l, $l = i$, denoted as input (l, k) of the switch. Moreover, Nodes#i, $1 \leq i \leq 8$, from the even-numbered boards#j, $j = 2,4,$ ..,32, connect to the input#k, $k = j/2$, of Plane#l, $l = 8 + i$. The proposed port-allocation scheme groups into the respective contention resolution stages of the switch packets from 2 adjacent boards, that in conjunction with the on-board switching layer ensures minimum contention between the different packets. It should be noted that every node can accommodate either computing resources, as illustrated on the example of Fig. 3, as well as memory, storage and accelerator resources.

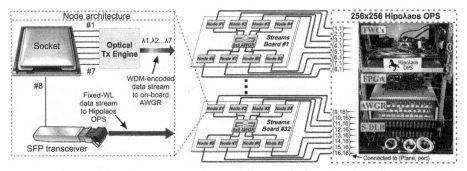

Fig. 3. Illustration of a locality-aware Rack interconnection scheme employing 32 Streams boards, with 8 nodes each, interconnected to a 256 × 256 Hipoλaos switch. On the left inset, the internal node architecture is presented, while on the right an actual photo of the Hipoλaos experimental prototype is presented.

Having already demonstrated the performance credentials of each constituent interconnection scheme in [17] and [18], we have proceeded with the evaluation of the network throughput and latency performance in a DC system incorporating the proposed dual-layer interconnection architecture. A simulation analysis has been performed for the 256-node system illustrated in Fig. 3, using the Omnet++ discrete event platform. A synchronous slotted network operation has been modelled where the packets are generated at predefined packet-slots, each one lasting for 57.6 ns. The traffic profile was customized to distribute a certain percentage of the total traffic generated by every node, uniformly to nodes of the same board (intra-board traffic), while the rest of the traffic was uniformly distributed to nodes from the other 31 boards (inter-board traffic). In order to offer a thorough evaluation of the architecture's performance, in terms of latency, both mean packet delay, as well as p99 delay metrics were collected by the simulation. The switch port allocation to the network nodes was performed according to the procedure described in the previous paragraph and illustrated in the layout of Fig. 3.

The modelled DC system featured node-to-switch and node-to-AWGR channel datarate of 10 Gb/s, along with fixed size packet-length of 72 bytes, comprising 8-bytes for header, synchronization and guard-band requirements and 64 bytes data payload, matching the size of a single cache-line transfer. Regarding the Hipoλaos processing latency, it was modelled to 456 ns in accordance with the experimental results [17], while the propagation latency for the various optical components of the switch (fibers, amplifiers, AWGRs), excluding the optical delay lines, was modelled to be 35 ns.

In order to perform a versatile evaluation of the proposed architecture under different traffic locality patterns, we have considered in our analysis two different cases for the percentage of the intra-/inter-board traffic; 50/50 and 75/25. Performance has been evaluated as a function of the available packet-buffers in the Hipoλaos switch, with the number of buffers ranging for 0 to 4 and corresponding to the maximum number of buffers experimentally demonstrated in [18].

Figure 4(a) to (c) present the simulation results for the case of 50/50 intra-/inter-board traffic distribution. Figure 4(a) presents the respective throughput versus the offered load results, concerning the total network traffic (both intra- and inter-board) for different numbers of buffers per Hipoλaos DLB. As expected, throughput increases almost linearly with increasing buffer size, approaching 100% for 100% offered load as long as the buffer size equals to more than 2 packet slots. Figure 4(b) presents the mean packet delay versus the offered load results, showing that latency ranges between 295 ns and 330 ns for a buffer size between 0 and 2 packet slots and for loads until 100%. Mean latency increases slightly as the buffer size increases reaching a maximum value of 335 ns for a buffer size of 4 packet slots where throughput reaches also its maximum value. Figure 4(c) presents the p99 delay results vs. the offered load, revealing a p99 value of 610 ns for maximum load and 4 buffers per DLB. As can be observed, the p99 delay metrics perform a step-wise "jump" as contention occurs due to the fact that packets are forwarded to longer DLB buffers that introduce delays in packet duration granularity. It is important to note that the only point of congestion in the architecture was identified at the Hipoλaos switch, since the intra-board AWGR switching scheme is able to offer 100% throughput and minimum latency values originating just from the signal's propagation delay.

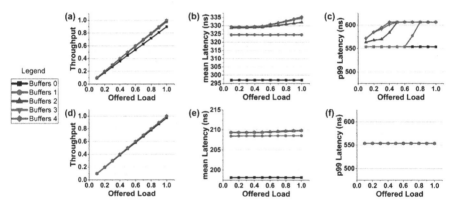

Fig. 4. Simulation results for different number of buffers per DLB (a) Throughput – 50/50, (b) Mean latency – 50/50, (c) P99 latency – 50/50, (d) Throughput – 75/25, (e) Mean latency – 75/25, (f) P99 latency – 75/25

Figure 4(d) to (f) present the simulation results for the case of 75/25 intra-/inter-board traffic distribution. As expected, throughput is slightly higher, reaching 100% in all cases, due to the fact that a lower percentage of traffic is headed towards the Hipoλaos switch, where congestion occurs. At the same time mean packet latency is decreased to 210 ns, while p99 latency now presents a maximum value of 550 ns, as less delay lines have to be utilized in the Hipoλaos DLB blocks.

The vital information that can be easily extracted from Fig. 4(b)–(c) and (e)–(f), is that the proposed dual-layer switching topology does not induce any additional latency compared to the conventional Hipoλaos architecture [17], but rather decreases the mean and p99 packet latency, due to the fact that the 2 switching layers operate in a parallel and functionally isolated manner. With sub-μsec latency considered as the main performance target for current memory disaggregated systems [9], the mean and p99 latency values of this novel Hipoλaos-STREAMS-based architecture with clustered optically-enabled 8-Socket MSBs reveals an excellent potential for a practical interconnect solution that can bring latency down to just a few 100's of nanosecond. Allowing on-board nodes to cluster in single-hop configurations over AWGR-based interconnects can yield minimized latency when combined with proper workload allocation for strengthening board-level traffic localization, while off-board traffic benefits from the latency-optimized dynamic switch characteristics of the Hipoλaos design.

4 Conclusion

The emergence of resource disaggregation in DC architectures is imposing stringent requirements on the interconnection architecture that has to support low-latency, high-throughput and high-radix connectivity, while at the same time accommodating efficient delivery of traffic with different locality characteristics. To this end we have demonstrated a dual-layer locality-aware optical interconnection architecture by combining the ICT-STREAMS silicon-photonics on-board communication paradigm with the intra-DC Hipoλaos high-port count switch. Simulation analysis of a 256-node dis- aggregated system, comprising 32 optically-interconnected 8-socket boards, revealed up to 100% throughput and mean, p99 latencies not higher than 335 nsec and 610 nsec, respectively, when a 50:50 ratio between on- and off-board traffic is employed. Finally, this layout could in principle form the basis for replacing the massive QPI "island" interconnection supported by a number of switch technologies like Bixby's [23] and PCI express, yielding a powerful network of cache-coherent islands at a maximum p99 latency value just above 600 nsec even when a balanced 50/50 traffic locality pattern is followed.

Acknowledgment. This work has been partially supported by the European H2020 projects ICT-STREAMS (Contract No. 688172) and L3MATRIX (Contract No. 688544).

References

1. Jones, N.: How to stop data centres from gobbling up the world's electricity. Nature **561**, 163–166 (2018)
2. Di, S., Kondo, D., Cappello, F.: Characterizing cloud applications on a Google data center. In: 2013 42nd International Conference on Parallel Processing (2013)
3. Reiss, C., Tumanov, A., Ganger, G., Katz, R., Kozuch, M.: Heterogeneity and dynamicity of clouds at scale. In: Proceedings of the Third ACM Symposium on Cloud Computing - SoCC 2012 (2012)
4. Intel® Rack Scale Design. http://www.intel.com/content/www/us/en/architecture-and-technology/rack-scale-design-overview.html
5. Open Compute Project. The Open Compute server architecture specifications. http://www.opencompute.org
6. Bielski, M., et al.: dReDBox: Materializing a full-stack rack-scale system prototype of a next-generation disaggregated datacenter. In: 2018 Design, Automation & Test in Europe Conference & Exhibition (DATE) (2018)

7. Tencent Explores Datacenter Resource Pooling Using Intel® Rack Scale Architecture (In-tel® RSA). https://www.intel.com/content/dam/www/public/us/en/documents/white-pa-pers/rsa-tencent-paper.pdf

8. Disaggregated Servers Drive Data Center Efficiency and Innovation. https://www.intel.com/content/www/us/en/it-management/intel-it-best-practices/disaggregated-server-ar-chitecture-drives-data-center-efficiency-paper.html

9. Gao, P.X., et al.: Network requirements for resource disaggregation. In: 12th {USENIX} Symposium on Operating Systems Design and Implementation (OSDI) (2016)

10. Roy, A., Zeng, H., Bagga, J., Porter, G., Snoeren, A.: Inside the social network's (Datacenter) network. In: Proceedings of the 2015 ACM Conference on Special Interest Group on Data Communication - SIGCOMM 2015 (2015)

11. Delimitrou, C., Sankar, S., Kansal, A., Kozyrakis, C.: ECHO: recreating network traffic maps for datacenters with tens of thousands of servers. In: 2012 IEEE International Symposium on Workload Characterization (IISWC) (2012)

12. Kandula, S., Sengupta, S., Greenberg, A., Patel, P., Chaiken, R.: The nature of data center traffic. In: Proceedings of the 9th ACM SIGCOMM Conference on Internet Measurement Conference - IMC 2009 (2009)

13. S Series Optical Circuit Switch|CALIENT Technologies. https://www.calient.net/prod-ucts/s-series-photonic-switch/

14. Glimmerglass Intelligent Optical Systems|Glimmerglass. http://www.glimmer-glass.com/index.php/products/intelligent-optical-systems/

15. Polatis SERIES 7000 – 384 × 384 port Software-Defined Optical Circuit Switch. https://www.polatis.com/series-7000-384x384-port-software-controlled-optical-circuit-switch-sdn-enabled.asp?

16. Chen, Q., Mishra, V., Parsons, N., Zervas, G.: Hardware programmable network function service chain on optical rack-scale data centers. In: Optical Fiber Communication Conference (2017)

17. Terzenidis, N., Moralis-Pegios, M., Mourgias-Alexandris, G., Vyrsokinos, K., Pleros, N.: High-port low-latency optical switch architecture with optical feed-forward buffering for 256-node disaggregated data centers. Opt. Express **26**, 8756 (2018)

18. Terzenidis, N., Moralis-Pegios, M., Mourgias-Alexandris, G., Alexoudi, T., Vyrsokinos, K., Pleros, N.: High-port and low-latency optical switches for disaggregated data centers: the hipoλaos switch architecture [Invited]. J. Opt. Commun. Networking **10**, B102 (2018)

19. Moralis-Pegios, M., Terzenidis, N., Mourgias-Alexandris, G., Vyrsokinos, K., Pleros, N.: A 1024-Port optical uni- and multicast packet switch fabric. J. Lightw. Technol. **37**, 1415–1423 (2019)

20. Moralis-Pegios, M., et al.: Multicast-enabling optical switch design employing Si buffering and routing elements. IEEE Photonics Technol. Lett. **30**, 712–715 (2018)

21. Terzenidis, N., Moralis-Pegios, M., Mourgias-Alexandris, G., Vyrsokinos, K., Pleros, N.: Multicasting in a high-port sub-μsec latency hipoλaos optical packet switch. IEEE Photonics Technol. Lett. **30**, 1535–1538 (2018)

22. An Introduction to the Intel® QuickPath Interconnect. https://www.intel.com/con-tent/www/us/en/io/quickpath-technology/quick-path-interconnect-introduction-paper.html

23. Wicki, T., Schulz, J.: Bixby: the scalability and coherence directory ASIC in Oracle's highly scalable enterprise systems. In: 2013 IEEE Hot Chips 25 Symposium (HCS) (2013)

24. Maniotis, P., et al.: Application-oriented on-board optical technologies for HPCs. J. Lightw. Technol. **35**, 3197–3213 (2017)

25. Kanellos, G., Pleros, N.: WDM mid-board optics for chip-to-chip wavelength routing inter-connects in the H2020 ICT-STREAMS. Opt. Interconnects XVII **10109**, 101090D (2017)

26. Pitris, S., et al.: A 40 Gb/s chip-to-chip interconnect for 8-socket direct connectivity using integrated photonics. IEEE Photonics J. **10**, 1–8 (2018)

27. Moralis-Pegios, M., et al.: On-chip SOI delay line bank for optical buffers and time slot interchangers. IEEE Photonics Technol. Lett. **30**, 31–34 (2018)
28. Spyropoulou, M., et al.: 40 Gb/s NRZ wavelength conversion using a differentially-biased SOA-MZI: theory and experiment. J. Lightw. Technol. **29**, 1489–1499 (2011)
29. Pitris, S., et al.: O-band energy-efficient broadcast-friendly interconnection scheme with SiPho Mach-Zehnder Modulator (MZM) & Arrayed Waveguide Grating Router (AWGR). In: Optical Fiber Communication Conference (2018)
30. Alexoudi, T., et al.: Optics in computing: from photonic network-on-chip to chip-to-chip inter-connects and disintegrated architectures. J. Lightw. Technol. **37**, 363–379 (2019)
31. Leijtens, X., Kuhlow, B., Smit, M.: Arrayed waveguide gratings. In: Venghaus, H. (ed.) Wavelength Filters in Fibre Optics, pp. 125–187. Springer, Heidelberg (2006)
32. Grani, P., Liu, G., Proietti, R., Yoo, S.B.: Bit-parallel all-to-all and flexible AWGR-based optical interconnects. In: Optical Fiber Communication Conference (2017)
33. Lamprecht, T., et al.: EOCB-platform for integrated photonic chips direct-on-board assembly within Tb/s applications. In: 2018 IEEE 68th Electronic Components and Technology Conference (ECTC) (2018)
34. Dangel, R., et al.: Polymer waveguides enabling scalable low-loss adiabatic optical coupling for silicon photonics. IEEE J. Sel. Top. Quantum Electron. **24**, 1–11 (2018)
35. Gough, C., Steiner, I., Saunders, W.: Energy Efficient Servers: Blueprints for Data Center Optimization. Apress, New York (2015)
36. Moralis-Pegios, M., et al.: 52 km-long transmission link using a 50 Gb/s O-band silicon microring modulator co-packaged with a 1 V-CMOS driver. Photonics J. **11**(4), 1–7 (2019)

Network-Wide Localization
of Optical-Layer Attacks

Marija Furdek[1]([⊠]) [iD], Vincent W. S. Chan[2] [iD], Carlos Natalino[1] [iD],
and Lena Wosinska[1] [iD]

[1] Department of Electrical Engineering, Chalmers University of Technology,
Gothenburg, Sweden
furdek@chalmers.se
[2] Electrical Engineering and Computer Science, Massachusetts Institute
of Technology, Cambridge, USA

Abstract. Optical networks are vulnerable to a range of attacks targeting service disruption at the physical layer, such as the insertion of harmful signals that can propagate through the network and affect co-propagating channels. Detection of such attacks and localization of their source, a prerequisite for secure network operation, is a challenging task due to the limitations in optical performance monitoring, as well as the scalability and cost issues. In this paper, we propose an approach for localizing the source of a jamming attack by modeling the worst-case scope of each connection as a potential carrier of a harmful signal. We define binary words called attack syndromes to model the health of each connection at the receiver which, when unique, unambiguously identify the harmful connection. To ensure attack syndrome uniqueness, we propose an optimization approach to design attack monitoring trails such that their number and length is minimal. This allows us to use the optical network as a sensor for physical-layer attacks. Numerical simulation results indicate that our approach obtains network-wide attack source localization at only 5.8% average resource overhead for the attack monitoring trails.

Keywords: Optical network security · Physical-layer attack detection · Attack monitoring trails

1 Introduction

Optical networks are critical communication infrastructure supporting a range of vital societal services and stakeholders. As such, they can be a target of deliberate attacks aimed at service disruption (SD) or eavesdropping by exploiting the inherent vulnerabilities of the optical devices [9]. While protection

This work was supported by the CelticPlus project SENDATE-EXTEND and COST Action 15127 RECODIS.

from eavesdropping relies on various methods for encryption at different layers of the networking stack, including the recent efforts in Quantum Key Distribution(QKD) systems, service disruption attacks threatening the advanced physical-layer paradigms, have not been adequately addressed so far. A plethora of physical-layer SD attack methods differs in terms of their level of sophistication, ease of implementation, damaging effects, their scope, extent, and persistence, ease of discovery, etc. For example, fiber cuts are relatively straightforward to implement, they affect all connections traversing the cut link, with the effect confined to that link, and are easy to discover.

One of the most harmful attack methods identified in the literature is power jamming. It is performed by inserting a harmful signal of excessive power into the fiber (e.g., by bending it [11]), which reduces the amount of gain allocated to co-propagating optical channels and aggravates the physical-layer impairments in the fiber. The damaging effects of this attack technique are not necessarily confined to the primarily intruded link but may propagate through the network. Combined with the lack of accurate attack models, as well as limited availability of physical-layer information due to the high cost and sparse placement of Optical Performance Monitoring (OPM) devices, identification and source localization of attacks at the optical layer is very challenging.

Recent advancements in commercially available coherent receivers that provide a rich set of OPM parameters to the Network Management System (NMS), paired with the proliferation of machine learning (ML) techniques, enable a breakthrough in physical-layer security management. Instead of relying on strategic deployment of OPM devices to help localize security breaches, which is expensive and unscalable, attack management can now leverage the ample OPM information obtained from the receivers at the destination of each connection, where they need to be detected anyway. This extensive set of OPM data can then be exhaustively analysed by applying ML techniques which allow to identify intricate relationships among the various parameters under different security regimes.

In our previous work, we have experimentally investigated the detection of harmful signals to identify signatures of jamming attacks of varying intensities. To this end, we developed machine learning approaches based on supervised [5] and unsupervised learning [3], that analyzed the OPM data obtained for a particular connection, and identified whether it has been affected by a jamming attack. The approaches based on supervised learning were able to achieve 100% accuracy in attack identification [5], while previously unseen (zero-day) attack scenarios were detected in up to 92% of occurrences [3]. In spite of the favorable performance of these approaches for detecting disruption at the connection level, localizing the source of a harmful signal at the network level requires a network-wide approach.

To this end, we propose an approach for network security diagnostics based on correlating the health of multiple connections upon their detection at the receiver and localizing the attack source according to the subset of degraded connections. We focus on the worst-case jamming attacks where we assume that any individual connection can carry a jamming signal, which can then affect the co-propagating connections along its entire physical path (i.e., there is no mechanism of thwarting the harmful signal propagation). This allows us to provide a general model for localizing the source of a harmful signal, which can easily be adapted to more specific cases by fine-tuning the assumptions. The scope of the damage from a jamming signal is modeled by defining binary words which we refer to as attack syndromes. Attack syndromes, if unique, provide a way of using the network as a sensor capable of diagnosing the security status of the network and identifying the harmful connection. To support such functionality, we develop an approach for generating unique attack syndromes in the network by sparse addition of attack monitoring probes such that their number and length is minimal.

The remainder of the paper is organized as follows. Section 2 overviews the related work. Section 3 explains the concept of proposed attack syndromes, their significance and formation. The problem of designing attack monitoring trails that ensure unique attack syndromes is formulated as an integer linear program in Sect. 4. Section 5 evaluates the performance of the proposed approach, while Sect. 6 outlines the remaining challenges and concludes the paper.

2   Related Work

Studies [4,8,14] focus on the detection of jamming attacks. In [4], the authors leverage alarms raised by the network components. Binary trees are formed based on the established channels and the deployed devices to reduce the time needed to analyze an alarm received by the centralized NMS. In [14], another centralized approach is proposed, relying on monitors and diagnostic lightpaths to improve attack detection efficiency. A distributed approach from [8] detects jamming attacks by tracking power levels of each connection at every port of each node in the network and forwarding the diagnostic procedure upstream until the source node of the harmful signal is located. The effectiveness of these procedures heavily depends on the assumptions of a particular attack method (e.g., monitoring only power to detect power jamming). Moreover, alarming the components for all types of attacks is costly, while monitoring all signals at all ports is expensive and unscalable. A mechanism based on constant sensing and reporting of numerous individual active monitors does not scale well with the size and the agility of future optical networks. In addition, such procedures increase the NMS complexity and stress the limited capability of network processing units, as the total amount of monitored information and signalling grows linearly with the number and size of network elements, and the number of connections. Therefore, we propose an approach that leverages only the information about connection health available at the receiver to form attack syndromes, while sparsely adding attack monitoring trails to resolve potential syndrome ambiguity.

The concept of monitoring trails has been thoroughly investigated in the context of link failure detection. In [12], the authors applied information theory to derive a tight lower bound on the minimum number of probes per network edge needed for failure diagnostics. The optimal design of monitoring trails using Integer Linear Programming (ILP) for single-link failures was presented in [13]. [1,2,10] proposed monitoring trail design to detect shared risk link group (SRLG) failures. While these approaches enable cost-efficient detection of failures of single or multiple geographically correlated links, our approach is concerned of detecting harmful connections that can traverse multiple links and affect different connections along their paths, requiring a connection-based approach.

3   Attack Syndromes for Unambiguous Localization of an Attack Source

The main idea of the proposed approach for attack source localization is to model the mutual attacking relations among the connections in the network, and deduce the source of an attack based on the subset of connections registered as degraded upon an attack occurrence. We use a simple example shown in Fig. 1 depicting a network with 6 nodes (A to F) and 4 connections (c_1 to c_4) to explain the basic concepts and structures used in the proposed approach. The attacking relations among connections are modeled using an attack graph (AG) and the corresponding attack diagnostic matrix A. Each connection c_i in the network is represented by an AG node. The AG element c_i is adjacent to all other connections c_j that are affected in case c_i carries a harmful signal.

The dimensions of the attack diagnostic matrix A match the number of connections in the network. Element $A[i, j]$ is equal to 1 if a harmful signal inserted on connection c_i can affect connection c_j (i.e., if they are adjacent in AG), and 0 otherwise. In this way, row i represents the binary attack syndrome (AS) of connection c_i. If the syndromes are unique, when NMS receives alarms reporting degradation of connections c_j that are adjacent to c_i in the AG, the received attack syndrome will match the one of c_i, which will identify c_i as the harmful connection. This is the case for the attack syndromes of all connections shown in Fig. 1.

However, attack syndromes of different individual connections can match and, hence, fail to provide unambiguous attack localization. Figure 2(a) illustrates such a scenario using the same network topology as in Fig. 1, and a different set of connections. As can be seen in the attack matrix, the attack

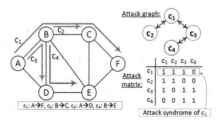

Fig. 1. An illustrative example with unique attack syndromes for all connections.

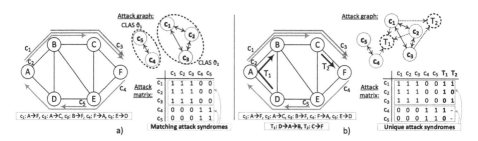

Fig. 2. An illustrative example with ambiguous attack syndromes (a), resolved by adding two attack monitoring trails T_1 and T_2 (b).

syndromes of connections $\{c_1, c_2, c_3\}$ are identical, as well as those of $\{c_4, c_5\}$. We refer to the set of connections with matching attack syndromes as a Cluster of Ambiguous Attack Syndromes (CLAS). As can be seen from the attack graph in Fig. 2(a), there are two CLASes, denoted with ϑ_1 and ϑ_2, and connections inside each CLAS form a clique (not necessarily maximal) in the AG. In general, a CLAS may be a part of a larger clique in the AG, where the attack syndromes of the CLAS non-members are differentiated due to their adjacency to other connections outside of the clique.

Attack syndrome disambiguation can be aided through judicious resource assignment, aimed at avoiding the creation of CLASes, minimizing their number or size [7]. However, such approaches cannot guarantee complete elimination of CLASes as a prerequisite for unambiguous identification of harmful connections. Therefore, we propose an approach for adding attack monitoring trails in the network which guarantee to break the ambiguity of indistinguishable attack syndromes, while minimizing the number and the length of added trails.

The example in Fig. 2(b) illustrates how to resolve attack syndrome ambiguity through sparse addition of dedicated attack monitoring trails. In general, in order to distinguish among attack syndromes of $|\vartheta|$ connections in CLAS ϑ, $\lceil log_2|\vartheta| \rceil$ distinguishing bits need to be added to their respective attack syndromes, i.e., we need to probe $\lceil log_2|\vartheta| \rceil$ individual network links. Any link to be probed for AS disambiguation needs to be traversed by one up to $|\vartheta| - 1$ connections from the CLAS ϑ (otherwise it does not provide any extra information about the harmful connection). For the example in Fig. 2(b), disambiguation of CLAS ϑ_1 requires probing $\lceil log_2|\vartheta_1| \rceil = \lceil log_2 3 \rceil = 2$ links (candidate links: A-B and C-F), while disambiguation of CLAS ϑ_2 requires probing $\lceil log_2|\vartheta_2| \rceil = \lceil log_2 1 \rceil = 1$ link (candidates: F-E and D-A).

In order to be resource-efficient, the total number of attack monitoring trails in the network, as well as their length, should be minimized. Therefore, each trail should traverse multiple individual links selected for probing. When deciding which candidate links to select for probing, and how to establish the attack monitoring trails over those links, two main constraints must be taken into account:

- The binary suffixes formed by the bits added to the attack syndromes of connections in the same CLAS by the established attack monitoring trails must be unique, and
- A monitoring trail should not include multiple candidate links intended to break attack syndrome ambiguity of connections in the same CLAS.

A feasible solution with two attack monitoring trails, denoted as T_1 and T_2 is shown in Fig. 2(b). T_1 is a multi-link trail that traverses link D-A to disambiguate the syndromes of connections in CLAS ϑ_1, and link A-B to disambiguate the syndromes in CLAS ϑ_2. As there are 3 connections in ϑ_2, link C-F is used for trail T_2. The suffixes added by T_1 and T_2 in the attack matrix in Fig. 2(b) are shown in bold. In the next section, we present an ILP for the establishment of attack monitoring trails that ensure unique attack syndromes and, hence, unambiguous identification of the harmful connection, while minimizing the number and the length of the trails.

4   Design of Probing Trails for Attack Localization

4.1   Problem Definition

Given is a physical network topology and a set of routed optical connections. The network topology is modeled as a graph $\mathcal{G}=(\mathcal{V},\mathcal{E})$, where $\mathcal{V}$ denotes a set of vertices representing network nodes, and $\mathcal{E}$ denotes a set of edges, representing directed network links. The set of routed optical connections is denoted as $\mathcal{C}$, where each connection $c \in \mathcal{C}$ traverses a set of links P_c along its path from the source node s_c to the destination node d_c. Based on the assignment of resources to the connections, the mutual attacking relations among them are identified *a priori* and given in form of an attack graph and a corresponding attack matrix, that allows for derivation of the attack syndromes. Consequently, the set of Clusters of Ambiguous Attack Syndromes CLASes, denoted with Θ, is also given. Our objective is to set up attack monitoring trails in the network which will ensure disambiguation among matching attack syndromes of the connections in such a way that the number and the length of the added trails is minimal. To do so, we must first determine the individual links in the network whose probing enables attack syndrome disambiguation, followed by the routing of the attack monitoring trails over the links identified in the previous step.

4.2   ILP Formulation

Input parameters

- $\mathcal{G}(\mathcal{V},\mathcal{E})$: a directed graph where $\mathcal{V}$ is the set of vertices that represent the network nodes, and $\mathcal{E}$ is the set of arcs that represent the network links. Each link e is defined by its source node o_e and destination node t_e;
- $\mathcal{C}$: a set of connections, where each connection $c \in \mathcal{C}$ is defined by its source node s_c, destination node d_c and physical route π_c;

- Φ: connection routing, where ϕ_e^c is equal to 1 if connection c traverses link e;
- Θ: a set of CLASes. Each CLAS $\vartheta \in \Theta$ comprises connections that have matching attack syndromes. In order to disambiguate the attack syndromes of lightpaths in CLAS ϑ, $\lceil log_2 |\vartheta| \rceil$ links need to be probed;
- F: probe-CLAS mapping matrix, where $F_{\vartheta,p}$ is equal to 1 if probing link p contributes to the disambiguation of attack syndromes for CLAS ϑ.
- H: probe-connection mapping matrix, where $H_{c,p}$ is equal to 1 if probing link p contributes to the disambiguation of the attack syndrome for connection c;
- $\mathcal{P}$: set of links that need to be probed, and may be concatenated into attack monitoring trails;
- $\mathcal{T}$: set of attack monitoring trails, $|\mathcal{T}|$ initiated to $|\mathcal{P}|$;
- M: a large constant, set to 1000.

Variables

- $\alpha_p^c \in \{0,1\}$: equal to 1 if a harmful signal carried by connection $c \in \mathcal{C}$ can affect probed link $p \in \mathcal{P}$, and 0 otherwise;
- $\overline{\alpha}_e^{c,p} \in \{0,1\}$: equal to 1 if connection c uses link e which matches probe p, and 0 otherwise;
- $\beta_p^t \in \{0,1\}$: equal to 1 if attack monitoring trail $t \in \mathcal{T}$ encompasses probed link p, and 0 otherwise;
- $\gamma_e^p \in \{0,1\}$: equal to 1 if probed link p matches link $e \in \mathcal{E}$, and 0 otherwise;
- $\overline{\gamma}_e^t \in \{0,1\}$: equal to 1 if attack monitoring trail t traverses link $e \in \mathcal{E}$, and 0 otherwise;
- $\delta_v^t \in \{0,1\}$: equal to 1 if node $v \in \mathcal{V}$ is the source node of trail t, and 0 otherwise;
- $\overline{\delta}_v^t \in \{0,1\}$: equal to 1 if node v is the destination node of trail t, and 0 otherwise;
- $\epsilon_e^{t,p} \in \{0,1\}$: equal to 1 if probed link p encompassed by trail t matches link e, and 0 otherwise;
- $\overline{\epsilon}_e^{t,p} \in \{0,1\}$: equal to 1 if probed link p matches link e, but is not encompassed by t, and 0 otherwise;
- $\eta^t \in \{0,1\}$: equal to 1 if trail t is active;
- $\Delta_c \in \mathbb{Z}^+$: decimal representation of the connection c's attack syndrome suffix formed by added probes;
- $x_p^t, z_p^t, y_p^t \in \{0,1\}$: control variables;

Objective function

$$\text{Minimize} \quad \sum_{t \in \mathcal{T}} \eta^t + \sum_{t \in \mathcal{T}} \overline{\gamma}_e^t \tag{1}$$

The objective of the approach is to minimize the total number of attack monitoring trails established in the network, and their total length in terms of link count.

Constraints

$$\Delta_c = \sum_p 10^p \cdot \alpha_p^c \cdot H_{c,p}, \quad \forall c \in \mathcal{C}. \tag{2}$$

Constraint (2) calculates the decimal value of the attack syndrome binary suffix formed by the probed links.

$$\Delta_c \neq \Delta_d, \quad \forall c, d \in \mathcal{C} : c, d \in \vartheta, c \neq d. \tag{3}$$

Constraint (3) ensures distinctive attack syndrome suffixes of any two connections c and d in the same CLAS ϑ.

$$\overline{\alpha}_e^{c,p} = \phi_e^c \cdot \gamma_e^p, \quad \forall c \in \mathcal{C}, \forall p \in \mathcal{P}, \forall e \in \mathcal{E}. \tag{4}$$

$$M \cdot \alpha_p^c \geq \sum_{e \in \mathcal{E}} \overline{\alpha}_e^{c,p}, \quad \forall c \in \mathcal{C}, \forall p \in \mathcal{P}. \tag{5}$$

$$\alpha_p^c \leq \sum_{e \in \mathcal{E}} \overline{\alpha}_e^{c,p}, \quad \forall c \in \mathcal{C}, \forall p \in \mathcal{P}. \tag{6}$$

Constraints (4)–(6) ensure that probed link p is marked as affected by connection c if they share any common link e.

$$\sum_{t \in \mathcal{T}} \beta_p^t \geq 1, \quad \forall p \in \mathcal{P}. \tag{7}$$

$$M \cdot \eta^t \geq \sum_{p \in \mathcal{P}} \beta_p^t, \quad \forall t \in \mathcal{T}. \tag{8}$$

$$\beta_p^t \leq \eta^t, \quad \forall p \in \mathcal{P}, \forall t \in \mathcal{T}. \tag{9}$$

$$\beta_p^t + \beta_r^t \leq 2 - F_{\vartheta,p} \cdot F_{\vartheta,r}, \quad \forall t \in \mathcal{T}, \tag{10}$$

$$\forall \vartheta \in \Theta, \forall p, r \in \mathcal{P} : F_{\vartheta,p} = F_{\vartheta,r} = 1, p \neq r.$$

Constraints (7)–(9) make sure that each probed link is included in an active attack monitoring trail. Constraint (10) guarantees that two probed links p and r which are used for disambiguation of attack syndromes within the same CLAS ϑ are not included in the same trail.

$$\sum_{v \in \mathcal{V}} \delta_v^t = \eta^t, \quad \forall t \in \mathcal{T}. \tag{11}$$

$$\sum_{v \in \mathcal{V}} \overline{\delta}_v^t = \eta^t, \quad \forall t \in \mathcal{T}. \tag{12}$$

$$\delta_v^t + \overline{\delta}_v^t \leq 1, \quad \forall t \in \mathcal{T}, \forall v \in \mathcal{V}. \tag{13}$$

Constraints (11)–(13) assign a source and a destination node to each active trail t.

$$\epsilon_e^{t,p} = \gamma_e^p \wedge \beta_p^t, \quad \forall T \in \mathcal{T}, \forall p \in \mathcal{P}, \forall e \in \mathcal{E}. \tag{14}$$

$$\bar{\epsilon}_e^{t,p} = \gamma_e^p \wedge (1 - \beta_p^t), \quad \forall t \in \mathcal{T}, \forall p \in \mathcal{P}, \forall e \in \mathcal{E}. \tag{15}$$

Constraints (14) and (15) model the relation between trail t and probe p that matches link e. Symbol $\wedge$ represents the logical *AND* operation in a compact form. Relation $a = b \wedge c$ is linearized as $a \geq b + c - 1; a \leq b; a \leq c$.

$$M \cdot \bar{\gamma}_e^t \geq \sum_{p \in \mathcal{P}} \epsilon_e^{t,p}, \quad \forall t \in \mathcal{T}, \forall e \in \mathcal{E}. \tag{16}$$

$$M \cdot (1 - \bar{\gamma}_e^t) \geq \sum_{p \in \mathcal{P}} \bar{\epsilon}_e^{t,p}, \quad \forall t \in \mathcal{T}, \forall e \in \mathcal{E}. \tag{17}$$

$$\bar{\gamma}_e^t \leq \eta^t, \quad \forall t \in \mathcal{T}, \forall e \in \mathcal{E}. \tag{18}$$

Constraints (16) and (17) model the dependency of the attack monitoring trail routing on the arrangement of probed links which they include or exclude. According to (16), trail t must traverse link e if there exists a probe p which matches e and is included in t. Correspondingly, t is not allowed to traverse link e if it is used by probe p that is excluded from t. Constraint (18) ensures that only active trails use links.

$$\sum_{e \in \mathcal{E}: v = o_e} \bar{\gamma}_e^t - \sum_{e \in \mathcal{E}: v = t_e} \bar{\gamma}_e^t - 1 + M \cdot x_v^t \geq 0, \tag{19}$$

$$\forall t \in \mathcal{T}, \forall v \in \mathcal{V}.$$

$$\delta_v^t \leq M \cdot (1 - x_V^t), \quad \forall t \in \mathcal{T}, \forall v \in \mathcal{V}. \tag{20}$$

$$\sum_{e \in \mathcal{E}: v = t_e} \bar{\gamma}_e^t - \sum_{e \in \mathcal{E}: v = o_e} \bar{\gamma}_e^t - 1 + M \cdot y_v^t \geq 0, \tag{21}$$

$$\forall t \in \mathcal{T}, \forall v \in \mathcal{V}.$$

$$\bar{\delta}_v^t \leq M \cdot (1 - y_v^t), \quad \forall t \in \mathcal{T}, \forall v \in \mathcal{V}. \tag{22}$$

$$\sum_{e \in \mathcal{E}: v = o_e} \bar{\gamma}_e^t - \sum_{e \in \mathcal{E}: v = t_e} \bar{\gamma}_e^t + M \cdot z_v^t \geq 0, \tag{23}$$

$$\forall t \in \mathcal{T}, \forall v \in \mathcal{V}.$$

$$1 - \delta_v^t \wedge \bar{\delta}_v^t \leq M \cdot (1 - z_v^t), \quad \forall t \in \mathcal{T}, \forall v \in \mathcal{V}. \tag{24}$$

Constraints (19)–(24) ensure flow conservation of attack monitoring trails. Constraints (19) and (20) relate to the source node of trail t. If node v is the source of t, i.e., $\delta_v^t = 1$, then the control variable x_v^t in (20) takes on the value of 0, forcing the number of outgoing links from node v carrying t to be greater than the number of incoming links. Similar observations apply to constraints (21)–(22) and (23)–(24) which relate to the destination node and the intermediate nodes of t, respectively.

Assuming $|\mathcal{T}|$ is upper-bounded by $|\mathcal{P}|$, which is in turn upper-bounded by $log_2|\mathcal{C}|$, the number of variables is upper-bounded by $|\mathcal{V}|D(|\mathcal{C}|log_2|\mathcal{C}| + log_2^2|\mathcal{C}|)$, where D is the maximum nodal degree. The number of constraints is upper-bounded by $|\mathcal{C}|^2 + log_2^2|\mathcal{C}|(\mathcal{V}D\mathcal{C} + log_2|\mathcal{C}|)$.

5   Numerical Results

We evaluate the performance of the proposed approach in terms of the generated CLASes and the resources needed for attack diagnostics. The ILP was implemented in Optimization Programming Language (OPL) and solved with CPLEX v12.8 running on a Red Hat Enterprise Linux workstation with 16-cores Intel Xeon processor and 64 GB of RAM. The investigated topologies, shown in Fig. 3, were a dummy network with 6 nodes and 18 unidirectional links (Fig. 3(a)), Polish network with 12 nodes and 36 links [6] (Fig. 3(b)), and the NSF network with 14 nodes and 42 links (Fig. 3(c)).

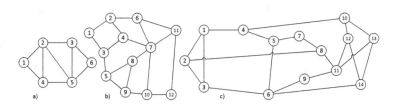

Fig. 3. Test topologies used in simulations: (a) 6-node dummy network, (b) Polish network, and (c) NSF network.

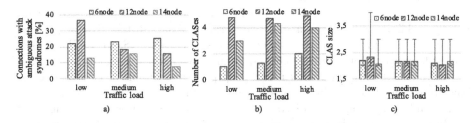

Fig. 4. The percentage of connections with ambiguous attack syndromes (a), the number or CLASes in the network (b), and their size (c).

For each topology, we considered a low, medium and high traffic load, by randomly generating uniformly distributed traffic matrices with $\{2, 3, 5\}$ connection requests per node for the 6-node network, {4, 6, 11} for the Polish, and {5, 7, 13} for the NSF network, respectively. The requests were routed over the shortest physical path, the resulting CLASes were extracted using a C++ script, and fed to the ILP solver. The reported results are averaged over 10 traffic matrices.

To illustrate the need for attack syndrome disambiguation, Fig. 4(a) shows the percentage of connections whose attack syndromes are not unique. For the 6-node and the Polish 12-node network, attack syndromes of 23% connections on average are ambiguous, while this value for the NSF network is 12%. The percentage of AS-ambiguous connections in the 6-node and Polish network decreases for higher loads, which can be explained by a greater number of diverse connections disambiguating each other's syndromes. The average number of CLASes and their respective size are shown in Fig. 4(b) and (c), respectively. The number of CLASes in the 6-node network ranges between 1 and 2, while the Polish and the NSF network test cases have between 3 and 4.9 CLASes. The 6-node and the NSF network have between 2 and 3 connections in each CLAS (denoted with the error bars in Fig. 4(c)), while the maximum CLAS size in the Polish network equals 4, yielding an average CLAS size of just above 2 for all networks.

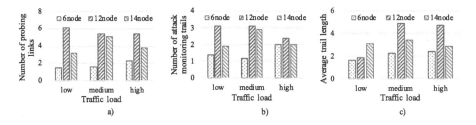

Fig. 5. The number of individual links that need to be probed to resolve attack syndrome ambiguity (a), the number of attack monitoring trails established over those links (b), and the trail length (c).

The number of links which must be probed in order to resolve the ambiguity of the attack syndromes is shown in Fig. 5(a). For the 6-node network, probing on average 1.8 links over all scenarios provides the necessary distinguishable suffixes in the attack syndromes of the connections inside each CLAS. In the Polish and the NSF network, on average 5.6 and 4 links need to probed, respectively. If we assume that only single-link monitoring probes are applied, i.e., there is no concatenation of the probing links into attack monitoring trails, probing each link would require one pair of transponders, and the number of probing links would translate into the number of necessary transponder pairs. Concatenating the probing links into monitoring trails reduces this cost. As shown in Fig. 5(b), our approach requires 1.5, 2.87, and 2.3 attack monitoring trails on average for the three networks, respectively. Establishing multi-link monitoring trails reduces the respective number of necessary transponder pairs by 15.2%, 49.1%, and 44%. The hop count of the established trails is shown in Fig. 5(c). On average over all test cases, attack monitoring trails traverse 2.09, 3.8, and 3.1 links in the 6-node, Polish, and NSF network, respectively. The trails incurred a resource usage overhead of 9.45%, 5.72% and 2.25% for the three networks, respectively, or 5.8% on average over all instances. For the 6-node network, the ILP was solved in less than 1 s, while the average running times for the Polish and the NSF network were 32.8 s and 28.9 s, respectively.

6   Conclusions and Future Work

This paper investigated scalable and resource-efficient localization of harmful connections inserted in the network with the goal of disrupting co-propagating optical channels. The proposed approach is based on leveraging OPM data available from the receivers and forming binary attack syndromes that reflect the health of each connection. To ensure the attack syndromes are unique, which is essential for correct identification of the harmful connection, we developed an ILP for sparse addition of attack monitoring probes of minimal number and length. The simulation results indicate that complete attack syndrome disambiguation can be achieved at only a minor resource overhead for the probes. For future work, we plan to investigate diagnostics of a broader range of attacks with different effects, while also incorporating the uncertainty of ML approaches in the detection of connection degradation caused by attacks. To enhance the scalability of the framework, low-complexity heuristic solutions will be developed.

References

1. Ali, M.L., et al.: M-burst: a framework of SRLG failure localization in all-optical networks. IEEE/OSA J. Opt. Commun. Networking 4(8), 628–638 (2012). https://doi.org/10.1364/JOCN.4.000628
2. Babarczi, P., et al.: Adjacent link failure localization with monitoring trails in all-optical mesh networks. IEEE/ACM Trans. Networking 19(3), 907–920 (2011). https://doi.org/10.1109/TNET.2010.2096429
3. Furdek, M., et al.: Experiment-based identification of service disruption attacks in optical networks. In: Proceedings of Photonics West, pp. 10946-12.1–10, February 2019. https://doi.org/10.1117/12.2509613
4. Mas, C., et al.: Failure location algorithm for transparent optical networks. IEEE J. Sel. Areas Commun. 23(8), 1508–1519 (2005). https://doi.org/10.1109/JSAC.2005.852182
5. Natalino, C., et al.: Field demonstration of machine-learning-aided detection and identification of jamming attacks in optical networks. In: Proceedings of ECOC, pp. We2.58.1–3, September 2018. https://doi.org/10.1109/ECOC.2018.8535155
6. Orlowski, S., Wessäly, R., Pióro, M., Tomaszewski, A.: SNDlib 1.0—Survivable network design library. Networks 55(3), 276–286 (2010). https://doi.org/10.1002/net.20371. https://onlinelibrary.wiley.com/doi/abs/10.1002/net.20371
7. Pederzolli, F., et al.: Towards secure optical networks: a framework to aid localization of harmful connections. In: Proceedings of OFC, p. Th2A.42, March 2018. IEEEXplore

8. Rejeb, R., et al.: Multiple attack localization and identification in all-optical networks. Opt. Switch. Netw. **3**(1), 41–49 (2006). https://doi.org/10.1016/j.osn.2005.12.001
9. Skorin-Kapov, N., et al.: Physical-layer security in evolving optical networks. IEEE Commun. Mag. **54**(8), 110–117 (2016). https://doi.org/10.1109/MCOM.2016.7537185
10. Tapolcai, J., et al.: Neighborhood failure localization in all-optical networks via monitoring trails. IEEE/ACM Trans. Netw. **23**(6), 1719–1728 (2015). https://doi.org/10.1109/TNET.2014.2342222
11. Uematsu, T., et al.: Design of a temporary optical coupler using fiber bending for traffic monitoring. IEEE Photonics J. **9**(6), 1–13 (2017). https://doi.org/10.1109/JPHOT.2017.2762662
12. Wen, Y., et al.: Efficient fault-diagnosis algorithms for all-optical WDM networks with probabilistic link failures. IEEE/OSA J. Lightwave Technol. **23**(10), 3358–3371 (2005). https://doi.org/10.1109/JLT.2005.855695
13. Wu, B., et al.: Monitoring trail: on fast link failure localization in mesh all-optical networks. IEEE/OSA J. Lightwave Technol. **27**(18), 4175–4185 (2009). https://doi.org/10.1109/JLT.2009.2022769
14. Wu, T., Somani, A.: Crosstalk attack monitoring and localization in all-optical networks. IEEE/ACM Trans. Networking **13**(6), 1390–1401 (2005). https://doi.org/10.1109/TNET.2005.860103

Analytical Modeling of Survivable Anycast Communication in Optical Networks

Yan Cui and Vinod M. Vokkarane[✉]

University of Massachusetts Lowell, Lowell, MA 01854, USA
Yan_Cui@student.uml.edu, Vinod_Vokkarane@uml.edu

Abstract. Network resources are imperfect and vulnerable to failure from a wide variety of sources. Survivability is a well-researched field that focuses on strategies to prevent or reduce the harm inflicted when network elements fail. Solutions tend to either provision resources, such as backup paths, proactively so that traffic can be switched to the alternative route after a failure, or quickly find new resources to provision after failure event occurs. Current survivability solutions guarantee protection against these failures, but there is no mathematical model to calculate the network blocking probability for survivability solutions of anycast communication. In this paper, we developed new analytical models to calculate network-wide blocking performance for anycast survivability approaches. Performance results show that our models are accurate and are verified by extensive simulation results.

Keywords: Survivability · Analytical model · WDM networks · Anycast

1 Introduction

In recent years, with rapid growth in demands on network connections, the optical network, acting as the foundation of network connectivity, have been becoming more and more indispensable and important to our daily life. Hence, failures in optical networks may cause catastrophic disasters. Those network failures happen on both network nodes and network links are common due to the human error, such as fiber cuts during construction accidents [1] and natural disasters. The arrival of Hurricane Sandy in New York and New Jersey in October 2012 resulted in the failure of three hundred Verizon facilities along the eastern seaboard [2]. Other unavoidable natural disasters, such as the catastrophic destruction brought about by 2011 Tohoku earthquake and tsunami in Japan [3], can occur, often without warning. Therefore, the ability of recovery of network connectivity, which is called network survivability [4], is of significance in the design of modern networks.

Regarding traffic engineering strategies, it can be beneficial to use different transmission techniques with respect to the characteristics of realized demands. Nowadays, the conventional transmission paradigm is unicast, i.e., data transmits from a source node to a destination node. However, the unicast paradigm cannot accommodate the novel distributed network applications, e.g., content distribution and Data Center (DC).

© IFIP International Federation for Information Processing 2020
Published by Springer Nature Switzerland AG 2020
A. Tzanakaki et al. (Eds.): ONDM 2019, LNCS 11616, pp. 323–335, 2020.
https://doi.org/10.1007/978-3-030-38085-4_28

In the distributed network applications, available network services are provided by more than one network service providers (e.g., the DCs). In order to support these services, anycast could be applied which refers to the transmission of data from a source node to any one member in the candidate destination set [5]. The anycast client can establish a connection with any of the available DCs and selects the target DC based on different network performance criteria (e.g., DC response time, distance to DC, DC load, etc.). As a consequence, anycast is capable of improving network performance, remarkably reduce the network load and may also provide protection against the selected the target DC failure [6].

The designs of survivable networks are often modeled as the linear programming problem with graph theory, wherein, the nodes represent the network components (such as computers, routers, etc.), and edges represent the communication links between the components. Therefore, the survivable network design problem can be modeled as a problem of finding a subgraph satisfying certain connectivity constraints, or augmenting a given network to certain connectivity requirements [7]. In particular, the input is an undirected graph (or digraphs) with weights on the edges or nodes and prescribed demands on connectivity between nodes in the graph with the objective being the computation a subgraph of minimum weight that satisfies the connectivity demands.

There are mainly a drawback in the existing works on design of survivable networks, (1) authors are mainly focused on the design of optimal network survivability algorithms without considering the negative effects caused by new designed survivability algorithms. For instance, by selecting a subgraph for a pair of source and destination, there will be less available network resources for other traffics. This might cause severe network congestion when the amount of traffics is large.

In this work, we provide the theoretical analysis demonstrating the network-wide block rate with considering the survivability algorithms for anycast traffics. We assume two protection policies for anycast traffic networks. One is called survivable routing policy (SRP); The other is called survivable routing with relocation policy (SRRP). In the first scheme, two link-disjointed path are allocated to each pair of traffic source and destination. For efficient resource provision, in the second scheme, the Anycast connection is composed of two link disjoint routing paths between an anycast client and two same content DCs, wherein one path is used as the backup path just in case the primary path that carries the data fails.

The remainder of this paper is organized as follows: Sect. 2 introduces the network model and assumptions, and we describe the proposed blocking probability analytical model in Sect. 3. Numerical evaluation and model verification are discussed in Sect. 4, and Sect. 5 concludes this paper.

2   Network Model and Assumptions

We consider a stochastic connection request arrival process and model connection arrivals in the network as a Poisson process. We also assume that the holding time of connection requests is exponentially distributed. In the analysis, the total offered load of the network is uniformly distributed between different anycast client.

We adopt the first-fit wavelength assignment (FF-WA) policy. In this scheme, all wavelengths are indexed and lowest indexed available wavelength is assigned before a higher indexed wavelength. We also assume that the resource provisioning and allocation for the dynamic connection request starts as soon as the request arrives into the network. The connection requests are holding-time-aware, each providing an exact duration.

Moreover, we assume that full wavelength conversion between all input and output links at all intermediate optical cross-connects is available. This provide the ability of fully making use of available wavelength spectrum for every link in a path.

2.1 Survivable Routing Policy (SRP)

We denote a anycast connection request as $R(s, D)$. Where s is anycast connection request node, and $D = (d_1, d_2, \ldots, d_m)$ is a destination set and all candidate destinations are numbered. We assume that a source node s is randomly chosen from a node set and a candidate destination set is randomly chosen from the same node set except the source node for each incoming connection request.

For each source and candidate destination pair, we use Dijkstra's algorithm to find the optimal link-disjointed primary path and backup path. We denote the primary path as $p(s, d_{ip})$, and the backup path as $p(s, d_{ib})$, wherein i is the index of candidate destination. For example, Fig. 1 shows for the anycast client located at node 1, the destination set includes two destinations: node 2 and node 5. For the first destination node 2, the primary path generated by Dijkstra's algorithm is $p(s, d_{1p})$ and the related link-disjointed backup is $p(s, d_{1b})$. For the second destination node 5, the primary path and backup path are $p(s, d_{2p})$ and $p(s, d_{2b})$.

Anycast service requires selection of a destination for the candidate destinations. We use a first-fit destination selection (FF-DS) policy. In the FF-DS, all candidate destinations are numbered. Each destination will be checked one by one to verify if there are any available wavelengths for the incoming request. If at least one wavelength is available on each link along the primary and backup paths at a destination, the reservation is successful. Otherwise, the next destination will be checked. If there are no available wavelength on any link along all destinations, the connection request will be blocked. As an example a anycast client at node 1, the first destination node 2 will be checked first, followed by the second destination node 5. If there are no available wavelengths on any link all the two destinations, the anycast request will be blocked.

2.2 Survivable Routing with Relocation Policy (SRRP)

We denote an connection request as $R(s, D)$, where s is the anycast connection request node, $D = (d_p, d_b)$ and d_p is the selected target DC node, and d_b is backup data center node with same content. We assume that each node may be a source node s or a data center node d_p for the incoming connection request. We assume there are n DC nodes provide same content as backup choice. The backup data center node is generated randomly among of the n same DC nodes.

For each source – target DC- backup DC pair, we use Dijkstra's algorithm to find the optimal link-disjointed primary path and backup path. We denote the primary path as $p(s, d_p)$, and the backup path as $p(s, d_b)$. For example, Fig. 2 shows for the anycast client located at node 1, the primary path generated by Dijkstra's algorithm is $p(n_1, n_2)$ and the related link-disjointed backup path is $p(n_1, n_5)$.

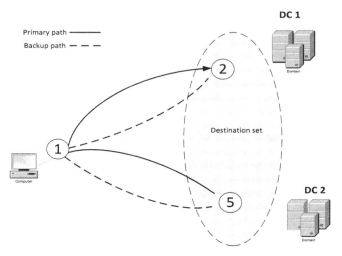

Fig. 1. Anycast connection with primary and backup paths for each DC.

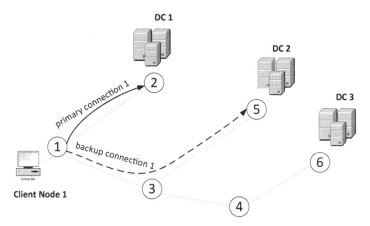

Fig. 2. Anycast connection with primary and backup paths.

In order to cope with link failures, a connection needs to be allocated with a primary path and a backup path. The primary path $p(s, d_p)$ is the working path used to transfer its data from the source s to the destination d_p. The data is rerouted through the backup path in case of a failure on the primary path. We adopt dedicated path protection scheme to define the blocking problem for incoming connection request. When a connection request arrival at the network, the request tries to get resource allocation on the primary path and backup path, if currently there are available resource on each link traversed by primary path or backup path, we call this connection request is allocated successfully. Otherwise, the connection request will be blocked.

3 Analytical Blocking Model

There are two parts in this section. In the first part, we give the computation process of link arrival rates to calculate the link blocking probability. We present our theoretical model on how to calculate the average network blocking probability in the second part.

3.1 Computation of Link Arrival Rate

Survivable Routing Policy (SRP)
Link arrival rate when $|D| = 1$
    This is called unicast traffic, when only one destination is included in destination set for incoming request. Since each node may be a source node or a candidate destination node, we can find that the total number of combinations of source-candidate destination pairs is $v \cdot (v - 1)$, if the network has v nodes. Since the total offered load to the network is uniformly distributed among source-candidate destination set pairs, we can derive the arrival rate between a source and a destination as

$$\lambda^{s,D} = \lambda^{s,d} = \frac{\lambda}{v(v - 1)} \tag{1}$$

We obtain the arrival rate λ^j for link j by combining the contributions of requests from all primary and backup paths that traverse such a link. Hence,

$$\lambda^j = \sum_{s,d \,|\, j \epsilon rp(s,d_p) \text{ or } j \in p(s,d_b)} \lambda^{s,d}. \tag{2}$$

Link arrival rate when $|D| >= 2$
    Each source-candidate destination set pair includes a source node and two destination nodes, which means the size of the route set is 2. As each node in an anycast network may be a source node or a destination node, if a network graph includes v nodes, the number of combinations of source-candidate destination set pairs is $v(v - 1)(v - 2)$. Since the total offered load to the network is uniformly distributed among source-candidate destination set pairs, we can derive the arrival rate of a route set between a source and candidate destination set as

$$\lambda^{s,D} = \frac{\lambda}{v \cdot (v - 1)(v - 2)} \tag{3}$$

The request to the destination set will arrive at the first destination and attempt resource allocation, so the arrival rate of the first destination is the same as the arrival rate of the route set. However, if the request coming to first destination set is blocked, the request then arrives to the second destination and tries to receive resource allocation. So the contributed arrival rate to the second route is from the requests which are already blocked on the first destination.
    In summary, we can derive the arrival rate of each source-destination pair by combining the contributions of requests that arrive at the destination set as

$$\lambda^{s,d} = \sum_{s,D} \lambda^{s,D} + \sum_{s,D} \lambda^{s,D} P^{sd^1}. \tag{4}$$

In above equation, the first term is the sum of the arrival rate of source-candidate destination set pairs in which the destination d is the first destination in a destination set. The second term is the sum of the arrival rate of destination sets in which the d is the second destination, as shown in Fig. 3. Considering that the blocking probability P^{sd^1} that one source destination pair is blocked has already been computed in unicast network, we can compute the arrival rate of a source-candidate destination pair using the above equation. We can use Eq. (2) to calculate the link arrival rate after having computed the route arrival rate.

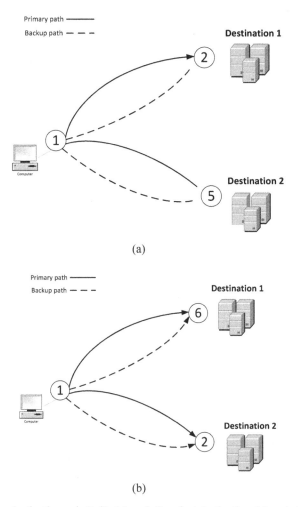

Fig. 3. A source destination pair (1,2): (a) node 2 as first destination (b) node 2 as second one

Survivable Routing with Relocation Policy (SRRP)

We denote the total mean arrival rate to the network as λ, the arrival rate for each primary-backup paths set as λ^{s,d_p,d_b}, the arrival rate of primary path between source s

and destination d_p as λ^{s,d_p} and the arrival rate of backup path as λ^{s,d_b}. We will derive the link j arrival rate λ^j based on the connection request traversed by link j.

Since each node may be an anycast client node or a target DC node and the backup DC node is fixed based on the target DC node, we can find that the total number of combinations of client-DC pairs is $v \cdot (v-1)$, if the network has v nodes. Since the total offered load to the network is uniformly distributed among client-DC pairs, we can derive the arrival rate between a client node and DC node as

$$\lambda^{s,d_p,d_b} = \lambda^{s,d_p} = \lambda^{s,d_b} = \frac{\lambda}{v(v-1)}. \tag{5}$$

The connection request will go to primary path and backup path and try to get resource allocation. For a route (source-destination pair) in a network generated by route algorithm, as shown in Fig. 4, the route may be as a primary path or as backup path to do the resource allocation. We denote a route in a network as $p(s,d)$ and the cumulated arrival rate going through this route as $\lambda^{s,d}$. We can get the arrival rate of a route (source-destination pair) generated by routing algorithm as

$$\lambda^{s,d} = \lambda^{s,d_p} + \lambda^{s,d_b} \tag{6}$$

We obtain the arrival rate λ^j for link j by combining the contributions of requests from all routes $p(s,d)$ that traverse such a link. Hence,

$$\lambda^j = \sum_{s,d \mid j \epsilon r(s,d)} \lambda^{s,d}. \tag{7}$$

3.2 Network-Wide Blocking Model

The average generalized network blocking model is obtained in three steps. First, we provide a link blocking model based on Erlang-B model. We then present the primary and backup path set blocking computation. After having computed primary and backup path set blocking, we can calculate the average network blocking probability.

Link Blocking Analysis
If there is no available wavelength for incoming request on a link, the request is called blocked on this link.

We can model a link as a queuing system. We consider the number of wavelengths for each link to be equal and denoted as W and the average holding time of request is τ. We can calculate the blocking probability of link j, denoted as B_j, which is equal to the Erlang loss formula [9],

$$B^j = B\left(W, \lambda^j \tau\right) = \frac{\frac{(\lambda^j \tau)^W}{w!}}{\sum_{k=0}^{W} \frac{(\lambda^j \tau)^k}{k!}}. \tag{8}$$

In the above equation, λ^j represents the arrival rate of link j.

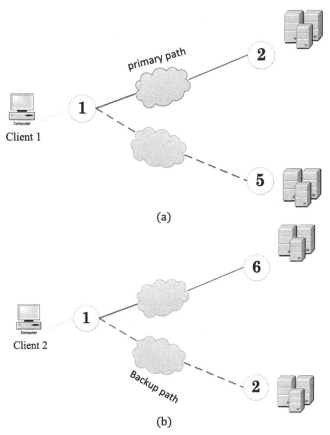

Fig. 4. A path $p(n_1, n_2)$ generated by routing algorithm: (a) as a primary path (b) as backup path for different connection request.

Primary - Backup Path Set Blocking Computation
Under SRP

- For Anycast $|D| = 1$

One destination node means only one pair of primary and backup paths. We can assume that the wavelength allocation on a path is independent between the links which are traversed by this path. With wavelength converters, different wavelength can be assigned on different links along a path. For survivability, there is at least one available wavelength on each link traversed by primary path and backup path for incoming request to get resource allocation. Considering link disjoint constrain, the probability that a connection request gets blocked which means at least one link along a primary path or backup path has no available wavelength when the connection request arrives to the network is equal to 1 minus the probability that the connection is not blocked in any of the corresponding link j along the primary path $p(s, d_p)$ and backup path $p(s, d_b)$, Hence, we can derive the probability that a primary-backup set is blocked as

$$B_{s,D} = 1 - \prod_{\substack{j:j \in p(s,d_p) \\ or\ j \in p(s,d_b)}} \left(1 - B^j\right). \tag{9}$$

- For Anycast $|D| = 2$

If the candidate destination set size is two, there are one primary backup path for each destinations. We know there are no common link between primary and backup paths going to same destination. However common links probably happen between paths belongs to different destinations. We classify the links traversed by the all paths of this anycast traffic as three sets: set CL includes common links traversed by the first and second destinations; set L_1 includes links going to the first destination only; set L_2 includes links going to the second destination only. If any link belongs to CL has no available wavelength, the incoming request will be blocked, because the traffic cannot go the first or second destinations. We define this blocking probability as

$$B_1 = 1 - \prod_{j \in CL} \left(1 - B^j\right). \tag{10}$$

If all links belongs to CL has at least one available wavelength, but any link belongs to set L_1 and any link belongs to set L_2 has no available wavelength. The incoming traffic is still blocked. We define this blocking probability as

$$B_2 = \left(1 - \prod_{j \in L_2} \left(1 - B^j\right)\right)\left(1 - \prod_{j \in L_1} \left(1 - B^j\right)\right) \prod_{j \in CL} \left(1 - B^j\right). \tag{11}$$

In the above, the two cases are mutually exclusive, so we can sum the probability that each case happens to affect the primary-backup path set blocking probability:

$$B_{s,D} = B_1 + B_2. \tag{12}$$

Under SRRP
We can assume that the wavelength allocation on a route is independent between the links which are traversed by this route. With wavelength converters, different wavelength can be assigned on different links along a route. For survivability, there is at least one available wavelength on each link traversed by primary path and backup path for incoming request to get resource allocation. Considering link disjoint constrain, the probability that a connection request gets blocked which means at least one link along a primary path or backup path has no available wavelength when the connection request arrives to the network is equal to 1 minus the probability that the connection is not blocked in any of the corresponding link j along the primary path $p(s, d_p)$ and backup path $p(s, d_b)$, Hence, we can derive the probability that a primary-backup set is blocked as

$$B_{s,d_p,d_b} = 1 - \prod_{\substack{j:j \in p(s,d_p) \\ or\ j \in p(s,d_b)}} \left(1 - B^j\right). \tag{13}$$

Network-Wide Blocking Probability

We can calculate the network wide blocking probability after having computed every individual primary-backup path set blocking probability, which is simply defined as

$$N = \frac{\sum_{s,d_p,d_b} \lambda^{s,d_p,d_b} \cdot \tau \cdot B_{s,d_p,d_b}}{\sum_{s,d_p,d_b} \lambda^{s,d_p,d_b} \cdot \tau}. \tag{14}$$

4 Numerical Results and Analysis

In this section, we assess the analytical blocking model proposed in Sect. 3 and compare its performance with simulation results on the 14-node National Science Foundation network (NSFnet) shown in Fig. 5.

In the simulations, we assume a Poisson arrival process with an average arrival rate of λ and an exponential distribution for request holding time with average holding time τ equal to 1. The total offered load is uniformly distributed among source-candidate destination set pairs. For a given simulation set, we change the arrival rate in order to generate the desired offered load ($\rho = \lambda\tau$). The resource provisioning and allocation for a connection request starts as soon as the call arrives into the network. We use the first-fit wavelength assignment and fixed route policy (Dijkstra's shortest path) to determine the link- disjointed primary and backup path for one source-destination pair or one source-target DC-backup DC pair. We use first-fit destination selection (FF-DS) policy for anycast requests to do the simulation. We assume 8 wavelengths on each link to do the simulation. The simulation results were averaged over 30 seeds of 10^6 connection demands each.

Reduced load [8] is a scientific method for the purpose of making theoretical model more close to reality. It is widely adopted in theoretical model of optical networks. To make our work valuable, we all involve reduced load in our analytical models.

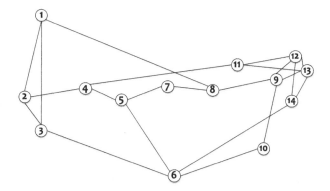

Fig. 5. NSF network.

Figure 6 shows the average network blocking probability performance as a function of different offered load for unicast traffic ($|D| = 1$) in survivability NSFnet. We can observe that the analytical results accurately match the simulation results. As expected, the blocking probability increases as the offered load increases. If the offered load is fixed, the blocking rate for unicast traffic with survivability is much higher than that unicast traffic without survivability algorithm. This is because two link-disjointed paths are provided for each source-destination pair in survivability networks, which needs much more network resource to allocate one single traffic, However the network resource provided are same.

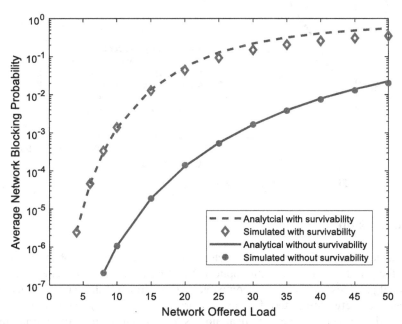

Fig. 6. Network blocking comparison between uncast paradigm $|D| = 1$ without survivability and unicast paradigm with survivability.

Figure 7 shows the average network blocking probability as a function of different offered load under SRP and under SRRP in NSFnet. We can observe that the analytical results accurately match the simulation results. It is worth noting that comparing the results between $|D| = 1$ and $|D| = 2$ under SRP for the NSFnet with same offered load, and same number of wavelengths on each link, the blocking probability on the latter is lower. This is because increasing the number of candidate destinations means increasing the size of the route set for anycast, providing more opportunities for a request to succeed in resource allocation based on FF-DS policy. To gain more insight in the efficiency of survivable routing with relocation scheme, We can observe that performance under survivable routing with relocation scheme are much better than that of under survivable routing for anycast ($|D| = 2$) paradigm, with same offered load.

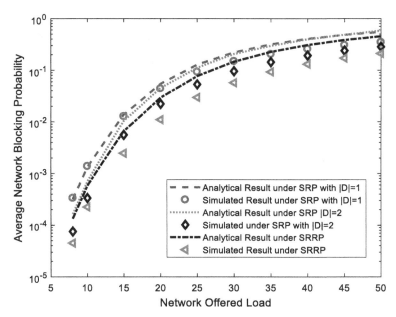

Fig. 7. Network blocking probability under SRP and SRRP

5 Conclusion

We presented analytical models to compute network-wide blocking probability for any-cast traffic paradigm in survivability optical WDM networks. Results demonstrate that our model provides good accuracy compared to simulation results. The models can be considered a useful design tool for anycast survivability optical WDM networks. For future work, we will work on analytical models for many-to-many traffic paradigms in survivability networks [7].

References

1. Modiano, E., Narula, A.: Survivable lightpath routing: a new approach to the design of WDM-based networks. IEEE J. Sel. Areas Commun. **20**(4), 800–809 (2002)
2. Kwasinsk, A.: Hurricane sandy effects on communication systems. The University of Texas at Austin, Technical report PR-AK-0112-2012, December 2012
3. Adachi, T., Ishiyama, Y., Asakura, Y., et al.: The restoration of telecom power damages by the Great East Japan Earthquake. In: 2011 IEEE 33rd International Telecommunications Energy Conference (INTELEC), pp. 1–5, October 2011
4. Ellison, R.J., Fisher, D.A., Linger, R.C., et al.: Survivable network systems: an emerging discipline. Carnegie-Mellon Software Engineering Institute, Technical report CMU/SEI-97-TR-013 (1999)
5. Walkowiak, K., Rak, J.: Shared backup path protection for anycast and unicast flows using the node-link notation. In: Proceedings of the IEEE International Conference on Communication (ICC 2011), Kyoto, Japan, 5–9 June 2011 (2011)

6. Goścień, R., Walkowiak, K., Tornatore, M.: Survivable multipath routing of anycast and unicast traffic in elastic optical networks. IEEE/OSA J. Opt. Commun. Networking **8**(6), 343–355 (2016)
7. Davis, D.A.P., Vokkarane, V.M.: Failure-aware protection for many-to-many routing in content centric networks. IEEE Trans. Netw. Sci. Eng. (2019)
8. Cui, Y., Vokkarane, V.M.: Analytical blocking model for anycast RWA in optical WDM networks. IEEE/OSA J. Opt. Commun. Networking **8**(10), 787–799 (2016)

Network Coding for Security Against Eavesdropping Attacks in Elastic Optical Networks

Giannis Savva[✉], Konstantinos Manousakis, and Georgios Ellinas

Department of Electrical and Computer Engineering and KIOS CoE,
University of Cyprus, 1678 Nicosia, Cyprus
savva.giannis@ucy.ac.cy

Abstract. In this work, routing and spectrum allocation (RSA) algorithms together with network coding (NC) are proposed for elastic optical networks. NC has been used in optical networks for protection against link failures and also in multicasting to improve spectral efficiency. In this work, NC is used to protect confidential connections against eavesdropping attacks. The confidential signals are XOR-ed with other signals at different nodes in their path while transmitted through the network. These signals can be combined either at the source node and/or at intermediate nodes. To implement NC for confidential connections, a set of constraints for the NC problem in addition to the constraints of the RSA problem are incorporated to the algorithms. The combination of signals through network coding significantly increases the security of confidential connections, since an eavesdropper will receive a combination of signals from different connections, making it extremely difficult for the confidential signal to be decrypted. A number of RSA strategies are examined in terms of confidentiality, spectrum utilization, and blocking probability. Performance results demonstrate that network coding provides an additional layer of security for confidential connections with only a small increase in the spectrum usage.

Keywords: Network coding · Eavesdropping · Elastic Optical Network (EON) · Routing and Spectrum Allocation (RSA)

1 Introduction

Elastic optical networks (EONs) based on orthogonal frequency division multiplexing have been proposed to address the growth of traffic in backbone networks. EONs can handle traffic demands more efficiently than wavelength division multiplexed (WDM) networks due to the orthogonality of the spectrum slices used. In EONs, the C-band can be separated in slices (frequency slots) of 25, 12.5, and 6.25 GHz. Therefore, each requested connection can be allocated to a number of spectrum slots in order to be established in the network [1].

© IFIP International Federation for Information Processing 2020
Published by Springer Nature Switzerland AG 2020
A. Tzanakaki et al. (Eds.): ONDM 2019, LNCS 11616, pp. 336–348, 2020.
https://doi.org/10.1007/978-3-030-38085-4_29

In order to solve the routing and spectrum allocation (RSA) problem in EONs and establish a connection for a given demand, the following three constraints must be satisfied: (i) the *spectrum continuity constraint* - each demand must be allocated to the same frequency slots (FS) on each link of the selected path, (ii) the *non-overlapping constraint* - a frequency slot can only be allocated to one demand at a time, and (iii) the *spectrum contiguity constraint* - the frequency slots serving each demand must be contiguous [2].

In EONs, even short attacks can still compromise large amounts of data leading to serious security issues. For this reason, optical layer security (OLS) has received considerable attention in the last few years. Security threats for optical networks include the observation of the existence of communications (privacy), the unauthorized use of spectrum (authentication), the manipulation or destruction of data (integrity), denial of service (availability), and unauthorized access to information (confidentiality) [3–5]. In this work, the focus is on confidentiality, where an adversary tries to make sense of accessed confidential data from an optical communication channel (eavesdropping). For example, in optical networks, an attacker can eavesdrop by physically tapping into the optical fiber or by observing the crosstalk interference emitted in adjacent spectrum by confidential signals [4,6], and can potentially go undetected for a prolonged period of time.

Authors in [7] utilize network coding (NC) for multicasting connections to improve network throughput. In [8] authors propose a proactive protection scheme that combines both the advantages of EONs and NC, in order to enable network resilience against optical link failures while also reducing the optical spectrum utilization. Further, authors in [9] study the effectiveness of linear network coding (LNC) in optical networks to protect connections from security threats such as eavesdropping and jamming attacks. In [10], authors propose an eavesdropping-aware RSA algorithm where demands use several paths to establish a connection based on the probability of eavesdropping. This probability however cannot be always known. In [11] authors propose an RSA algorithm with a spectrum reallocation technique to increase security in EONs, while works in [12], [13] focused on the development of algorithms for the enhancement of physical layer security by using spread spectrum techniques over EONs. These works, however, require additional spectrum resources to establish all connections.

In this work, the focus is again on security against confidential attacks in EONs, but this time novel RSA algorithms are proposed in combination with network coding. New constraints are defined to implement NC and are used as additional constraints to the RSA problem. To the best of our knowledge, this is the first time that NC has been integrated with RSA in order to provide security against eavesdropping attacks in EONs. When NC is utilized, it is extremely difficult for the attacker to compromise any confidential connection, since a number of different connections that traverse several routes will have to be compromised, in order for the attacker to make sense of the accessed confidential data.

The rest of the paper is organized as follows. NC in optical networks is discussed in Sect. 2, followed by the problem description in Sect. 3. Then, the proposed algorithm that uses NC during the solution of the RSA problem is presented in Sect. 4, followed by the performance results in Sect. 5. Finally, Sect. 6 concludes the paper.

2   The Concept of Network Coding in Optical Networks

In NC, to enhance network security, a confidential connection can transmit an encrypted version of its data by combining it (via an XOR operation) with other co-propagated connections. Thus, in the case of an eavesdropping attack, the attacker must have knowledge of both the encrypted version of the signal and the co-propagated connections used to perform the XOR operations in order to decrypt the confidential data. It is important to note that very few works study the concept of NC for security in optical networks [9] and none considers jointly solving the NC and RSA problems.

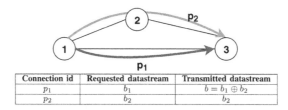

Connection id	Requested datastream	Transmitted datastream
p_1	b_1	$b = b_1 \oplus b_2$
p_2	b_2	b_2

Fig. 1. Example of network coding involving two connections.

Figure 1 presents a simple example where NC can be used to secure a confidential demand (connection p_1). In this example, it is assumed that connection p_1 is allocated to spectrum slots 1–3 on path 1–3 and the requested datastream is represented as b_1. Also, connection p_2 transmits datastream b_2 through path 1–2–3. To provide confidentiality for connection p_1, source node 1 transmits an encrypted version of the datastream, denoted as b, where $b = b_1 \oplus b_2$, while connection p_2 transmits datastream b_2. This way, even if an adversary eavesdrops on any intermediate link along the path of confidential connection p_1, confidential data cannot be decrypted, since, in this example, the eavesdropper must also gain access to connection p_2 and datastream b_2. In this case, since both connections have the same destination, node 3 can acquire both b and b_2 signals and therefore the XOR operation can be performed between the two datastreams ($b \oplus b_2 = b_1$) to decrypt datastream b_1. Note that in this work the assumption is that an attacker can gain access to the signals by tapping individual links but cannot access the signals at network nodes as these are securely placed within the telecom providers' sites.

In opaque optical networks, the process of NC could be easily implemented, since optical signals can be received, combined, and transmitted at intermediate nodes. However, for such a technique to work in transparent optical networks, the nodes must be equipped with additional hardware in order to perform the XOR operation at the physical layer. In addition, the involved signals must use the same spectrum resources in order for NC to be enabled. Thus, the deployment of NC schemes in EONs assumes the usage of all-optical XOR gates. A review of all-optical XOR gate technology has been performed in [14]. All-optical XOR gates are typically based on semiconductor optical amplifiers and the execution of XOR operations can be performed at line speed for transmissions up to 100 Gbps, with different modulation schemes, signifying that a practical implementation of optical XOR operations for processing optical signals is indeed possible [15].

3   Problem Description

In this work, the problem of routing and spectrum allocation and network coding is jointly solved in EONs so as to also offer security for confidential demands against eavesdropping. Using NC, each confidential connection combines its data with the data from other connections and designs a network code that changes based on the data that the aforementioned connections transmit. In this work, in order for a confidential connection to be considered secure, its data must be combined with the data of other connections in the same spectrum slots in each of the links that the confidential connection traverses. Specifically, the following additional constraints must now be satisfied when solving the combined NC-RSA problem to ensure security against eavesdropping for a confidential demand:

- **Encrypted Transmission (ET):** All links of the selected path must transmit an encrypted version of their data with at least one XOR operation with other established connections.
- **Frequency Slot Matching (FSM):** At least a subset of the frequency slots utilized by the confidential connection must have the same id with the slots of the rest of the established connections used in the XOR operations.

To satisfy the ET constraint, an established connection must have at least two common nodes with the confidential connection (the first node will be used to encrypt the confidential connection and the second node will be used to decrypt it). Thus, an established connection with at least two common nodes with the confidential connection can either provide security for the entire path of the confidential demand (source and destination as common nodes), or it can provide security for part of the connection (source/intermediate node to intermediate/destination node). For a confidential connection to be considered secure, the selected established connections must collectively secure all links of that connection.

To satisfy the FSM constraint, at least a subset of the frequency slots utilized by the confidential connection must have the same id with the frequency slots of the rest of the established connections used in the XOR operations. This is the case, since it is assumed that no frequency conversion is performed at intermediate nodes, and therefore, the signals used for the XOR operation must be on the same frequency. However, the confidential connection is considered as secure even if only part of the signal is XOR-ed, since the eavesdropper would still have to access all connections used in the encryption process in order to decrypt the transmitted data.

Figure 2 illustrates an example where several connections can be used in order to secure a confidential demand, extending the simple example shown in Fig. 1.

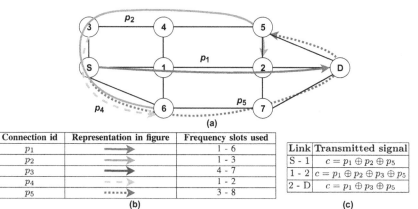

Fig. 2. Example of NC in a 9-node network topology utilizing 5 connections.

In this example, it is assumed that connections p_2, p_3, p_4 and p_5 are currently established in the network (Fig. 2(a)) using paths $6-S-3-4-5-2$, $1-4-5-D$, $3-S-6$, and $S-6-7-D-5$, respectively. Also, for simplicity, assume that each connection is assigned to the frequency slots shown in Fig. 2(b). For provisioning confidential connection request p_1, it is assumed that the $S-1-2-D$ route is selected, along with spectrum slots 1–6. Since p_2 is utilized on part of the same frequency slots and has two common nodes with p_1, it can be used to encrypt the confidential signal by enabling NC on node S and decrypting the signal at node 2, providing security for links $S-1$ and $1-2$. Similarly, connections p_3 and p_5 can be further used to encrypt p_1. Note that p_4 cannot be utilized to encrypt connection p_1, since connections using routes p_1 and p_4 have only one node in common. The transmitted signals along all links of connection p_1 are presented in Fig. 2(c).

As previously mentioned, in this work, a confidential connection is considered secure if it satisfies constraints ET and FSM, which is the case in this example. Also, it is noted that all spectrum slots are XOR-ed at links $S-1$ and $1-2$, whereas only a part of the signal (frequency slots 3–6) is XOR-ed at link $2-D$. Nevertheless, the connection is still considered as secure, since an eavesdropper would still have to access the signal of all individual connections used at each link (i.e., p_1, p_3, and p_5 for link $2-D$) in order to decrypt confidential data.

4   RSA with Network Coding

The proposed NC-RSA algorithm is divided into the routing and spectrum allocation sub-problems. A network planning scenario is considered, where all demands are known a priori and each demand is described by a 4-tuple (s, d, B, c), denoting the source, destination, bit-rate, and confidentiality, respectively. Confidentiality in this case is defined as a binary variable which describes the demand as confidential (1) or non-confidential (0).

4.1   Routing

For the routing sub-problem, k-shortest candidate paths that are able to satisfy a requested connection are found. These k-shortest paths can be subsequently sorted based on a number of metrics, such as the number of hops, the modulation format, or the most/least used nodes/links. Also, different routing strategies can apply for the confidential and the non-confidential connections. Specifically, in this work, each node (n) and link (l) are characterized by the number of established connections that use them (denoted as U_n and U_l respectively). Further, each path takes the value of the node/link with the highest U_n/U_l among all the nodes/links it traverses ($U_{p,n}, U_{p,l}$). The paths of the non-confidential connections can then be sorted based on the following three criteria:

- **Most used nodes/links (MUN/MUL):** The candidate paths for each s-d pair are sorted in descending order based on the value $U_{p,n}/U_{p,l}$ of each path. By selecting the path which comprises of the most used nodes/links, the number of XOR operations for a confidential connection will potentially increase.
- **Least used nodes/links (LUN/LUL):** In this case, the candidate paths of each connection are sorted in ascending order based on the value $U_{p,n}/U_{p,l}$. Thus, the connections will be distributed in the network in a balanced manner, and therefore confidential connections will more likely find paths that satisfy the NC constraints.
- **Maximum spectrum efficiency (MSE):** The candidate paths are sorted in descending order based on the number of hops and the modulation format used (hybrid metric [16]). Thus, connections are established having as an aim to maximize the spectrum efficiency of the network rather than maximizing the number of XOR operations.

After sorting the paths, the non-confidential connections are established using the first path that has available spectrum resources, based on one of the three aforementioned sorting strategies. For the confidential connections, the candidate path that produces the most number of XOR operations is used, which also depends on the spectrum slots selected. To achieve this, the XOR spectrum slot metric (XOR-SSM) is introduced that counts the minimum number of XOR operations that can be performed on each link for the selected group of frequency slots. Thus, for each candidate path, XOR-SSM is calculated, and the path and frequency slots that provide the highest XOR-SSM are used to establish the confidential connection.

4.2   Spectrum Allocation

For the spectrum allocation sub-problem, available spectrum resources must be allocated for a requested connection satisfying the slot *continuity, contiguity,* and *non-overlapping* constraints [2]. For the non-confidential connections, the spectrum allocation is performed in a first-fit manner, where the first group of frequency slots from the sorted candidate paths that is able to establish the connection is allocated.

For the confidential connections, the process of allocating spectrum resources is based on maximizing the number of XOR operations that can be performed for the selected path and group of frequency slots, utilizing the XOR-SSM metric. Algorithm 1 describes the NC-RSA approach for a given confidential demand. Also, the example in Fig. 3 is subsequently used to better explain the proposed algorithm.

Algorithm 1. NC-RSA for a given confidential demand

Input: $G(V, E)$, *Candidate paths P, Paths currently established P_e, Confidential demand D $(s, d, B, 1)$*

Output: Connection Establishment

1: **for** each candidate path $p \in P_{s,d}$ **do**
2:     Find a set of paths $P_{used} \in P_e$ that are used by the established connections and have at least two common nodes with path p
3:     Create temporary matrix $t = L \times F$, where L = number of links in path p and F = overall number of freq. slots. Initialize all matrix entries to 0.
4:     **for** each path $p_u \in P_{used}$ **do**
5:         Calculate the set of links in p that can be covered by p_u and increase by one the values for the links and spectrum slots that are covered by p_u within t
6:     **end for**
7:     Initialize XOR-SSM$_p = 0$
8:     **for** each group $(a - b)$ of available spectrum slots in p that can be allocated to D **do**
9:         $c_z^{a-b} = \sum_{n=a}^{b} t_{z,n}$, for $z = 1$ to L
10:        $\mathcal{C}^{a-b} = min(c_1^{a-b}, ..., c_L^{a-b})$
11:        XOR-SSM$_p = max(\text{XOR-SSM}_p, \mathcal{C}^{a-b})$
12:    **end for**
13: **end for**
14: Select p with max XOR-SSM$_p$ and establish connection

For a given confidential connection, the XOR-SSM$_p$ is calculated for each candidate path p. To do this, a temporary matrix (denoted as t in the algorithm) is used, with size $L \times F$, where L denotes the number of links of the candidate path and F denotes the overall number of frequency slots of each link in the network. Next, the set of the already established paths with at least two common nodes with the path under investigation is found (denoted as P_{used} in the algorithm). This set of paths can be used to satisfy the ET constraint.

Subsequently, the values for the links and spectrum slots that are covered by p_u within t are increased by 1.

Next, for each available group of frequency slots $(a - b)$, the number of XOR operations performed on each link z of path p are calculated using the following equation: $c_z^{a-b} = \sum_{n=a}^{b} t_{z,n}$, where a and b are the starting and ending slots selected. From these computed values the minimum $\mathcal{C}^{a-b} = min(c_1^{a-b}, ..., c_L^{a-b})$ is selected (i.e., the weakest link in terms of the number of XOR operations performed to secure that link is considered). Then, for path p, the group of frequency slots with the maximum $\mathcal{C}$ is selected and is considered as the value of XOR-SSM for that path. The value of the XOR-SSM metric signifies that for any value greater than zero (i.e., x), at least x XOR operations are used to secure the confidential connection in each link. This also implies that the ET and FSM constraints are satisfied for that confidential connection. On the other hand, if XOR-SSM is zero, there is at least one link in the path where none of the spectrum slots utilized can be XOR-ed, and therefore the connection is not considered secure. Finally, when the XOR-SSM is the same for two candidate paths, the one with the least number of hops is selected, so as to increase spectrum efficiency whenever possible.

In Fig. 3, assume a network with $F = 5$, candidate path p_4 requiring 3 frequency slots, and set P_{used} consisting of paths $\{p_1, p_2, p_3\}$, where each connection is allocated spectrum slots as shown in Fig. 3(a). The resulting t using all paths in P_{used} is shown in Fig. 3(b) (for example, p_1 contributes to cells $t_{(1,3)}$, $t_{(1,4)}$, $t_{(2,3)}$, $t_{(2,4)}$, since it can cover spectrum slots 3 and 4 in both links in p_4). To calculate the number of XOR operations on link 2, if the group of frequency slots selected is 3–5, $c_2^{3-5} = t_{(2,3)} + t_{(2,4)} + t_{(2,5)} = 1 + 2 + 1 = 4$. The results for each link and group of spectrum slots are presented in Fig. 3(c). Also, $\mathcal{C}^{2-4} = min(c_1^{2-4}, c_2^{2-4}) = min(2,3) = 2$, and $\mathcal{C}^{1-3}$ and $\mathcal{C}^{3-5}$ are equal to 1

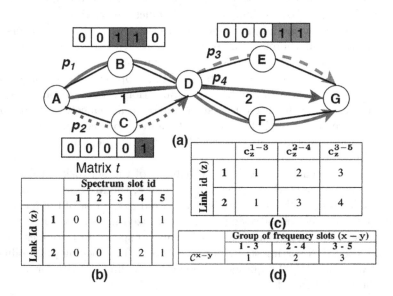

Fig. 3. Example of NC-RSA algorithm for a given confidential connection.

and 3, respectively (Fig. 3(d)). Thus, XOR-SSM$_{p_4}$ = $max(\mathcal{C}^{1-3}, \mathcal{C}^{2-4}, \mathcal{C}^{3-5})$ = $max(1, 2, 3) = 3$, using frequency slots 3–5.

5   Performance Evaluations

The simulation setup used to evaluate the proposed algorithm is as follows: an EON is implemented using bandwidth variable transponders that operate using multiple modulation formats: BPSK, QPSK, 8-QAM, and 16-QAM. The transmission reach for each modulation format is given by 9300, 4600, 1700, and 800 km respectively. Moreover, a flexible grid is implemented with channel spacing of 12.5 GHz which results in a total of 320 spectrum slots for each link in the network with a baud rate of 10.7 Gbaud for each frequency slot. Further, the Telefonica network [17] with 30 nodes and 56 bidirectional links is used for all experiments. In all cases, demands are randomly generated using a uniform distribution for all s-d pairs, where each demand size varies from 10 to 100 Gbps. Also, 20 candidate paths are calculated offline for each s-d pair. It is noted that a large number of candidate paths is used so as to provide the confidential connections with several candidate paths that could maximize the XOR-SSM metric. Moreover, each presented result is the average of 10 experiments performed with different generated sets of demands. Finally, for all simulations, the number of demands designated as confidential is set to 40% of the overall number of requests.

First, the percentage of confidential connections that are securely established (have XOR-SSM metric greater than 1) is presented in Fig. 4 for the different sorting strategies of the candidate paths as described in Sect. 4. As shown in Fig. 4, using different sorting techniques has a significant effect on the number of confidential connections that can be provisioned securely in the network. Clearly, the MUN or MUL techniques provide much better results compared to the rest of the sorting techniques, since connections are forced to traverse the same node/links, and therefore, more connections with at least two common nodes can be found to perform the XOR operation with the confidential connection. Further, as shown from the results, the MUN approach outperforms MUL, with approximately 95% of the confidential connections securely established. The reader should note that for the established confidential connections that cannot be secured, extra (dummy) lightpaths can be added to accommodate the links where XOR operations are not performed just for the sole purpose of securing all confidential connections.

Next, Fig. 5 presents the blocking probability of the network when different sorting techniques are used. As shown in the figure, the MUL sorting approach provides the highest blocking probability compared to the rest of the techniques, since the paths chosen aim at using the most utilized links in order to increase security rather than maximizing the efficient use of spectrum resources. On the other hand, the MUN sorting strategy provides only 3% blocking probability for a large network load (1500 requests), while also providing security for almost all of the confidential demands.

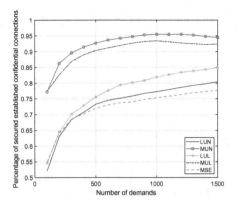

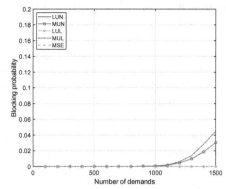

Fig. 4. Percentage of established confidential connections that are secured.

Fig. 5. Blocking probability using different sorting techniques.

To quantify the amount of security provided for the confidential connections, the number of XOR operations performed on each link of a confidential connection can be calculated. As discussed above, increasing the number of XOR operations performed on each link reduces the probability that an eavesdropper can decrypt confidential data, since the eavesdropper would have to access, for each link of the confidential path, all connections that were used during the XOR process. Figure 6 presents the average number of XOR operations per link per confidential connection in the network, when using different sorting techniques for the candidate paths.

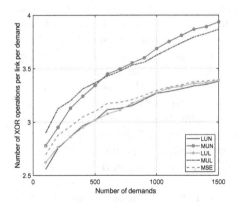

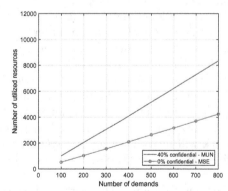

Fig. 6. Number of XOR operations per link per confidential connection.

Fig. 7. Utilized spectrum resources for the MUN and MSE sorting techniques.

Using the MUN approach maximizes the number of XOR operations performed for each confidential connection compared to the rest of the sorting approaches. For MUN, up to 4 XOR operations can be performed on each link of a confidential connection, on average, compared to the least used and MSE cases, where 3.4 XOR operations are performed on each link. This means that, when MUN is utilized, an eavesdropper would have to simultaneously gain access to information from 4 other connections that traverse different links and nodes in the network in order to decrypt the data traversing a single link of the confidential connection.

Selecting different routing and spectrum allocation strategies for each confidential connection will, on the one hand secure the confidential connections against an eavesdropping attack, but, on the other hand, could force the algorithm to deviate from an efficient spectrum utilization solution. Figure 7 presents the number of utilized spectrum slots when using the MUN strategy, (which outperforms all other sorting approaches in terms of the number of XOR operations per confidential connection), versus the case where all connections are designated as non-confidential and the candidate paths are sorted based on the MSE technique (which maximizes spectrum efficiency). In this case, the blocking probability is set to 0% in order to obtain the exact number of spectrum resources utilized for each set of demands. As shown in the figure, the MUN sorting strategy requires more spectrum resources than MSE to establish all connections. This is to be expected and is mainly due to the usage of paths that maximize the number of XOR operations for the confidential connections, rather than using the best paths in terms of spectrum efficiency.

6   Conclusions

In this work, a novel joint NC-RSA approach is presented in EONs to increase physical layer security against eavesdropping attacks. The proposed technique uses network coding to combine connections already established in the network with the confidential ones in order to transmit encrypted versions of their confidential data. Using this approach, an eavesdropper must now access multiple connections in the network in order to compromise any confidential information. The performance results obtained demonstrate that the MUN sorting approach for routing the candidate paths can be used to securely provision almost all (95%) of the confidential demands, while providing the best security against an eavesdropping attack with multiple connection combinations per link. Future work will investigate routing techniques for minimizing the number of dummy lightpaths required to securely provision all confidential demands.

Acknowledgment. This work has been supported by the European Union's Horizon 2020 research and innovation programme under grant agreement No. 739551(KIOS CoE) and from the Government of the Republic of Cyprus through the Directorate General for European Programmes, Coordination and Development. This article is based upon work from COST Action CA15127 ("Resilient communication services protecting end-user applications from disaster-based failures RECODIS") supported by COST (European Cooperation in Science and Technology).

References

1. Gerstel, O., Jinno, M., Lord, A., Yoo, S.J.B.: Elastic optical networking: a new dawn for the optical layer? IEEE Commun. Mag. **50**(2), s12–s20 (2012). https://doi.org/10.1109/MCOM.2012.6146481
2. Christodoulopoulos, K., Tomkos, I., Varvarigos, E.A.: Routing and spectrum allocation in OFDM-based optical networks with elastic bandwidth allocation. In: 2010 IEEE Global Telecommunications Conference GLOBECOM 2010, pp. 1–6 (2010). https://doi.org/10.1109/GLOCOM.2010.5684008
3. Fok, M.P., Wang, Z., Deng, Y., Prucnal, P.R.: Optical layer security in fiber-optic networks. IEEE Trans. Inf. Forensics Secur. **6**(3), 725–736 (2011). https://doi.org/10.1109/TIFS.2011.2141990
4. Skorin-Kapov, N., Furdek, M., Zsigmond, S., Wosinska, L.: Physical-layer security in evolving optical networks. IEEE Commun. Mag. **54**(8), 110–117 (2016). https://doi.org/10.1109/MCOM.2016.7537185
5. Manousakis, K., Ellinas, G.: Attack-aware planning of transparent optical networks. Opt. Switch. Netw. **19**, 97–109 (2016). https://doi.org/10.1016/j.osn.2015.03.005. http://www.sciencedirect.com/science/article/pii/S1573427715000302. Advances in Availability and Survivability in Optical Networks
6. Kitayama, K., et al.: Security in photonic networks: threats and security enhancement. J. Lightwave Technol. **29**(21), 3210–3222 (2011). https://doi.org/10.1109/JLT.2011.2166248
7. Agarwal, A., Charikar, M.: On the advantage of network coding for improving network throughput. In: Information Theory Workshop, pp. 247–249 (2004). https://doi.org/10.1109/ITW.2004.1405308
8. Ramirez, W., Masip-Bruin, X., Yannuzzi, M., Montero, D., Martinez, A., Lopez, V.: Network coding-based protection scheme for elastic optical networks. In: 2014 10th International Conference on the Design of Reliable Communication Networks (DRCN), pp. 1–8 (2014). https://doi.org/10.1109/DRCN.2014.6816136
9. Engelmann, A., Jukan, A.: Balancing the demands of reliability and security with linear network coding in optical networks. In: 2016 IEEE International Conference on Communications (ICC), pp. 1–7 (2016). https://doi.org/10.1109/ICC.2016.7511590
10. Bai, W., et al.: Eavesdropping-aware routing and spectrum allocation based on multi-flow virtual concatenation for confidential information service in elastic optical networks. Opt. Fiber Technol. **40**, 18–27 (2018). https://doi.org/10.1016/j.yofte.2017.10.004. http://www.sciencedirect.com/science/article/pii/S1068520017303085
11. Singh, S.K., Bziuk, W., Jukan, A.: Balancing data security and blocking performance with spectrum randomization in optical networks. In: 2016 IEEE Global Communications Conference (GLOBECOM), pp. 1–7 (2016). https://doi.org/10.1109/GLOCOM.2016.7841622
12. Savva, G., Manousakis, K., Ellinas, G.: Eavesdropping-aware routing and spectrum allocation in eons using spread spectrum techniques. In: 2018 IEEE Global Communications Conference (GLOBECOM), pp. 1–6 (2018). https://doi.org/10.1109/GLOCOM.2018.8647253
13. Savva, G., Manousakis, K., Ellinas, G.: Spread spectrum over OFDM for enhanced security in elastic optical networks. In: 2018 Photonics in Switching and Computing (PSC), pp. 1–3 (2018). https://doi.org/10.1109/PS.2018.8751442
14. Zhang, M., Wang, L., Ye, P.: All optical XOR logic gates: technologies and experiment demonstrations. IEEE Commun. Mag. **43**(5), S19–S24 (2005). https://doi.org/10.1109/MCOM.2005.1453421

15. Kong, D., et al.: All-optical XOR gates for QPSK signal based optical networks. Electron. Lett. **49**(7), 486–488 (2013). https://doi.org/10.1049/el.2013.0010

16. Savva, G., Ellinas, G., Shariati, B., Tomkos, I.: Physical layer-aware routing, spectrum, and core allocation in spectrally-spatially flexible optical networks with multicore fibers. In: 2018 IEEE International Conference on Communications (ICC), pp. 1–6 (2018). https://doi.org/10.1109/ICC.2018.8422782

17. Savva, G., Manousakis, K., Shariati, B., Tomkos, I., Ellinas, G.: Connection provisioning in spectrally-spatially flexible optical networks with physical layer considerations. In: 2018 20th International Conference on Transparent Optical Networks (ICTON), pp. 1–4 (2018). https://doi.org/10.1109/ICTON.2018.8473872

Resilient Cloud-RANs Adopting Network Coding

Arash Farhadi Beldachi[1]([✉]), Markos Anastasopoulos[1], Alexandros Manolopoulos[2],
Anna Tzanakaki[1,2], Reza Nejabati[1], and Dimitra Simeondou[1]

[1] High Performance Networks Group, University of Bristol, Bristol, UK
Arash.Beldachi@bristol.ac.uk
[2] Department of Physics, University of Athens, Athens, Greece

Abstract. This study focuses on the provisioning of resilient Cloud Radio Access Network (C-RAN) services employing optical transport networks. In response to the high bandwidth requirements necessary for the protection of the C-RAN architecture from optical transport network and/or BBU failures, a novel approach based on Network Coding (NC) is proposed. A novel architectural and hardware framework to enable NC are also provided and a suitable implementation addressing the problem of fast NC-related operations processing at the edge is demonstrated. A global time stamping solution that can be used to address the strict synchronization requirements of FH flows arriving at the BBUs, keeping buffering at the edge as low as possible, has been developed. The performance of the proposed solution has been experimentally evaluated demonstrating negligible penalties. Network level modeling results demonstrate a reduction of the total optical network capacity required for this type of applications by 33%.

Keywords: Cloud-RAN · Resilience · Network Coding · Synchronization · Optical networks · Mobile edge

1 Introduction

Cloud-Radio Access Networks (C-RANs) have been recently proposed as a key concept to address the inefficiencies of traditional RAN systems and support services requiring very low latency, high reliability, density and mobility. In C-RAN, Remote Units (RUs), are connected to the Central Unit (CU) where the Baseband Unit (BBU) pool is located through high bandwidth transport links, transmitting I/Q streams, known as fronthaul (FH) [1]. Through its pooling and coordination gains, C-RAN addresses the increased capital and operational costs, as well as the limited scalability and flexibility of traditional RAN. However, C-RAN requires tremendous transport bandwidth and impose strict latency and synchronization constraints [1, 2]. To address the need for a flexible transport network offering the required capacity levels we have proposed the Time-Shared Optical Network (TSON) solution [1]. However, the transport capacity problem is further exaggerated under survivable C-RAN deployments (see i.e. [3–8]).

© IFIP International Federation for Information Processing 2020
Published by Springer Nature Switzerland AG 2020
A. Tzanakaki et al. (Eds.): ONDM 2019, LNCS 11616, pp. 349–361, 2020.
https://doi.org/10.1007/978-3-030-38085-4_30

In many protection schemes, the optical network capacity is duplicated in size [8] to make possible realistic survivable C-RAN deployments.

A typical example of systems offering protection to any kind of failures (either at the optical transport or the compute domain where BBUs are hosted) is shown in Fig. 1(a). Specifically, in case of failure of the main paths interconnecting the RUs with the BBUs (i.e. paths 1-6, 3-5), FH flows are routed to their destination through a set of secondary (protection) paths (1-2-4-5, 3-2-4-6). A similar approach is taken for the C-RAN protection against BBU failures [6]. It is clear that under this scenario, multiple FH flows need to be transferred over a set of links introducing even higher transport bandwidth requirements.

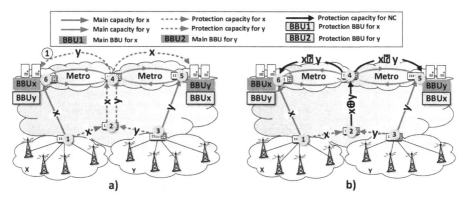

Fig. 1. Protection of a C-RAN network from failures of compute and/or network elements. (a) In the traditional approach, working and protection capacity for regions x, y are establishes over common links causing bottleneck (b) Protection of C-RAN adopting NC. FH flows from regions x, y are multiplexed ($x \oplus y$) at ingress edge node and replicated at the reducing bandwidth requirements by half.

To address this issue the concept of Network Coding (NC) [9] is proposed with the aim offer resilient FH services by multiplexing FH flows and therefore reducing the volume of the transmitted I/Q streams. Using NC, 2 different FH traffic streams with the same source and destination nodes are routed through the network following diverse paths. These can be protected through their modulo-two sum that is generated at the source node and forwarded to the common destination node. This allows reconstruction of each one of the two initial streams at the destination node, in case of the occurrence of a failure along one of the two paths that the initial two streams are traversing. This approach offers $1 + 1$ protection capabilities without having to transfer separately the working and protection copies of the two FH streams across the optical transport network. This reduces the overall protection bandwidth requirement by half (see link 2-4 in Fig. 1b). Through this approach, simultaneous protection against optical network and/or compute elements can be achieved.

Although NC has been extensively used to protect networks against link failures, its application in resilient FH networks has not been proposed before. This can be attributed mainly to the overhead that the application of the modulo-two sum and the replication operations of NC introduce in practical systems that may degrade the performance of C-RANs. At the same time, the operation of the decoding process at the edge imposes significant buffering requirements due to the high data rate of FH streams. To address these limitations, we propose the extension of TSON with an architecture and a hardware implementation that manage to execute the coding and decoding processes at line rate. This solution minimises at the same time buffering requirements adopting a purposely developed synchronization scheme to make it suitable for C-RAN implementations. To quantify the benefits of the proposed approach at a network level and further improve performance, an optimization framework is proposed. The proposed scheme focuses on optimally placing the NC-enabled edge nodes to minimize the overall deployment cost and protect the system from possible network or compute element failures. The performance of the proposed scheme is experimentally validated over the Bristol city test-bed considering the requirements imposed by an operating open source LTE platform.

The rest of the paper is organized as follows: The implementation of the NC enabled edge nodes is provided in Sect. 2. Section 3 provides a brief description of the resilience 5G network design problem with and without NC considerations. Experimental and theoretical evaluation is also carried out whereas Sect. 4 concludes the paper.

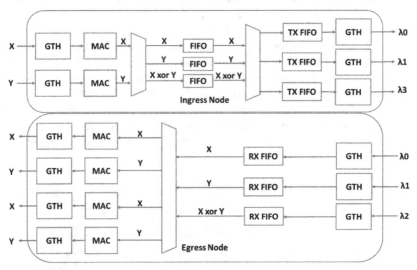

Fig. 2. Implemented architecture of the TSON technology to solve the 5G network design problem with resilience considerations

2 Implementation Aspects

To apply NC in 5G operational environments, two main practical aspects should be resolved: (1) implementation of the modulo-two sum and the replication operations at the FH line rate and, (2) synchronization between flows reaching decode nodes (flows $x, x \oplus y$ and flows $y, x \oplus y$ of Fig. 1b). In the following subsections, the implementation details together with experimental demonstration of an NC-enabled optical edge node is presented.

2.1 NC Operations Implementation at TSON

TSON [12, 13] is a multi-wavelength fully bi-directional synchronous, and flexible active optical transport network technology. Its network implementation consists of Field Programmable Gate Array (FPGA) optoelectronics platforms integrated with advanced optical components to enable high performance processing and transparent switching and transport. TSON provides a multiple protocol programable interface that meets 5G Key Performance Indicators (KPIs) such as high bandwidth and sub-millisecond end-to-end latency [13]. Although natively TSON allows handling Ethernet frames, its configuration can support a broad range of framing structures and communication protocols including CPRI, either natively or through their packetized versions.

In this paper we propose the use of TSON technology to address the 5G optical transport network requirements with resilience considerations. Figure 2 shows the TSON architecture implemented to solve this problem. The ingress TSON node is responsible for traffic coding and mapping. Its ports consist of two clients: X and Y. The output ingress node contains three different wavelengths that can be configured on the fly using Software Defined Networking (SDN) to address different programmable parameters. The egress edge nodes include the reverse functionality and ports. For the implementation of our experimental configuration we have employed two Xilinx VC709 evaluation boards. These contain 4XSFP/SFP+ cages. FM-S18 modules are used to expand the number of SFP+ cages as more than 4X10Gbs ports are required for the experiment. The FM-S18 is an FPGA Mezzanine Card (FMC) module that provides up to eight SFP/SFP+ module interfaces directly into Multi-Gigabit Transceivers of the FPGA. Figure 3 shows the implementation architecture for the evaluation of the proposed concept with two TSON nodes. Each TSON node emulates three source nodes of a butterfly network, with the aim to create a proof of concept experiment and showcase the concept of linear network coding. TSON node 1 receives two different traffic streams (A and B) and sends the

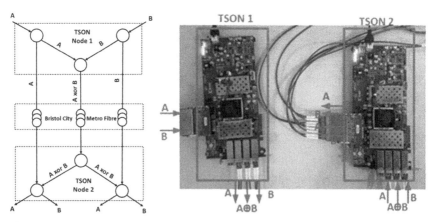

Fig. 3. (a) TSON Implementation architecture for evaluation concept, (b) TSON edge node setup for the experimental implementation

streams A, B, and their modulo 2 sum (XOR) of both traffic streams to TSON node 2. TSON node 2 receives the three traffic streams and transmits each traffic stream A and B simultaneously to two destinations of TSON node 2.

2.2 Synchronization of Network Coded Flows

To reduce buffering requirements during the coding/decoding phase of the FH flows, high synchronization accuracy across the network is needed. An early TSON prototype with local synchronization capabilities is described in [10]. To address the system wide strict synchronization requirements of the NC implementation, a subsystem relying on separate developed time stamper has been developed. Figure 4 shows the Subsystem architecture for the NC-enabled TSON nodes. The time stamper unit is located between the MAC and PCS/PMA IP cores, uses the Timer Syns clock and follows the IEEE 1588 [11] protocol. In addition, the time stamper considers the physical layer delay for stamping.

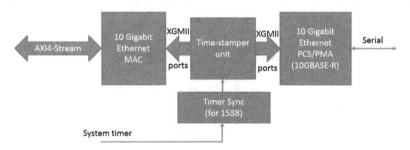

Fig. 4. Synchronization subsystem for the NC implementation

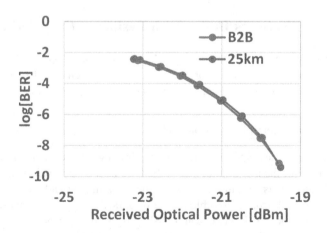

Fig. 5. BER measurements

2.3 Subsystem Experimental Validation

Two different scenarios are considered for experimental evaluation of the subsystems responsible for the NC-operations, including the modulo-two sum and synchronization accuracy. The first scenario includes both FPGAs connected back-to-back with short fibre lengths. In the second scenario, the proposed technologies are evaluated over the Bristol City test-bed Fibre with 25 km of standard single-mode fibre (SSMF). An Anritsu traffic analyser generates two Ethernet traffic streams to the TSON edge node 1 at 9 Gbps. The traffic is received from the TSON node 2. The performance parameters under consideration include Bit Error Rate (BER) and latency. Latency is defined as the time difference between the arrival of a frame at the analyser, and its departure from the analyser.

Figure 5 shows the BER measurements as a function of received optical power for the different scenarios under consideration. The BER curves show that the penalty observed for the case of 25 km of SSMF transmission over the Bristol City Infrastructure compared to the back-to-back (B2B) performance is less than 1 dB. Table 1 displays the end-to-end latency for the transmitted flows. The TSON nodes latency for the 25 km transmission is less than 2% of total latency.

Table 1. End-to-end flow latency

Latency	μs
B2B	1.979
25 km	125.4

3 Optimal 5G Network Design with Resilience Considerations

In the previous section, the implementation details of NC-enabled TSON nodes have been described. In this section, the problem of optical placement of these nodes at a metro environment to support resilient operation of C-RANs is provided.

3.1 Traditional Optimization Framework

This section provides a description of the modeling framework used to identify the optical network resources for the interconnection of the RUs with the compute resources where the BBU are hosted. This formulation extends the work in [1] to address resilience and protect the 5G network from a possible failure of optical and/or DC network elements. Taking into account both FH network and BBU processing demands, let $\mathcal{P}_r$ be the set of paths interconnecting RU $r \in \mathcal{R}$ with server s where BBUs are hosted with $p \in \mathcal{P}_r$. Now let x_{rp} be the rate at which FH demand originating from r flows through path p.

The following demand constraints should be satisfied:

$$\sum_{s\in S}\sum_{p\in P_r} \alpha_{rs}x_{rp} = h_r, \quad \forall r \in \mathcal{R} \tag{1}$$

where α_{rs} is a binary coefficient taking values equal to 1 if RU $r \in \mathcal{R}$ is supported by server s.

In order to protect the planned network from a possible server failure hosting the BBU, a backup mechanism is introduced. This mechanism ensures that in case of failure of the primary server s, FH flows are routed to an alternative server s' $(s' \neq s)$ through the candidate path p' $(p' \in P_r)$ with corresponding flow $x_{rp'}$. To formulate this requirement the binary coefficient $\alpha_{rss'}$ is introduced to indicate whether FH flow originating from RU r is assigned to servers s, s' or not. This coefficient equals to 1, if BBU of RU r is processed at server s or in case of its failure on server s'; 0 otherwise. In order to protect the operation of an RU from a possible server s failure, the following FH flow protection constraints should be satisfied:

$$\sum_{\substack{s',\, s' \neq s \\ s,\, s' \in S}} \sum_{p' \in P_r} \alpha_{rss'}x_{rp'} = h_r, \quad \forall r \in \mathcal{R}, s \in S \tag{2}$$

Summing all FH flows over the optical network link $e(e \in \mathcal{E})$, the necessary link e capacity, denoted as u_e, is determined:

$$\sum_{r\in R}\sum_{s\in S}\left[\sum_{p\in P_r} \beta_{erp}x_{rp} + \sum_{\substack{s' \in S, \\ s' \neq s}} \sum_{p'\in P_r} \beta'_{erp'}x_{rp'} \right] \leq u_e, \quad \forall e \in \mathcal{E} \tag{3}$$

$$u_e \leq C_e, \quad \forall e \in \mathcal{E} \tag{4}$$

In (3), β_{erp} and $\beta'_{erp'}$ are binary coefficients taking values equal to 1 if link e belongs to path p and p', respectively, realizing FH flow r at server s or s'; 0 otherwise. In (4), C_e is an upper bound of the capacity of link e.

Apart from server failures, optical network link failures are also addressed by forwarding FH flows to their destination via alternative paths. In order to protect the network from a possible link failure, a mechanism routing flows through alternative paths is introduced. Now, let Q_{rp} be the set of paths that can be used to protect a path $p \in P_r$ from a possible failure, y_{rq} the rate at which FH demand originating from r flows through path $q_p \in Q_{rp}$ protecting main path $p \in P_r$ (with p, q being disjoint) and $u'_e = C_e - u_e$ the remaining link e capacity. Adopting the same rationale as in Eqs. (1)–(4), the following path-protection constraints are introduced:

$$\sum_{s\in S}\sum_{q\in Q_{rp}} \alpha_{rs}y_{rq} = h_r, \quad \forall r \in \mathcal{R}, p \in P_r \tag{5}$$

$$\sum_{\substack{s', s' \neq s \\ s, s' \in S}} \sum_{q' \in Q_{rp}} \alpha_{rss'} y_{rq'} = h_r, \ \forall r \in \mathcal{R}, \ s \in \mathcal{S}, p \in \mathcal{P}_r \tag{6}$$

$$\sum_{r \in \mathcal{R}} \sum_{s \in \mathcal{S}} \left[\sum_{q \in Q_{rp}} \beta_{erq} y_{rq} + \sum_{\substack{s' \in S, \\ s' \neq s}} \sum_{q' \in Q_{rp}} \beta'_{erq'} y_{rq'} \right] \leq u'_e, \ \forall e \in \mathcal{E}, p \in \mathcal{P}_r \tag{7}$$

So far, the proposed model ensures that the network capacity is adequate to support the transmission of the FH flows to the servers where BBUs are hosted. However, once the information arrives at its destination, server s should have adequate capacity to support of BBU processing. To evaluate this capacity, h_r is mapped from a network type of requirement to a computing resource through the introduction of parameter $\mathcal{M}_{rs}$. This parameter specifies the computational requirements (usually in Instructions Per Second - IPS) to support FH flow r on server s.

To evaluate this parameter, an extensive benchmarking campaign utilizing OpenAir-Interface (OAI) has been carried out. OAI is an open source software-based implementation of the LTE architecture for 5G experimentation and prototyping that encompasses the full protocol stack both in the E-UTRAN and the Evolved Packet Core (EPC) that runs in a commodity x86-based Linux Personal Computer or data center. In this system, the transceiver functionality is realized via a software radio frontend (such as the Ettus USRP B210). The combination of the open-source software and the inexpensive hardware involved, makes OAI a very attractive platform for experimentation and research towards the forthcoming 5th Generation. The platform comprises two components: (i) openairinterface5g which implements the E-UTRAN, that is, eNodeB and UE and, (ii) openair-cn which implements the Core Network, that is, the MME HSS, S-GW and P-GW. Based on OAI, the parameters $\mathcal{M}_{rs}$ for various wireless access network configurations has been evaluated. The total volume of BBU processing performed at s is given by:

$$v_s(x) = \sum_{r \in \mathcal{R}} \sum_{p \in P_r} \alpha_{rs} \mathcal{M}_{rs}, \ s \in S \tag{8}$$

Besides the working capacity, a spare set of resources should be reserved at each server s for protection purposes. Servers' capacity protection constrains are expressed through

$$v'_{s\prime}(x) = \sum_{r \in \mathcal{R}} \sum_{p\prime \in P_r} \sum_{\substack{s \in S \\ t \neq s}} \alpha_{rss\prime} \mathcal{M}_{rs\prime}, \quad s' \in S \tag{9}$$

As already mentioned, the primary objective of the proposed scheme is to minimize the total power consumption of the resulting network configuration. Let k_e being the cost of the capacity of link e of the optical network and PC_s the power consumed at server s. The following cost function should be minimized:

$$min \, \mathcal{O}(\boldsymbol{p}, \boldsymbol{x}) = \sum_{e \in \mathcal{E}_o} k_e(u_e(\boldsymbol{x}) + u'_e(\boldsymbol{x})) + \sum_{s \in \mathcal{S}} PC_s(v_s(\boldsymbol{x}) + v'_s(\boldsymbol{x})) \qquad (10)$$

subject to constraints (1)–(9).

3.2 Extension: Integration of NC

In the Sect. 3.1, a modeling framework enabling resilient operation of the C-RAN system by protecting it from possible optical network and/or compute failure has been proposed. To address the very high bandwidth requirements that are imposed by this approach, an alternative formulation employing NC is proposed. To demonstrate the potential of NC in resilient C-RAN networks let us consider the simple 5G topology of Fig. 1. Adopting the traditional approach, multiple source-destination paths must be established double-sizing the necessary network bandwidth is some parts of the optical network (i.e. links interconnecting nodes 2-4, 4-5 and 4-6 in Fig. 1a). This may act as bottleneck considering that in FH networks this capacity may be extremely high. The adoption of NC, however, resolves this issue as it multiplexes FH streams originating from the two RUs. At the edge, FH streams are replicated (nodes 1, 3) and transmitted through disjoint paths 1-2, 1-3. Then, at node 2 instead of forwarding protection FH flows from regions x and y, the modulo-two sum $x \oplus y$ is transmitted over links 2-4, 4-6 and 4-5. At the egress nodes where BBUs are connected, the operations $x \oplus (x \oplus y)$ and $y \oplus (x \oplus y)$, are performed for BBU1 and BBU2, respectively, recovering FH flows y and x, respectively. Thus, by enabling encoding and decoding processes at the edge, throughput in survivable C-RAN architectures can be increased by a factor of 2.

An architectural decision in NC-enabled C-RANs is associated with the placement of the modulo-two sum and replication operations at the edge nodes. To optimize the operation of resilient NC-enabled C-RANs, Eqs. (5)–(7) of the original problem are dropped and replaced by a suitable set of constraints enabling NC. Let $\mathcal{N}_1, \mathcal{N}_2$, be the set of nodes where the modulo sum and replication operations are performed. To keep the analysis tractable, we assume that RUs are located in regions, x, y, as shown in Fig. 1(b), however, it can be easily extended to multiple nodes. Now, let $\mathcal{R}_x, \mathcal{R}_y$ be the set of RUs belonging to regions x, y, respectively with $\mathcal{R} = \mathcal{R}_x \cup \mathcal{R}_y$ and δ_{n1} a binary variable taking value equal to 1 if the protection flows of RUs originating from regions x, y are multiplexed at node $n_1 \in \mathcal{N}_1$. The following flow constraints should be satisfied:

$$\sum_{n_1 \in \mathcal{N}_1} \sum_{q \in \mathcal{Q}_{rn_1}} \delta_{n1} y_{rq} = h_z, \quad \forall r \in \mathcal{R}_z, z = x, y \qquad (11)$$

$$\sum_{r \in \mathcal{R}_x} \sum_{\substack{k \in \mathcal{R}_y, \\ k \neq r}} \sum_{n_1 \in \mathcal{N}_1} \delta_{n1} = 1 \qquad (12)$$

where $\mathcal{Q}_{rn_1}$ denotes the set of paths interconnecting an RU r with node n_1. Equation (12) indicates that the encoding process of all RUs will be performed at a single node.

The encoded multiplexed stream $y_{n1} = y_{rq} \oplus y_{kq}$ is then forwarded to node $n_2 \in \mathcal{N}_2$ where the replication operation is performed. Flows are transmitted over candidate paths $q \in \mathcal{Q}_{n1n2}$ interconnecting nodes n_1 and n_2 with capacity $z_q, q \in \mathcal{Q}_{n1n2}$. Introducing the binary variable γ_{n2} taking value equal to 1 if the output of node $n1$ is forwarded to node $n2 \in \mathcal{N}_2$ or not, the following equations yields:

$$\sum_{n_2 \in \mathcal{N}_2} \sum_{q \in \mathcal{Q}_{n1n2}} \gamma_{n2} z_q = y_{n1}, \quad \forall n_1 \in \mathcal{N}_1 \tag{13}$$

with $\sum_{n2 \in \mathcal{N}_2} \gamma_{n2} = 1$.

The replicated flows z_q are then routed to the locations where BBU are hosted over the shorted available paths. Finally, taking the summation of all FH flows over the optical network link e, the necessary protection capacity at e, u'_e, is determined adopting a similar approach to Eqs. (3), (7). Finally, the NC-enabled C-RAN network is optimized by minimizing the cost function (10) subject to the constraints mentioned above.

3.3   Network Level Evaluation

To evaluate the performance of the overall system, the processing requirements of the virtualized BBUs, and, consequently parameter $\mathcal{M}_{rs}$, are determined. To achieve this, an extensive set of experiments has been carried out using OAI. Performance analysis includes CPU Utilization and instructions' measurement for different data rates as well as the application profiling. The measurements where performed with the use of the top command, which monitors the running processes in Linux systems and perf which is a collection of tools for system profiling. More specifically, the OAI profiling was done with the record command, which summarizes where CPU time is spent. Measurements were performed in the idle mode (LTE device phone not connected) and while downloading with different data rates (100 Kbps, 200 Kbps, 500 Kbps, 1 Mbps and 2 Mbps). The results are given in Fig. 6. The measurement was performed with the perf stat command. As we can see, the instructions are clearly increasing in proportion to the data rate.

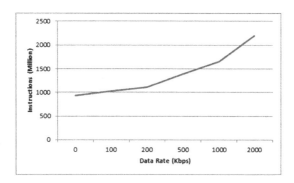

Fig. 6. Total instructions per second for OAI as a function of access data rate

Once BBU requirements have been determined, the performance of the overall system with and without NC considerations is examined for the Bristol City topology shown in Fig. 7. In this topology, RUs are attached to the edge node through point to point links. For this topology, BBU processing for Regions A and D will be provided by Server 1 whereas BBU processing for Regions B and C by Server 2. At the same time, the main FH connectivity will be provided through links 1-5 and 3-6 for regions A, B, respectively. Protection of FH flows will be provided through paths 1-2-4-6 for Region A, 3-2-4-5 for region B, 5-4-6 for region D and 6-4-5 for region C. The encoding (replication) processes for regions A, B will be performed at node 2 (4), while for Regions C and D decoding and replication operations will be both formed at node 4.

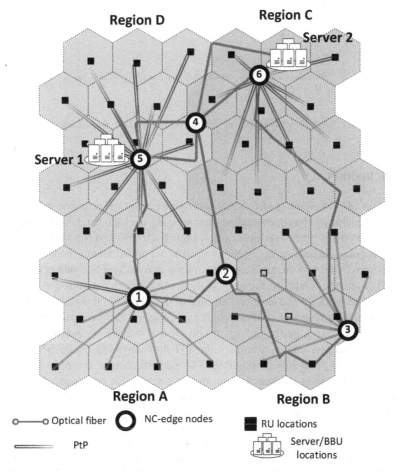

Fig. 7. Modified Bristol City topology with NC enabled nodes.

A comparison of the optical network power consumption for the Bristol City network for the provisioning of resilient C-RAN services is shown in Fig. 8, with and without the adoption of NC. It is observed that when NC is adopted, the protection capacity of the optical network is reduced by approximately 33% leading to an overall reduction of the power consumption.

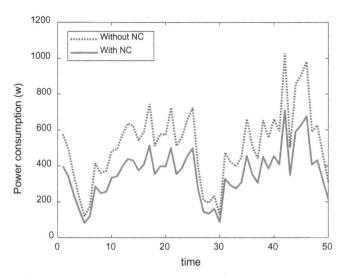

Fig. 8. Bristol City optical network power consumption for the provisioning resilient C-RAN services.

4   Conclusions

The problem of provisioning of C-RAN services over optical transport networks with resilient considerations has been studied. Recognizing the high bandwidth requirements that emerge from this type of services, a novel approach based on Network Coding (NC) has been proposed. In order to apply NC in realistic 5G network environments, execution of the modulo-2 sum and the replication operation at fronthaul line rate is required. An additional challenge relates to the very high storage capacity required at the edge of the transport network for the temporal storage of the FH flows that arrive from disjoint protection paths. In response to these challenges, a novel architectural framework and a hardware implementation have been proposed that manage to perform NC-related operations at line rate and synchronize the FH flows arriving at the BBUs keeping buffering at the edge as low as possible. The performance of the proposed solution has been experimentally evaluated demonstrating negligible penalties. Network level modeling results demonstrate a reduction of the total optical network capacity required for this type of applications by 33%.

Acknowledgment. This work has been financially supported partially by the EU Horizon 2020 project 5G-PICTURE under grant agreement No. 762057 and The U.K. Engineering and Physical Sciences Research Council (EPSRC), grant number EP/L020009/1, TOUCAN. We would also like to thank Prof. Andreas Polydoros, NKUA, for providing the USRPs used for OAI benchmarking.

References

1. Tzanakaki, A., et al.: 5G infrastructures supporting end-user and operational services: the 5G-XHaul architectural perspective. In: IEEE ICC (2016)

2. Ruffini, M.: Multi-dimensional convergence in future 5G networks. JLT **35**(3), 535–549 (2017)
3. Khorsandi, B., Tonini, F., Raffaelli, C.: Design methodologies and algorithms for survivable C-RAN. In: ONDM 2018, pp. 106–111 (2018)
4. Khorsandi, B.M., Raffaelli, C., Fiorani, M., Wosinska, L., Monti, P.: Survivable BBU hotel placement in a C-RAN with an optical WDM transport. In: DRCN 2017, pp. 1–6 (2017)
5. Shehata, M., Ayoub, O., Musumeci, F., Tornatore, M.: Survivable BBU placement for C-RAN over optical aggregation networks. In: 2018 20th ICTON, Bucharest, pp. 1–4 (2018)
6. Mohamed, S., et al.: Resilient BBU placement in 5G C-RAN over optical aggregation networks. Photon Netw. Commun. **37**(3), 388–398 (2019)
7. Wong, E., Grigoreva, E., Wosinska, L., Machuca, C.M.: Enhancing the survivability and power savings of 5G transport networks based on DWDM rings. J. Opt. Commun. Networking **9**(9), D74–D85 (2017)
8. Colman-Meixner, C., Figueiredo, G.B., Fiorani, M., Tornatore, M., Mukherjee, B.: Resilient cloud network mapping with virtualized BBU placement for cloud-RAN. In: Proceedings of ANTS, Bangalore, pp. 1–3 (2016)
9. Dikaliotis, T.K., Dimakis, A.G., Ho, T., Effros, M.: On the delay of network coding over line networks. In: IEEE ISIT, pp. 1408–1412 (2009)
10. 5G-XHaul Project, Deliverable D2.2: System Architecture Definition, submitted 1 July 2016
11. IEEE Standard for a Precision Clock Synchronization Protocol for Networked Measurement and Control Systems. IEEE Std 1588-2008
12. Yan, Y., et al.: FPGA-based optical network function programmable node. In: Proceedings of the OFC (2014)
13. Beldachi, A.-F., et al.: Experimental demonstration of 5G fronthaul and backhaul convergence based on FPGA-based active optical transport. In: Proceedings of ECOC (2018)

A Novel Carrier-Cooperation Scheme with an Incentive for Offering Emergency Lightpath Support in Disaster Recovery

Sugang Xu[1]([⊠]), Noboru Yoshikane[2], Naoki Miyata[3], Masaki Shiraiwa[1],
Takehiro Tsuritani[2], Xiaocheng Zhang[3], Yoshinari Awaji[1], and Naoya Wada[1]

[1] NICT, 4-2-1, Nukui-Kitamachi, Koganei, Tokyo 184-8795, Japan
{xsg,shiraiwa,yossy,wada}@nict.go.jp
[2] KDDI Research, Inc., 2-1-15 Ohara, Fujimino-shi, Saitama 356-8502, Japan
{yoshikane,tsuri}@kddi-research.jp
[3] NTT Communications Corporation, 3-4-1 Shibaura, Minato-ku, Tokyo 108-8118, Japan
{naoki.miyata,xiaocheng.zhang}@ntt.com

Abstract. To achieve the fast recovery of optical transport networks following a disaster, we investigate a novel scheme to enable cooperation between carriers. Carriers can take advantage of their surviving or recovered optical resources to aid one another with emergency lightpath support to reduce efficiently the burden of recovery, which is heavy immediately after disasters. These lightpaths can be employed exclusively by the counterpart carriers to satisfy their highest priority traffic demands, such as safety confirmation and victim relief. In addition, we introduce an incentive to carriers to prompt cooperation. The carrier cooperation-planning problem is decomposed into eight tasks, and distributed to individual carriers and a third-party organization. During cooperation, the carriers' confidential information can be strictly protected by employing a carrier optical network abstraction mechanism. The evaluation results reveal that our proposal can significantly reduce the burden on recovery and the corresponding cost for carriers, resulting in fast and efficient disaster recovery.

Keywords: Carrier cooperation · Disaster recovery · Emergency lightpath support · Incentive

1 Introduction

In modern transport networks, sophisticated protection and restoration schemes are taken into account in both the network design phase and operation phase to enhance the resiliency of networks and to protect services from failures [1–5]. In addition to schemes based on a proactive approach, the fast and efficient restoration of damaged networks following disasters is critical for network carriers (hereinafter called carriers). Major disasters have demonstrated that it is costly and time-consuming to independently recover individual original optical transport networks [6].

© IFIP International Federation for Information Processing 2020
Published by Springer Nature Switzerland AG 2020
A. Tzanakaki et al. (Eds.): ONDM 2019, LNCS 11616, pp. 362–376, 2020.
https://doi.org/10.1007/978-3-030-38085-4_31

To achieve fast and efficient disaster recovery, sparsely located surviving network resources should first be used. In a single-carrier recovery scenario, interconnection mechanisms between the surviving resources in multi-vendor networks have been investigated [7, 8]. To further take advantage of surviving resources in the networks of various carriers, and to perform well-balanced recovery tasks among carriers, in [9] and [10], we have investigated a carrier-cooperation scheme. In this scheme, carriers collaborate to construct an emergency common packet transport network in the disaster area with their surviving optical resources; this emergency common transport network is shareable among carriers.

In this paper, we propose an alternative cooperation approach and a scheme (to provide more options to meet different situations in disaster recovery) in which carriers offer one another emergency lightpath support (lightpath support for short) employed exclusively by the counterpart carriers. In addition, we introduce an incentive to carriers that supply emergency lightpaths. In this scheme, the planning problem for carrier cooperation-based recovery is decomposed and distributed to carriers and a third-party organization, and the carriers' confidential topology information is strictly protected during cooperation. Simulation results reveal that our proposal can significantly reduce the number of recovery tasks undertaken by each carrier, and the corresponding cost.

The remainder of this paper is organized as follows. Section 2 introduces the carrier-cooperation network model and an incentive mechanism for prompting lightpath support between carriers. Section 3 presents the distributed planning for disaster recovery based on carrier cooperation. Section 4 presents simulations and results, and Sect. 5 summarizes the paper.

2 Model of Recovery Based on Carrier Cooperation

2.1 Network Model

Figure 1 illustrates the optical transport networks of two carriers, Carrier-A and Carrier-B, which overlap in a disaster area. To hide the confidential topology information during cooperation, carriers perform an abstraction of their topologies to a common reference topology. It should be noted that the reference topology in a disaster area is assumed available prior to disasters. The details of the preparation of the reference topology are beyond the scope of this paper.

The numbered circles in the reference topology in Fig. 1 represent nodes in major cities. Each node contains an underlying optical node (e.g., reconfigurable optical add/drop multiplexer [ROADM]) and an upper-layer packet switch/router. Nodes in different carriers' abstracted networks with the same number are located in the same city. Nodes A0 and B0 (for Carrier-A and Carrier-B, respectively) are abstracted nodes that represent nodes outside of the disaster area. Nodes A1–A11 and B1–B11 are in the disaster area; of these, A1–A2 and B1–B2 are candidate borders for relaying packet traffic between the disaster area and outside network. The lines between adjacent nodes in this reference topology represent the segments that traverse the underlying individual carriers' optical networks. Solid lines between nodes represent the surviving segments, dotted lines are damaged ones that are candidates for restoration.

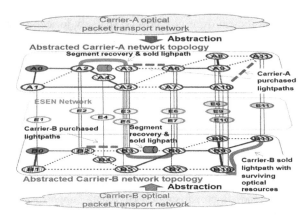

Fig. 1. Network model of disaster recovery based on carrier cooperation.

In Fig. 1, between the two carriers' abstracted topologies, the third-party nodes, E1–E11, are selected points in an emergency shareable exchange network (ESEN) that are employed to connect the nodes of different carriers within a city, e.g., performing optical-electrical-optical (OEO) conversion. Details of the ESEN nodes are omitted herein due to space limitations. The thin vertical lines between the ESEN nodes and carrier nodes represent short-distance fibres for carrier interconnection. Because these fibres are short, the cost of the interconnection of closely located nodes of different carriers in a city is lower than the cost of a long-distance optical network restoration. For simplicity, short-distance fibre costs are omitted from this paper.

2.2 Emergency Lightpath Support with an Incentive

To achieve fast and efficient recovery, carriers can cooperate and offer lightpath support to their counterpart carriers. In this paper, an emergency lightpath is a wavelength path. Besides the lightpaths which are employed by carriers themselves, the emergency lightpaths are offered to and employed exclusively by the counterpart carriers through the ESEN nodes (e.g., via OEO conversion), creating the temporary connectivity between the packet switches/routers in the packet layer. To offer an incentive to carriers that supply the emergency lightpaths, we assume that lightpath support is offered at a fee. Lightpath support is performed in two scenarios: (i) carriers can establish lightpaths with their surviving optical network resources and sell the lightpaths to their counterpart carrier; (ii) carriers can initially recover some of the damaged segments and establish/sell the lightpaths over the recovered segments for the counterpart carrier. Due to the high cost of segment recovery, the fee of the lightpath support (ii) is high. For instance, in Fig. 1, Carrier-B sells a scenario (i) lightpath between B10–B11 to Carrier-A with its surviving resources. Additionally, two carriers recover damaged segments A2–A3 and B3–B6, respectively, and sell the scenario (ii) lightpaths to one other.

Figure 2 presents a negotiation model in carrier cooperation. In addition to carriers, a third-party entity is introduced (hereinafter referred to as ESEN). First, the ESEN collects and exchanges the price information of the candidate emergency lightpaths (scenario [i]) among carriers; these lightpaths are based on surviving optical network resources. Based on the price information, each carrier evaluates the minimum requests necessary for its counterpart carrier's lightpath support, which can reduce its recovery tasks and the cost of satisfying its highest priority traffic demands (e.g., safety confirmation and victim relief). Second, when there is a set of damaged segments that both carriers wish to recover, the ESEN acquires information pertaining to these shared segments from the carriers, including the price for lightpath support (scenario [ii]). Based on this information, the ESEN performs segment recovery task matching between carriers to balance the segment recovery and reduce the recovery tasks and costs for individual carriers. For instance, as illustrated in Fig. 1, there are shared damaged segments, A2–A3/B2–B3 and A3–A6/B3–B6, which must be recovered. After the ESEN performs recovery task matching, Carrier-A and Carrier-B perform the recovery of segments A2–A3 and B3–B6, respectively, which is simply a part of the original recovery task. Both carriers aid one another with the lightpath support scenario (ii), and both receive income and rewards to compensate for their expenses. Thus, the segment recovery task and costs are significantly reduced, resulting in fast and efficient recovery.

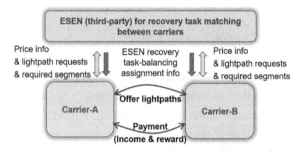

Fig. 2. Negotiation model in carrier cooperation-based disaster recovery.

3   Planning of Carrier Cooperation

To enable carrier cooperation and prompt the lightpath support among carriers during disaster recovery, the recovery planning problem is decomposed into eight tasks, as displayed in Fig. 3. These tasks are distributed to carriers and a third-party organization; the latter does not require the confidential information (e.g., topology) of any carrier. For simplicity, only segment recovery costs are taken into account here; the problem of nodal recovery cost is left for future work.

3.1   Modeling of Carrier-Side Planning Tasks (CSPTs)

For Tasks 3, 4, and 6 performed by carriers and shown in Fig. 3, we propose a generalized integer linear programming (ILP) model CSPT to carriers as a reference model. For each task, the values of the given information are adjusted; the information is summarized as follows. The constraints are presented in Appendix 1.

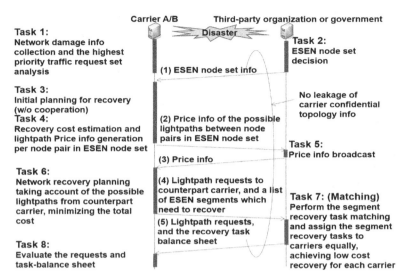

Fig. 3. Planning process in disaster recovery based on carrier cooperation.

G	$G = (V, E)$, graph of carrier network
V	Set of nodes. Each node consists of a ROADM and an electrical switch/router
E	Set of long-haul fibre links, i.e., the set of all edges in graph G
Δ	Set of all carrier identifications, e.g., integer 0, 1, 2, etc.
S	Set of abstracted outside source nodes. $S \subset V$
B	Set of candidate border nodes. $B \subset V$
Ω	Set of ESEN nodes. $\Omega \subset V - S$
$G^* = (\Omega, E^*)$	Common reference ESEN network topology abstracted from graph G. E^* is the set of optical network segments between nodes (each in a major city)
Ψ	Set of possible lightpaths (scenario [i]) between ESEN nodes declared by counterpart carrier
Π	Set of lightpaths (scenario [i]) between ESEN nodes required by counterpart carrier
R	Set of node pairs with traffic demands in the upper-layer packet network
$\Gamma_{s,d}$	Packet traffic volume (e.g., 10 Gbps) between node pair $(s, d) \in R$
$A_{s,d}$	Profit of traffic between node pair (s, d). A large value indicates a high priority
W	Set of wavelengths
$U_{m,n}^{w}$	Indicator of the existing wavelength utilization of w ($w \in W$) in the long-haul fibre link from nodes m to n. 0: free, 1: occupied. ($m, n \in V$)
$L_{m,n}$	Indicator of the long-haul fibre link between nodes m, n; 0: does not exist, 1: exists. ($m, n \in V$)

(continued)

(*continued*)

$T_{m,n}$	Recovery cost of damaged long-haul fibre between nodes m, n. The cost can be defined with a positive value or inf (infinite). $T_{m,n} \neq$ inf is considered the candidates for restoration. (m, $n \in V$)
$C_{i,j}$	Recovery cost of ESEN segments in the abstracted ESEN topology, which is estimated by the carrier itself. ($(i, j) \in E^*, i, j \in \Omega$)
p_{ij}	Price when selling emergency lightpath between ESEN node pair (i, j), estimated by the carrier itself, e.g., by employing surviving optical network resources (scenario [i]) or recovered ESEN segments (scenario [ii]). ($(i, j) \in E^*, i, j \in \Omega$)
p'_{ij}	Price when purchasing the emergency lightpath between ESEN node pair (i, j) estimated by the counterpart carrier, e.g., by employing surviving optical network resources (scenario [i]) or recovered ESEN segments (scenario [ii]). ($(i, j) \in E^*, i, j \in \Omega$)
O_{ij}	Request for emergency lightpath (scenario [i]) between ESEN node pair (i, j), which is required by the counterpart carrier after evaluation. 0: not required, 1: required. ($(i, j) \in E^*, i, j \in \Omega$)
F_i^w	Number of free transponders at node i ($i \in V$) with wavelength w ($w \in W$)
G_m	Number of free transponders at node m ($m \in V$)
D_m	Degree limitation imposed on node m ($m \in V$)
C	Data rate of each lightpath (e.g., 100 Gbps)
a_{opt}	Weight for suppressing wavelength consumption in underlying optical networks
a_{IP}	Weight for suppressing bandwidth consumption in upper-layer packet networks

Binary Variables:

$\alpha^{s,d}$	1: indicates the satisfied traffic demands between node pair $(s, d) \in R$; 0: otherwise
u_b	1: indicates the border node at $b \in B$; 0: otherwise
$\beta_{m,n}$	1: indicates the selected long-haul fibre link (m, n) for repair; 0: otherwise. (m, $n \in V$)
$P_{m,n}^{(i,j),w}$	1: routing and wavelength assignment (RWA) for the lightpath between nodes i and j passing through long-haul fibre link (m, n) with wavelength w; 0: otherwise. ($w \in W$; $i, j \in V$; $m, n \in V$)
$v_{i,j}^w$	1: indicates lightpath between nodes i and j using wavelength w; 0: otherwise. ($w \in W$; $i, j \in V$)
$\lambda_{i,j}^{s,d}$	1: indicates packet traffic routing. Traffic between source s and destination d passing through the lightpath between nodes i and j; 0: otherwise. ($i, j \in V$, $[s, d] \in R$)
σ_{ij}	1: indicates request for purchasing counterpart carrier's lightpath between ESEN node pair (i, j); 0: otherwise. $[(i, j) \in \Psi, i, j \in \Omega]$. Note that $\sigma_{ij} = 1$ indicates that $O_{ij} = 1$ for the counterpart carrier

Objective:
The concern in (1) are summarized as follows. (Portion 1) Satisfy the highest priority traffic demands as many as possible; (Portion 2) Select the minimum necessary border nodes to reduce management cost; (Portion 3) Select the minimum necessary (a) long-haul fibre links for restoration in the carrier's underlying optical network and (b) the purchase of the emergency lightpaths (scenario [i]) between the ESEN node pairs from the counterpart carrier; (Portion 4) Minimize the wavelength consumption in the carrier's optical layer network for all necessary lightpaths; (Portion 5) Solve the packet routing in the upper layer, minimizing the total logical link bandwidth consumption. We converted the profits in the first portion, the border creation cost in the second portion, the recovery cost in the third portion, the wavelength consumption (e.g., energy consumption) in the fourth portion, and the logical link bandwidth consumption in the fifth portion to currency, using a specified unit in order to unify the dimensions. The detailed conversion method, however, is outside the scope of this paper. Coefficients B_1, B_2, B_3, a_{opt}, and a_{IP} separate different portions into non-overlapping value ranges.

$$\min\left[-B_1 \sum_{(s,d)\in R} \Gamma_{s,d} A_{s,d} \alpha^{s,d} + B_2 \sum_{b\in B} \mu_b + B_3 \left(\sum_{m,n\in V | T_{m,n}\neq inf} T_{m,n}\beta_{m,n} \right.\right.$$
$$\left. + \sum_{(i,j)\in \Psi} p'_{i,j}\sigma_{i,j} \right) + a_{opt} \sum_{i,j\in V} \sum_{w\in W} \sum_{m,n\in V | U^w_{m,n}=0, or T_{m,n}\neq inf} P^{(i,j),w}_{m,n} \quad (1)$$
$$\left. + a_{IP} \sum_{(s,d)\in R} \sum_{i,j\in V} \lambda^{s,d}_{i,j} \right]$$

3.2 Modeling of Third-Party-Side Matching Task (TSMT)

For the matching task, Task 7 (see Fig. 3), performed by a third-party organization (ESEN), we propose an ILP model. The given information is summarized as follows. The TSMT is described as below. The constraints are shown in Appendix 2.

X^a	Set of damaged ESEN segments that must be recovered by Carrier a to satisfy Carrier a's highest priority traffic. ($a \in \Delta$)
X_{common}	Set of common ESEN segments that must be recovered to satisfy the highest priority traffic by both carriers in Δ
p^a_{ij}	Price for selling an emergency lightpath (scenarios [i] and [ii]) between an ESEN node pair (i, j), which is estimated and declared by Carrier a. ($a \in \Delta, i, j \in \Omega$)

Linear Variable:

λ_{max}	Greatest sum paid by individual carriers

Binary Variables:

$\gamma^a_{i,j}$	1: indicates that the task for ESEN segment (i, j) recovery and lightpath (scenario [ii]) creation is assigned to Carrier a; 0: otherwise. ($a \in \Delta, i, j \in E^*$)

Objective:

$$\min(\lambda_{\max}) \tag{2}$$

When carriers have damaged ESEN segments need to recovery (X^a), the third-party organization identifies the jointly desired ESEN segments for both carriers (X_{common}). For X_{common}, the third-party organization performs the matching of the ESEN segment recovery task to individual carriers. To achieve well-balanced task matching, the objective in (2) is to minimize the greatest sum paid by any carrier. Upon receiving a recovery task assignment, individual carriers perform ESEN segment recovery and sell the lightpaths over the recovered ESEN segment to their counterpart carriers. The corresponding payment received from the counterpart carrier is treated as a reward in compensation for performing the ESEN segment recovery task, as part of the cooperation between carriers.

3.3 Distributed Task Implementations

In Task 1, the carriers collect the damage information and traffic demands which are of the highest priority for safety confirmation and victim relief [8]. In Task 2, the third-party ESEN identifies the disaster area and selects the major cities and ESEN nodes. The implementations of Tasks 3, 4, 6, 7, and 8 (see Fig. 3) are described as follows and considered to be a reference guideline. Task 3, 4, 6, and 8 are performed by carriers. Task 7 is performed by a third-party organization. Details of the simple Task 5 are omitted due to space limitations.

(1) Task 3: Initial planning for standalone recovery (by carrier)

> **Step-1:** Assign highest priority traffic requests R and $\Gamma_{s,d}$;
> **Step-2:** Set $\Psi = \{\}, \Pi = \{\}$;
> **Step-3:** Solve **CSPT**; Record the fibre links that must necessarily be recovered ($\beta_{m,n} = 1$);

(2) Task 4: Recovery cost and price estimation (by carrier)

> **Step-1:** Assume that there is dummy traffic between nodes 0 and 1;
> **Step-2:** For each node pair (i, j), where $i, j \in \Omega$ estimate cost,
>
> Assign $\Pi = \{(i,j)\}$, and solve **CSPT** (with surviving fibre links and the damaged fibre links recorded in Task 3);
> Record recovery cost $C_{i,j} = \sum\limits_{m,n \in V | T_{m,n} \neq \inf} T_{m,n}\beta_{m,n}$;
>
> **Step-3:** For the damaged ESEN segments $(i, j) \in E^*$, where $C_{i,j} > 0$, the carrier generates price $p_{i,j}^a$ for offering the scenario (ii) emergency lightpath. For example, $p_{i,j}^a = b * C_{i,j}$, $(b > 1)$, or a flat price, $p_{i,j}^a = H$, $(H > C_{i,j})$ for all of the

damaged ESEN segments to conceal the detailed damage information; For the scenario (i) lightpaths, where $C_{i,j} = 0$, generate price $p_{i,j}^a$. For example, $p_{i,j}^a = b *$ normal_price$_{i,j}$, $(b > 1)$, or a flat price, $p_{i,j}^a = r * H$, $(r > 0)$ to conceal the detailed information;

Step-4: Send the price of the emergency lightpaths for both scenarios (i) and (ii) to the third-party ESEN.

(3) Task 6: Evaluation of the candidate emergency lightpaths support (scenario [i]) of the counterpart carrier (by carrier)

Step-1: Assign highest priority traffic requests R and $\Gamma_{s,d}$;
Step-2: Set $\Psi = \{(i,j) | p_{i,j}^a \text{ is disclosed by counterpart Carrier } a\}$ $(i, j \in \Omega)$, $\Pi = \{\}$;
Step-3: Solve **CSPT**;
Step-4: Send the emergency lightpath (i, j) request solution, where $\sigma_{ij} = 1$, and X^a, including the ESEN segment (i, j), with recovery cost $C_{i,j} = \sum_{m,n \in V | T_{m,n} \neq \inf} T_{m,n} \beta_{m,n}$, where $C_{i,j} > 0$, to the third-party organization.

(4) Task 7: The third-party organization performs ESEN segment recovery matching (by the ESEN)

Step-1: Based on X^a received from the carriers, identify the maximum even number of jointly desired ESEN segments for both carriers, X_{common};
Step-2: Based on the carriers' price information for offering the scenario (ii) emergency lightpaths received after Task 4, solve **TSMT** for recovery task matching;
Step-3: Collect all solutions where $\gamma_{i,j}^a = 1$, namely, the segment recovery and lightpath (scenario [ii]) creation task-balance result and the emergency lightpath request list (after Task 6); send to individual carriers.

(5) Task 8: Evaluation of the required emergency lightpaths and ESEN segment recovery task matching (by carrier)

Step-1: Carrier calculates its costs;

C_1: Total payment for counterpart's lightpath support (scenario [i]);
C_2: Total payment for counterpart's lightpath support (scenario [ii]);
C_3: Total segment recovery cost, which is assigned by the third-party organization in recovery task matching;
C_4: Total remaining cost for segment recovery that is not involved in carrier cooperation; namely, those that cannot be balanced and must be performed by this carrier;

Step-2: Carrier calculates its incomes and rewards;

I_1: Total income received from counterpart carrier for offering lightpath support with surviving optical resources (scenario [i]);

I_2: Total income received from counterpart carrier for offering the lightpath support with recovered ESEN segments (scenario [ii]);

Step-3: Carrier calculates its profit as the sum of the income and reward minus the sum of the costs. If the profit in cooperation is larger than that of standalone recovery, carrier cooperation is deemed beneficial and will be adopted.

In the cases where some required emergency lightpaths cannot be satisfied, e.g., due to the changes in resource availability according to after-shock etc., the failed lightpath(s) can be marked and repeat the aforementioned process for refinement.

4 Simulations and Numerical Results

4.1 Evaluation Model

Evaluations were conducted to observe the effects of the aforementioned carrier-cooperation scheme. With respect to the shared ESEN abstracted network topology in the disaster area, a network topology that is a subset of the Japan photonic network model [11] was employed, as shown in Fig. 1. For simplicity, the topologies of the original networks of Carrier-A and Carrier-B were identical to this reference topology. Namely, the ESEN segments were identical to the fibre links of the carriers' original networks. Note that theoretically, an identical topology is not required. Each carrier's network consisted of 12 nodes, including one outside node, two border node candidates, and another nine inside nodes (i.e., one node per city, and 17 bidirectional fibre links). At each node i, F_i^w was set to 7 for each wavelength w, and $G_i = 7$. Eleven ESEN nodes from nodes 1 to 11 were co-located with the carriers' nodes in the cities, and the data rate of the lightpath was set to $C = 100$ Gbps. The number of surviving long-haul fibre links in each carrier's original network was changed as 5 and 10 (these surviving links were assigned as $L_{m,n} = 1$). For both carriers' networks, the distribution pattern of the surviving fibre links was selected such that they had a strong correlation [8]. For example, the fibre links of both the Carrier-A/B networks between two cities had a high probability to have survived or have been damaged together. In this study, this probability was set to 0.8 to represent the strong correlation between link (segment) failures in different carriers' networks. The cases with a probability 0.4 had similar performance, which is omitted due to space limitations.

For simplicity, for all damage situations, the value of $T_{m,n}$ was set to 10 for restoring the damaged long-haul fibre links; therefore, the ESEN segment restoration cost $C_{i,j} = 10$. A flat price for emergency lightpaths was adopted; that is, for the scenario (ii) lightpath, $p_{i,j}^a = H$, and H was fixed at 10 for all cases. For the scenario (i) lightpath, $p_{i,j}^a = r * H$ to conceal the detailed information. The coefficient r was set to 0.3, 0.5, 0.7, and 1.1 to observe the effect on the pricing of the scenario (i) lightpath. A non-flat pricing scheme is beyond the scope of this paper and left for future work.

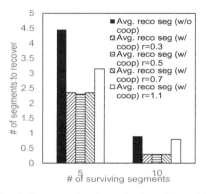

Fig. 4. Recovery burden reduction effect with identical damage level.

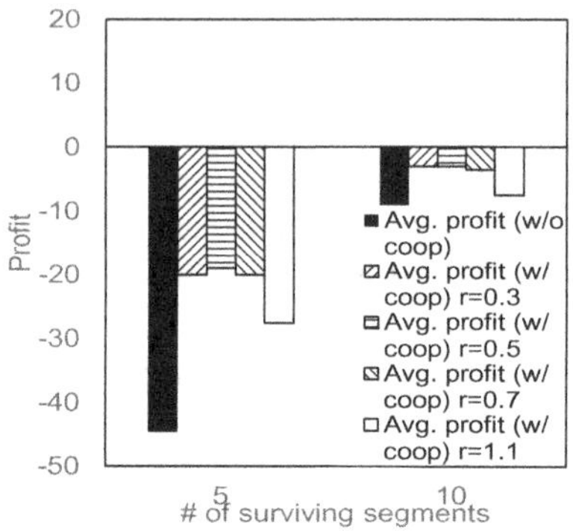

Fig. 5. Improved profit via cooperation with identical damage level.

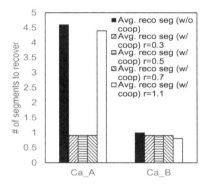

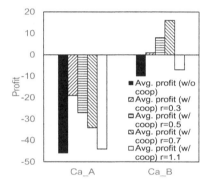

Fig. 6. Recovery burden reduction effect in unequal damage situation.

Fig. 7. Improved profit via cooperation in unequal damage situation.

For the Carrier-A and Carrier-B networks, it is assumed that each of the nine inside nodes, d, has the highest priority packet traffic demand to/from the outside node (node 0) for safety confirmation and victim relief (with the same value, $A_{0,d} = 10$, $\Gamma_{0,d} = 10$ Gbps). For each carrier's network, the number of wavelengths $|W| = 4$ was adequate for all high-priority traffic requests in the evaluation. $U_{m,n}^{w}$ is set to 0 for all of the surviving links. For the coefficients in (1), $B_1 = 1000000$, $B_2 = 10000$, $B_3 = 100$, $a_{opt} = 10$, and $a_{IP} = 1$. The optimization of the aforementioned network planning models (CSPT, TSMT) is solved by CPLEX [12], on a PC (Xeon Gold 5115 2.4-GHz 20-core CPU, 128 GB memory).

4.2 Numerical Results

We simulated three damage situations, namely, with surviving fibre links 5:5, 10:10, and 5:10 between the networks of Carrier-A and Carrier-B. The first two ones reflect an identical damage level, whereas the last situation reflects unequal damage among carriers. For each situation, we generated 50 cases of damage patterns. For all cases, the traffic demands of carriers were satisfied. Major results are selected and plotted in Figs. 4, 5, 6 and 7. The average computational time for each case is less than 15 min.

For the identical damage situations, we first observed the effect of our proposal on the recovery burden reduction. Figure 4 plots the average number of ESEN segments recovered per carrier, which was yielded by standalone single-carrier recovery (w/o coop) and our proposal of carrier cooperation (w/ coop). With price coefficient $r = 0.3, 0.5$, and 0.7, in comparison to standalone recovery, a nearly 50% reduction of the recovery burden can be achieved via carrier cooperation due to the surviving resource use and recovery task balancing among carriers. With a significantly reduced burden on recovery, a fast recovery of communication can be expected. However, when we increased the price of the scenario (i) emergency lightpath (e.g., $r = 1.1$), which exceeds the cost of segment recovery, the carrier does not purchase the scenario (i) lightpath support from the counterpart carrier because it is even more costly than the segment recovery performed by carrier itself. The burden reduction effect is decreased.

Figure 5 plots the profits calculated in Task 8 (see Sect. 3.3). The results clearly indicate that with carrier cooperation and an appropriate price of the scenario (i) lightpath, income and reward can be achieved in cooperation, and carriers can significantly improve their profits compared to single-carrier standalone recovery. This demonstrates the strong incentive for carriers to offer lightpath support to one another in both heavy and lightweight disasters. However, when we increased the price of the scenario (i) emergency lightpath (e.g., $r = 1.1$), the profit decreases, especially in lightweight disaster cases. Few surviving resources can be utilized due to the high price.

For an unequal damage situation with a differing amount of surviving fibre links (e.g., 5:10) between the Carrier-A (Ca_A) and Carrier-B (Ca_B) networks, Fig. 6 plots the average number of ESEN segments recovered per carrier, and Fig. 7 plots the corresponding profits. For Carrier-A, which was heavily damaged, given an appropriate price of the lightpath (scenario [i]), the recovery task performed by Carrier-A was dramatically reduced, owing to lightpath support from Carrier-B (in particular, scenario [i]). Accordingly, with the income and reward received from each other, Carrier-A and Carrier-B experienced larger profits than that of single-carrier standalone recovery. Because Carrier-B was the supplier of the emergency lightpath, its profit was much higher than that of Carrier-A. When the price was increased (e.g., from $r = 0.3$ to 0.7), the profit of Carrier-B increased accordingly. Meanwhile, when we further increased the price, namely with $r = 1.1$, because Carrier-A would not purchase the lightpath support (scenario [i]), the income from Carrier-A were not acquired. Thus, Carrier-B's profit was low. This indicates that an appropriate price also plays an important role. For further investigation, a non-fixed recovery cost and non-flat pricing scheme, and the observations with wide parameter ranges and more situations, e.g., where there is less co-location of nodes between carriers, should be considered and left as future work.

5 Conclusions

In this paper, we propose a novel planning scheme for disaster recovery based on carrier cooperation, in which carriers aid one another by offering emergency lightpath support. The lightpaths are employed exclusively by the counterpart carriers to satisfy the highest priority traffic demand, such as safety confirmation and victim relief with a significantly reduced recovery burden. In addition, we introduce an incentive in the planning scheme to stimulate carrier cooperation. Importantly, during cooperation, the confidential information of the carriers can be protected by introducing a carrier optical network abstraction mechanism. The evaluation results reveal that our proposal can significantly reduce the number of recovery tasks undertaken by each carrier and the corresponding costs, resulting in a fast and efficient recovery.

Appendix 1: Constraints in CSPT

The constraints of available transponders are shown from (3) to (6). RWA constraints in the underlying optical network are from (7) to (9). The constraints that each lightpath can utilize at most is one wavelength on a surviving long-haul fibre link are shown in (10), including the constraints for using the co-route and the same wavelength for both directions. Expression (11) implies that wavelength utilization can also be possible if there is a restored fibre link. The degree-limitation constraints at each node are given in (12). In case of emergency interconnection between ROADMs, there will be a limitation on the degree of ROADM. Constraints on upper-layer packet routing are shown from (13) to (15). The constraints on bandwidth consumption of packet traffic in lightpaths that are not for sale or purchase in carrier cooperation are shown in (16). The traffic constraints on the emergency lightpaths that are to be sold to the counterpart carrier and are the candidates for purchase from the counterpart carrier in carrier cooperation are shown in (17) and (18), respectively. Constraints (19) indicate that the lightpaths $(i, j) \in \Pi$ should be created and sold to the counterpart carrier. The constraints on border specification are shown in (20) and (21).

$$\sum_{j \in V} \sum_{n \in V | (U_{i,n}^w = 0, \text{or} T_{i,n} \neq \inf)} P_{i,n}^{(i,j),w} \leq F_i^w, \forall i \in V; \forall w \in W \tag{3}$$

$$\sum_{i \in V} \sum_{m \in V | (U_{m,j}^w = 0, \text{or} T_{m,j} \neq \inf)} P_{m,j}^{(i,j),w} \leq F_j^w, \forall j \in V; \forall w \in W \tag{4}$$

$$\sum_{j \in V} \sum_{w \in W} \sum_{n \in V | (U_{i,n}^w = 0, \text{or} T_{i,n} \neq \inf)} P_{i,n}^{(i,j),w} \leq G_i, \forall i \in V \tag{5}$$

$$\sum_{i \in V} \sum_{w \in W} \sum_{m \in V | (U_{m,j}^w = 0, \text{or} T_{m,j} \neq \inf)} P_{m,j}^{(i,j),w} \leq G_j, \forall j \in V \tag{6}$$

$$\sum_{m \in V | (U_{m,k}^w = 0, \text{or} T_{m,k} \neq \inf)} P_{m,k}^{(i,j),w} = \sum_{n \in V | (U_{k,n}^w = 0, \text{or} T_{k,n} \neq \inf)} P_{k,n}^{(i,j),w},$$

$$\forall i, j, k \in V | (i \neq j \neq k); \forall w \in W \tag{7}$$

$$\sum_{n \in V | (U_{i,n}^w = 0, \text{or} T_{i,n} \neq \inf)} P_{i,n}^{(i,j),w} = v_{i,j}^w, \forall i, j \in V | (i \neq j); \forall w \in W \tag{8}$$

$$\sum_{m \in V | (U_{m,j}^w = 0, \text{or} T_{m,j} \neq \inf)} P_{m,j}^{(i,j),w} = v_{i,j}^w, \forall i, j \in V | (i \neq j); \forall w \in W \tag{9}$$

$$\sum_{i,j \in V} [P_{m,n}^{(i,j),w} + P_{n,m}^{(i,j),w}] \leq 1, \forall w \in W; \forall m, n \in V | U_{m,n}^w = 0 \tag{10}$$

$$\sum_{i,j \in V} [P_{m,n}^{(i,j),w} + P_{n,m}^{(i,j),w}] \leq \beta_{m,n}, \forall w \in W; \forall m, n \in V | T_{m,n} \neq \inf \tag{11}$$

$$\sum_{n \in V | T_{m,n} \neq \inf} \beta_{m,n} + \sum_{n \in V | L_{m,n}=1} L_{m,n} \leq D_m, \forall m \in V | (\exists n \in V, T_{m,n} \neq \inf) \tag{12}$$

$$\sum_{i \in V | i \neq k \neq s \neq d} \lambda_{i,k}^{s,d} = \sum_{j \in V | j \neq k \neq s \neq d} \lambda_{k,j}^{s,d}, \forall (s, d) \in R, \forall k \in V \tag{13}$$

$$\sum_{j \in V | (j \neq s \neq d)} \lambda_{s,j}^{s,d} = \alpha^{s,d}, \forall (s, d) \in R \tag{14}$$

$$\sum_{i \in V | (i \neq s \neq d)} \lambda_{i,d}^{s,d} = \alpha^{s,d}, \forall (s, d) \in R \tag{15}$$

$$\sum_{(s,d) \in R} \Gamma_{s,d} \lambda_{i,j}^{s,d} \leq C \sum_{w \in W} v_{i,j}^w, \forall i, j \in V | (i \neq j) \, and \, (i, j) \notin (\Psi \cup \Pi) \tag{16}$$

$$\sum_{(s,d) \in R} \Gamma_{s,d} \lambda_{i,j}^{s,d} \leq C \left[\left(\sum_{w \in W} v_{i,j}^w \right) - O_{i,j} \right], \forall (i, j) \in \Pi \tag{17}$$

$$\sum_{(s,d) \in R} \Gamma_{s,d} \lambda_{i,j}^{s,d} \leq C \left[\left(\sum_{w \in W} v_{i,j}^w \right) + \sigma_{i,j} \right], \forall (i, j) \in \Psi - \Pi \tag{18}$$

$$\sum_{w \in W} v_{i,j}^w \geq O_{i,j}, \forall (i, j) \in \Pi \tag{19}$$

$$\lambda_{s*,b}^{s*,d} \leq u_b, \forall s* \in S, \forall d \in (V - S) | (s*, d) \in R; \forall b \in B \tag{20}$$

$$\lambda_{b,k}^{s*,d} \leq u_b, \forall s* \in S, \forall d \in (V - S) | (s*, d) \in R; \forall b \in B; \forall k \in V - S - B \tag{21}$$

Appendix 2: Constraints in TSMT

The constraint on the maximum cost experienced by individual carriers is shown in (22). The constraint assuring task assignment in X_{common} among carriers is in (23).

$$\sum_{(i,j) \in X_{\text{common}}} p_{i,j}^a \gamma_{i,j}^a \leq \lambda_{\max}, \forall a \in \Delta \tag{22}$$

$$\sum_{a \in \Delta} \gamma_{i,j}^a = 1, \forall (i, j) \in X_{\text{common}} \tag{23}$$

References

1. Sivakumar, M., et al.: A hybrid protection-restoration mechanism for enhancing dual-failure restorability in optical mesh-restorable networks. In: Proceedings of the 4th Annual SPIE International Conference on Optical Networking and Communications 2003, pp. 37–48 (2003)
2. Ramasubramanian, S., Chandak, A.: Dual-link failure resiliency through backup link mutual exclusion. IEEE/ACM Trans. Networking **16**(1), 157–169 (2008)
3. Saito, H.: Analysis of geometric disaster evaluation model for physical networks. IEEE/ACM Trans. Networking **23**(6), 1777–1789 (2015)
4. Saito, H., Kawahara, R., Fukumoto, T.: Proposal of disaster avoidance control. In: Proceedings of the Networks 2014 (2014)
5. Habib, M.F., Tornatore, M., De Leenheer, M., Dikbiyik, F., Mukherjee, B.: Design of disaster-resilient optical datacenter networks. IEEE J. Lightwave Technol. **30**(16), 2563–2573 (2012)
6. Technical Report on Telecommunications and Disaster Mitigation: ITU-T FG-DR&NRR, Version 1.0, June 2013
7. Xu, S., et al.: Emergency optical network construction and control with multi-vendor interconnection for quick disaster recovery. IEICE Trans. Commun. **E99–B**(2), 370–384 (2016)
8. Xu, S., et al.: Emergency optical network planning with multi-vendor interconnection and portable EDFAs. Ann. Telecommun. **73**, 127–138 (2018)
9. Xu, S., et al.: Multi-carrier interconnection-based emergency packet transport network planning in disaster recovery. In: Proceedings of the 13th International Conference on Design of Reliable Communication Networks (DRCN 2017), Munich, Germany (2017). 8 pages
10. Xu, S., et al.: Multicarrier-collaboration-based emergency packet transport network construction in disaster recovery. In: Proceedings of the 10th International Workshop on Resilient Networks Design and Modeling (RNDM 2018), Norway, vol. Ta, no. 3 (2018)
11. Sakano, T., et al.: A study on a photonic network model based on the regional characteristic of Japan. Tech. Rpt. IEICE, PN2013-01 (2013). (in Japanese)
12. IBM CPLEX Optimizer. https://www.ibm.com/products/ilog-cplex-optimization-studio. Accessed 12 Apr 2019

State-of-the-Art and Future of Submarine Cable System Technology

Hidenori Takahashi$^{(\boxtimes)}$ (iD)

KDDI Research, Inc., 2-1-15, Ohara, Fujimino-shi, Saitama 356-8502, Japan
takahashi@kddi-research.jp

Abstract. The FASTER cable system has been developed as the first trans-pacific optical submarine cable system designed for digital-coherent transmission at the initial state. With this significant change for submarine cables, the design capacity is continuously being upgraded following the improvement of the state-of-the-art modulation format to maximize spectral efficiency even at the limited optical signal-to-noise ratio (OSNR). For the next generation, the novel technologies are expected to increase the capacity per cable under the conditions of limited feeding power and space in a cable. This report reviews some technologies from the current to the promising future submarine cable systems such as the introduction of space-division-multiplexing (SDM) technologies.

Keywords: Submarine cable · Optical communication · Digital coherent transmission

1 Introduction

The demand for increasing the capacity of optical submarine cable systems for global communication is steadily growing. The traffic increase rate is maintained at around 40% per year for transpacific segments. To support the traffic growth, over 10 submarine cable systems have been built and operated following the technology evolutions. Nowadays, digital-coherent transmission technology is considered as the default for a transponder at the initial design stage of optical submarine cables. For example, in the FASTER cable system whose ready-for-service (RFS) launch was June 2016, the initial design capacity is 60 Tbit/s consisting of 6 fiber pairs (FP) $\times$ 100 ch $\times$ 100 Gbit/s utilizing wavelength-division-multiplexing (WDM) technology [1–3]. This trend never seems to change, so the higher capacity optical submarine cable system will be indispensable for future global communication. This paper reviews the evolution of telecommunication technology for submarine cable systems, explains the currently available state-of-the-art technologies, and finally describes the promising technologies that are expected to overcome some significant issues and be applicable for future optical submarine cable systems.

© IFIP International Federation for Information Processing 2020
Published by Springer Nature Switzerland AG 2020
A. Tzanakaki et al. (Eds.): ONDM 2019, LNCS 11616, pp. 377–388, 2020.
https://doi.org/10.1007/978-3-030-38085-4_32

2 Evolution of Submarine Cables for Communication

2.1 Transpacific Submarine Cable Systems

Table 1 shows the evolution of the once in-service transpacific submarine cable system for communication by RFS year, including those already retired. Typical cable length of transpacific systems is around 10,000 km. The "TPC-1" was the first telephone cable between Japan and the US, consisting of a coaxial cable, whose initial design capacity was just 128 phone lines. Assuming the bit rate of a phone line as 64 kbit/s, the initial design capacity has increased ~560 million times that of the original 50 years ago, leading to the introduction of FASTER.

Table 1. In-service transpacific submarine cable systems

System	RFS [Year]	Tech.	Ini. des. Rx	Ini. des. signals/FP [bit/s]	FP	Initial design capacity
TPC-1	1964	Coax.	–	–	–	128 lines[*1]
TPC-2	1976	Coax.	–	–	–	845 lines[*2]
TPC-3	1989	Regen.	DD	$1 \times 280M$	2	560 Mbit/s
TPC-4	1992	Regen.	DD	$1 \times 560M$	2	1.1 Gbit/s
TPC-5	1995	EDFA	DD	$1 \times 5G$	2	10 Gbit/s
China-US	2000	EDFA	DD	$8 \times 2.5G$	4	80 Gbit/s
PC-1	2001	EDFA	DD	$16 \times 10G$	4	640 Gbit/s
Japan-US	2001	EDFA	DD	$16 \times 10G$	4	640 Gbit/s
TGN-P	2002	EDFA	DD	$64 \times 10G$	8	5.12 Tbit/s
TPE	2008	EDFA	DD	$64 \times 10G$	4	2.56 Tbit/s
Unity	2010	EDFA	DD	$96 \times 10G$	5	4.8 Tbit/s
FASTER	2016	EDFA	DC	$100 \times 100G$	6	60 Tbit/s
NCP	2018	EDFA	DC	$N \times 100G$	7	80 Tbit/s

[*1]Assuming the bitrate for a telephone line as 64 kbit/s, it will be 8.2 Mbit/s.
[*2]Assuming the bitrate for a telephone line as 64 kbit/s, it will be 54 Mbit/s.
RFS: Ready for Service
Coax: Copper cable
Regen.: Regenerator as the repeater for the optical fiber cables
EDFA: Optical amplifier as the repeater for the optical fiber cables
Ini. des.: Initial design
Rx: Receiver
DD: Direct detection
DC: Digital coherent

The optical fiber communication has been introduced with TPC-3 as the first transpacific optical submarine cable system. A regeneration repeater was used so the signal quality was independent of the total transmission distance; however, the capacity had never changed from the initial design stage. TPC-5 was the first transpacific cable to introduce an erbium-doped fiber amplifier (EDFA) for the re-amplifying scheme with the initial design capacity of 10 Gbit/s (5 Gbit/s × 2FP) in 1995. With its larger capacity, the mainstream of international video broadcasting was shifted from satellites to submarine cables after the Atlanta Olympic games in 1996. Thanks to the physical characteristics of EDFA, it is independent of the modulation format of optical signals. Even though it has the drawback of noise accumulation being generated in EDF, it is possible to increase the design capacity by changing the signal modulation format, known as upgrading. This means that the evolution of the transponder increases the value of the deployed cable. In other words, the limitation is determined by the usable bandwidth of a repeater. For example, already deployed cables seem obsolete when a new generation cable is constructed with a wider bandwidth. This is because the operation and maintenance cost for submarine cables is not so different between the old and the newly deployed version. Therefore, the narrower bandwidth cable has relatively higher running costs. Even if the design lifespan of submarine cables is typically 25 years, the actual "business" lifespan tends to be shortened with traffic migration to a higher capacity cable because of the previously described reason. For example, the China-US cable as shown in Table 1 was retired in Dec. 2016 even 16 years after RFS [4].

2.2 Technology Trend of Optical Submarine Cable

The repeatered system with EDFA is widely adopted currently. Figure 1 shows the historical evolution of the initial design capacity per one FP for transpacific optical submarine cable systems.

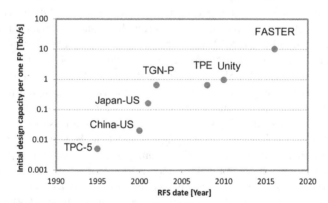

Fig. 1. Historical evolution of the initial design capacity per one FP for transpacific optical submarine cable systems.

The TCP-5 used a dispersion shifted fiber (DSF) cable designed for single channel transmission. After that, the non-zero DSF (NZ-DSF) cable was introduced for WDM transmission such as the Japan-US cable network, etc. Furthermore, the dispersion managed fiber (DMF) cable was introduced for dense WDM (DWDM) systems such as Unity. For these cable types, the direct-decision (DD) receiver was considered as the transmission method. On the other hand, the digital-coherent transmission technology was considered at the initial design stage for FASTER. This enables the cable to only consist of positive dispersion fibers (D+ fiber).

3 State-of-the-Art Technologies

This section explains the cutting-edge submarine cable technologies that are currently available. There are two types of application: that for new cable deployment, and that for the upgrading of already deployed cables by simply replacing the submarine line terminal equipment (SLTE).

3.1 +D Fiber Transmission Line

The newly deployed cable can support digital-coherent transmission since the introduction of FASTER for transpacific cables. This change has led to the introduction of the dual-polarization (DP), phase and amplitude modulation to increase the spectral efficiency (SE). Compared to DSF, NZ-DSF and DMF cables, the +D fiber cable gives increments of accumulated dispersion monotonously, which contributes to the reduction of the signal quality degradation caused by the nonlinear effect such as self-phase modulation (SPM), cross-phase modulation (XPM) and four-wave mixing (FWM), etc. However, the quantity of accumulated dispersion becomes huge, e.g., it hits 200,000 ps/nm when the signal transmits over 10,000-km fiber with +20 ps/nm/km dispersion. For the digital coherent transmission, the dispersion is compensated by digital signal processing (DSP). Thanks to the development of the high-performance DSP, which had an ability to compensate such a huge dispersion, it has become possible to introduce +D fiber for transoceanic submarine cables. Moreover, the evolution of +D fiber is rapidly proceeded in terms of the larger effective area (A_{eff}) and lower attenuation. Compared to the standard single mode fiber (SSMF) whose A_{eff} is 80 μm^2, the ultra-low-loss 130 μm^2 fiber is used in FASTER [2]. Furthermore, the fiber with 0.152-dB/km attenuation has been commercialized recently [5]. The large A_{eff} fiber contributes to the reduction of the nonlinear effect, and low loss fiber is effective for increasing the signal-to-noise ratio (SNR) or extension of the repeater span, which gives a higher capacity or lower cost with fewer required numbers of repeaters. At R&D bases, as a loss of 0.1419 dB/km is reported with an A_{eff} of 147 μm^2, further improvement can be expected [6].

Additionally, this evolution leads to significant changes not only for the transmission capacity, but for the operation and maintenance works. In the case of cable repairment, it is required to insert additional cables whose length must be twice as long as the water depth. For example, if a cable fault happens at a water depth of 6,000 m, a 12-km cable at least must be inserted. This means that the accumulated dispersion is changed according to the length of the inserted cable. In the cable of NZ-DSF and/or DMF types, the transmission line is composed of at least 2 types of fiber, so the repair procedure depends on the type and the length of fiber at the faulty point with precise calculation of the accumulated dispersion. However, for the +D fiber cable, basically only one type of fiber is required to prepare the spare cable; additionally, the operator no longer has to pay heed to the change of the accumulated dispersion utilizing the DSP function in the transponder. This contributes to simplifying the operation and maintenance procedures.

3.2 Advanced Modulation Formats

As shown in Fig. 1, the initial design capacity has increased 10-fold from Unity to FASTER with the introduction of digital coherent transmission technology. Furthermore, it can achieve higher SE with the advanced modulation formats. This progress is applicable both to new cable systems and all of the already deployed cables such as DSF, NZ-DSF, DMF and +D fiber types. By upgrading the design capacity of the existing cable, the "business" lifespan of the cable can be extended. Especially, it is more effective to apply the format for +D fiber cables than the other fiber types. As +D fiber cables give smaller nonlinearity, they are suitable for the typical higher SE modulation format that is weak for nonlinear effects. In the case of FASTER, while the initially designed modulation format is dual-polarization (DP)-quadrature phase shift keying (QPSK) with SE of 2.5 bit/s/Hz between the Japan and US segment, the DP-8QAM (quadrature amplitude modulation) signals have been introduced in 37.5-GHz spacing with SE of 4.0 bit/s/Hz [2]. Additionally, at the MAREA for transatlantic cables with a length of 6,644 km, it has been reported that the SE of 6.21 bit/s/Hz is achievable with DP-16QAM, which indicates that it will contribute to the upgrading of the design capacity from the initial one of 160 Tbit/s/cable to 200 Tbit/s/cable [7]. Furthermore, recently the commercialization of the constellation shaping modulation format has proceeded which can approach the theoretical limit, the so-called Shannon limit [3, 8]. Even these are offline processing, SE of 7.46 bit/s/Hz is confirmed at AEC-1 of transatlantic cables (5,523 km) with probabilistic constellation shaping (PS)-64QAM modulation [8]. Additionally, it has been confirmed that 5.5 bit/s/Hz is achievable with a Q-margin of 0.45 dB without the application of the nonlinear compensation function at the Taiwan to US segment of FASTER with 11,000 km [3]. Still, the decision about the availability of these SE should be defined by operators according to their policies in light of the communication sustainability and reliability.

3.3 C+L Band Transmission Technologies and Raman Amplification

One of the restrictions for submarine cables is the limited number of fibers in a cable, therefore the technologies to increase the transmission bandwidth is attractive. A typical submarine cable system is designed for C-band transmission, but recently, C+L band transmission has been introduced. For example, PLCN, which is under construction at this moment, will be the first transpacific system with C+L band transmission between Hong Kong and the US of over 12,917 km [9]. Roughly, L-band can support almost the same capacity as C-band, so the C+L band can be treated as virtually double the number of FPs compared to the C-band only system. However, as shown in the schematic view of Fig. 2, the C- and L-band must be separated in a repeater, so twice the number of EDFAs is required, and therefore it does not contribute to the reduction of power consumption per signal basically. Another case of L-band application is the hybrid type with Raman amplification. As shown in the actual case of ARBR (2,700 km with 4 FPs) between Argentina and Brazil, even though the initial design capacity is 12 Tbit/s per FP, the potential capacity can be extended to 44 Tbit/s per FP utilizing the 70 nm of C+L band transmission bandwidth [10, 11].

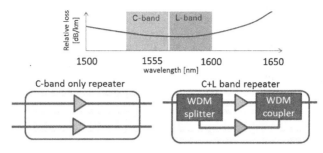

Fig. 2. Schematic view of C-band only and C+L band repeaters.

4 Restrictions for Optical Submarine Cables

Submarine cable systems have particular restrictions compared to terrestrial ones. In this section, the two main limitations are explained.

4.1 Power Feeding Limitation for Submarine Cable

First, there is only one type of power supply for optical submarine cables. In the case of a typical point-to-point configuration, the electrical power is supplied from both ends of the cable by the power feeding equipment (PFE) in the cable landing station (CLS). For the transpacific cables, it supplies electrical power to 100 repeaters. The electric potential difference is mainly determined by the power consumption of repeaters and power loss at cables. The voltage of each side of the cable is set to be positive and negative half that of the required electric potential difference. For example, when the required potential difference is 15 kV, the voltage of each side is set to be +7.5 kV and −7.5 kV, respectively. So, the voltage in the middle point becomes virtual earth of 0 V, the same as ground (earth) shown in Fig. 3, even if the conductor is not electrically connected to the ground. This configuration is a remedy for cable fault types called shunt faults. When the conductor of a cable is partly exposed in the water caused by scratch, the faulty point is forced to be grounded (earthed) as 0 V. It means that it becomes impossible to supply power from the initially assigned PFE to the repeaters that are located on the far side of the faulty point. To repair this situation, the PFE on the other side of the cable increases the output power to provide sufficient power to the repeater. If a shunt fault happens near the shore, all of the required power must be supplied from one side. It seems like a single-end feeding that needs twice the power as that of the normal setting. Therefore, typically the maximum voltage for PFE is specified as twice the voltage for the normal setting. Note that the maximum voltage of current commercialized PFE is 15 kV, so a limited number of EDFAs can be activated. Especially, the transatlantic and/or transpacific cables must be equipped with a large number of repeaters, so the usable power is relatively small for each repeater, and accordingly, the number of implementable FPs is limited. The other design is to reduce the power of the pump laser or to use fewer numbers of repeaters to increase the supportable number of FPs; however, the achievable OSNR will be decreased, and accordingly, the ultimate capacity per FP becomes smaller.

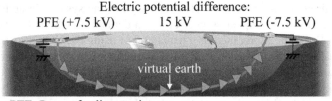

PFE: Power feeding equipment

Fig. 3. Schematic view of double-end feeding for a submarine cable.

The cable capacity with the utilization of dual-polarization (DP) transmission is restricted by the Shannon limit as shown in Eq. (1):

$$C = N \times B \times 2log_2(1 + SNR) \tag{1}$$

where C is the maximum capacity in theory, N, B and SNR are the number of FP, bandwidth and signal-to-noise ratio (SNR), respectively. The SNR is related to OSNR in the optical fiber communication field, so usually:

$$OSNR = P_{sig}/P_{ASE} \tag{2}$$

P_{sig} and P_{ASE} are the power per signal within the signal bandwidth of BW_{sig} and amplified spontaneous emission (ASE) noise power density, respectively. The noise power density is defined with the bandwidth BW_{noise}. In the case of the bandwidth of P_{sig} and P_{ASE} are equalized, the $OSNR$ can be treated as SNR. The P_{sig} can be assigned by the output power setting of the repeater; on the other hand, the P_{ASE} depends on span loss, which also means gain, noise figure (NF) of the repeater, and the number of repeaters. Therefore, the OSNR is decreased as the number of repeaters increases, so the theoretical maximum capacity becomes smaller for longer distances.

While the ultimate performance of submarine cables is determined by Eqs. (1) and (2), the existence of nonlinear effect cannot be disregarded with the introduction of digital coherent transmission. So, the characteristics of optical submarine cables should be defined by the generalized OSNR (GOSNR) that includes the nonlinear effect as follows [12]:

$$GOSNR = P_{sig}/(P_{NL} + P_{ASE}) \tag{3}$$

where P_{NL} is the noise caused by the nonlinear effect. Additionally, Generalized SNR (GSNR) is also proposed which is independent of signal bandwidth [29]:

$$GSNR = GOSNR - 10\log_{10}(BW_{sig}/BW_{noise}) \tag{4}$$

As described previously, the +D fiber type cable gives smaller P_{NL} than the other types such as DSF, NZ-DSF and DMF, and this is one of the main reasons why +D fiber can have higher potentials than the other types in terms of the capacity.

Conventionally, the optical submarine cable is procured for both wet and dry plants including SLTE at the same time. Therefore, it is common sense to use the Q-factor to show signal quality as the criteria for acceptance of the system. In addition to this condition, FASTER has adopted another criterion defined by OSNR for the first time in the world [2]. Furthermore, there is a new trend of using the GOSNR (or GSNR) as the criteria instead of the Q-factor [13]. The background to this trend is that recently the style of procurement has changed to the so-called "Open cable", which is contracted for wet plants only. It is advantageous because operators can choose SLTE freely. However, it also means no SLTE introduction at the initial stage, so it is impossible to define the criteria with Q-factor for acceptance. Therefore, there are some difficulties to be resolved, for example, how to confirm the reliability of estimated GOSNR (or GSNR) before making a contract, and how to measure GOSNR (or GSNR) after construction, etc. Currently, the GN-model is used for the estimation of GOSNR (or GSNR) at the design stage [14], while the measured nonlinear coefficient can be correlated with the value of the fiber specification that is obtained by the transmission performance of an actual real-time transponder [13]. The result contributes to the strategy of the cable system acceptance test.

4.2 Limitation of Fiber Counts for Submarine Cables

Another constraint for optical submarine cables is the implementable number of fibers, which is significantly less compared to terrestrial cables and/or unrepeatered systems. As shown in Table 1 and the case of MAREA, the number of FPs is equal to or less than 8. This restriction is related to the limitation of the power supply described in the previous section. Even if it is difficult to define the limitation of implementable fiber counts per cable, the cable capacity can reach several 100 Tbit/s per cable considering these limitations such as GOSNR, power supply and fiber counts [12].

5   Policy and Technologies for Next Generation

5.1 Maximum Power Operation for Double-End Feeding

The normal setting for PFE is typically half that of the required electric potential difference on both ends to repair shunt faults at double-end feeding configuration. In other words, these PFEs have potentials to support double the capacity utilizing maximum power even in normal situations, if accepted by operators. However, as this configuration is quite weak for shunt faults, it means that communication can fail suddenly. To make matters worse, the cable cannot be used until the completion of the cable repairment. Therefore, this operational policy will be one of choices if the operator has robustness with diversity using the other cables. Note that the repair period for a submarine cables will take a few weeks or more [15]. So, it is important for operators to keep in mind the estimated duration for recovery.

5.2 Shared Pumping for Multiple EDFA with Multicore Fiber (MCF) of Space-Division-Multiplexing (SDM) Technologies

Related to the issues described previously, it is important to reduce the power consumption per FP or channel. To provide the same gain for all of the WDM channels, each

EDFA has a gain flattening filter (GFF) at the output side of EDF. However, The GFF reduces the total output power because the transmission profile of GFF is designed to highly attenuate around the higher gain band to equalize the power or OSNR among all WDM channels. Recently, however, it is considered to be one of the causes of wasted energy. So, a novel configuration is proposed to increase capacity that utilizes a higher number of fiber cores with narrow bandwidth EDFA [16, 17]. The attractive point of Ref. [16] is the introduction of multicore fiber (MCF) as a method of space-division multiplexing (SDM) technologies. In that report, WDM signals are transmitted via a 12-core fiber with 12 EDFAs in parallel whose pump light power is provided and shared from a pump laser output of 800 mW. As a result, it is confirmed that 105.1 Tbit/s signals successfully transmit over 14,350 km of a 12-core fiber transmission line. The drawback of this proposal is that the required number of cores becomes 12 times, so it seems difficult to install in a submarine cable just by utilizing the multiple conventional single core single-mode fibers (SC-SMF). Therefore, the introduction of MCF is feasible with the reduction of the fiber counts. Moreover, the multiple parallel EDFA can be replaced by multicore-EDFA (MC-EDFA) as explained in the following section.

5.3 Uncoupled-Core MCF and Coupled-Core MCF

The MCF is regarded as a possible candidate for an applicable technology for optical submarine cable systems in terms of its energy and space-saving efficiencies. The MCFs are categorized into two groups: uncoupled MCF (UC-MCF) and coupled-core MCF (CC-MCF), depending on the quantity of crosstalk (XT) between cores. The first advantage of UC-MCF is the easier upgradability from the current conventional SC-SMF based system. With the minimized XT, it can be treated as multiple SC-SMFs virtually. To reduce the XT, each core is surrounded by a lower refractive index layer [18, 19]. It contributes to the application of the conventional transponder without any modification, so it seems easier to realize.

One of the topical merits of CC-MCF is lower attenuation. For example, the attenuation of 0.158 dB/km is achieved even if its cladding diameter is the standard size of 125 μm for a 4-core fiber [20]. The value of attenuation is approaching the value of SC-SMF with a pure-silica core that is commonly used for submarine cable systems, so it is effective for system design in terms of maintaining the repeater span, etc. Furthermore, it is indicated that CC-MCF gives lower nonlinearity compared to SC-SMF that has equivalent A_{eff}, as confirmed by the transmission experiment [21]. This means that CC-MCF may contribute to the increase in GOSNR or reduction of the number of repeaters.

5.4 Multicore EDFA

Regardless of the multi-fiber or MCF cases, the required number of EDFAs in a repeater is increased as a function of the number of cores. Because of the space limitation in a repeater, it is required to minimize the size of an EDFA unit. From this perspective, multicore EDFA (MC-EDFA) is attractive to decrease the number of EDFs and then amplify multiple cores with one MC-EDF. The low XT characteristics have been confirmed and the applicability for transoceanic distance transmission is demonstrated experimentally

[22–25]. Moreover, the cladding pump MC-EDFA (CP-MC-EDFA) method is proposed to excite multiple cores at once [24–27]. First, it has a further space saving efficiency utilizing some optical components that can handle multiple cores at once. Additionally, it contributes to reduction of the power consumption per core with the introduction of double cladding MC-EDF and a multimode laser diode (LD) for a pump laser instead of multiple single mode pump LDs. The drawback is the difficulty in increasing the excitation efficiency because of the huge difference of the mode field diameters between MM-LD and each core of MC-EDFA. Basically, the excitation efficiency is increasing as a function of the length of CP-MC-EDFA. Typically, the length of EDF is longer for L-band than C-band, therefore, in the case of cladding pumping, L-band CP-MC-EDFA is intrinsically energy efficient [25]. It is confirmed that 50×256 Gbit/s can be transmitted over 5,040 km of a 7-core fiber with CP-7C-EDFA [26]. To increase the excitation efficiency, it is proposed to recycle the remaining pump lightwave from output to input of CP-MC-EDFA [27, 28]. It is reported that the pump power can be decreased by 14% compared to the no-recycling case at the same output power condition [27], and the other report shows that a 32% reduction in power consumption is observed in the same gain condition [28]. Regarding these results, CP-MC-EDFA is expected to be a possible means of reducing the power consumption of a repeater.

6 Summary

This paper reviewed the evolution of transpacific communication cables, current cutting-edge technologies and promising technologies for future optical submarine cable systems. The typical design lifespan of submarine cable systems is as long as 25 years, so technical evolution is progressed for new cables and for already deployed cables with new type fibers and advanced modulation format in parallel. The main issues are limitation of power feeding for submarine cables and space for a cable and a repeater. So, MCF and MC-EDFA of SDM technologies are expected to overcome these limitations. It seems that the traffic demands will never abate for global networking; therefore, the technical evolution will continue into the future for optical submarine cable systems.

Acknowledgment. This work is partly supported by the national project of the Ministry of Internal Affairs and Communications of Japan (#0155-0041).

References

1. KDDI Corporation: FASTER Cable System is Ready for Service, Boosts Trans-Pacific Capacity and Connectivity (2016). https://global.kddi.com/company/news/detail/faster-cable-system-is-ready-for-service-boosts-trans-pacific-capacity-and-connectivity.html
2. Kamalov, V., et al.: FASTER open submarine cable. In: ECOC 2017, Th2E.5 (2017)
3. Kamalov, V., et al.: Evolution from 8QAM live traffic to PS 64-QAM with neural-network based nonlinearity compensation on 11000 km open subsea cable. In: OFC 2018, PDP, Th4D.5 (2018)
4. FCC (2016). https://docs.fcc.gov/public/attachments/DA-16-1221A1.pdf

5. Yamaguchi, H., Yamamoto, Y., Hasegawa, T., Kawano, T., Hirano, M., Koyano, Y.: Ultra-low loss and large Aeff pure-silica core fiber advances. In: SubOptic 2016, EC07 (2016)
6. Tamura, Y., et al.: Lowest-ever 0.1419-dB/km loss optical fiber. In: Proceedings of the Optical Fiber Communication Conference (OFC 2017), Th5D.1 (2017)
7. Infinera Corporation: Infinera Breaks Real-time Subsea Spectral Efficiency Records with 6.21 b/s/Hz on 6,644 km MAREA Trans-Atlantic Cable (2018). https://www.infinera.com/wp-content/uploads/pr-infpspectral-efficiency-records-marea-trans-atlantic-cable.pdf
8. Cho, J., et al.: Trans-Atlantic field trial using high spectral efficiency probabilistically shaped 64-QAM and single-carrier real-time 250-Gb/s 16-QAM. J. Lightwave Technol. **36**(1), 103–113 (2018)
9. Pacific Light Data Communication Co., Ltd.: http://pldcglobal.com/
10. Seaborn Networks: https://www.seabornnetworks.com/seaborn-networks-systems/arbr/
11. Xtera (2018). https://www.xtera.com/2018/05/01/seaborn-selects-cl-band-design-arbr-serve-needs-icp-community/
12. Mateo, E., Inada, Y., Ogata, T., Mikami, S., Kamalov, V., Vusirikala, V.: Capacity limits of submarine cables. In: SubOptic 2016, TH1A.1 (2016)
13. Mateo, E., Nakamura, K., Inoue, T., Inada, Y., Ogata, T.: Nonlinear characterization of fiber optic submarine cables. In: ECOC 2017, Th2E4 (2017)
14. Poggiolini, P., Bosco, G., Carena, A., Curri, V., Jiang, Y., Forghieri, F.: The GN-model of fiber non-linear propagation and its applications. J. Lightwave Technol. **32**(4), 694–721 (2014)
15. The International Cable Protection Committee: Submarine Cables and BBNJ (2016). http://www.un.org/depts/los/biodiversity/prepcom_files/ICC_Submarine_Cables_&_BBNJ_August_2016.pdf
16. Turukhin, A., et al.: 105.1 Tb/s power-efficient transmission over 14,350 km using a 12-core fiber. In: OFC 2016, Th4C.1 (2016)
17. Turukhin, A., et al.: Power-efficient transmission using optimized C+L EDFAs with 6.46 THz bandwidth and optimal spectral efficiency. In: ECOC 2018, Mo4G.4 (2018)
18. Hayashi, T., Taru, T., Shimakawa, O., Sasaki, T., Sasaoka, E.: Uncoupled multi-core fiber enhancing signal-to-noise ratio. Opt. Express **20**(26), B94–B103 (2012)
19. Gonda, T., Imamura, K., Sugizaki, R., Kawaguchi, Y., Tsuritani, T.: 125 μm 5-core fibre with heterogeneous design suitable for migration from single-core system to multi-core system. In: ECOC 2016, W.2.B.1 (2016)
20. Hayashi, T., Tamura, Y., Hasegawa, T., Taru, T.: 125-μm-cladding coupled multi-core fiber with ultra-low loss of 0.158 dB/km and record-low spatial mode dispersion of 6.1 ps/km$^{1/2}$. In: OFC 2016, PDP, Th5A.1 (2016)
21. Ryf, R., et al.: Long-haul transmission over multi-core fibers with coupled cores. In: ECOC 2017, M2E1 (2017)
22. Takahashi, H., et al.: First demonstration of MC-EDFA-repeatered SDM transmission of 40 x 128-Gbit/s PDM-QPSK signals per core over 6,160-km 7-core MCF. In: ECOC 2012, PDP, Th.3.C.3 (2012)
23. Igarashi, K., et al.: 1.03-Exabit/s.km Super-Nyquist-WDM transmission over 7,326-km seven-core fiber. In: ECOC 2013, PDP, PD3.E.3 (2013)
24. Takeshima, K., et al.: 51.1-Tbit/s MCF transmission over 2,520 km using cladding pumped 7-core EDFAs. In: OFC 2015, W3G.1 (2015)
25. Tsuchida, Y., et al.: Cladding pumped seven-core EDFA using an absorption-enhanced erbium doped fibre. In: ECOC 2016, M.2.A.2 (2016)
26. Kawaguchi, Y., Tsuritani, T.: Ultra-long-haul multicore fiber transmission over 5,000 km using cladding pumped seven-core EDFA. In: OECC 2017, 3-1K-3 (2017)

27. Takasaka, S., Maeda, K., Kawasaki, K., Yoshioka, K., Sugizaki, R., Tsukamoto, M.: Cladding pump recycling in 7-core EDFA. In: ECOC 2018, We1E3 (2018)
28. Takeshita, H., Matsumoto, K., de Gabory, E.L.T.: Transmission of 200Gbps PM-16QAM signal through 7-core MCF and MC-EDFA using novel turbo cladding pumping scheme for improved efficiency of the optical amplification. In: ECOC 2018, We2.35 (2018)
29. Mateo, E., Inoue, T., Nakamura, K., Mikami, S., Inada Y., Ogata, T.: Linear vs nonlinear submarine systems. In: SubOptic 2019, OP8-3 (2019)

Modeling Long-Haul Optical Networks with Quasi-single-mode Fibers

Ioannis Roudas[1(✉)] , Xin Jiang[2] , and Luis Miranda[1,3]

[1] Department of Electrical and Computer Engineering, Montana State University,
Bozeman, MT 59717, USA
ioannis.roudas@montana.edu

[2] Department of Engineering and Environmental Science, College of Staten Island,
CUNY, Staten Island, NY 10314, USA
jessica.jiang@csi.cuny.edu

[3] Department of Electrical and Electronic Engineering, Public University of Navarra,
Pamplona, Spain
luis.miranda@unavarra.es

Abstract. Few-mode fibers (FMFs) with weak mode coupling which are used to transmit signals predominantly in the fundamental mode are referred to as quasi-single-mode (QSM) fibers. QSM fibers can be designed to have much larger effective areas for the fundamental propagation mode than conventional single-mode fibers (SMFs). Signal transmission over the fundamental mode of QSM fibers can reduce distortion arising from the fiber Kerr nonlinearity. Random light coupling, however, among QSM fiber modes leads to multipath interference (MPI). Simultaneous reduction of nonlinear distortion and MPI can be achieved by using hybrid fiber spans, each composed of a QSM fiber segment to restrict nonlinear distortion, followed by an ultra-low-loss, large-effective-area SMF segment to suppress MPI.

In this invited paper, we review modeling and simulation tools that can be used for the design and optimization of coherent optical communication systems and networks with hybrid QSM fiber/SMF spans. We show that the precise selection of the fiber splitting ratio per span is not critical for the system performance and can be calculated with sufficient accuracy using a modified version of the nonlinear Gaussian noise model for hybrid fiber spans.

Keywords: Multipath interference (MPI) · Optical communications · Optical fiber · Quasi-single-mode (QSM) transmission

1 Introduction

Kerr nonlinearity in single-mode fibers (SMFs) places a ceiling on the spectral efficiency of contemporary optical communication systems [7]. To overcome this limitation, several techniques for nonlinear distortion mitigation and compensation in long-haul optical communications systems have been proposed over the past few years [1,2].

© IFIP International Federation for Information Processing 2020
Published by Springer Nature Switzerland AG 2020
A. Tzanakaki et al. (Eds.): ONDM 2019, LNCS 11616, pp. 389–397, 2020.
https://doi.org/10.1007/978-3-030-38085-4_33

A promising nonlinear distortion mitigation strategy uses the fundamental propagation mode of FMFs to establish single-mode links with reduced nonlinear distortion due to the Kerr effect [5,6,8,13,15–19]. This technique is called quasi-single-mode (QSM) transmission. By extension, FMFs with weak mode coupling which are used to transmit signals predominantly in the fundamental mode are referred to as quasi-single-mode (QSM) fibers.

Launching light in the fundamental mode of an ideal, straight, perfectly-cylindrical FMF results, in principle, in pure single-mode propagation without coupling to higher-order modes. In practice, however, there always exists random coupling from the fundamental mode to higher-order modes and vice versa because of fiber irregularities. This leads to the generation and propagation of a multitude of copies of the signal waveform across the fiber link. Due to modal dispersion, these echoes propagate at various group velocities and interfere either constructively or destructively with the main signal propagating on the fundamental mode. This effect is referred to as multipath interference (MPI) [10,14].

A compromise between fiber nonlinearities and MPI can be achieved by resorting to a combination of a large effective mode area QSM fiber and a smaller effective mode area SMF [4,15,19]. The QSM fiber is placed at the beginning of the span where signal power is greatest to restrict nonlinear distortion, followed by an SMF segment to suppress MPI. We can adjust the splitting ratio between QSM fiber and SMF to maximize the system performance.

Monte Carlo simulation can be commonly used to compute the optimum fiber splitting ratio. The main drawback of this approach is that it often requires excessive computational resources to evaluate the performance of a large number of candidate fiber configurations and select the best among them. This is due to the high computational complexity of the numerical solution of the Manakov equation using the split-step Fourier algorithm. A preferable alternative would be to use an approximate analytical model to either compute the optimum fiber splitting ratio directly or, at least, to limit the parameter space prior to running Monte Carlo simulations.

The nonlinear Gaussian noise model [11,12] provides an analytical first-order perturbation solution of the Manakov equation in the absence of polarization mode dispersion (PMD) and polarization-dependent loss (PDL). In this regime, signal distortion due to the Kerr nonlinearity resembles a zero-mean, complex Gaussian additive noise. The variance of the latter is calculated in closed-form from fiber and system parameters [11,12].

In its original formulation [11,12], the nonlinear Gaussian noise model is restricted to coherent optical communication systems using a single fiber type per span. Recently, we extended this formalism to model coherent optical communication systems with hybrid fiber spans [4] comprising a combination of QSM fiber and SMF per span. In [9], we used Monte Carlo simulation to validate this model. We showed that it can predict the optimum hybrid fiber configuration per span with sufficient accuracy.

The purpose of this article is to review modeling and simulation tools that can be used for the performance evaluation and optimization of coherent optical communication systems with hybrid QSM fiber/SMF spans. Using these tools, we show that the optimum fiber splitting ratio per span increases with the percentage of MPI compensation at the coherent optical receiver. The peak system performance, however, is a slowly-varying function of the fiber splitting ratio. Therefore, the precise selection of the fiber splitting ratio per span is not critical and can be calculated with sufficient accuracy using the above-mentioned modified version of the nonlinear Gaussian noise model for hybrid fiber spans.

2 Theoretical Model

2.1 System Topology

Figure 1 depicts the block diagram of a representative long-haul coherent optical communication system for QSM transmission with hybrid fiber spans. The transmission link of total length L is composed of a concatenation of N_s identical spans. Each span has length ℓ_s and comprises two fiber types. Each fiber type is characterized by its LP_{01} mode effective area A_{eff}, its nonlinear index coefficient n_2, its group velocity dispersion (GVD) parameter β_2 or, equivalently, its chromatic dispersion parameter D, and its attenuation coefficient a. In what follows, indices 1, 2 stand for the first and second fiber segment per span, respectively. For instance, the optical fiber lengths of the two segments are ℓ_{s_1}, ℓ_{s_2}, and their effective mode areas are $A_{\text{eff}_1}, A_{\text{eff}_2}$, respectively. The three splices between dissimilar optical fibers denoted by $\otimes$ in Fig. 1 have losses χ_1, χ_2, and χ_3, respectively. The optical fiber is followed by an optical amplifier of gain equal to the span loss $G = \chi_1^{-1}\chi_2^{-1}\chi_3^{-1}e^{a_1\ell_{s_1}+a_2\ell_{s_2}}$ and noise figure F_A.

We consider wavelength division multiplexing (WDM) and polarization division multiplexing (PDM) based on ideal Nyquist channel spectra. The latter are created using square-root raised cosine filters with zero roll-off factor at the transmitter and the receiver. Furthermore, we assume that the WDM signal is a superposition of an odd number N_{ch} wavelength channels with spacing $\Delta f = R_s$. We denote by P the total average launch power per channel (in both polarizations) and by R_s the symbol rate. We want to evaluate the performance of the center WDM channel at wavelength λ.

2.2 Analytical Performance Evaluation

Effective Optical Signal-to-Noise Ratio (OSNR). The performance of coherent optical systems without in-line chromatic dispersion compensation is related to the *effective* optical signal-to-noise ratio (OSNR_{eff}) at the receiver input. This quantity takes into account the amplified spontaneous emission (ASE) noise, the MPI, and the nonlinear distortion. All the above effects can be modeled as independent, zero-mean, complex Gaussian noises with a good degree of accuracy. More specifically, the OSNR_{eff} at a resolution bandwidth $\Delta\nu_{\text{res}}$ can be well described by the analytical relationship [10]

$$\text{OSNR}_{\text{eff}} = \frac{P}{\tilde{a} + \tilde{\beta}P + \tilde{\gamma}P^3}, \tag{1}$$

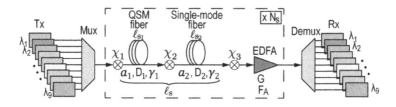

Fig. 1. Representative long-haul coherent optical communications system with hybrid fiber spans.

where $\tilde{a}$ is the ASE noise variance, $\tilde{\beta}P$ is the crosstalk variance due to MPI, and $\tilde{\gamma}P^3$ is the nonlinear noise variance. The coefficients $\tilde{a}, \tilde{\beta}, \tilde{\gamma}$ depend on the fiber and system parameters.

Noise Variances for Systems with Hybrid Fiber Spans. Nonlinear noise accumulation for coherent optical communication systems using hybrid fiber spans can be modeled by extending the perturbation formalism of [11,12]. Here, we consider ideal Nyquist PDM WDM signals with channel spacing equal to the symbol rate R_s. We obtain the following expression for the nonlinear noise coefficient $\tilde{\gamma}$

$$\tilde{\gamma} \cong \frac{16}{27} \frac{N_s^{1+\epsilon} \Delta \nu_{\text{res}}}{R_s^3} \chi_1^2 \int_{-\frac{B_0}{2}}^{\frac{B_0}{2}} \int_{-\frac{B_0}{2}}^{\frac{B_0}{2}} \left| \gamma_1 \frac{1 - e^{-(a_1 + i\Delta\beta_1)\ell_{s_1}}}{a_1 + i\Delta\beta_1} \right. $$
$$\left. + \chi_2 \gamma_2 e^{-(a_1 + i\Delta\beta_1)\ell_{s_1}} \frac{1 - e^{-(a_2 + i\Delta\beta_2)\ell_{s_2}}}{a_2 + i\Delta\beta_2} \right|^2 df_1 df_2. \tag{2}$$

In (2), γ_m are the nonlinear coefficients, $\Delta\beta_m$ are the propagation constant mismatches of the two fiber segments per span, $m = 1, 2$, and ϵ is a fitting parameter.

For modeling MPI, we assume that the QSM fibers under consideration exhibit weak coupling between the fundamental mode group LP_{01} and the higher-order mode group LP_{11}, i.e., the power coupling coefficient κ satisfies the relationship $\kappa \ell_{s_1} \ll 1$. Then, the MPI coefficient $\tilde{\beta}$ is given by [10] (with a sign correction)

$$\tilde{\beta} = N_s \frac{\Delta\nu_{\text{res}}}{R_s} \frac{(\Delta\alpha\ell_{s_1} - 1 + e^{-\Delta\alpha\ell_{s_1}})\kappa^2}{\Delta\alpha^2}, \tag{3}$$

where $\Delta\alpha$ is the differential mode attenuation (DMA).

Finally, the ASE noise variance for arbitrary span lengths is given by [3]

$$\tilde{\alpha} = hf_0 N_s (GF_A - 1) \Delta\nu_{\text{res}}, \tag{4}$$

where h is Planck's constant and f_0 is the center WDM channel carrier frequency.

2.3 Numerical Simulations

In numerical simulations, we consider hybrid fiber spans composed of a hypothetical QSM fiber and a representative commercially-available, large-effective-area SMF. We assume an ideal Nyquist WDM signal composed of 9 wavelength channels, each carrying PDM 16-QAM. The simulation parameters are listed in Table 1. For simplicity, splice losses and splice-induced MPI are neglected.

Table 1. Simulation parameters

Parameter	Symbol	Value
Modulation format		PDM-16QAM
Symbol rate	R_s	32 GBd
WDM channels	N_{ch}	9
WDM channel spacing	Δf	R_s
Link length	L	6,000 km
Span length	ℓ_s	80 km
Attenuation coefficients	α_1, α_2	0.155 dB/km
QSM fiber LP_{01} mode effective area	A_{eff_1}	350 μm²
SMF LP_{01} mode effective area	A_{eff_2}	150 μm²
Power coupling coefficient	κ	10^{-3} km^{-1}
Differential mode attenuation (DMA)	$\Delta\alpha$	2 dB/km
Nonlinear refractive index	n_2	2.1×10^{-20} m²/W
GVD parameter	$|\beta_2|$	26.6 ps²/km
EDFA noise figure	F_A	5 dB

We evaluate the Q-factor vs. launch power for the central WDM channel using two different methods: (a) Monte Carlo simulation using direct error counting; and (b) The nonlinear Gaussian noise model for hybrid fiber spans described earlier.

3 Results and Discussion

In this section, we compute the optimal fiber splitting ratio per span that maximizes system performance. In particular, we investigate how this ratio depends on the degree of MPI equalization at the coherent optical receiver.

System Performance for 80 km Spans. At the beginning, we examine the variation of the Q-factor as a function of the launched power per WDM channel for a coherent optical system composed of 80 km spans. Figure 2a and b show numerical results for two extreme MPI cases: (i) when MPI is not compensated; and (ii) when complete elimination of the MPI-induced intersymbol interference (ISI) is achieved using adaptive equalization at the coherent receiver, respectively. Different color curves correspond to different length combinations of QSM fiber and large-effective-area SMF. In Fig. 2a, the best combination of optical fibers leading to optimal system performance consists of about 40 km of QSM fiber at the beginning of each span, followed by 40 km large-effective-area SMF at the end of each span. The use of this fiber combination yields an optimal Q-factor $Q_0 = 8.3$ dB, which is better than that achieved with the two other displayed fiber configurations. In Fig. 2b, where we assume that there is complete equalization of MPI-induced ISI at the coherent optical receiver, the best system performance is achieved using only QSM fiber at each span. The optimal Q-factor obtained by this fiber configuration is 9.5 dB.

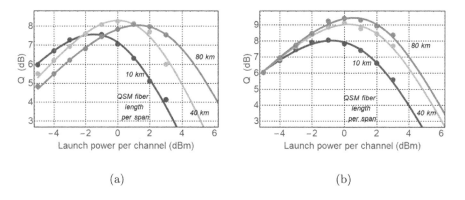

(a)   (b)

Fig. 2. Q-factor as a function of the total launch power per channel. (a) No MPI compensation; (b) 100% MPI compensation. (Symbols: Points: Monte Carlo simulations; Lines: Least squares fitting using (1) with $\tilde{a}, \tilde{\beta}, \tilde{\gamma}$ as unknown parameters.)

System Performance for Various MPI Compensation Levels. Figure 3 shows plots of the optimum Q-factor Q_0 as a function of the QSM fiber length per span ℓ_{s_1}. Curves from bottom to top correspond to progressively larger levels of MPI compensation at the coherent optical receiver. For 0% MPI compensation, about 50% of each span is QSM fiber. As MPI compensation increases, the fraction of QSM fiber per span increases. At 100% compensation, the best system performance is achieved by using exclusively QSM fiber. We observe that the proposed nonlinear Gaussian noise model given by (1)–(4) describes fairly well the numerical results.

It is worth noting that Q_0 is a slowly-varying function of the QSM fiber length ℓ_{s_1} in a wide region around the peak. For instance, in the absence of MPI compensation, the system performance changes by only 0.1 dBQ when the QSM fiber length varies in the range 22–61 km. This weak dependence of Q_0 on the QSM fiber length implies that it is not critical to determine the fiber splitting ratio per span with utmost accuracy. The nonlinear Gaussian noise model can be used to compute the fiber splitting ratio per span with sufficient accuracy even without exact knowledge of the value of the fitting parameter ϵ. For instance, in the absence of MPI compensation, using the nonlinear Gaussian noise model with $\epsilon = 0$ yields an optimum QSM fiber length $\ell_{s_1} = 31$ km, which results in less than 0.1 dBQ decrease from the maximum performance.

These general trends persist independent of the choice of the QSM fiber LP_{01} mode effective area and the fiber span length. The above results reveal that, in spite of the generation of MPI, the use of QSM fiber is beneficial.

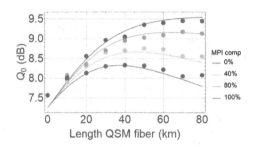

Fig. 3. Optimum Q-factor Q_0 as a function of the QSM fiber length ℓ_{s_1} per span. (Symbols: Points: Monte Carlo simulations; Lines: Least squares fitting using (1)–(4) with ϵ as an unknown parameter. Here $\epsilon \simeq 0.2$.)

4 Conclusion

The aim of this article was to review modeling and simulation tools that can be used for the performance evaluation and optimization of coherent optical communication systems with hybrid fiber spans, comprising a combination of QSM fiber and a large-effective-area SMF per span. Monte Carlo simulation was used to compute the optimum hybrid fiber configuration per span with high accuracy. We showed that the optimum fiber splitting ratio per span increases with the percentage of MPI compensation at the coherent optical receiver. For instance, for a transatlantic system with 80 km spans, in the absence of MPI compensation, it is best to use equal lengths of QSM fiber and SMF per span. In contrast, for full MPI compensation, the optimum system performance is achieved by using exclusively QSM fiber.

In addition, we analytically evaluate the performance of the aforementioned optical communication systems with hybrid QSM fiber/SMF spans. Nonlinear distortion and multipath interference are represented as additive white Gaussian noises. We extended the original nonlinear Gaussian noise formalism to model systems with hybrid fiber spans. The analytical model predictions qualitatively explain the numerical simulation results. The value of the analytical model lies in its simplicity. It helps us understand the interplay among various physical parameters. Most importantly, it can be used to compute the fiber splitting ratio per span with sufficient accuracy.

Acknowledgment. The authors would like to thank J. D. Downie, M. Mlejnek, and W. A. Wood of Corning Research and Development Corporation for fruitful discussions.

References

1. Cartledge, J.C., Guiomar, F.P., Kschischang, F.R., Liga, G., Yankov, M.P.: Digital signal processing for fiber nonlinearities. Opt. Express **25**(3), 1916–1936 (2017). https://doi.org/10.1364/OE.25.001916. http://www.opticsexpress.org/abstract. cfm?URI=oe-25-3-1916

2. Dar, R., Winzer, P.J.: Nonlinear interference mitigation: methods and potential gain. J. Lightwave Technol. **35**(4), 903–930 (2017). http://jlt.osa.org/ abstract.cfm?URI=jlt-35-4-903

3. Desurvire, E.: Erbium-doped fiber amplifiers: principles and applications. Wiley, New York (2002). https://books.google.com/books?id=6UJGAAAAYAAJ

4. Downie, J.D., et al.: Quasi-single-mode fiber transmission for optical communications. IEEE J. Sel. Top. Quantum Electron. **23**(3), 1–12 (2017). https://doi.org/ 10.1109/JSTQE.2016.2617208

5. Downie, J.D., Hurley, J.E., Kuksenkov, D.V., Lynn, C.M., Korolev, A.E., Nazarov, V.N.: Transmission of 112 Gb/s PM-QPSK signals over up to 635 km of multimode optical fiber. Opt. Express **19**(26), B363–B369 (2011). https://doi.org/10.1364/ OE.19.00B363. http://www.opticsexpress.org/abstract.cfm?URI=oe-19-26-B363

6. Downie, J.D., Li, M.J., Mlejnek, M., Roudas, I.G., Wood, W.A., Zakharian, A.R.: Optical transmission systems and methods using a QSM large-effective-area optical fiber. US Patent 9,841,555, 12 December 2017

7. Ellis, A.D., McCarthy, M.E., Khateeb, M.A.Z.A., Sorokina, M., Doran, N.J.: Performance limits in optical communications due to fiber nonlinearity. Adv. Opt. Photon. **9**(3), 429–503 (2017). https://doi.org/10.1364/AOP.9.000429. http://aop.osa.org/abstract.cfm?URI=aop-9-3-429

8. Li, M.J., Mishra, S.K., Mlejnek, M., Wood, W.A., Zakharian, A.R.: Quasi-single-mode optical fiber with a large effective area. US Patent 9,846,275, 19 December 2017

9. Miranda, L., Roudas, I., Downie, J.D., Mlejnek, M.: Performance of coherent optical communication systems with hybrid fiber spans. In: European Conference on Optical Communication (ECOC), Gothenburg, Sweden, September 2017. https:// doi.org/10.1109/ECOC.2017.8345972. Paper P2.SC6.18

10. Mlejnek, M., Roudas, I., Downie, J.D., Kaliteevskiy, N., Koreshkov, K.: Coupled-mode theory of multipath interference in quasi-single mode fibers. IEEE Photon. J. **7**(1), 1–16 (2015). https://doi.org/10.1109/JPHOT.2014.2387260

11. Poggiolini, P.: The GN model of non-linear propagation in uncompensated coherent optical systems. J. Lightwave Technol. **30**(24), 3857–3879 (2012). https://doi.org/ 10.1109/JLT.2012.2217729

12. Poggiolini, P., Bosco, G., Carena, A., Curri, V., Jiang, Y., Forghieri, F.: The GN-model of fiber non-linear propagation and its applications. J. Lightwave Technol. **32**(4), 694–721 (2014). https://doi.org/10.1109/JLT.2013.2295208

13. Ryf, R., et al.: Mode-multiplexed transmission over conventional graded-index multimode fibers. Opt. Express **23**(1), 235–246 (2015). https://doi.org/10.1364/OE. 23.000235. http://www.opticsexpress.org/abstract.cfm?URI=oe-23-1-235

14. Sui, Q., et al.: Long-haul quasi-single-mode transmissions using few-mode fiber in presence of multi-path interference. Opt. Express **23**(3), 3156–3169 (2015). https://doi.org/10.1364/OE.23.003156.   http://www.opticsexpress.org/abstract.cfm?URI=oe-23-3-3156

15. Yaman, F., et al.: First quasi-single-mode transmission over transoceanic distance using few-mode fibers. In: Optical Fiber Communications Conference (OFC), Los Angeles, CA, March 2015. https://doi.org/10.1364/OFC.2015.Th5C.7. Paper Th5C.7

16. Yaman, F., et al.: 10× 112 Gb/s PDM-QPSK transmission over 5032 km in few-mode fibers. Opt. Express **18**(20), 21342–21349 (2010). https://doi.org/10.1364/OE.18.021342. http://www.opticsexpress.org/abstract.cfm?URI=oe-18-20-21342

17. Yaman, F., Bai, N., Zhu, B., Wang, T., Li, G.: Long distance transmission in few-mode fibers. Opt. Express **18**(12), 13250–13257 (2010). https://doi.org/10.1364/OE.18.013250. http://www.opticsexpress.org/abstract.cfm?URI=oe-18-12-13250

18. Yaman, F., Mateo, E., Wang, T.: Impact of modal crosstalk and multi-path interference on few-mode fiber transmission. In: Optical Fiber Communication Conference (OFC), Los Angeles, CA (2012). https://doi.org/10.1364/OFC.2012.OTu1D.2. http://www.osapublishing.org/abstract.cfm?URI=OFC-2012-OTu1D.2. Paper OTu1D.2

19. Zhang, S., Yaman, F., Huang, Y., Downie, J.D., Zou, D., Wood, W.A., Zakharian, A., Khrapko, R., Mishra, S., Nazarov, V., Hurley, J., Djordjevic, I.B.: Capacity-approaching transmission over 6375 km using hybrid quasi-single-mode fiber spans. J. Lightwave Technol. **35**(3), 481–487 (2017). https://doi.org/10.1109/JLT.2016.2631151

Crosstalk Mitigation in Long-Reach Multicore Fiber Communication Systems Using RKHS Based Nonlinear Equalization

Sandesh Jain[1], Anuj Agrawal[1(✉)], Vimal Bhatia[1], and Shashi Prakash[2]

[1] Signals and Software Group, Discipline of Electrical Engineering, Indian Institute of Technology Indore, Indore 453552, India
{phd1501202003,phd1601202004,vbhatia}@iiti.ac.in
[2] Photonics Laboratory, Devi Ahilya University, Indore 452017, India
sprakash@ietdavv.edu.in

Abstract. The transmission reach of multi-core fiber (MCF) communication systems is severely affected by inter-core crosstalk (IC-XT), which limits its application for long-reach core optical network. One of the major factors limiting the transmission reach of MCF is nonlinear IC-XT interference, which makes the overall system nonlinear, thereby resulting in a poor bit error rate (BER) performance. Conventional Volterra series based nonlinear equalizer are computationally complex, and impaired by modeling error due to the truncation of polynomial kernel. In this paper, for the first time, we propose multivariate kernel least mean square (KLMS) based adaptive nonlinear equalizer for mitigating IC-XT impairments in MCF communication systems. The proposed scheme is inspired from reproducing kernel Hilbert space (RKHS) based machine learning algorithms. Simulations are performed for different multi-core structures, fiber lengths, and modulation schemes, which show that the proposed KLMS algorithm exhibit superior BER performance over the existing Volterra series equalizer.

Keywords: Multicore fiber · Crosstalk · Adaptive · Nonlinear · Equalizer · Reproducing kernel Hilbert space

1 Introduction

Telecommunication traffic generated by mobile and fixedline users is aggregated through metro and access networks into the core optical fiber communication

---

A. Agrawal—Student Member, IEEE, OSA.
S. Jain—Student Member, IEEE.
V. Bhatia—Senior Member, IEEE.
S. Prakash—Senior Member, IEEE, OSA.

© IFIP International Federation for Information Processing 2020
Published by Springer Nature Switzerland AG 2020
A. Tzanakaki et al. (Eds.): ONDM 2019, LNCS 11616, pp. 398–411, 2020.
https://doi.org/10.1007/978-3-030-38085-4_34

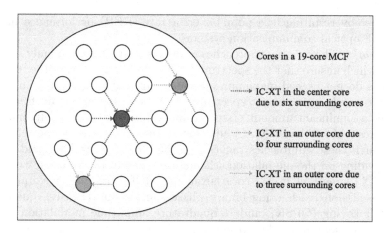

Fig. 1. IC-XT in different cores in a 19-core MCF (the value of $h_{i,j}$ given by (1) in channel matrix **H** depends on the number of surrounding cores shown above, and other MCF parameters specified in (2), causing non-linear IC-XT interference) (Color figure online)

networks. Currently, optical fibers carry about 99% of global Internet traffic [1]. Cisco forecasted a compound annual growth rate of 26% in global IP traffic from 2017 to 2022 [2]. Currently deployed single-core fibers (SCFs) will not be able to support the continuously increasing bandwidth demands in future. Thus space division multiplexing (SDM) technology has been proposed to further increase the optical fiber capacity in spatial dimension using multicore fibers (MCFs) and/or multimode fibers (MMFs) [3–6]. This work is focussed on MCF optical communication systems.

MCFs can increase the capacity of optical communication systems, however, the transmission reach in such systems is severely affected by inter-core crosstalk (IC-XT) [3–6]. The IC-XT increases with increase in fiber length. Hence, it is difficult to perform all-optical transmission in core networks, where transmission reach of the order of thousands of kilometers is required. With the ever-increasing traffic demands, the amount of traffic in the core optical networks aggregated through metro/access networks will increase. Thus, to support the increasing bandwidth demands using MCFs in long-reach core networks, use of digital signal processing (DSP) at the receiver end is unavoidable [3].

IC-XT in an MCF depends on the core arrangement, number of cores, and fiber length along with other specific parameters related to fiber manufacturing [3–6]. Thus, IC-XT for different cores in an MCF is different, and is dependent of the number of surrounding cores. For instance, in a 19-core MCF shown in Fig. 1, the cores shown in red, green, and blue color will be affected by IC-XT due to six, four, and three number of cores, respectively. Moreover, the IC-XT between any two cores in an MCF is nonlinearly related to the core pitch, bending radius, coupling coefficient, propagation constant, and the fiber length [3–6]. This results in nonlinear IC-XT interference, which increases with fiber length, thereby resulting in a poor bit error rate (BER) performance in long-reach MCF optical communication systems.

Related Works: The existing approaches to deal with IC-XT are mainly based on methods which ensure that the spectrum is allocated in a way that the transmitted signals do not exceed maximum allowable threshold XT levels [5,6]. These approaches result in inefficient spectrum utilization, and spectrum fragmentation since a significant amount of spectrum in different cores is left unused to ensure threshold XT levels [6]. In addition to this, the transmission reach possible through these approaches ranges from hundreds to few thousand kilometers, depending on the modulation scheme used. For instance, using worst-case XT (WC-XT) method in a 7-core hexagonal MCF structure, maximum possible transmission reach using binary phase shift keying (BPSK), quadrature phase shift keying (QPSK), and 16-quadrature amplitude modulation (QAM) is 1118 km, 397 km, and 89 km, respectively [5]. Thus, these existing approaches are not applicable for long-reach core optical networks, where shortest routes amongst different node pairs exceed these reach values. For example, in UBN24 network topology, the maximum length of shortest paths among node pairs is 6650 km [7] (i.e., between the nodes at San Diego and Ithaca [8]).

To enable communication through MCFs in high-capacity core networks such that long-reach using higher modulation formats can be obtained, an effective nonlinear equalization mechanism is required at the receiver for mitigating nonlinear IC-XT impairments. Volterra series based nonlinear equalizers have been proposed in the literature for compensating nonlinear distortions [9,10], however, they are suitable only for short reach optical transmissions [9]. Furthermore, Volterra series based approaches are computationally complex, and impaired by modeling error due to abrupt truncation of Taylor's series till second/third order terms [11,12].

Conventional linear adaptive filtering algorithms [13] like least mean square (LMS) algorithm, recursive least squares (RLS) algorithm, and their variants deliver sub-optimal performance for nonlinear systems [14]. Recently, reproducing kernel Hilbert space (RKHS) based machine learning algorithms have shown promise in the area of nonlinear channel equalization/estimation, system identification, time series prediction, wind forecasting, and pattern classification. Hence, linear adaptive filters have been combined with the RKHS framework to yield a class of kernel adaptive filters (KAFs) [15] like kernel LMS (KLMS) [14] and kernel RLS (KRLS) algorithms [16].

In this paper, we propose RKHS inspired KLMS based nonlinear equalizer for compensating the nonlinear distortions introduced by nonlinear IC-XT. Proposed RKHS based equalizer have the following advantages over the existing polynomial (like Volterra) series based nonlinear equalization; First, it transforms a non-convex optimization problem in lower dimensional input space to a convex optimization problem in RKHS, which guarantees the global optimal Wiener solution [17]. Secondly, the proposed equalizer has the ability to model any arbitrary nonlinearity without its *apriori* knowledge by using reproducing kernel. This property of the proposed equalizer stems from Riesz representation theorem [18]. Third, the proposed equalizer does not suffer from modeling error, which is not the case with Volterra equalizers. Fourth, the proposed equalizers are computationally efficient, which can be achieved by using sparsification techniques like the novelty criterion (NC), the coherence criterion, the quantization criterion, surprise criterion, and fixed budget models [15]. In this work, we incorporate NC in the proposed equalizer to yield sparse KLMS-NC algorithm, which makes the proposed equalizer suitable for practical deployments.

The organization of the rest of this paper is as follows: Sect. 2 gives brief overview of the system model considered in this work. Proposed RKHS based nonlinear equalizer is detailed in Sect. 3. Simulation results are provided in Sect. 4 to illustrate the performance of the proposed algorithm. Finally, Sect. 5 concludes the paper.

Notations: Following terminology is used throughout the paper: $\mathbb{R}$ and $\mathbb{C}$ denote field of real and complex numbers respectively. Matrices are denoted by capital bold-face letters like $\mathbf{H}$ with dimensions $\mathbb{R}^{m \times n}$, where m and n indicate the row and column dimension, respectively. Vectors at k^{th} time instant are denoted by small bold-face letters like $\mathbf{x}_k$ with dimensions $\mathbb{C}^n$ while scalars are represented by simple lower-case letters. $\mathbf{I}_N$ denotes a $N \times N$ identity matrix, and $\mathbf{O}$ denotes null matrix. $(\cdot)^H$ denotes Hermitian transpose of $(\cdot)$. The operator $\mathbb{E}\{\cdot\}$ denotes statistical expectation. Inner product in RKHS $\mathscr{H}$ is represented by $< \cdot, \cdot >_{\mathscr{H}}$, and $||\cdot||_{\mathscr{H}}$ denotes norm in RKHS $\mathscr{H}$. Gradient of x with respect to y is denoted by $\nabla_y(x)$.

2   System Model

In this Section, system model considered in this work is described. Data bits are first modulated by using QPSK/QAM schemes to generate modulated symbols. Let $\mathbf{x}_k = [x^{(1)}, x^{(2)}, \ldots, x^{(l)}, \ldots, x^{(N_c)}]^T \in \mathbb{C}^{N_c}$ denotes the modulated input symbol vector at k^{th} time instant, where $x^{(l)}$ denotes the signal corresponding to l^{th} core of MCF, and N_c indicates number of cores in MCF. Input symbols $\mathbf{x}_k$ are then transmitted through multi-core optical fiber. The cross-talk channel matrix $\mathbf{H}$ for MCF is modeled as [19]

$$\mathbf{H} \in \mathbb{R}^{N_c \times N_c} = \begin{bmatrix} h_1 & h_{1,2} & \cdots & h_{1,N_c} \\ h_{2,1} & \ddots & & h_{2,N_c} \\ \vdots & & \ddots & \vdots \\ h_{N_c,1} & h_{N_c,2} & \cdots & h_{N_c} \end{bmatrix},$$

where $h_{i,j}$ represents the cross-talk between i^{th} and j^{th} core. Based on coupled-power theory, $h_{i,j}$ is expressed as [3,6]

$$h_{i,j} = \frac{1 - e^{-2 \cdot L \cdot r_{i,j}}}{1 + e^{-2 \cdot L \cdot r_{i,j}}} \quad \forall i \neq j,$$

$$h_i = 1 - \sum_{i \neq j} h_{i,j} \tag{1}$$

where L is the length of optical fiber, and $r_{i,j}$ represents the mean XT increase per unit length of the fiber, which is given by

$$r_{i,j} = \frac{2 \cdot \kappa_{i,j}^2 \cdot R}{\beta \cdot \Lambda}, \tag{2}$$

where $\kappa_{i,j}$, R, β, and Λ are MCF parameters called coupling coefficient between i^{th} and j^{th} core, bending radius, propagation constant, and the core pitch, respectively. The received signal $\mathbf{y}_k = [y^{(1)}, y^{(2)}, \ldots, y^{(l)}, \ldots, y^{(N_c)}]^T \in \mathbb{C}^{N_c}$ (where $y^{(l)}$ denotes the received signal corresponding to l^{th} core of MCF) at k^{th} time instant can be written as

$$\mathbf{y}_k = \mathbf{H}\mathbf{x}_k + \mathbf{n}_k, \tag{3}$$

where $\mathbf{n}_k = [n^{(1)}, n^{(2)}, \ldots, n^{(l)}, \ldots, n^{(N_c)}]^T \in \mathbb{C}^{N_c} \sim \mathcal{CN}(0, \sigma_n^2 \mathbf{I}_{N_c})$ is independent and identically distributed (i.i.d) complex additive white Gaussian noise (AWGN) vector with mean 0 and co-variance matrix $\sigma_n^2 \mathbf{I}_{N_c}$, $n^{(l)}$ denotes the noise in l^{th} core of MCF. (3) can be decomposed as follows:

$$y^{(1)} = h_1.x^{(1)} + \underbrace{(h_{1,2}.x^{(2)} + \ldots + h_{1,N_c}.x^{(N_c)})}_{\text{IC-XT interference}} + n^{(1)}$$

$$y^{(2)} = h_2.x^{(2)} + \underbrace{(h_{2,1}.x^{(1)} + \ldots + h_{2,N_c}.x^{(N_c)})}_{\text{IC-XT interference}} + n^{(2)}$$

$$\vdots \qquad\qquad \vdots$$

$$y^{(N_c)} = h_{N_c}.x^{(N_c)} + \underbrace{(h_{N_c,1}.x^{(1)} + \ldots + h_{N_c,N_c-1}.x^{(N_c-1)})}_{\text{IC-XT interference}} + n^{(N_c)} \tag{4}$$

The terms inside the parenthesis in (4) represents the additive IC-XT interference. The nonlinear expression for cross-talk $h_{i,j}$ in (1) makes the mapping between received symbol $\mathbf{y}_k$ and transmitted symbol $\mathbf{x}_k$ nonlinear, which results in nonlinear distortions at the receiver. To circumvent, received symbol $\mathbf{y}_k$ is given as an input to the proposed RKHS based nonlinear equalizer detailed in Sect. 3.

3 Proposed RKHS Based Nonlinear Equalizer

In this Section, RKHS based nonlinear equalizer is proposed for mitigating IC-XT interference in MCFs. Further, NC based sparsification and computational complexity is discussed in the next subsections. As inferred from (1) and (3), received symbols $\mathbf{y}_k$ are impaired by nonlinear IC-XT interference, therefore, received observations $\mathbf{y}_k$ are mapped from finite dimensional input space to the high dimensional feature space such as RKHS, denoted by $\mathscr{H}$ by using a nonlinear transformation $\Psi(\cdot)$ [20]. Mapping to RKHS is essential because a nonlinear problem in original input space is converted to a linear problem in high dimensional RKHS (from Cover's theorem). Let $\mathbf{\Omega}_k$ denote the implicit weight matrix in RKHS at k^{th} time instant. Using training observations $\{\mathbf{x}_k, \psi(\mathbf{y}_k)\}_{k=1}^{N_{\mathrm{tr}}}$ (where N_{tr} is the number of training observations), the empirical loss function for multivariate KLMS algorithm[1] is formulated according to minimum mean square error (MMSE) criterion in RKHS as [14,15].

Algorithm 1. Proposed nonlinear equalizer in RKHS for IC-XT mitigation in MCF

Input: Received observations $\mathbf{y}_k$
Output: Equalized symbols $\hat{\mathbf{x}}_k$
% *Initialization:*
Choose $k = 1$, maximum iterations: MAXITER, η, σ, δ_o, δ_e, $\mathbf{e}_1 \leftarrow \mathbf{s}_1$, $\mathscr{D}[1] \leftarrow \{\mathbf{y}_1\}$, and $\mathscr{Q}[1] \leftarrow \{\mathbf{e}_1\}$
% *Computation:*
while $k \leq$ MAXITER **do**
    % Computation of estimated output
    $\hat{\mathbf{x}}_k = \mu_{\mathrm{KLMS}} \sum_{j=1}^{|\mathscr{D}_k|} \mathscr{Q}_k^j \mathscr{K}_{\mathrm{G},\sigma}(\mathscr{D}_k^j, \mathbf{y}_k)$
    % Computation of error vector
    $\mathbf{e}_k = \mathbf{x}_k - \hat{\mathbf{x}}_k$
    % Sparsification by NC
    if $\min\limits_{\forall j} \|\mathbf{y}_k - \mathscr{D}_k^j\| \geq \delta_o$ and $\|\mathbf{e}_k\| \geq \delta_e$ **then**
        $\mathscr{D}_{k+1} = \{\mathscr{D}_k \cup \mathbf{y}_k\}$
        $\mathscr{Q}_{k+1} = \{\mathscr{Q}_k \cup \mathbf{e}_k\}$
    else
        $\mathscr{D}_{k+1} = \{\mathscr{D}_k\}$
        $\mathscr{Q}_{k+1} = \{\mathscr{Q}_k\}$
    end if
    $k = k + 1$
end while

$$\mathscr{L}_{\mathrm{KLMS}}(\mathbf{\Omega}_k) = \min_{\mathbf{\Omega}_k} \quad \mathbb{E}\left\{\frac{1}{2}\|\mathbf{x}_k - \mathbf{\Omega}_k\Psi(\mathbf{y}_k)\|_{\mathscr{H}}^2\right\} \tag{5}$$

where $\mathbf{e}_k = \mathbf{x}_k - \mathbf{\Omega}_k\Psi(\mathbf{y}_k)$ is the prediction error vector in RKHS. Weight update equation for the proposed multivariate KLMS based equalizer can be written by applying stochastic gradient descent algorithm as follows [21]

$$\mathbf{\Omega}_{k+1} = \mathbf{\Omega}_k - \mu_{\mathrm{KLMS}}\nabla_{\mathbf{\Omega}_k}(\mathscr{L}_{\mathrm{KLMS}}(\mathbf{\Omega}_k)) = \mathbf{\Omega}_k + \mu_{\mathrm{KLMS}}\mathbf{e}_k\Psi^H(\mathbf{y}_k), \tag{6}$$

where μ_{KLMS} is the step-size for KLMS algorithm. The recursive weight update equation can be written as (assuming $\mathbf{\Omega}_k = \mathbf{O}$)

$$\mathbf{\Omega}_{k+1} = \mu_{\mathrm{KLMS}} \sum_{i=1}^{k} \mathbf{e}_i\Psi^H(\mathbf{y}_i), \tag{7}$$

---

[1] Multivariate KLMS algorithm is the generalization of classical univariate KLMS algorithm [14] for vector-valued desired data [17].

Estimated output of the proposed KLMS based equalizer can be written as [17]

$$\hat{\mathbf{x}}_k = \mathbf{\Omega}_k \Psi(\mathbf{y}_k) = \mu_{\mathrm{KLMS}} \sum_{i=1}^{k-1} \mathbf{e}_i < \Psi(\mathbf{y}_i), \Psi(\mathbf{y}_k) >_{\mathscr{H}} \tag{8}$$

Inner product in (8) is difficult to compute as $\Psi(\cdot)$ is not known apriori. However, according to Mercer's theorem, inner product in RKHS can be evaluated by using Mercer kernel as follows [15,20]

$$\mathscr{K}(\mathbf{y}_i, \mathbf{y}_k) = <\Psi(\mathbf{y}_i), \Psi(\mathbf{y}_k)>_{\mathscr{H}} \tag{9}$$

Invoking (9) in (8) we get

$$\hat{\mathbf{x}}_k = \mu_{\mathrm{KLMS}} \sum_{i=1}^{k-1} \mathbf{e}_i \mathscr{K}_{\sigma,\mathrm{G}}(\mathbf{y}_i, \mathbf{y}_k), \tag{10}$$

where $\mathscr{K}_{\sigma,\mathrm{G}}(\mathbf{y}_i, \mathbf{y}_k) = \exp\left(-\dfrac{\sum_{\forall q}(\mathbf{y}_i^q - \mathbf{y}_k^{q*})^2}{2\sigma^2}\right)$ is the complex Gaussian kernel [15] with σ as the kernel width, and superscript q denotes q^{th} entry of the vector. The main advantage of the proposed nonlinear equalizer in RKHS is that it does not require weights $\mathbf{\Omega}_k$ and nonlinear function $\Psi(\cdot)$ to be known apriori as long as the kernel function $\mathscr{K}(\cdot, \cdot)$ is specified.

3.1   NC Based Sparsification

The main issue with the proposed KLMS based nonlinear equalizer in RKHS is that its computational complexity linearly increases with each observation as $O(k)$, which hinders the practical viability of the proposed algorithm. However, all the observations are not required for training and equalization. Hence, a dictionary based sparsification technique based on Platt's novelty criterion (NC) [15] is incorporated in the proposed KLMS based equalizer to yield sparse KLMS-NC algorithm [15]. We introduce the notion of dictionary of observations (denoted by $\mathscr{D}_k$) which keeps track of all the input regressors used for training the system, and dictionary of error terms (denoted by $\mathscr{Q}_k$). Initially, dictionary starts from the first observation as $\mathscr{D}_k = \{\mathbf{y}_1\}$ and $\mathscr{Q}_k = \{\mathbf{e}_1\}$, and the incoming observations are selectively added to the dictionary according to the following two rules of Platt's NC as: (1) First, the Euclidean distance of the incoming observation is computed with the existing dictionary as $\min_{\forall j} ||\mathbf{r}_k - \mathscr{D}_k^j||_2 \ \forall j = 1, 2, \cdots S$, where S denotes number of observations in the current dictionary $\mathscr{D}_k$. If it is less than some pre-defined threshold δ_o then the current incoming observation is discarded and not added to the dictionary. However, if $\min_{\forall j} ||\mathbf{r}_k - \mathscr{D}_k^j||_2 \geq \delta_o$ then second rule is checked; (2) If $||\mathbf{e}_k|| \geq \delta_e$ then the current observation is added to the dictionary as $\mathscr{D}_{k+1} = \{\mathscr{D}_k, \mathbf{y}_k\}$ and size of the dictionary gets increased by one. Otherwise, dictionary remains unchanged as $\mathscr{D}_{k+1} = \{\mathscr{D}_k\}$. The pseudo code for the proposed equalizer based on KLMS-NC algorithm is detailed in Algorithm 1.

3.2   Computational Complexity

Computational complexity of the Volterra series equalizer is $O(M^P)$ [9], where M is the number of filter taps used for P^{th} order Volterra filter. Computational complexity of the Volterra equalizer increases with the increase in order P. Hence, lower order (upto second or third) Volterra series filter are generally used for real time implementation [9]. After incorporating NC based sparsification, the computational complexity of the proposed KLMS-NC algorithm get reduced from $O(k)$ to $O(|\mathscr{D}_k|)$ [22–24], where $|\mathscr{D}_k|$ indicates cardinality of the dictionary (dictionary-size), i.e., the number of observations present in the dictionary at convergence.

4   Simulations

In this Section, simulations are presented to demonstrate the performance of the proposed algorithm. QPSK and 16-QAM modulation schemes are considered. An ensemble of 10^4 symbols are considered over 100 independent Monte-carlo trials. Two different core structures, i.e., 12-core dual ring structure (DRS)-MCF structure, and 19-core hexagonal MCF structure are considered with the following parameters: $\kappa = 3.5 \times 10^{-3}$, $R = 80$ mm, $\beta = 4 \times 10^6$, and Λ is chosen as 40 μm, and 35 μm for 12-core, and 19-core MCF, respectively [3]. Proposed KLMS based nonlinear equalizer is compared with the conventional Volterra series based nonlinear equalizer. Volterra series equalizer with 65 first order, and 45 second order filter taps are chosen. Out of 10^4 symbols, 1000 symbols are used for training. Kernel width $\sigma = 5$ is set by Silverman's rule [15], step-size $\mu_{\mathrm{KLMS}} = 0.45$ ($0 < \mu_{\mathrm{KLMS}} < 2$ as given in [15,25]), observation-quantization constant $\delta_o = 10^{-3}$, and error-quantization constant $\delta_e = 0.1$ is set according to the rules given in [15].

First, the SNR vs BER performance, and evolution of dictionary-size for 12-core MCF with fiber length 1000 km, are shown in Figs. 2 and 3, respectively, using QPSK and 16-QAM modulation schemes. It can be observed from Fig. 2 that the proposed KLMS equalizer delivers 3–5 dB gain at an approximate BER of 10^{-4} over the conventional Volterra series equalizer for QPSK and 16-QAM constellations. It can be also observed from Fig. 2 that the Volterra series equalizer has a BER error floor in high SNR regime due to the truncation error. Further, it is observed from Fig. 3 that, out of 1000 observations, proposed algorithm requires only 360 observations for QPSK, and 400 observations for 16-QAM, which highlights the computational simplicity of the proposed algorithm. Computational complexity details are given in Table 1.

Next, the SNR vs BER performance is evaluated by varying the length of the fiber in Fig. 4 for 12-core MCF using 16-QAM modulation scheme. The mean IC-XT values corresponding to different fiber lengths are shown in Fig. 4, which exceed the threshold IC-XT for 16-QAM modulation scheme [5]. It can be observed from Fig. 4 that the BER performance degrades with increase in fiber length since IC-XT increases with increase in fiber length. However, using the proposed nonlinear equalizer, longer reach using higher modulation schemes

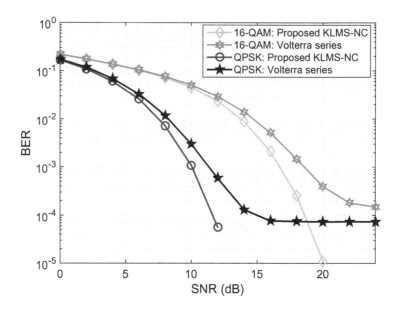

Fig. 2. SNR vs BER performance for Volterra series and the proposed KLMS algorithm for 12-core MCF using QPSK and 16-QAM modulation schemes

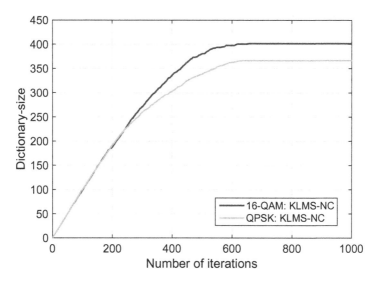

Fig. 3. Evolution of dictionary-size for the proposed KLMS algorithm for 12-core MCF using QPSK and 16-QAM modulation schemes

(i.e., 16-QAM) can be achieved, which demonstrates the practical viability of the proposed equalizer for core optical communication networks. Further, dictionary-size performance for the proposed algorithm is analyzed in Fig. 5 for 12-core MCF using 16-QAM modulation scheme. As inferred from Fig. 5, the dictionary-size also increases with the increase in fiber length, i.e., more number of regressors/observations are required for equalization of increased IC-XT levels.

Table 1. Comparison of computational complexity for Volterra series, KLMS, and KLMS-NC based equalizers for 12-core MCF using 16-QAM

Equalization algorithm	Number of multiplications	Complexity order
Volterra series	2025	$O(M^P)$
KLMS	1000	$O(k)$
KLMS-NC	400	$O(|\mathscr{D}_k|)$

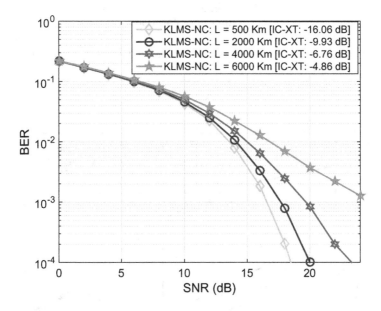

Fig. 4. SNR vs BER performance for the proposed KLMS algorithm for 12-core MCF using 16-QAM for different optical fiber lengths

To study the variation of nonlinear IC-XT on different core arrangements, the BER performance of the proposed algorithm is compared for 12-core DRS-MCF and 19-core hexagonal MCF structures in Fig. 6 using 16-QAM. It can be observed from Fig. 6 that the BER for 19-core MCF is higher than that for the 12-core MCF. This is due to the difference in core arrangement in the 12-core DRS-MCF, and 19-core hexagonal MCF structure. In a 12-core DRS-MCF, the maximum number of surrounding cores is 4 (for internal ring), whereas, in a

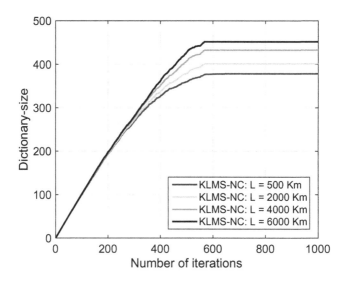

Fig. 5. Evolution of dictionary-size for the proposed KLMS algorithm for different lengths of 12-core MCF using 16-QAM

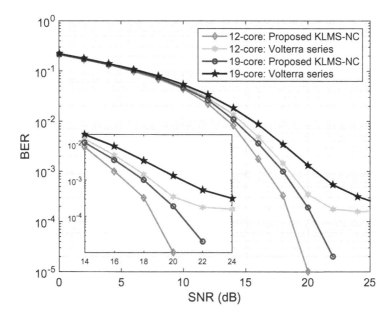

Fig. 6. SNR vs BER performance for the proposed KLMS algorithm for 12-core and 19-core MCF using 16-QAM

19-core MCF, the maximum number of surrounding cores is 6 (for central and inner hexagon cores). This increase in the number of surrounding cores leads to increase in the number of non-zero elements $h_{i,j} \forall i \neq j$ in the channel matrix **H**. In addition to this, due to smaller core pitch in 19-core hexagonal MCF, the value of $h_{i,j} \forall i \neq j$ increases, thereby resulting in increased nonlinear IC-XT interference, and hence increased BER in the 19-core MCF as compared to the 12-core MCF.

5   Conclusion

In this paper, the problem of nonlinear IC-XT interference in long-reach MCF optical communication systems is addressed. KLMS based supervised machine learning algorithm in RKHS is proposed for mitigating IC-XT impairments in MCF. Further, novelty criterion based sparsification is incorporated in the proposed equalizer to reduce its computational complexity. Simulations are performed for 12-core DRS-MCF, and 19-core hexagonal MCF structures, which shows the nonlinear IC-XT variation with core arrangement. The proposed algorithm is evaluated by varying modulation schemes, and fiber length. Simulation results indicate that the proposed KLMS based nonlinear equalizer outperforms the existing Volterra series based nonlinear equalizer. This indicates that the proposed equalizer is a viable approach for mitigating nonlinear IC-XT impairments in long-reach MCF optical communication systems.

In future, we plan to demonstrate the proposed KLMS based nonlinear equalizer experimentally for long-reach core optical networks. In addition to this, other nonlinear impairments in MCF due to Kerr effect and splicing will be addressed in future work.

Acknowledgment. This publication is an outcome of the R&D work under the Visvesvaraya Ph.D. Scheme of the Ministry of Electronics & Information Technology (MeitY), Government of India (GoI), being implemented by Digital India Corporation. The authors would like to thank the Indian Institute of Technology (IIT) Indore for all the support and resources.

References

1. Msongaleli, D.L., Dikbiyik, F., Zukerman, M., Mukherjee, B.: Disaster-aware submarine fiber-optic cable deployment for mesh networks. J. Lightwave Technol. **34**(18), 4293–4303 (2016)
2. Cisco white paper: Cisco Visual Networking Index: Forecast and Trends, 2017–2022 (2018)
3. Saridis, G.M., Alexandropoulos, D., Zervas, G., Simeonidou, D.: Survey and evaluation of space division multiplexing: from technologies to optical networks. IEEE Commun. Surv. Tutor. **17**(4), 2136–2156 (2015)
4. Tode, H., Hirota, Y.: Routing, spectrum, and core and/or mode assignment on space-division multiplexing optical networks. J. Opt. Commun. Netw. **9**(1), A99–A113 (2017)

5. Klinkowski, M., Walkowiak, K.: Impact of crosstalk estimation methods on the performance of spectrally and spatially flexible optical networks. In: 2018 20th International Conference on Transparent Optical Networks (ICTON). IEEE, pp. 1–4 (2018)

6. Yang, M., Zhang, Y., Wu, Q.: Routing, spectrum, and core assignment in SDM-EONS with MCF: node-arc ILP/MILP methods and an efficient XT-aware heuristic algorithm. J. Opt. Commun. Netw. **10**(3), 195–208 (2018)

7. Agrawal, A., Bhatia, V., Prakash, S.: Spectrum efficient distance-adaptive paths for fixed and fixed-alternate routing in elastic optical networks. Opt. Fiber Technol. **40**, 36–45 (2018)

8. Yu, X., et al.: Migration from fixed grid to flexible grid in optical networks. IEEE Commun. Mag. **53**(2), 34–43 (2015)

9. Stojanovic, N., Karinou, F., Qiang, Z., Prodaniuc, C.: Volterra and Wiener equalizers for short-reach 100G PAM-4 Applications. J. Lightwave Technol. **35**(21), 4583–4594 (2017)

10. Wu, X., Huang, C., Xu, K., Zhou, W., Shu, C., Tsang, H.K.: 3× 104 Gb/s single-λ interconnect of mode-division multiplexed network with a multicore fiber. J. Lightwave Technol. **36**(2), 318–324 (2018)

11. Mitra, R., Miramirkhani, F., Bhatia, V., Uysal, M.: Mixture-kernel based Post-distortion in RKHS for Time-varying VLC Channels. IEEE Trans. Veh. Technol. **68**, 1564–1577 (2018)

12. Mitra, R., Bhatia, V.: Low complexity post-distorter for visible light communications. IEEE Commun. Lett. **21**(9), 1977–1980 (2017)

13. Haykin, S.S., et al.: Adaptive Filter Theory, vol. 2. Prentice-Hall, Englewood Cliffs (1986)

14. Liu, W., Pokharel, P.P., Principe, J.C.: The kernel least-mean-square algorithm. IEEE Trans. Signal Process. **56**(2), 543–554 (2008)

15. Liu, W., Principe, J.C., Haykin, S.: Kernel Adaptive Filtering: A Comprehensive Introduction, vol. 57. Wiley, Hoboken (2011)

16. Engel, Y., Mannor, S., Meir, R.: The kernel recursive least-squares algorithm. IEEE Trans. Signal Process. **52**(8), 2275–2285 (2004)

17. Tobar, F.A., Kung, S.-Y., Mandic, D.P.: Multikernel least mean square algorithm. IEEE Trans. Neural Netw. Learn. Syst. **25**(2), 265–277 (2014)

18. Schölkopf, B., Herbrich, R., Smola, A.J.: A generalized representer theorem. In: Helmbold, D., Williamson, B. (eds.) COLT 2001. LNCS (LNAI), vol. 2111, pp. 416–426. Springer, Heidelberg (2001). https://doi.org/10.1007/3-540-44581-1_27

19. Abouseif, A., Ben-Othman, G.R., Jaouën, Y.: Multi-core fiber channel model and core dependent loss estimation. In: Signal Processing in Photonic Communications, p. SpW1G-3. Optical Society of America (2018)

20. Bouboulis, P., Theodoridis, S.: Extension of Wirtinger's calculus to reproducing kernel Hilbert spaces and the complex kernel LMS. IEEE Trans. Signal Process. **59**(3), 964–978 (2011)

21. Boyd, S., Vandenberghe, L.: Convex Optimization. Cambridge University Press, Cambridge (2004)

22. Chen, B., Zhao, S., Zhu, P., Principe, J.C.: Quantized kernel recursive least squares algorithm. IEEE Trans. Neural Netw. Learn. Syst. **24**(9), 1484–1491 (2013)

23. Mitra, R., Bhatia, V.: Kernel-based parallel multi-user detector for massive-MIMO. Comput. Electr. Eng. **65**, 543–553 (2018)

24. Singh, U., Mitra, R., Bhatia, V., Mishra, A.: Kernel LMS based estimation techniques for radar systems. IEEE Trans. Aerosp. Electron. Syst. **55**, 2501–2515 (2019)
25. Mitra, R., Bhatia, V.: Adaptive sparse dictionary-based kernel minimum symbol error rate post-distortion for nonlinear LEDs in visible light communications. IEEE Photonics J. **8**(4), 1–13 (2016)

Physical Layer Security in Optical Networks

Dimitris Syvridis[1]($\boxtimes$), Evangelos Pikasis[2], and Charidimos Chaintoutis[2] 🔟

[1] Department of Informatics and Telecommunications,
National and Kapodistrian University of Athens, Athens, Greece
dsyvridi@di.uoa.gr
[2] Eulambia Advanced Technologies Ltd., Ag., Paraskevi, Greece

Abstract. In this paper we'll discuss technological alternatives related to physical layer security of optical communication systems and networks. In the introduction, an overview of confidentiality and availability issues of the optical networks will be discussed, focusing mainly in the physical layer-related solutions. In the following paragraphs we'll provide two distinct approaches for the physical layer encryption. The first is based on a One-Time-Pad implementation using synchronized true random sequences. The second uses cryptographic keys generated by Photonic Physical Unclonable Function devices for scrambling the Orthogonal Frequency Division Multiplexing subcarriers.

Keywords: Physical layer · Optical chaos · Physical Unclonable Function · OFDM scrambling

1 Introduction

Nowadays communication networks support all crucial human activities from personal communications to financial transactions, massive data management, industrial processes, energy infrastructures, health/medical data exchange, transport, etc. Military communications is another highly demanding area in terms of security. Although a lot of attention has been given to the performance of the networks, such as bandwidth and latency, security aspects become more and more crucial for obvious reasons. Since the communication systems and networks, especially those based on fiber-optic media, were not designed from the ground up taking security aspects into account, the current solutions are mainly applied at the upper network layers rather than employing a holistic new approach. Particularly in the physical layer of the networks insufficient progress in security has been made. Facing the potential threats at the lower network levels, will significantly impact the security aspects at the higher layers as well.

There are different types of threats related to the physical layer of the optical network. A first group of threats are those related to availability, targeting at performance degradation or even complete interruption of the network operation. Fiber infrastructure disasters, unintentional (e.g. natural disaster related) or intentional (malicious human actions aiming at interruption of communication links or injection jamming signals) are among the physical layer threats to be considered [1]. Electromagnetic pulse (EMP)

A. Tzanakaki et al. (Eds.): ONDM 2019, LNCS 11616, pp. 412–424, 2020.
https://doi.org/10.1007/978-3-030-38085-4_35

attack is also another possible threat. Although the communication channel (optical fiber) will not be affected by EMP, all electronic/optoelectronic components related to the network operation will be damaged or malfunction depending on the strength of the electromagnetic field.

Another potential threat is related to the confidentiality, targeting at accessing data by unauthorized users for eavesdropping or even traffic monitoring/analysis. Although optical fiber is considered safer compared to wireless channels, possible means that could be used by an eavesdropper is optical fiber tapping or information extraction based on adjacent channel interference/crosstalk. Encryption and coding [2] are means for ensuring confidentiality in an optical network. Encryption is either at the optical or electronic level and it requires cryptographic key distribution/sharing between transmitter and receiver. In general, an XOR operation between the key and the data is the means for encrypting the data with the cryptographic key. There are different methods to implement optical XOR gates such as Four Wave Mixing in a SOA, cross gain modulation, cross phase modulation, etc. In the electrical domain, the most commonly used means of encryption rely on AES ciphers. These symmetrical encryption schemes are based on substitution-permutation networks and have several efficient software and hardware implementations [3]. Concerning coding, optical CDMA [4] is the most common approach, following the principles of the corresponding method used in the wireless systems. Alternative solutions based on chaos encrypted communications have been also proposed and demonstrated [5].

Key generation is based on specific software implementations or employing different types of random processes. Software based implementations rely on pseudorandom number generators whereas those obtained by statistically random physical phenomena such as thermal noise, photoelectric effect, amplified spontaneous emission [6] or other quantum phenomena are true random number sequences. Concerning key distribution, quantum technologies appear to provide the ultimate security [6–9], either in the form of DV-QKD or CV-QKD, exploiting the particle or the wavelength nature of light respectively. However, although QKD may provide an effective way to achieve unconditional security, a number of successful hacking on commercial QKD has been reported [10] as well as deficiencies in the theory behind the specific implementations [11, 12]. At the same time, Britain's National Cyber Security Centre disclosed a document in 2016 about security risks of QKD and its inefficient cost performance, and possible future threats being yet unknown [13].

In this paper we present two different approaches targeting at the physical layer encryption. The first demonstrates a photonic implementation of the "One-Time Pad" encryption scheme based on mutually injected semiconductor lasers, operating in the chaotic regime and continuously generating synchronized ultrafast true random number sequences. These sequences are then used for encryption of the data to be transmitted [14]. The second is based on a cryptographic key generation using a novel Photonic Physical Unclonable Function device. These keys are used for scrambling the modulation parameters of transceivers included in the communication system.

2   One-Time-Pad Data Encryption Using Synchronized True Random Sequences

2.1   One-Time-Pad Encryption System

The proposed One-Time-Pad encryption system capable to operate at Gb/s rates is based on synchronized broadband chaotic analog signals that are the seed for ultrafast TRBS generation. Each user's transceiver has access to this locally generated TRBS that is synchronized with the TRBSs generated by other users, through a background fiber network that supports broadband chaotic signal generation and synchrony. User #1 encodes the data that wishes to send with the appropriate FEC convolutional code and applies a XOR operation with the locally generated TRBS (Fig. 1). The encrypted data follows the desired transmission path in the network to reach the legitimate recipient (user #2), where the decoding process takes place. User's #2 locally generated TRBS participates also to a XOR operation in order to provide the initially encoded data to the decoder and obtain finally the initial data. Contrariwise, the opposite communication from user #2 to user #1 is supported using the same methodology and the same TRBS generators. Convolutional coding in forward error correction (FEC) methods is included to minimize or eliminate synchronization error between analog chaotic signals that results in errors in TRBSs' synchrony.

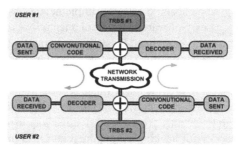

Fig. 1. One-time-pad bi-directional encryption system using synchronized ultrafast TRBS generators and FEC methods for error-free secure communications.

2.2   Optical System for the Chaos Synchronization

Each user participates in the optical network configuration with the appropriate hardware equipment; its specifications and properties can guarantee broadband chaotic signal emission, which can be potentially converted to a TRBS under a pre-determined methodology. At the same time, through the appropriate network bi-directional topology, it can guarantee very high level of chaotic signal synchronization. In the mutual optical injection topology of Fig. 2, users hold at their premises identical DFB semiconductor lasers (SLs) and photodetectors. (PDs). The SLs are interactively coupled with an identical DFB SL hub at the other edge of the network, through polarization control, optical routing and amplification. Its location can be at km distance as demonstrated by the inclusion of a 3.5 km fiber transmission spool. The SL hub offers a drive force for mutual injection and operation of the users' SLs at the coherence collapse regime. Although the process is polarization sensitive using a polarization scrambler or polarization tracker could be a possible solution to the polarization problem.

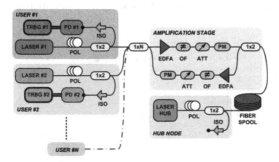

Fig. 2. Optical system of mutually injected semiconductor DFB lasers for broadband and synchronized chaotic signal emission. POL: polarization controller, 1×2 and $1 \times N$: optical coupler with 2 or N equal splitting ratio inputs, ISO: optical isolator, PD: 10 GHz photoreceiver, EDFA: 25 dB-gain erbium-doped fiber amplifier, OF: optical filter with FWHM $= 0.36$ nm, ATT: optical attenuator, PM: inline power monitor, TRBG: true random bit generator. Black line connections are fiber-optic links; red line connections are high-frequency electrical links. (Color figure online)

2.3   True Random Bit Generation

At the next level, the synchronized photo-detected signals at each user's premises are converted from their analog form to binary sequences in order to support one-time-pad encryption. The emerging digital sequences shall meet the criteria of randomness in order to play the role of encryption random key generators. Each measured sample is digitized under a single-bit or a multi-bit methodology via analog-to-digital (A/D) conversion. In order to obtain identical true random sequences from all users participating in the network tow conditions are required: (i) the chaotic analog signals emitted by the different users shall preserve high-quality synchronization, and (ii) these analog signals shall lead after digitization verified TRBSs. These prerequisites imply identical steps and parameterization of the post-processing procedures, as well as identical hardware modules used by all users.

2.4   One-Time-Pad Performance

Each legitimate user that coupled to the optical network, fulfilling some predetermined conditions, can generate the synchronized and random key sequences. The level of synchrony error of the users' analog signals attained at the optical layer is translated as an error rate of the generated digital keys. The larger the cross-correlation value between the two analog signals is, the smaller the error rate between the two TRBSs will be. As it can be seen from Fig. 3, for sufficiently low error rate between the keys generated by the two users, extremely high-quality synchronization is needed. For example, and assuming FEC (1/2), the required cross correlation between the chaotic signals is in the order of 0.999. This is exactly the key point for the security of the proposed system. If an eavesdropper attempts to intervene and tap even a minor fraction of the chaotic signal shared between the legitimate users, the synchronization quality will immediately degrade and the communication between the two users will collapse.

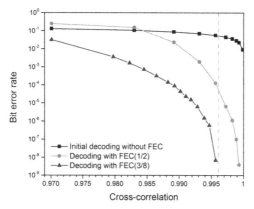

Fig. 3. Error rate for the key generation vs. cross-correlation between the chaotic signals of the two users.

3   Photonic PUFs as Physical Root of Trust for OFDM-Based Optical Communication Systems

PUFs have been recently proposed as a physical root of trust that uniquely combines key storage and generation procedures. Thus, the CIA triad of security objectives (Confidentiality, Integrity, and Authentication) can be achieved by exploiting cryptographic primitives that are hardened by properties of the actual physical world. Essentially, a PUF is the physical analogue of a one-way mathematical function, based on an unclonable, non-reproducible and complex physical mechanism. Combined with their deterministic operation, PUFs are appropriate for cryptographic key generation on demand, eliminating the need for key storage (no key-at-rest property) in secure Non-Volatile Memory modules (NVM). In this way, keys cannot be found by an attacker who has accessed the device and compromised all the memory contents. Additionally, in this way, it is possible to provision keys for devices that are rapidly scaling in numbers, year after year. The basic concept behind PUFs has been materialized in various different implementations with the main differentiation being between optical/photonic PUFs as introduced in [16]. and silicon-based PUFs as introduced in [17]. The idea behind PUFs is to use unavoidable, implicit defects present in the manufacturing process of a hardware token in order to make a digital 'fingerprint' of the token. In general, when an extrinsic excitation (Challenge) is presented to a PUF, a corresponding output (Response) is generated. This response is determined by a complex physical function that is unique to each token or PUF instance, as shown in Fig. 4. Using the same challenge, different PUFs produce a different response. The combination of the challenge and its corresponding response lead to the creation of unique challenge–response pairs (CRPs). The uniqueness of the responses of different PUFs under the same challenge (unclonability) and the uniqueness of the responses of the same PUF under different challenge (unpredictability) have made PUFs useful for a wide variety of applications, spanning from authentication and secret key storage [17, 18], cryptographic key generation [19], software–hardware interconnection [20], and tamper detection [21] to shielding systems against code-reuse attacks [12] and cyber-hardening blockchain applications [23]. So far, the spotlight of attention has been mainly focused on silicon-cast PUFs, whose principle of operation is based on exploiting uncontrollable variations in operational parameters [17, 24]. Existing implementations include ring-oscillators [17, 25], arbiter PUFs [26], static random-access memory (SRAM) PUFs [27] to mention a few. Despite their merits in terms of integration, unclonability, and robustness, the underlying physical scrambling mechanism, in most cases, is rather simplistic, resulting to enhanced vulnerability to modelling attacks [28, 29]. The arsenal of adversaries is enhanced through various side-channel attacks [30, 31]. Emerging PUF implementations based on nanofabrication procedures [32], hold great promise, but current results are focused on providing proof of concept and do not evaluate their cryptographic performance.

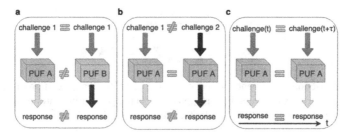

Fig. 4. Representation of the typical PUF properties. (a) Unclonability: same challenges but different PUFs provide different responses, (b) Unpredictability: different challenges to the same PUF provide different response, (c) Robustness: time-invariant operation

Photonic PUF implementations are based on the combination of the coherent interaction of a laser beam with the randomness of a disordered physical medium (Fig. 5). The medium could be a material containing randomly positioned micro-structures that act as scatterers [16], or an optical fiber [34, 35]. A laser source illuminates a transparent, inhomogeneous medium (PUF's token), the goal being to produce unique interference patterns (speckle) which are subsequently captured as images (responses). The recorded images undergo a post-processing procedure, via hashing algorithms, and every hashed response is mapped to a **unique bit-string output**. In this way unique **Challenge-Response Pairs** are acquired. While the physical characteristics of the PUF token, that enable the extraction of the unique responses, are permanent in nature, the information extraction from PUFs (and other noisy sources, like biometrics) is a probabilistic procedure; on a single challenge, a different response may be produced, due to the uncontrollable and random evaluation noise. In order to ensure robust operation under the effect of noise, the mapping of each image to a unique bit-string and its recovery is achieved through fuzzy extractor algorithms [36].

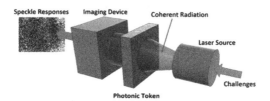

Fig. 5. Conceptual representation of a p-PUF

The fuzzy extractor scheme comprises two phases: the enrolment and the verification phase. The former corresponds to the first time that a challenge is applied whereby the output string is generated along with a set of public helper data, while the latter represents the noisy rerun of the measurement during which the same result is recreated by using the helper data produced in the enrolment phase. A simple schematic of the described procedure is depicted in Fig. 6.

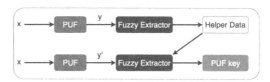

Fig. 6. Fuzzy extraction: enrolment and reconstruction phase for the generation of PUF keys. x represents a challenge; y is the initial PUF response for challenge x during enrolment and y' is the PUF's response for the same challenge under the presence of noise

The security properties of the p-PUFs are based on the complexity of the underlying physical mechanism, with its complexity rendering p-PUFs more secure than their electronic counterparts. For example, a modelling attack would require partitioning the PUF token into wavelength-sized voxels and solving Maxwell's equations for each possible arrangement [33]. We should mention here that secret keys provide security based on the fact that they are completely random (and thus unpredictable). PUF responses, have a high degree of randomness, but are usually not completely random. Fuzzy extraction algorithms, apart from accurate key reproduction, also remedy the uniformity problem by employing "randomness extractors". Randomness extractors (i.e., universal hash functions) convert a high entropy input into a shorter, uniformly distributed output. Following this procedure, some of the source's entropy is "sacrificed" to acquire uniformly distributed random keys. We should mention here that the public nature of the fuzzy extractor's helper data (the pieces of information used for accurate response reproduction) poses no security risk; helper data do not contain any useful information for an adversary that could take hold of them.

3.1   PUF-Enabled Subcarrier Scrambler Module, to Cyber-Harden OFDM-Based Communications

The three primary 5G NR diverse use cases which defined by 3GPP [37] are: Ultra Reliable Low Latency Communications (URLLC), Enhanced Mobile Broadband (eMBB) and Massive Machine Type Communications (mMTC). Some potential applications for 5G networks include gaming, Virtual reality applications, Vehicle to vehicle, Internet of Things (IoT) and machine to machine communications (M2M). Some of the key requirements that need to be achieved by a modulation scheme, in order to support all the aforementioned applications are [38]:

- Capable of handling high data rate wide bandwidth signals
- Able to provide low latency transmissions
- Capable of fast switching between uplink and downlink for TDD systems
- Interworking between high and low frequency bands
- Enable the possibility of energy efficient communications

Orthogonal Frequency Division Multiplexing (OFDM) has been an outstanding choice for 4G networks providing significant spectrum efficiency and performance improvement in frequency-selective channels. The Cyclic-Prefix (CP) OFDM is the predominant candidate for 5G networks for the cases of downlink and uplink in the sub-6 GHz frequency band and for the mmWave range [39]. A typical block diagram of an OFDM RF transceiver with the subcarrier scrambler module is depicted in Fig. 7. In the case of the OFDM transmitter, a high bit rate stream after the parallel to serial converter is driven to QAM mapper and the mapping process forms the buffered bit stream to QAM symbols. In a conventional OFDM system, the complex stream is given as input to the IFFT stage, modulating each subcarrier with QAM symbols. In this scheme, an extra stage, a **PUF-based scrambler**, is added performing re-distribution of the subcarriers across the frequency domain. The scrambler module performs the subcarrier scrambling operation exploiting the unique responses of the p-PUF module. The unique bit-string responses are used as seeds that feed a pseudo RNG (pseudo-Random Number Generator). Thus, a scrabbling number sequence is produced, and the subcarriers are scrabbled accordingly. A Cyclic Prefix (CP) in order to combat the multipath is added

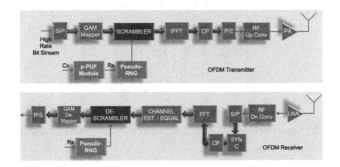

Fig. 7. A typical block diagram of an OFDM transceiver

and afterwards the produced complex OFDM signal is RF up-converted, amplified by power amplifier (PA) and radiated from the antenna.

At the receiver side, the reverse operations include synchronization, frequency domain estimation/equalization and de-scrambling. It must be noted that the process of the frequency estimation and equalization is not affected from the scrambling method. Under this scheme, the bit and power loading methods cannot be used. After the handshaking process, the net bit rate of the proposed system is the OFDM net bit rate. Given that the PUF response (used as seed for the pseudo-RNG) is precisely reproduced, and the pseudo-RNG algorithm is known, the de-scrambling sequence would precisely follow the scrabbling one.

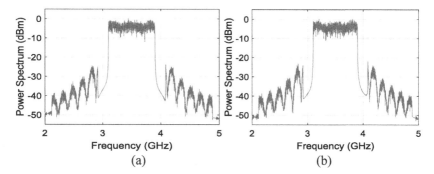

Fig. 8. The power spectrum of the RF up-converted of the (a) unscrambled and (b) scrambled OFDM signal

The power spectrum of an (a) un-scrambled and (b) scrambled OFDM up-converted signal to 3.5 GHz carrier frequency, as well as the time traces for these two cases are shown in Figs. 8 and 9 respectively. As can be observed, the power spectra of the up-converted OFDM signals are different as well as the time traces for the two cases.

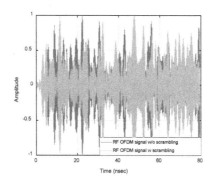

Fig. 9. Un-scrambled and scrambled up-converted OFDM time traces

In order to quantify the difference between the unscrambled and scrambled OFDM signals we employ the cross-correlation metric, as is depicted in Fig. 10. As can be seen, the maximum of the cross-correlation of the OFDM signal with itself is 0.97, while in the second case is 0.023. Compared with single carrier schemes, OFDM systems exhibit high peak-to-average power ratio (PAPR). The high value of PAPR is one of the detrimental aspects of OFDM systems since the OFDM signal is greatly affected by the non-linear effects of RF power amplifier (PA), causing serious in-band distortions as well as adjacent channel interference. The scrambling process doesn't affect the PAPR distribution as depicted in Fig. 11, where complementary cumulative distribution function (CCDF) denotes that a probability distribution of the PAPR of OFDM symbols is over a certain threshold.

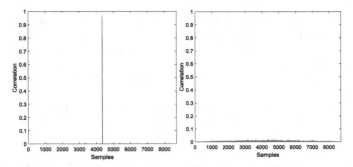

Fig. 10. Cross-correlation of the OFDM signal with itself and between the un-scrambled and scrambled up-converted OFDM signal

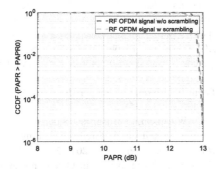

Fig. 11. CCDF curves for the scrambled and unscrambled scheme.

As can be seen from all the above graphs, the effect of the scrambling process on the basic characteristics of an OFDM signal is negligible, providing the security of the communication system.

4 Conclusion

In this paper we presented two different approaches for the physical layer encryption. The first is based in an optical implementation of the One-Time-Pad cryptographic scheme. We have shown that almost perfect synchronization between mutually injected chaotic lasers placed at the premises of two communicating users leads to the continuous generation of synchronized true random number sequences. These sequences can be used for encrypting/decrypting the data streams exchanged between the two users. The second is based on optical implementation of a Physical Unclonable Function and its application a key generator for scrambling the OFDM subcarriers in a typical 5G communication scheme.

References

1. Rejeb, R., Leeson, M.S., Green, R.J.: Fault and attack management in all-optical networks. IEEE Commun. Mag. **44**(11), 79–86 (2006)
2. Wang, Z., Fok, M.P., Prucnal, P.R.: Physical encoding in optical layer security. J. Cyber. Secur. Mob. **1**, 83–100 (2012)
3. Schneier, B., et al.: The twofish team's final comments on AES selection. AES Round **2**(1), 1–13 (2000)
4. Wang, Z., Xu, L., Chang, J., Wang, T., Prucnal, P.R.: Secure optical transmission in a point-to-point link with encrypted CDMA codes. IEEE Photonics Technol. Lett. **22**(19), 1410–1412 (2010)
5. Argiris, A., Syvridis, D., Larger, L., Lodi, V.A., Colet, P., Fischer, I., et al.: Chaos-based communications at high bit rates using commercial fibre-optic links. Nature **438**(17), 343–346 (2006)
6. Argyris, A., Pikasis, E., Deligiannidis, S., Syvridis, D.: Sub-Tb/s physical random bit generators based on direct detection of amplified spontaneous emission signals. J. Lightwave Technol. **30**(9), 1329–1334 (2012)
7. Rosenberg, D., Harrington, J.W., Rice, P.R., Hiskett, P.A., Peterson, C.G., Hughes, R.J., et al.: Long-distance decoy-state quantum key distribution in optical fiber. Phys. Rev. Lett. **98**, 010503-1–010503-4 (2007)
8. Hadfield, R.H., Habif, J.L., Schlafer, J., Schwall, R.E., Nam, S.W.: Quantum key distribution at 1550 nm with twin superconducting single-photon detectors. Appl. Phys. Lett. **89**, 241129-1 (2006)
9. Scheuer, J., Yariv, A.: Giant fiber lasers: a new paradigm for secure key distribution. Phys. Rev. Lett. **97**, 140502-1–140502-4 (2006)
10. Lydersen, L., Wiechers, C., Wittmann, C., Elser, D., Skaar, J., Makarov, V.: Hacking commercial quantum cryptography systems by tailored bright illumination. Nat. Photon. **4**(10), 686–689 (2010). https://doi.org/10.1038/nphoton.2010.214
11. Yuen, H.P.: Universality and The Criterion 'd' in Quantum Key Generation arXiv:0907. 4694v1 (quant-ph) (2009)
12. Yuen, H.P.: Fundamental quantitative security in quantum key generation. Phys. Rev. A **82**(6), 062304 (2010). https://doi.org/10.1103/PhysRevA.82.062304
13. The British governmental white paper, "Quantum Key Distribution," National Cyber Security Centre, a part of GCHQ in Britain, 4th Oct (2016)
14. Wu, B.B., Narimanov, E.E.: A method for secure communications over a public fiber-optical network. Opt. Express **14**(9), 3738–3751 (2006)
15. Argyris, A., Pikasis, E., Syvridis, D.: Gb/s one time pad data encryption with synchronised chaos based true random bit generation. J. Lightwave Technol. **34**(22), 532–5331 (2016)
16. Pappu, R., Recht, B., Taylor, J., et al.: Physical one-way functions. Science **297**, 2026–2030 (2002)

17. Gassend, B., Clarke, D., Van Dijk, M., et al.: Silicon physical random functions. In: Proceedings of the 9th ACM Conference on Computer and Communications Security, pp. 148–160. ACM (2002)
18. Ruhrmair, U., Devadas, S., Koushanfar, F.: Security based on physical unclonability and disorder. In: Tehranipoor, M., Wang, C. (eds.) Introduction to Hardware Security and Trust, pp. 65–102. Springer, New York (2012). https://doi.org/10.1007/978-1-4419-8080-9_4
19. Suh, G.E., Devadas, S.: Physical unclonable functions for device authentication and secret key generation. In: 2007 44th ACM/IEEE Design Automation Conference DAC 2007, pp. 9–14 (2007)
20. Tuyls, P.: Towards Hardware-Intrinsic Security: Foundations And Practice. Springer, Heidelberg (2010). https://doi.org/10.1007/978-3-642-14452-3
21. Kursawe, K., Sadeghi, A.-R., Schellekens, D., et al.: Reconfigurable physical unclonable functions-enabling technology for tamper-resistant storage (2009)
22. Qiu, P., Lyu, Y., Zhai, D., et al.: Physical unclonable functions-based linear encryption against code reuse attacks. In: 2016 53rd ACM/EDAC/IEEE Design Automation Conference (DAC) (2016)
23. Chaintoutis, C., et al.: Optical PUFs as physical root of trust for blockchain-driven applications. IET Software 13, 182–186 (2018)
24. Suh, G.E., Devadas, S.: Physical unclonable functions for device authentications and secret key generation. In: Proceedings of 44th Annual Conference on Design Automation, pp. 9–14 (2007)
25. Maiti, A., Schaumont, P.: Improving the quality of a physical unclonable function using configurable ring oscillators. In: Proceedings of the International Conference on Field Programmable Logic and Applications, pp. 703–707. IEEE (2009). https://doi.org/10.1109/FPL.2009.5272361
26. Lee, J.W., et al.: A technique to build a secret key in integrated circuits for identification and authentication applications. In: Proceedings of the IEEE Symposium on VLSI Circuits. Digest of Technical Papers, pp. 176–179. IEEE (2004). https://doi.org/10.1109/VLSIC.2004.1346548
27. Xu, X., Rahmati, A., Holcomb, D.E., Fu, K., Burleson, W.: Reliable physical unclonable functions using data retention voltage of SRAM cells. IEEE Trans. Comput. Des. Integr. Circuits Syst. 34, 903–914 (2015)
28. Nguyen, P.H., Sahoo, D.P., Chakraborty, R.S., Mukhopadhyay, D.: Efficient attacks on robust ring oscillator PUF with enhanced challenge-response set. In: Proceedings of the Design, Automation & Test in Europe Conference & Exhibition (DATE), pp. 641–646. IEEE (2015)
29. Hospodar, G., Maes, R., Verbauwhede, I.: Machine learning attacks on 65 nm Arbiter PUFs: accurate modeling poses strict bounds on usability. In: Proceedings of the 2012 IEEE International Workshop on Information Forensics and Security (WIFS), pp. 37–42 (2012)
30. Tajik, S., Ganji, F., Seifert, J.P., Lohrke, H., Boit, C.: Laser fault attack on physically unclonable functions. In: Proceedings of 2015 Workshop on Fault Diagnosis and Tolerance in Cryptography (FDTC), pp. 85–96. IEEE (2016). https://doi.org/10.1109/FDTC.2015.19
31. Mahmoud, A., Ruhrmair, U., Majzoobi, M., Koushanfar, F.: Combined Modeling and Side Channel Attacks on Strong PUFs. IACR Cryptology ePrint Archive (2013)
32. Gao, Y., Ranasinghe, D.C., Al-Sarawi, S.F., Kavehei, O., Abbott, D.: Emerging Physica unclonable functions with nanotechnology. IEEE Access 4, 61–80 (2016)
33. Ruhrmair, U., Hilgers, C., Urban, S., et al.: Optical pufs reloaded. Eprint Iacr.org (2013)
34. Akriotou, M., Mesaritakis, C., Grivas, E., et al.: Random number generation from a secure photonic physical unclonable hardware module. In: Proceedings of the 2018 ISCIS Security Workshop, Imperial College London (2018)
35. Mesaritakis, C., Akriotou, M., Kapsalis, A., et al.: Physical unclonable function based on a multi-mode optical waveguide. Sci. Rep. 8(1), 9653 (2018)

36. Armknecht, F., Maes, R., Sadeghi, A.-R., et al.: A formalization of the security features of physical functions. In: 2011 IEEE Symposium on Security and Privacy, pp. 397–412 (2011)
37. ITU-R SG05. Draft new Report ITU-R M. - Minimum requirements related to technical performance for IMT-2020 radio interface(s), February 2017
38. Lin, X., et al.: 5G new radio: Unveiling the essentials of the next generation wireless access technology. IEEE Commun. Stand. Mag. **3**(3), 30–37 (2019)
39. TS 38.211. NR; Physical channels and modulation. V15.1.0, April 2018. http://www.3gpp.org/ftp//Specs/archive/38_series/38.211/38211-f10.zip. Accessed 18 June 2018

A Gated Service MAC Protocol for 5G Fiber-Wireless Cloud-Radio Access Networks

Agapi Mesodiakaki[1]([✉])(iD), Pavlos Maniotis[1], Georgios Kalfas[1](iD),
Christos Vagionas[1](iD), John Vardakas[2](iD), Elli Kartsakli[2](iD),
Angelos Antonopoulos[3](iD), Eftychia Datsika[2](iD), Christos Verikoukis[3](iD),
and Nikos Pleros[1](iD)

[1] Department of Informatics, Aristotle University of Thessaloniki,
Thessaloniki, Greece
{amesodia,ppmaniot,gkalfas,chvagion,npleros}@csd.auth.gr
[2] Iquadrat Informatica, Barcelona, Spain
{jvardakas,ellik,edatsika}@iquadrat.com
[3] Telecommunications Technological Centre of Catalonia, Castelldefels, Spain
{aantonopoulos,cveri}@cttc.es

Abstract. Next generation, i.e., fifth generation (5G), networks will leverage both fiber and wireless (FiWi) technology to meet the challenging 5G traffic demands. Moreover, a Cloud-Radio Access Network (C-RAN) architecture will be mainly adopted, which places the BaseBand Units (BBUs) at centralized locations, thus offering cost-efficient energy supply and climate control. To this end, efficient Medium Transparent-Medium Access Control (MT-MAC) protocols are needed to ensure the optimal exploitation of both media. In this paper, we propose a gated service MT-MAC protocol (gMT-MAC) for Millimeter Wave (mmWave) Analog Radio-over-Fiber (A-RoF) C-RANs. GMT-MAC grants a transmission window to each user equal to the time needed for its requested traffic to be successfully sent. A mean packet delay model is also proposed and verified by means of simulation. The performance of gMT-MAC is evaluated for different network load conditions, number of Remote Radio Heads (RRHs) and optical availability values. The provided results prove the suitability of gMT-MAC to meet the sub-ms delay requirements of latency-critical 5G services.

Keywords: Fifth Generation (5G) networks · Mean packet delay model · Fiber-Wireless (FiWi) · Millimeter Wave (mmWave) · Cloud-radio access networks (C-RANS) · Analog Radio-over-Fiber (A-ROF) · Medium Transparent-MAC (MT-MAC)

Supported by H2020-5G PPP 5G-PHOS (grant agreement 761989), MSCA ITN 5G STEP-FWD (grant agreement 722429), SPOT5G (TEC2017-87456-P) and AGAUR (2017 SGR 891).

© IFIP International Federation for Information Processing 2020
Published by Springer Nature Switzerland AG 2020
A. Tzanakaki et al. (Eds.): ONDM 2019, LNCS 11616, pp. 425–436, 2020.
https://doi.org/10.1007/978-3-030-38085-4_36

1   Introduction

Next generation, i.e., Fifth Generation (5G), networks increase peak data rate and cell edge data rate needs to 20 Gbps and 1 Gbps, respectively, compared to Forth Generation (4G) networks. In parallel, latency-critical 5G applications, also known as Ultra-Reliable Low Latency Communication (URLLC) applications, require lower than 1 ms end-to-end delay [1]. In order to meet these ever-increasing capacity and latency demands, the exploitation of higher spectrum bands, e.g., Millimeter Wave (mmWave), is expected to play a key role due to the huge bandwidth availability they offer. This trend is also reflected in Rel. 15 of 5G New Radio (NR) standard by 3GPP, which refers to the exploitation of spectrum bands up to 52.6 GHz, with Rel. 16 including even higher frequencies [2]. Nevertheless, mmWave bands experience high propagation losses, and therefore, enable shorter link ranges than traditional sub-6 GHz networks. As a result, when used in the Radio Access Network (RAN) part, they stress the need for antenna densification.

Hence, centralized architectures are favored, e.g., Cloud-RANs (C-RANs) [3], which separate BaseBand Units (BBUs) from Remote Radio Heads (RRHs), placing the former at centralized locations. Thereby, efficient network management as well as energy supply and climate control are achieved. Centralization, however, sets challenging capacity requirements for the BBU-RRH connection, also known as fronthaul, which should be able to support a massive number of broad mmWave channels. In parallel, the protocol specification used for the BBU-RRH communication, also known as Common Public Radio Interface (CPRI) [4], is highly inefficient in this case as it imposes up to two orders of magnitude bandwidth penalty compared to the IP rate. In this context, the need to design new efficient protocol solutions is imperative.

To that end, Analog-Radio-over-Fiber (A-RoF) technology has received increased attention from the research community mainly by virtue of its capability to meet both the centralization and high fronthaul capacity needs [5–8]. This is achieved by placing all main hardware, i.e., sampling and digital-to-analog conversion components, within the BBU, hence significantly simplifying the RRHs compared to Digital-Radio-over-Fiber (D-RoF) technology [9]. As a result, no bandwidth penalty is imposed on the fronthaul link, since no radio waveform digitization takes place and hence the full fiber bandwidth can be exploited to carry the mmWave channels [10]. On the other hand, by removing the inter-mediate digitization at the RRH, the optical and the wireless domains get completely separated one from the other. Thus, controlling both the optical and wireless resources from the centralized BBU pool, while meeting the strict 5G C-RAN delay requirements becomes a challenging problem to face.

A Medium Transparent-MAC (MT-MAC) scheme has been proposed to efficiently manage both the optical and wireless resources in Fiber-Wireless (FiWi) networks that employ A-RoF [11,12]. In MT-MAC, the users have a direct communication with the BBU, while the RRHs perform solely the Radio Frequency (RF)/optical signal conversion. An enhanced MT-MAC version has been also proposed aiming at optimizing the size of the transmission window allocated to each RRH. In particular, contrary to the fixed allocation included in the traditional MT-MAC version, a more sophisticated allocation based on the number of active users, i.e., users that have traffic to be sent, located in the range of each RRH is performed. In other words, an RRH with a higher number of active users will be allocated a longer transmission window. Due to its client-weighted data wavelength allocation, this protocol version is also known as Client-Weighted MT-MAC [13,14]. Client-Weighted MT-MAC was shown to achieve improved performance in terms of throughput and mean packet delay fairness compared to the fixed allocation of the traditional MT-MAC. Specifically, the fact that the size of the transmission window allocated to each user was the same regardless of the number of users that were sharing the same RRH resources, results in improved service equalization.

Although the aforementioned schemes achieve fairness either among RRHs (traditional MT-MAC, where the same transmission window size is allocated to each RRH), or among users (client-weighted MT-MAC, where the transmission window size allocated to each RRH is proportional to its number of active users), more sophisticated schemes are needed that will offer service equalization on a packet basis. To this end, the gated service scheme addresses this challenge by allocating transmission windows proportional to the number of packets located at the buffer of each user during the reporting phase. This scheme has received great research attention and has been also studied in the context of the Interleaved Polling with Adaptive Cycle Time (IPACT) protocol for Ethernet Passive Optical Networks (EPONs) [15,16]. As shown in [17], gated service IPACT achieves considerable lower delay compared to fixed-service IPACT. Nonetheless, despite its unquestionable benefits, to the best of our knowledge, the gated service has never been exploited to MT-MAC protocol design for A-RoF FiWi C-RANs.

To that end, in this paper, we propose a gated service MT-MAC protocol (gMT-MAC), i.e., a protocol that grants a transmission window to each user equal to the amount of time needed to successfully send its reported traffic. An analytical model for the mean packet delay is also proposed and verified by means of simulation. The protocol performance is also evaluated for different network load conditions, number of RRHs and optical wavelength availability levels. Part of this work is based on the analysis of gated IPACT scheme for EPONs, presented in [17]. It has been appropriately adapted though for A-RoF FiWi C-RANs to account for the additional delay induced by the wavelength allocation and contention periods during the joint optical and wireless gMT-MAC time cycle. Thereby, the proposed work constitutes the first gated service model that addresses the joint wireless and optical resource allocation problem for FiWi C-RANs. On the contrary, the state-of-the-art either consists of RoF models addressing only the wireless resource allocation problem [18–20] or operates with fixed transmission window allocation [12]. The proposed model is shown to be in a very good agreement with the simulation results, thus proving the validity of both. Our results also prove the suitability of gMT-MAC for 5G C-RANs, since it is shown to be able to meet the sub-ms mean packet delay requirements of 5G latency-critical applications.

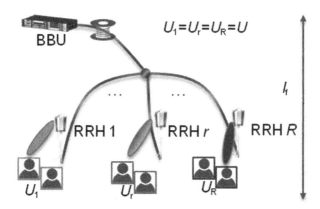

Fig. 1. System model under study composed of a BaseBand Unit (BBU) located at a distant location and R Remote Radio Heads (RRHs) forming a Passive Optical Network (PON). Wavelength Division Multiplexing (WDM) is also employed in case more than one data wavelengths are available.

The rest of the paper is organized as follows. In Sects. 2 and 3, the system model and the gMT-MAC operation are described, respectively. In Sect. 4, the mean packet delay analytical model for is presented. Section 5 refers to the model validation by means of simulation. Specifically, the simulation scenario as well as the evaluation results are given, while useful insights are gained for the performance of gMT-MAC. Finally, Sect. 6 concludes the paper.

2   System Model

As shown in Fig. 1, the system model under study consists of a C-RAN network, in which a BBU is placed at a centralized location l_f meters away from R RRHs. A Passive Optical Network (PON) topology is also employed for the RRH interconnection. The parameter U_r refers to the number of users served by the RRH r. Poisson packet arrivals are assumed with bit rate equal to λ_U bps and a fixed packet length of l_p. The buffer size of each user is B packets.

In order to tackle the increased complexity, a symmetric network in terms of number of users is assumed, i.e., $U_1 = U_2 = ... = U_r = U_R = U$. Hence, all RRHs have the same average packet arrival rate (bps), i.e., $\lambda = U\lambda_U$. Nevertheless, it is worth pointing out that the number of packets located at the buffer of each user at a specific instant is a random parameter, although it follows the same distribution for all users and RRHs. Consequently, the same holds for the number of active users per RRH. These instantaneous changes are exploited by gated service schemes, which grant transmission windows proportional to the number of packets that each user requests at a specific time period.

We also assume W data wavelengths which can be transmitted through the same fiber link exploiting Wavelength Division Multiplexing (WDM). Another wavelength is also assumed, which is dedicated for control information exchange.

The BBU-user communication over the FiWi link follows the gMT-MAC protocol, which will be detailed in Sect. 3. Finally, uplink and downlink operate at different frequencies, i.e., a node can receive and transmit concurrently.

3   Gated Service MT-MAC Protocol (gMT-MAC)

The proposed protocol comprises two parallel procedures, the allocation of data wavelength to the RRHs with active users and the allocation of resources to their users. For the data wavelength assignment, the BBU should initially be informed for the RRHs with users that have traffic to send. Therefore, it transmits a short pulse which is broadcasted to all users through their RRHs [12]. The users with pending traffic reply with the same pulse to their respective RRHs and from there the pulses are transmitted back to the BBU. For the identification of the RRHs that contain users with pending traffic, the difference in the distance between the BBU and each RRH is exploited, as it eventually leads to time difference between the reception of the pulses originated by different RRHs. Once the RRHs with pending traffic have been identified, a round robin allocation of the data wavelengths takes place among them. Specifically, a list is created including the RRHs with active users that have not been served yet. The RRH located first in the list has the highest priority in case a new data wavelength becomes available. On the other hand, in case a new RRH becomes active, it will be placed last.

Regarding the resource allocation to the active users of an RRH that has been assigned a data wavelength, it includes Request Resource Frames (RRFs) and data exchange frames. The first type of frames refers to the identification of the active users, while the second to the exchange of data information.

During an RRF, each active user picks up a random number between $[0, s_{RRF} - 1]$, which represents the number of slots it has to wait until it transmits its ID packet to the BBU. The parameter s_{RRF} denotes the number of RRF slots. Hence, in each slot, the BBU transmits a POLL and the user with the respective chosen number replies with its ID, including its buffer (BF) status. Upon successful reception of the ID packet by the BBU, an ACK packet is transmitted to the user. In case more than one users choose the same number, a collision occurs and the BBU does not send an ACK. In this case, the collided users will participate to another RRF by choosing a new number from the set $[0, s_{RRF} - 1]$. The RRF procedure will be repeated until either the maximum number of RRFs has been reached or all users have been successfully identified.

As for the data frame exchange process, each one of the identified users is being sequentially polled by the BBU to send its data. The polling sequence follows the user identification order. Due to the gated service employed by gMT-MAC, the transmission window allocated to each user is proportional to the number of reported packets located at its buffer during the identification process. Upon successful reception of the data packets of a polled user, the BBU sends an ACK packet following a procedure similar to the RRF process.

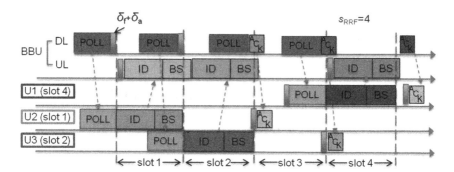

Fig. 2. Example of Request Resource Frame (RRF) process with 3 active users and $s_{RRF} = 4$ RRF slots.

3.1 Operational Example of gMT-MAC

For a better understanding of gMT-MAC operation, an operational example referring (i) to the RRF process and (ii) to the data exchange process is given.

Request Resource Frame (RRF) Process. As shown in Fig. 2, we consider a simple example with 3 active users and $s_{RRF} = 4$ RRF slots. At the beginning of the RRF, each user selects a random number from the set $[0, 3]$. In the considered example, U1 selected number 3, U2 number 0 and U3 number 1. As a result, U1 will send its ID packet after waiting 3 slots, i.e., at slot 4, U2 without waiting at all, i.e., at slot 1 and U3 at slot 2. In each slot, the BBU transmits a POLL packet. Upon receiving the POLL, i.e., after $T_{POLL} + \delta_f + \delta_a$, the user that selected the respective slot replies with its ID packet including its buffer status, BF. The parameters T_{POLL}, δ_f and δ_a stand for the time duration of a POLL packet and the propagation delay in the fiber and in the wireless medium, respectively. The next POLL, which corresponds to slot 2, is scheduled $T_{POLL} + \delta_f + \delta_a$ before the end of slot 1. As a result, U3 that is scheduled to send its ID packet at slot 2, transmits it at the beginning of slot 2. The same procedure is repeated for the rest of the slots. Notice that slot 3 corresponds to an empty slot, since no user has selected it. Regarding the acknowledgment of the ID packet reception, ACK packets are sent together with the next POLL frames for higher bandwidth efficiency. In particular, an ACK is sent together with the next scheduled POLL frame as long as (i) the ID packet has been successfully received by the BBU, and (ii) there is another POLL packet to be sent. Hence, in the considered example, the ACK for the ID packet of U2 is sent together with the third POLL, while the ACK for the ID packet of U3 is sent together with the forth POLL. For the ID packet of U1, however, the ACK is sent immediately after the ID packet reception by the BBU, given that there is no other scheduled POLL frame left.

Thus, the RRF process duration can be given by

$$T_{RRF} = T_{POLL} + s_{RRF}T_{ID} + T_{ACK} + 3\delta_f + 3\delta_a, \tag{1}$$

where T_{ID}, T_{ACK} is the time duration of an ID and an ACK packet, respectively.

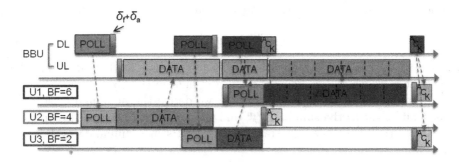

Fig. 3. Example of data exchange process between the BBU and the 3 active users that have been identified based on the RRF process example of Fig. 2.

Data Frame Exchange Process. Regarding the data frame exchange process, a simple example is given in Fig. 3, assuming the same users that have been identified in the previous RRF example of Fig. 2. During the data frame exchange, a POLL packet is transmitted by the BBU for each active user sequentially in the order that they have been previously identified. Hence, initially U2 will be polled, then U3 and finally U1. For each user that is being polled, a transmission window is being granted based on the buffer status it reported during the identification process. Thus, a transmission window equal to the duration of 4 data packets is being granted to U2, of 2 data packets to U3 and of 6 data packets to U1. After each polled user has successfully sent its reported data to the BBU, an ACK is sent to the user. For higher bandwidth efficiency, similar to the RRF process, the ACK is sent together with the next POLL packet, as long as there is one. Hence, the ACK for the data packets of U2 is transmitted together with the third POLL. In the case there is no other POLL packet left, i.e., after all identified users have been polled, a single ACK is sent in the end of the process, which contains acknowledgement information for all the remaining data packets of the users. Moreover, given that there is no need to wait for the ACK packet to be received by the users, the duration of the data exchange process equals

$$T_{DE} = T_{POLL} + \sum_{i=1}^{U_{act}} T_{DATA_i} + T_{ACK} + 2\delta_f + 2\delta_a, \tag{2}$$

with U_{act} denoting the number of active users that have been successfully identified in the previous RRF process.

4   Mean Packet Delay Analysis

We focus our analysis on the time period between two successive transmission windows of a specific RRH, denoted by T_{cyc}. This parameter increases with the traffic load, since in gMT-MAC all users send as many data packets as they requested during the identification process. To calculate the average T_{cyc}, we first derive its minimum value that equals a round-trip time in the fiber. Hence,

$$T_{cyc}^{min} = 2\delta_f, \tag{3}$$

where $\delta_f = l_f/c_f$ is the propagation delay in the fiber, with l_f denoting the average fiber length and c_f being the speed of light in the fiber.

Thereafter, based on T_{cyc}^{min} calculation, we derive the minimum cycle time under traffic load as the sum of T_{cyc}^{min} and the amount of time needed to send the packets that have been generated by all RRHs in a minimum cycle time, i.e.,

$$T_{cyc}^{min'} = T_{cyc}^{min} + (\Lambda/l_p)T_{cyc}^{min}T_p + T_{POLL} + T_{ACK} + 2\delta_f + 2\delta_a, \tag{4}$$

where $\Lambda = (R/W)\lambda$ denotes the total packet arrival rate (bps) of all RRHs. The parameters T_p, T_{POLL}, T_{ACK} refer to the duration of a data packet, a POLL and an ACK packet, respectively. In general, the duration of a packet x of l_x bits is given by $T_x = l_x/D_u$, with D_u being the uplink channel capacity (bps).

The properties of the Poisson traffic enable us to derive an approximate distribution of cycle times. Given that the number of packets is an integer number, the duration of a cycle m can take solely discrete values, i.e.,

$$T_{cyc}^m = \frac{R}{W}(T_{POLL} + T_{ACK} + 2\delta_f + 2\delta_a) + T_{RRF} + mT_p, \quad m \geq 0, \tag{5}$$

with T_{RRF} being the RRF duration, given by (1).

By solving (5) in terms of m and setting $T_{cyc}^m = T_{cyc}^{min'}$, we derive the minimum value of m, denoted by m_{min}. We then model the evolution of cycle times as a discrete Markov chain and calculate the matrix of transition probabilities from a cycle to another, denoted by $\mathbf{P}$. The longest cycle corresponds to the case where all user buffers are full. In this case, the total number of packets is $B_{max}^{all} = B \cdot U \cdot (R/W)$. Hence, the transition probability to cycle times that are longer than the minimum cycle time under traffic load can be calculated as

$$p_{i,j} = Pr[T_{cyc}^{m_{min}+j} | T_{cyc}^{m_{min}+i}] = e^{-\frac{\Lambda}{l_p}T_{cyc}^{m_{min}+i}}\frac{\left(\frac{\Lambda}{l_p}T_{cyc}^{m_{min}+i}\right)^j}{j!}, i \geq 0, j > 0. \tag{6}$$

The transition probability to the minimum cycle time under traffic load equals

$$p_{i,0} = Pr[T_{cyc}^{m_{min}} | T_{cyc}^{m_{min}+i}] = \sum_{n \in [0, m_{min}]} e^{-\frac{\Lambda}{l_p}T_{cyc}^{m_{min}+i}}\frac{\left(\frac{\Lambda}{l_p}T_{cyc}^{m_{min}+i}\right)^n}{n!}, i \geq 0. \tag{7}$$

Table 1. Simulation parameters.

Parameter	Value	Parameter	Value
Speed of light in the fiber (c_f)	$2 \cdot 10^8$ m/s	ID packet size (l_{ID})	72 bytes
Air propagation delay (δ_a)	0.2 µs	POLL packet size (l_{POLL})	72 bytes
Number of RRF slots (s_{RRF})	10	Bit rate per data wavelength (D_u)	1 Gbps
ACK packet size (l_{ACK})	16 bytes	Maximum consecutive RRF frames	1
Data packet size (l_p)	2000 bytes	User buffer size (B)	40 packets

Thus, we derive the steady state probabilities by solving the following system.

$$\pi \mathbf{P} = \pi \tag{8}$$

$$\sum_{i=0}^{B_{max}^{all}} \pi_i = 1, \tag{9}$$

where π is the eigenvector reflecting the steady state transition probabilities to cycle time i, with i ranging from 0 to B_{max}^{all}. The average cycle time then equals

$$\overline{T_{cyc}} = \sum_{i=0}^{B_{max}^{all}} \pi_i T_{cyc}^{m_{min}+i}. \tag{10}$$

Considering that a packet is more likely to arrive at a longer cycle time, we can conclude that the probability that a packet arrives at a specific cycle is proportional to its length. Hence, the steady state probabilities are rewritten as

$$\widetilde{\pi}_i = \frac{\pi_i T_{cyc}^{m_{min}+i}}{\sum_{n=0}^{B_{max}^{all}} \pi_n T_{cyc}^{m_{min}+n}}. \tag{11}$$

It is also worth pointing out that a packet that arrives on a specific cycle will not be sent during the first transmission window, given that the user has first to notify the BBU for its buffer status and successfully receive the POLL packet before initiating the data transmission. Moreover, packet arrivals take place on average half-way between two transmission windows due to non-bursty nature of Poisson traffic. Hence, a packet stays in the queue on average for one-and-a-half cycles, and consequently the mean packet delay can be approximated by

$$\overline{X} = \frac{3}{2} \sum_{i=0}^{B_{max}^{all}} \widetilde{\pi}_i T_{cyc}^{m_{min}+i}. \tag{12}$$

5   Model Validation

5.1   Simulation Scenario

The proposed mean packet delay model was developed in MATLAB®, whereas for the simulations the Java discrete-event simulator, presented in [12], was modified accordingly so as to consider the gated service related features of gMT-MAC.

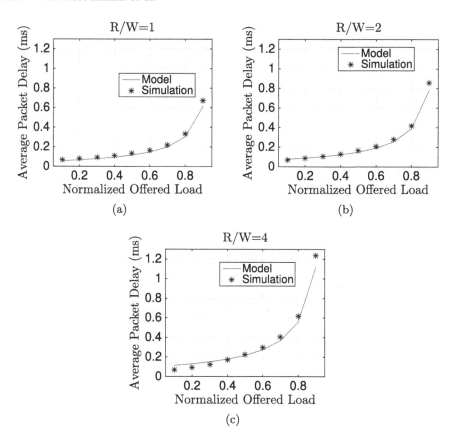

Fig. 4. Mean packet delay versus normalized offered load for different R/W ratio values: Comparison of analytical model (presented in Sect. 4) with simulation results (Sect. 3).

In our results, we study different R/W ratio values due to the high impact of this parameter on the system performance. Per RRH, $U = 5$ users are considered, while the fiber length has a mean value of $l_f = 1$ km and variance 5 m. The rest of the simulation parameters are summarized in Table 1.

5.2   Results

In Fig. 4, the mean packet delay versus the normalized offered load is shown for different R/W ratio values for both the analytical model and the simulations. Please note that the system operates under stable conditions for normalized offered load up to 0.8. In other words, the network throughput is equal to the offered load and consequently there are no dropped packets. However, above this value, the network becomes unstable, i.e., with non-zero packet drops.

The analytical model is shown to be in a very good agreement with the simulation results for all R/W ratio values, which proves the validity of both.

Nevertheless, for 0.9 normalized offered load, the network becomes unstable, making the queues susceptible to small variations caused by the probabilistic Poisson traffic, which accounts for the small model-simulations gap.

We can also observe that the mean packet delay increases with the offered load and R/W ratio value increase. It is worth pointing out, however, that in all cases, when the system operates under stable conditions, the mean packet delay remains below 1 ms. Thereby, the suitability of gMT-MAC is proved to satisfy the challenging 5G delay requirements e.g., of URLLC services.

6   Conclusions

In this paper, we proposed gMT-MAC, an MT-MAC protocol for mmWave A-RoF C-RANs, which employs gated service for maximum bandwidth efficiency. We also proposed a mean packet delay model, which was verified by means of simulation for different R/W ratio values and network load conditions. Our results showed: (i) that the proposed model closely matches the simulations, which proves the validity of both, and (ii) that gMT-MAC can be considered a promising 5G protocol able to address the challenging requirements of 5G C-RANs by offering sub-ms delay performance.

References

1. Chen, H., et al.: Ultra-reliable low latency cellular networks: use cases, challenges and approaches. IEEE Commun. Mag. **56**(12), 119–125 (2018). https://doi.org/10.1109/MCOM.2018.1701178
2. Parkvall, S., Dahlman, E., Furuskar, A., Frenne, M.: NR: the new 5G radio access technology. IEEE Commun. Stand. Mag. **1**(4), 24–30 (2017). https://doi.org/10.1109/MCOMSTD.2017.1700042
3. Agiwal, M., Roy, A., Saxena, N.: Next generation 5G wireless networks: a comprehensive survey. IEEE Commun. Surv. Tutor. **18**(3), 1617–1655 (2016). https://doi.org/10.1109/COMST.2016.2532458. Thirdquater
4. CPRI Specification: Common Public Radio Interface (CPRI); Interface Specification. IEEE Communications Standards Magazine V7.0, October 2015
5. Liu, X., Zeng, H., Chand, N., Effenberger, F.: Efficient mobile fronthaul via DSP-based channel aggregation. J. Lightwave Technol. **34**(6), 1556–1564 (2016). https://doi.org/10.1109/JLT.2015.2508451
6. Ishimura, S., Bekkali, A., Tanaka, K., Nishimura, K., Suzuki, M.: 1.032-Tb/s CPRI-equivalent rate IF-over-fiber transmission using a parallel IM/PM transmitter for high-capacity mobile fronthaul links. J. Lightwave Technol. **36**(8), 1478–1484 (2018). https://doi.org/10.1109/JLT.2017.2787151
7. Giannoulis, G., et al.: Analog radio-over-fiber solutions for 5G communications in the beyond-CPRI era. In: 2018 20th International Conference on Transparent Optical Networks (ICTON), pp. 1–5, July 2018. https://doi.org/10.1109/ICTON.2018.8473886
8. Delmade, A., et al.: Performance analysis of analog IF over fiber fronthaul link with 4G and 5G coexistence. IEEE/OSA J. Opt. Commun. Netw. **10**(3), 174–182 (2018). https://doi.org/10.1364/JOCN.10.000174

9. Novak, D., et al.: Radio-over-fiber technologies for emerging wireless systems. IEEE J. Quantum Electron. **52**(1), 1–11 (2016). https://doi.org/10.1109/JQE. 2015.2504107

10. Miyamoto, K., Kuwano, S., Terada, J., Otaka, A.: Split-PHY processing architecture to realize base station coordination and transmission bandwidth reduction in mobile fronthaul. In: 2015 Optical Fiber Communications Conference and Exhibition (OFC), pp. 1–3, March 2015. https://doi.org/10.1364/OFC.2015.M2J.4

11. Kalfas, G., Pleros, N.: An agile and medium-transparent MAC protocol for 60 GHz radio-over-fiber local access networks. J. Lightwave Technol. **28**(16), 2315–2326 (2010). https://doi.org/10.1109/JLT.2010.2046394

12. Kalfas, G., Vardakas, J., Alonso, L., Verikoukis, C., Pleros, N.: Non-saturation delay analysis of medium transparent MAC protocol for 60 GHz fiber-wireless towards 5G mm wave networks. J. Lightwave Technol. **35**(18), 3945–3955 (2017). https://doi.org/10.1109/JLT.2017.2723521

13. Kalfas, G., et al.: Client-weighted medium-transparent MAC protocol for user-centric fairness in 60 GHz radio-over-fiber WLANs. IEEE/OSA J. Opt. Commun. Netw. **6**(1), 33–44 (2014). https://doi.org/10.1364/JOCN.6.000033

14. Mesodiakaki, A., et al.: Medium-transparent dynamic bandwidth allocation for 5G fiber wireless dense fronthaul networks. In: 2018 IEEE 23rd International Workshop on Computer Aided Modeling and Design of Communication Links and Networks (CAMAD), pp. 1–6, September 2018. https://doi.org/10.1109/CAMAD. 2018.8514953

15. Ngo, M.T., Gravey, A., Bhadauria, D.: A mean value analysis approach for evaluating the performance of EPON with gated IPACT. In: 2008 International Conference on Optical Network Design and Modeling, pp. 1–6, March 2008. https://doi.org/ 10.1109/ONDM.2008.4578407

16. Miyata, S., Baba, K., Yamaoka, K.: Exact mean packet delay for delayed report messages multipoint control protocol in EPON. IEEE/OSA J. Opt. Commun. Netw. **10**(3), 209–219 (2018). https://doi.org/10.1364/JOCN.10.000209

17. Lannoo, B., Verslegers, L., Colle, D., Pickavet, M., Gagnaire, M., Demeester, P.: Analytical model for the IPACT dynamic bandwidth allocation algorithm for EPONs. J. Opt. Netw. **6**(6), 677–688 (2007). https://doi.org/10.1364/JON. 6.000677. http://jon.osa.org/abstract.cfm?URI=jon-6-6-677

18. Fan, Y., et al.: Performance analysis for IEEE 802.11 distributed coordination function in radio-over-fiber-based distributed antenna systems. Opt. Express **21**(18), 20529–20543 (2013). https://doi.org/10.1364/OE.21.020529. http://www.opticsexpress.org/abstract.cfm?URI=oe-21-18-20529

19. Pal, A., Nasipuri, A.: Performance analysis of IEEE 802.11 distributed coordination function in presence of hidden stations under non-saturated conditions with infinite buffer in radio-over-fiber wireless LANs. In: 2011 18th IEEE Workshop on Local Metropolitan Area Networks (LANMAN), pp. 1–6, October 2011. https://doi.org/ 10.1109/LANMAN.2011.6076921

20. Mjeku, M., Gomes, N.J.: Analysis of the request to send/clear to send exchange in WLAN over fiber networks. J. Lightwave Technol. **26**(15), 2531–2539 (2008). https://doi.org/10.1109/JLT.2008.927202

12 Gb/s Multiband Fiber-Wireless Link Using Coherent IFoF and V-band mmWave Radio

Nikos Argyris[1]([✉]), Giannis Giannoulis[2], Konstantina Kanta[2], Panagiotis Toumasis[2], Dimitrios Apostolopoulos[2], and Hercules Avramopoulos[2]

[1] Mellanox Technologies Ltd., Hakidma 26, 2069200 Yokneam, Israel
nikosa@mellanox.com

[2] National Technical University of Athens, Iroon Polytechniou 9, 15780 Zografou, Greece

Abstract. We experimentally demonstrate two Analog Mobile Fronthaul concepts exploiting coherent optical systems technology. Single Sideband generation and coherent detection of a 12 Gb/s signal with 6 subcarriers using an IQ modulator is presented along with an extended reach Fiber-Wireless transmission concept using IQM-DD system and V-band radio.

Keywords: Coherent communications · Radio frequency photonics · Fiber optics communications

1 Introduction

The 5G hype continues to grow; Targeting the use case of Gigabit connectivity to the user, early deployments focus on the Fixed Wireless Access (FWA) scenarios, while their first commercialization stages continue to gain momentum as a potential investment [1]. In order to meet the high traffic densities, peak data rates and low-latency requirements of 5G mobile connections, the fiber-based Mobile Fronthaul (MFH) needs to be revisited through cost-efficient optical transport solutions [2]. To this end, analog Intermediate Frequency and Analog Radio-over-Fiber (IFoF/A-RoF) solutions have been intensively promoted from the research community as a path to overcome the low bandwidth efficiency of the Common Public Radio Interface (CPRI), which lacks scalability in high-capacity interconnections between the Baseband Unit (BBU) and a high number of mmWave Remote Radio Heads (RRHs). The Digital Signal Processing (DSP)-assisted IFoF has been investigated as an option for spectrally efficient FH architectures, employing Intensity Modulation/Direct Detection (IM/DD) schemes over linear low-bandwidth optoelectronics [3]. Moreover, as network operators are focusing on a more demand-driven network planning through centralized architectures and network densification [4], has led to research activities towards unlocking the bandwidth of mmWave bands for Gigabit capacity fiber/wireless fronthaul links to multiple pico/femto cells [5].

Entering the beyond-CPRI era, optical IQ Modulation (IQM) carrying native radio waveforms could also be considered as an approach to further support the above-mentioned capacity increase. By introducing a second dimension on the modulation

A. Tzanakaki et al. (Eds.): ONDM 2019, LNCS 11616, pp. 437–443, 2020.
https://doi.org/10.1007/978-3-030-38085-4_37

space, which results in doubling the link capacity, a link featuring higher immunity to transmission impairments is also feasible. Since both magnitude and phase components of the optical field are modulated, effects such as chromatic dispersion can be pre-compensated, thus improving power and noise margins of the link [6]. Moreover, modulation of the optical carrier in both dimensions has been widely investigated as it offers extended dynamic ranges compared to schemes based solely on the modulation of optical intensity and significant gains on the driving RF signals can be obtained, compared to IM/DD schemes [7]. Leveraging the penetration of coherent systems, even for the last mile of optical access, the transmission of coherent analog RoF signals over coherent Passive Optical Network (PON) infrastructure, can be nowadays considered as a competitive MFH solution for specific 5G-related concepts [8]. Their proven coexistence with baseband optics, allows for sharing existing fiber infrastructure dedicated for coherent PON links and coherent Tx/Rx equipment allowing for generate/detect wideband RoF waveforms [9]. Such equipment reuse enables for further cost savings lowering installation expenses of new equipment for the fronthaul deployment [10].

Within this paper we present two experimental demonstrations which introduce the Coherent IFoF transport into FWA scenarios with Gb/s capacity. First, we validate the feasibility of Single Sideband (SSB) IFoF transmission using IQM and coherent detection on a 12 Gb/s Digital Subcarrier Multiplexed (SCM) signal with 6 bands. It is shown that the performance of the SSB scheme exceeds its Double Sideband (DSB) counterpart in terms of Error Vector Magnitude (EVM). Our presented transport scheme can be also adopted in centralized radio access topologies where all the digital stages are removed from the RRHs. To this end we demonstrate a second scenario for a downlink Fiber-Wireless interconnection (Fi-Wi) in which SSB IFoF using an IQM-DD scheme is combined with V-band radio equipment for wireless indoor transmission. Raw capacity of 12 Gb/s with EVM below the 3GPP specification is achieved for 25-km and 50-km long fiber and 5-m wireless links showcasing the immunity to chromatic dispersion induced power fading.

2 Multi-band SSB IFoF Using IQ Modulation and Coherent Detection

In the context of exploiting existing coherent optical link topology, we demonstrate transmission of an IFoF signal using IQ modulation (IQM) and coherent detection. In addition to its cost-efficient features, due to existing hardware reuse, the proposed implementation allows for mitigation of chromatic dispersion induced power fading of the IFoF signals. The IQ modulators at the coherent transmitter side can provide an optical SSB (OSSB) signal using Hilbert transformation (HT) in the driving signals on the RF domain [11]. The analytical signal (SSB equivalent) is defined as a complex signal with real and imaginary parts consisting of the signal itself and its Hilbert transform respectively. Feeding the two signals (real and imaginary part) into the In-phase and Quadrature inputs of the modulator, the resulting optical spectrum at the transmitter output consists only of its lower sideband. The experimental setup is illustrated in Fig. 1a.

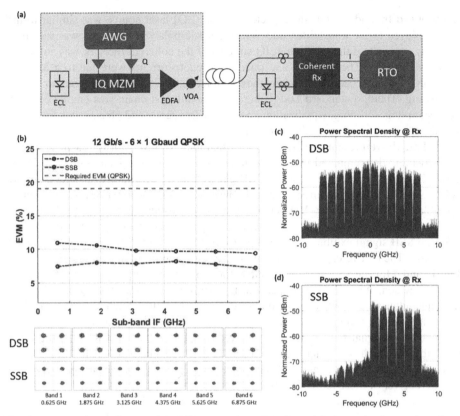

Fig. 1. (a) Experimental setup of the SSB generation using IQ modulation and coherent detection. (b) EVM Diagram per band and respective constellations for the DSB and SSB transmission in back-to-back configuration. (c) Recovered spectra after coherent reception of DSB and (d) SSB generated multiband schemes.

As a reference signal, we are considering a SCM signal consisting of 6 bands at equidistant IF carriers, with a total bandwidth of 7.2 GHz. An Arbitrary Waveform Generator (AWG) was used to provide the data signals for both In-phase and Quadrature streams for the multiband scheme. The SCM signal and its Hilbert transform were digitally synthesized and loaded into the Generator's memory. Each subcarrier was Quadrature Phase Shift Keying (QPSK) modulated at 1 Gbd, while the subcarrier frequencies were at 0.625 GHz, 1.875 GHz, 3.125 GHz, 4.375 GHz, 5.625 GHz and 6.875 GHz. Pulse shaping using Root Raised Cosine (RRC) shaping filters with roll-off factor $\alpha = 0.2$ and digital linear pre-distortion of the optoelectronic components' frequency response were also performed. Both RF streams were amplified by two linear drivers to achieve voltage levels of ~5 Vpp at the RF inputs of the modulator. An External Cavity Laser (ECL) with ~100 kHz linewidth, provided the optical carrier at 1545.45 nm to the IQ MZM while an EDFA followed by a Variable Optical Attenuator (VOA) was employed to set the launch power of the optical transmitter. A polarization diversity coherent receiver was used for intradyne detection, with input signal and Local Oscillator (LO) power levels at 0 dBm and +10 dBm respectively. The (LO) laser source was similar to the one employed at the transmitter side. Since a single polarization signal was transmitted, only one pair of the two output IQ streams of the coherent receiver was sufficient for demodulation. The in-phase and quadrature photocurrents were fed to a 33 GHz Real Time Oscilloscope (RTO) where they sampled at 80 GSa/s and digitized for offline processing. There, a standard DSP coherent demodulation chain was employed, with downsampling, retiming, equalization and carrier frequency and phase recovery stages yielding the final estimate of the received signal.

In Fig. 1b we present the Error Vector Magnitude (EVM) plot for each subcarrier after coherent detection and DSP for both the Single (SSB) and Dual Sideband (DSB) cases. It should be noted that for the DSB generation the quadrature channel from the AWG was switched off, while the optical power at the EDFA output was tuned using a Variable Optical Attenuator (VOA) in order to keep constant the same optical power at the transmitter output as in the SSB case. It is observed that after coherent reception and DSP the SSB signal exhibits improved performance of ~2.26% EVM compared to the DSB case. The recovered spectra after coherent reception for both cases are depicted in Fig. 1c and d for the SSB signal, as well as for its DSB counterpart, are also depicted.

It is evident that the SSB property at the RF domain before the IQ modulator at the transmitter side is also preserved after coherent detection. Such a feature could be a potential solution to interconnect IFoF/RoF links with IQ baseband Radio frontends, without any external mixing stages at the radio equipment of an RRH. On the other hand, this approach comes at the cost of using an additional laser source for the coherent receiver, which in turn poses increased processing demands for carrier recovery on a digital receiver of these radio signals.

3   25 km/50 km Fiber and 5 m V-band Wireless Transmission with SSB Using IQM-DD

The robust performance of the SSB scheme against the optical power fading, induced by the interplay of fiber's chromatic dispersion and the chirp of analog RoF transmitters [5], is a prerequisite for transmitting IFoF and RoF signals without imposing limits on the range of the possible fiber link lengths but extending them to longer distances. As presented in [3] the performance of a DSB multi-band IFoF signal is strongly limited by the chromatic dispersion fading for a 25 km link, with the bands close to 8 GHz being the ones exhibiting severe degradation. In the previous section, we proved that an optical IQ modulator facilitated SSB generation of such multiband radio signals. By modifying the topologies presented in [3] and [12] from IM-DD to IQM-DD, as shown in the testbed of Fig. 2, we implemented an extended-reach Fi Wi link with up to 50 km fiber and 5 m wireless distances.

Similarly to Sect. 2, we consider the same reference signal to be a SCM scheme consisting of 6 similar bands at equidistant IF carriers to be SSB generated by the IQ Modulator. After the fiber link (25 km or 50 km SSMF) we employ Direct Detection using a 10 GHz photoreceiver composed of a PIN photodiode (0.7 A/W responsivity) and a low noise Transimpedance Amplifier (TIA of 20 dB gain). The output fed into a mmWave upconverter (Noise Figure of 8 dB) connected to a V-band directional Tx

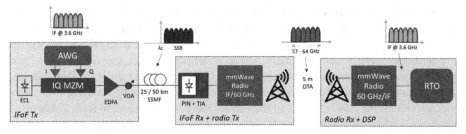

Fig. 2. Experimental setup for the 50 km fiber and 5 m V-band wireless transmission using IQM-DD for OSSB generation.

antenna. The signal was received by an identical antenna (Rx), located at a 5 m horizontal distance from the Tx-antenna. Standard pyramidal gain horn V-band antennas of 23 dBi gain and 10° beamwidth were employed to realize the Over The Air (OTA) transmission link. After the mmWave-to-IF downconversion, we evaluated the Fiber-Wireless (Fi-Wi) link on the receiver side by performing offline DSP on the digitized data acquired by the above-mentioned real time oscilloscope. At the receiver side DSP, downsampling to 2 samples/symbol, retiming and carrier recovery and equalization stages were employed to mitigate for the transmission impairments of the combined Fi-Wi link.

The EVM performance of the proposed Fi-Wi scheme is illustrated in Fig. 3. For the 25 km fiber and 5 m wireless link, the performance of all 6 subcarriers of the multiplexed signal were well below the EVM threshold of 3GPP, achieving an average 6% EVM margin. For the FiWi transmission on the 50 km fiber and 5 m wireless link the margin is reduced to minimum values however achieving acceptable performance [13]. The above EVM performance achieved for all the different bands after the fiber/wireless

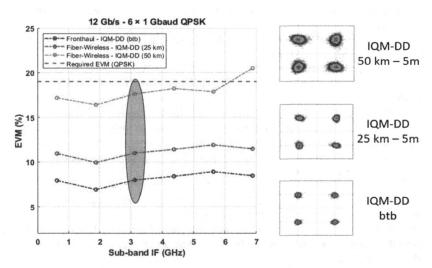

Fig. 3. EVM diagram per band for the FiWi transmission of the SSB signal using IQM-DD RoF transmission. Constellation diagrams are included for the 3.125 GHz IF.

transmission for both cases reveal the immunity of the analog IFoF transport against the fiber transmission impairments, compared to the results shown in [3]. It is also evident that the EVM penalty for the longer fiber transmission (50 km SSMF) is associated only with the lower received optical power which approaches the sensitivity of the photoreceiver. Therefore, it is evident that an IFoF link, using an IQM-DD scheme, achieves cancelation of the chromatic dispersion induced fading even for long fiber links, given that the power budget of the link supports transmission to such distances.

4 Conclusion

We have demonstrated two experimental concepts where the use of coherent optical transceivers supports high capacity FWA connectivity through IFoF. SSB generation of a 12 Gb/s signal with 6 QPSK subcarriers using an IQ modulation is successfully detected using a coherent receiver, allowing for possible coexistence between Analog MFH and coherent PON infrastructure. On top of this, a Fiber-Wireless Fronthaul scenario with extended fiber reach (50 km) capabilities is showcased by an IQM-DD system where the SSB IFoF signal exhibits high tolerance against fading impairments due to fiber chromatic dispersion. Successful Fiber-Wireless transmission using V-band radio equipment is verified with EVM performance within the specifications of the 3GPP standards.

Acknowledgement. This work was supported by the H2020 5G-PPP Phase 2 project 5G PHOS (761989).

References

1. 5G Fixed Wireless Gigabit Services Today: An Industry Overview, Open license white paper, November 2017
2. Lim, C.: Evolution of radio-over-fiber technologies: past and present. In: Proceedings of ECOC 2018, Rome, Italy, September 2018 (2018)
3. Argyris, N., et al.: DSP enabled fiber-wireless IFoF/mmWave link for 5G analog mobile fronthaul. In: Proceedings of IEEE 5G World Forum, Santa Clara, CA, USA, July 2018 (2018)
4. China Mobile: C-RAN: The Road Towards Green RAN, White Paper (2011)
5. Argyris, N., et al.: A 5G mmWave fiber-wireless IFoF analog mobile fronthaul link with up to 24 Gb/s multi-band wireless capacity. J. Lightwave Technol. **37**, 2883–2891 (2019)
6. Killey, R.I., et al.: Electronic dispersion compensation by signal predistortion. In: 2006 Optical Fiber Communication Conference and the National Fiber Optic Engineers Conference, Anaheim, CA, p. 3 (2006). https://doi.org/10.1109/ofc.2006.215449
7. Zibar, D., et al.: DSP based coherent receiver for phase-modulated radio-over-fiber optical links. In: Proceedings of OFC 2008, San Diego, CA, USA, February 2008 (2008)
8. Schrenk, B.: Full-duplex coherent radio-over-fiber transmission over 1:128 split PON using an EML as bidirectional RRH optics. In: Proceedings of OFC 2018, San Diego, CA, USA, March 2018 (2018)
9. Prince, K., et al.: Converged wireline and wireless access over a 78-km deployed fiber long-reach WDM PON. IEEE Photon. Technol. Lett. **21**(17), 1274–1276 (2009)

10. Arevalo, G.V., et al.: Techno-economics for optimal deployment of optical fronthauling for 5G in large urban areas. In: Proceedings of ICTON 2018, Bucharest, Romania, July 2018 (2018)
11. Smith, G.H., et al.: Overcoming chromatic-dispersion effects in fiber-wireless systems incorporating external modulators. IEEE Trans. Microw. Theory Tech. **45**(8), 1410–1415 (1997)
12. Vagionas, C., et al.: A 6-band 12 Gb/s IFoF/V-band fiber-wireless fronthaul link using an InP externally modulated laser. In: Proceedings of ECOC 2018, Rome Italy, September 2018 (2018)
13. GPP, TS 38.104 V15.0.0, Table 9.6.2.3-1, December 2017

System Innovations in Inter Data Center Transport Networks

Loukas Paraschis[1]([⊠]) [ID], Harald Bock[2], Parthiban Kandappan[1],
Bernd Sommerkorn-Krombholz[2], Joao Pedro[3], Abhinava Sadasivarao[1] [ID],
Sharfuddin Syed[1], Jeff Rahn[1], Paul Doolan[1], and Biao Lu[1]

[1] Infinera Corporation, Sunnyvale, USA
lparaschis@infinera.com
[2] Infinera Corporation, Munich, Germany
[3] Infinera Corporation, Lisbon, Portugal

Abstract. We review the most important WDM DCI system innovations. State-of-the-art coherent transmission has already exceeded 6 b/s/Hz, using subcarrier modulation. The adoption of software innovations in automation and programmability, that DCI pioneered in transport networks, has also simplified operations and enables the emergence of "open" transport architectures. Combining these advancements with emerging network analytics frameworks allows exciting innovations in network design and management optimization.

Keywords: DCI · WDM · SDN · Coherent · Optical transport · Network design · Analytics

1 Introduction

Traffic on the networks interconnecting data centers (DC), referred to as data center interconnect (DCI) networks, has grown more than any other transport network traffic type [1–3], and has been projected to grow by at least two more orders of magnitude [3, 4]. The economics associated with this growth have motivated the building of dedicated DCI networks, and of a new class of purpose-built systems that are optimized for the DCI requirements [5, 6]. In many respects, the growth of DCI has been the most significant development in optical transport networking this decade, and its most significant evolution since the major transitions from TDM to IP/MPLS and WDM [6, 7].

While DCI has a few things in common with traditional telecommunication transport, for example most of the current WDM technology employed in DCI is the same as that used in telecom networks, the DCI transport networks have a substantial number of unique characteristics (both architectural and operational) that have motivated the development of a new class of DCI-optimized packet and optical transport systems [5, 6]. More specifically, DCI-optimized transport systems have been developed to address the DC operational environment, with requirements for lower power and cost per Gb/s, for simpler DCI routing that focus on maximizing throughput rather than routing scale,

© IFIP International Federation for Information Processing 2020
Published by Springer Nature Switzerland AG 2020
A. Tzanakaki et al. (Eds.): ONDM 2019, LNCS 11616, pp. 444–451, 2020.
https://doi.org/10.1007/978-3-030-38085-4_38

and for high capacity, typically point-to-point, WDM systems that maximize spectral efficiency by employing state-of-the-art coherent transmission (summarized in Sect. 2) [4–6].

Moreover, DCI transport networking has also pioneered the extensive adoption of significant software innovations [6, 8–13] in programmability, automation, management abstraction, and control-plane disaggregation, typically referred collectively as SDN (summarized in Sect. 3). This new DCI-optimized infrastructure is increasingly being deployed globally and has leveraged SDN to enable important innovations in open transport network architectures. In addition these new networks account for some of the most spectrally-efficient fiber deployments, that already exceed 6 b/s/Hz even in very long subsea routes, leveraging digital subcarriers and advancements in photonic-integration [14, 15] and will, by 2020, improve by an additional 20% leveraging constellation shaping [16] and further advancements in photonic-integration [17]. This paper summarizes the main WDM system innovations that have facilitated this explosive DCI evolution, and then presents (in Sect. 4) some important recent innovations in optical transport design achieved by combining the advancements in coherent open WDM with extensible software/SDN infrastructure. More specifically, this novel networking paradigm usually couples recent advancements in streaming-telemetry methodologies [10, 13] with emerging network analytics frameworks [13, 18]. These are often combined with machine-learning [18], to improve capacity (e.g. optical margin) optimization [18, 19], as well as enhancing (e.g. predictive) management and control [13, 20].

2 Coherent WDM Transmission

Widespread adoption of coherent communication in WDM networks has enabled significant increases in per-fiber capacities. A decade ago, on-off keying modulation could support 1–2 Tb/s on a single fiber. This increased to 5 Tb/s using the first generation of coherent signaling, and further expanded to 30–40 Tb/s with the best available technology today.

First-generation coherent systems supported QPSK modulation and hard-decision forward error correction. Fiber capacity was increased using two orthogonal polarizations of the optical signal. In addition, the ability to use coherent mixing to select a single channel enabled inexpensive colorless de-multiplexing. Dispersion compensation could also be accomplished using digital signal processing (DSP). As a result, flexible add/drop line systems have changed dramatically to leverage the capabilities of coherent systems. Since the initial introduction, significant improvements have made their way into coherent systems. The use of DSP has expanded to the transmitter, enabling higher order modulation(s) than QPSK, and introducing near-Nyquist shaping to improve spectral efficiency. ADC and DAC technology have both improved dramatically. Lasers have been tailored for low linewidth to support higher order modulation. Advanced signal processing such as Nyquist subcarriers have further improved nonlinear performance and tolerance to dispersion. All these improvements have helped increase bandwidth and drive down cost per bit.

The most spectrally-efficient deployed fiber networks today already exceed 6 b/s/Hz, leveraging digital subcarriers and advancements in photonic integration [14, 15]. By 2020, constellation shaping [16] and further advancements in photonic-integration [17] will provide an additional 20% improvement of spectral density for a given reach performance.

3 Software Innovations and SDN

The unique operational characteristics of the cloud DCs have also given rise to novel software requirements, and innovation opportunities for DCI [5, 6, 8–11]. More specifically, DC operators pioneered the pervasive use of DevOps and software automation techniques, initially to serve their hyperscale compute infrastructure needs [8, 11, 21, 22]. Incorporating equivalent software innovations to advance the functionality of DCI networks has led to the introduction of network programmability, automation, management abstraction, and control-plane disaggregation, often referred collectively as SDN transport [6, 8–13]. While many of these SDN innovations were initially introduced in DCI packet transport, their more recent adoption in DCI optical systems has been an even more radical innovation because traditional optical network management has previously been based on proprietary (vendor-specific) NMS [5, 9]. The most notable example has been the use of extensive API frameworks based on YANG data models, and the related NETCONF, RESTCONF, and gRPC interfaces, which we identify as model-driven networking (MDN) [9–13]. These APIs enable DCI network operators to develop new transport automation and abstraction frameworks [10, 11]. OpenConfig is one such widely adopted API [10] and is currently supported by all major DCI transport system vendors [3, 12, 13]. Other, more recent, important MDN efforts are also in progress, aiming for enhancements in the MDN robustness and functionality, beyond OpenConfig [11, 13].

MDN innovations have also catalyzed newer forms of performance monitoring, particularly streaming telemetry which was pioneered in DCI transport and aimed to resolve the limitations of the traditional SNMP data pull approaches [8, 10, 11]. These new telemetry frameworks, have enabled two important innovations in WDM systems: First, they facilitate more manageable reporting of a greater number of network and system parameters, such as transmit and receive optical power, Pre-FEC and Post-FEC statistics, amplifier parameters, dispersion, severity of alarms, client and line side laser temperatures, device/port up/down status, etc. Second, and even more important, MDN based non-proprietary frameworks allow the end-user extensive flexibility in defining the desired content (more or less info), the method (e.g. data encoding mechanism), and the granularity (from milliseconds to hours) of the network monitoring mechanisms; e.g. [12]. Such advanced monitoring flexibility also allows transport to be more effectively integrated in to the network management and control planes, and more easily combined with machine-learning techniques [21], towards advanced network analytics [13, 19]. Network analytics aims to identify, based on operator defined trigger points, potential drifts in parameters and notify network operations for actionable remedial steps that would allow for sufficient time to anticipate and plan repair maintenance and recovery, minimizing potential down times [11, 20–22]. For DCI operators such new network analytics frameworks, based on innovations in streaming telemetry methodologies, are being increasingly considered an important evolution of network management and mediation and have recently been combined with cognitive systems [11, 20]. A typical cognitive system, comprising of utilizing PM telemetry streaming, along with policy-based operations and maintenance, was demonstrated in a proof-of-concept by a leading North American service provider [20]. In that example, the system continually monitors the bandwidth utilization and based on real-time analytics, takes policy defined action to increase the available bandwidth by creating additional services automatically.

Along with the increased openness and programmability comes the need to advance the system control-plane and network management abstraction beyond vendor specific, usually proprietary, implementations. This effort is part of a much wider networking effort to adopt intent-based configuration frameworks [8], which is not specific to transport. It requires that network layers are controlled by an SDN Controller or NMS that maintains global network state and monitors the entire network (including optical transport) for changes. Based on this global state (and the operator intent), the Controller decides when the network needs to transition from one state to another. In the simplest scenario of optical capacity expansion *(State A to State B)*, where A is a steady-state optical network operating at capacity X, and B is the optical network with increased capacity $X' > X$, the Controller sends the entire configuration (including ones that don't need change) to each NE. In such a declarative configuration management (DCM) scenario, the NEs identify and apply only the required change e.g., turn-up extra wavelengths, with the (combined) end-result being the increase in network capacity to X'. Much like the other such SDN innovations, DCM has been initially introduced in network switching and routing systems. However, we consider the recent extension of DCM, and more generally intent-based networking to WDM transport, which was again pioneered in next generation DCI WDM systems [13], to be very exciting because it enables network operations and capacity to be optimized (potentially dynamically) based on network parameters and operator policy rules [13].

Finally, DCI network element MDN programmability is now being enhanced to accommodate third-party software agent extensibility, which would allow applications developed by a network operator to interact with the DCI transport system NEs [11, 13]. For example, [13] described the first to our knowledge, implementation in a WDM system of such SW-agent based operational extensibility, which specifically focused on network analytics applications. Note that the advancements in MDN, including the DCM, and SW agent extensibility, benefit all transport use-cases, not just DCI, becoming particularly valuable in improving the operational efficiency (OpEx) of large-scale deployments [20].

Moreover, while the first explicit goal of these software innovations has been to improve operational efficiency, and thus reduce OpEx, these innovations can also improve CapEx by enabling open and vendor-agnostic network management. In this sense, they are becoming the first important step towards open line-system (OLS) architectures, which can then be combined with emerging network analytics and machine-learning, to improve capacity (e.g. optical margin) optimization [18, 19, 23, 24], which we discuss in the next section.

4 Innovations in Network Design and Optimization

Recently, for network planning purposes, system providers and even more DCI operators have moved away from vendor agnostic, offline planning tools towards novel strategies to optimize the capacity-reach trade-off of their network. The original approach of stacking margins within traditional planning tools that reflect component performance variations, system aging, network evolution and other network level effects is truly not efficient. In order to cope with the outlined need for OpEx and CapEx reductions a new paradigm in planning is required. Leveraging new technologies such as performance, baud- and bit-rate flexible transponders, and leveraging the ability of streaming telemetry data enable live monitoring and *Current State of Life* determination of the optical performance, providing the current present margin in the network.

In a very recent field trial in Telia Carrier, a Tier 1 European service provider, the benefit of this paradigm has been demonstrated [25], and Infinera Aware technology has proven to address it in combination with a new class of transponder [26]. We refer to this transponder class as autonomous intelligent transponder (AIT) as it takes advantage a host of information of information today's digital signal processors provide such as signal-to-noise ratio (SNR), accumulated chromatic dispersion and differential group delay, to name a few, in order to autonomously adapt transmission parameters to the current quality of the transmission link. The main benefit of this approach is that channel capacity (or any other suitable metric) is maximized at every point in time without manual setup or configuration. We conducted the field trial in Telia Carrier's production European backbone network. The link connects Munich, Zürich, Strasbourg, and Frankfurt over Infinera's hiT 7300 multi-haul optical line system. The link consists of 20 spans of standard single mode fiber (SSMF) with a total link length of 1500 km, 14 inline amplifiers (half pure EDFA and half hybrid EDFA Raman), and 7 ROADMs. The AITs were installed in Munich, simplifying configuration and operation during the trial. Apart from other live traffic channels our channels under test occupied the spectrum from 191.6 THz to 192.0 THz in both directions with 50 GHz channel spacing. The AIT channel was placed in the middle with four 100 Gb/s DP-4QAM neighbor channels on either side.

The BER of the neighbor channels, which were provided by Infinera's Groove G30 platform, were monitored during the whole trial to capture any impact from their adaptively switching AIT neighbor. We discovered that in its current implementation the standalone AIT capacity solution does not achieve optimum efficiency in the presence of nonlinearities coming mainly from direct neighbor channels, i.e. it provides an OSNR margin larger than necessary. We conclude that with different slopes of the BER vs. OSNR curves in the presence of non-linearities, the actual margin is underestimated. We chose to estimate the amount of nonlinear distortion and real OSNR as a result of running the Infinera Aware Technology solution [18]. We gained 1.0 dB in OSNR and 20% higher bit rate by combination of AIT and Aware in the field trial scenario (Fig. 1).

This example clearly demonstrates how this new approach to optimizing optical performance in a network can help increase available bandwidth in a given installation and so maximize network utilization. Combining this performance analytics approach with machine learning techniques will open an additional range of functions and possibilities that will support planning and operations within an open networking environment.

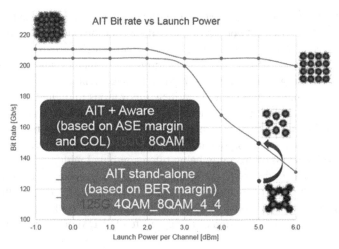

Fig. 1. Optimum AIT bit rate vs. launch power per channel after 1500 km plus additional 50 km NZDSF span. The curves show AIT stand-alone results with 0.5 dB OSNR margin (blue curve with and orange curve without neighbor channels). Red markers show AIT stand-alone result with 1.5 dB OSNR margin (circle) and AIT + Aware result with 1.5 dB ASE margin (star). (Color figure online)

One specific use-case that is relevant in this context is the prediction of the optical reach of new lightpaths in disaggregated and open DWDM line systems. Usually, there is no agreed and truly valid performance model for such a multi-vendor and sometimes even multi-technology environment. Upgrading these networks with additional capacity is not straightforward as optical performance of new channels can only be predicted with very limited accuracy.

This challenge can be overcome by the combination of optical performance monitoring on the installed system with machine learning techniques. The accuracy of such predictions will obviously improve over time as the number of installed lightpaths increases, generating more training data to retrain a machine learning-based performance estimator. and can significantly simplify operational and planning procedures in open DWDM networking.

In particular, the information generated by the Infinera Aware Technology during a network optimization cycle, can be used successfully by machine learning tools to accurately predict performance of new lightpaths in an open line system with disaggregated transponders [19, 24].

5   Conclusion

This paper summarized the evolution and innovations of purpose-built DCI transport systems that enable some of the most spectrally-efficient fiber networks deployed today. Most notably, state-of-the-art coherent WDM transmission has leveraged subcarrier modulation to exceed 6 b/s/Hz even in subsea routes. Also, it will soon incorporate real-world implementations of constellation shaping to enhance the system performance by an additional 1 dB and offer finely granular optimization of channel capacity per optical link. At the same time, DCI networks are leading the way in the extensive adoption of software innovations to simplify operations and enable open transport architectures. Often collectively referred to as SDN, these innovations really include major steps towards increased network programmability, automation, management abstraction, and control-plane disaggregation. Moreover, important new innovations in optical transport design are achieved combining the advancements in coherent WDM with an open and extensible software/SDN infrastructure. This novel networking paradigm usually combines recent advancements in streaming-telemetry methodologies with emerging network analytics frameworks, and more recently being often combined with machine-learning, to improve capacity (e.g. optical margin) optimization, as well as network operations based on enhanced (e.g. predictive) management and control. More specifically, the example use-cases discussed here demonstrate the promise of analytics tools as well as machine learning technology in the operation of disaggregated DWDM environments.

Acknowledgement. We would like to acknowledge insightful interactions related to this work with many colleagues in the industry and academia, and especially Anders Lindgren and Stefan Melin at Telia Company.

References

1. Holzle, U.: A ubiquitous cloud requires a transparent network. In: IEEE/OSA Conference on Optical Fiber Communications (OFC), Plenary (2017)
2. Vusirikala, V.: SDN enabled programmable, dynamic optical layer. In: European Conference on Communications (ECOC), Plenary (2017)
3. Global Cloud Index. www.cisco.com/c/en/us/solutions/collateral/service-provider/global-cloud-index-gci/white-paper-c11-738085.html. Accessed 21 Mar 2019
4. Hamilton, J.: How Many Data Centers Needed World-Wide. https://perspectives.mvdirona.com/2017/04/how-many-data-centers-needed-world-wide. Accessed 24 Mar 2019
5. Koley, B., et al.: Future needs of WDM transport for inter-datacenter interconnections. In: IEEE/OSA Conference on Optical Fiber Communications (OFC), M2E1 (2014)
6. Paraschis, L., Kannan, R.: Innovations in inter data center transport networks, chap. 17. In: Optical Fiber Telecommunications VII, Elsevier (2019). ISBN 978-0128165027
7. Paraschis, L.: Advancements in metro regional and core transport network architectures for the next-generation internet, chap. 18. In: Optical Fiber Telecommunications VI Volume B, Systems and Networks, Elsevier, pp. 793–817 (2016). ISBN 978-0123969606
8. Koley, B.: The zero touch network. In: IEEE 12th International Conference on Network and Service Management, Keynote (2016)
9. Paraschis, L.: SDN innovations in WAN. In: Optical Internetworking Forum (OIF), Plenary presentation (oif2015.083) (2015)
10. Shaikh, A., et al.: Vendor-neutral network representations for transport SDN. In: IEEE/OSA Conference on Optical Fiber Communications (OFC), Th4G.3 (2016)
11. Symposium on "Transport Network Management and Analytics innovations", IEEE/OSA Conference on Optical Fiber Communications (OFC) Tu3H (2018)
12. Sadasivarao, A., et al.: High performance streaming telemetry in optical transport networks. In: IEEE/OSA Conference on Optical Fiber Communications (OFC), Tu3D.3 (2018)

13. Sadasivarao, A., et al.: Demonstration of advanced open WDM operations and analytics, based on an application-extensible, declarative, data model abstracted instrumentation platform. In: IEEE/OSA Conference on Optical Fiber Communications (OFC), M3Z.1 (2019)
14. Rahn, J., et al.: DSP-enabled frequency locking for near-Nyquist spectral efficiency superchannels utilizing integrated photonics. In: IEEE/OSA Conference on Optical Fiber Communications (OFC), W1B.3 (2018)
15. Grubb, S., et al.: Real-time 16QAM transatlantic record spectral efficiency of 6.21 b/s/Hz enabling 26.2 Tbps capacity. In: IEEE/OSA Conference on Optical Fiber Communications (OFC), M2E.6 (2019)
16. Maher, R., et al.: Constellation shaped 66 GBd DP-1024QAM transceiver with 400 km transmission over standard SMF. In: Proceedings of European Conference on Communications (ECOC), PDPB2 (2017)
17. Going, R., et al.: Multi-channel InP-based coherent PICs with hybrid integrated SiGe electronics operating up to 100 GBd, 32QAM. In: Proceedings of European Conference on Optical Communication (ECOC) Th.PDP.C.3 (2017)
18. Slovak, J., et al.: Aware optical networks: leaving the lab. J. Opt. Commun. Netw. (JOCN) 11(2), A134 (2018)
19. Morais, R.M., Pedro, J.: Machine learning models for estimating quality of transmission in DWDM networks. J. Opt. Commun. Netw. (JOCN) 10(10), D84 (2018)
20. Infinera Press Release. https://www.infinera.com/centurylink-and-infinera-on-the-path-toward-the-cognitive-network. Accessed 24 Mar 2019
21. Barroso, L.A., et al.: The Datacenter as a Computer - An Introduction to the Design of Warehouse-Scale Machines. Morgan & Claypool, San Rafael (2009)
22. Gill, V., et al.: Worse is better. In: NANOG 49, San Francisco, June 14 (2010)
23. Wu, X., et al.: Applications of artificial neural networks in optical performance monitoring. J. Lightwave Technol. (JLT) 27(16), 3580–3589 (2009)
24. Singh, R., et al.: RADWAN: rate adaptive wide area network. In: Proceedings of SIGCOMM (2018)
25. Telia Carrier Press Release. https://www.teliacarrier.com/Press-room/Press-releases/Mar-13-2018.html. Accessed 24 Mar 2019
26. Infinera Press Release. https://www.infinera.com/telia-carrier-infinera-demonstrate-industry-first-autonomous-intelligent-transponder-live-network-field-trial. Accessed 25 Mar 2019

SDN Control of Disaggregated Optical Networks with OpenConfig and OpenROADM

Ramon Casellas[ID], Ricard Vilalta[✉][ID], Ricardo Martínez[ID], and Raúl Muñoz[ID]

CTTC/CERCA, Av. Carl Friedrich Gauss, 7, 08860 Castelldefels, Spain
ramon.casellas@cttc.es

Abstract. Most deployed optical transport networks are proprietary, behaving as a closed, highly coupled, single-vendor managed domain. Although their control planes and management systems may export high-level and open northbound interfaces (NBI), the internal details and interfaces are not disclosed to the network operator. However, driven by the requirements of telecommunication and data-center operators and the need to keep costs down while supporting sustained traffic increase, a trend known as disaggregation has steadily emerged during the past years. It involves composing and assembling open and available components, devices and sub-systems into optical infrastructures and networks, combining "best-in-class" devices, tailored to the specific needs of the aforementioned operators. It has been motivated by factors such as an increase in hardware commoditization, a perceived different rate of innovation of the different components, a promised acceleration in service deployment, or the consequent reduction in operational and capacity expenses. In practice, disaggregation brings multiple challenges, depending on the level that applies (e.g., partial or total, down to each of the optical components) and is taking place in stages. It is commonly accepted that disaggregation implies a trade-off between: (i) the opportunities due to the new degree of flexibility provided by component migration and upgrades without vendor lock-in and (ii) the potential decrease in performance compared to fully integrated systems and the underlying complexity – including interoperability -, critical in full disaggregation scenarios. From the point of view of control and management, disaggregation heavily relies on the adoption of open interfaces exporting hardware programmability. Disaggregated optical networks are an important use case for the adoption or a unified, model-driven development. In this paper, tutorial in nature, we will introduce the main concepts behind Software Defined Networking (SDN) for disaggregated optical networks, presenting reference architectures and industry common practices related to the adoption of a unified, model driven approach. The second part will cover an overview of selected deployment models (e.g., addressing transceiver and OLS disaggregation) as well as the OpenConfig and OpenROADM optical device models and Transport API (TAPI) interfaces, which constitute the main elements of the implemented SDN control plane. Such control plane targets mainly the metro segment, as defined within the EC Metro-Haul and ONF ODTN projects.

Keywords: SDN · Disaggregated optical networks · NETCONF/YANG · RESTConf · OpenROADM · OpenConfig

© IFIP International Federation for Information Processing 2020
Published by Springer Nature Switzerland AG 2020
A. Tzanakaki et al. (Eds.): ONDM 2019, LNCS 11616, pp. 452–464, 2020.
https://doi.org/10.1007/978-3-030-38085-4_39

1 Introduction

A main requirement for the operation of optical transport networks is the automation of the service provisioning process, minimizing manual intervention and across the whole network. This involves setting up connections and configuring the forwarding and switching behavior of intermediate nodes, with increasing traffic dynamicity requiring frequent and complex re-arrangement in an environment of increasing complexity. This complexity comes from the underlying technology – including not only the inherent complexity of the optical technology but also the increasing programmability of the DWDM systems and devices – and the need to provision such services with multiple technological layers and in networks spanning multiple segments and across administrative domains [1].

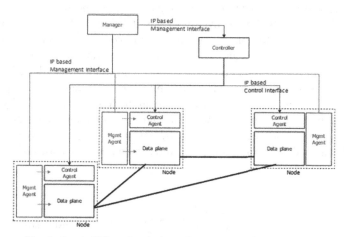

Fig. 1. Logical Functional view of a Centralized control plane.

A "Control plane" is a system and a set of functions especially dedicated to the provisioning of connectivity services, with higher abstractions, refined functional architectures, better addressing the (evolving) requirements, specially designed for and focusing on the configuration and specifics of the forwarding and switching operations, with standard interfaces operating across domains ensuring vendor inter-operability. A control plane that adopts a centralized deployment model (as is the case when following SDN principles) relies on a logical centralized controller, enabling an application layer and separating the control plane from the data plane, avoiding the complexity of distributed control planes and exploiting the programmability of network devices for greater flexibility and control (see Fig. 1).

Considering the southbound interface (SBI), and in the scope of disaggregated optical networks, it would be desirable to have a common and unified protocol and underlying switch model, similar to the role of OpenFlow [2] in packet switched networks. In practice, this is not straightforward. On the one hand, OpenFlow is a low level, byte-oriented protocol, complex to extend and, in the optical domain, there seems to be little support, despite having published normative documents [3]. On the other hand, there is a need to interact with multiple elements using multiple (legacy) protocols, there is a significant heterogeneity in terms of optical devices capabilities, and developing a common interface protocol would likely require agreed-upon hardware models and extensions. In general, a SBI protocol should be extensible, remaining future-proof and enabling generic configuration for existing and new devices. This is accomplished, in part, by decoupling the protocol to transport information and messages between entities from the way information is structured. The community seems to favor approaches based on a unified data modeling language and a standard transport protocol.

2   Model Driven Development

In simple terms, model driven development can be defined as an approach to design SDN controlled networks based on the systematic use of (ideally open and standard) data models. Such models should cover most aspects of network operation and control (e.g., service models, control plane constructs as topologies, connections and devices, e.g., "everything-as-model"…), and be specified using open and standard data modelling languages. In this way, such models can be automatically validated and used – including automated code and stub generation – and application logic can be developed around them. In general, for a given e.g. device, its Information Model macroscopically describes the device capabilities, in terms of operations and configurable parameters, using high level abstractions without specific details on aspects such as a particular syntax or encoding and its Data Model determines the structure, syntax and semantics of the data that is externally visible.

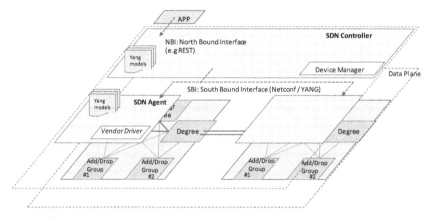

Fig. 2. SDN-based centralized control plane for a disaggregated network

To adopt a model driven development for disaggregated optical networks (see Fig. 2), there are a set of basic requirements. First, a unified information and data modelling language, to describe a device capabilities, attributes, operations to be performed on a device or system and notifications; a common language with associated tools enabling complex models with complex semantics, flexible, supporting extensions and augmentation, a set of "best-practice" and guidelines for model authors. Next, an architecture for remote configuration and control, adopting a client/server paradigm, supporting multiple clients, access lists, transactional semantics and rollback. Then, an associated transport protocol, which provides primitives to view and manipulate the data, providing a suitable encoding as defined by the data-model, which needs to be flexible, efficient, secure. Finally, interoperability is easier given standard, agreed upon models for devices. This area is a huge activity one, where it is hard to reach consensus (given the controversial aspects) and with Standards Defining Organizations (SDOs) competing and overlapping. Next, we elaborate more on the different requirements and choices.

2.1 The Yang Modeling Language

A Yang [4] module defines a data model; it includes a header, imports, and include statements, type definitions, configurations and operational data declarations as well as actions (RPC) and notifications. The language is expressive enough to structure data into data trees within the so-called datastores, by means of encapsulation of containers and lists. It is possible to define constrained data types (e.g. following a given textual pattern), to condition the presence of specific data to the support of optional features and, finally, to allow the refinement of models by extending and constraining existing models (by inheritance/augmentation), resulting in a hierarchy.

2.2 The NETCONF Architecture and Protocol

The NETCONF [5] protocol offers primitives to view and manipulate data, providing a suitable encoding as defined by the data-model. Data is arranged into one or multiple configuration datastores (set of configuration information that is required to get a device from its initial default state into a desired operational state). The protocol thus enables remote access to a device, and provides the set of rules by which multiple clients may access and modify a datastore within a NETCONF server (e.g., device). The protocol is, in simple terms, based on the exchange of XML-encoded RPC messages over a secure (commonly Secure Shell, SSH) connection. Out of the different messages and operations, the <get-config> allows retrieving part or the configuration data, the <edit-config> allows changing (creating, deleting, merging or replacing) that data (including adding elements to a container, or adding elements to a list, as allowed by the model) and, <get> allows to retrieve device state information and operational data.

It is worth mentioning that NETCONF typically requires an "XML over SSH" protocol stack, and a lightweight protocol also exists, more adopted to API consumers. A common web/HTTP approach to design services is based on the Representational State Transfer (REST) paradigm, an architectural style that defines a set of constraints to be used for creating Web services. RESTful Web services allow their clients to access and manipulate textual representations of Web resources by using a uniform and predefined set of stateless operations. RESTCONF [6–8] relies on REST and provides a HTTP-based API to access the hierarchical data within the running datastore. RESTCONF thus maps NETCONF operations to HTTP operations (such as POST, PUT, and DELETE) used to create and replace resources in the web, and supports two main encodings: XML and JSON.

2.3 Common Network and Device Models

From the point of view of control and management, disaggregated optical networks are an important use case for the use of open interfaces exporting programmability. However, optical networks are particularly challenging to model due to the lack of agreed-upon hardware models, and this is critical for the development of an interoperable ecosystem around disaggregated hardware. Regarding interoperability across multiple vendors, which is a key requirement in a disaggregated network, having common and agreed-upon device and network models simplifies development and integration. There are several SDOs working on this aspect. In this work, we focus on two main groups, which are suitable for the goal of demonstrating the ideas and concepts. OpenROADM MSA [7, 8] defines vendor-neutral specifications for ROADMs as well as transponders and pluggable optics. Specifications consist of both interoperability and data models. OpenConfig [9] is a collaborative effort by network operators, has published a set of models providing a configuration and state model for terminal optical devices within a DWDM system, including both client- and line-side parameters.

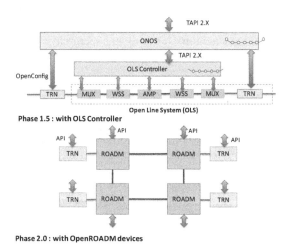

Fig. 3. ODTN phases for the two partial disaggregation models (src: ONF ODTN project)

3 Targeted Use Cases and Disaggregation Models

An in-depth discussion of the different options regarding disaggregation is provided in [10] including partial and full models. Here, we cover mainly: (i) partial disaggregation with transceiver and Open Line System (OLS) and (ii) partial transceiver and network element disaggregation (see Fig. 3), as the main use cases in the scope of the Metro-Haul [11] and the ODTN projects [12]. The Metro-Haul project goal is to design cost-effective, energy-efficient, agile and programmable metro networks, scalable for 5G access and future requirements, including the design of all-optical metro nodes (including full compute and storage capabilities) that interface with both 5G access and multi-Tbit/s elastic core networks. The ODTN (Open and Disaggregated Transport Networks) is an ONF project that aims to rally service providers, hardware vendors and system integrators, to build a reference implementation using open source software, open and common data models. Both projects deal with disaggregated DWDM systems, including but not limited to transponders and Open Line Systems, amplifiers, multiplexers, all-optical switches and ROADMs, covering the extension of an open source network operating system (ONOS SDN Controller) for control.

4 Selected Data Models and Protocols

4.1 Transport API (T-API)

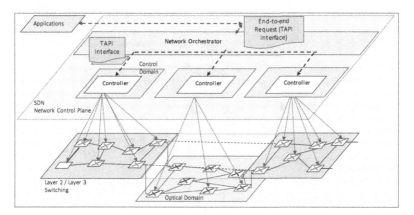

Fig. 4. TAPI SDN controller NBI for Network Orchestration

As stated earlier, SDN Controllers offer proprietary interfaces to applications (or Network Orchestrators), an approach commonly referred to as "vendor domains or islands". This heterogeneity, due to having different controllers interfaces in a multi-domain context, forces the use of "plugins" and it is difficult and expensive to extend (with the so-called umbrella management systems, used by the operators to deploy services spanning multiple domains). As a driving motivation and clear problem statement, there is a need for a standard interface, with common models, to act as a controller NBI (see Fig. 4). The Transport API (T-API) [13] published by the ONF meets the main requirements to be a protocol and interface used between an orchestrator and multiple domain controllers. In our case, it constitutes the Optical controller NBI (or the OLS). Of particular interest is the TAPI 2.1 release, given the support for the photonic media and its use to request (network) media channels in either disaggregated model. The main concepts within TAPI are detailed next. A TAPI based interface offers multiple services; in the scope of this paper, we consider the topology and connectivity.

(1) **Common Context**. The TAPI context is the shared information between a TAPI client (user) and the TAPI server (SDN controller). The model defines a TAPI domain as being able to provide services between Service Interface Points (or SIPs) mainly

characterized by their universally unique identifiers (UUIDs). A basic operation for a client is to "retrieve" the context in order to obtain the list of SIPs, so connectivity services are requested between two (or more) exported SIPs. (**2**) **Topology context and models**. If a given TAPI server supports topology model, it augments the TAPI shared context with a (list of) topology(ies). Each topology is composed of a list of nodes, which, in turn, have Node Edge Points (NEPs). Links connect two NEPs. The model is flexible enough to support recursive topologies and different levels of abstraction. The level of detail exported is configurable by policy. A client is thus able to obtain an (abstracted) view of the topology and map TAPI SIPs to external NEPs. (**3**) **Connectivity context and models.** Finally, the third model augments the shared context in order to support Connectivity Services. The instantiation of a connectivity service relies on the instantiation of several connections (e.g. one end-to-end and internal at each TAPI node). For this, Connection End Points (CEPs) are instantiated over NEPs (and contain information about the connections) and connections involve two or more CEPs (Fig. 5).

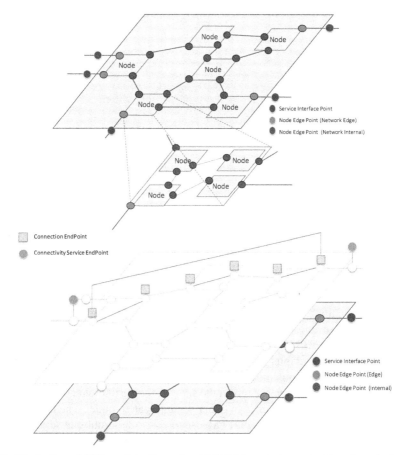

Fig. 5. Illustration of TAPI models: the notion of TAPI domain (recursive) topology [up] and the Connectivity Service/Connection concepts [bottom].

The user is able to specify, within a request, the desired protocol and layer as well as attributes and applicable constraints (e.g. path constrains, including or excluding elements etc.). Being NBI and expected to be easily consumed by users and applications, most TAPI implementations rely on RESTCONF as transport protocol.

4.2 OpenConfig Terminal Device

OpenConfig focuses on compiling a consistent set of vendor-neutral YANG data models. These data models cover a variety of network elements, from routers to optical switch. We use both the platform and the terminal-device models. The former defines a platform as having software and hardware components (such as line cards, ports, transceivers or optical channels). The latter allowing the activation of optical channels – in terms of frequency, power and operational mode – within line ports and the association (mapping) of client signals to optical channels in a quite flexible way.

4.3 OpenROADM Device Model

The device model proposed by OpenROADM is sketched in Fig. 6. A ROADM is composed of a given number (N) of directions or degrees (DEG) and a given number of add/drop stages (named Shared Risk Groups or SRGs in OpenROADM terminology). A degree has in and out amplifiers and a WSS to mux/demux the signals, towards other degrees or towards add/drop stages. In simple terms, the Yang mode defines a first section related to the device information (node identifiers, vendor, model, serial number, geolocation, etc.) followed by a section that includes a list of circuit-packs, describing the physical architecture including their components ports and naming, as well as the correspondence in terms of actual racks and shelves.

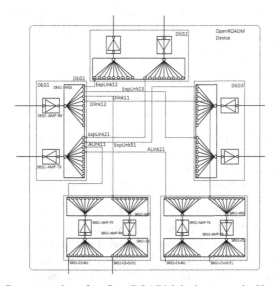

Fig. 6. Representation of an OpenROADM device as per its Yang model

The next section details the set of ROADM interfaces (which can be supported over either logical interfaces or physical ports). Another section lists the internal links (links between ports of a given component or circuit pack), the physical links (links between different components, such as a link between Degree 1 and 2, named ExpLink12 or the drop link between Degree 3 and SRG1 named DLink31) and external links (between ROADMs). In either case, links are listed keyed by their name and the associated circuit pack ports. Next, the model also includes two lists for the main component blocks: a list of degrees, numbered, saying how many optical channels are supported as well as flexi-grid capabilities and a list of SRGs (Add/Drop groups), numbered, with a list of add drop port pairs. Finally, the roadm-connection list includes the connections that are active (that have been established) in the device. It is worth noting that each connection is identified by its name (a string, but OpenROADM papers provide guidelines on how to name them) along with two references to existing interfaces.

5 Network Operations and Service Workflow

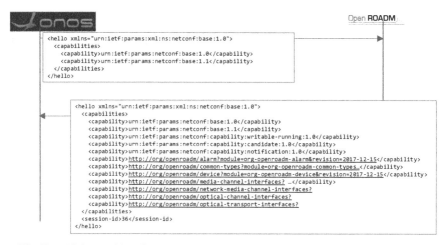

Fig. 7. Initial capability discovery between the SDN controller and the OpenROADM.

Network Discovery: From the point of view of networks operation, the procedure is as follows: first, the network operator configures the SDN controller (in our case, the implementation is based on ONOS) with the list of devices, and the NETCONF credentials. This means IP addresses, Netconf ports (default is 830), user credentials, etc.

The SDN controller establishes a persistent NETCONF session with the device. Let us focus on the OpenROADM devices. First, there is an initial capability exchange, in which the NETCONF client (ONOS) discovers what models and features are supported (Fig. 7) using a HELLO. Next, the SDN controller issues <get> and <get-config> messages as needed to retrieve info about the devices. Typically, a <get> operation with a subtree filter of <org-openroadm-device><info/> allows retrieving basic data to add the device into the SDN controller device manager. Similar operations on the circuit packs and ports are used to retrieve internal connectivity and to discover port capabilities (Fig. 8). For example, we query the list of circuit packs and their ports, e.g. the DEGREE1 AMPRX and see the DEG1-AMPRX-IN, this is a multi-wavelength port, external, and its partner port is DEG1-AMRTX-OUT. We can also see a logical connection point, the DEG1 Trail Termination Point for RX for that degree.

Fig. 8. NETCONF <get> operation to retrieve the list of circuit packs of the OpenROADM.

If the device supports it, we can retrieve external links to discover how Open-ROADMs are inter-connected. This allows the SDN controller to construct a network topology view. If this is not supported, other means of topology discovery need to be defined, including, if need be, manual provisioning at the SDN controller. The result is that the SDN controller is aware of the network topology and end-to-end services may be requested, using, for example, the GUI (Fig. 9).

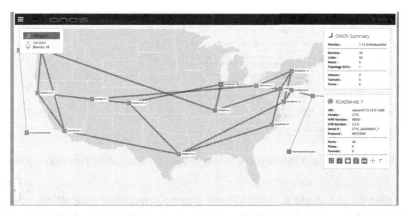

Fig. 9. ONOS GUI with NSFNET topology (14 OpenROADM and 2 OpenConfig devices).

Service Creation: In order to request a service, the user or operator retrieves the list of available Service Interface Points (SIPs) using the TAPI NBI and proceeds to request a connectivity service between a pair of SIPs (for a point-to-point connection). The request can specify if it applies e.g. to a digital signal between two transceiver client ports or, alternatively a network media channel between two transceiver line ports (or two OLS ports for an OLS controller). The SDN controller maps those SIPs to node edge points, and performs a routing and spectrum assignment process that finds the k-shortest path between the devices and performs first fit spectrum allocation. Once completed, flow and forwarding rules are configured at each device: for the Terminal Device, a logical channel association is instantiated within the device between a client (transceiver) port and an optical channel component bound to the line port of the device. For each of the OpenROADM devices across the path, a ROADM internal connection is requested: (i) OTS and OMS (optical transport and optical multiplex) interfaces are created within each degree (if not existing), (ii) Supporting Media Channel and NMC interfaces are created, (iii) Followed by the creation of a roadm-connection object.

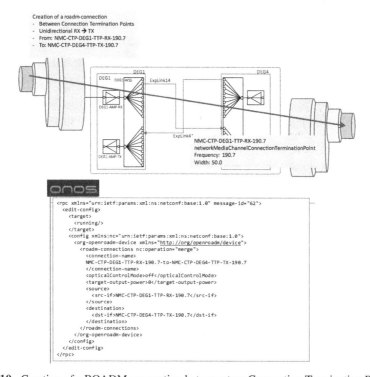

Fig. 10. Creation of a ROADM connection between two Connection Termination Points.

For example, to create a unidirectional express connection supporting a 50 GHz signal centered at 190.7 GHz from degree 1 to degree 4 (Fig. 10), the SDN controller proceeds as follows. First, assume that the OTS and OMS interfaces are configured at the ROADM degrees; these interfaces correspond to the lower layers of the OTN model; OTS corresponds to the Optical Transmission Section, e.g. between amplified fiber sections and OMS to the Optical Multiplex section. Next, create Media Channel (MC) interfaces (via a <edit-config> operation) over the OMS interfaces (by convention named MC-TTP-DEG1-TTP-RX-190.7 and MC-TTP-DEG1-TTP-RX-190.7, with a min-freq: 190.675 and max-freq: 190.725, which specifies the supporting media channel. Next, create Network Media Channel (NMC) interfaces over the MC interface, specifying a center frequency and width, inducing Connection Termination Points (CTPs). Finally, establish the unidirectional connection between CTPs, from the interface NMC-CTP-DEG1-TTP-RX-190.7 to NMC-CTP-DEG4-TTP-TX-190.7. Once the cross-connections have been provisioned at all the nodes along the path and the transceivers configured with the appropriate transmission parameters, the service is active.

6   Conclusions

We have given an introduction to model driven development, the adopted framework for SDN for transport networks, leveraging on the increase of device programmability. We have introduced the main concepts behind SDN for disaggregated optical networks, presenting reference architectures and industry common practices, the use of the Yang data modelling language and the NETCONF/RESTCONF protocols, covering a subset of deployment models in partial and full disaggregation. We have focused on a clear use case for model driven development, i.e., disaggregated optical networks, with emphasis on the use of TAPI interfaces and OpenROADM device models. Even if the trend is perceived as positive, model driven development will not reach its full potential unless the framework, languages, etc. can use a set of common, agreed- upon models.

Acknowledgements. We would like to thank Alessio Giorgetti (CNIT) and Roberto Morro (TIM) for contributions to the development of OpenROADM ONOS drivers. This paper has been funded by the EC through the H2020-METRO-HAUL (671598) and by the Spanish MICINN AURORAS (RTI2018-099178-B-I00) projects.

References

1. Casellas, R., Martinez, R., Vilalta, R., Munoz, R.: Control, management, and orchestration of optical networks: evolution, trends, and challenges. J. Lightwave Technol. **36**(7), 1390–1402 (2018)
2. Open Networking Foundation (ONF) Technical Specification TS-025, OpenFlow Switch Specification v1.5.1, 26 March 2015
3. Open Networking Foundation (ONF) Technical Specification TS-022, Optical Transport Protocol Extensions, Version 1.0, 15 March 2015
4. Bjorklund, M. (ed.): The YANG 1.1 Data Modeling Language, IETF Request for Comments 7950, August 2016
5. Enns, R. (ed.): Network Configuration Protocol NETCONF, IETF Request for Comments 6241, June 2011
6. Bierman, A., Bjorklund, M., Watsen, K.: RESTCONF protocol, IETF Request for Comments 8040, January 2017

7. The Open ROADM Multi-Source Agreement (MSA). http://www.openroadm.org
8. Morro, R., Lucrezia, F., Gomes, P., et al.: Automated end to end carrier ethernet provisioning over a disaggregated WDM metro network with a hierarchical SDN control and monitoring platform. In: 2018 European Conference on Optical Communication (ECOC)
9. OpenConfig project and data models. http://openconfig.net, https://github.com/openconfig/public/tree/master/release/models
10. Riccardi, E., et al.: An operator view on the introduction of white boxes into optical networks. JLT **36**(I15), 3062–3072 (2018)
11. The Metro-haul project. http://metro-haul.eu
12. Open Networking Foundation (ONF), The Open Disaggregated Transport Network (ODTN) project. https://www.opennetworking.org/odtn/
13. Open Networking Foundation (ONF), Transport API project. https://wiki.opennetworking.org/display/OTCC/TAPI

Poster Papers

Self-learning Routing for Optical Networks

Yue-Cai Huang[1]($\boxtimes$)(iD), Jie Zhang[2], and Siyuan Yu[3,4]($\boxtimes$)(iD)

[1] School of Physics and Telecommunication Engineering,
South China Normal University, Guangzhou, China
huangyuecai@scnu.edu.cn
[2] XenLink Co. Ltd., Guangzhou, China
[3] State Key Laboratory of Optoelectronic Materials and Technologies,
School of Electronics and Information Technology, Sun Yat-sen University,
Guangzhou, China
[4] School of Computer Science, Electronic and Electrical Engineering and Engineering
Mathematics, University of Bristol, Bristol BS8 1UB, UK
s.yu@bristol.ac.uk

Abstract. It is generally very difficult to optimize the routing policies in optical networks with dynamic traffic. Most widely-used routing policies, e.g., shortest path routing and least congested path (LCP) routing, are heuristic policies. Although the LCP is often regarded as the best-performing adaptive routing policy, we are often eager to know whether there exist better routing policies that surpass these heuristics in performance. In this paper, we propose a framework of reinforcement learning (RL) based routing scheme, that learns routing decisions during the interactions with the environment. With a proposed self-learning method, the RL agent can improve its routing policy continuously. Simulations on a ring-topology metro optical network demonstrate that, the proposed scheme outperforms the LCP routing policy.

Keywords: Optical networks · Routing · Self-learning

1 Introduction

Routing of optical networks has been under research for more than two decades [4,9,17]. There are basically three approaches: fixed routing, fixed-alternative routing [6,14], and adaptive routing [3,11]. For the fixed routing, one pre-determined route is always chosen for a given source-destination pair. If the route is unavailable, the call request is blocked. For the fixed-alternative routing, there is an ordered list of fixed candidate routes for each source-destination pair. Upon call request, each route is tried following the order until a route is found available; if no route is available, the request is blocked. For the adaptive routing, the path is chosen dynamically depending on the network status upon the request arrival. Among all routing policies, adaptive routing generally gives the best performance [17].

© IFIP International Federation for Information Processing 2020
Published by Springer Nature Switzerland AG 2020
A. Tzanakaki et al. (Eds.): ONDM 2019, LNCS 11616, pp. 467–478, 2020.
https://doi.org/10.1007/978-3-030-38085-4_40

Most well-known adaptive routing policies are heuristic policies. For example, the adaptive shortest-cost-path routing tries to minimize the resources used for each connection upon its arrival, aiming to hold more simultaneous connections. The least congest path (LCP) routing balances the load over the network, so as to avoid bottlenecks. Among the adaptive routing policies, the LCP routing is generally regarded to have the best performance [11]. These heuristic adaptive routing policies can be regarded as to capture some features of the network status and then intuitively exploit the features to achieve good performance. For instance, the LCP policy considers the feature of load on each available path and select the least congested path. As known, besides the load, there are many other features that may affect the network performance, e.g., the number of hops, the link availability, the traffic in service, the topology, etc. From this perspective, A good adaptive policy needs to include enough features and properly exploit them, while on the other hand, in a realistic situation, the variations of network status are often too many to be summarized. These variations come from the change of spectrum availability of each link, the change of remaining holding time of each call, etc. Even if we only consider a simplified version of network status with only the spectrum availability and source-destination pairs, a huge number of network status still exit. Consider the following example. For a five-node bi-directional ring-topology network, with five wavelengths on each link, and only four source-destination pairs (1-2, 2-1, 1-3, 3-1), there are over four billion simplified network status. Therefore, making good adaptive routing policies is challenging, which is a major reason that heuristic algorithms were popular over the past decades.

Recently, Google successfully applied reinforcement learning in playing Atari games and achieved above-human-level performance [12]. The RL-based agent can derive efficient representations of the environment, and use these to generalize past experience to new situations. This gives us a possible way to overcome the difficulty of feature extraction for adaptive routing. In [2,8,10,13], the authors apply reinforcement learning to the routing of optical networks. These methods allow the RL-based agent to learn a routing policy during the interaction with the network environment. In a more recent work [5], a Deep Q-Network (DQN) algorithm is used to capture the features inspired by [12] and obtain some performance improvement compared to the shortest path routing policy. While we still have the following open question: whether there are better routing policies than the existing ones, and how can we find the best routing policies. This paper tries to answer these questions.

In this paper, we propose a RL-based self-learning method. It is based on the following observation: suppose we already have one routing policy, if we can change this policy with just one better action under one specific circumstance, we should have a better policy. With our proposed method, the RL agent changes its current policy according to the competition result of the current policy and a reference policy. In this way, the RL agent should be able to learn for a policy that is no worse than the reference policy. Then, the reference policy is periodically updated with the learnt policy. By repeating the above learning process iteratively, the RL agent can improve its policy continuously.

2   RL for Optical Network Routing

In this section, we first model the optical network routing problem into an RL problem with self-learning (Subsects. 2.1 and 2.2). Then, we introduce how to apply DQN algorithm to the routing problem in Subsect. 2.3. Due to space limitation, the basic knowledge of RL will not be covered in this paper, and readers are strongly recommended to refer [16] for better understanding of this paper.

2.1   Mathematical Representation of State and Action

We consider the RL state only at the time when a new connection request arrives. That means at time $t, t + 1, t + 2, \ldots$, there is one and only one connection request arriving, and there is no connection request arrivals in the time periods between.

The state at time t, denoted by S_t is composed of two parts: the network state S_t^{net} and the arrival traffic state S_t^{tra}. $S_t = \left[S_t^{\text{net}}, S_t^{\text{tra}} \right]$.

The network state S_t^{net}, representing the resource occupation state at time t, is defined as,

$$S_t^{\text{net}} = \begin{bmatrix} b_{11}(t), & \cdots, & b_{1w}(t), & \cdots, & b_{1W}(t) \\ & \cdots \\ b_{l1}(t), & \cdots, & b_{lw}(t), & \cdots, & b_{lW}(t) \\ & \cdots \\ b_{L1}(t), & \cdots, & b_{Lw}(t), & \cdots, & b_{LW}(t) \end{bmatrix}, \tag{1}$$

where,

$$b_{lw}(t) = \begin{cases} 1, & \text{if wavelength } w \text{ of link } l \text{ is} \\ & \text{available at time } t \\ -1, & \text{if wavelength } w \text{ of link } l \text{ is} \\ & \text{unavailable at time } t. \end{cases} \tag{2}$$

From Eqs. (1) and (2), network state S_t^{net} is an $L \times W$ matrix, with element $b_{lw}(t)$ denoting the availability of wavelength w on link l. W is the total number of wavelengths and L is the total number of links.

The arrival traffic state at time t (i.e., upon new traffic arrival) is S_t^{tra}, which is defined as Eq. (3). K is the total number of paths for the newly arrived traffic under study.

$$S_t^{\text{tra}} = \begin{bmatrix} b'_{11}(t), & \cdots, & b'_{1k}(t), & \cdots, & b'_{1K}(t) \\ & \cdots \\ b'_{l1}(t), & \cdots, & b'_{lk}(t), & \cdots, & b'_{lK}(t) \\ & \cdots \\ b'_{L1}(t), & \cdots, & b'_{Lk}(t), & \cdots, & b'_{LK}(t) \end{bmatrix}, \tag{3}$$

where,

$$b'_{lk}(t) = \begin{cases} 1, & \text{if link } l \text{ is not included by path } k \\ -1, & \text{if link } l \text{ is included by path } k. \end{cases} \qquad (4)$$

S_t^{net} is an $L \times W$ matrix, and S_t^{tra} is an $L \times K$ matrix. S_t is to connect the two matrix along the rows, and therefore an $L \times (W + K)$ matrix.

The action of the routing problem is to choose one path from the K paths under study. Therefore, action $A_t \in \{1, 2, \ldots, K\}$.

2.2   Reward

The choice of reward is essential for RL, since the objective of RL is to maximize the expected cumulative reward. Well-designed reward setting should be in consistent with the objective of the routing, i.e., to minimize the call blocking probabilities. As for the routing problem, the evaluation of a routing policy is not determined by one routing decision, but by a sequence of routing decisions. Therefore, the reward should reflect the performance of an action within a sequence. Although we have feed-back from future rewards by discounting, this kind of reward cannot fit well with the objective to minimize the blocking probabilities.

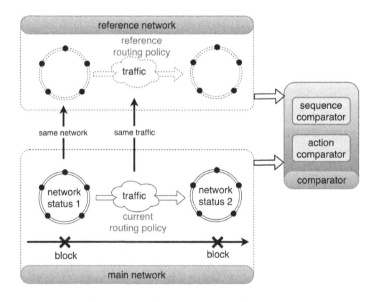

Fig. 1. The illustration of self learning.

In this paper, the reward is set based on the concept of self-learning, which is inspired by the method of "self-play" used by Alpha Zero [15]. The reward is set by a comparison of the network running a learning routing policy with a reference network running a reference routing policy, as illustrated in Fig. 1. It includes three parts: the main network, the reference network and the comparator.

The main network is the optical network adopting the learning routing policies, with ϵ-greedy approach used to balance the exploration and exploitation. When an arrival is blocked, the network state is recorded and the traffic till the next block is also recorded.

The reference network is a virtual optical network for comparison. It is configured following the recorded network state from the main network, and the recorded traffic is injected to this network. A reference routing policy is adopted. The performance of the saved network can be evaluated by simulations from the initial network state and traffic injected with the given policy.

The comparator compares the two networks with its two components: sequence comparator and action comparator:

1. *Sequence comparator* compares the sequence of actions, by considering which sequence incurs a blocking state earlier. There are three kinds of comparison outputs: "better", "same", and "worse". If the main network incurs blocking earlier than the reference network, we regard the sequence of actions from the learning routing policy performs worse than the reference, then the comparator outputs "worse". Similarly, if the main network incurs blocking at the same time with the reference network, the comparator outputs "same". Finally, if the main network incurs blocking later than the reference network, the comparator outputs "better".

2. *Action comparator* compares each action in the sequence. The sequence comparator gives a general impression of the performance of the actions within a sequence, while not every action is better than (worse than/same with) the actions in the reference policy. Therefore, we should compare them one by one. The action comparator considers each state-action pairs from the reference network. It compares the same state but with action from the learning policy. It outputs two results: same action or different action.

Finally, based on the comparison results, the reward can be set, as given by Table 1. An intuitive explanation on this kind of setting is as follow. (1) If action comparator outputs "same" or the sequence comparator outputs "same", the actions of the main network and that of the reference network tend to have little difference in affecting the performance, therefore, a relatively small and positive reward 0.1 is given. (2) If actions of the two networks are different, and the sequence in the main network performs better, the action of the main network is potentially a key action to lead to a better sequence, therefore, a relatively big and positive reward 1.0 is given. (3) If actions of the two networks are different, and the sequence in the main network performs worse, this action is potentially a key action to lead to a worse sequence, therefore, a relatively big but negative reward -1.0 is given. (4) If blocking occurs, give a very big negative reward -10. Since the rewards are set by comparisons, policies better than the reference policy can be obtained, when maximizing the cumulative reward.

Table 1. The setting of reward

	Sequence comparison	Action comparison	Reward
Accept	Better than ref	=	1.0
		≠	0.1
	Same with ref	=	0.1
		≠	0.1
	Worse than ref	=	0.1
		≠	−1.0
Block	NA	NA	−10.0

= means same actions, ≠ means different actions.

Another question is how to choose the reference policy. It can be a well-known policy, e.g., shorted path routing or least congest path routing, or it can be the learning policy as well. When the reference policy is some known policy, the learner is learning a policy no worse than the known policy. If the reference policy is the learning policy itself, then it becomes "self-learning". In this case, the reference policy is the learnt policy with greedy action, and in the main network, the ϵ-greedy policy can be used to explore the state space. After some time, the reference policy can be updated with the newly learnt policy. In this way, the RL-agent improves itself continuously.

2.3   Learning with Deep Q-Network

Due to the curse of dimensionality, we use a neural network (NN) shown by Fig. 2 as the Q-value function approximator. The input of the neural network is the state at each time step, S_t, and the output is the predicted action-value (Q-value) for each individual action for the input state. In this way, the Q-values of all actions is computed with a single forward pass at the same time for a given state.

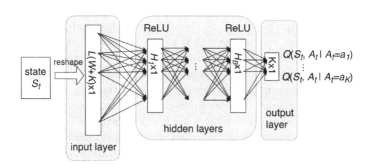

Fig. 2. The NN for Q-value approximation (dropout ignored).

The neural network with weights Θ is used as the Q-network. Denote $Q(s, a; \Theta)$ as the parameterized Q-value for state s and action a. Denote $Q(s', a'; \Theta)$ as the parameterized Q-value for the next state s' and the next action a'. The NN can be trained by adjusting Θ_i at iteration i to reduce the mean-squared error in the Bellman equation, where the optimal target value is given by:

$$\text{Target: } y = r + \gamma \max_{a'} Q(s', a'; \Theta),$$

r is the instantaneous reward, γ is the discount factor, $\gamma < 1$. \hfill (5)

Then, the loss function at each iteration i is given by the mean-squared error of between the Q-network and the Q-learning targets,

$$L_i(\Theta_i) = \mathop{\mathbb{E}}_{s,a,r,s'} \left[(y_i - Q(s, a; \Theta_i))^2 \right]$$

$$= \mathop{\mathbb{E}}_{s,a,r,s'} \left[\left(r + \gamma \max_{a'} Q(s', a'; \Theta_i^-) - Q(s, a; \Theta_i) \right)^2 \right].$$

\hfill (6)

A gradient descent can be applied to minimize the loss function. Besides, experience replay [12] is adopted, to randomly sample previous transitions, so as to smooth the training sample distribution over past behaviors. Moreover, several techniques are also used to facilitate the learning, including mini batch gradient descent, dropout in NN, and Adam optimizer [7]. The DQN algorithm is shown by Algorithm 1. The experience replay technique is shown. For simplicity, the reward setting part is ignored. To get a full picture, Algorithm 1 and Fig. 1 need to be combined.

In the Algorithm 1, two steps are taken recursively: the *sampling* and the *training*. During the sampling, samples of transitions are stored to the replay memory. During the training, samples are randomly chosen from the replay memory to train the neural network. Since the samples are chosen with reward given by self-comparing, the samples are generally better than the current routing policy. Therefore, the routing policies becomes better and better. The learnt policy is embedded in the trained Q-networks, $\arg\max_a Q(s, a; \Theta)$. The policy in the reference network is updated periodically.

3   Simulations

A discrete event simulator written in Python is used to simulate the traffic and the resource provision of the optical network. The DQN reinforcement learning part is written based on TensorFlow [1].

3.1   Parameter Settings

Consider a five-node bidirectional-ring-topology metro network. The key notations are listed in Table 2 for convenience, and they are also explained in the context. The total number of wavelength is five. The traffic pattern is non-uniform

---

Algorithm 1. Reinforcement learning algorithm

---

1 #INITIALIZATION
2 Create and initialize the optical network
3 Create and initialize the neural network
4 Initialize replay memory D
5 **while** *not stopping criterion* **do**
6   **while** *not policy update criterion* **do**
7   #SAMPLING
8   **while** *not sampling stopping criterion* **do**
9   Upon traffic coming, store state to S_t
10   With probability ϵ select a random action A_t
11   Otherwise select $A_t = \arg\max_A Q(S_t, A; \Theta)$
12   Execute action A_t and wait until new traffic coming, get new state S_{t+1}
13   Get reward r_{t+1}
14   Store transition $(S_t, A_t, r_{t+1}, S_{t+1})$ in D
15   **end while**
16   #TRAINING
17   **while** *not training stopping criterion* **do**
18   Sample a random minibatch of transitions (s, a, r, s') from D
19   Set $y = r + \gamma \max_{a'} Q(s', a'; \Theta)$
20   Perform a gradient step on $(y - Q(s, a; \Theta))^2$ with respect to the neural network parameters Θ
21   **end while**
22   **end while**
23   Policy is $\arg\max_a Q(s, a; \Theta)$
24   Update policy in the reference network
25 **end while**
26 Policy is $\arg\max_a Q(s, a; \Theta)$

---

with traffic matrix given as follows:

$$T = \lambda \begin{bmatrix} 0,1,1,0,0 \\ 1,0,0,0,0 \\ 1,0,0,0,0 \\ 0,0,0,0,0 \\ 0,0,0,0,0 \end{bmatrix}. \tag{7}$$

This means, traffic only exists for source-destination pair $(1, 2)$, $(1, 3)$, $(2, 1)$, and $(3, 1)$. The arrival processes are independent Poisson processes, with arrival rate λ, and the service time distributions follow exponential distributions with average service time μ. In this bidirectional ring topology, routing can be done clockwise or anti-clockwise. Therefore, for each accepted request, only two actions can be chosen: routing clockwise or anti-clockwise. For wavelength assignment, the first-fit strategy is used.

Table 2. Key parameters

	Notation	Meaning	Value
Optical network	N	Number of nodes	5
	L	Number of links	$L = 2N = 10$
	W	Number of wavelengths	5
	K	Number of routing paths	2
Traffic	λ	Arrival rate	0.4
	μ	Average service time	1.0
RL agent	γ	Discount rate	0.99
	α	Learning rate	1×10^{-5}
	ϵ	Explore rate	0.1
	B	Number of hidden layers of the Q-network	3
	H	Number of neurons for each hidden layer same number for each hidden layer	$\{32, 256, 1024\}$
	P	Dropout probability for NN	0.5

A five-layer forward feed fully-connected neural network is chosen as the function approximator for the state-action value function. The neural network is illustrated in Fig. 2. Recall that the state of the RL algorithm is a $L \times (W + K)$ matrix. With total number of link $L = 10$, total number of wavelength $W = 5$, and total number of paths $K = 2$, the state is a 10×7 matrix. This matrix is reshaped to a 70×1 array and forms the input layer of the neural network. Then it is followed by three hidden layers with number of nodes H_1, H_2, H_3. The ReLU activation function is chosen for all hidden layers. Besides, not shown in Fig. 2, the dropout technique is introduced in the neural network to avoid overfitting, with the dropout probability 0.5. Besides, the discount rate γ is 0.99, the explore rate ϵ is 0.1, and the learning rate α is 1×10^{-5}.

3.2 Learning for a Reference Policy

With the aim of outperforming the existing routing policies, we should check first whether the RL-routing can learn to be a given policy, i.e., policy-fitting. Therefore, we run a set of simulations to fit the RL-routing to be the best-performed LCP routing. We compare the actions given by the Q-network and those given by the LCP policy. If the actions are the same, then give reward 1, otherwise, give reward -1. The simulation results are shown in Figs. 3 and 4. In the two figures, the x-axis is the number of arrivals batches (1 arrival batch includes 1000 arrivals), i.e., the results are collected every arrival batches (every 1000 arrivals). Figure 3 shows the blocking probabilities of LCP and three RL-based policies with different number of nodes in the hidden layer of the Q-networks. The accuracy shown by Fig. 4 representing the portion that the actions

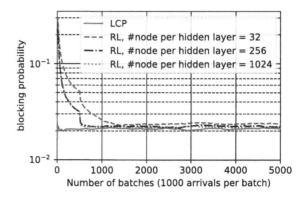

Fig. 3. Performance of RL-routing with LCP fitting.

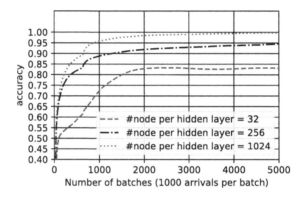

Fig. 4. The accuracy of fitting LCP by RL routing.

from RL routing are the same with those from LCP policy. From Fig. 3, we can see that the blocking probabilities become similar with LCP soon (after 2000 bathes) for all Q-networks. While from Fig. 4, it is revealed that only the case with number of hidden layer nodes 1024 fits the LCP after 4000 batches. We can make two points here: (1) To fit even a simple policy such as LCP, we need a large enough neural network. (2) There are many different policies that give similar performance with the LCP.

3.3   Self learning

Taking the RL-routing policy that is already fit to the LCP, we apply the self-learning process to pursue better policies. The simulation results are shown in Fig. 5. It is demonstrated by Fig. 5 that the RL-routing, incurs some degradation at the beginning of the training, gradually it outperforms LCP and maintains the advantage over LCP during the training. This demonstrate that, by the self-learning method, indeed better routing policies can be learnt. We should also notice that, the performance of the learnt policies incurs some variations.

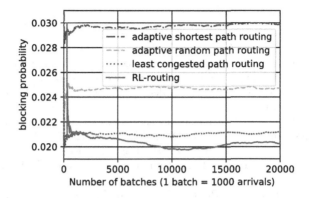

Fig. 5. Performance of RL-routing with self-learning.

These variations may come from the exploration and the variations of the reference policy to be compared.

4   Discussion

This is an early work for applying reinforcement learning to the optical network resource allocation, there are some limitations that need to be investigated for future research. One challenge is the scalability. For the simulated 5-node-5-wavelength ring metro network, a five layer fully-connected neural network with 1024 nodes per hidden layer is already required. Some efforts need to be paid to reduce the complexity of the neural networks as the size of the optical network scales up. One potential approach is to use convolutional neural networks, leveraging the locality of the network status. There are also plenty of open problems for future research, including the impact of traffic variations and network topologies, and the spatial/spectral resource assignment.

5   Conclusion

This paper provides a new direction to optimize the routing of optical networks. The proposed reinforcement learning algorithm is able to continuously improve its routing policy with self learning method. Simulation on a ring-topology metro network demonstrate that the learnt policy outperforms the least congest path routing policy which was regarded the best routing policy. With the computation power increasing rapidly, this RL method can be a scalable approach for dynamic resource allocation and control for optical networks. It can also be combined with software defined network to achieve an agile control plane.

Acknowledgment. This work is supported by: National Natural Science Foundation of China (61490715, U1701661); Local Innovative and Research Teams Project of Guangdong Pearl River Talents Program (2017BT01X121); Fundamental Research Funds for the Central Universities of China (SYSU:17lgpy51).

References

1. Abadi, M., et al.: TensorFlow: large-scale machine learning on heterogeneous systems (2015). https://www.tensorflow.org/. software available from tensorflow.org
2. Alyatama, A.: Dynamic routing and wavelength assignment using learning automata technique [all optical networks]. In: Proceedings of IEEE GLOBECOM, vol. 3, pp. 1912–1917 (2004)
3. Chan, K.M., Yum, T.S.P.: Analysis of least congested path routing in WDM lightwave networks. In: Proceedings of INFOCOM, pp. 962–969 (1994)
4. Chatterjee, B.C., Sarma, N., Oki, E.: Routing and spectrum allocation in elastic optical networks: a tutorial. IEEE Commun. Surv. Tutorials **17**(3), 1776–1800 (2015)
5. Chen, X., Guo, J., Zhu, Z., Proietti, R., Castro, A., Yoo, S.: Deep-RMSA: a deep-reinforcement-learning routing, modulation and spectrum assignment agent for elastic optical networks. In: Proceedings of Optical Fiber Communication Conference, pp. W4F–2 (2018)
6. Harai, H., Murata, M., Miyahara, H.: Performance of alternate routing methods in all-optical switching networks. In: Proceedings of INFOCOM, vol. 2, pp. 516–524 (1997)
7. Kingma, D.P., Ba, J.: Adam: a method for stochastic optimization. arXiv preprint arXiv:1412.6980 (2014)
8. Kiran, Y., Venkatesh, T., Murthy, C.S.R.: A reinforcement learning framework for path selection and wavelength selection in optical burst switched networks. IEEE J. Sel. Areas Commun. **25**(9), 18–26 (2007)
9. Klinkowski, M., Lechowicz, P., Walkowiak, K.: Survey of resource allocation schemes and algorithms in spectrally-spatially flexible optical networking. Opt. Switching Netw. **27**, 58–78 (2018)
10. Koyanagi, I., Tachibana, T., Sugimoto, K.: A reinforcement learning-based lightpath establishment for service differentiation in all-optical WDM networks. In: Proceedings of IEEE GLOBECOM, pp. 1–6 (2009)
11. Li, L., Somani, A.K.: Dynamic wavelength routing using congestion and neighborhood information. IEEE/ACM Trans. Netw. (TON) **7**(5), 779–786 (1999)
12. Mnih, V., et al.: Playing Atari with deep reinforcement learning. arXiv:1312.5602 [cs.LG] (2013)
13. Pointurier, Y., Heidari, F.: Reinforcement learning based routing in all-optical networks. In: Proceedings of IEEE Fourth International Conference on Broadband Communications, Networks and Systems, pp. 919–921 (2007)
14. Ramamurthy, R., Mukherjee, B.: Fixed-alternate routing and wavelength conversion in wavelength-routed optical networks. IEEE/ACM Trans. Netw. **10**(3), 351–367 (2002)
15. Silver, D., et al.: Mastering the game of go without human knowledge. Nature **550**(7676), 354 (2017)
16. Sutton, R.S., Barto, A.G.: Reinforcement Learning: An Introduction (2018). http://incompleteideas.net/
17. Zang, H., Jue, J.P., Mukherjee, B.: A review of routing and wavelength assignment approaches for wavelength-routed optical WDM networks. Opt. Netw. Mag. **1**, 47–60 (2000)

Deterministic Contention Management for Low Latency Cloud RAN over an Optical Ring

Dominique Barth[1], Maël Guiraud[1,2(✉)], and Yann Strozecki[1]

[1] DAVID Laboratory, UVSQ, Versailles, France
{dominique.barth,mael.guiraud,yann.strozecki}@uvsq.fr
[2] Nokia Bell Labs, Nozay, France

Abstract. The N-GREEN project has for goal the design of a low cost optical ring technology with good performance (throughput, latency...) without using expensive end-to-end connections. We study the compatibility of such a technology with the development of the Cloud RAN, a latency critical application which is a major aspect of 5G deployment. We show that deterministically managing Cloud RAN traffic minimizes its latency while also improving the latency of the other traffics.

1 Introduction

Telecommunication network providers have to design inexpensive networks supporting an increasing amount of data and online applications. Many of these applications require QoS guarantees, like minimal throughput and/or maximal latency. The N-GREEN project aims to design a high performing optical ring while ensuring a minimal cost for providers. The current solutions with good QoS [1,2], establish end-to-end direct connections between the nodes, which is extremely expensive. The N-GREEN optical ring, offering any-to-any connections, is designed to ensure good performance at low cost: beyond the advantages of WDM technology adopted, the hardware it requires scales linearly with the number of nodes while direct connection scales quadratically making it impractical for more than a few nodes. The WDM technology of the N-GREEN optical ring is different of existing technologies or protocols like SDH/SONET and DQBD [3,4].

In this article, we study a Cloud RAN (C-RAN) application based on the N-GREEN optical ring described in [5,6]. C-RAN is one of the major area of development for 5G; it consists in centralizing or partially centralizing the computation units or **BaseBand Units** (BBU) of the **Remote Radio Heads** (RRH) in one datacenter [7]. Periodically, each RRH in the field sends some

This work was developed for the N-GREEN project. The authors thank the National Agency of Research (ANR) for partial funding in the frame of the N-GREEN project and the partners of the project for fruitful discussions.

A. Tzanakaki et al. (Eds.): ONDM 2019, LNCS 11616, pp. 479–491, 2020.
https://doi.org/10.1007/978-3-030-38085-4_41

uplink traffic to its associated BBU in the datacenter, then, after a computation, the BBU sends some downlink traffic back to the RRH. In this paper, we assume that the quantity of uplink and downlink traffic is the same. The latency of the messages between the BBU and the RRH is critical since some services need end-to-end latency as low as 1 ms [8,9].

Nowadays, the traffic is managed by statistical multiplexing [10]. Here, we propose an SDN approach to **deterministically** manage the periodic C-RAN traffic by choosing emission timing. Indeed, Deterministic Networking is one of the main method considered to reduce the end-to-end latency [11]. In a previous work [12], the authors have studied a similar problem for a star shaped network. In contrast with our previous work, finding emission timings so that different periodic sources do not use the same resource is easy in the context of the N-GREEN optical ring with a single data-center. However, we deal with two additional difficulties arising from practice: the messages from RRHs are scattered because of the electronic to optic interface and there are other traffics whose latency must be preserved. It turns out that the deterministic management of CRAN traffic we propose reduces the latency of CRAN traffic to the physical delay of the routes, while reducing the latency of the other traffics by smoothing the load of the ring over the period. To achieve such a good latency, our solution needs to reserve resources in advance, which slightly decreases the maximal load the N-GREEN optical ring can handle. Such an approach of reservation of the network for an application (CRAN in our context) relates to network slicing [13] or virtual-circuit-switched connections in optical networks [14,15].

In Sect. 2, we model the optical ring and the traffic flow. In Sect. 3, we experimentally evaluate the latency when using stochastic multiplexing to manage packets insertion on the ring, with or without priority for C-RAN packets. In Sect. 4, we propose a deterministic way to manage C-RAN packets without buffers, which guarantees to have zero additional latency from buffering in the optical ring. We propose several refinements of this deterministic sending scheme to spread the load over time, which improves the latency of best effort packet, or in Sect. 4.3, to allow the ring to support a maximal number of antennas at the cost of a very small latency for the C-RAN traffic.

2   Model of C-RAN Traffic over an Optical Ring

N-GREEN Optical Ring. The unidirectional optical ring is represented by an oriented cycle. The vertices of the cycle represent the nodes of the ring, where the traffic arrives. The arcs (u, v) of the cycle have an integer weight $\omega(u, v)$ which represents the time to transmit a unit of information from u to v. By extension, if u and v are not adjacent, we denote by $\omega(u, v)$ the size of the directed path from u to v. The **ring size** is the length of the cycle, that is $\omega(u, u)$ and we denote it by RS. A **container**, of capacity C expressed in bytes, is a basic unit of data in the optical ring.

The time is discretized: a unit of time corresponds to the time needed to fill a container with data. As shown in Fig. 1, the node u can fill a container with a data packet of size less than C bytes at time t if the container at position u at time t is *free*. If there are several packets in a node or if a node cannot fill a container, because it is not free, the remaining packets are stored in the **insertion buffer** of the node. A container goes from u to v in $\omega(u, v)$ units of time. The ring follows a **broadcast and select scheme with emission release policy**: When a container is filled by some node u, it is freed when it comes back at u after going through the whole cycle.

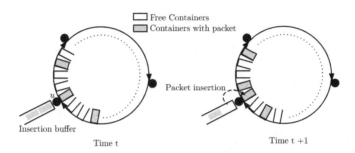

Fig. 1. Dynamic behavior of the ring.

C-RAN Traffic. The RRHs are the source of the **deterministic and periodic** C-RAN traffic. There are k RRHs attached to the ring and several RRHs can be attached to the same vertex. An RRH is linked to a node of the ring through an electronic interface of bit rate R Bps. The ring has a larger bit rate of $F \times R$ Bps. The integer F is called the **acceleration factor** between the electronic and the optical domains. A node aggregates the data received on the electronic interface during F units of time to create a packet of size C and then puts it in the insertion buffer. In each period P, an RRH emits data during a time called **emission time** or ET. Hence the RRH emits ET/F packets, i.e. requires a container of size C each F units of time during the emission time, as shown in Fig. 2.

At each period, the data of the RRH i begins to arrive in the insertion buffer at a time m_i called **offset**. The offsets can be determined by the designer of the system and can be different for each RRH but must remain the same over all periods. We assume that all BBUs are contained in the same data-center attached to the node v. The data from u is routed to its BBU at node v through the ring and arrives at time $m_i + \omega(u, v)$ if it has been inserted in the ring upon arrival. Then after some computation time, which w.l.o.g. is supposed to be zero, an answer is sent back from the BBU to the RRH. The same quantity of data is emitted by each BBU or RRH during any period.

In this paper, the **latency** of a data packet is defined as the time it waits in an insertion buffer. In other words, it is the logical latency into the optical ring. Indeed, because of the ring topology, the routes between RRHs and BBUs are fixed, thus we cannot reduce the physical transmission delay of a data which depends only on the size of the arcs used. Moreover, there is only one buffering point in the N-GREEN optical ring, the insertion buffer of the node at which the data arrives. Hence, in this context, to minimize the end-to-end delay, we need to minimize the (logical) latency. More precisely, we want to reduce the latency of the C-RAN traffic to **zero**, both for the RRHs (uplink) and the BBUs (downlink). In Sect. 4 we propose a deterministic mechanism with zero latency for C-RAN which also improves the latency of other data going through the optical ring. We shortly describe the nature of this additional traffic in the next paragraph.

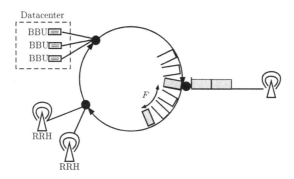

Fig. 2. Insertion of C-RAN traffic in the N-GREEN optical ring.

Best Effort Traffic. The optical ring supports other traffics, corresponding to the internet flow. We call this traffic **Best Effort** (BE). We want it to have the best possible distribution of latency, but since BE traffic is less critical than C-RAN traffic, we impose no hard constraint on its latency. At each node of the ring, a **contention buffer** is filled by a batch arrival process of BE data. This batch arrival process consists in generating, at each unit of time, a quantity of data drawn from a bimodal distribution to modelize the fact that internet traffic is bursty. Then, according to the fill rate of the contention buffer and the maximum waiting time of the data, a packet of size at most C may be created by aggregating data in the contention buffer. This packet is then put in the insertion buffer of the node. Hence, the arrival of BE messages can be modeled by a temporal law that gives the distribution of times between two arrivals of a BE packet in the insertion buffer. The computation of this distribution for the parameters of the contention buffer used in the N-GREEN optical ring is described in [16]. We use this distribution in our experiments to modelize BE packet arrival in the insertion buffer.

3   Evaluation of the Latency on the N-GREEN Optical Ring

We first study the latency of the C-RAN and BE traffics when the ring follows an opportunistic insertion policy: When a free container goes through a node,

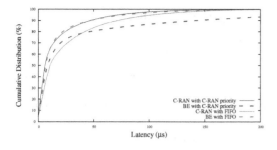

Fig. 3. Distribution of latencies for FIFO and C-RAN first.

Table 1. Parameters of the N-GREEN architecture.

Bit rate of an electronic interface R	10 Gbps
Optical ring bit rate $F \times R$	100 Gbps
Acceleration factor F	10
Container size C	100 kb
Unit of time (UoT) $C/(F \times R)$	1 μs
Length traveled during one UoT	200 m
Time to go through the cycle RS	100 UoT
Emission time ET	500 UoT
Period P	1,000 UoT
Number of RRH	5
Number of nodes k	5
Load induced by C-RAN traffic	50%
Load induced by BE traffic	40%

it is filled with a packet of its insertion buffer, if there is one. Two different methods to manage the insertion buffer are experimentally compared. First, the **FIFO** rule, which consists in managing the C-RAN and BE packets in the same insertion buffer. Then, when a free container is available, the node fills it with the oldest packet of the insertion buffer, without distinction between C-RAN and BE. This method is compared to a method called **C-RAN priority** that uses two insertion buffers: one for the BE packets, and another for the C-RAN packets. The C-RAN insertion buffer has the priority and is used to fill containers on the ring while it is non empty before considering the BE insertion buffer.

We compare experimentally these two methods in the simplest topology: The lengths of the arcs between nodes are equal and there is one RRH by node. The experimental parameters are given in Table 1 and chosen following [5]. In each experiment, the offsets of the RRHs are drawn uniformly at random in the period. The results are computed over 1,000 experiments in which the optical ring is simulated during 1,000,000 units of time. Figure 3 gives the cumulative distribution of both C-RAN and BE traffics latencies for the FIFO and the C-RAN priority methods. The source code in C of the experiments can be found on one of the authors' webpage [17].

Unsurprisingly, the latency of the C-RAN traffic is better when we prioritize the C-RAN messages, while the BE traffic is heavily penalized. Furthermore, there is still 10% of the C-RAN traffic with a latency higher than 50 μs, a problem we address in the next section.

Remark that, due to the broadcast and select mode, a message coming from any node induces the same load for all the nodes of the ring. Hence the latency of the traffics coming from any RRHs or from the BBUs are the same, which may seem couterintuitive knowing that all BBUs share the same node on the ring. This is why in Fig. 3 we do not distinguish between uplink C-RAN traffic (RRH to BBU) and downlink C-RAN traffic (BBU to RRH).

4   Deterministic Approach for Zero Latency

4.1   Reservation

Finding good offsets for the C-RAN traffic is a hard problem even for simple topologies and without BE traffic, see [12]. In this section, we give a simple solution to this problem in the N-GREEN optical ring, and we adapt it to minimize the latency of the BE traffic.

Let u be the node to which is attached the RRH i. To ensure zero latency for the C-RAN traffic, then the container which arrives at u at time m_i must be free so that the data from the RRH can be sent immediately on the optical ring.

To avoid latency between the arrival of the data from the RRH and its insertion on the optical ring, we allow nodes to **reserve** a container one round before using it. A container which is reserved cannot be filled by any node except the one which has reserved it (but it may not be free when it is reserved). If u reserves a container at time $m_i - RS$, then it is guaranteed that u can fill a free container at time m_i with the data of the RRH i. In the method we now describe, the C-RAN packets never wait in the node: The message sent by the RRH i arrives at its BBU at node v at time $m_i + \omega(u, v)$ and the answer is sent from the BBU at time $m_i + \omega(u, v) + 1$.

Recall that an RRH fills a container every F units of time, during a time ET. Thus if we divide the period P into **slots** of F consecutive units of time, an RRH needs to fill at most one container each slot. If an RRH emits at time m_i, then we say it is at **position** $m_i + \omega(u, v)$ (mod F). The position of an RRH corresponds to the position in a slot of the container it has emitted, when it arrives at v, the node of the BBU. If an RRH is at position p, then by construction, the corresponding BBU is at position $p + 1$ (mod F). For now, we do not allow waiting times for C-RAN traffic, hence each RRH uses a container at *the same position during all the emission time*.

Given a ring, a set of RRH's, a period and an acceleration factor F, the problem we solve here is to find an **assignment** of values of the offsets m_i's which is **valid**: two RRHs must never use the same container in a period. Moreover we want to preserve the latency of the BE traffic. It means that the time a BE packet waits in the insertion buffer must be minimized. To do so, we must minimize the time a node waits for a free container at any point in the period, by spreading the C-RAN traffic as uniformly as possible over the period.

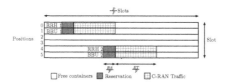

Fig. 4. A valid assignment with $F = 6$.

Figure 4 represents an assignment of two couples of RRH and BBU by showing the containers going through the node of the BBU during a period. Each slot has a duration of F unit of times, and, since an RRH/BBU emits a packet each F UoT during ET UoT, if we take the granularity of a slot to represent the time, the emission of a BBU/RRH is continuous in our representation, during ET/F slots. A date t in the period corresponds in Fig. 4 to the slot t/F and is at position $t \mod F$.

4.2 Building Valid Assignment with Zero C-RAN Latency

Remark that two RRHs which are not at the same position never use the same containers. Moreover, if we fix the offsets of the RRHs to even positions so that they do not reserve the same containers, then, because the answers of the BBU are sent without delay in our model, it will fix the offsets of the BBUs to odd positions which do not reserve the same containers. Hence, we need to deal with the RRHs only. The next proposition gives a simple method to find an assignment.

Proposition 1. *There is a valid assignment of the offsets $m_1, \ldots, m_k$ on the same position if $kET + RS \leq P$.*

Proof. W.l.o.g we fix m_1 to 0 and all the other offsets will then be chosen at position 0. Let $u_1, \ldots, u_k$ be the nodes attached to the RRHs $1, \ldots, k$. We assume that $u_1, \ldots, u_k$ are in the order of the oriented cycle. The last message emitted by the RRH 1 arrives at u_2 at time $ET - 1 + \omega(u_1, u_2)$. Therefore we can fix $m_2 = ET + \omega(u_1, u_2)$. In general we can set $m_i = (i - 1) \times ET + \omega(u_1, u_i)$ and all RRHs will use different containers at position 0 during a period. Since $k \times ET + \omega(u_1, u_1) \leq P$ by hypothesis, the containers filled by the kth RRH are freed before P. Hence when the RRH 1 must emit something at the first unit of time of the second period, there is a free container.

Remark that reserving free containers make them unusable for BE traffic which is akin to a loss of bandwidth. However, with our choice of emission times of the RRHs in the order of the cycle, most of the container we reserve are used by the data from some RRH. If all containers at some position are used, that is $kET + RS = P$, then there are only RS free containers wasted. In the worst case, less than $2RS$ containers are wasted by the assignment of Proposition 1.

It is now easy to derive the maximal number of antennas which can be supported by an optical ring, when using reservation and the same position for an RRH for the whole period.

Corollary 1. *There is a valid assignment with $\lfloor \frac{P-RS}{ET} \rfloor \times \frac{F}{2}$ antennas and zero latency.*

Proof. Following Proposition 1, the maximal number of antennas for which there is an assignment on the same position is $k = \lfloor \frac{P-RS}{ET} \rfloor$. In such an assignment, we need a second position to deal with the traffic coming from the BBUs coming back to those k antennas. Since we got F positions in the slot, the number of antennas supported by the ring is thus equal to $k \times \frac{F}{2}$.

With the parameters of the N-GREEN ring given in Table 1, we can support 5 antennas, while stochastic multiplexing can support 10 antennas albeit with extreme latency. There are two sources of inefficiency in our method. The first comes from the reservation and cannot be avoided to guarantee the latency of the C-RAN traffic. The second comes from the fact that an RRH must emit at the same position during all the emission time (to guarantee zero latency). We relax this constraint in Sect. 4.3 to maximize the number of antennas supported by the ring, while minimizing the loss of bandwith due to reservation.

We now present an algorithm using reservation as in Proposition 1 to set the offsets of several RRHs at the same position. In a naive assignment, we put each RRH in an arbitrary position, for instance one RRH by position. We then propose three ideas to optimize the latency of the BE traffic, by spacing as well as possible the free containers in a period.

Balancing Inside the Period. With the parameters of the N-GREEN ring given in Table 1 ($ET = \frac{P}{2}$, $F = 10$ and $n = 5$), there are no unused position. Any assignment has exactly one BBU or RRH at each position. If all the RRHs start to emit at the first slot, then during ET there will be no free container anywhere on the ring, inducing a huge latency for the BE traffic. To mitigate this problem, in a period, the time with free containers in each position must be uniformly distributed over the period as shown in Fig. 5.

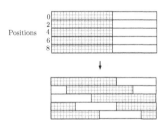

Fig. 5. Balancing inside the period.

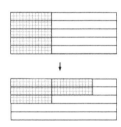

Fig. 6. Compacting positions.

Compacting Positions. For each position which is used by some RRH, and for each period, at least RS free containers are reserved which decreases the maximal load the system can handle. Therefore to not waste bandwidth, it is important to put as many RRHs as possible on the same position as shown in Fig. 6. Indeed, for any position which is not used at all, no container needs to be reserved. This strategy is also good to spread the load during the period since it maximizes the number of unused positions and for each unused position there is a container free of C-RAN traffic each F unit of times.

Balancing Used Positions. The free positions can be distributed uniformly over a slot, to minimize the time to wait before a node has access to a container from a free position, as shown in Fig. 7. To do so, compute the number of needed positions $x = \lceil k \times \frac{ET}{P-RS} \rceil$, with k the number of antennas using the previous strategy. Then, set the x used positions in the following way: $\lfloor \frac{F}{x} \rfloor - 1$ free positions are set between each used positions. If $\frac{F}{x}$ has a reminder r, then we set the r free remaining positions uniformly over the interval in the same way and so on until there are no more free position. It is a small optimization, since it decreases the latency by at most $F/2$.

Experimental Evaluation. Our algorithm *combines the three methods* we have described to spread the load over the period. In order to understand the interest of each improvement, we present the cumulative distribution of the latency of the BE traffic using them either alone or in conjunction and we compare our algorithm to stochastic multiplexing with C-RAN priority.

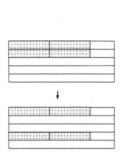

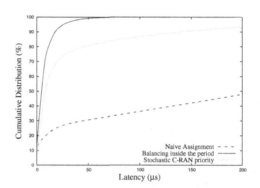

Fig. 7. Balancing used positions.   **Fig. 8.** BE latencies of a naive assignment and balancing inside the period for 5 antennas.

Figure 8 shows the performance of balancing the C-RAN traffic inside the period against a naive assignment in which all the RRH begin to emit at the same slot. We keep the same parameters as in Sect. 3 (see Table 1). As expected, the BE traffic latency is much better when we balance the C-RAN traffic inside the period and already much better than stochastic multiplexing.

To show the interest of compacting the positions, we must be able to put several RRHs at the same position. Hence, we change the emission time to $ET = 200$ and the number of antennas to $k = 12$ to keep the load around 90% as in the experiment of Fig. 3. This is not out of context since the exact split of the C-RAN (the degree of centralization of the computation units in the cloud) is not fully determined yet [7].

As shown in Fig. 9, the performance of the naive assignment is really bad. Compacting the RRHs on a minimal number of positions decreases dramatically the latency. If in addition, we balance over a period, we get another gain of latency of smaller magnitude: the average (respectively maximum) latency for BE traffic goes from $4.76\,\mu s$ (resp. $48\,\mu s$) to $3.28\,\mu s$ (resp. $37\,\mu s$). We did not represent the benefit of balancing used positions because the reduction in latency it yields is small as expected: the average (respectively maximum) latency for BE traffic goes from 4.76 μs (resp. 48 μs) to 4.43 μs (resp. 44 μs).

In Fig. 10, we compare the cumulative distribution of the latency of the BE traffic using the FIFO rule to our reservation algorithm with the three proposed improvements. The parameter are the same as in the previous experiment. The performance of our reservation algorithm is excellent, since the C-RAN traffic has *zero latency* and the BE traffic has a *better latency* than with the FIFO rule despite the cost of reservation. It is due to the balancing of the load of the C-RAN traffic over the period, that guarantee a more regular bandwidth for the BE traffic.

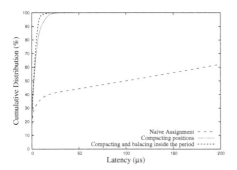
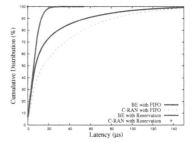

Fig. 9. BE latencies of compacting positions and balancing inside the period for 12 antennas.

Fig. 10. FIFO buffer compared to the best method with reservation for 12 antennas.

4.3   Building Valid Assignment with Some C-RAN Latency

The previous approach limits the number of antennas supported by the ring when $P - RS \mod ET \neq 0$, which is the case with N-GREEN parameters. The method we present in this section enables us to support more antennas and improves the latency of BE traffic (it reserves less free containers) by *allowing the data from an RRH to use two positions*. It is at the cost of a slightly worse latency for C-RAN traffic and it also requires in practice to implement some buffering for the C-RAN packets.

In order to support as much antennas as possible on the ring, we use *all* containers in a given position, improving on the compacting position heuristic.

Proposition 2. *There is a valid assignment for* k *antennas when* $k \leq \lfloor \frac{P-RS}{ET} \times \frac{F}{2} \rfloor$.

Proof. We consider the RRHs in the order of the ring. Let $l = \lfloor \frac{P-RS}{ET} \rfloor$, then we set the offsets of the first l RRHs as in Proposition 1. These RRHs are at position zero and the $(l + 1)$th RRH first emits at position zero, with offset $m_{l+1} = l * ET + \omega(u_0, u_{l+1})$.

The $(l+1)$th RRH emits up to time $P - \omega(u_{l+1}, u_0)$ at position zero, so that there is no conflict with RRH 0 during the next period. Hence, it has used the position zero during $x = P - \omega(u_{l+1}, u_0) - l * ET - \omega(u_0, u_{l+1}) = P - l * ET - RS$. From time $P - \omega(u_{l+1}, u_0) + 2$, the $(l+1)$th RRH emits at position 2 and during a time $ET - x$. Then the next RRH in the order is assigned to position 2, and begins to emit at time $P - \omega(u_{l+1}, u_0) + ET - x$ instead of zero. The rest of the assignment is built in the same way filling completely all first positions, until there are no more RRH.

Figure 11 illustrates the construction of Proposition 2 for the N-GREEN parameters. The loss due to reservation is exactly RS containers by used positions. Hence, it is possible to support 9 antennas (but no BE traffic in this extreme case), rather than 5 with the method of Sect. 4.2.

We call this new reservation algorithm **saturating positions** since it improves on compacting positions of the previous subsection. Moreover, there are no free slots in used positions, hence the idea of balancing into the period is not relevant. The only possible optimisation would be to balance the used positions, but it is not worth it since it adds additional latency for the RRHs using two different positions.

Fig. 11. Valid assignment for 9 antennas and the N-GREEN parameters.

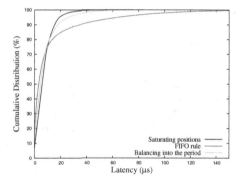

Fig. 12. Latencies of saturating positions, balancing into the period and FIFO rule for 5 antennas.

Figure 12 represents the cumulative distribution of the latency of BE traffic for the FIFO rule, saturating position, and balancing into the period using the N-GREEN parameters. Saturating positions reduces the BE traffic latency more than balancing into the period. This is easily explained by its lesser use of reservation. It is at the cost of a maximal latency of 2 µs for C-RAN traffic, so the designer can chose to use any of the two algorithms, according to what latency must be guaranteed to C-RAN or BE traffic.

5   Conclusion

As a conclusion, we want to stress the fact that to deal with a deterministic dataflow as C-RAN, we must use a deterministic policy rather than a classical stochastic one. By using a simple practical SDN scheme, which requires only to set the emission timing of the RRHs and to allow reservation on the optical ring, we remove all logical latencies. It also improves significantly the latencies of the BE traffic by spreading the load of the C-RAN traffic uniformly over the period. We are currently working on a prototype implementing this method on the NGREEN ring. We also plan to deal with the case of several data-centers containing the BBUs instead of one. The algorithmic methods to find good emission timings in this generalization are more complicated and similar to what was proposed in [12], but while the load due to the C-RAN traffic is not too high it should work very well. The results obtained show that te N-GREEN network architecture has a high potential in term of minimization of the end-to-end latency, in a multi-QoS environment. This study complete several studies demonstrating that the broadcast and select mechanism is extremely powerful to lead to deterministic networks, since it minimize the latency to its minimum feasible.

References

1. Pizzinat, A., Chanclou, P., Saliou, F., Diallo, T.: Things you should know about fronthaul. J. Lightwave Technol. **33**(5), 1077–1083 (2015)
2. Tayq, Z., et al.: Real time demonstration of the transport of ethernet fronthaul based on vRAN in optical access networks. In: OFC 2017. IEEE (2017)
3. Siller, C.A., Shafi, M.: SONET/SDH: A Sourcebook of Synchronous Networking. Wiley-IEEE Press, New York (1996)
4. Zukerman, M., Potter, P.G.: The DQDB protocol and its performance under overload traffic conditions. Comput. Netw. ISDN Syst. **20**(1–5), 261–270 (1990)
5. Chiaroni, D.: Network energy: problematic and solutions towards sustainable ICT. Invited paper, International Commission of Optics (ICO-24), August 2017
6. Uscumlic, B., et al.: Scalable deterministic scheduling for WDM slot switching Xhaul with zero-jitter. In ONDM 2018. IEEE (2018)
7. China Mobile: C-RAN: the road towards green RAN. White Paper, ver (2011)
8. 3GPP, 3rd Generation Partnership Project; Technical Specification Group Services and System Aspects; Service requirements for the 5G system;. Stage 1 (Release 16)
9. Boccardi, F., Heath, R.W., Lozano, A., Marzetta, T.L., Popovski, P.: Five disruptive technology directions for 5G. IEEE Commun. Mag. **52**(2), 74–80 (2014)
10. Kern, A., Somogyi, G., Cinkler, T.: Applying statistical multiplexing and traffic grooming in optical networks jointly (2006)
11. Finn, N., Thubert, P.: Deterministic Networking Architecture. Internet-Draft draft-finn-detnet-architecture-08, Internet Engineering Task Force (2016)
12. Barth, D., Guiraud, M., Leclerc, B., Marce, O., Strozecki, Y.: Deterministic scheduling of periodic messages for cloud RAN. In: ICT 2018, Saint Malo, France (2018)
13. Jiang, M., Condoluci, M., Mahmoodi, T.: Network slicing management & prioritization in 5G mobile systems. In: European Wireless, pp. 1–6 (2016)

14. Cadéré, C., Izri, N., Barth, D., Fourneau, J.-M., Marinca, D., Vial, S.: Virtual circuit allocation with QoS guarantees in the ECOFRAME optical ring. In: 2010 14th Conference on ONDM. IEEE (2010)
15. Szymanski, T.H.: An ultra-low-latency guaranteed-rate internet for cloud services. IEEE/ACM Trans. Netw. **24**(1), 123–136 (2016)
16. Ait El Mahjoub, Y., Castel-Taleb, H., Fourneau, J.-M.: Performance and energy efficiency analysis in NGREEN optical network. In: 2018 14th International Conference on Wireless and Mobile Computing, Networking and Communications (WiMob) (WiMob 2018), Limassol, Cyprus, October 2018 (2018)
17. Yann Strozecki's website. http://www.prism.uvsq.fr/%7Eystr/textesmaths.html

Resource Analysis and Cost Modeling for End-to-End 5G Mobile Networks

Hilary Frank[1]($\boxtimes$) ![ORCID], Rodrigo S. Tessinari[1], Yuqing Zhang[1], Zhengguang Gao[1,2], Carlos Colman Meixner[1], Shuangyi Yan[1], and Dimitra Simeonidou[1]

[1] High Performance Networks Group, University of Bristol, Bristol, UK
hilary.frank@bristol.ac.uk
[2] State Key Lab of Information Photonics and Optical Communications, Beijing University of Post and Telecommunications, Beijing 100876, China

Abstract. 5G network demands massive infrastructure deployment to meet its requirements. The most cost-effective deployment solution is now a challenge. This paper identifies a cost implementation strategy for 5G by reformulating existing cost models. It analyses three geo-type scenarios and calculates the total cost of ownership (TCO) after estimating the Capex and Opex. The calculations are narrowed to specific cities for clearer understanding instead of the usual generic estimates. An end-to-end 5G network resource analysis is performed. Our result shows that by the end of first year Capex constitutes over 90% of TCO for urban scenarios. Also uniform capacity deployment across geo-types impose severe investment challenges.

Keywords: 5G · Capex · Opex · TCO · End-to-End · Fiber · Microwave · CRAN · Backhaul · Core Network

1 Introduction

The growth of mobile communications since inception in the 1980s indicates that capacity is increasing along with rising demands for higher data rates. This trend has now witnessed four generations of mobile networks. Current research anticipates the next generation of mobile networks (NGMN) around 2020 [1]. The rate of revenue growth from wireless networks has not been proportional to the exponential increase in the networks over the years. Telecommunication companies in the UK suffered revenue fall in 2017 [2] despite raising demand. The impact of continuous traffic upsurge on network infrastructure has been a challenge for Mobile Network Operators (MNOs) [3]. Balancing the capacity needs of the networks with profitability is now a growing source of concern for MNOs.

MNOs must devise innovative ways to bring down cost while providing enhanced services to customers [4]. The crucial challenge of realizing 5G is becoming more economic than technological [5].

© IFIP International Federation for Information Processing 2020
Published by Springer Nature Switzerland AG 2020
A. Tzanakaki et al. (Eds.): ONDM 2019, LNCS 11616, pp. 492–503, 2020.
https://doi.org/10.1007/978-3-030-38085-4_42

It is important that suitable cost models are devised and applied to ensure an efficient use of resources to optimize Capital expenditure (Capex) and Operational expenditure (Opex). A detailed discussion on the TCO model for backhaul deployment was done by [6]. The study identified critical cost factors in order to achieve a cost-efficient strategy after considering two technology options: fiber and microwave. Our study shares some similarities with this work as it relates to cost models for wireless network. We extended the analysis to cover an end-to-end of the network and narrowed our discussion to three geo-type scenarios.

The idea of Centralized or Cloud Radio Access Network (CRAN) has been proposed by many studies. [7] shows that centralized Baseband Unit (BBU) is a viable option to save cost. Their considerations comprise cost comparisons in relation to baseband pooling and virtualization gains. This method is important for cost reduction towards TCO. But our analysis extend beyond the CRAN to encompass the entire mobile network end-to-end. We explored the deployment of 5G network by analyzing the key performance indicators. The number of small cells and macro cells were calculated for our case study cities - Lucca, Bristols and London.

Our paper reformulated earlier models to estimate the Capex, Opex, and TCO for the different geo-type scenarios. Some assumptions were considered in applying our model. Based on the results we recommend a 5G deployment strategy that would improve network cost efficiency.

The rest of the paper is structured as follows. Section 2 describes 5G Networks in detail. In Sect. 3, we present our cost model with analysis on the different aspects of the formulations. In Sect. 4 our case study is discussed with results while Sect. 5 concludes the paper and presents our future work.

Table 1. 5G disruptive capabilities [3,8]

KPI	Requirement	Description
Peak data rate	≥ 10 Gbps	Low mobility
Peak data rate	≥ 1 Gbps	High mobility
Availability	99.999%	Reliability
Data traffic density	≥ 10 Tbps/km^2	Network throughput per km^2
Device density	≥ 1 Million/km^2	Connected devices per km^2
Energy consumption	$\leq 10\%$ of 4G	Total energy consumption
Latency	< 1 ms	10x reduction in 4G latency
Mobility	Up to 500 km/h	Speed between Rx and Tx
Network Opex	$\leq 20\%$ of 4G	Total network management Opex

2   5G Network Architecture

To achieve the target of 1000x capacity, 5G networks will adopt ultra-dense small cell, millimeter wave (mm-wave), and massive MIMO [9]. The NGMN would converge diverse technology types to deliver the key performance indicators (KPIs) as shown in Table 1. It describes 5G disruptive potentials and the superior KPIs.

2.1   Wireless Access Networks in 5G

5G will consist of 3 spectrum layers namely - Lower, Middle and Upper frequency bands, corresponding to 700 MHz, 3.5 GHz and 26 GHz respectively. The use of higher frequency for future mobile networks has become imperative for small cells. The mm-wave spectrum range of 30 GHz to 300 GHz is attractive for 5G cost reduction strategy because it opens more room for spectrum and permits higher data rates [10]. However, mm-wave suffers increased path loss beyond 200 m [3]. Experimental results show that the compression of higher order antenna elements against the shorter wavelength of the mm-wave bands compensates for the path loss. Massive antenna elements are projected to be as much as 10x the number of streams in service to all terminals, compared to present MIMO [9].

2.2   Cloud Radio Access Networks

The concept of Cloud or Virtualized RAN is one that basically divides the functions of the gNodeB (gNB) and centrally positions it at greater distance (up to kilometers) from the Remote Radio Head (RRH), to a shared pool of virtualized BBU [4]. This increases spectral efficiency, throughput and reduces equipment and power cost at cell sites. In 5G New Radio (NR) transport architecture, BBU is split into RRH, Distributed Unit (DU) and Central Unit (CU). CRAN is viewed as an enabler for 5G dense networks. It benefits the ultra-dense cell structure by the avoidance of inter-cell interference through centralized management and distribution of intelligent resource [11].

5G Fronthaul and Midhaul have evolved with the concept of CRAN. The portion of wireless architecture referred to as fronthaul is the link between DU or radio controller and the RRHs. The DU interfaces with the RRH through an optical fiber connection called enhanced Common Public Radio Interface (eCPRI). The eCPRI link forms the fronthaul of the Network as Fig. 1 shows. This imposes strict latency and synchronization requirements [12,13]. Different options of functional splits are now being proposed [14].

According to [4], BBU centralization can provide as much savings as 50% Opex and 15% Capex. Also, MNOs expend as much as 80% Capex on RAN. This implies that gNB infrastructure constitute significant cost component for RAN [3], which could reduce considerably with the use of CRAN and substantially decrease TCO.

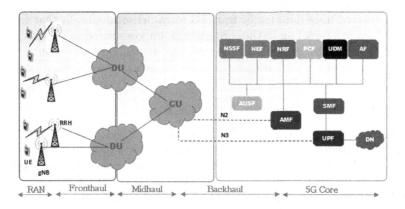

Fig. 1. End-to-end 5G mobile network architecture

2.3   Multi-access Edge Computing

Multi-access Edge Computing (MEC) is an innovative concept that converges telecom and information technology applications by orchestrating cloud-based services at the edge of computing networks [15]. MEC run applications nearer the edge of the network. It brings the system closer to the end users and hence reduces latency, network congestion and creates an efficient backhaul and core networks. 5G latency dependent applications and services would benefit from this strategy, when distributed around the network edge. MEC is a promising innovation for 5G success and would reduce the cost of its implementation.

2.4   Backhaul for 5G Network

Backhaul or transport network, is the connection that transports data between the CU and 5G Core based on the N2 and N3 interfaces. The backhaul link is dimensioned to meet the required peak data rates and high-speed applications. This connection can be either wired or wireless. Different backhaul solutions include microwave, fiber optics, meshed wireless, copper cable and Free Space Optical communication (FSO). Contemporary 4G networks mostly use either fiber or Line of Sight (LOS) solutions.

The topology of fiber backhaul deployment has a structure of either in a tree or point-to-point (PtP) topology. In PtP the central office (CO) connects one optical line terminal (OLT) through a devoted fiber to an optical network unit (ONU) in the user/client premises. These devices perform signal conversions from electrical to optical and vice versa.

In a tree-based approach, such as Passive Optical Network (PON) or Active Optical Network (AON), one OLT is linked to multiple ONUs through splitting and switching devices located in street cabinets [6]. Fiber optics are transmitted across long distances starting from the transponder and existing the node at designated port. Amplifiers are installed about every 80 km to amplify fiber links that suffers attenuation over those distances.

The expected huge data traffic from 5G ultra-dense small cells that would be connected via the backhaul to the core network imposes extreme requirements in terms of capacity, energy, latency, and cost [12]. It becomes important to devise innovative backhaul provisioning to cater for these extreme requirements.

2.5   Core Network

The Core Network is the control hub of a telecom network infrastructure. Mainly it performs aggregation, authentication, charging, switching, service invocation and gateway functions. This involves the control plane such as the Access and Mobility Management Function (AMF), Session Management Function (SMF) or Authentication Server Function (AUSF) and the data plane involving User Plane Function (UPF).

Two key innovations are being proposed that are timely for 5G network architecture. These are software defined networking (SDN) and network function virtualization (NFV) [3]. SDN basically separates the forwarding of data function from the control using software. This makes a dynamic architecture that is much easier to adapt, manage and cost-effective to implement [12]. New developments are likely to come about due to SDN capabilities, one of which is the possibility of a reduced core network infrastructure [3].

NFV technology enables key network functions to be executed in software environment by enabling scalability and flexibility in programmable network slices. NFV creates the possibility of shorter deployment time and the use of commercial off the shelf (COTS) based solutions instead of proprietary hardware that are usually vendor specific [3]. The availability of COTS solutions will lead to reduce deployment cost.

2.6   5G Use Cases

The NGMN will witness much higher bandwidth with lower latency and massive interconnection of devices. The use cases can be classified into three main categories - massive Machine Type Communication (mMTC), enhance Mobile Broadband (eMBB) and Ultra-Low Latency Communications (URLLC). Most of these 5G use cases depend on computing intelligence requiring sensor networks and driven by virtual reality and tactile internet. The capabilities of these uses cases are described in Table 1. Their implementation would pave the way for diverse business concepts at various levels of connectivity [8]. This will enrich the prospects of commercial involvement in the deployment of the NGMN.

3   Cost Model

The 5G objective calls for considerable planning. The usual resource over-provisioning strategy often result in network resource under utilization and high energy consumption [5]. We devised our model based on the following assumptions:

Table 2. Demographic, cell site and traffic capacity calculations

	Lucca	Bristol	London
Population	92,155	452,790	8,850,000
Area (km^2)	185.5	110.0	1,572.0
Population density (per km^2)	496	4116	5629
User density (per km^2)	50	412	563
Traffic capacity (Gbps per km^2)	25	206	282
Mean traffic capacity (Mbps)	510	500	501
Number of users per cell	4.9	41.2	56.3
Small Cell (SC)	1850	1100	15720
Macro Cell (MC)	71	42	605

- 5% of subscribers simultaneous usage of network;
- 50:50 wired to wireless backhaul deployment ratio;
- 2.5% annual inflation rate;
- Fiber deployment option: cascaded splitter;
- Cost of Core network upgrade is 10% of RAN deployment cost [3];
- Small and Macro cell radius 200 m and 2 km.

3.1 Capacity Planning Estimation

The network coverage and capacity analysis will include the following, type of information, coverage area available spectrum, subscriber forecast and traffic density. The demographics for the three cities in our case study from where other calculations such as cell range, number of cells, users per cell arise are presented in Table 2.

3.2 Coverage, Cell Site and Traffic Capacity (TC) Calculation

Area of the hexagonal shape is given by the following equation:

$$\left[\left(3\sqrt{3} \right) / 2 \right] . d^2 \tag{1}$$

TC = Pop. density × 10% subscription × 5% usage × data rate. Hence number of small and macro cells for coverage, traffic capacity and mean traffic capacity are shown in Table 2.

The mean traffic capacity per user (MTC) equals to the cell capacity divided by the number of users. MTC is approximately 500 Mbps.

3.3 Total Cost of Ownership

Our research calculates the total cost of 5G deployment to equal the summation of the total cost of Capex and Opex. A cost model summary of non-sharing infrastructure is presented

$$TCO_{5G} = \sum_{i=1}^{N_c} Capex_{5G} + \left(\sum_{i=1}^{N_o} Opex_{5G_{[/yr/infl]}} \right) N_{yrs} \qquad (2)$$

TCO_{5G} = Total cost of 5G network deployment

$Capex_{5G}$ = Sum of capital expenditures

$Opex_{5G}$ = Sum of operational expenditures plus inflation

N_{yrs} = Number of years used for Opex calculation

The Total Cost of Ownership for 5G network consist of Capex and Opex for the end-to-end stretch of wireless network. Reflecting the network portions in the TCO is given as follows

$$TCO = Capex_{[Acc+BH+CN]} + Opex_{[Acc+BH+CN]} \qquad (3)$$

Where Acc, BH and CN denotes the Access, Backhaul and Core portions in the wireless network. Our model performs joint calculations for the Access and Backhaul segments of the network, particularly for some Opex cost factors such as energy consumption, maintenance and reparation cost. This is an error avoidance strategy. At points of convergence, such as cabinets, the distinction between Access and Backhaul for the purpose of Opex calculation diminishes greatly. In calculating the cost of Core network upgrade, we followed [3], which assumes 10% of RAN deployment cost as the cost of Core network upgrade.

3.4 Capex Calculations

Capex is the capital expenditure which refers to a one-off-investment cost used to acquire or upgrade physical assets or infrastructure. Our formulation comprises the summation of equipment, infrastructure and installation cost plus spectrum licence fee.

$$Capex = \sum_{i=1}^{N_{Eq}} Cost_{Eq} + \sum_{i=1}^{N_{Infra}} Cost_{Infra} + \sum_{i=1}^{N_{Insta}} Cost_{Insta} + \sum_{i=1}^{N_L} Cost_{Lfee} \qquad (4)$$

Equipment Cost. This refers to all cost connected to the acquisition of equipment both for fiber and microwave cost components. Fiber and microwave equipment cost are modelled as follows

$$Cost_{Eq}^{F} = \sum_{i=1}^{N_{OLT}} Cost_{OLT} + \sum_{i=1}^{N_{ONT}} Cost_{ONT} + \sum_{i=1}^{N_s} Cost_s \qquad (5)$$

$$Cost_{Eq}^{Mw} = 2N_{Mwlink}.Pr_{ant} + N_{sw}.Pr_{sw} \qquad (6)$$

Equation 4 follows that of [6]. Where $Cost_{OLT}$, $Cost_{ONT}$ and $Cost_s$ denotes cost of OLTs, ONTs and Splitters. Also, N_{Mwlink}, Pr_{ant}, N_{sw} and Pr_{sw} represents the number of links used for microwave, antenna price, number of switches and unit price of switches.

Infrastructure Cost. This refers to the total cost needed to deploy or lease communication infrastructure. We have associated fiber cost to the infrastructure component because the fiber length determines the duct and trenching length. It works better when these components are factored in common. On the part of microwave, the infrastructure cost include cost associated with microwave hubs, masts and antennas.

$$Cost^F_{Infra} = L.\,(Cost_F + Cost_{CW}) \tag{7}$$

Where L denotes length of trenches, whereas $Cost_F$ and $Cost_{CW}$ represents cost of fiber and civil works. The formulation for microwave is as follows

$$Cost^{Mw}_{Infra} = \sum_{i=1}^{N_{hub}} (N_{Mwhub}.Pr_{hub}) \tag{8}$$

Where N_{Mwhub} denotes number of microwave hubs and Pr_{hub} its unit price.

Installation Cost. The installation component captures man-hours required to perform the necessary installations, wiring, preparation of sites, technician salary and travel time to and from site locations. The formulation is given by [5].

$$Cost_{Insta} = \left[\sum_{i=1}^{N_{link}} (IT_i + 2T_i).TS \right] NT_i \tag{9}$$

Where IT_i and T_i, denotes installation and travel time, TS and NT_i represents technician salary and number of technicians respectively.

3.5 Opex Calculations

Opex translates to operational expenditure, which means the recurring cost needed to continuously operate the business daily. One of the key cost components for network operators is power consumption. We have formulated our Opex cost by remodelling that given by [16]. The major Opex cost components are energy consumption, maintenance and fault management or reparation cost. Our model for the Opex calculation is given as follows

$$Opex = 365 \left[\sum_{i=1}^{N} (24P_h.C_E).N_C \right] + \sum_{i=1}^{N_m} C_M.C_{F_c} \tag{10}$$

Energy Consumption. Electricity consumption is an important Opex cost driver. Between 70%–80% of energy requirement of the network is projected to be consumed by the access network [8]. In view of the expected ultra-dense network, innovative energy management schemes are needed to cut operating cost of 5G network. We have derived the energy cost by adding the consumption cost of every electrical equipment in the different locations within the network such as those in the central office, cell sites and street cabinets.

$$Cost_{En} = 365 \left(\sum_{i=1}^{N} 24P_h.C_E.N_C \right) \tag{11}$$

Where P_h, C_E and N_C represents electric power needed per hour, cost of one kWh of energy and number of cabinets, which in this case could mean, Central Office, cell sites or street cabinet.

Maintenance expenses are regularly incurred to keep the network running at optimal performance. This may consist of routine system upgrade, equipment testing, and software licence renewal among others. Our maintenance cost model is given by [6].

Maintenance Cost

$$Cost_M = \sum_{i=1}^{N} (Co_m + Cab_m + M_{Mw} + Sw_{lic}) \tag{12}$$

Where Co_m, Cab_m and M_{Mw} denotes the cost incurred from maintaining central offices, street cabinets and microwave links. Sw_{lic} reflects licence fee for periodic software upgrade. Details of this formulation can be obtained in [6].

Fault Management/Reparation Cost. Reparation of system failures such as fiber cut, and other natural or man-made faults incur cost. We have remodelled this cost component to reflect the probability of failure employing the Weibull distribution which is mainly applied in reliability engineering from [5].

$$Cost_{F_m} = \left[\sum_{i=1}^{N} (FR + Pen) \right] P_f \tag{13}$$

Where FR and Pen denotes failure reparation and penalty cost respectively. P_f represents probability of failure following Weibull's distribution.

$$FR = \left[\sum_{i=1}^{N_f} (MTTR_f + 2T_i).TS \right] NTR_f \tag{14}$$

Where $MTTR_f$ reflects mean time to repair failure and NTR_f denotes number of people to repair failure. Further details can be obtained in [5].

4   Case Study

Table 3 presents cost values used.

Our result in Fig. 2(a) shows that fiber is consistently the most capital intensive cost factor in all scenarios. The result reveals significant cost difference between fiber and microwave for Lucca than Bristol and London.

Table 3. Values used for cost calculations

Components/parameters	Price (Euros)	Source
OLT core shell	5000	[17]
OLT cross connect	8000	[17]
OLT service shell	5000	[17]
ONT	150	[17]
Technician salary (hour)	52	[6]
Small/large microwave antenna	200/2000	[6]
Power splitter (1:16/1:32)	170/340	[6]
Fiber (km)	80	[6]
Trenching (km)	45000	[6]
Microwave link	400	[13]
Yearly cell site rent	8000	[13]
Microwave hub	800	[13]
Electricity cost	0.2 per kWh	[16]
Energy consumption per hour	1.4 kW	[16]

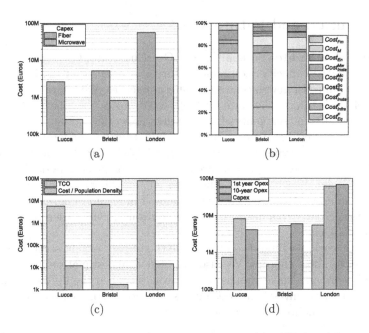

Fig. 2. (a) Capex comparison for fiber and microwave. (b) TCO breakdown across all scenarios. (c) TCO and cost per population density comparison showing Bristol with a higher TCO but much lower cost per population density than Lucca. (d) Capex, 1st year Opex, and 10 years cumulative Opex comparison.

Whereas the later two cities have 16% and 21% difference respectively, Lucca has as much as 56%. It is relatively more expensive to deploy fiber in Lucca than in the other two cities. This identifies the most cost-effective backhaul deployment for the NGMN.

The cost breakdown in Fig. 2(b) presents infrastructure as the most dominant cost component constituting at least 30% of TCO in all scenarios.

The TCO as in Fig. 2(c) shows that London has the highest deployment cost and Lucca the lowest. Bristol has the lowest cost per user, which validates the result that Lucca is relatively more expensive in comparison. Also Lucca with approximately 1% of London's population requires as much as 12% of London's TCO. This is due to the role of area and population density in the economies of scale.

Figure 2(d) shows the result of three comparisons. The ten years Opex has been calculated with compounding inflation rate. It shows that capital expenditure constitutes over 90% of TCO for Bristol and London by the end of first year, while Lucca's operational expenditure was as much as 15% for the same period. But after ten years, while Opex was still below Capex by 12% for Bristol and 10% for London, Lucca's Opex exceeds Capex by 50%. This trend depicts increasing operational expenditure cost as population density of the scenario decreases.

5   Conclusion and Future Work

We conducted an end-to-end analysis of 5G architecture. Given the 5G KPI's, we also calculated capacity requirements for three selected cities, including the number of small cells, macro cells and traffic capacities. We reformulated exiting cost models to estimate the total cost of ownership by calculating Capex and Opex for the different segments of the wireless network.

Based on the results, we conclude that investment consideration should be a function of the geo-type scenarios. As a result, 5G system capacity should be adjusted in less densely populated areas to allow for profitable deployment. In such areas wireless backhaul option becomes a compelling economic choice. Consideration should be given to a capacity trade-off in favour of coverage. However, the benefits accruable to a network when ubiquitous services are rendered should not be overlooked.

As future work, we intend to investigate the impact of infrastructure sharing in under neutral host concept. We also aim at revenue estimation for a projected number of years and make similar comparisons between the different scenarios. Finally, we aim to investigate the effects of application related cost on cost savings and revenue forecast for the NGMN.

Acknowledgments. We thank TETFUND, Ken Saro-Wiwa Polytechnic, Nigeria, EU H2020 Metro-Haul and 5GCity grant agreement No. 761727 and No. 761508 for their support.

References

1. Frank, H., Iaeng, P.B.: Mobile networks beyond 4G. In: Proceedings of the World Congress on Engineering, vol. 1 (2015)
2. Ofcom Technology Tracker. https://www.ofcom.org.uk/about-fcom/latest/media/facts
3. 5G infrastructure requirements in the UK. Technical report (2017)
4. Checko, A., et al.: Cloud RAN for mobile networks - a technology overview. IEEE Commun. Surv. Tutor. **17**(1), 405–426 (2015)
5. Charni, R., Maier, M.: Total cost of ownership and risk analysis of collaborative implementation models for integrated fiber-wireless smart grid communications infrastructures. IEEE Trans. Smart Grid **5**(5), 2264–2272 (2014)
6. Mahloo, M., Monti, P., Chen, J., Wosinska, L.: Cost modeling of backhaul for mobile networks. In: IEEE International Conference on Communications Workshops (ICC), pp. 397–402 (2014)
7. De Andrade, M., Tornatore, M., Pattavina, A., Hamidian, A., Grobe, K.: Cost models for baseband unit (BBU) hotelling: from local to cloud. In: IEEE International Conference on Cloud Networking (CloudNet), pp. 201–204 (2015)
8. Agyapong, P.K., Iwamura, M., Staehle, D., Kiess, W., Benjebbour, A.: Design considerations for a 5G network architecture. IEEE Commun. Mag. **52**(11), 65–75 (2014)
9. Frank, H.: Interference mitigation for femto deployment in next generation mobile networks. In: Proceedings of the International MultiConference of Engineers and Computer Scientists, vol. 2 (2016)
10. Siddique, U., Tabassum, H., Hossain, E., Kim, D.I.: Wireless backhauling of 5G small cells: challenges and solution approaches. IEEE Wirel. Commun. **22**(5), 22–31 (2015)
11. Taufique, A., Jaber, M., Imran, A., Dawy, Z., Yaacoub, E.: Planning wireless cellular networks of future: outlook, challenges and opportunities. IEEE Access **5** (2017)
12. Jaber, M., Imran, M.A., Tafazolli, R., Tukmanov, A.: 5G backhaul challenges and emerging research directions: a survey. IEEE Access **4**, 1743–1766 (2016)
13. Lisi, S.S., Alabbasi, A., Tornatore, M., Cavdar, C.: Cost-effective migration towards C-RAN with optimal fronthaul design. In: IEEE International Conference on Communications (ICC), pp. 1–7 (2017)
14. Pelekanou, A., Anastasopoulos, M., Tzanakaki, A., Simeonidou, D.: Provisioning of 5G services employing machine learning techniques. In: International Conference on Optical Network Design and Modeling (ONDM), pp. 200–205 (2018)
15. Taleb, T., Samdanis, K., Mada, B., Flinck, H., Dutta, S., Sabella, D.: On multi-access edge computing: a survey of the emerging 5G network edge cloud architecture and orchestration. IEEE Commun. Surv. Tutor. **19**(3), 1657–1681 (2017)
16. Chiaraviglio, L., et al.: Bringing 5G into rural and low-income areas: is it feasible? IEEE Commun. Stand. Mag. **1**(3), 50–57 (2017)
17. Davim, J.P., Ziaie, S., Pinto, A.N.: CAPEX model for PON technology using single and cascaded splitter schemes. In: IEEE EUROCON-International Conference on Computer as a Tool (EUROCON), pp. 1–4 (2011)

Analog IFoF/mmWave 5G Optical Fronthaul Architecture for Hot-Spots Using Multi-channel OFDM-Based WDM Signals

Charoula Mitsolidou[1]([✉]) [ID], Christos Vagionas[1], Agapi Mesodiakaki[1],
Pavlos Maniotis[1], George Kalfas[1], Chris G. H. Roeloffzen[2], Paulus W. L. van Dijk[2],
Ruud M. Oldenbeuving[2], Amalia Miliou[1], and Nikos Pleros[1]

[1] Department of Informatics, Aristotle University of Thessaloniki, Thessaloniki, Greece
cvmitsol@csd.auth.gr
[2] LIONIX International B.V., Enschede, The Netherlands

Abstract. An analog Intermediate-Frequency-over-Fiber (IFoF) – based fronthaul 5G architecture for high traffic hot-spot environments is presented. The proposed optical fronthaul link utilizes Photonic Integrated Circuit (PIC) Wavelength Division Multiplexing (WDM) Externally Modulated Laser (EML) - based optical transmitters at a centralized Base Band Unit (BBU) and Reconfigurable Optical Add-Drop Multiplexers (ROADMs) at the Remote Radio Head (RRH) side located in the hot-spot area. By employing two WDM links, where each wavelength carries six 0.5 Gbaud IF bands of Orthogonal Frequency Division Multiplexing (OFDM) with 16 – QAM Sub-Carrier (SC) modulation, a total data rate of 96 Gb/s was achieved. Error Vector Magnitude (EVM) measurements were carried out, exhibiting acceptable performance below the EVM FEC limit of 12.5%. A power budget study was also performed, suggesting up to 9.5 km fiber lengths between the BBU and the hot-spot network. The proposed architecture complies with the high capacity and low latency requirements of the 5G vision, thus may be an efficient solution for 5G fronthauling of heavy traffic hot-spot areas.

Keywords: 5G networks · Analog fronthaul · Intermediate Frequency over Fiber · OFDM · Photonic Integrated Circuit · ROADM

1 Introduction

The insatiable mobile data traffic growth in combination with the exponential proliferation of smart mobile devices [1], have created a new set of bandwidth and latency requirements beyond the capabilities of the legacy 4G mobile networks. To this end, Fifth Generation (5G) networks have already stepped in as the next generation technology for broadband mobile connectivity [2]. Towards satisfying user's experience, 5G broadband access has been defined by expert alliances through Key Performance Indicators (KPIs) that foresee user rates of 1 Gb/s and peak rates up to 10 Gb/s at latencies less than 10 ms,

© IFIP International Federation for Information Processing 2020
Published by Springer Nature Switzerland AG 2020
A. Tzanakaki et al. (Eds.): ONDM 2019, LNCS 11616, pp. 504–515, 2020.
https://doi.org/10.1007/978-3-030-38085-4_43

resulting in high area connection densities up to 10^6 devices per km^2 [3]. To address the 5G goals, intense research efforts have directed on the development of New Radio (NR) systems [4] and the introduction of millimeter Wave (mm-Wave) spectral bands of 28 GHz and 60 GHz in the access networks [5].

The initial 5G trials are expected to be deployed at densely populated areas and overcrowded hotspots, such as stadiums, airports etc., where the density of the users may result on financially viable installations [6]. However, moving to the New Radio systems comes with the need for densification of the Access Points (APs), in order to cope with the high propagation losses of the mm-Wave band [7], bringing at the same time increased deployment costs. To alleviate the densification costs, operators gradually focus on the Centralized RAN (C-RAN) technology [8] that shifts the demanding operations at the Central Office (CO), while simplifying the hardware of the APs.

However, the cost-reduction due centralization does not alleviate on its own the upcoming fronthaul explosion [9], which necessitates the transmission of ultra-broadband mm-Wave channels at a small latency and energy envelope. Towards developing 5G NR systems capable to follow this explosion, research and industry efforts have been directed on the adoption and optimization of specific key technologies.

One of the directions is to employ the technology that can seamlessly combine the wireless access networks with the optical transport. Since optical fiber has chosen as the means to transport data to the centralized Base-Band Units (BBUs), analog Intermediate Frequency over Fiber (IFoF) technology [10] is currently investigated as an efficient fronthaul technique for distributing data from the BBU to a large number of Remote Radio Heads (RRHs) in a bandwidth- and cost-efficient manner. The advantage of IFoF is that it utilizes aggregation of mobile signals in intermediate frequencies and modulation with cost-efficient and low bandwidth devices [11], without adding any extra delay due to digital procedures as in the equivalent Common Public Radio Interface (CPRI)-based schemes [12]. Up to now, most of the analog IFoF-based demonstrations have been mainly evaluated for single carrier data signals with bandwidth up to 1 Gb/s [11], or for OFDM signals with channel bandwidth less than 200 MHz [10, 13, 14].

Another physical-layer key technology for cost efficient fronthauling, is the Photonic Integrated Circuit (PIC) technology that has already proved beneficial for optical communications [15]. Based on already developed PIC technologies which mainly include linear analog transceivers with high peak data rates beyond the 10 Gb/s [16] and low-loss integrated Reconfigurable Add/Drop Optical Multiplexer (ROADMs), 5G networks can be evolved into larger-scale and denser topologies utilizing the cost, energy and size benefits of PICs. So far, the advantages of using PIC - based transceivers and wavelength multiplexing devices have been investigated only for metro-rings and PON networks [17].

Finally, another key direction for achieving efficient fronthauling is the development of Medium Access Control (MAC) protocols capable to allocate all available optical, wireless and time-domain resources of a converged Fiber-Wireless (FiWi) network, while simultaneously satisfying the low latency KPI constraints [18]. Recently, we investigated the employment of a Medium-Transparent resource allocation scheme in a hotspot FiWi 5G network, achieving adequate throughput and latency values [19]. However, this analysis was based on certain physical - layer assumptions since the hardware specifications were not available at that time.

Although significant research advances have been reported for each of the above key technologies individually, yet it remains a research gap on defining the physical – layer specifications of a fronthaul architecture that will incorporate all distinct technological aspects in the same scheme, while simultaneously meet the 5G KPI requirements. Towards addressing this research gap, we extend our previous MAC-layer related work [19], by providing a detailed physical – layer study of the proposed analog IFoF 5G fronthaul architecture for hot-spot areas. The architecture employs photonic integrated Indium Phosphide (InP) transmitters at the BBU and optical busses of WDM-ROADMs at the hot-spot area. Our analysis relies on experimentally verified simulation models of the optical transceivers as well as the signal degradation induced by the fiber-propagation, while WDM functionalities are leveraged by a low-loss photonic integrated Si_3N_4/SiO_2 ROADM design. The transmission of 6-IF band OFDM 16-QAM signals was successfully confirmed by Error Vector Magnitude (EVM) measurements, revealing performance above the commonly acceptable limits.

This paper is organized as follows: Sect. 2 presents the concept of the proposed 5G hot-spot architecture, while Sect. 3 shows the simulation modeling of the employed building blocks. The physical - layer evaluation of optical fronthaul link is presented in Sect. 4. Section 5 provides the conclusion of the work.

2   5G Fronthaul Architecture for Stadiums

The concept of the proposed 5G fronthaul architecture, serving a typical sport-stadium is depicted in Fig. 1. In this architecture, the BBU is located in a centralized location outside the hot-spot area of the stadium and is interconnected with the RRH units which are dispersed around the stadium, through fiber links.

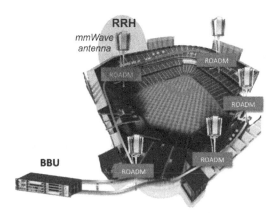

Fig. 1. Conceptual representation of the 5G IFoF/mmWave fronthaul architecture for hot-spot stadiums.

WDM optical transmitters based on photonic integrated Externally Modulated Laser (EML) modulators are employed at the BBU side, in order to generate and transmit the IFoF signals to the hot-spot area where the RRHs are placed at different regions of the stadium in an optical bus topology. Each RRH consists of an optical ROADM that either drops any of the wavelengths at the connected RRH or sends it to the next RRH of the bus. Moreover, each RRH incorporates a number of antennas that are responsible for optical - to - IF and subsequently IF - to - mmWave conversion before the wireless transmission to the clients. It should be noted that multi - IF bands transmission per wavelength is supported, allowing in this way each wavelength to carry different user channels on different IF bands.

Based on this concept, our goal is to design a fronthaul architecture according to the requirements of the 5G vision by identifying what is the optimum set of resources in terms of fiber-lengths, optical losses, number of wavelengths, modulation etc., while simultaneously complying with the physical layer performance metrics of the available hardware and providing a low cost and power consumption solution.

3   Simulation Modeling

In order to ensure that the simulation results used for the physical layer performance evaluation of the proposed fronthaul are reliable, we created experimentally-verified simulation models of the main building blocks employed in the simulation setup. Particularly, the response of the employed optical modulator was matched with the respective experimental characterized behavior of a high – power linear InP - based EML [16], while the signal impairments (losses, chromatic dispersion) caused by the fiber transmission, were matched with the respective response of a Standard Single Mode Fiber (SMF) [20]. The simulation model of the ROADM was also matched with the estimated spectral response of a MZI - based ROADM design being currently fabricated on the TriPleX platform [21]. Figure 2 depicts the simulation model results of the EML, perfectly matched with the experimentally-verified response of a fabricated InP - based linear EML operating in the C – band and comprising a laser source co-integrated with an Electro Absorption Modulator (EAM) [16].

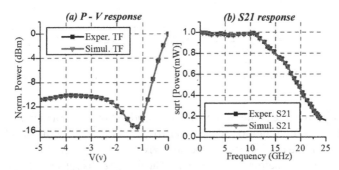

Fig. 2. EML modeling: (a) Power versus Volts experimental and simulated transfer functions, (b) experimental and simulated S21 curves.

More specifically, Fig. 2(a) shows the experimentally - measured and the simulated curve of the normalized output optical power versus the input voltage, revealing identical responses for both curves with a linear regime between −1 V and −0.2 V and an Extinction Ratio (ER) of 12 dB. The experimentally – measured and the simulated electro - optic S21 curves of the EML are illustrated in Fig. 2(b) exhibiting identical characteristics with a flat - top spectral response up to 11 GHz.

Figure 3(a) presents the cascaded MZI-based ROADM design [22] that is currently fabricated on the Si_3N_4/SiO_2 TriPleX platform [21] and its estimated spectra response was used for the matching procedure of the ROADM simulation model. The employed ROADM that was designed by Lionix International [23] for operation in the C – band, is capable to add or drop four wavelengths spaced with 100 GHz channel spacing. The four wavelengths (λ_1, λ_2, λ_3, λ_4) are inserted into the first cascaded block of MZIs depicted in Fig. 3(a) with the green color, having a Free Spectral Range (FSR) of 200 GHz. Wavelengths λ_1 and λ_3 separated with 200 GHz channel spacing are exiting output port 1 of the MZI cascade, while wavelengths λ_2 and λ_4 again spaced with 200 GHz are exiting output port 2. The WDM signal carrying λ_1 and λ_3 is fed into the brown block of MZIs of the ROADM upper arm that has a FSR of 400 GHz. As it is shown in Fig. 3(a) the first cascade of 400 GHz FSR drops λ_1, while the second block of MZIs with 400 GHz FSR drops λ_3. In a similar manner, the WDM signal carrying λ_2 and λ_4 is directed at the lower arm of the ROADM, where the first brown cascade of MZIs having a FSR of 400 GHz drops λ_4 at its output port 1 and the second cascade drops λ_2 at its respective output port 1.

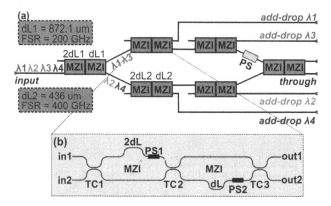

Fig. 3. (a) ROADM design based on cascaded MZIs, (b) building block of the cascaded MZIs.

Figure 3(b) shows the configuration of the cascaded MZIs used as a building block in the ROADMs. This configuration consists of two MZIs connected with Tunable Couplers (TCs) whose coupling coefficients can be properly adjusted in order to obtain the proper spectral response at the output of the cascade. The first MZI has an arm length difference of 2dL, while the arm length difference of the second MZI is equal to dL. The longer arms of 2dL and dL of the respective MZIs are placed on the opposite sides of the waveguides in order to minimize the dispersion effect. Phase Shifters (PSs) are employed in the longest arm of each MZI to control the spectral position of the MZI's filter, allowing in this way to drop each time the proper wavelength.

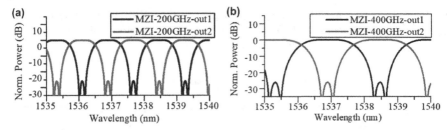

Fig. 4. ROADM modeling: simulated spectral response of the cascaded MZIs' filters with: (a) FSR = 200 GHz (green MZIs), (b) FSR = 400 GHz (brown MZIs). (Color figure online)

The arm difference dL1 for the cascade of MZIs with FSR equal to 200 GHz, was chosen to be 872.1 μm, while the arm difference dL2 for the cascaded MZIs of 400 GHz FSR, was chosen to be equal to 436 μm. The total losses of the ROADM were calculated to be up to 3.1 dB, taking into account the fiber in/out interfaces and the propagation losses of the waveguides.

Figure 4(a) depicts the spectral response for the output ports of the cascaded MZIs with the FSR of 200 GHz, which is responsible for splitting λ_1 (1536.9 nm), λ_3 (158.46 nm) from λ_2 (1537.67 nm), λ_4 (1539.25 nm) at its output ports 1 and 2, respectively. Figure 4(b) illustrates the spectral response for both outputs of the cascade of MZIs that has a FSR equal to 400 GHz and is depicted with the brown color in Fig. 3(a). The filtering response of the cascade shown in Fig. 4(b) allows for separating λ_1 from λ_3 and λ_2 from λ_4. It is worth mentioning that both spectral responses, shown in Fig. 4, exhibit flat-top filter shape by properly setting the values of the coupling coefficients TC1, TC2, TC3 equal to 0.9248, 0.28 and 0.5, respectively.

4   Optical Fronthaul Performance Evaluation

In this section, we present the physical - layer simulations performed with the aid of VPI photonics software [24], in order to evaluate the performance of the proposed analog optical fronthaul link when a multi-IF band WDM signal with OFDM - based format and SC modulation of 16 - QAM is transmitted. The employed setup of the WDM hot-spot link as well as the physical layer results will be presented. It should be mentioned that the matched simulation models, described in the previous section were employed in order to provide a reliable performance evaluation study.

4.1   Simulated Setup

Figure 5 illustrates the setup employed for the performance evaluation of the optical WDM downlink transmission from the BBU to the RRH side comprising four ROADMs interleaved in an optical bus for serving half of hot-spot area (e.g. sports stadium). The other half of the stadium is served by another independent and identical transmission link, thus without loss of generality we focus only on one of the two transmission links. As shown in Fig. 5, the BBU consists of a WDM transmitter that employs four EML modules, modulating the respective Continues Waves (CWs) at the peak wavelengths of

1536.9 nm, 1537.67 nm, 1538.46 nm and 1539.25 nm. Each EML is driven by a different multi - IF band electrical signal consisting of six OFDM waveforms that are generated and up-converted to six different IF frequencies.

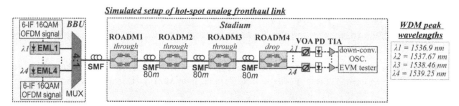

Fig. 5. Simulated setup of the analog multi - IFoF optical fronthaul, comprising the WDM EML-based transmitter at the BBU side and the ROADM bus at the stadium side.

Table 1 summarizes the waveform parameters of the aggregated multi – IF band OFDM signal. Particularly, six IF bands with peak frequencies at 3.8 GHz, 4.4 GHz, 5 GHz, 5.6 GHz, 6.2 GHz and 6.8 GHz were employed, with each of them occupying a bandwidth of 0.5 GHz and consisting of 256 SCs. Each SC has a baud rate of 1.953 Mbd and a modulation format of 16 - QAM, resulting on a data rate of 2 Gb/s per IF channel. The six IF bands are separated by a guard band of 100 MHz. Thus, the aggregated data rate of all IF bands fed into the EML is equal to 12 Gb/s for a total occupied bandwidth of 3.5 GHz.

Table 1. Waveform parameters

Parameter	Value	Parameter	Value
Modulation	OFDM 16-QAM	SC baud-rate	1.953 MBaud
IF bands	6	Data rate per IF	2 Gb/s
IF center frequencies	3.8, 4.4, 5, 5.6, 6.2, 6.8 (GHz)	Channel guard band	100 MHz
BW per IF band	0.5 GHz	BW per λ	3.5 GHz
SC per IF band	256	Data rate per λ	12 Gb/s

The voltage swing of the electrical signal entering the EAM section of the respective EML is adjusted to the value of 0.7 Vpp and the bias voltage is set to −0.4 V achieving in this way operation in the linear region of the EAM. The laser section of each EML was set to its maximum optical power, resulting on an optical signal with an average modulated power of 2.8 dB [16] for each of the WDM channels exiting the respective EML. The outputs of the four EMLs are multiplexed by a 4:1 optical Multiplexer (MUX) and the resultant WDM stream is transmitted through a SMF to the ROADM bus located in the stadium hot-spot area (half part of the stadium). The data rate of the transmitted WDM signal is equal to 48 Gb/s (12 Gb/s per λ), resulting in a total data rate of 96 Gb/s when two identical optical links are used, as it is proposed in our fronthaul network. At the stadium side, the employed four ROADMs are capable to add or drop any of the four WDM channels originated by the BBU. The four ROADMs are placed around the stadium's periphery in a bus topology with the neighboring ROADMs equally spaced at 80 m. The distance between the ROADMs was chosen based on the actual diameter of a typical football - stadium [25]. In this setup, we focused on the worst case scenario, where all the WDM channels crossed through the first three ROADMs of the bus and dropped by the longest reach forth ROADM. The dropped demultiplexed optical signals are fed into an array of four photo-receivers for optical-to-electrical conversion by the Photo-Diode (PD) and amplification by the Transimpedance Amplifier (TIA). The outputs of the TIAs are down-converted and captured by the EVM tester. VOAs were used for controlling the received optical power entering the PD.

4.2   Results

In this sub-section, we present the physical-layer performance evaluation study of the optical fronthaul link, considering that the WDM multi-IF data signal crosses through the three first ROADMs and is received by the last 4th ROADM of the optical bus. The length of the SMF connecting the BBU with the 1st ROADM was set equal to 500 m and the minimum Received Optical Power (ROP) corresponding to the first IF band was equal to −13 dBm, calculated by taking into account the maximum losses of all building blocks of the evaluated link. Figure 6(a) presents the EVM value per SC index of all IF bands for the first WDM channel at the $\lambda 1 = 1536.9$ nm. As it can be observed, the first IF band at 3.8 GHz exhibited the worst performance with the EVM values of the SCs ranging from 7.3% to 9.4%, while the last IF of 6.8 GHz showed the best performance with EVMs between 4.6%–5.9%. Figure 6(b) and (c) depicts the constellation diagrams for the worst performing SCs of the outermost IF bands of 3.8 GHz and 6.8 GHz, exhibiting EVMs equal to 9.4% and 5.9%, respectively. This non-equal performance of the 6 IF channels, is attributed to the filtering effect that the signal experiences as it crosses through the hot-spot link, resulting to partially uneven losses and not ideally flat channel response. Similar performance was obtained for all the other WDM channels with EVM values below the 3GPP threshold of 12.5% [26].

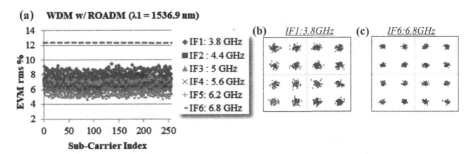

Fig. 6. (a) EVM per sub-carrier for all IF bands for $\lambda 1 = 1536.9$ nm at a minimum received optical power of −13 dBm, (b) constellation diagram for the first IF band at 3.8 GHz and (c) the last IF band at 6.8 GHz.

Figure 7 depicts the EVM measurements for the worst performing 16-QAM modulated SC of each WDM channel versus the ROP of the data signal inserted into the array of PDs connected with the drop ports of the fourth ROADM. The WDM signal was transmitted from the BBU to the hot-spot stadium area through a 500 m SMF, crossed the first three ROADMs and dropped by the 4th ROADM. As it is shown, all wavelengths (λ_1, λ_2, λ_3, λ_4) exhibit similar performance, achieving an EVM below the 12.5% threshold for a ROP value of -15 dBm. This measurement indicates that the dropped data signals reaching the PDs of the longest-reach ROADM should have an optical power higher than -15 dB for exhibiting adequate performance.

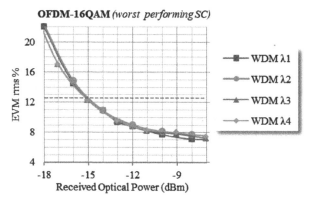

Fig. 7. EVM versus ROP (dBm) for the worst performing SC of each WDM channel.

Thus, in order to investigate the feasibility of the proposed fronthaul link with the employed hardware, we performed a power budget study for calculating the actual optical power entering the PDs of the fourth ROADM, based on the losses of the individual devices. Table 2 presents the power budget parameters of all building blocks incorporated in the link, with the EML exhibiting a modulated average output optical power (P_{OUT}) of 2.8 dBm [16], the MUX (L_{MUX}) and the ROADM (L_{ROADM}) adding 1.5 dB and 3.1 dB losses, while the SMF (L_{SMF}) inserting propagation losses of 0.25 dB/km [20]. The actual ROP is calculated as by subtracting the sum of the losses from the output power of the signal exiting the EML, as shown in (1):

Table 2. Power budget parameters

Building block	Value
EML modulated average output power (P_{OUT})	2.8 dBm
MUX losses (L_{MUX})	1.5 dB
SMF propagation losses (L_{SMF})	0.25 dB/km
ROADM losses (L_{ROADM})	3.1 dB (max.)

$$\text{actual } ROP = P_{OUT} - L_{MUX} - N * L_{ROADM} - length * L_{SMF} \qquad (1)$$

where N is the number of the ROADMs in the optical bus and *length* the total SMF
length including both the fiber connecting the BBU with the first ROADM and the fiber
links connecting the neighboring ROADMs.

By considering a number of 4 ROADMs, a fiber link of 500 m between the BBU-
first ROADM and fiber links of 80 m between the adjacent ROADMs and utilizing the
parameter values shown in Table 2, the actual ROP was calculated equal to −11.3 dBm.
Since this value is higher than the required ROP of −15 dBm derived by the EVM measurements in Fig. 7, the applicability of the proposed 5G fronthaul link was successfully
confirmed for WDM signals with OFDM waveform and 16-QAM SC modulation.

Towards investigating the longest distance between the BBU and the hot-spot area,
we performed a fiber length study with the main criteria being the actual ROP calculated
from the power budget analysis of the system (Eq. 1) to be higher than the ROP required
in order to achieve an EVM value less than 12.5%. In this study we employed the setup
shown in Fig. 5, using different values for the length of the SMF interconnecting the
BBU with the first ROADM.

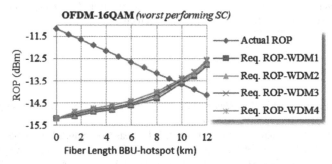

Fig. 8. *ROP* versus the length of the SMF fiber connecting the BBU with the first ROADM.
Curve of the actual *ROP* deriving from the power budget of the hot-spot link and curves of the
ROP required to achieve an EVM = 12.5% (3GPP threshold) for all WDM channels.

Figure 8 illustrates the *ROP* versus the SMF *length* connecting the BBU and the first
ROADM, where the red line corresponds to the actual *ROP* in dBm reaching the PDs of
the 4th ROADM, calculated by Eq. 1. By substituting the values of Table 2 and varying
the length parameter from 0 km to 12 km, the actual *ROP* was linearly decreased from
−11.1 dB at 0 km to −14.1 dB at 12 km. The other four curves show the ROP required
at the input of the PDs connecting with the fourth ROADM, in order to achieve an EVM
value bellow the acceptable limit of 12.5%. Each of these curves corresponds to the
worst performing SC of a different WDM channel. As it can be observed, the EVM
degrades for all channels as the fiber length increases due to the signal impairing effect
of the chromatic dispersion. By comparing the actual and the required *ROP*, it can be
seen that these curves cross at a length of 9.5 km. Before this crossing point the actual
ROP stemming from Eq. 1 is higher than the required *ROP*, revealing that the longest
reach to place the BBU from the hot-spot area is equal to 9.5 km. Considering that the

proposed fronthaul architecture targets on hot-spot networks where all the clients are gathered to a specific geographical area, the BBU box is expected to be placed not more than a few km from the hot-spot, with the fiber length of 9.5 km satisfying the above requirement.

5 Conclusion

We designed and evaluated an analog optical 5G fronthaul architecture for serving the bandwidth - demanding needs of hot-spot areas, such as sport-stadiums. The proposed cost-effective fronthaul scheme comprises a centralized Baseband Unit (BBU) with low cost WDM PIC-based optical transmitters and Remote Radio Heads (RRHs) on bus topology equipped with wavelength selective PIC-based ROADMs. By exploiting the WDM technology and using 6-band OFDM with 0.5 Gbaud 16-QAM modulation format, an aggregate capacity up to 96 Gb/s was achieved when two WDM links were employed. We also carried out a power budget study, showing the feasibility to locate the BBU equipment in a distance up to 9.5 km from the hot-spot area.

Acknowledgment. This work is supported by H2020-5G PPP 5G-PHOS (grant agreement 761989) and MSCA ITN 5G STEP-FWD (grant agreement 722429).

References

1. Ericsson: Ericsson Mobility Report. https://www.ericsson.com/en/mobility-report/reports/november-2018. Accessed 12 Apr 2019
2. Andrews, L., et al.: What will 5G be? IEEE J. Sel. Areas Commun. **32**(6), 1065–1082 (2014)
3. NGMN: NGMN 5G White paper. https://www.ngmn.org/fileadmin/ngmn/content/downloads/Technical/2015/NGMN_5G_White_Paper_V1_0.pdf. Accessed 12 Apr 2019
4. Lien, S., et al.: 5G new radio: waveform, frame structure, multiple access, and initial access. IEEE Commun. Mag. **55**(6), 64–71 (2017)
5. Rappaport, T.S., et al.: Millimeter wave mobile communications for 5G cellular: it will work! IEEE Access **1**, 335–349 (2013)
6. 5G Infrastructure Association, 5G Trials Roadmap. https://5g-ppp.eu/5g-trials-roadmap/. Accessed 12 Apr 2019
7. Ge, X., Tu, S., Mao, G., Wang, C., Han, T.: 5G ultra-dense cellular networks. IEEE Wirel. Commun. **23**(1), 72–79 (2016)
8. Checko, A., et al.: Cloud RAN for mobile networks—a technology overview. IEEE Commun. Surv. Tutor. **17**(1), 405–426 (2014)
9. Kani, J., et al.: Solutions for future mobile fronthaul and access-network convergence. J. Lightwave Technol. **35**(3), 527–534 (2017)
10. Sung, M., et al.: Demonstration of IFoF based 5G mobile fronthaul in 28 GHz millimeter wave testbed supporting giga-bit mobile services. In: Optical Fiber Communications Conference and Exhibition (OFC), Los Angeles, CA, USA (2017)
11. Vagionas, C., et al.: A 6-band 12 Gb/s IFoF/V-band fiber-wireless fronthaul link using an InP externally modulated laser. In: European Conference on Optical Communication (ECOC), Tu4B.6, Rome, Italy (2018)
12. Common Public Radio Interface. Interface Specification v7.0., October 2015

13. Martin, E., et al.: 28 GHz 5G radio over fibre using UF-OFDM with optical heterodyning. In: International Topical Meeting on Microwave Photonics (MWP), Beijing, China (2017)
14. Shibata, N., et al.: 256-QAM 8 wireless signal transmission with DSP-assisted analog RoF for mobile front-haul in LTE-B. In: OECC/ACOFT, Melbourne, Australia, 6–10 July 2014 (2014)
15. Winzer, P.J., Neilson, D., Chraplyvy, A.: Fiber-optic transmission and networking: the previous 20 and the next 20 years. Opt. Express **26**(18), 24190–24239 (2018)
16. Debregeas, H., et al.: Record 6 dBm electroabsorption modulated laser for 10 Gb/s and 25 Gb/s high power budget access networks. In: Optical Fiber Communications Conference and Exhibition (OFC), Los Angeles, CA, USA (2017)
17. Marom, D., et al.: Survey of photonic switching architectures and technologies in support of spatially and spectrally flexible optical networking. IEEE/OSA J. Opt. Commun. Netw. **9**(1), 1–26 (2017)
18. Shokri-Ghadikolaei, H., Fischione, C., Fodor, G., Popovski, P., Zorzi, M.: Millimeter wave cellular networks: a MAC layer perspective. IEEE Trans. Commun. **63**(10), 3437–3458 (2015)
19. Kalfas, G., et al.: Medium-transparent packet-based fronthauling for 5G hot-spot networks. In: International Conference on Transparent Optical Networks (ICTON), Bucharest, Romania (2018)
20. Corning, LEAF Optical Fiber. https://www.corning.com/au/en/products/communication-networks/products/fiber/leaf-fiber.html. Accessed 12 Apr 2019
21. Roeloffzen, C.G., et al.: Low-loss Si3N4 TriPleX optical waveguides: technology and applications overview. J. Sel. Top. Quant. Electron. **24**(4), 1–21 (2018)
22. Horst, F., et al.: Cascaded Mach-Zehnder wavelength filters in silicon photonics for low loss and flat pass-band WDM (de-) multiplexing. Opt. Express **21**(10), 11652–11658 (2013)
23. LioniX International. https://www.lionix-international.com/. Accessed 12 Apr 2019
24. VPIphotonics. http://vpiphotonics.com/index.php. Accessed 12 Apr 2019
25. Toumba stadium. https://www.stadiumguide.com/toumba/. Accessed 12 Apr 2019
26. 3GPP, TS 38.104 V15.0.0, Table 9.6.2.3-1, December 2017

Hybrid and Optical Packet Switching Supporting Different Service Classes in Data Center Network

Artur Minakhmetov[(✉)], Cédric Ware, and Luigi Iannone

LTCI, Télécom Paris, Institut Polytechnique de Paris, 91120 Palaiseau, France
artur.minakhmetov@telecom-paris.fr

Abstract. Optical Packet Switching is a prominent technology proposing not only a reduction of the energy consumption by the elimination
of numerous optical-electrical-optical conversions in electronic switches,
but also a decrease of network latencies due to the cut-through nature of
packet transmission. However, it is adversely affected by packet contention, preventing its deployment. Solutions have been proposed to
tackle the problem: addition of shared electronic buffers to optical
switches (then called hybrid opto-electronic switches), customization of
TCP protocols, and use of different service classes of packets with distinct switching criteria.

In the context of data center networks we investigate a combination of
said solutions and show that the hybrid switch, compared to the optical
switch, boosts the performance of the data center network. Furthermore,
we show that introducing a "Reliable" service class improves performance
for this class not only in the case of the hybrid switch, but also brings
the optical switch to performance levels comparable to that of the hybrid
switch, all the while keeping other classes' performance on the same level.

Keywords: Optical Packet Switching · Packet Switching · TCP
Congestion Control · Optical switches · Hybrid switches · Classes of
Service · Packet preemption

1 Introduction

The Optical Packet Switching (OPS) technology regained public interest in the
mid-2000s [8] in the face of demand for high reconfigurability in networks, made
possible through statistical multiplexing along with efficient capacity use and
limiting the energy consumption of the switches [15]. However, with traffic being
asynchronous and in the absence of technology that would make practical optical
buffers in switches, the contention issue arises, leading to poor performance in
terms of Packet Loss Ratio (PLR) [10], thus making the OPS concept impractical. To the present moment, several solutions have been proposed to bring the
OPS technology to functional level, among which: adding a shared electronic

Published by Springer Nature Switzerland AG 2020
A. Tzanakaki et al. (Eds.): ONDM 2019, LNCS 11616, pp. 516–527, 2020.
https://doi.org/10.1007/978-3-030-38085-4_44

buffer, thus making hybrid opto-electronic switches [17, 19, 21]; intelligent routing of packets of different priorities in the hypothesis that not all of them would need the same requirements for PLR [16]; and a network-level solution without changing the OPS hardware, introducing special TCP Congestion Control Algorithms (CCA) for packet transmission in order to increase overall network throughput, thus negating the still high PLR [5]. These three solutions are detailed below.

First, the hybrid switch consists in coupling an all-optical bufferless packet switch with an electronic buffer. Several implementations of the idea were already proposed in the last decade [17, 19, 21]. The concept of the hybrid switch considered in this study is: when contention occurs on two (or more) packets, i.e. when a packet requires using an output that is busy transmitting another packet, it is diverted to a shared electronic buffer through Optical-Electrical (OE) conversion. When the destination output is released, the buffered packet is emitted from the buffer, passing Electrical-Optical (EO) conversion. However, in the absence of contention, the hybrid switch works as an all-optical switch, without any wasteful OE and EO conversions. Adding a shared buffer with only a few input-output ports lets us considerably decrease PLR compared to an all-optical switch, and bring its performance up to the level of an electronic switch, but now with an important reduction in energy consumption, since one would save the OE/EO (OEO) conversions for most packets [16].

Second, highlighting an important question of the existence of classes of service in a network, Samoud et al. [16] propose handling packets depending on their class: high priority packets can preempt low priority ones from being buffered or transmitted. It was shown that the demand for low PLR may be met for high priority packets and relaxed for others, achieving sustainable operation with a number of buffer input/output ports less than half that of optical links in a switch.

Third, Argibay-Losada et al. [5] propose to use all-optical switches in OPS networks along with special TCP CCAs, in order to bring the OPS network throughput up to the same levels as in Electrical Packet Switching (EPS) networks with conventional electronic switches. Particularly noteworthy in protocol design is the Retransmission Timeout (RTO). This parameter controls how long to wait for the acknowledgment after sending a packet until the packet is considered lost and re-sent. When a transmission is successful and without losses, RTO is set to a value close to the Round-Trip-Time (RTT), i.e. the time elapsed between the start of sending a packet and reception of its acknowledgment. By simple tweaking of initialization value of RTO and reducing it from conventional 1 s to 1 ms, it was shown that both custom and conventional TCP CCAs will boost the performance of the optical packet switched network.

In our previous works we analyzed the gain from use of the hybrid switch in a Data Center (DC) network by introducing Hybrid Optical Packet Switching (HOPS): we showed that HOPS with a custom designed TCP can outperform OPS and EPS in throughput [12, 13]. Furthermore, in [11] we have managed to show the possibility of 4 times reduction in DC energy consumption for data transport coming from OEO conversions while using HOPS compared to EPS.

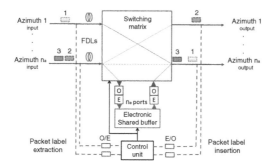

Fig. 1. General architecture of hybrid optical packet switch

In this study we aim to investigate not only a combination of HOPS with custom design of TCP, but also the influence of the introduction of Classes of Service, i.e. switching and preemption rules for packets of different priorities.

Considering the general interest in the scientific and industrial communities to implement different packets priorities in Data Centers (DCs), as well as the problem of traffic isolation for tenants in DC [14], we implement the idea presented by Samoud et al. [16] and investigate the benefits of application of such technology in a DC network. We successfully show that one can considerably improve the performance of network consisting of hybrid switches with a small number of buffer inputs for high priority connections while keeping it on a good level for default connections. Additionally, we show that high priority connections in OPS network also can profit from the introduction of classes of service, matching or even surpassing the performance of the network consisted of hybrid switches with a small number of buffer inputs without classes of service.

The paper is composed as follows: Sect. 2 presents hybrid switch's architecture and packets preemption policy, Sect. 3 outlines simulation conditions, Sect. 4 discusses the results obtained and, finally, Sect. 5 offers our main conclusions.

2   Hybrid Switch Architecture and Packets Preemption Policy

2.1   Hybrid Switch Architecture

The first concept of a hybrid switch was proposed in 2004 by Takahashi et al. [20], and the scientific community has kept its attention on the implementation of the idea since then [17]. In 2010 Ye et al. [21] presented a Datacenter Optical Switch (DOS), an optical packet switch, that could be seen as a prototype of a hybrid switch: switching was performed through a combination of Arrayed Waveguide Gratings switching matrix with Tunable Wavelength Converters (TWC), contentions were managed through the shared electronic buffer, storing contending packets. In 2012 Takahashi et al. [19] presented a similar concept, called Hybrid

Optoelectronic Packet Router (HOPR). DOS and HOPR, despite the name, are not quite what we call hybrid switches, as all the packets undergo OEO conversions by TWCs.

In 2016 Segawa et al. [17] proposed a switch that performs switching of optical packets through a broadcast-and-select switching matrix and then re-amplification by Semiconductor Optical Amplifiers (SOAs). This switch splits the incoming optical packet into several ways corresponding to output ports, blocks those that don't match the packet's destination, and then re-amplifies the passed packet with a SOA. A shared electronic buffer is there to solve packet contention. The OEO conversion is made only for contending packets, unlike DOS or HOPR where all the packets undergo OEO conversions.

All of the presented solutions above have common main blocks, that we are emulating in our study in order to approach hybrid switch functions. The general structure of a hybrid switch is presented in Fig. 1 with the following main blocks: an optical switching matrix; an electronic shared buffer; and a control unit that configures the latter two according to the destination of the packets, carried by labels. The hybrid switch has n_a inputs and n_a outputs, representing non-wavelength-specific input and output channels, or Azimuths, thus making n_a channels for a switch. Another important parameter is n_e: n_e inputs and n_e outputs of a buffer. These are the channels through which a packet is routed/emitted to/from a buffer.

In our study we make the following assumptions. The optical matrix has a negligible reconfiguration time, on the ns scale [7]. The labels can be extracted from the packet and processed without converting the packet itself to electronic domain, e.g. by transmitting them out of band on dedicated wavelengths as in the OPS solution presented by Shacham et al. [18]. This solution allows label extraction via a tap coupler, requiring an OE conversion only for the label, and short Fiber Delay Lines at the inputs of the optical switch. We are not considering any particular technology for the Control Unit, and implement our simulations focusing on the supposed ideal optical matrix, and on a store-and-forward buffer.

2.2 Packets Preemption Policy

The switching algorithm for a hybrid switch is adopted from [16] and implements different bufferization and preemption rules for different packets classes. We consider three of them: Reliable (R), Fast (F) and Default packets (D). R packets are those that attempted to be saved by any means, even by preemption of F or D packets on their way to buffer or switch output. F packets could preempt only D packets on their way to the switch output. D packets cannot preempt other packets.

The priority distribution in the DC network is adopted from [16] and taken from the real study on core networks [1]. This may seem improper for DCs, however, we seek to study the performance of the hybrid switch in the known context. Also, it will be shown below that the distribution considered lets us organize a pool of premium users (10%) of R connections in DCs that could

---

Algorithm 1. Preemption Policies in a Hybrid Switch

1: **procedure** ROUTE (PACKET p)
2:      $prio \leftarrow p.priority\_class$
3:      $switch\_out \leftarrow$ get_destination_azimuth(p)
4:      **if** $switch\_out$.is_free() **then**
5:          $switch\_out$.receive(p)
6:      **else if** $buffer\_in$.is_free() **then**
7:          $buffer\_in$.receive(p)
8:      **else if** $prio ==$**R and** $buffer\_in$.receiving(**D**) **then**
9:          $buffer\_in$.preempt_last_packet(**D**)
10:         $buffer\_in$.receive(p)
11:     **else if** $prio ==$**R and** $switch\_out$.receiving(**D**) **then**
12:         $switch\_out$.preempt_last_packet(**D**)
13:         $switch\_out$.receive(p)
14:     **else if** $prio ==$**R and** $buffer\_in$.receiving($\tilde{\mathbf{F}}$) **then**
15:         $buffer\_input$.preempt_last_packet($\tilde{\mathbf{F}}$)
16:         $buffer\_input$.receive(p)
17:     **else if** $prio ==$**R and** $switch\_out$.receiving($\tilde{\mathbf{F}}$) **then**
18:         $switch\_out$.preempt_last_packet($\tilde{\mathbf{F}}$)
19:         $switch\_out$.receive(p)
20:     **else if** $prio ==$$\tilde{\mathbf{F}}$ **and** $switch\_out$.receiving(**D**) **then**
21:         $switch\_out$.preempt_last_packet(**D**)
22:         $switch\_out$.receive(p)
23:     **else**
24:         drop(p)

---

profit from the best performance, while other users almost wouldn't be influenced by performance loss. F packets can preempt D packets only on the way to switch output, while R packets first would consider preemption of D packet being buffered. Thus F packets had lower delay than R packets [16]. However, further it will be shown that this device-level gain doesn't translate to network-level gain in a DC network in terms of Flow Completion Time (FCT), and R connections perform better than F. That's why here we refer to Fast (F) as Not-So-Fast ($\tilde{F}$) packets and connections. Eventually, in this study we consider, that 10% of connections have R priority, 40% of connections have $\tilde{F}$ priority, 50% of connections have D priority.

When a packet enters the switch it checks if required Azimuth output (i.e. switch output) is available. If yes, the packet occupies it. Otherwise, the packet checks if any of buffer inputs are available. If yes, it occupies one and starts bufferization. If none of the buffer inputs are available, in the case of absence of preemption policy in a switch the packet would be simply dropped. Here, we consider a switch with preemption policy that would follow the steps of algorithm presented in Algorithm 1. If a packet of any type is buffered, it is re-emitted FIFO, as soon as required switch output is available.

3   Study Methodology

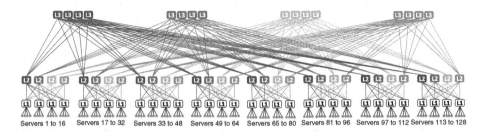

Fig. 2. Fat-tree topology network, interconnecting 128 servers with three layers of switches.

As in our previous work [12,13], we simulate the communications of DC servers by means of optical packets. We study DC network performance for two groups of scenarios: DC with classes of service using preemption policy outlined in Sect. 2.2, and DC with switches that don't have any preemption rules. For each scenario we consider OPS and HOPS case.

Communications consist of transmitting files between server pairs through TCP connections. The files' size is random, following a lognormal-like distribution [3], which has two modes around 10 MB and 1 GB. We simulate transmission of 1024 random files (on the same order as 1000 in [5]), i.e. 8 connections per server. File transmission is done by data packets using jumbo frames with a size of 9 kB. This value defines the packet's payload and corresponds to Jumbo Ethernet frame's payload.

In our study we also use SYN, FIN, and ACK signaling packets. We choose for them to have the minimal size of the Ethernet frame of 64 B [2]. We assume that this minimal size would contain only the relevant information about Ethernet, TCP/IP layers. As we still need to attach to the jumbo frames all the information of these layers, for simplicity, we just attach to it a header of 64 B discussed previously. Thus we construct a packet of maximum size 9064 B to be used in our simulations, with a duration τ dependent on the bit-rate. Servers have network interface cards of 10 Gb/s bit-rate. Buffer inputs and outputs used by a hybrid switch support the same bit-rate.

The actual transmission of each data packet is regulated by the DCTCP CCA [6], developed for DCs, which decides whether to send the next packet or to retransmit a not-acknowledged one. CCA uses next constants: $DCTCP_{threshold} = 27192$ B, $DCTCP_{acks/pckt} = 1$, $DCTCP_g = 0.06$, as favorable for HOPS. We apply the crucial reduction of the initialization value of RTO towards 1 ms, as advised in [5]. To be realistic, the initial 3-way handshake and 3-way connection termination are also simulated.

We developed a discrete-event network simulator based on an earlier hybrid switch simulator [16], extended so as to handle whole networks and include TCP emulation. The simulated network consists of hybrid switches with the following architecture: each has n_a azimuths, representing the number of input/output optical ports, and n_e input/output ports to the electronic buffer, as shown in Fig. 1. The case of the bufferless all-optical switch (OPS) corresponds to $n_e = 0$, for the case of the hybrid switch (HOPS) we consider $n_e = 2$.

We study the DC fat-tree topology, interconnecting 128 servers by means of 80 identical switches with $n_a = 8$ azimuths, presented in Fig. 2, a sub-case of a topology deployed in a Facebook's DCs [4]. All links are bidirectional and of the same length $l_{link} = 10$ m as typical link lengths for DC. The link plays the role of device-to-device connection, i.e. server-to-switch, switch-to-server or switch-to-switch. The link is supposed to represent a non-wavelength-specific channel. Paths between servers are calculated as a minimum number of hops, which offers multiple equal paths for packet transmission allowing load-balancing and thus lowering the PLR.

The network is characterized by the network throughput (in Gb/s) and average FCT (in µs) for each type of connections and general case as a function of the arrival rate of new connections, represented by the Poissonian process. We have chosen FCT as a metric considered to be the most important for network state characterization [9].

4 Evaluation Results

We present here the results of our study and their analysis. To reduce statistical fluctuations, we repeated every simulation a hundred times with different random seeds for $n_e = 0$ (OPS) and $n_e = 2$ (HOPS). The mean throughput and mean FCT are represented in Fig. 3 and in Fig. 4 with 95% t-Student confidence intervals, for three types of connections: R, F and D connections. We take as a reference results from the network without packet preemption policy: the division of connections to classes is artificial and just represent corresponding to classes' percentage of connections in the network. We define high load as more than 10^5 connections per second.

While comparing just OPS and HOPS, it is seen that in general HOPS outperforms or has the same performance as OPS, but with the cost of only $n_e = 2$ buffer inputs.

R connections benefit the most from the introduction of the Classes of Service and preemption policy as it seen on Figs. 3a and 4a, both in the cases of OPS and HOPS. Throughput for R connections in HOPS network rises by around 25% (Fig. 3a), while in OPS case it rises by a factor 2.5 at least on high load, matching the performance of HOPS network. We would like to bring readers attention on the fact that it seems to be low throughput, compared to other classes of service, but this is the mere effect of the fact that in the network only 10% of connections are of type R. However, if one considers the FCT, which is comparable with other types of classes and lowest among them, then the preemption policy's benefits are more evident: on the highest considered load OPS reduces its FCT almost by a factor of 8, while HOPS reduces it by at least

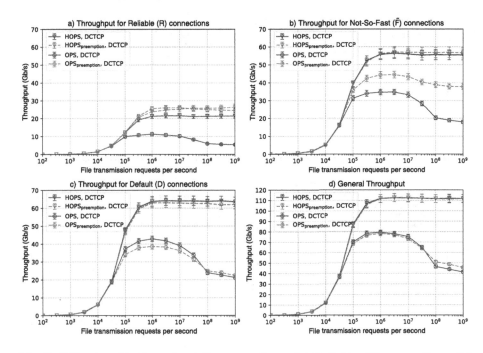

Fig. 3. DC network's throughput for connections: (a) Reliable (R) connections, (b) Not-So-Fast (F̃) connections, (c) Default (D) connections, (d) Overall network performance

a factor of 2, keeping it on the level of tens of μs. Even if OPS's FCT doesn't match FCT in the case of HOPS while considering Classes of Service, it does match the FCT in the case of HOPS without Classes of Service. While applying preemption policy, connections are indeed Reliable: in Fig. 5 we can see that PLR (ratio of packets lost due to preemption or dropping to packets emitted by servers) decreases by around factor of 10, while for F̃ and D PLR remains around the same level (not shown here).

F̃ traffic benefits less than R traffic from introduction of Classes of Service, but the gain is still there. For OPS we managed to boost the throughput by almost 30–100% on the high load, while for HOPS the gain is less evident. However, when we consider FCT on Fig. 4b we can see that OPS decreases its FCT by almost a factor of 2 for high load, and HOPS around 25%. HOPS FCT for F̃ packets is bigger than for those of reliable (R), contrary to what may be induced from [16], where they are labeled as Fast (F). This may be explained by the fact that the delay benefits for F packets are on the order of a μs, while here FCT is of an order of tens and hundreds of μs, and is defined mostly by TCP CCAs when contention problem is solved.

D traffic does not benefit from the introduction of Classes of Service, and it is on its account the gains for R and F̃ traffic exists. However, while considering the performance reductions, we notice almost unchanged throughput for HOPS

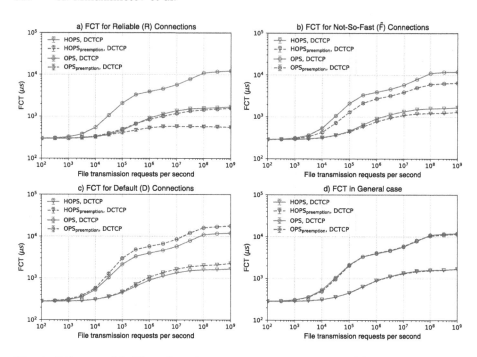

Fig. 4. DC network's Flow Completion Time for connections: (a) Reliable (R) connections, (b) Not-So-Fast ($\tilde{F}$) connections, (c) Default (D) connections, (d) Overall network performance

case, and for OPS the drop of only 10% at most, which could be seen as a beneficial trade-off in R and $\tilde{F}$ traffic favor with their boost of performance both in throughput and FCT.

The network as a whole, regardless of the presence of Classes of Service, performs the same, which is expected, as connections occupy limited network resources. We can observe that the gain due to introduction of Classes of Service for R and $\tilde{F}$ traffic decreases with the increase of number of buffer inputs/outputs (i.e. from $n_e = 0$ towards $n_e = 2$), and for fully-buffered switch ($n_e = n_a = 8$) the gain would be 0, because no packet would ever require preemption, only bufferization. However, there are technological benefits to use small number of buffer input/outputs as it directly means simplification of switching matrix ($n_a = 8$, $n_e = 2$ means 10×10, $n_a = n_e = 8$ means 16×16 matrix) and reduction of number of burst receivers (inputs) and transmitters (outputs) for buffers. In the case of EPS, the gain would be also 0, but in general EPS entails an increase in energy consumption for OEO conversions compared to HOPS by a factor of 2 to 4 [11] on high load.

While observing the network performance overall, it's seen that introduction of Service of Classes both in OPS and HOPS helps to boost the performance for the R and $\tilde{F}$ connections, while keeping the performance of D connections relatively on the same level. This fact could lead to economic benefits in a Data

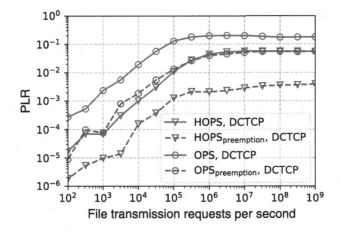

Fig. 5. Mean PLR of reliable (R) connections

Center: charge more priority clients for extra performance, almost without loss of it for others. Furthermore, using pure OPS instead of HOPS in DCs may be economically viable, as OPS delivers the best possible performance to R connections, on the level of HOPS performance for $\tilde{F}$ connections, and relatively low performance for D connections, since high performance may be not needed for D connections.

5   Conclusions

In this study we enhanced the analysis of HOPS and OPS DC networks by applying classes of service in terms of preemption policy for packets in optical and hybrid switches, while solving the contention problem. In the case of HOPS we demonstrated that with custom packet preemption rules, one can improve the performance for Reliable and Not-So-Fast class connections, almost without losing it for Default connections. Furthermore, we showed that Classes of Service can boost the performance of OPS for Reliable and Not-So-Fast class connections, match or bring it on the level of those in HOPS. This proves that OPS could be used in DCs, delivering high performance for certain connections, while Default class connections are still served on an adequate level.

It remains to be seen whether these results remain with a different service class distribution; and whether an actual low-latency service class can be implemented (e.g. using another protocol than TCP).

References

1. 100Gb/s Réseau Internet Adaptative (100GRIA) FUI9 project. Technical report, December 2012
2. IEEE standard for ethernet. IEEE Std 802.3-2015 (Revision of IEEE Std 802.3-2012), pp. 1–4017, March 2016
3. Agrawal, N., Bolosky, W.J., Douceur, J.R., Lorch, J.R.: A five-year study of file-system metadata. ACM Trans. Storage **3**(3), 9–es (2007). https://dl.acm.org/doi/10.1145/1288783.1288788
4. Andreyev, A.: Introducing data center fabric, the next-generation Face-book data center network, November 2014. https://code.fb.com/production-engineering/introducing-data-center-fabric-the-next-generation-facebook-data-center-network/. Accessed 17 July 2018
5. Argibay-Losada, P.J., Sahin, G., Nozhnina, K., Qiao, C.: Transport-layer control to increase throughput in bufferless optical packet-switching networks. IEEE J. Opt. Commun. Netw. **8**(12), 947–961 (2016)
6. Bensley, S., Thaler, D., Balasubramanian, P., Eggert, L., Judd, G.: Data center TCP (DCTCP): TCP congestion control for data centers. RFC 8257, RFC Editor, October 2017
7. Cheng, Q., Wonfor, A., Wei, J.L., Penty, R.V., White, I.H.: Low-energy, high-performance lossless 8 × 8 SOA switch. In: Optical Fiber Communication Conference, p. Th4E.6. Optical Society of America (2015)
8. de Almeida Amazonas, J.R., Santos-Boada, G., Solé-Pareta, J.: Who shot optical packet switching? In: International Conference on Transparent Optical Networks (ICTON), p. Th.B3.3, July 2017
9. Dukkipati, N., McKeown, N.: Why flow-completion time is the right metric for congestion control. SIGCOMM Comput. Commun. Rev. **36**(1), 59–62 (2006)
10. Kimsas, A., Øverby, H., Bjornstad, S., Tuft, V.L.: A cross layer study of packet loss in all-optical networks. In: Proceedings of AICT/ICIW (2006)
11. Minakhmetov, A., Ware, C., Iannone, L.: Data center's energy savings for data transport via TCP on hybrid optoelectronic switches. IEEE Photonics Technol. Lett. **31**(8), 631–634 (2019)
12. Minakhmetov, A., Ware, C., Iannone, L.: Optical networks throughput enhancement via TCP stop-and-wait on hybrid switches. In: Optical Fiber Communication Conference, p. W4I.4. Optical Society of America (2018)
13. Minakhmetov, A., Ware, C., Iannone, L.: TCP congestion control in datacenter optical packet networks on hybrid switches. IEEE J. Opt. Commun. Netw. **10**(7), B71–B81 (2018)
14. Noormohammadpour, M., Raghavendra, C.S.: Datacenter traffic control: understanding techniques and tradeoffs. IEEE Commun. Surv. Tutor. **20**(2), 1492–1525 (2018)
15. Rouskas, G.N., Xu, L.: Optical packet switching. In: Sivalingam, K.M., Subramaniam, S. (eds.) Emerging Optical Network Technologies, pp. 111–127. Springer, Boston (2005). https://doi.org/10.1007/0-387-22584-6_5
16. Samoud, W., Ware, C., Lourdiane, M.: Performance analysis of a hybrid optical-electronic packet switch supporting different service classes. IEEE J. Opt. Commun. Netw. **7**(9), 952–959 (2015)
17. Segawa, T., Ibrahim, S., Nakahara, T., Muranaka, Y., Takahashi, R.: Low-power optical packet switching for 100-Gb/s burst optical packets with a label processor and 8 × 8 optical switch. J. Lightw. Technol. **34**(8), 1844–1850 (2016)

18. Shacham, A., Small, B.A., Liboiron-Ladouceur, O., Bergman, K.: A fully implemented 12×12 data vortex optical packet switching interconnection network. J. Lightwave Technol. **23**(10), 3066 (2005)
19. Takahashi, R., Nakahara, T., Suzaki, Y., Segawa, T., Ishikawa, H., Ibrahim, S.: Recent progress on the hybrid optoelectronic router. In: 2012 International Conference on Photonics in Switching (PS), pp. 1–3, September 2012
20. Takahashi, R., et al.: Ultrafast optoelectronic packet processing for asynchronous, optical-packet-switched networks, Invited. J. Opt. Netw. **3**(12), 914–930 (2004)
21. Ye, X., Mejia, P., Yin, Y., Proietti, R., Yoo, S.J.B., Akella, V.: DOS - a scalable optical switch for datacenters. In: 2010 ACM/IEEE Symposium on Architectures for Networking and Communications Systems (ANCS), pp. 1–12, October 2010

Reduction of Delay Overfulfillment in IP-over-DWDM Transport Networks

Uwe Bauknecht, Tobias Enderle[✉], and Arthur Witt

Institute of Communication Networks and Computer Engineering,
University of Stuttgart, Stuttgart, Germany
{uwe.bauknecht,tobias.enderle,arthur.witt}@ikr.uni-stuttgart.de

Abstract. The traffic in today's transport networks is increasing dramatically due to more demanding applications like video on demand and improving access technologies like 5G. Additionally, the quality of service requirements are becoming more stringent while network operators are seeking new ways for revenue creation. We propose a multi-layer network reconfiguration approach that reduces the overfulfillment of service delay requirements. In that way it provides an incentive to customers with low-delay services to acquire a more expensive service class for their traffic. Additionally, it relieves highly utilized links for services with very strict delay requirements. We provide an ILP formulation that solves this multi-layer network problem by performing a cross-layer optimization. Further, we evaluate our approach for two nationwide backbone networks. We show that a reduction of service delay overfulfillment is possible and how that affects other network metrics.

Keywords: Delay · ILP · Network reconfiguration · Optimization · Overfulfillment · QoS

1 Introduction

Since its inception, the Internet has changed significantly from a best-effort network of low-rate data exchange services into a ubiquitous and indispensable service delivery infrastructure for individuals and businesses alike. Trends like software as a service and video on demand, fueled by more potent access technologies such as FTTx and 5G, allow Internet-based business models such as cloud and content delivery services to thrive. These so-called over-the-top (OTT) services rely on the availability and quality of the underlying connection services rendered by Internet service providers (ISPs). Therefore, OTT providers require connection services that provide higher data rates and also adhere to guarantees on quality of service (QoS) metrics codified in service level agreement (SLAs). In order to ensure their fulfillment and avoid contract penalties, ISPs typically resort to overprovisioning QoS parameters on such SLA-based services. This practice translates to the ISPs' multi-layered core networks as well, where the packet forwarding layer and the optical transport layer are both subject to overdimensioning and further safety margins.

© IFIP International Federation for Information Processing 2020
Published by Springer Nature Switzerland AG 2020
A. Tzanakaki et al. (Eds.): ONDM 2019, LNCS 11616, pp. 528–539, 2020.
https://doi.org/10.1007/978-3-030-38085-4_45

Matching the continuous growth in traffic volume of currently 26% annually[1] [5] becomes increasingly expensive, especially due to improvements of core network transmission equipment approaching the limits of the deployed fiber infrastructure [6]. To avoid or at least defer costly investments for commissioning new fibers, ISPs try to reduce operational costs and explore new avenues of revenue creation. Important means towards cost reduction are improving the utilization of existing equipment and reducing safety margins. Several works have been published which address this and related issues. For example, the authors of [8] introduce an approach which increases the network utilization by exploiting the fact that some service requests can temporarily tolerate lower bandwidth. This frees resources in high load situations and allows more services to be accepted in the long run. In [1] we presented a latency-aware network reconfiguration approach that minimizes the amount of active network hardware. In [11], ways to reduce safety margins that compensate physical layer impairments and aging are discussed. Techniques like these can be employed by a software-defined networking (SDN) approach which exploits global knowledge of the network state to dynamically adjust the network's configuration such that light path and traffic routing precisely fit the QoS requirements of the services to be realized and thereby reduce overprovisioning [13].

In addition to cost reduction, a more differentiated service level agreement (SLA) portfolio can help increase an ISP's revenue [14]. On the side of individual end customers with low-rate best-effort contracts, ISPs have already instated so-called "data caps", where the bandwidth is throttled by rate shaping if a customer exceeds a predetermined data volume. This way, they capitalize on heavy users by offering uncapped services at increased rates [12]. For business clients who use their connections beyond the limits of their SLA contracts up to the maximum overprovisioning, rate shaping is also an option to control the data rate. Other QoS parameters are harder to limit with inexpensive measures, leaving business customers with little to no incentive to acquire contracts with more stringent guarantees, given that they are well aware of their contracts' overfulfillment. Among these parameters especially delay requirements are imperative to the aforementioned services.

Sanctioning customers by actively limiting delay overfulfillment could be realized on both, the packet layer and the optical layer. On the packet layer, incoming traffic could simply be queued in buffers for a preconfigured amount of time. However, since the buffer size necessary for delaying scales directly with the data rate and typical line cards have limited buffer memory, additional hardware would be needed given the large data rates of some business customer connections. Moreover, this also raises concerns when considering availability requirements since additional active hardware also harbors additional points of failure. On the optical layer, latency can be artificially introduced by simple fiber delay lines. Due to the low cost and deterministic delay, this approach seems superior, but also requires custom delay lines for each service and a more complicated fiber routing to match services to delays.

---

[1] Compound Annual Growth Rate 2017 to 2022.

Rather than introducing additional hardware to artificially reduce quality, a differentiated service routing on the existing infrastructure enables reduced operational cost, provides means of sanctioning customers and allows for increased revenue services by exploiting the overprovisioning of existing hardware. Traffic of customers under sanction can be shifted to physically longer and therefore delay-inducing paths where switching equipment is otherwise underutilized while the shorter routes can be dedicated to premium services increasing revenue.

The main part of this work is organized as follows. In Sect. 2, we formulate the considered network architecture and reconfiguration problem. In Sect. 3, we describe our proposed path generation and optimization approach. Simulation setup and results are presented in Sect. 4. Eventually, we conclude the work in Sect. 5.

2   Problem Statement

We consider a two-layer transport network which receives aggregated client traffic demands from earlier stages of the ISP's aggregation network. We assume a controller of global knowledge on all state of the transport network. This could be realized by an SDN-controlled IP-over-DWDM architecture. Our prototypical network therefore consists of a circuit-oriented optical layer and a packet-oriented electrical layer on top. The physical topology is given as the directed graph $G = (V, E)$, where V is the set of nodes and E is the set of directed fiber links. Each node consists of an optical switch and a packet router connected to it. The optical switch acts as a contentionless, directionless and colorless reconfigurable optical add-drop multiplexer (ROADM), such that arbitrary optical circuits can be established between any fiber, which connects to another node, and any of the tunable ports in the line cards of the router. Each fiber link can provide a capacity in terms of data rate, defined by the maximum number of wavelengths multiplied by their individual data rates. We focus on the single line rate case.

Further, we are given a set of demands K that need to be routed in the network. Each demand $k \in K$ is an aggregation of services. It connects a node pair $(s, t) \in U = \{(u, v) \in V \times V : u \neq v\}$ with a fixed data rate h_k and a maximum allowed end-to-end delay $\tau_{k,\max}$, also referred to as target delay. A node pair can also be connected by multiple demands.

Demands are routed in the virtual topology which in turn is defined by optical circuits in the optical layer. An optical circuit requires one line port at the router of its source node and one at the router of its target node. Intermediate nodes are bypassed, i.e., the circuit is switched in the ROADM without conversion to the electrical domain. Depending on the path on which a demand k is routed through the network it experiences a certain delay τ_k. We denote the difference between $\tau_{k,\max}$, the maximum delay a demand is allowed to experience, and its actual delay τ_k as *delay overfulfillment*. Further we denote

$$\Delta \tau_k = \frac{\tau_{k,\max} - \tau_k}{\tau_{k,\max}} \tag{1}$$

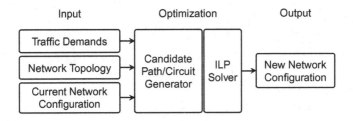

Fig. 1. Overview of the solution approach

as *relative delay overfulfillment*. We focus on core networks that span large geographical distances which in turn lead to significant propagation delays. In the core, these are the largest contributor to overall delay [15], followed by queuing delay. While queuing delay in routers can generally result in large delay spikes, these occur only rarely in the core where client traffic had already been subject to prior rate shaping. Together with traffic engineering sufficient link capacity to avoid excessive congestion can be ensured, such that we assume that queuing delays can be controlled in regular operation. Since existing studies show typical queuing delays to vary significantly between different networks from a few micro- [3] to a few milliseconds [2], which typically remains below the propagation delay in our scenario, we choose to focus on the deterministic part of the delay by modeling a demand's delay τ_k on a path by its propagation delay.

In [7], we already presented a delay-aware routing approach that minimizes the amount of active hardware in the network. This approach yields short paths for most demands which results in high delay overfulfillment. Our goal is to find a routing approach that reduces the delay overfulfillment compared to a resource optimization as shown in [7]. To be more precise, we find a network configuration, i.e., a set of circuits and a corresponding routing, for a given set of demands K that minimizes the average relative delay overfulfillment for a certain subset $K_S \subseteq K$ of those demands. We study the effects on the blocking behavior for a continuous reconfiguration of the network with demands that change over time. Furthermore, we consider the effects on the amount of network hardware that is needed. We focus on router line cards because they are the lion's share of the operator's capital expenditure (CAPEX) [10].

3   Solution Approach

We solve the problem introduced in the previous section with the help of an integer linear program (ILP). The ILP is based on a link-path formulation, i.e., it selects optimal routes out of a precomputed set of candidate paths. The whole process is depicted in Fig. 1. As input the algorithm receives the network topology, the set of demands as well as the current configuration of the network. In the first step, candidate paths are generated for each of the demands. Subsequently, the demands are routed using the ILP. The result is a new network configuration. We employ a make before break migration approach meaning that if the

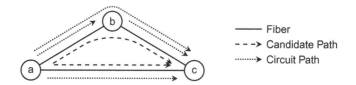

Fig. 2. Candidate path generation for a demand from node a to node c

routing of a demand changes from the previous to the current configuration, then the new path must be completely set up before the old one is torn down. Consequently, we need to ensure that enough capacity is available to realize old and new path simultaneously. The details are explained in the following sections.

3.1 Path Generation

The ILP selects optimal routes out of a set of precomputed candidate paths. The generation of these paths consists of two steps. In the first step, we find paths for the demands in the physical topology. In the second step, we create corresponding circuit realizations for each of the previously found paths. With this approach, a joint optimization of electrical and optical layer is possible.

For every demand $k \in K$ that connects nodes s and t we use the first m shortest simple paths between s and t in the physical layer $G = (V, E)$ as candidate paths. If the demand allows a maximum delay of $\tau_{k,\max}$, then only the subset of the m paths that fulfill this delay requirement is used. We denote the set of these valid paths by L_k.

We represent a candidate path $l \in L_k$ as a tuple of physical links, i.e., $l = (e_1, e_2, \ldots)$ where $e_i \in E$. In order to realize such a candidate path l one or more consecutive optical circuits need to be set up. An optical circuit can span one or more physical links; therefore, if we split l into several sub-tuples we obtain a sequence of optical circuit paths that realize l. We find all possible sequences of optical circuit paths and denote them by $R_{k,l}$. Sequences containing circuit paths that are longer than a predefined transparent optical reach are excluded. We denote the set of all individual circuit paths by C.

An example is given in Fig. 2 where we assume a demand from node a to c. Two simple paths, a–c and a–b–c, connect the two nodes. The path a–c can only be realized by a circuit connecting nodes a and c directly. The path a–b–c can be realized by a single circuit that bypasses node b or by two consecutive circuits, a–b and b–c.

3.2 ILP Formulation

The goal of the ILP is the joint minimization of demand blocking, delay over-fulfillment and required router line cards. To this end, we define variables that encode the selected candidate paths as well as the resulting amount of circuits and hardware that is required. Specifically, we define

- $g_{k,l,r} \in \{0,1\}$ ($k \in K, l \in L_k, r \in R_{k,l}$) as path selector, i.e., $g_{k,l,r}$ is one if demand k is routed over path l using circuit realization r;
- $b_k \in \{0,1\}$ ($k \in K$) as indicator for a blocked demand;
- $w_c \in \mathbb{N}$ ($c \in C$) as the number of parallel circuits on circuit path c where C is the set of all circuit paths in the network;
- $w'_c \in \mathbb{N}$ ($c \in C$) as the number of circuits on circuit path c taking migration into account;
- $p_{v,t} \in \mathbb{N}$ ($(v,t) \in U$) as the number of ports at v for connections with t;
- $q_v \in \mathbb{N}$ ($v \in V$) as the number of line cards at node v;
- $i_e \in \{0,1\}$ ($e \in E$) as indicator for a highly utilized link.

The objective function is

$$\min \left(\alpha \sum_{k \in K} b_k + \beta \sum_{v \in V} q_v + \frac{\gamma}{|K_S|} \sum_{k \in K_S, l \in L_k, r \in R_{k,l}} g_{k,l,r} \cdot \Delta\tau_{k,l} + \frac{\mu}{|E|} \sum_{e \in E} i_e \right). \quad (2)$$

The first term penalizes blocked demands while the second term is responsible for the minimization of active line cards. The third term penalizes the average relative delay overfulfillment of the demands in $K_S \subseteq K$. The parameter $\Delta\tau_{k,l}$ is demand k's relative delay overfulfillment if it takes path l. The last term penalizes links that are highly utilized. This is important for the make before break migration approach because it encourages the optimizer to leave some free link capacity for later migration steps.

The following constraints complete the ILP.

$$\sum_{l \in L_k, r \in R_{k,l}} g_{k,l,r} = 1 - b_k \quad \forall k \in K \tag{3}$$

$$\sum_{k \in K, l \in L_k, r \in R_{k,l}} \rho_{c,k,l,r} \cdot h_k \cdot g_{k,l,r} \leq \xi \cdot w_c \quad \forall c \in C \tag{4}$$

$$\sum_{k \in K, l \in L_k, r \in R_{k,l}} \rho_{c,k,l,r} \cdot h_k \cdot g_{k,l,r} + \sum_{k \in \widehat{K}, l \in L_k, r \in R_{k,l}} \rho_{c,k,l,r} \cdot h_k \cdot \widehat{g}_{k,l,r}$$
$$- \sum_{k \in K \cap \widehat{K}, l \in L_k, r \in R_{k,l}} \rho_{c,k,l,r} \cdot h_k \cdot g_{k,l,r} \cdot \widehat{g}_{k,l,r} \leq \xi \cdot w'_c \quad \forall c \in C \tag{5}$$

$$\sum_{c \in C} \delta_{e,c} \cdot \xi \cdot w'_c \leq \pi_e \quad \forall e \in E \tag{6}$$

$$\frac{1}{\pi_e} \sum_{c \in C} \delta_{e,c} \cdot \xi \cdot w_c \leq \psi + i_e \quad \forall e \in E \tag{7}$$

$$\sum_{c \in C} w_c \cdot \varphi_{c,v,t} \leq p_{v,t} \quad \forall (v,t) \in U \tag{8}$$

$$\sum_{c \in C} w_c \cdot \varphi_{c,t,v} \leq p_{v,t} \quad \forall (v,t) \in U \tag{9}$$

$$\sum_{t \in V \setminus \{v\}} p_{v,t} \leq \kappa \cdot q_v \quad \forall v \in V \tag{10}$$

In these constraints the set $\widehat{K}$ contains the demands of the previous reconfiguration step. Additionally, we define the parameters

- $\xi \in \mathbb{R}$ as the capacity of a single optical circuit;
- $\pi_e \in \mathbb{R}$ as the capacity of link e;
- $\psi \in [0, 1]$ as the utilization threshold for highly utilized links;
- $\kappa \in \mathbb{N}$ as the number of router ports a line card can maximally hold;
- $\rho_{c,k,l,r} \in \{0, 1\}$ as indicator showing whether circuit realization r of demand k's candidate path l uses circuit path c;
- $\delta_{e,c} \in \{0, 1\}$ as indicator showing whether circuit path c traverses link e;
- $\varphi_{c,u,v} \in \{0, 1\}$ as indicator showing whether circuit path c connects nodes u and v with u as source node;
- $\widehat{g}_{k,l,r} \in \{0, 1\}$ as the optimal path selector of the previous configuration.

Equation (3) ensures that a demand is either routed on exactly one path or blocked. Constraints (4) and (5) ensure that enough circuits are installed depending on the chosen paths. In contrast to Constraint (4), which only considers the demands of the current reconfiguration step, Constraint (5) also takes the routing of the previous reconfiguration step into account allowing the make before break migration. (6) is a link capacity constraint and (7) triggers the indicator i_e if the utilization of link e exceeds a certain limit $\psi \in [0, 1]$. Constraints (8) and (9) reserve a sufficient amount of router ports to accommodate the optical circuits. Finally, (10) ensures that enough line cards are present to hold the ports.

4   Evaluation

In this section we evaluate our approach. We first present the topologies and traffic demands as well as the parameters we studied. Then we discuss our results.

4.1   Network Topologies and Architecture

We selected the two backbone networks Abilene and Géant, found in the SNDlib [9], to evaluate the behavior of our routing approach in different wide-area networks. We only show details for the Géant topology here since the results for Abilene are very similar.

Géant is a research network connecting various countries in Europe. As we neglect the connection to New York, we end up with 21 nodes and 68 directed links. The topology is shown in Fig. 3(a). We assume that the ports operate at a data rate of $\xi = 100$ Gbps with a transparent reach of 2500 km and that a router line card can hold a single port, i.e., $\kappa = 1$ [4]. Further, we assume that the number of wavelengths on a link is limited such that $\pi_e = 40 \cdot \xi$.

4.2   Traffic Demand

We synthetically generated traffic demands whose arrival and holding times follow a negative exponential distribution. We assume that the demands have wavelength granularity, i.e., the traffic value of a demand h_k equals the capacity ξ

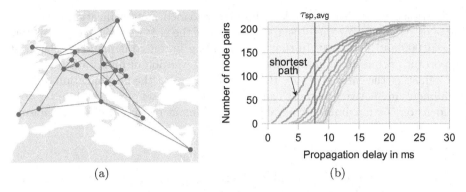

Fig. 3. Logical fiber topology (a) and propagation delay distributions of the 10 shortest paths (b) for the European research network Géant [9] without the node in New York. The path length index in (b) increases from left to right, i.e., the red curve on the left corresponds to the shortest path. The average delay of the shortest path at $\tau_{\mathrm{sp,avg}} = 7.7\,\mathrm{ms}$ is depicted with the red vertical line. (Color figure online)

of an optical circuit. We distinguish two traffic demand classes, namely *delay-sensitive* and *delay-insensitive* demands. The delay-insensitive demands do not have a delay requirement meaning that they can be routed on arbitrary routes. The delay-sensitive demands do have a certain delay requirement $\tau_{k,\mathrm{max}}$. In the ILP optimization they form the set K_S, i.e., their delay overfulfillment is minimized. Delay-sensitive demands were generated only between those node pairs for which the shortest connecting path satisfies the delay requirement. Varying the delay requirement therefore also changes the number of node pairs with delay-sensitive traffic. Figure 3(b) shows the delay distribution for the ten shortest paths between all node pairs. Additionally, the average shortest path delay $\tau_{\mathrm{sp,avg}}$ considering all node pairs is depicted. It is visible that for a delay requirement $\tau_{k,\mathrm{max}}$ equal to the average shortest path delay $\tau_{\mathrm{sp,avg}}$, 128 node pairs can be connected with a delay-sensitive demand. 98 of them have at least one alternative path. The remaining 30 node pairs can be connected on the shortest path only. Our approach tries to avoid the blocking of demands between those node pairs by routing demands with less strict delay requirements on circumjacent links.

4.3   Reconfiguration

The reconfiguration is triggered at regular intervals where the ratio of the interval duration and the mean holding time of the traffic demands equals 0.05. In each reconfiguration step we route the demands that will arrive in the following interval while taking the present configuration of the current interval into account. We employ a make before break migration to transition between two configurations. For the candidate path generation we consider the $m = 10$ shortest paths between each node pair. For each path we consider all possible circuit realizations. We consider a link to be highly loaded if its utilization exceeds a value of $\psi = 0.95$. For the objective function of the ILP we used the parameters $\alpha = 10\,000$ and $\mu = 1000$. In that way, avoiding unrouted demands is the most important optimization goal followed by the prevention of highly utilized links. By adjusting the ratio of β to γ the trade-off between the minimization of over-fulfillment and active line cards can be controlled. We set $\beta = 0.0001$ and $\gamma = 10$ to focus on the maximum achievable overfulfillment reduction in this scenario.

4.4   Varied Scenario Parameters

For the evaluation of the introduced reconfiguration approach we adjusted a number of parameters relevant for the traffic generation.

The *offered load* describes the amount of traffic that needs to be transported through the network in relation to its capacity. Therefore, on the one hand, the offered load depends on the demand values themselves. But on the other hand it also depends on the path length of a routed demand. Demands between nodes with a physical connection can be routed single-hop whereas demands between distant nodes necessarily occupy resources on several links. We therefore introduce an offered load metric which, to a certain extent, takes these differences in the path length into account. For each demand k we compute the shortest possible path and count the number of physical links ζ_k it traverses. In our model, this value ζ_k is equivalent to the number of wavelengths the demand occupies when it is routed on the shortest path. We multiply the occupied wavelengths with the demand value h_k and relate it to the total network capacity, i.e., the sum of all link capacities. The offered load is then given by

$$A = \frac{\sum_{k \in K} \zeta_k \cdot h_k}{\sum_{e \in E} \pi_e}. \tag{11}$$

An additional parameter is the *share of delay-sensitive demands* in the total number of demands $\phi = |K_S|/|K|$. Lastly, we vary the target delay $\tau_{k,\max}$ of the delay-sensitive demands. In order to compare networks with different geographical layouts we relate the target delay to the average shortest path delay $\tau_{\mathrm{sp,avg}}$ of the network. We introduce a *target delay factor* χ_τ which adjusts the target delay according to $\tau_{k,\max} = \chi_\tau \cdot \tau_{\mathrm{sp,avg}}, \forall k \in K_S$.

Using the introduced parameters we have determined demand inter-arrival and holding times. Based on these, we generated a traffic demand series of 200 demand sets for each parameter combination of offered load A, share of delay-sensitive demands ϕ and target delay factor χ_τ as depicted in Fig. 4.

4.5   Results

The presented approach on the reduction of delay overfulfillment is compared to a resource optimization. The resource optimization routes the traffic load such that the amount of active line cards is minimized while the delay requirements are satisfied. This is realized by setting $\gamma = 0$ in the ILP's objective function.

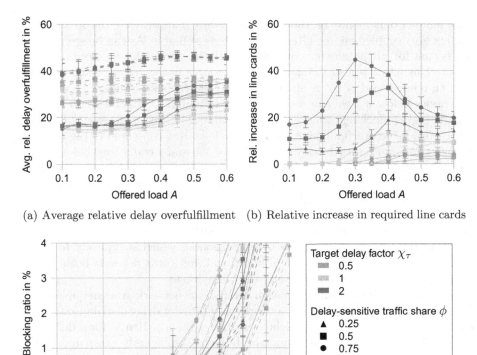

(a) Average relative delay overfulfillment   (b) Relative increase in required line cards

(c) Blocking ratio

Fig. 4. Results of the introduced reconfiguration approach for wavelength demands with Poisson arrivals and departures. Shown metrics are the average relative delay overfulfillment (a), the relative increase in required line cards compared to a delay-aware resource optimization (b) and the blocking ratio (c). The error bars represent one standard deviation.

Figure 4 shows the results of our investigation as introduced for the Géant topology for an offered load ranging from 0.1 to 0.6 in steps of 0.05. Each data point represents the average of a series of 200 reconfigurations including migration. The error bars show one standard deviation. Figure 4(a) shows the relative delay overfulfillment averaged over all delay-sensitive demands K_S. As can be seen, our approach is able to reduce the relative overfulfillment by up to 60% compared to the resource optimization for the case that the target delay factor is 2. Even for a delay factor of 0.5, for which alternative paths for delay-sensitive demands are scarce, an overfulfillment reduction is possible. The share of delay-sensitive demands has only a small impact on the delay overfulfillment. Figure 4(c) shows the blocking ratio, i.e., the ratio of unrouted demands to the total number of demands K. Blocking occurs only if all wavelengths on an physical link are occupied and no alternative route is available. As can be seen, blocking occurs for all parameter combinations if the offered load exceeds a value of 0.4. This effect is also visible with the resource optimization which suggests that an offered load of 0.4 is already close to the capacity limit of the network. For values below 0.4 we can see that the overfulfillment minimization exhibits slightly higher blocking ratios. Figure 4(b) shows the relative increase in required line cards for the overfulfillment reducing optimization compared to the resource optimization. For a target delay factor of $\chi_\tau = 0.5$ and a traffic load below 0.3 no increase in the number of line cards is visible. Also for $\chi_\tau = 1$ and traffic loads up to 0.2 this number stays the same for both optimization approaches. This means that the delay overfulfillment can be reduced without the need to invest more line cards. For a target delay of twice the average shortest path delay additional line cards are necessary. However, we assume that this hardware overhead is within the margin of hardware overprovisioning which is typically found in transport networks. The amount of additional line cards depends both on the share of delay-sensitive demands and the offered load.

We have conducted the evaluation for the US network Abilene [9] as well. Compared to Géant, the Abilene network has a broader delay distribution resulting in less alternative paths for delay-sensitive demands. Hence, for a delay factor of 0.5 the overfulfillment cannot be reduced significantly compared to the resource optimization. For higher target delays the results are very similar to those presented for the Géant topology. In particular, they confirm that the delay overfulfillment can be significantly reduced by our approach while the blocking behavior is only slightly affected.

5   Conclusions

In this paper we presented a new routing and network reconfiguration approach which addresses the overfulfillment of delay requirements in transport networks. The approach routes traffic on paths other than the shortest path to reduce the delay overfulfillment of traffic demands. In that way, customers experience service delays closer to the limits specified in their SLA providing an incentive to acquire a more expensive service class if necessary. For the ISP this provides a new opportunity for revenue creation. As a secondary goal, our approach relieves highly utilized links for those demands that have no alternative to the shortest path due to their strict delay requirements.

We presented a parameterizable ILP that jointly optimizes routing in the optical and electrical layer of the transport network. We evaluated our proposed approach for two nationwide transport networks. The results show that the delay overfulfillment can be reduced by up to 60% without a significant increase in the blocking ratio compared to a resource optimization. The number of required line cards naturally increases because longer routes are taken. However, we assume it to remain within the margin of hardware overprovisioning by ISPs. Furthermore, the trade-off between the minimization of overfulfillment and required hardware depends on adjustable parameters which allows the ISP to adapt our approach to its business models and networking hardware.

Acknowledgements. This work has been performed in the framework of the CELTIC EUREKA project SENDATE-TANDEM (Project ID C2015/3-2), and it is partly funded by the German BMBF (Project ID 16KIS0458). The authors alone are responsible for the content of the paper.

References

1. Bauknecht, U.: Resource efficiency and latency in dynamic IP-over-WSON networks utilizing flexrate transponders. In: Photonic Networks; 18. ITG-Symposium, pp. 36–41, May 2017
2. Bozkurt, I.N., et al.: Dissecting latency in the internet's fiber infrastructure. arXiv preprint arXiv:1811.10737, November 2018
3. Choi, B.Y., Moon, S., Zhang, Z.L., Papagiannaki, K., Diot, C.: Analysis of point-to-point packet delay in an operational network. Comput. Netw. **51**(13), 3812–3827 (2007). https://doi.org/10.1016/j.comnet.2007.04.004
4. Cisco: CRS 1-port 100 Gigabit Ethernet Coherent DWDM Interface Module (2013)
5. Cisco: Visual Networking Index: Forecast and Trends, 2017–2022, November 2018
6. Ellis, A.D., McCarthy, M.E., Khateeb, M.A.Z.A., Sorokina, M., Doran, N.J.: Performance limits in optical communications due to fiber nonlinearity. Adv. Opt. Photonics **9**(3), 429–503 (2017). https://doi.org/10.1364/AOP.9.000429
7. Enderle, T., Bauknecht, U.: Modeling dynamic traffic demand behavior in telecommunication networks. In: Photonic Networks; 19th ITG-Symposium, pp. 18–25, June 2018
8. Lourenço, R.B., Tornatore, M., Martel, C.U., Mukherjee, B.: Running the network harder: connection provisioning under resource crunch. IEEE Trans. Netw. Serv. Manage. **15**(4), 1615–1629 (2018). https://doi.org/10.1109/TNSM.2018.2875103
9. Orlowski, S., Pióro, M., Tomaszewski, A., Wessäly, R.: SNDlib 1.0-survivable network design library. In: Proceedings of the 3rd International Network Optimization Conference (INOC 2007), Spa, Belgium, April 2007
10. Papanikolaou, P., Christodoulopoulos, K., Varvarigos, M.: Multilayer flex-grid network planning, pp. 151–156 (2015). https://doi.org/10.1109/ONDM.2015.7127290
11. Pointurier, Y.: Design of low-margin optical networks. IEEE/OSA J. Opt. Commun. Netw. **9**(1), A9–A17 (2017). https://doi.org/10.1364/JOCN.9.0000A9
12. Sen, S., Joe-Wong, C., Ha, S., Chiang, M.: A survey of smart data pricing: past proposals, current plans, and future trends. ACM Comput. Surv. **46**(2), 15:1–15:37 (2013). https://doi.org/10.1145/2543581.2543582
13. Velasco, L., Castro, A., King, D., Gerstel, O., Casellas, R., Lopez, V.: In-operation network planning. IEEE Commun. Mag. **52**(1), 52–60 (2014). https://doi.org/10.1109/MCOM.2014.6710064
14. Walrand, J.: Economic models of communication networks. In: Liu, Z., Xia, C.H. (eds.) Performance Modeling and Engineering, pp. 57–89. Springer, Boston (2008). https://doi.org/10.1007/978-0-387-79361-0_3
15. Xiao, P., Li, Z., Guo, S., Qi, H., Qu, W., Yu, H.: A K self-adaptive SDN controller placement for wide area networks. Front. Inf. Technol. Electron. Eng. **17**(7), 620–633 (2016). https://doi.org/10.1631/FITEE.1500350

Design of a Real-Time DSP Engine on RF-SoC FPGA for 5G Networks

Vasileios Kitsakis[1], Konstantina Kanta[2], Ioannis Stratakos[3],
Giannis Giannoulis[2], Dimitrios Apostolopoulos[2], George Lentaris[3],
Hercules Avramopoulos[2], Dimitrios Soudris[3], and Dionysios I. Reisis[1(✉)]

[1] Electronics Laboratory, Department of Physics, National and Kapodistrian
University of Athens, Physics Building. IV, Panepistimiopolis, 15784 Athens, Greece
{bkits,dreisis}@phys.uoa.gr

[2] Photonics Communication Research Laboratory, Department of Electrical
and Computer Engineering (Old Building), National Technical University of Athens,
15773 Athens, Greece
{kkanta,jgiannou,apostold,hav}@mail.ntua.gr

[3] Microprocessors and Digital Systems Lab, School of Electrical
and Computer Engineering, National Technical University of Athens,
15780 Athens, Greece
{istratak,glentaris,dsoudris}@microlab.ntua.gr

Abstract. 5G advances the wireless communications by providing a significant improvement to the data rate, capability of connected devices and data volumes compared to the previous generations. While these advantages combine along with a wider range of applications to merit the end-user, the technologies to be used are not specified. Considering this problem and in order to efficiently support the 5G deployment researchers and engineers turned their attention on FPGA base band architectures that keep the implementation cost relatively low and at the same time they are reprogramable to provide solutions to the emerging requirements and their consequent modifications. Aiming at the contribution to the 5G technologies the current paper introduces the design of a base band DSP architecture that targets the required real time performance. Moreover, the proposed architecture is scalable by efficiently parallelizing and/or pipelining the corresponding data paths. The paper presents the pilot FPGA designs of the IFFT/FFT and Sampling Frequency Offset (SFO) functions that achieve a 500 Msps performance on a RF-SoC Xilinx ZCU111 board.

Keywords: 5G Networks · 5G-PHOS · DSP engine · FPGA

1 Introduction

Even though the number of 5G technology demonstrations that are presented by the system vendors and telecom operators is increasing [1], the transition from

A. Tzanakaki et al. (Eds.): ONDM 2019, LNCS 11616, pp. 540–551, 2020.
https://doi.org/10.1007/978-3-030-38085-4_46

4G-Long Term Evolution (LTE) will be a long process, while the final 5G specifications are not defined yet. This transition is enforced by the network demands of increasingly popular emerging technologies such as virtual/augmented reality and 4K video, low latency, reliability and device/network energy efficiency, will be addressed by 5G networks by exploiting existing technologies that include millimeter waves (mmWave), massive multiple input – multiple output (MIMO), beamforming [2], [3] and multi-carrier modulation formats [4]. The prevailing network architectures are the centralized and ultra-dense network topologies at the mobile fronthaul (MFH), providing higher data rates in a new radio-band (30–300GHz) [5] through the use of mmWave (radiofrequency) RF carriers. However, the high attenuation of mmWave transmission, due to atmospheric absorption, will anchor optical fiber as the main transmission link between the Base Band Unit (BBU) and the Remote Radio Head (RRH) side, bringing Radio-over-Fiber (RoF) technology to the core of future 5G implementations [5].

The MFH with digital fiber-optic interfaces, such as the Common Public Radio Interface (CPRI), with high data rates cannot be supported by the CPRI-formatted frame specifications [6]. Moreover, the latency of RRH processing [7] makes Analog RoF (A-RoF) a strong 5G candidate, without digitization penalty but with high throughput eliminating the optical hardware demands.

In this context, the EU funded H2020 5G-PHOS project, will exploit results in the area of photonics in order to architect centralized A-RoF 5G networks for dense, ultra-dense and Hot-Spot areas incorporating Photonic Integrated Circuits (PICs) in optical mmWave signal generation, DSP-assisted optical transmission, reconfigurable optical add/drop multiplexing (ROADM) and optical beamforming functionalities. 5G-PHOS expects to release a seamless, interoperable, RAT-agnostic and SDN-programmable FiWi 5G network that supports 64×64 MIMO antennas in the V-band.

BBUs involve computationally demanding DSP functions and have to be reprogrammable because the standards are still open. Moreover, the transition from Distributed-RAN (D-RAN) topologies towards Cloud-RAN (C-RAN) architectures, where a pool of BBUs accommodate the needs of several RRHs, will use reconfigurable processors and FPGAs [11]. Besides the cloudification of the mobile fronthaul, fully elastic optical transceivers will operate in dual mode supporting both D-RoF and A-RoF transport, and allow for distance-adaptive modulation [12]. These elastic FPGA-based BBUs facilitate also the transition towards Ethernet-based fronthaul [13]. Through this Radio-over-Ethernet (RoE) approach, FPGAs can offer solutions that cope with the inherent jitters of the CPRI traffic over standard Ethernet [14].

In the current work within the context of 5GPHOS [23], we design a proof-of-concept datapath to transmit and receive data according to the aforementioned ideas of C-RAN and A-RoF, with potential use even in future MEC scenarios. More specifically, we consider here data streams e.g., via Ethernet, as input to our system consisting of: (a) CPU/smartNIC handling MAC layer tasks, (b) FPGA handling the digital baseband processing, (c) DAC/ADC for signal conversion to an IF, (d) fiber optics for ARoF transmission/reception to the RRH, and (e) mmWave RRH for establishing new radio-band links. Aiming at providing an effective solution to the BBU, this paper focuses on the design of a System-on-Chip (SoC) FPGA-based architecture realizing parts (b) and (c). To this end, we capitalize on state-of-the-art chips integrating processors, FPGA resources, DAC/ADC with digital-up/down-conversion and hard-IPs for the FEC functions, to provide a scalable embedded solution with low cost/power but real-time performance. We research for developing the BBU DSP functions and their fine tuning by the use of simulations and implement these on Xilinx RF-SoC FPGA of the ZCU111 board [21]. The proposed custom VHDL circuits are based on pipelining and parallelization techniques to achieve the required real-time performance. The following sections present an overview of our envisaged final system, details regarding our functions at algorithmic level, as well as the FPGA architectures of the IFFT/FFT and Sampling Frequency Offset (SFO) designed during the ongoing development stage of our DSP chain.

The paper is organized with the following section presenting related FPGA architectures. Section 3 describes the DSP algorithmic design and details. Section 4 presents the DSP architecture. Section 5 gives the details of the design on the FPGA and the corresponding performance results and finally, Sect. 6 concludes the paper.

2   State of the Art and Related Results

The main challenge in A-RoF transmission is the transport of mmWave signals over the optical link achieving high performance. In order to overcome signal impairments, the proposed methods include the impact of chromatic dispersion through RF power fading and distortion due to nonlinearity within the link [8]. A-IFoF is gaining momentum on the verge of 5G release, while DSP-enabled A-IFoF/mmWave transmission is shown in laboratory scale [11]. Using IF frequencies can mitigate the distortion caused by optical links without fully compensating for the Fi-Wi channel impairments. Consequently, DSP technics on FPGAs improve the signal quality based on pre-emphasis and post-equalization technics [9]. DSP-enabled channel aggregation methods used in MFH systems achieve high bit-rates and multiple-user connectivity [10].

There is a plethora of works for OFDM transceivers on FPGA devices for specific communication standards. The work in [15] shows FPGAs with a full processing chain for an OFDM transceiver for the IEEE 802.11, IEEE 802.16 and IEEE 802.22 standards. In [17] a non-continuous OFDM FPGA-based baseband architecture utilizes dynamic partial-reconfiguration to adapt its processing datapath and [18] gives the adaptable FFT core. Finally, [16] presents a pilot-based channel estimation technique for a system consisting of a 16-QAM mapper/demapper, 1024-point IFFT/FFT with 798 data samples, 56 pilots and 170 zeros.

3   DSP Algorithm

3.1   Centralized DSP Engine

Figure 1 shows the single band Tx and Rx DSP block chain designed to support the centralized, analog RoF based network architecture targeted in 5GPhos. Multiplexing of multiple bands will be performed in the DACs driving the centralized transceiver's unit optical interface. The DSP blocks represented with red color, are used for the generation and demodulation of f-OFDM signals. Specifically, the operations of these blocks are the modulation of the QAM symbols, their mapping to orthogonal sub-carriers, the CP insertion and the filtering at the transmitter side and the corresponding operations at the receiver side. Considering 5G specifications [22], the 5GPHOS waveform parameters are: 400MHz band-size, 256-point FFT and 32-samples cyclic prefix (cp). In the literature the candidate filters are: the soft-truncated sinc filters, including hann and rrc window, and the equiripple filters based on the Remez exchange algorithm. Given that equiripple filtered signals are prone to ISI and the extended use of rrc filters, the latter was the filter of choice in 5GPhos.

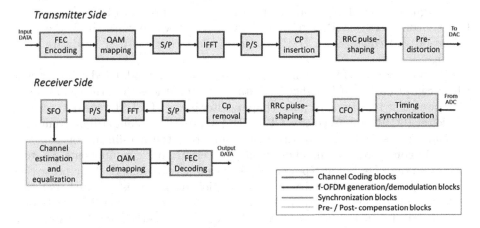

Fig. 1. Block diagrams of typical f-OFDM optical transmitter and receiver DSP chain

3.2   Algorithmic Treatment of Timing and Frequency Synchronization

Both FFT window alignment and carrier frequency offsets (CFO) correction are dealt with in time domain, as depicted in Fig. 1. The operating principle of the two block relies on identifying in the received signal an expected time domain sequence or some form of repetition. For this purpose, a preamble is used and correlation algorithms executed at the receiver side track the f-OFDM symbols and the local oscillator induced frequency offsets.

Possible inaccuracies in the receiver and transmitter sampling clocks could lead to ICI. Sampling frequency offsets (SFO) causes slow drift of the FFT window, hence loss of the sub-carriers orthogonality. In contrast to the CFO, the effect of SFO depends on the individual sub-carriers' characteristics, therefore most DSP techniques for SFO compensation are applied in frequency domain, thus after the FFT block. Both pilot-aided and blind methods can be adopted for the algorithmic treatment of the effect. In 5G-PHOS, we will use a blind algorithm based on the fourth power of the phase of the received sub-carriers for extracting a mean value of the constellation rotation. Then, we apply the estimated phase to the signal.

3.3   A-IFoF Tx Pre-compensation and Rx Equalization

To achieve correct demodulation of the received signal, an estimation of the inverted channel response must be calculated and applied to the signal, minimizing the impact of the channel noise and frequency selectivity. The term "channel" refers to the whole transmission link that includes the length of the sSMF fiber, the wireless link, any electro/optical amplification and up/down-conversion required. The above processes are implemented either at the receiver, by an equalization filter, or at the transmitter by a pre-distortion filter. For a C-RAN compatible DSP engine, an FPGA board will perform both the pre-distortion and equalization DSP functions, alleviating end-user hardware processing.

Multi-carrier waveforms consist of a large number of modulated sub-carriers, which can result in much higher instantaneous amplitudes than the signal average power. The insertion of a pulse shaping filter in the f-OFDM waveform results in a lower PAPR, compared to a CP-OFDM approach [19], but still high enough to render the signal prone to distortion caused by the non-linear components of the A-IFoF transmission. Those include all electro-optic components, i.e. the EMLs and the PDs, but also power amplifiers and passive mixers. To improve the f-OFDM transmission linearity, a pre-distortion technique is required. For the respective algorithm generation, the memory effects of high PAPR caused non-linearity are taken into account. A widely discussed method for modeling the nonlinearity in literature is the Volterra series memory polynomial. However, since extracting the inverse of the Volterra system is complicated, an adaptive pre-distorter scheme seems to be preferable than a post-compensation scenario. This algorithm can be implemented by an adaptive filter fed by a one-tap RLS or LMS algorithm [20].

An advantage of multi-carrier waveforms is their robustness to chromatic dispersion and wireless link multipath effects. Thanks to the cyclic prefix insertion to the transmitted f-OFDM symbols, the time-domain signal presents periodicity which allows for a simpler channel estimation in frequency domain. Thus, the receiver equalization can be performed by a single-tap filter, as in the pre-distortion case. The equalization schemes are selected by taking into account the wireless channel transmission effects, since the optical link is static and adds insignificant distortion to the signal.

4   Base Band Digital Architecture

The 5G-PHOS project will use a ZCU111 board hosting a Xilinx's Zynq Ultra-scale+ RF-SoC device [21], which integrates a quad-core Cortex-A53 APU, a dual-core Cortex-R5 RPU, an FPGA fabric and dedicated ADCs/DACs. Moreover, each ADC/DAC component has its own digital datapath that offers real or complex signal processing, digital-up/down conversion units and mixing to digital IF frequencies in the order of GHz. Furthermore, specialized soft-decision FEC (SD-FEC) hard-blocks support the processing requirements.

Currently, similar deployed systems use an FPGA device along with external DACs/ADCs to implement the required functionality. These systems adopt the JESD204B standard as the link between converters and the receiver/transmitter. The downside of this approach is the development time needed to optimize the communication, as well as the power consumed. On the other hand, the RF-SoC device offers an embedded hardware platform for the deployment of the proposed DSP engine, alleviating extra development or performance costs. In the presented setup, the RF-SoC device includes the DSP blocks for the transmitter and the receiver. The board communicates with an ethernet switch utilizing the 25GBASE-SR standard through an SFP28 connector and by SMA cables it interfaces the ADCs/DACs with the analogue front-end.

The transmitter gets data from the ethernet switch and forwards these into four independent processing paths that handle a 500 MHz band each. The bands are processed independently (Fig. 1 transmitter) and their data are forwarded to four distinct DAC units configured in pairs to merge their respective bands and to produce two dual-band signals digitally up-converted to 1.5 GHz digital IF and converted to analog. These analog signals are transmitted through SMA cables in an analog synthesizer, capable to up-convert the received signals to their analog IF of 5 GHz and from there drive the next stage, which consists of the optoelectronics components. In the receiver, optical signals are converted to electrical on the optoelectronics components. These analog signals have an analog IF of 5 GHz and are down-converted to 1.5 GHz analog IF by the analog synthesizer, that feeds the ADCs of the RF-SoC device. A single ADC digitizes the received signal and it further digitally down-converts a dual-band signal to baseband, separates it to two single bands and sets apart the I/Q parts of the signals. The output of an ADC is then processed by the FPGA DSP blocks of the receiver subsystem (Fig. 1 receiver) and the results are transmitted through the ethernet IP core to the external ethernet switch. Figure 2 illustrates the high-level architecture of the DSP engine on RF-SoC device. Note that the dual-band creation on the DACs is simplified for illustrative purposes.

We illustrate the design of the DSP algorithms of the RF-SoC device by the description of the receiver processing chain for a single band signal. An ADC provides to the FPGA a 2Gsps single band signal separated to its I/Q parts. First, a timing synchronization algorithm on two streams of samples locates the frame start. The output rate will be 500 Msps. Next, the CFO correction block corrects any frequency offset on the received signal and then each I/Q stream drives through an RRC pulse-shaping filter to minimize ICI and ISI effects and

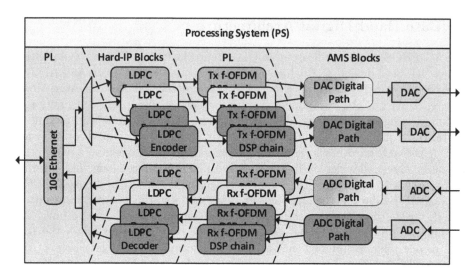

Fig. 2. High-level architecture of DSP processing on Zynq Ultrascale+ RF-SoC device.

it removes the samples of the CP. The fourth step is the FFT decimation in frequency radix-2 FFT algorithm; it processes 256 complex points since every OFDM symbol consists of 256 I/Q samples (191 carriers, 17 pilots and 48 zeros) and produces results with ~470 Msps. The fifth step implements the SFO correction block based on the Viterbi Fourth Power Estimator algorithm. The block receives the complex output points from the FFT block and corrects the frequency offsets.

At this stage, after completing the correction of the possible errors introduced during the transmission of the signals through the channel, the DSP chain performs the channel estimation and equalization. This procedure takes as input the results calculated by the SFO correction block and uses the 17-pilots samples present in each OFDM symbol to perform its operation. The results of this block are forwarded to a soft-decision QAM demodulation block. The QAM demodulator can demodulate 4/16/64-QAM constellations and implements the approximate log-likelihood ratio (ALLR) algorithm to give an estimate on the value of the data bits received. Finally, the ALLR values are given as input to the soft-decision FEC block at ~350 Msps. The FEC processing block performs LDPC decoding, and based on the ALLR values gives the final stream of data. This stream of data is the input to the ethernet IP block.

5   FPGA Design and Results

The proposed FPGA architectures are scalable with respect to the throughput by parallelizing and/or pipelining the data paths. For efficiently supporting the data stream we opted to include all the modules as a pipelined chain architecture.

Currently, we have complete the FPGA design and the testing of its two major modules: the *FFT* and the *phase shift estimation and compensation (SFO)*.

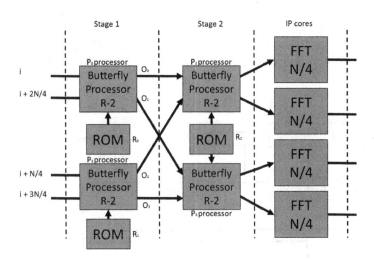

Fig. 3. The FFT module

5.1 FFT Module

Off-the-self IPs can be used for the radix-2 decimation in frequency (DIF)FFT. To achieve though the required throughput we have to include more than one cores into a parallel design: it has a throughput proportional to the number of cores, that is the parallel architecture of k parallel smaller FFT blocks, the parallel design achieves k times greater throughput than a single block design. For a relatively small k the parallel design will achieve the same clock frequency with the single core. The proposed design is based on a scalable k block N-point FFT. The initial study showed that the four blocks should suffice with respect to the required throughput (Fig. 3). The four blocks N-FFT design accomplishes four times the throughput and operates with four $N/4$-point FFT blocks. Two additional stages must be implemented before the $N/4$-FFT blocks, to complete the two first stages of the DIF-FFT algorithm. The first stage consists of two radix-2 processors (P_0 and P_1) and two ROM memories (one memory per processor, R_0 and R_1). The first processor P_0 receives as inputs the FFT points with indexes i and $i + 2N/4$ (where $i = [0, 1, 2, \ldots, N/4 - 1]$) and produces two outputs O_0 and O_1. The phase factors of this processor are stored in the first ROM (R_0) in the following order $[0, 1, 2, \ldots, N/4 - 1]$. The second processor ($P_1$) receives as inputs the FFT points with indexes $i + N/4$ and $i + 3N/4$ (where $i = [0, 1, 2, \ldots, N/4 - 1]$) and produces two outputs O_2 and O_3. The phase factors of this processor are stored in the second ROM (R_1) in the following order $[N/4, N/4+1, N/4+2, \ldots, N/2-1]$. The second stage also consists of two radix-2 processors (P_2 and P_3) but one ROM (R_3) since the processors in this stage use the same factors. The inputs of P_2 are O_0 and O_2 while the inputs of P_3 are O_1 and O_3. The phase factors of this stage are stored in R_3 in the following order $[0, 2, 4, \ldots, N/2 - 2]$. Each processor output is the input of each $N/4$-FFT block. The output of the first $N/4$-FFT block are the FFT points with indexes $[0, 4, 8, \ldots, N - 4]$, the output of the second are the FFT points with indexes $[1, 5, 9, \ldots, N - 3]$, the output of the third are the FFT points with indexes $[2, 6, 10, \ldots, N - 2]$ and the output of the fourth are FFT points with indexes $[3, 7, 11, \ldots, N - 1]$.

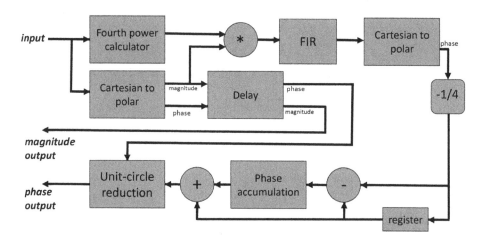

Fig. 4. The phase shift estimation and compensation module

5.2 Phase Shift Estimation and Compensation

The phase shift estimation and compensation module consists of six basic components: the fourth power calculator block, two cartesian to polar conversion blocks, the FIR filter block, the delay block, the phase accumulation block and the unit-circle reduction block (Fig. 4). The fourth power calculator block computes the fourth power of the complex input as follows: the complex input is routed to both input-ports of a complex multiplier; this multiplier computes the second power of the complex number. Similarly, a second complex multiplier computes the fourth power of the complex number. The cartesian to polar conversion block uses the Cordic algorithm to calculate the magnitude and the phase of the cartesian input. The fir block is a transposed Finite Impulsive Response (FIR) filter with L-taps and all the coefficients are equal to $1/L$. The delay block is a FIFO memory with depth $L/2$, the input is delayed for $L/2$ cycles. The phase accumulation block receives as input the phase of a complex number, which has a real number representation. The input is multiplied by the number $2/\pi$. The product of the multiplication is subtracted from the number $1/2$ and the product of this subtraction is floored. Then the floored numbers are multiplied by $\pi/2$ and the product (FN) must be accumulated each clock cycle. If the accumulated output is greater than 2π then the accumulation input is $FN - 2\pi$ instead of FN. This method subtracts the unit-circles (note that $e^{2\pi i} = 1$) from the accumulation. The unit-circle reduction block receives as input a phase and compares it with π. If the phase is greater than π then 2π is subtracted from the phase. This method ensures that the values are between $-\pi$ and π. The product of this operation is added with the output of the delay block and the final correction is performed. The product of the addition is compared with $-\pi$ and π. If the product is greater than π then 2π is subtracted from the product; else if the product is smaller than $-\pi$ then 2π is added to the product. The output is the corrected phase and the phase values are between $-\pi$ and π. The input to the module is a complex number; this number is the input of the fourth power calculator block and the first cartesian to polar conversion block. The product of the first block is the fourth power of the module input, while the product of the second block is the magnitude and the phase of the module input. The fourth power is multiplied by the magnitude and the product is the input of the FIR block. The magnitude and the phase are the inputs of the delay block. The output of the FIR block is the input of the second cartesian to polar conversion block. The output of the cartesian to polar conversion block is negated and divided by four; then, the product is subtracted with the product of the previous clock cycle (delayed product). The result of the subtraction is the input of the phase accumulation block. Then, the output of the phase accumulation block is added to the delayed product. The product of this addition and the output of the delay block are the inputs of the unit-circle reduction block. Finally, the output of this block and the magnitude output of the delay block are the outputs of the module.

5.3 FPGA Results

The demonstration prototype required a 2 Gsps throughput design on the KCU105 board. The aforementioned FPGA achieves this throughput with the four FFT core design. The FFT was configured to process 256 points with 16-bit accuracy for the real part and 16-bit for the imaginary part for each input and output point. The scaling factor of the output points is 8-bits ($2^8 = 256$). The module achieves clock frequency 0.5 GHz and utilizes the following FPGA resources: 4286 LUTs (1.77% of the available), 1311 LUTRAMs (1.16%), 8379 FFs (1.73%), 2 BRAMs (0.33%) and finally 96 DSPs (5%).

The phase shift estimation and compensation module implementation achieve the target throughput (500 Msps on the RFSoC (XCZU28DR) board) with minimum calculation complexity and minimum accuracy loss. The unit-circle reduction method was used to avoid the implementation of divisions and the scaling of the data. The proposed method is advantageous, because it utilizes comparisons and additions/subtractions, which keep the implementation cost lower than the corresponding divisions and have no impact on accuracy. This method is also safe regarding the overflow, since the design keeps the data values inside specific intervals (e.g. $[-\pi, \pi]$). The design was configured to process 32-bit words; 16-bits real part and 16-bits imaginary part for the input data, 16-bits magnitude and 16-bits phase for the output data. As noted above the data are unscaled. The module achieves clock frequency approximately 0.5 GHz and utilizes the following FPGA resources: 2235 LUTs (0.56% of the available), 126 LUTRAMs (0.06%), 2546 FFs (0.3%) and finally 13 DSPs (0.3%).

6   Concluding Remarks

The current paper summarized key requirements/directions in emerging 5G technologies that will benefit from FPGA platforms and, subsequently, in the context of the ongoing European project 5GPHOS, it presented our proof-of-concept design of a scalable baseband processor supporting ARoF links in 5G networks. The proposed design exploits a state-of-the-art system-on-chip FPGA tailored for RF applications, namely the XCZU28DR RFSoC. We utilized its integrated set of DAC, ADC, FEC, CPU, and FPGA resources, to assemble processing pipelines realizing high-performance OFDM transmitters and receivers for mmWave telecommunications. In our scalable FPGA architecture, 4+4 distinct pipelines at 500 Msps will operate in parallel to input+output 4+4 streams of data comprising four bidirectional bands. Each pipeline will accelerate multiple DSP functions via efficient VHDL circuit design and customized configuration of the relevant RFSoC components. Our future work will advance the architectural design and development of each DSP function on FPGA, its optimization and integration to the system, and the testing of the final FPGA module, in-the-field. Our final FPGA module targets approximately 8+8 Gbps throughput, in total, with low-latency, low-power, and real-time performance.

Acknowledgement. This work has been supported by the European Commission through H2020 5GPPP Phase II project 5G PHOS [23], Contract Number 761989.

References

1. https://alertify.eu/154-operators-in-66-countries-have-demonstrated-testing-or-trialling-5g-technologies/
2. Bogale, T.E., Le, L.B.: Massive MIMO and mmWave for 5G wireless HetNet: potential benefits and challenges. IEEE Veh. Technol. Mag. **11**(1), 64–75 (2016)
3. Keysight Technologies: MIMO and Beamforming in the 5G Context, SBr T (2017)
4. Schaich, F., Wild, T.: Waveform contenders for 5G – OFDM vs. FBMC vs. UFMC. In: 2014 6th International Symposium on Communications, Control and Signal Processing (ISCCSP), Athens, 2014, pp. 457–460 (2014)
5. Giorgi, L., et al.: Subcarrier multiplexing RF plans for analog radio over fiber in heterogeneous networks. J. Lightw. Technol. **34**(16), 3859–3866 (2016)
6. Kim, H.: RoF-based optical fronthaul technology for 5G and beyond. In: 2018 Optical Fiber Communications Conference and Exposition (OFC). San Diego, CA (2018)
7. Chen, D.: FronthaulBandwidth Analysis and Latency Constraint Considerations. IEEE 802.1, San Diego, July 2016

8. Lim, C., Nirmalathas, A., Bakaul, M., Lee, K., Novak, D., Waterhouse, R.B.: Mitigation strategy for transmission impairments in millimeter-wave radio-over-fiber networks [Invited]. J. Opt. Networking **8**, 201–214 (2009). https://doi.org/10.1364/JON.8.000201

9. Shibata, N., et al.: 256-QAM 8 wireless signal transmission with DSP-assisted analog RoF for mobile front-haul in LTE-B. In: 2014 OptoElectronics and Communication Conference and Australian Conference on Optical Fibre Technology, Melbourne, VIC, pp. 129–131 (2014)

10. Liu, X., Zeng, H., Chand, N., Effenberger, F.: Efficient mobile fronthaul via DSP-based channel aggregation. J. Lightw. Technol. **34**(6), 1556–1564 (2016)

11. Argyris, N., et al.: DSP enabled fiber-wireless IFoF/mmWave link for 5G analog mobile fronthaul. In: Proceedings of 2018 IEEE 5G World Forum, 9–11 July 2018, Santa Clara, CA, USA (2018)

12. Osorio, C., et al.: Dual-mode distance-adaptive transceiver architecture for 5G optical fiber fronthaul. In: Proceedings of Advances in Wireless and Optical Communications 2018 (RTUWO 2018), 15-16 November 2018, Riga, Latvia (2018)

13. Chitimalla, D., et al.: 5G fronthaul-latency and jitter studies of CPRI over ethernet. IEEE/OSA J. Opt. Commun. Networking **9**(2), 172–182 (2017)

14. Paulo, J., et al.: FPGA-based testbed for synchronization on ethernet fronthaul with phase noise measurements. In: Proceedings of 1st International Symposium on Instrumentation Systems, Circuits and Transducers (INSCIT 2016), 29 August–03 September 2016, Belo Horizonte, Brazil (2016)

15. Pham, T.H., Fahmy, S.A., McLoughlin, I.V.: An end-to-end multi-standard OFDM transceiver architecture using FPGA partial reconfiguration. IEEE Access **5**, 21002–21015 (2017)

16. Deng, R., et al.: SFO compensation by pilot-aided channel estimation for real-time DDO-OFDM system. Opt. Commun. **355**, 172–176 (2015)

17. Ferreira, M.L., Ferreira, J.C.: Reconfigurable NC-OFDM processor for 5G communications. In: 2015 IEEE 13th International Conference on Embedded and Ubiquitous Computing (EUC), IEEE (2015)

18. Ferreira, M.L., Barahimi, A., Ferreira, J.C.: Reconfigurable FPGA-based FFT processor for cognitive radio applications. In: Bonato, V., Bouganis, C., Gorgon, M. (eds.) ARC 2016. LNCS, vol. 9625, pp. 223–232. Springer, Cham (2016). https://doi.org/10.1007/978-3-319-30481-6_18

19. Di Stasio, F., et al.: Multirate 5G downlink performance comparison for F-OFDM and W-OFDM schemes with different numerologies. In: 2018 International Symposium on Networks, Computers and Communications (ISNCC), pp. 1-6 (2018)

20. Jian, W., Yu, C., Wang, J., Yu, J., Wang, L.: OFDM adaptive digital predistortion method combines RLS and LMS algorithm. In: 2009 4th IEEE Conference on Industrial Electronics and Applications, Xi'an, 2009, pp. 3900–3903 (2009). https://doi.org/10.1109/ICIEA.2009.5138938

21. https://www.xilinx.com/products/boards-and-kits/zcu111.html

22. 3GPP, TS 38.104 V15.0.0, Table 9.6.2.3-1, December 2017

23. http://www.5g-phos.eu/

Performance of Underwater Wireless Optical Link Under Weak Turbulence and Pointing Errors Using Heterodyne QAM Technique

Argyris N. Stassinakis[✉], Hector E. Nistazakis, George K. Varotsos, and George S. Tombras

Department of Electronics, Computers, Telecommunications and Control, Faculty of Physics, National and Kapodistrian University of Athens, Athens 15784, Greece
{a-stasinakis,enistaz,georgevar,gtombras}@phys.uoa.gr

Abstract. Underwater optical wireless communications (UOWC) have gained attention due to the advantages they offer that can greatly alter the performance of a link. But such systems are affected by absorption and non predictable factors that may decrease the availability and the reliability of the system. In this work, the bit error rate (BER) of an underwater optical link with heterodyne detection modulated with M-QAM technique in presence of turbulence and pointing errors will be investigated. This investigation will lead to a closed form mathematical expression for the BER as a function of link parameters, that is very important in order to deploy an effective link. Various numerical results will also be presented for the reliability of the system.

Keywords: Underwater optical communications · BER · Gamma distribution · Turbulence · Pointing errors

1 Introduction

Optical wireless communications have attracted research and commercial interest due to the plenty advantages they offer that fulfill the requirements of modern networks [1–3]. Such advantages are the high bit rate they can achieve in low operational and installation cost. Such systems are point to point links that use a laser beam in order to transmit a signal between a receiver and a transmitter. So, the use of narrow beamwidth laser for transmitting information creates a license free communication link. Such systems were mostly used for terrestrial and satellite communications (FSO/sat-FSO) [1, 2, 4], but during the last few years, optical wireless communications have also been applied for underwater communications in order to solve the problem of low bit rate in relative short distances [5–11]. On the other hand, the laser beam that propagates along the water is affected by various factors that decrease the performance of the system. The main factor that decreases the possibilities of UOWC systems is the strong power absorption of the laser beam. Another important and non predictable factor that affects underwater OWC systems is the presence of turbulence that creates power fluctuations at the receiver due to

A. Tzanakaki et al. (Eds.): ONDM 2019, LNCS 11616, pp. 552–559, 2020.
https://doi.org/10.1007/978-3-030-38085-4_47

the local variations of the refractive index, a phenomenon called scintillation [5, 8–15]. In order to investigate how the link is affected by turbulence, various statistical distributions are used depending on the turbulence strength [13, 16]. In this work, that weak turbulence is assumed, gamma statistical distribution is suitable to model the channel [17]. Another factor that deteriorates the performance of an underwater OWC system is the misalignment between the transmitter and the receiver due to vibrations that come from various sources mostly from internal mechanisms of the vessel. The statistical distribution of Beckman's model is used in order to model the fluctuations of pointing errors [18–21]. The modulation technique that will be used in this OWC system, is the quadrature amplitude modulation (QAM), that is an extensively used modulation scheme in modern communication systems [22–25]. The demodulation of QAM system will be deployed using heterodyne detection, a technique that presents many advantages as high sensitivity and better frequency selectivity in case of wavelength division multiplexing [8]. In order to investigate how turbulence and pointing errors affect the performance of the system described, a closed form mathematical expression for the bit error rate (BER), will be extracted. BER is an important metric for the reliability of a communication system [16, 23]. In Sect. 2, the underwater channel will be analyzed and in Sect. 3 the BER of the system will be calculated. Finally in Sect. 4 the corresponding numerical results will be presented.

2 Underwater Channel Modeling

Main unpredictable factor that affects UOWC communications is the oceanic turbulence that is the chaotic change of pressure and flow velocity of the water. This phenomenon is responsible for variation of several characteristics of water through which the laser beam of an UOWC system propagates, creating lack of homogeneity of the refraction index. So the power that the receiver intercepts presents fluctuations, a phenomenon called scintillation. Such fluctuations may lead to deterioration of the performance of the system depending on its impact. A parameter that measures the strength of this effect is turbulence structure constant, C_n^2, that can be calculated using the following equation [5, 8]:

$$
C_n^2 = 16\pi^2 k^{-7/6} L^{-11/6} \text{Re} \left\{ \int_0^L ds \int_0^\infty \omega d\omega [E(s, \omega, L) \right.
$$

$$
\left. \times E(s, -\omega, L) + |E(s, \omega, L)|^2 \right] \Phi_n(\omega) \right\}
\tag{1}
$$

where ω is the magnitude of the spatial frequency, $E(\alpha_1, \alpha_2, \alpha_3) = ik \cdot \exp(-0.5 \cdot i \cdot s \cdot (L - s)\omega^2 / kL)$, k is the wave number, L is the distance between the transmitter and the receiver and $\Phi_n(\omega)$ is given as [5, 8]:

$$
\Phi_n(\omega) = 0.388 \cdot 10^{-12} \varepsilon^{-1/3} \omega^{-11/3} \left(1 + 2.35\omega^{2/3} \cdot v^{1/2} \varepsilon^{-1/6}\right)
$$

$$
\times w^{-2} \left(w^2 \exp(-1.863 \cdot 10^{-2} \varphi) + \exp(-1.9 \cdot 10^{-4} \varphi)\right.
$$

$$
\left. -2w \exp(-9.41 \cdot 10^{-3} \varphi)\right)
\tag{2}
$$

where ε is the rate of dissipation of kinetic energy per unit mass of the fluid, w provides the ratio of temperature to salinity contributions to the refractive index spectrum, v is the kinematic viscosity and $\varphi = 8.284\omega^{4/3}v\varepsilon^{-1/3} + 12.978\omega^2 v^{3/2}\varepsilon^{-0.5}$, [5, 8].

In order to investigate how the turbulence affects the performance of the system, various statistical models are used to model the channel depending on the turbulence strength [10–13]. A suitable model for weak turbulence is the gamma distribution and the pdf as a function of irradiance, I_t, is given by the following equation, [17]:

$$f_{I_t}(\mathrm{I}_t) = \mathrm{I}_t^{\zeta-1} \cdot \exp(-\mathrm{I}_t\zeta) \cdot \frac{\zeta^\zeta}{\Gamma(\zeta)} \tag{3}$$

where $\Gamma(.)$, signifies the Gamma function and parameter ζ can be estimated as [17]:

$$\zeta = \frac{1}{\sigma_p^2} \tag{4}$$

with σ_p^2 being the power scintillation index which is the normalized variance of the received optical power, I, and can be calculated using the following equation [13, 17, 22]:

$$\sigma_p^2 = \frac{1}{a} + \frac{1}{b} + \frac{1}{ab} \tag{5}$$

$$a = \left(\exp\left(\frac{0.49\delta^2}{\left(1 + 0.18d^2 + 0.56\delta^{12/5}\right)^{7/6}}\right) - 1\right)^{-1} \tag{6}$$

$$b = \left(\exp\left(\frac{0.51\delta^2\left(1 + 0.69\delta^{12/5}\right)^{-5/6}}{\left(1 + 0.9d^2 + 0.62\delta^{12/5}\right)^{5/6}}\right) - 1\right)^{-1} \tag{7}$$

where $d = \sqrt{kD^2/(4L)}$, $k = 2\pi/\lambda$ is the optical wave number, λ is the operational wavelength of the link, D is the aperture diameter of the receiver and L is the distance between the transmitter and the receiver. Parameter δ^2, is the Rytov variance given as, [13]:

$$\delta^2 = 1.23C_n^2 k^{7/6}L^{11/6} \tag{8}$$

Due to the narrow beamwidth of the laser beam that UOWC systems use, there must be a precision in the alignment between the receiver and the transmitter. But several phenomena like mechanical vibrations of the system or rip currents in the water may cause pointing errors that lead to power fluctuations at the receiver. In order to investigate this pointing errors, Beckmman's model is suitable and accurate to model the channel and its pdf as a function of Irradiance, I_p, is given by the following equation [18–20]:

$$f_{I_p}(\mathrm{I}_p) = \frac{g^2}{A_0^{g^2}}\mathrm{I}_p^{g^2-1}, \quad 0 \le I_p \le A_0 \tag{9}$$

with g being the ratio between the equivalent beam radius at the receiver, w_{zeq}, and the pointing error displacement standard deviation, σ_s, and is given by the following equation [15–17]:

$$g = \frac{w_{zeq}}{2\sigma_s} \tag{10}$$

The parameter w_{zeq} can be calculated using [18–20]:

$$w_{zeq}^2 = \frac{w_z \sqrt{\pi} \, erf(u)}{2u \cdot \exp(-u^2)} \tag{11}$$

where w_z is the beam waist, $u = \sqrt{\pi} r / \sqrt{2} w_z$ and $A_0 = (erf(u))^2$ with w_z represents the radius of the Gaussian beam on the receiver plane.

In order to investigate both turbulence and pointing errors effect, a combined pdf will be extracted using the following mathematical property [19]:

$$f_I(I) = \int f_{I|I_t}(I|I_t) f_{I_t}(I_t) dI_t \tag{12}$$

where $I = I_t I_p$.

Substituting Eqs. (3) and (9) in (12), the combined pdf for weak turbulence strength and pointing errors will be given as [18]:

$$f_I(I) = \frac{g^2 \zeta}{A_0 \Gamma(\zeta)} G_{1,2}^{2,0} \left(\frac{\zeta I}{A_0} \middle| \begin{matrix} g^2 \\ g^2 - 1, \zeta - 1 \end{matrix} \right) \tag{13}$$

The combined pdf can be expressed as a function of the instantaneous SNR, μ, and the average SNR, ξ, using the following equation for the case of heterodyne detection systems, [8, 19]:

$$I = \frac{\mu}{\xi} \tag{14}$$

So applying random variable transformation in Eq. (13) using Eq. (14), the combined pdf as a function of SNR will be given by the following equation:

$$f_\mu(\mu) = \frac{g^2 \zeta}{A_0 \Gamma(\zeta) \xi} G_{1,2}^{2,0} \left(\frac{\zeta}{A_0} \frac{\mu}{\xi} \middle| \begin{matrix} g^2 \\ g^2 - 1, \zeta - 1 \end{matrix} \right) \tag{15}$$

3 Bit Error Rate Calculation

A very important metric concerning the performance of a link is the bit error rate that represents the probability of receiving an error bit at the receiver. The modulation technique that is assumed to be applied in the underwater link will be M-QAM with heterodyne detection.

The BER for the received M-QAM signal is given by [22, 24]:

$$P(\mu) = \frac{2(1 - M^{-1/2})}{\log_2(M)} \cdot erfc\left(\sqrt{\frac{3 \cdot \mu}{4(M-1)}}\right) \tag{16}$$

Using Eq. (16), the average BER can be obtained by averaging over the combined distribution of Eq. (15):

$$P_{av}(\xi) = \frac{2(1 - M^{-1/2})g^2\zeta}{\log_2(M)A_0\Gamma(\zeta)\xi}$$

$$\times \int_0^\infty erfc\left(\sqrt{\frac{3 \cdot \mu}{4(M-1)}}\right) G_{1,2}^{2,0}\left(\frac{\zeta}{A_0}\frac{\mu}{\xi}\bigg| \begin{matrix} g^2 \\ g^2 - 1, \zeta - 1 \end{matrix}\right) \tag{17}$$

The above integral can be solved by expressing the erfc(.) function using Meijer G function and after some mathematical manipulations [26] the BER of an underwater optical link in a channel with weak turbulence and pointing errors using M-QAM modulation will be given as:

$$P_{av}(\xi) = \frac{8(1 - M^{-1/2})(M-1)g^2\zeta}{3\sqrt{\pi}\log_2(M)A_0\Gamma(\zeta)\xi}$$

$$\times G_{3,3}^{2,2}\left(\frac{4\zeta(M-1)}{3 \cdot A_0\xi}\bigg| \begin{matrix} 0, -\frac{1}{2}, g^2 \\ g^2 - 1, \zeta - 1, -1 \end{matrix}\right) \tag{18}$$

4 Numerical Results

In this section the results of the average BER, *Pav*, will be presented for an underwater optical communication system using M-QAM modulation technique according to Eq. (18). We have chosen three to values for the modulation index M = 4 and 16 and three values for the ratio of temperature to salinity contributions to the refractive index, w = [− 0.05, −1, −3], the rate of dissipation of kinetic energy per unit mass ε = [10⁻¹, 10⁻², 10⁻⁴] m²/s³ and the viscosity, v = [0.01, 0.002, 10⁻⁵]. All values were chosen for low values of the scintillation index m^2 [5]. The wavelength of the laser beam is assumed to be λ = 532 nm, the aperture diameter of the receiver D = 1 cm and the distance L = 80 m. Concerning the pointing errors, we assume normalized spatial jitters with equal to $\sigma_x/r = 0.05$ and $\sigma_y/R = 0.1$.

In Fig. 1, the BER of the underwater OWC system for 4-QAM is presented as a function of links parameters. It is clear that as parameters w, ε and v are not stable, the BER of the system may change even for 2 orders of magnitude. More precisely, as the absolute value w increases, the performance of the system decreases, as the BER becomes higher. Furthermore, the reliability of the system increases when parameter ε, decreases. Viscosity also affects the BER of the systems as the systems performs better for lower values of v.

In Fig. 2, the corresponding results of BER are presented in case of 16-QAM. It is clear that the system's performance deteriorates as the BER increases and as in Fig. 1, the system's BER strongly depends on link's and channel's parameters.

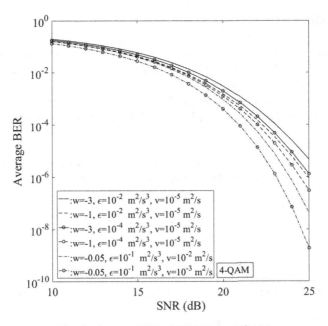

Fig. 1. Average BER of UOWC for 4-QAM

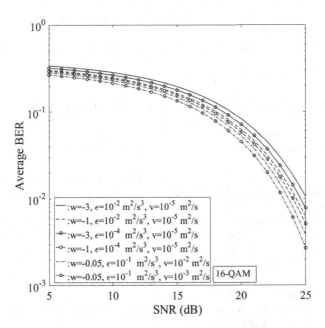

Fig. 2. Average BER of UOWC for 4-QAM

5 Conclusions

In this work we derived a closed form mathematical expression for the BER of an underwater optical link modulated with M-QAM with heterodyne detection that is affected by weak turbulence and pointing errors. According to the results presented, UOWC systems are strongly depended on oceanic turbulence and pointing errors, so the choice of link parameters must be careful in order to deploy a communication system with high performance.

Acknowledgment. This project has received funding from the European Union's Horizon 2020 research and innovation program under grant agreement No: 777596.

References

1. Ghassemlooy, Z., Popoola, W.O.: Terrestrial Free-Space Optical Communications. Network Layer and Circuit Level Design. Eds S. Ait Fares and F. Adachi (2010)
2. Henniger, H., Wilfert, O.: An introduction to free-space optical communications. Radioengineering **19**(2), 203–212 (2010)
3. Alzenad, M., Shakir, M.Z., Yanikomeroglu, H., Alouini, M.: FSO-based vertical Backhaul/Fronthaul framework for 5G + wireless networks. IEEE Commun. Mag. **56**(1), 218–224 (2018). https://doi.org/10.1109/MCOM.2017.1600735
4. Gopal, P., Jain, V.K., Kar, S.: Performance analysis of ground to satellite FSO system with DAPPM scheme in weak atmospheric turbulence. In: 2012 International Conference on Fiber Optics and Photonics (PHOTONICS), Chennai 2012, pp. 1–3 (2012). https://doi.org/10.1364/photonics.2012.wpo.43
5. Baykal, Y.: Scintillations of LED sources in oceanic turbulence. Appl. Opt. **55**, 8860–8863 (2016)
6. Arnon, S.: Underwater optical wireless communication network. Opt. Eng. **49**(1), 015001 (2010)
7. Kaushal, H., Kaddoum, G.: Underwater optical wireless communication. IEEE Access **4**, 1518–1547 (2016). https://doi.org/10.1109/ACCESS.2016.2552538
8. Fu, Y., Du, Y.: Performance of heterodyne differential phase-shift-keying underwater wireless optical communication systems in gamma-gamma-distributed turbulence. Appl. Opt. **57**, 2057–2063 (2018)
9. Peppas, K.P., Boucouvalas, A.C., Ghassemloy, Z.: Performance of underwater optical wireless communication with multi-pulse pulse-position modulation receivers and spatial diversity. IET Optoelectron. (2017). https://doi.org/10.1049/iet-opt.2016.0130
10. Peppas, K.P., Boucouvalas, A.C., Ghassemloy, Z., Khalighi, M., Yiannopoulos, K., Sagias, N.: Semiconductor optical amplifiers for underwater optical wireless communications. IET Optoelectron. **11**(1), 15–19 (2017). https://doi.org/10.1049/iet-opt.2016.0010
11. Boucouvalas, A.C., Peppas, K.P., Yiannopoulos, K., Ghassemloy, Z.: Underwater optical wireless communications with optical amplification and spatial diversity. IEEE Photonics Technol. Lett. **28**(22), 2613–2616 (2016)
12. Andrews, L., Phillips, R., Hopen, C., Al-Habash, M.: Theory of optical scintillation. J. Opt. Soc. Am. A **16**, 1417–1429 (1999)
13. Majumdar, A.K.: Free-space laser communication performance in the atmospheric channel. Opt. Fiber Commun. Rep. **2**, 345–396 (2005)

14. Muhammad, S.S., Kohldorfer, P., Leitgeb, E.: Channel modeling for terrestrial free space optical links. In: ICTON 2005, vol. Tu.B3.5, pp. 407–410 (2005)
15. Zhu, X., Kahn, J.M.: Free-space optical communication through atmospheric turbulence channels. IEEE Trans. Commun. **50**(8), 1293–1300 (2002)
16. Nistazakis, H.E., Tsiftsis, T.A., Tombras, G.S.: Performance analysis of free-space optical communication systems over atmospheric turbulence channels. IET Commun. **3**, 1402–1409 (2009)
17. Epple, B.: Simplified channel model for simulation of free-space optical communications. IEEE/OSA J. Opt. Commun. Netw.g **2**(5), 293–304 (2010). https://doi.org/10.1364/JOCN.2.000293
18. Ninos, M., Nistazakis, H.E., Sandalidis, H.G., Stassinakis, A.N., Tombras, G.S.: Block error rate performance of OOK free-space optical links over gamma–gamma turbulence channels with generalised non-zero boresight pointing errors. IET Optoelectron. (2018). https://doi.org/10.1049/iet-opt.2018.5055
19. Sandalidis, H.G., Tsiftsis, T.A., Karagiannidis, G.: Optical wireless communications with heterodyne detection over turbulence channels with pointing errors. J. Lightwave Technol. **27**, 4440–4445 (2009)
20. Yang, F., Cheng, J., Tsiftsis, T.A.: Free-space optical communication with nonzero boresight pointing errors. IEEE Trans. Commun. **62**(2), 713–725 (2014)
21. Boluda-Ruiz, R., García-Zambrana, A., Castillo-Vázquez, C., Castillo-Vázquez, B.: Novel approximation of misalignment fading modeled by Beckmann distribution on free-space optical links. Opt. Express **24**, 22635–22649 (2016)
22. Bekkali, A., Naila, C.B., Kazaura, K., Wakamori, K., Matsumoto, M.: Transmission analysis of OFDM-based wireless services over turbulent radio-on-FSO links modeled by gamma-gamma distribution. IEEE Photonics J. **2**(3), 510–520 (2010). https://doi.org/10.1109/JPHOT.2010.2050306
23. Djordjevic, G.T., Petkovic, M.I.: Average BER performance of FSO SIM-QAM systems in the presence of atmospheric turbulence and pointing errors. J. Mod. Opt. **63**(8), 715–723 (2016). https://doi.org/10.1080/09500340.2015.1093662
24. Nistazakis, H.E., Stassinakis, A.N., Sandalidis, H.G., Tombras, G.S.: QAM and PSK OFDM RoFSO over M-turbulence induced fading channels. IEEE Photonics J. **7**(1), 1–11 (2015). https://doi.org/10.1109/jphot.2014.2381670. Art no.7900411
25. Nistazakis, H.E., Stassinakis, A.N., Tombras, G.S., Muhammad, S.S., Tsigopoulos, A.D.: K modeled turbulence and nonlinear clipping for QAM OFDM with FSO and fiber serially linked. In: 2014 20th International Conference on Microwaves, Radar and Wireless Communications (MIKON), Gdansk, 2014, pp. 1–4 (2014)
26. Adamchik, V.S., Marichev, O.I.: The algorithm for calculating integrals of hypergeometric type function and its realization in reduce system. In: Proceedings of the International Conference on Symbolic and Algebraic Computation, Japan, 1990, pp. 212–224 (1990)

MCF Skew Estimation at the Receiver for ARoF Antenna Beamforming

Thomas Nikas[1]([:envelope:]) [iD], Evangelos Pikasis[2], Sotiris Karabetsos[3] [iD],
and Dimitris Syvridis[1]

[1] Department of Informatics and Telecommunications, National and Kapodistrian
University of Athens, 15784 Athens, Greece
tnikas@di.uoa.gr
[2] Eulambia Advanced Technologies Ltd., 15342 Agia Paraskevi, Greece
[3] Department of Electrical and Electronics Engineering, University of West Attika,
12241 Egaleo, Greece

Abstract. Multicore fibers can be used for Radio over Fiber transmission of mmwave signals for phased array antennas in 5G networks. The inter-core skew of these fibers distorts the radiation pattern and has to be measured and compensated. We propose a method to accurately measure the differential delays remotely, after installation, without intervening heavily with the transmitter setup. The properties of the phase response measured at a distant receiver are exploited to acquire the differential delays among the antenna array elements.

Keywords: Multicore fiber · Inter-core skew · Radio over fiber · Phased arrays · Beam steering

1 Introduction

Antenna beam forming is adopted in a wide area of radio applications and recently in 5G wireless technology. In 5G, coverage and bandwidth requirements push the operating frequencies to mmwave, deploying dense pico- and femto-cell networks [1]. Orthogonal Frequency Division Modulation (OFDM) with its variants is the most prominent modulation scheme proposed for 5G [2]. Beam-forming (BF) is utilized to alleviate the free space path loss and through wall attenuation, important factors for efficient radio coverage at mmwave frequencies. Base station to vehicle communication quality is also enhanced using a steerable beam that tracks the mobile user. Commonly, the phase shifting process takes place at the transmitter, just before power amplification and feeding of the individual antenna elements. Manufacturing tolerances, aging of components and temperature variations at outdoor installations generate phase alignment errors which distort the radiation pattern. Furthermore, the component phase responses and transmission line path lengths after the phase shifting stage must be identical in order to preserve the beam quality. These factors and requirements become more critical in higher operating frequencies and in a multi-beam antenna, which is fed by some form of fixed or configurable phase shifting network, like Blass or Butler matrices.

A. Tzanakaki et al. (Eds.): ONDM 2019, LNCS 11616, pp. 560–569, 2020.
https://doi.org/10.1007/978-3-030-38085-4_48

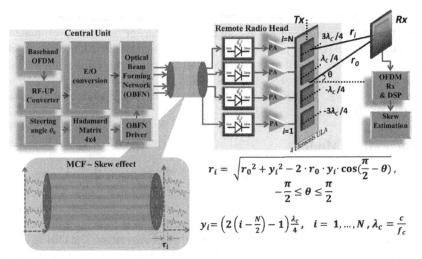

Fig. 1. The ARoF system with OBFN, MCF link, RRH with $N = 4$ element, $\lambda_c/2$ spaced array and radio propagation model.

A promising technique to serve network densification and flexible resource allocation in 5G is Radio over Fiber (RoF). The analog variant of RoF (ARoF) is especially suited for remote antenna beam forming. The phase shifting process can be performed using Optical Beam Forming Networks (OBFNs) which are True Time Delay (TDD) devices and provide squint free beams [3]. The OBFNs are preferably located at the Central Unit (CU) and multi-core fibers (MCFs) are used to convey the phase shifted optical signals to the Remote Radio Heads (RRHs) [4]. The RF modulated, phase shifted optical carriers are detected, amplified and feed the antenna array elements, greatly simplifying the RRHs. MCF fibers present both static and dynamic differential delays among the fiber cores [5], which must be equalized to prevent severe RF beam pattern distortion. The full equalization of the effective path lengths is cumbersome and energy inefficient, mainly involving manual calibration. An automatic partial equalization method has been proposed [6] in which the remainder modulo $2\,k\pi$ of the differential phase shifts is equalized. In either case of full or partial equalization, the differential delays must be accurately measured and compensated.

The static inter-core skew can be measured with optical means, like time domain or correlation reflectometers [7] before fiber installation. Dynamic MCF skew and any additional differential delays due to optical connectors and electronic path inequalities in various points of the CU and RRH subsystems, as well as aging and manufacturing tolerances are not measured. These stray delays might be large enough to distort the antenna radiation pattern. On the other hand, it is preferable to characterize the RoF and RF transmission system as a whole, using a single method. Advanced techniques, like pseudo-noise gating [8, 9] using orthogonal sequences have been proposed for satellite antenna beamforming alignment and characterization.

In this paper, we propose a novel method for measuring the differential delays among the antenna elements, emerged either from optical or electrical length inequalities or both.

It is based on the OFDM frequency domain equalization process at the receiver and exploits the phase response of the acquired system transfer function to estimate each antenna element delay. The process is mainly performed on installation, as an initial calibration procedure, as well as at periodic maintenance periods, involving minimum modifications in standard OFDM transmitter and receiver. Moreover, it is tolerant to multipath propagation. The resolution of the measured delays depends on the bandwidth of the OFDM signal.

2 Theoretical Model

The architecture of the ARoF system is shown in Fig. 1, depicting the model for the followed analysis. The baseband OFDM signal is formed using pilot QAM symbols known to the receiver in all used subcarriers, in order to acquire with maximum resolution the system transfer function. The baseband signal is then up-converted to the required radio frequency and modulates linearly the optical carrier. The OBFN imposes the appropriate phase shifts for steering the antenna beam and launches N optical signals to N cores of the MCF. At the RRH, each core feeds the corresponding photodiode and RF amplification chain leading to the antenna element. The antenna consists of N, $\lambda_c/2$ spaced elements, forming a uniform linear array (ULA). The inter-core skew imposes differential time delays τ_i, $i = 1, ..., N$ to the signals arriving at RRH which have to be compensated partially or completely. At RRH, the N photocurrents are expressed as $I(i, t) = I_{0,i} \cdot s(t - \tau_i) \cdot e^{j2\pi f_c t}$, $i = 1, ..., N$ where $s(t - \tau_i)$ are the baseband OFDM signals delayed by τ_i per core, $I_{0,i}$ is the complex value of the i-th photocurrent and $I_{0,i} = |I_{0,i}| e^{-j(i-1)\pi \sin\theta_0}$. The phase delay step $\pi \sin\theta_0$ is imposed by the OBFN to steer the beam to θ_0 and the amplitude of the photocurrent is set to $|I_{0,i}| = 1/\sqrt{N}$ using uniform excitation, normalized to unity power. At the receiver antenna located at distance r_0 and azimuthal angle θ_0, the summation of the electrical fields produced by each antenna element is expressed as $E_R(t) = \sum_{i=1}^{N} a I_{0,i} s(t - \tau_i) e^{j2\pi f_c t} e^{-j2\pi f_c r_i/c}$, where a is a factor expressing the linear relation of the electrical field and antenna current as well as line of sight path loss. The factor a is assumed time invariant and frequency independent within the signal bandwidth.

After reception, analog to digital conversion and FFT, the received signal $R(t)$ is transformed to the discrete frequency domain $R_k = ab \sum_{i=1}^{N} I_{0,i} X_k e^{-j2\pi(f_c+k/T_s)\tau_i} e^{-j2\pi f_c r_i/c}$, where X_k, R_k are the transmitted and received QAM pilot symbols of the k-th OFDM subcarrier and the factor b expresses the linear electrical field – antenna current relation, assumed to have the same time invariability and frequency independence properties of a. Then, the discrete frequency domain transfer function is

$$H_k = \frac{R_k}{X_k} = ab \sum_{i=1}^{N} I_{0,i} e^{-j2\pi(f_c+k/T_s)\tau_i} e^{-j2\pi f_c r_i/c} \tag{1}$$

As the receiver is located at the transmitter antenna far field $r_i \cong r_0 - y_i \cdot \sin\theta_0$ (Fig. 1) and taking into account the phase shifts imposed by the OBFN to steer the antenna main lobe to θ_0, the transfer function is expressed as

$$H_k = \frac{ab}{\sqrt{N}} e^{-j\left[\frac{2\pi f_c r_0}{c} + \frac{\pi}{2} \cdot \sin\theta_0 \cdot (N-1)\right]} \sum_{i=1}^{N} e^{-j2\pi(f_c+k/T_s)\tau_i} \tag{2}$$

Setting the constant terms $abe^{-j\left[\frac{2\pi f_c r_0}{c}+\frac{\pi}{2}\cdot\sin\theta_0\cdot(N-1)\right]}$, equal to unity, the transfer function becomes

$$H_k = \frac{1}{\sqrt{N}}\sum_{i=1}^{N} e^{-j2\pi(f_c+k/T_s)\tau_i} = \sum_{i=1}^{N} h_k^i \qquad (3)$$

In (3), the complex value of H_k in every OFDM subcarrier k is the vector sum of the $h_k^i = \frac{1}{\sqrt{N}}e^{-j2\pi(f_c+k/T_s)\tau_i}$ terms, contributed from all N transmitter antenna elements with various τ_i delays. The h_k^i terms can be seen as the individual transfer functions at subcarrier k from each transmitter antenna element i to the receiver. The phase $-2\pi(f_c+k/T_s)\tau_i$ of h_k^i as a function of k is linear, with slope $-2\pi\tau_i/T_s$, from which the time delays τ_i can be calculated.

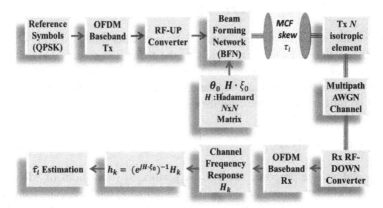

Fig. 2. The simulation model. The $\boldsymbol{H}\cdot\xi_0$ phase shifts are imposed via the BFN prior to MCF transmission.

The problem is to determine the individual element transfer function h_k^i from the received sum in (3). For this reason, we impose additional, known to the receiver phase shifts $\xi_{i,m}$ via the beam forming network to every m-th OFDM symbol, $m = 1\ldots N$, of N successive symbols. Then, the transfer function for the m-th OFDM symbol in the time series of N symbols is expressed as

$$H_{k,m} = \sum_{i=1}^{N} e^{j\xi_{i,m}} h_k^i \qquad (4)$$

The phase shifts are set to $\xi_{i.m} = H_{i,m}\cdot\xi_0$, where $H_{i,m}$ are elements of a non-singular matrix $\boldsymbol{H}_{NxN}$ and ξ_0 is a constant. In matrix form, (4) is written as

$$\boldsymbol{H_k} = e^{j\boldsymbol{H}\cdot\xi_0}\boldsymbol{h_k} \qquad (5)$$

In order to calculate $\boldsymbol{h_k}$ from the N successive values of $\boldsymbol{H_k}$, we have to solve the $N\cdot N$ linear system in (5) for all subcarriers. The matrix $e^{j\boldsymbol{H}\cdot\xi_0}$ must be invertible, so we choose $\boldsymbol{H}_{NxN}$ to be a Hadamard matrix and $\xi_0 \neq \pi$. The obtained values for all MCF cores and antenna elements are

$$\boldsymbol{h_k} = (e^{j\boldsymbol{H}\cdot\xi_0})^{-1}\boldsymbol{H_k} \qquad (6)$$

from which the time delays τ_i can be calculated. Recalling that the phase of h_k^i as a function of k is linear, with a slope of $-\frac{2\pi\tau_i}{T_s} = -\omega_s\tau_i$, then the delays can be estimated as the mean value of $\angle h_{k+1}^i - \angle h_k^i$,

$$\widehat{\tau_i} = -\frac{\sum_{k=-\frac{N_{F_u}}{2}}^{\frac{N_{F_u}}{2}-1}\left(\angle h_{k+1}^i - \angle h_k^i\right)}{N_{F_u}\omega_s} \tag{7}$$

N_{F_u} being the number of the used OFDM subcarriers. Alternatively, the phase slope of h_k^i can be estimated by applying linear least squares regression to the $\varphi_k^i = \angle h_k^i$ samples. The a (rad/Hz) coefficient of the fitted function

$$\widehat{\varphi_k^i} = a \cdot k/T_s + b, \qquad \widehat{\tau_i} = -a/2\pi \tag{8}$$

is the phase slope, while the constant term b is the remainder modulo 2π of $-2\pi f_c\tau_i$. In this sense, the carrier frequency is not affecting the estimation process. On the contrary, wider signal bandwidth provides sufficient phase information both for the mean value estimation in (7) and the linear regression and is expected to influence the accuracy. This factor shall be further studied in the following section.

3 Numerical Analysis

In order to evaluate the proposed method, we performed simulations of ARoF, multipath wireless and skew estimation systems. The simulation model is depicted in Fig. 2. At first, N successive baseband OFDM pilot symbols are generated and up-converted to the carrier frequency. Each time domain symbol is split to N identical streams and appropriate phase shifts for steering the main lobe to θ_0 along with the $\xi_{i.m}$ phase offsets are applied by passing through the OBFN. The MCF skew delays are inserted to the N streams and the signals are transmitted to the multi-path radio channel. Gaussian white noise of variable power spectral density is added and the summation of electrical fields is calculated at the receiver antenna. After down-conversion and FFT, the system transfer functions H_k for the N successive OFDM symbols are acquired. The linear system is solved using (6) and the time delays $\widehat{\tau_i}$ are calculated using (7) and (8). Then, the absolute estimation error $|\tau_i - \widehat{\tau_i}|$ is computed in both cases.

The simulation parameters are listed in Table 1, chosen so as to follow 5G New Radio numerology and beyond. The generated OFDM signal bandwidth is roughly 400 MHz centered at a carrier frequency of 26 GHz. The non-linearity of electro-optical conversion and photodiode shot noise contribution is not included in the model. Instead, the overall ARoF transmission, free space radio propagation and receiver noise figure are characterized by the final signal to noise ratio (SNR) at the receiver.

The multipath propagation model is static, not involving Doppler shift and comprises the strong line of sight component, which is dominant in higher microwave and mmwave frequencies. Except line of sight, two more propagation paths are considered, with relative to line of sight delays not exceeding the OFDM cyclic prefix. The offset angle ξ_0 was set to $\pi/2$ imposing $\pm\pi/2$ phase offset, in order to achieve the maximum possible

Table 1. Simulation Model Parameters

Parameter	Value
Modulation per subcarrier	QPSK (4-QAM)
Sampling frequency Fs	983.04 MHz
FFT/IFFT size NF	4096
Number of used subcarriers NFu	416–2500
OFDM symbol duration Ts (w/o CP)	4.16 μs
Subcarrier spacing, 1/Ts	240 kHz
Cyclic Prefix (CP)	520 ns
Total symbol duration	4.68 μs
Signal bandwidth	100–600 MHz
Carrier frequency fc	26 GHz
Received signal SNR	10–30 dB
Offset angle ξ_0	π/2 rad
Azimuthal steering angle θ_0	0°
Multipath delay	80 ns, 400 ns
Multipath gain	−6 dB, −20 dB
Number of Tx antenna elements, N	8, 16
MCF skew delays, τ_i	Uniformly distributed, with maximum delay of 1 ns

phase shift of π radians when multiplied with opposite sign elements of the Hadamard matrix. The inter-core differential delays of the MCF are uniformly distributed samples with maximum value of 1 ns. The receiver could be located at any known to the transmitter azimuthal angle θ_0 and the beam forming network imposes the corresponding phase offsets to the antenna currents. These offsets do not affect the skew estimation as they are canceled out by the different propagation lengths from each transmitter element to the receiver. So, the beam steering angle θ_0 was set to 0° supposing that the OFDM receiver is located at this azimuthal angle.

At first, a set of delays was inserted in the MCF transmission model for $N = 4$ antenna elements and the proposed method was applied in the multipath radio propagation environment. The receiver SNR was set to 30 dB and the OFDM bandwidth to 400 MHz. The solution of the linear system $h_k = (e^{jH \cdot \xi_0})^{-1} H_k$ provided the phase estimation per antenna element depicted in Fig. 3, where the higher delay values result in steepest phase slope. The observed ripple is attributed to the multipath propagation.

Next, several random sets of skew delays for $N = 8$ antenna elements are considered in MCF transmission and estimated at the receiver with SNR of 20 dB and 400 MHz bandwidth, using both (7) and linear least squares regression (8). In all cases, the linear least squares regression performed better, minimizing the error between the estimated and actual delays. So, it is used throughout the following steps. Then, the offset angle ξ_0 was reduced from π/2 to π/3. The estimation error increased, attributed to the decreased

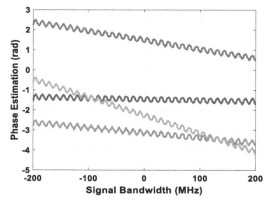

Fig. 3. The phase estimation per antenna element for $N = 4$ for $\tau_1 = 80$ ps (blue), $\tau_2 = 400$ ps (purple), $\tau_3 = 720$ ps (green), $\tau_4 = 1430$ ps (red). (Color figure online)

phase shift among the BFN imposed phase values, $2\pi/3$ instead of π. So, the initial assumption that maximum phase shift offers the best possible accuracy is confirmed and used throughout the following simulations.

In order to evaluate the measurement resolution of the proposed scheme, 100 sets of skew delays for $N = 8$ and $N = 16$ transmitting antenna elements are considered and estimated with variable SNR at the receiver. The mean error between the estimated and actual delays as well as the associated standard deviation is calculated and the results for $N = 8$ and $N = 16$ elements are depicted in Figs. 4 and 5 respectively. The estimation error is converging to roughly 3 ps for SNR higher than 20 dB. This value corresponds to 8% ambiguity compared to the period $1/f_c$ of the 26 GHz carrier frequency. Such a small value is not affecting the antenna radiation pattern, as will be confirmed in the following. For $N = 16$ antenna elements (Fig. 5), the estimation error is reduced for lower SNR and approaches the same value of roughly 3 ps for higher SNR.

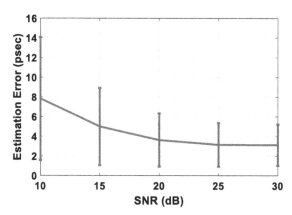

Fig. 4. The estimation error versus receiver SNR for $N = 8$ antenna elements.

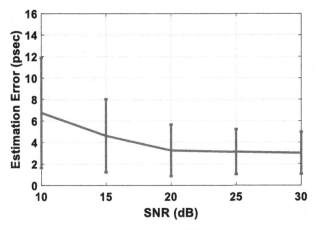

Fig. 5. The estimation error versus receiver SNR for $N = 16$ antenna elements.

As stated in Sect. 2, the carrier frequency is not affecting the estimation error, so the relative ambiguity can become significant in higher frequencies. For example at 60 GHz, 3 ps estimation error will result in 18% ambiguity, causing more severe radiation pattern distortion. On the other hand, wider bandwidth is assigned at higher frequencies, so it is important to investigate the performance of the method in variable bandwidth conditions. The bandwidth was varied from 100 MHz to 600 MHz by properly setting the number of the used subcarriers, for $N = 8$ and the receiver SNR was set to 30 dB. The results presented in Fig. 6, verify that increased bandwidth provides more accurate estimates of the skew delays. In this sense, the relative ambiguity at higher frequencies can be restricted to acceptable values.

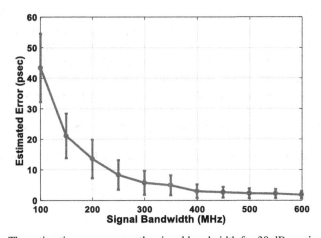

Fig. 6. The estimation error versus the signal bandwidth for 30 dB receiver SNR.

Finally, the radiation pattern distortion of the transmitter antenna array is evaluated. Using a random vector of skew delays for $N = 8$ elements, we estimated them and applied the obtained values for compensation. The compensation process is either complete, adding appropriate delays to equalize the propagation time in all cores, or partial, using the method described in [6]. The radiation patterns are depicted in Fig. 7. When using the actual delays ranging to hundreds of picoseconds, the radiation patterns coincide with the ones in Fig. 7, despite small estimation errors.

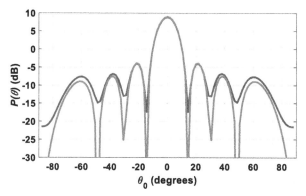

Fig. 7. Antenna array factor $P(\theta)$ for $N = 8$ elements and receiver SNR $= 30$ dB, using the estimated delay values in full (blue) and partial (red) compensation methods. (Color figure online)

4   Conclusion

An accurate and efficient method has been presented for skew estimation in MCF–ARoF beamforming arrangements in multipath propagation environment with variable SNR at the receiver. It can be used for skew compensation after the MCF link is installed, without any prior knowledge of the inter-core differential delays. The method can also be applied more generally, to any RF transmitter employing steerable antenna array, for initial estimation of possible main lobe misalignment and antenna pattern distortion as well as for periodic maintenance. Ongoing work involves the deployment of the ARoF system testbed and the experimental evaluation of the proposed method.

Acknowledgement. This work was (partly) funded by the EU H2020 blueSPACE (GA No 762055) project.

References

1. Shafi, M., et al.: 5G: a tutorial overview of standards, trials, challenges, deployment, and practice. J. Sel. Areas Commun. **35**(6), 1201–1221 (2017)

2. Berardinelli, G., Pajukoski, K., Lähetkangas, E., Wichman, R., Tirkkonen, O., Mogensen, P.E.: On the potential of OFDM enhancements as 5G waveforms. In: 79th Vehicular Technology Conference (VTC Spring), pp. 1–5, May 2014

3. Zhuang, L., Roeloffzen, C.G.H., Heideman, R.G., Borreman, A., Meijerink, A., van Etten, W.: Single-chip ring resonator-based 1X8 optical beam forming network in CMOS-compatible waveguide technology. IEEE Photon. Technol. Lett. **19**(15), 1130–1132 (2007)

4. Nagayama, T., Akiba, S., Tomura, T., Hirokawa, J.: Photonics-based millimeter-wave band remote beamforming of array-antenna integrated with photodiode using variable optical delay line and attenuator. J. Lightwave Technol. **36**(19), 4416–4422 (2018)

5. Puttnam, B.J., Rademacher, G., Luís, R.S., Sakaguchi, J., Awaji, Y., Wada, N.: Inter-core skew measurements in temperature controlled multi-core fiber. In: IEEE 2018 Optical Fiber Communications Conference and Exposition (OFC), pp. 1–3, March 2018

6. Nikas, T., Pikasis, E., Syvridis, D.: Static skew compensation in multi core radio over fiber systems for 5G Mmwave beamforming. In: Photonics in Switching and Computing (PSC), September 2018

7. Eiselt, M., Dochhan, A.: Single-ended fiber latency measurement with picosecond-accuracy using correlation OTDR. arXiv preprint arXiv:1808.00201 (2018)

8. Hounam, D., Schwerdt, M., Zink, M.: Active antenna module characterisation by pseudo-noise gating. In: Proceedings of 25th ESA Antenna Workshop Satellite Antenna Technology, Noordwijk, The Netherlands (2002)

9. Brautigam, B., Schwerdt, M., Bachmann, M.: An efficient method for performance monitoring of active phased array antennas. IEEE Trans. Geosci. Remote Sens. **47**(4), 1236–1243 (2009)

Core Arrangement Based Spectrum-Efficient Path Selection in Core-Continuity Constrained SS-FONs

Anuj Agrawal[1]([envelope]), Vimal Bhatia[1], and Shashi Prakash[2]

[1] Signals and Software Group, Discipline of Electrical Engineering,
Indian Institute of Technology Indore, Indore 453552, India
{phd1501202003,vbhatia}@iiti.ac.in
[2] Photonics Laboratory, Devi Ahilya University, Indore 452017, India
sprakash@ietdavv.edu.in

Abstract. In this work, we exploit the spatial dimension of spectrally-spatially flexible optical networks (SS-FONs) to perform path selection. The existing path selection schemes in SS-FONs predominantly use k-shortest paths (KSP) method. However, in this work, we demonstrate that in SS-FONs, consideration of core selection along with link selection between source and destination nodes can significantly increase the spectrum utilization efficiency. We propose a k-core arrangement based paths (KCAP) scheme that performs path calculation and prioritization on the basis of core arrangement in different multicore fiber (MCF) structures, threshold crosstalk (XT) values, distance adaptive modulation (DAM), and the number of MCF links. The proposed KCAP achieves better spectrum utilization than the existing XT-aware and predefined core-prioritization schemes.

1 Introduction

The introduction of elastic optical network (EON) [1] brought flexibility in the spectral domain, which significantly increased the spectrum efficiency of optical networks. The main enabling technologies of EON are distance adaptive modulation (DAM), bit-rate adaptive transceivers, flexible spectrum grids, and multi-carrier transmission techniques. EON has been accepted as a promising solution to satisfy the ever-increasing bandwidth demands in near-future. EON requires technology migration only at the nodes, while utilizing the existing fiber infrastructure. However, it is predicted that the bandwidth supported by the existing single-core fiber (SCF)/single-mode fiber (SMF) technology will soon fall short to satisfy the future bandwidth intensive applications in the 5G and beyond era [2–7]. Thus, with a view to further increase the optical network capacity, spectrally-spatially flexible optical networks (SS-FONs) (also known as space division multiplexed (SDM)-EONs) have been researched in the recent past. The SS-FONs expand the capacity of optical networks in the spatial domain

© IFIP International Federation for Information Processing 2020
Published by Springer Nature Switzerland AG 2020
A. Tzanakaki et al. (Eds.): ONDM 2019, LNCS 11616, pp. 570–583, 2020.
https://doi.org/10.1007/978-3-030-38085-4_49

(along with the spectral domain flexibility of EON) through multi-core and/or multi-mode fibers (MCF/MMF) [6]. This work is focussed on MCF SS-FONs.

The routing, spectrum, core and/or mode assignment (RSCMA) problem in SS-FONs is subdivided in to the routing (R), and spectrum, core and/or mode assignment (SCMA) sub-problems [2–7]. Various schemes have been proposed in the literature in recent past for SCMA to improve spectrum utilization and manage crosstalk (XT) levels in SS-FONs. However, for the routing sub-problem, k-shortest paths (KSP) routing has been predominantly used [2–7] in SS-FONs. To perform RSCMA, paths are first calculated and prioritized (on the basis of KSP) offline for different node-pairs in an optical network topology, and then SCMA is done on the calculated routes. In SCF/SMF optical networks, routing deals with the selection of fiber links to be used from source s to destination d nodes in a network. However, in SS-FONs, the added dimension (i.e., spatial dimension) can significantly affect the spectrum utilization efficiency of path selection schemes. In this work, for the first time, we exploit the spatial dimension of SS-FONs for path selection and prioritization.

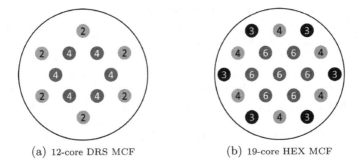

(a) 12-core DRS MCF   (b) 19-core HEX MCF

Fig. 1. Core grouping in MCFs on the basis of number of surrounding cores: (a) Two core groups with $\alpha = 4$, and $\alpha = 2$, shown by red, and green color, respectively; (b) Three core groups with $\alpha = 6$, $\alpha = 4$, and $\alpha = 3$, shown by red, green, and blue color, respectively. (Color figure online)

In different MCF structures [2–8], multiple cores are arranged in different pattern. Figure 1 above shows the core arrangement in a 12-core dual ring structure (DRS) MCF, and a 19-core hexagonal (HEX) MCF structure. A lightpath traveling between s to d in an SS-FON may be routed through any of the cores in MCF. Further, using fully non-blocking reconfigurable optical add/drop multiplexers (FNB-ROADMs) [9], lightpaths may switch cores at intermediate nodes. Thus, in SS-FONs, routing is not limited to the selection of only links between the s-d pair, rather it is two-dimensional, where selection of both links and cores is to be performed to define the end-to-end path between an s-d pair of nodes. Thus, in this work, we propose a k-core arrangement based paths (KCAP) scheme that calculates and prioritizes paths in terms of both links and cores on the basis of core arrangement, DAM, threshold XT levels, and number of links between s-d pairs in an SS-FON.

FNB-ROADMs require enormous node complexity and very high CAPEX, hence core-continuity constrained (CCC) SS-FONs (where core switching is not possible at intermediate nodes) have been proposed in the literature [9] as a solution to satisfy the increasing bandwidth demands in short- and mid-term future. Thus, in this work, we consider CCC SS-FONs. In an SCF optical network, if P number of possible paths exist between an s-d pair, the number of possible paths between that $s - d$ pair in an n-core CCC SS-FON will be $n \cdot P$ (one possible path through each core). In the existing RSCMA approaches, core selection is performed under SCMA sub-problem, however, in this work we show that consideration of core selection while calculating paths can significantly improve the spectrum utilization.

Related Work: Inter-core XT in SS-FONs is a major consideration to perform RSCMA. The existing RSCMA approaches ensure acceptable threshold XT levels through various SCMA schemes [2–7], and do not consider XT values during route calculation. Hence, we review the existing schemes used to manage XT levels in SS-FONs. In [10], an overview of existing XT estimation methods is given. A frequently used method to ensure acceptable XT levels performs worst case (WC)-XT calculations, where the maximum possible XT that can occur in any core of an MCF is calculated offline. Based on the WC-XT calculations for different modulation formats (MFs) and s-d pairs, SCMA is done. An straightforward approach to ensure acceptable XT levels is XT-avoid [11], where allocation of same frequency slot (FS) in any two adjacent cores in an MCF is avoided, thereby resulting in no XT amongst cores. Another approach to manage acceptable XT levels in SS-FONs is strict-XT [10,11], which require complex calculations for strict XT level check of all the existing lightpaths on the arrival of every new lightpath demand.

Both the WC-XT and XT-avoid methods are proactive approaches to deal with XT as they do not require any complex calculation depending on the dynamic changes in spectrum usage in different cores. The XT-avoid approach is highly spectrum inefficient as it leads to a large number of unused FSs in SS-FONs due to XT avoidance criteria [11]. However, the WC-XT approach has higher spectrum utilization efficiency as compared to XT-avoid method since WC-XT allows spectrum overlapping between adjacent cores considering acceptable XT levels. Hence, we consider WC-XT with KSP (referred to as KSP-WC-XT) as one of the benchmark schemes to compare its spectrum utilization efficiency with the proposed KCAP.

As we exploit the spatial flexibility and core arrangement in the proposed KCAP, we study another benchmark scheme (referred to as KSP-WC-XT-CP) that performs core-prioritization (CP). Figure 1 shows the number of surrounding cores α for each core in the 12-core DRS MCF and the 19-core HEX MCF. As the XT value in a core depends on the number of surrounding cores [6,10,11], a predefined CP approach can enhance spectrum utilization while ensuring acceptable XT levels. In [2], a CP scheme has been proposed for spectrum allocation

(SA) in SS-FONs, where non-adjacent cores with low α have been preferred first to allocate spectrum. However, as spectrum gets allocated in all the cores with increasing network load, effects of XT will be observed due to all surrounding cores, thereby making it difficult to allocate future lightpath demands with acceptable XT levels and/or efficient MFs. We apply a similar CP scheme for path selection in KSP-WC-XT-CP, where the cores with minimum α are preferred first for path prioritization. The proposed KCAP scheme is detailed in Sect. 2 with a comparative description with the benchmark KSP-WC-XT and KSP-WC-XT-CP schemes. It should be noted that all the three schemes, i.e., KSP-WC-XT, KSP-WC-XT-CP, and the proposed KCAP are the proactive schemes that do not require complex dynamic XT calculations depending on the spectrum information.

Notations: Let Z be the set of lightpath demands, with index z, in a given SS-FON mesh connected network graph $G(V, W, C, P)$, where V is the set of nodes, with index v, W is the set of fiber links present in a network, with index w, C is the set of cores available per fiber link, with index c, and P is the set of link distances, with index p. A lightpath request is denoted by $Z\{s_z, d_z, r_z\}$, where s_z, and d_z are the source and destination nodes, respectively, of request z, and r_z is the bitrate required by request z. Let I be the set of all possible paths between all $s - d$ pairs in a network, with index i. The FS granularity, and the number of guard slots per lightpath are denoted by Δf, and N_g, respectively. Let M (b/s/Hz) denotes the modulation spectral efficiency.

2   Proposed: *k*-core Arrangement Based Paths (KCAP)

The proposed KCAP leverages spatial flexibility of SS-FONs along with spectral flexibility (i.e., DAM and bit-rate adaptive SA) for path calculation and prioritization while ensuring acceptable XT levels of paths. In the proposed KCAP, core grouping is performed on the basis of the number of surrounding cores (α) for each core in an MCF. Cores with the same α are grouped in one core group G_i. For example, in Fig. 1(a), the 12 cores can be categorized into two core groups; G_1: consisting of the six cores of outer ring with $\alpha = 2$, and G_2: consisting of the six cores of inner ring with $\alpha = 4$. Similarly, the cores of 19-core HEX MCF, shown in Fig. 1(b), can be categorized into three core groups, G_1 (consisting of six cores with $\alpha = 3$), G_2 (consisting of six cores with $\alpha = 4$), and G_3 (consisting of seven cores with $\alpha = 6$).

In the analytical model based on coupled-power theory [6,10,11], the mean XT (XT_μ) value in an MCF is given by

$$XT_\mu = \frac{\alpha - \alpha \exp(-(\alpha + 1) \cdot h \cdot L)}{1 + \alpha \exp(-(\alpha + 1) \cdot h \cdot L)}, \tag{1}$$

where, L is the length of MCF, and h is a constant, which is calculated as

$$h = \frac{2 \cdot \kappa^2 \cdot R}{\beta \cdot \Lambda}, \tag{2}$$

Table 1. Transmission reach L (km) for different core groups in 12-core DRS MCF and 19-core HEX MCF

MCF-type		BPSK	QPSK	8QAM	16QAM
	XT_{th} (dB)	-21.7	-26.2	-28.7	-32.7
12-core	$L(G_1)$	3347.74	1189.11	668.86	266.33
DRS MCF	$L(G_2) = L_{wc}$	1672.45	594.38	334.37	133.16
19-core	$L(G_1)$	2230.57	792.58	445.86	177.55
HEX	$L(G_2)$	1672.45	594.38	334.37	133.16
MCF	$L(G_3) = L_{wc}$	1114.66	396.21	222.9	88.77

where, κ is the coupling-coefficient, R is the bending radius, β is the propagation constant, and Λ is the core pitch. To determine the transmission reach with acceptable XT levels given the value of threshold XT (XT_{th}), (1) can be rewritten as

$$L = \frac{1}{(\alpha + 1) \cdot h} \ln\left(\frac{\alpha(1 + XT_{\mu})}{\alpha - XT_{\mu}}\right). \tag{3}$$

Substituting the typical values of XT_{th} [10] for binary phase shift keying (BPSK), quadrature phase shift keying (QPSK), 8-quadrature amplitude modulation (8QAM), and 16QAM modulation schemes in (3), we calculate the transmission reach L for different core groups in 12-core DRS MCF and 19-core HEX MCF, as shown in Table 1. For BPSK, QPSK, 8QAM, and 16QAM MFs, $M = 1$, $M = 2$, $M = 3$, and $M = 4$, respectively. The value of h in (3) is calculated using (2) by substituting the MCF-specific values [10] specified in Table 5.

It can be observed from Table 1 that for different core groups, the value of L is different. Using DAM, the shortest physical path is preferred for lightpath establishment since it offers highest possible MF, thereby increasing spectrum efficiency. However, from Table 1, it can be observed that a lightpath of same physical distance, if routed through different cores in an MCF will result in selection of different MFs. Hence, the KSP scheme, where paths are calculated and prioritized on the basis on increasing physical lengths, will not be suitable for efficient spectrum utilization in SS-FONs.

In WC-XT method, the maximum possible XT value (i.e., the worst case transmission reach L_{wc}) in an MCF is considered. Hence, for 12-core DRS MCF, $L_{wc} = L(G_2)$, and for 19-core HEX MCF $L_{wc} = L(G_3)$, as shown in Table 1. Using, DAM and bit-rate adaptive SA, the number of FS N_i^w required on each $w \in |W(i)|$ is given by (4) for a lightpath demand z with required bit rate b_z (in Gbps) [12]. Here, $|W(i)|$ is the subset of links in path $i \in I$. Highest supported M is chosen according to the physical distance of the chosen path.

$$N_i^w = \left\lceil \frac{b_z}{\Delta f \cdot M} \right\rceil + N_g \tag{4}$$

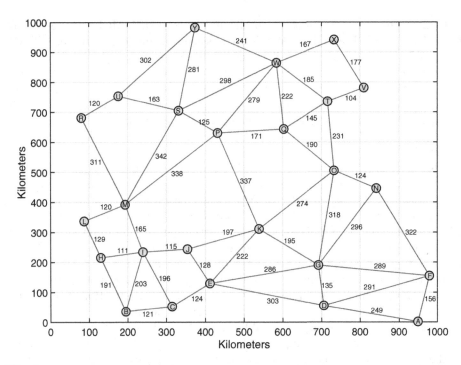

Fig. 2. A 25-node test network topology randomly generated in a 1000 km × 1000 km area using GG.

The number of FS required in the network (N_i^n) for different paths $i \in I$ can be obtained as the product of N_i^w and the number of links used in the ith path [13],

$$N_i^n = N_i^w \cdot |W(i)|. \tag{5}$$

Table 2. Path calculation and prioritization using KSP-WC-XT scheme

Demand		Path 1	Path 2	Path 3	Path 4
F-G	Path	FG	FDG	FADG	FNG
	Length (km)	289	426	540	618
	MF	8QAM	QPSK	QPSK	BPSK
	N_i^n	6 ①	14 ②	20 ③	26 ④
R-W	Path	RUSW	RUYW	RUSPW	RUSPQW
	Length (km)	581	663	687	801
	MF	QPSK	BPSK	BPSK	BPSK
	N_i^n	20 ①	38 ②	50 ③	62 ④

Consider the network topology shown in Fig. 2. The value of N_i^n for a light-path demand of $b_z = 150$ Gbps between F-G and R-W node pairs is calculated in

Table 2, 3 and 4 considering $k = 4$ paths and 12-core DRS MCF for the benchmark KSP-WC-XT and KSP-WC-XT-CP schemes, and the proposed KCAP scheme. In Table 2, highest possible MF has been selected as per L_{wc} such that the path length does not exceed L_{wc} for the selected MF. The encircled values denote path priority obtained by KSP-WC-XT, where paths are prioritized on the basis on physical fiber lengths. From Table 1, it is observed that the path priority obtained results in the increasing order of the value of N_i^n, which indicates that the path that requires minimum FS in the network has been preferred the most.

However, as we calculate N_i^n on the basis of core arrangement, i.e., depending on the value of α for different cores in Table 3, it is found that the obtained paths are not in the increasing order of N_i^n. It can be observed that for lightpath establishment through Path 4 using a core with $\alpha = 2$, the N_i^n required is 10, whereas for Path 3, N_i^n required is 14. Further, it can be observed that for Path 1 (with $\alpha = 4$), the N_i^n required is 6, and for Path 2 (with $\alpha = 2$), the N_i^n required is 10. This indicates that preferring the cores with lesser α for lightpath establishment until they are fully allocated is also not a spectrum-efficient approach. The encircled values denote path prioritization using KSP-WC-XT-CP, where predefined core prioritization on the basis of increasing values of α has been done for lightpath establishment. From Table 3, it can be observed that the paths prioritized using KSP-WC-XT-CP are not in the increasing order of the value of N_i^n. Thus, in SS-FONs, neither core prioritization, nor shortest path selection results in path prioritization in the increasing order of spectrum consumption (i.e., N_i^n).

Table 3. Path calculation and prioritization using KSP-WC-XT-CP scheme

Demand		Path 1	Path 2	Path 3	Path 4
F-G	Path	FG	FDG	FADG	FNG
	Length (km)	289	426	540	618
	MF($\alpha = 2$)	8QAM	8QAM	8QAM	8QAM
	$N_i^n(\alpha = 2)$	6 ①	10 ②	14 ③	10 ④
	MF($\alpha = 4$)	8QAM	QPSK	QPSK	BPSK
	$N_i^n(\alpha = 4)$	6 ⑤	14 ⑥	20 ⑦	26 ⑧
R-W	Path	RUSW	RUYW	RUSPW	RUSPQW
	Length (km)	581	663	687	801
	MF($\alpha = 2$)	8QAM	8QAM	QPSK	QPSK
	$N_i^n(\alpha = 2)$	14 ①	14 ②	26 ③	32 ④
	MF($\alpha = 4$)	QPSK	BPSK	BPSK	BPSK
	$N_i^n(\alpha = 4)$	20 ⑤	38 ⑥	50 ⑦	62 ⑧

The N_i^n required in SS-FONs depend on the value of α, the length of fiber, and the number of links between $s-d$. Hence, in the proposed KCAP, we perform core grouping on the basis of the value of α. Offline path calculation based on XT_{th}, core groups, DAM, and number of fiber links is performed in the proposed KCAP, and N_i^n is calculated for various possible paths between different $s - d$ pairs in an SS-FON. The routes are then prioritized on the basis of the increasing values of N_i^n, as shown in Table 4. The encircled values in Table 4 denote path prioritization using the proposed KCAP. It can be observed from Table 1 that G_1 (having $\alpha = 2$) of 12-core DRS MCF, offers twice the L as that obtained using G_2. Alternatively, it can be said that G_1 is more spectrum efficient as it allows the selection of higher MF than G_2 for a particular value of L. For example, to establish a lightpath of 1000 km in a 12-core DRS MCF SS-FON, QPSK can be used using G_1, however, BPSK has to be used if the lightpath is established using G_2 since it exceeds L possible with QPSK using G_2, as observed from Table 1. Hence, in case of a tie between the value of N_i^n for two paths with different core groups, the proposed KCAP prefers G_i with higher α in order to save the spectrum efficient cores for future lightpath demands. In case of a tie between the value of N_i^n for two paths of different physical length, the path with shorter physical length is preferred in the proposed KCAP.

It is worth noting that the existing RSCMA schemes first obtain the paths, and then XT-estimation, DAM, and CP is performed under the SCMA sub-problem for allocating spectrum on the chosen path/s. However, the proposed KCAP calculates the paths on the basis of core arrangement, threshold XT levels, DAM, and number of links used. It may also be noted here that though bit rate b_z appears in (4), KCAP can find the path preference without the knowledge of bit rate requirements of lightpath demands, and is thus applicable to perform dynamic lightpath provisioning. From (4), it can be seen that for a particular $s - d$ pair in a given SS-FON with certain MCF structure, the physical distance is constant, α is constant, and hence M corresponding to different $s - d$ pairs and core groups is also constant. FS granularity Δf is also fixed to a typical value of 12.5 or 6.25 GHz. The numbers of guard slots N_g per lightpath are also constant. The number of links $|L(i)|$ for a path between any $s - d$ pair is also constant. Thus, the N_i^n required in the network by a path $i \in I$ can be represented as $N_i^n = \lceil x_i \cdot b_z \rceil$, where x_i is constant for any route $i \in I$. Hence, route prioritization can be done using the proposed KCAP by sorting routes on the basis of increasing values of $N_i^n = \lceil x_i \cdot b_z \rceil$ considering any arbitrary value for b_z.

The proposed KCAP is summarized in the following steps as follows:

Step 1: Perform core grouping on the basis of α in MCF used.

Step 2: Calculate L for different core groups using (2), (3) on the basis of XT_{th} values corresponding to different MFs.

Step 3: Calculate N_i^n using (4), (5) for different possible paths, and prioritize them on the basis of increasing value of N_i^n.

Table 4. Path calculation and prioritization using the proposed KCAP

Demand		Path 1	Path 2	Path 3	Path 4
F-G	Path	FG	FDG	FADG	FNG
	Length (km)	289	426	540	618
	$MF(G_1)$	8QAM	8QAM	8QAM	8QAM
	$N_i^n(G_1)$	6 ②	10 ③	14 ⑥	10 ④
	$MF(G_2)$	8QAM	QPSK	QPSK	BPSK
	$N_i^n(G_2)$	6 ①	14 ⑤	20 ⑦	26 ⑧
R-W	Path	RUSW	RUYW	RUSPW	RUSPQW
	Length (km)	581	663	687	801
	$MF(G_1)$	8QAM	8QAM	QPSK	QPSK
	$N_i^n(G_1)$	14 ①	14 ②	26 ④	32 ⑥
	$MF(G_2)$	QPSK	BPSK	BPSK	BPSK
	$N_i^n(G_2)$	20 ③	38 ⑤	50 ⑦	62 ⑧

3   Performance Evaluation

In this section, a comparative performance evaluation of the proposed KCAP, and the benchmark KSP-WC-XT and KSP-WC-XT-CP schemes has been done. To perform a comprehensive assessment of the proposed KCAP on network topologies of different size and connectivity, we generate random network topologies based on Gabriel graph (GG) [14] instead of few standard network topologies. In this approach, a number of nodes are randomly located in a given geographical area following uniform distribution, and then the nodes are connected through fiber links using GG theory. As per GG theory, any two nodes o_1 and o_2 are connected by a link iff there is no other node lying in a circle obtained with center as the mid-point of the straight line joining o_1 and o_2, and diameter equal to the length of that straight line. We generate random network topologies, where the number of nodes is varied in each iteration, uniformly selected from the set specified in Table 5. Thus, network topologies of varying node/link density, link-lengths and connectivity is obtained in each iteration. The simulation results shown have been averaged over 100 iterations. One such instance of the random network topology for 25 nodes is shown in Fig. 2.

In each iteration, a total of 5000 lightpath demands for 12-core DRS MCF, and 10000 lightpath demands for 19-core HEX MCF, respectively, have been generated uniformly among different node pairs. The lightpaths with heterogeneous data rate requirement (given in Table 5) are established incrementally in the randomly generated network topologies. Each link in the network is assumed to be a MCF bidirectional link. For spectrum allocation, first-fit (FF) scheme has been employed in which for each core, all the available frequency slots are indexed, and then spectrum allocation is done starting from the lowest index of frequency slots. Lightpath establishment using all the considered schemes is subject to the

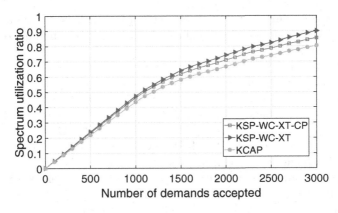

Fig. 3. Spectrum utilization ratio (SUR) with increase in the number of accepted lightpath demands in 12-core DRS MCF SS-FON.

Table 5. Simulation parameters

Parameter	Value
Number of lightpath demands for 12-core DRS MCF SS-FON	5000
Number of lightpath demands for 19-core HEX MCF SS-FON	10000
Heterogeneous data rate set	$\{40, 200, 500, 1000\}$ Gbps
Number of available FS per core	320
FS granularity	12.5 GHz
Geographical area where random network topology is obtained	1000 km $\times$ 1000 km
Set of number of nodes in random network topologies	$\{20, 30, 40\}$
κ	1.27×10^{-3}
β	4×10^{6} m^{-1}
R	50 mm
Λ	40 μm

spectrum continuity, spectrum contiguity, and non-overlapping spectrum allocation with CCC. Simulation parameters are summarized in Table 5.

Performance has been evaluated in terms of spectrum utilization ratio (SUR) versus the number of accepted lightpath demands. SUR is defined as the ratio of the number of FS utilized in the network to the total number of available FS in the network. Thus, a low value of SUR indicates better spectrum utilization for a certain number of accepted lightpath demands. In the literature [10, 15], modulation selection ratio has been used in SS-FONs for performance evaluation, where selection of higher MFs indicate better spectrum utilization. However, as we observe in Tables 3 and 4, the N_i^n depends on MF selection as well as core group selection. Hence, establishing lighpaths using high MF initially on cores with less values of α (such as in KSP-WC-XT-CP) may lead to much lower MF selection for future lightpath demands. To analyze the pattern of MF selection with varying network load, we analyze different path selection schemes on the basis of average modulation spectral efficiency (M_{avg}). It is defined as the ratio of the sum of M of all the accepted lightpath demands to the number of accepted lightpath demands.

Figure 3 shows the SUR with increase in the number of accepted lightpath demands. As more and more demands gets established in the network, spectrum consumption in all the cores and links increases. The proposed KCAP performs better than both the benchmark schemes, achieving an average improvement of 7.5%, and 11.55% in SUR as compared to the KSP-WC-XT-CP, and KSP-WC-XT schemes, respectively. The KSP-WC-XT-CP performs better than the KSP-WC-XT scheme since it considers core arrangement based CP utilizing the spatial dimension for path calculation and prioritization, whereas KSP-WC-XT does not utilize the core arrangement in MCFs.

In Fig. 4, SUR for 19-core HEX MCF has been evaluated. The increased number of cores offered acceptance of higher number of lightpath demands in SS-FONs. Further, the number of core groups in 19-core HEX MCF is three, as shown in Fig. 1 and Table 1. Thus, core grouping increases the average SUR improvement of the proposed KCAP to 9.66% and 14.35%, as compared to the KSP-WC-XT-CP, and KSP-WC-XT, respectively, in Fig. 4.

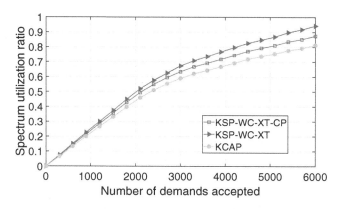

Fig. 4. Spectrum utilization ratio (SUR) with increase in the number of accepted lightpath demands in 19-core HEX MCF SS-FON.

In Fig. 5, M_{avg} for 12-core DRS MCF at different values of spectrum utilized is shown, which describes the pattern of MF selection by different path selection schemes. At 30% spectrum utilization, the KSP-WC-XT-CP scheme performs better than the KSP-WC-XT and the proposed KCAP in terms of M_{avg}, indicating higher MF selection. However, with the increase in spectrum utilization, M_{avg} for KSP-WC-XT-CP decreases, whereas for the proposed KCAP, M_{avg} increases slightly. This is because in KSP-WC-XT-CP, the spectrum efficient cores (with low α) have been preferred first for lightpath establishment. However, as the spectrum utilization increases, the lightpath establishment using cores with higher α increases, resulting in low MF selection for future demands.

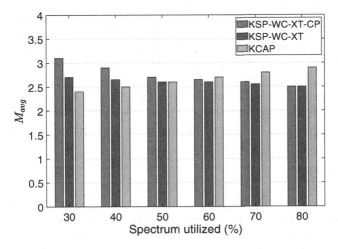

Fig. 5. Average modulation spectral efficiency (M_{avg}) with increase in spectrum utilization in 12-core DRS MCF.

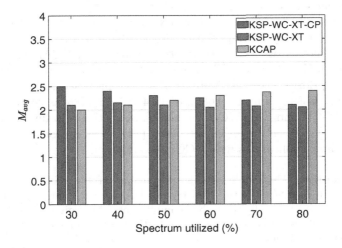

Fig. 6. Average modulation spectral efficiency (M_{avg}) with increase in spectrum utilization in 19-core HEX MCF.

Figure 6 shows M_{avg} for 19-core HEX MCF. The pattern of M_{avg} using different schemes in 19-core HEX MCF is similar to that observed in 12-core HEX MCF. However, the value of M_{avg} for all the schemes is lesser in 19-core HEX MCF as compared to that in 12-core DRS MCF. This is due the higher $\alpha = 6$ for the inner seven cores in the 19-core HEX MCF, which affects L, and hence MF selection. The value of M_{avg} for KSP-WC-XT almost remains the same with increase in spectrum utilization for both the 12-core DRS MCF, and 19-core HEX MCF. This is due to the reason that KSP-WC-XT does not prioritize routes on the basis of core arrangement.

As the demands arrive in the network, and the spectrum is utilized beyond 50%, it can be observed that the proposed KCAP performs better than both the KSP-WC-XT-CP and KSP-WC-XT schemes. It is worth noting that higher M_{avg} for KSP-WC-XT-CP at $30\% - 50\%$ spectrum utilization does not indicate a directly proportional relation with spectrum utilization efficiency. This can be observed from the lower values of SUR for KSP-WC-XT-CP as compared to the proposed KCAP for different number of demands accepted, since N_i^n depends on the core group selection and the number of links as well along with MF selection.

4   Conclusion

In SS-FONs, consideration of spatial dimension (i.e., core arrangement in MCF) during path selection can significantly improve the spectrum utilization efficiency, as demonstrated in this work. Hence, two-dimensional paths between $s - d$ pair should be calculated in SS-FONs that specify: (a) the fiber links to be used in the network, and (b) the core to be used in the MCF. The proposed KCAP calculates and prioritizes paths on the basis of core arrangement, XT_{th}, DAM, and the number of links between $s - d$ pair. The proposed KCAP performs better than the existing KSP-WC-XT scheme which does not consider core arrangement of MCFs. Furthermore, the proposed KCAP has also been compared with KSP-WC-XT-CP scheme that utilizes the core arrangement to perform core prioritization on the basis of α. The proposed KCAP achieves an average improvement of up to 9.66%, and 14.35% in SUR as compared to the KSP-WC-XT-CP, and KSP-WC-XT schemes, respectively. In future, we plan to show the effects of core arrangement based path selection for short-reach and intra-datacenter applications with CCC relaxation.

Acknowledgment. This publication is an outcome of the R&D work under the Visvesvaraya Ph.D. Scheme of the Ministry of Electronics & Information Technology (MeitY), Government of India (GoI), being implemented by Digital India Corporation. The authors would like to thank the Indian Institute of Technology (IIT) Indore for all the support and resources.

References

1. Jinno, M., Takara, H., Kozicki, B., Tsukishima, Y., Sone, Y., Matsuoka, S.: Spectrum-efficient and scalable elastic optical path network: architecture, benefits, and enabling technologies. IEEE Commun. Mag. **47**(11), 66–73 (2009)
2. Tode, H., Hirota, Y.: Routing, spectrum, and core and/or mode assignment on space-division multiplexing optical networks. J. Opt. Commun. Netw. **9**(1), A99–A113 (2017)
3. Shariati, B., Rivas-Moscoso, J.M., Marom, D.M., Ben-Ezra, S., Klonidis, D., Velasco, L., Tomkos, I.: Impact of spatial and spectral granularity on the performance of SDM networks based on spatial superchannel switching. J. Lightwave Technol. **35**(13), 2559–2568 (2017)

4. Zhang, L., Ansari, N., Khreishah, A.: Anycast planning in space division multiplexing elastic optical networks with multi-core fibers. IEEE Commun. Lett. **20**(10), 1983–1986 (2016)
5. Khodashenas, P.S., Rivas-Moscoso, J.M., Siracusa, D., Pederzolli, F., Shariati, B., Klonidis, D., Salvadori, E., Tomkos, I.: Comparison of spectral and spatial superchannel allocation schemes for SDM networks. J. Lightwave Technol. **34**(11), 2710–2716 (2016)
6. Saridis, G.M., Alexandropoulos, D., Zervas, G., Simeonidou, D.: Survey and evaluation of space division multiplexing: from technologies to optical networks. IEEE Commun. Surv. Tutor. **17**(4), 2136–2156 (2015)
7. Fujii, S., Hirota, Y., Tode, H., Murakami, K.: On-demand spectrum and core allocation for reducing crosstalk in multicore fibers in elastic optical networks. J. Opt. Commun. Netw. **6**(12), 1059–1071 (2014)
8. Sano, A., et al.: 409-Tb/s+ 409-Tb/s crosstalk suppressed bidirectional MCF transmission over 450 km using propagation-direction interleaving. Opt. Express **21**(14), 16777–16783 (2013)
9. Moreno-Muro, F.-J., Rumipamba-Zambrano, R., Pavón-Marino, P., Perelló, J., Gené, J.M., Spadaro, S.: Evaluation of core-continuity-constrained ROADMs for flex-grid/MCF optical networks. J. Opt. Commun. Netw. **9**(11), 1041–1050 (2017)
10. Klinkowski, M., Walkowiak, K.: Impact of crosstalk estimation methods on the performance of spectrally and spatially flexible optical networks. In: 20th International Conference on Transparent Optical Networks (ICTON), pp. 1–4 (2018)
11. Yang, M., Zhang, Y., Wu, Q.: Routing, spectrum, and core assignment in SDM-EONS with MCF: node-arc ILP/MILP methods and an efficient XT-aware heuristic algorithm. J. Opt. Commun. Netw. **10**(3), 195–208 (2018)
12. Castro, A., Velasco, L., Ruiz, M., Comellas, J.: Single-path provisioning with multipath recovery in flexgrid optical networks. In: Proceedings of ICUMT, pp. 745–751 (2012)
13. Agrawal, A., Bhatia, V., Prakash, S.: Spectrum efficient distance-adaptive paths for fixed and fixed-alternate routing in elastic optical networks. Opt. Fiber Technol. **40**, 36–45 (2018)
14. Szcześniak, I., Gola, A., Jajszczyk, A., Pach, A.R., Woźna-Szcześniak, B.: Itinerant routing in elastic optical networks. J. Lightwave Technol. **35**(10), 1868–1875 (2017)
15. Goścień, R., Walkowiak, K.: On the efficiency of survivable flex-grid SDM networks. J. Lightwave Technol. **36**(10), 1815–1823 (2018)

Topology and Failure Modeling for Optical Network Resilience Analysis Against Earthquakes

Anuj Agrawal[1]($\boxtimes$), Vimal Bhatia[1], and Shashi Prakash[2]

[1] Signals and Software Group, Discipline of Electrical Engineering,
Indian Institute of Technology Indore, Indore 453552, India
{phd1501202003,vbhatia}@iiti.ac.in
[2] Photonics Laboratory, Devi Ahilya University, Indore 452017, India
sprakash@ietdavv.edu.in

Abstract. In this paper, we propose a stochastic failure and optical network topology (SFONT) model that can be used to comprehensively analyze the resilience of optical networks against a large number of possible earthquakes. We study an optical network densification problem, where dense network topologies are generated using the proposed SFONT model. Further, a seismic-risk aware optical network densification (SRA-OND) scheme is proposed with a view to design the future optical networks robust against earthquakes. The proposed SFONT model has been evaluated at various stages of network densification. To validate the capability of the proposed SFONT model to emulate real-world networking and failure scenario, we also perform a similar analysis based on RailTel optical network topology, seismic hazard maps, and real past earthquake data from India. Simulations indicate that the proposed SFONT model can be used to estimate and analyze the impact of network-resilience schemes on optical networks for a large number of possible earthquakes.

1 Introduction

Earthquakes have been a major cause of optical fiber cable (OFC) destruction in the past. For instance, the 2008 China Sichuan earthquake of magnitude 8.0 destroyed around $30,000$ km of OFCs [1]. In a telecom-cloud infrastructure (TCI) supported by optical network, various nodes interconnect datacenters (DCs), multiprotocol label switching (MPLS) areas, and cable landing stations (CLS) through OFCs [2,3]. A rapid increase in the number of DC and OFC deployment has been observed in the recent past, and many more DCs and OFCs are planned to be deployed in future to enable beyond 5G telecommunication, and cloud services [4]. Moreover, to realize the maximum benefits of wireless network densification, backhaul optical networks also need to be densified [4,5]. Thus, with a view to make the future TCI resilient against earthquakes, the

---

V. Bhatia—Senior Member, IEEE
S. Prakash—Senior Member, IEEE, OSA

© IFIP International Federation for Information Processing 2020
Published by Springer Nature Switzerland AG 2020
A. Tzanakaki et al. (Eds.): ONDM 2019, LNCS 11616, pp. 584–597, 2020.
https://doi.org/10.1007/978-3-030-38085-4_50

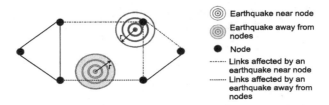

Fig. 1. Possibility of GCMFs in a mesh-connected optical network due to earthquakes at different epicenter locations around the network.

optical network components (nodes/links) should be physically located in the low seismic-risk regions.

To design robust future optical networks, a method for comprehensive and long-term analysis of various network-resilience schemes is required to assess optical networks against a large number of possible earthquakes. Thus, in this work, we propose a stochastic failure and optical network topology (SFONT) model that can be used to estimate and analyze the impact of various network-resilience schemes on optical networks.

Since large-scale natural disasters such as earthquakes affect a large geographical region, all the fiber cables lying in that region may fail simultaneously. Such a large-scale failure caused due to a common disaster occurrence is referred to as geographically correlated multi-link failure (GCMF). In the studies [1,6–9] that address the problem of robust physical network design, most of the works propose physical fiber route modification as a solution to achieve network robustness. However, in Fig. 1, we show that GCMFs are highly dependent on the physical location of nodes.

In Fig. 1, an example mesh-connected 6-node optical network is shown. Here, two earthquakes causing disaster in a circular area of radius r from their epicenters are shown. It can be observed that the earthquake that occur in the vicinity of node is vulnerable to a GCMF affecting three fiber links. However, the earthquake that occur far away from nodes is vulnerable to single-link failure that can be survived using the conventional dedicated path protection (DPP), or shared path protection (SPP) methods. Thus, for resilient network design against GCMFs, the locations of nodes are of utmost concern. For simulations, we consider GCMFs caused due to earthquakes having epicenters in the vicinity of nodes.

In this work, we study an optical network densification (OND) scenario with a view to design the future dense optical networks resilient against earthquakes. We propose a seismic-risk aware optical network densification (SRA-OND) scheme for robust physical network topology design that finds the low seismic-risk regions to locate the new nodes. We evaluate the proposed SFONT model by analyzing various OND stages using the proposed SRA-OND as well as a seismic-risk unaware (SRU)-OND approach (where nodes are randomly located without considering seismic risk). To verify the capability of the proposed SFONT model to emulate real-world network topologies and failure scenarios,

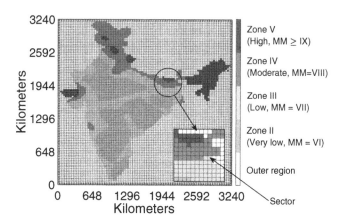

Fig. 2. Seismic hazard map of India [16] subdivided into sectors.

we compare the proposed SFONT model with a real-world case considering past real earthquakes [10], and real Indian RailTel optical network topology [11].

Related Work: The failure modeling and resilience analyses done by majority of the studies [6–8,12–15] are based on one/two network topology, arbitrary disaster zones, and few instances of disaster occurrence. However, for a comprehensive and rigorous assessment of any resilience-improvement scheme, they should be analyzed for a number of randomly obtained networks, since the performance may vary with changes in network topologies. In the proposed SFONT model, random network topologies of varying size and connectivity are obtained in each iteration. In [8,9], spatially uniform occurrence of disasters has been assumed in a given geographical region. However, practically, in a large geographical region, the probability of occurrence of natural disasters varies with different geographical locations. We incorporate this characteristic of spatially non-uniform disaster probability in the proposed SFONT model to generate earthquake epicenters. Moreover, we leverage the spatially non-uniform disaster probability in the proposed SRA-OND to locate the nodes in low seismic-risk regions. In [12], four arbitrary sample disaster zones have been assumed for resilience-analysis. Random disaster zones have been assumed in [14] without considering any disaster risk model. However, for a comprehensive and long-term assessment of any resilience-improvement scheme, it should be tested for a large number of possible disaster occurrences.

For the first time in the literature, in the proposed SFONT model, we perform optical network densification in a given geographical region using Matérn hard core point process (MHCPP) and Gabriel graphs (GGs). To generate large number of spatially non-uniformly distributed earthquakes as per seismic-risk, we employ Poisson point process (PPP). The proposed SFONT model is described in the next section. The notations used in this paper are summarized in Table 1.

2   Proposed Stochastic Failure and Optical Network Topology (SFONT) Model

To obtain network topology, and to generate failures in a geographical region, we consider a bounded set $\mathbf{G} \subset \mathbb{R}^2$ representing the geographical region of interest. In this paper, we consider a bounded region $\mathbf{G}$ of 3240 km × 3240 km representing India and the neighboring regions. The region lying outside the border of India is included in a set $_{\mathbf{n}}\mathbf{G}$ representing non-feasible regions for node placement. The objective is to obtain random network topology within the Indian terrestrial region $(\mathbf{G} \cap _{\mathbf{n}}\mathbf{G})$, and to generate spatially non-uniformly distributed earthquakes as per the seismic-risk. To obtain seismic-risk information, we consider the seismic hazard map of India [16] (shown in Fig. 2), which is classified in to four types of zones on the basis of maximum Modified Mercalli (MM) intensity of seismic shaking. In this work, to describe the proposed SFONT model and to validate the hypothesis, we consider the seismic hazard map of India. However, the proposed model is generic in the sense that it can be used to obtain failures and network topologies in any geographical region, given its seismic hazard map.

It can be observed from seismic hazard maps of various countries/continents [10,16] that seismicity does not change for small distances, and thus seismic-risk of a small local region can be considered as uniform throughout that region. We convert the geographical region $\mathbf{G}$ provided as an input into a grid-structure, as shown in Fig. 2, where the grid contains square shaped bounded regions of small area, which we refer as 'sectors'. The whole geographical region is subdivided into n number of sectors, where each sector of area $_{\mathbf{a}}|\mathbf{B}|$ represents a bounded region in $\mathbb{R}^2$, and the seismic risk (i.e., seismic zone type) does not change within a sector. We obtain the locations and density of earthquake epicenters in each $\mathbf{B}_i \in \mathbf{B}$ using the poisson point process (PPP) [17]. As per the definition of PPP $\mathbf{\Phi}$ of density λ, the number of points (q) in the bounded set $\mathbf{B} \subset \mathbb{R}^2$ has a poisson distribution with mean $_{\mathbf{a}}|\mathbf{B}|\lambda$, i.e.,

$$\mathbb{P}(\mathbf{\Phi}(\mathbf{B}) = q) = \exp\left(-_{\mathbf{a}}|\mathbf{B}|\lambda\right)\frac{(_{\mathbf{a}}|\mathbf{B}|\lambda)^q}{q!}, \tag{1}$$

where the density λ is given by

$$\lambda = \frac{\mathbb{E}[\Phi(\mathbf{B})]}{_{\mathbf{a}}|\mathbf{B}|}. \tag{2}$$

In PPP, the number of points (epicenters) in a given bounded area is given by (1), and the location of points $(\mathbf{X})$ is uniformly distributed in each $\mathbf{B}_i \in \mathbf{B}$. Since earthquakes are more frequent in high seismic zones [10], we generate different number of earthquake epicenters using different values of density (λ^s), as given in Table 2. Large number of earthquake epicenters obtained in the given geographical region are shown in Fig. 3. It can be observed from Fig. 3 that the number of earthquakes per unit area decreases with seismic-risk in the order: Zone V $\rightarrow$ Zone IV $\rightarrow$ Zone III $\rightarrow$ Zone II [16].

Table 1. Notations

Symbol	Description
Φ	point process (PP)
$\mathbb{R}^1 = \mathbb{R}$	field of real number
$\mathbb{R}^n$	n-dimensional Euclidean space
$\mathbb{N}$	set of natural numbers
$\mathbb{E}$	expectation
$\mathbb{P}$	probability
$\mathbf{dist}(a, b)$	Euclidean distance between points a and b, where $a, b \in \mathbb{R}^2$
$\mathbf{G}$	a bounded set representing the geographical region of interest, $\mathbf{G} \subset \mathbb{R}^2$
$_\mathbf{n}\mathbf{G}$	set of bounded regions non-feasible for node placement, $_\mathbf{n}\mathbf{G} \subset \mathbb{R}^2$, $_\mathbf{n}\mathbf{G} \subset \mathbf{G}$, index g (here, $\mathbf{n}$ is prescript)
$\mathbf{B}$	a bounded set representing the geographical region of sectors, $\mathbf{B} \subset \mathbf{G}$, $\mathbf{B} \subset \mathbb{R}^2$, index i (i.e., $\mathbf{B}_i$ denotes the bounded region of ith sector)
$_\mathbf{a}|\mathbf{G}|, _\mathbf{a}|\mathbf{B}|$	area of bounded regions represented by set $\mathbf{G}, \mathbf{H}$, respectively (here, $\mathbf{a}$ is prescript)
l_G	length of the area of $\mathbf{G}$
b_G	breadth of the area of $\mathbf{G}$
a_i	length of the edge of sector $\mathbf{B}_i$
$\Phi(\mathbf{B})$	number of points of PP in a bounded set $\mathbf{B}$
S	set of types of seismic zones, index s
λ	density of poisson point process (PPP)
λ^s	density of poisson point process (PPP) for zone type s
λ_m	density of MHCPP
$_\mathbf{a}|\mathbf{G}|\lambda$	mean number of points of PP in a bounded region $\mathbf{G}$
r_h	hard core parameter of MHCPP
$\mathbf{X}$	set of points denoting epicenter coordinates, $\mathbf{X} \subset \mathbb{R}^2$, $\mathbf{X} \subset \mathbb{G}$
$\mathbf{V}$	set of points representing node locations in original topology, $\mathbf{V} \subset \mathbb{R}^2$, $\mathbf{V} \subset \mathbb{G}$
$\mathbf{V}'$	set of points representing locations of nodes in the SRA-OND topology
V	set of nodes, index v, $V \subset \mathbb{N}$
W	set of links, index w, $V \subset \mathbb{N}$
D	set of link lengths, index w, $V \subset \mathbb{N}$
D'	set of link lengths in the SRA-OND topology, index w, $V \subset \mathbb{N}$
K	set of sectors, index k, $K \subset \mathbb{N}$
K^s	sector of type s seismic zone
$K(v)$	set of sectors to be searched for shifting of vth node (V_v), $K(v) \subset K$, index p
$K(n)$	set of sectors non-feasible for node placement, $K(n) \subset K$
$K(r)_k$	set of sectors used to calculate SR_k, $K(r)_k \subset K$
SR_k	seismic-risk associated with sector K_k
Ω	set of weights assigned to each sector as per their seismic zone type, index k (more weight is assigned to higher seismic zones)
$\Omega(V)$	set of weights of sectors in which nodes are located, index v
n	number of sectors in the region $\mathbf{G}$, $n = |K|$
n_k^r	number of sectors on the either sides of sector K_k used to calculate SR_k of sector K_k
n_k^f	number of sectors on the either sides of sector K_k (having earthquake epicenter) where if a node is located, multi-link failure will occur
c_k	center of sector K_k
M	magnitude of earthquake (on moment magnitude scale)

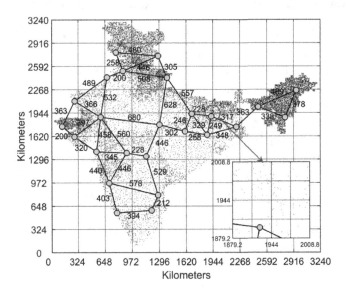

Fig. 3. Network topology and epicenters obtained using the proposed SFONT model. Link lengths are in km. (inset shows the epicenters obtained using PPP in different sectors).

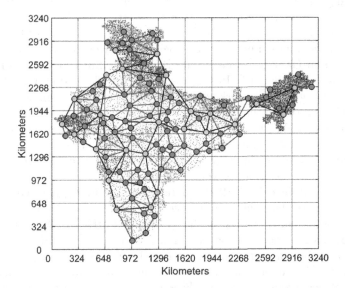

Fig. 4. Seismic risk unaware optical network densification (SRU-OND) of the network topology shown in Fig. 3. Here, the nodes of existing/initial network are represented by yellow color, and the new nodes (initially placed in the center of the desired region) to be deployed for network densification are shown in green color. (Color figure online)

Table 2. Values of parameters used to obtain earthquake epicenters in Figs. 2 and 3

Parameter	Value
Dimensions of bounded region $\mathbf{G}$, l_G, b_G	3240 km
Length of edge of sectors $\mathbf{H} \subset \mathbf{G}$, a_h	32.4 km
Set of types of seismic zones, S	$\{II, III, IV, V\}$
PPP density for K^V, λ^V	0.02
PPP density for K^{IV}, λ^{IV}	0.01
PPP density for K^{III}, λ^{III}	0.004
PPP density for K^{II}, λ^{II}	0.001
Range of M for K^V,	$[5, 10)$
Range of M for K^{IV},	$[5, 8)$
Range of M for K^{III},	$[5, 7)$
Range of M for K^{II},	$[5, 7)$
Hard core parameter, r_h	200 km

We consider significant earthquakes [10] ($M \geq 5$) for optical network resilience evaluation. To assign magnitude to the earthquake epicenters obtained in Fig. 3, we consider real statistics from the United States Geological Survey (USGS) [18], where the approximate percentage distribution of earthquakes of different range of magnitudes is: $(M \geq 8) = 0.0624\%$; $(7 \leq M < 8) = 0.8737\%$; $(6 \leq M < 7) = 8.3717\%$; and $(5 \leq M < 6) = 90.6922\%$. We denote the above ranges of magnitudes by M_{8+}, M_{7-8}, M_{6-7}, and M_{5-6}, respectively.

To design the physical network topology in the given geographical region, we generate random Gabriel graphs (GGs) [19,20], modified by Matérn hard core point process (MHCPP) [17]. In the literature [19,20], random GGs have been generated to design the network topologies, where a fixed number of nodes are located with uniform spatial distribution in a given geographical area. However, using uniform spatial distribution, it is possible that two or more nodes may get placed in the same location, which is impractical. Hence, we modify the GGs by MHCPP, that eliminates the impractical probability of two or more nodes being located at the same location, or very close to each other.

MHCPP is obtained from PPP, where points are first generated using PPP [17]. Then, some of the points are deleted such that no two points (nodes) with a separation less than r_h coexist in the constructed MHCPP. An instance of the proposed SFONT model is shown in Fig. 3, where $r_h = 200$ km, and $_a|\mathbf{G}|\lambda_m = 25$. It can be seen from Fig. 3 that there is at least a distance of r_h km amongst different nodes. The fiber-links amongst various node-pairs are considered to be of shortest physical route. To rigorously assess various network-resilience schemes for physical network design, logical topology design, protection, restoration, early warning data backup, survivable routing, etc., networks of different size and topology can be obtained by tuning different parameters, and evaluated for a large number of possible failures using the proposed SFONT model.

3   Proposed Seismic Risk Aware Optical Network Densification (SRA-OND) Scheme

The proposed SRA-OND scheme can be used to perform OND so as to make the future TCI robust against earthquake induced GCMFs. We assume that the desired region for each new node to be deployed is a square area of size 5×5 sectors. The randomly obtained node locations in the proposed SFONT model are assumed as the center of the desired regions for node deployment. Node shifting is then performed to calculate the seismic-risk (SR) for all the nodes to be placed within their desired regions. In the proposed SRA-OND, a bounded geographical region $\mathbf{G} \subset \mathbb{R}^2$ (square or rectangular) subdivided into sectors $\mathbf{B}$, and a network topology with locations of all the nodes, are provided as input. The current locations $\mathbf{V}$ of all the nodes are also provided as input. The proposed SRA-OND is described in the following steps as follows:

Step 1: The set of non-feasible sectors $K(n)$ is found, where all the sectors having a common region to that specified in $_n\mathbf{G}$, are included in the set $K(n)$.

Step 2: For each $V_v \in V$, node shifting is performed from the current (i.e., central) sector to all other sectors lying within the desired region (of size 5×5 sectors) for node deployment.

Step 3: The SR_k corresponding to each sector K_k is calculated. The SR_k for k^{th} sector is calculated using the seismic zone type of nearby n_k^r sectors, and the Euclidean distance of these sectors from the kth sector. We calculate SR_k using (3) as

$$SR_k = \sum \Omega_k \cdot \mathbf{dist}(c_k, c_l), \forall K_l \in K(r)_k, \tag{3}$$

where, c_l represents the center of sectors in $K(r)_k$.

Step 4: Amongst all the sectors in $K(v)$ for the node $V_v \in V$, the sector with minimum value of SR_k is chosen for node placement (provided a sector of lower seismic zone type is found in the desired region).

Step 5: The modified node locations $(\mathbf{V}')$, and link distances $(\mathbf{D}')$ are returned by the proposed SRA-OND scheme.

4   Performance Evaluation

In this section, resilience-evaluation of network topologies has been performed considering network densification in various stages. We consider four stages of network densification, namely, Stage 1 (S_1), Stage 2 (S_2), Stage 3 (S_3), and Stage 4 (S_4). At each stage, the number of nodes is gradually increased by varying the value of λ_m. We generate 100 instances of the proposed SFONT model for the parameter values given in Table 2, except r_h, which is considered as 180 km, 150 km, 120 km, and 100 km for S_1, S_2, S_3, and S_4, respectively. The decreasing values of r_h indicate the decrease in minimum link-length with increased network densification. The effect of generated earthquakes on various random network topologies is then calculated.

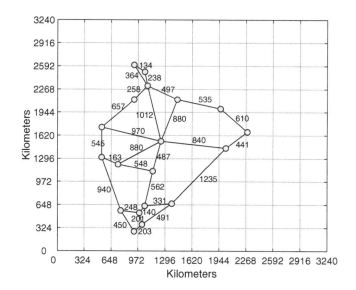

Fig. 5. 19-node RailTel network topology [11]. Link lengths are in km.

To compare the proposed SRA-OND, we study another scheme, namely, SRU-OND, where network densification is seismic-risk unaware (SRU). To realize SRU-OND, the nodes have been located in the central sector of the desired regions for each node to be deployed. To evaluate the proposed SRA-OND scheme under real-world network scenario, all the significant past earthquakes that occurred since the year 1900 in India [10] have been simulated. We use the Richter logarithmic scale to generate GCMFs based on the distance between epicenter and node [21]. Accordingly, we use the distance ratio $n_k^f : 3n_k^f : 6n_k^f : 10n_k^f$ to generate GCMFs due to various earthquakes of magnitude M_{5-6}, M_{6-7}, M_{7-8}, and M_{8+}, respectively. The average number of nodes corresponding to S_1, S_2, S_3, and S_4 are $_a|\mathbf{G}|\lambda_m = 40$, $_a|\mathbf{G}|\lambda_m = 60$, $_a|\mathbf{G}|\lambda_m = 80$, and $_a|\mathbf{G}|\lambda_m = 100$, which shows gradual network densification.

Figure 3 shows the initial network topology (which represents the existing network to be densified) obtained using the proposed SFONT model, and Fig. 4 shows the dense network obtained at S_4 by adding nodes in the initial topology shown in Fig. 3. The 19-node RailTel network topology is shown in Fig. 5, and the dense network at S_4 for the topology shown in Fig. 5 is shown in Fig. 6. The SRA-OND topology corresponding to Fig. 6 is shown in Fig. 7, where the nodes interconnected by blue solid lines represent the SRA-OND topology obtained by seismic-risk aware node shifting, whereas the initial randomly obtained nodes interconnected by black dashed lines represent the part of SRU-OND topology which has been modified in the SRA-OND topology. Here, the nodes which are either already located in the lowest seismic zone, or could not be relocated in a lower seismic zone within the desired region (of size 5×5 sectors) for that node

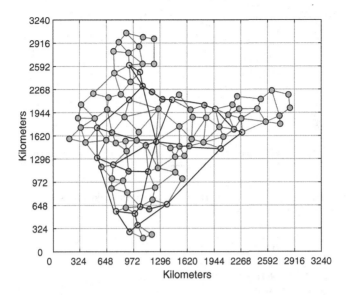

Fig. 6. Seismic risk unaware optical network densification (SRU-OND) of the 19-node RailTel network topology shown in Fig. 5. Here, the nodes of 19-node RailTel network are represented by yellow color, and the new nodes (initially placed in the center of the desired region) to be deployed for network densification are shown in green color. (Color figure online)

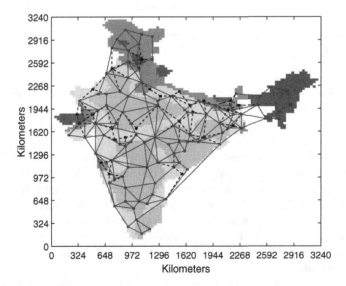

Fig. 7. Seismic risk aware optical network densification (SRA-OND) of the 19-node RailTel network topology (here, the location of new nodes are identified as the sector with minimum seismic risk (SR_k) within the desired region of node placement)

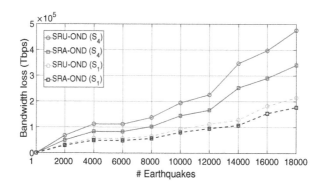

Fig. 8. Cumulative bandwidth loss (BL) due to earthquakes for SRU-OND and SRA-OND under the proposed SFONT model.

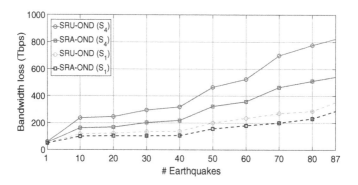

Fig. 9. Cumulative bandwidth loss (BL) due to past real earthquakes for SRU-OND and SRA-OND of 19-node RailTel network.

are kept at their original locations. Similar to Fig. 7, SRA-OND is performed for each of the 100 generated instances of the proposed SFONT model.

We perform routing, modulation, and spectrum allocation (RMSA) for each request in a set of 1000 randomly generated connection requests (in each topology) having heterogeneous bandwidth requirements uniformly selected from the set $\{40, 200, 500, 1000\}$ Gbps. We perform distance adaptive modulation, first-fit spectrum allocation, and k-shortest paths routing. After establishing all the requests, the spectrum state is frozen, and the effect of earthquakes is obtained (using $n_k^f = 1$) in terms of cumulative bandwidth loss (BL) in Tbps, and connection drop ratio (CDR). CDR is defined as the ratio of the number of connections dropped due to earthquake to the number of connections established before the earthquake arrival.

Figures 8, 9, 10 and 11 show the simulation results in terms of BL and CDR. In Fig. 8, BL due to a large number of earthquakes (18000) generated using the proposed SFONT model is shown. Simulations at the first (S_1) and the fourth (S_4) stage of network densification are shown to compare the proposed

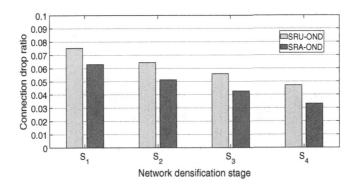

Fig. 10. Connection drop ratio (CDR) for SRU-OND and SRA-OND under the proposed SFONT model at different network densification stages.

SRA-OND with the SRU-OND. It can be observed from Fig. 8 that at both the S_1 and S_4 stages, significant reduction in BL due to earthquakes has been achieved. An average reduction of 14.3%, and 29.9% in BL at S_1, and S_4, respectively, has been achieved using the proposed SRA-OND, which demonstrates the advantage of seismic-risk aware physical network design. Besides, it is observed that with increased network densification, the improvement in BL using the proposed SRA-OND increases, which shows the long-term advantage of the proposed SRA-OND scheme.

Figure 9 shows the BL obtained due to the 87 past earthquakes occurred since the year 1900 in India at different locations. The initial topology considered in this case is the 19-node Indian RailTel network topology [11]. The earthquakes have been simulated randomly from the set of 87 earthquakes at each of the 100 iterations for every densification stage. Simulation results obtained in Fig. 9 show a similar trend with that obtained under the proposed SFONT model in Fig. 8. As the size of earthquake data set is smaller in Fig. 9, the amount of BL is also smaller as compared to that in Fig. 8. However, the average improvement in BL using the proposed SRA-OND is 17.1% and 38.2% at S_1 and S_4, respectively, which highlights the advantage of considering seismic-risk while densifying optical networks.

In Figs. 10 and 11, CDR has been evaluated at S_1, S_2, S_3, and S_4 after simulating all the earthquakes. In Fig. 10, CDR under the proposed SFONT model has been evaluated. It is observed from Fig. 10 that CDR decreases with increased network densification, since the percentage amount of traffic per unit node/link decreases with network densification (i.e., the number of connections dropped per unit node/link-failure decreases with network densification). It is also observed that at all the four stages, the proposed SRA-OND performs better than the SRU-OND. In Fig. 11, CDR for past real earthquakes in India for densification of 19-node RailTel network has been evaluated, where a similar trend of results has been observed as that obtained under the proposed SFONT model in Fig. 10.

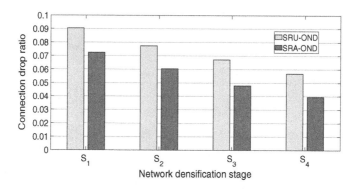

Fig. 11. Connection drop ratio (CDR) for SRU-OND and SRA-OND of the 19-node RailTel network at different network densification stages.

The similarity observed in the trend of results obtained under the proposed SFONT model and that obtained for the RailTel network densification and real past earthquakes show that the proposed SFONT model can be used to emulate earthquake failures and network topologies, given the seismic hazard map any region. Thus, the proposed SFONT model can be used to estimate the impact of various network-resilience schemes on optical networks for a large number of possible earthquakes.

5   Conclusion

We proposed an SFONT model using PPP, MHCPP, and GGs that can be used to comprehensively evaluate various network-resilience schemes for optical networks. Further, we proposed an SRA-OND scheme that can significantly reduce the BL due to earthquake induced GCMFs. The proposed SRA-OND scheme has been evaluated and compared with the SRU-OND scheme under the proposed SFONT model as well as for a real-world case from India. The similarity observed in the trend of results obtained under both the cases validates the capability of the proposed SFONT model to emulate real-world networks and failure scenarios. In future, we plan to design resilient DC interconnection network with a content-centric approach.

Acknowledgment. This publication is an outcome of the R&D work under the Visvesvaraya Ph.D. Scheme of the Ministry of Electronics & Information Technology (MeitY), Government of India (GoI), being implemented by Digital India Corporation. The authors would like to thank the Indian Institute of Technology (IIT) Indore for all the support and resources.

References

1. Tran, P., Saito, H.: Enhancing physical network robustness against earthquake disasters with additional links. J. Lightwave Technol. **34**(22), 5226–5238 (2016)

2. Velasco, L., Ruiz, M.: Provisioning, Recovery, and In-Operation Planning in Elastic Optical Networks. Wiley, Hoboken (2017)
3. Ciena webinar: Diving into the Data Center Interconnect (DCI) Seascape. https://mynetwork.ciena.com/webinar-diving-into-the-dci-seascape-tyou.html?aliId=54469151
4. Ciena webinar: 5G will need fiber and lots of it. http://www.ciena.com/insights/webinars/5G-Will-Need-Fiber-and-Lots-of-It.html
5. Bhushan, N., et al.: Network densification: the dominant theme for wireless evolution into 5G. IEEE Commun. Mag. **52**(2), 82–89 (2014)
6. Tran, P.N., Saito, H.: Geographical route design of physical networks using earthquake risk information. IEEE Commun. Mag. **54**(7), 131–137 (2016)
7. Msongaleli, D.L., Dikbiyik, F., Zukerman, M., Mukherjee, B.: Disaster-aware submarine fiber-optic cable deployment for mesh networks. J. Lightwave Technol. **34**(18), 4293–4303 (2016)
8. Saito, H.: Spatial design of physical network robust against earthquakes. J. Lightwave Technol. **33**(2), 443–458 (2015)
9. Cao, C., Zukerman, M., Wu, W., Manton, J.H., Moran, B.: Survivable topology design of submarine networks. J. Lightwave Technol. **31**(5), 715–730 (2013)
10. USGS Search Earthquake Catalog. https://earth-quake.usgs.gov/earthquakes/search
11. Pandya, R.J., Chandra, V., Chadha, D.: Simultaneous optimization of power economy and impairment awareness by traffic grooming, mixed regeneration, and all optical wavelength conversion with an experimental demonstration. J. Lightwave Technol. **32**(24), 4166–4177 (2014)
12. Bao, N.H., Tornatore, M., Martel, C.U., Mukherjee, B.: Fairness-aware degradation based multipath re-provisioning strategy for post-disaster telecom mesh networks. J. Opt. Commun. Netw. **8**(6), 441–450 (2016)
13. Agrawal, A., Vyas, U., Bhatia, V., Prakash, S.: SLA-aware differentiated QoS in elastic optical networks. Opt. Fiber Technol. **36**, 41–50 (2017)
14. Habib, M.F., Tornatore, M., De Leenheer, M., Dikbiyik, F., Mukherjee, B.: Design of disaster-resilient optical datacenter networks. J. Lightwave Technol. **30**(16), 2563–2573 (2012)
15. Agrawal, A., Sharma, P., Bhatia, V., Prakash, S.: Survivability enhancement of backbone optical networks leveraging seismic zone information. In: Proceedings of the IEEE Advanced Networks and Telecommunications Systems (ANTS), pp. 1–6 (2017)
16. Murty, C.V.R.: Where are the seismic zones in India? http://www.iitk.ac.in/nicee/EQTips/EQTip04.pdf
17. ElSawy, H., Hossain, E., Haenggi, M.: Stochastic geometry for modeling, analysis, and design of multi-tier and cognitive cellular wireless networks: a survey. IEEE Commun. Surv. Tut. **15**(3), 996–1019 (2013)
18. Earthquake Statistics, USGS. https://earthquake.us-gs.gov/earthquakes/browse/stats.php
19. Szcześniak, I., Gola, A., Jajszczyk, A., Pach, A.R., Woźna-Szcześniak, B.: Itinerant routing in elastic optical networks. J. Lightwave Technol. **35**(10), 1868–1875 (2017)
20. Cetinkaya, E.K., Alenazi, M.J., Cheng, Y., Peck, A.M., Sterbenz, J.P.: On the fitness of geographic graph generators for modelling physical level topologies. In: Proceedings of the Reliable Networks Design and Modeling (RNDM), Almaty, Kazakhstan, pp. 38–45 (2013)
21. Ammon, C.J.: Earthquake Size. http://eqseis.geosc.psu.edu/~cammon/HTML/Classes/IntroQuakes/Notes/earthquake_size.html

A Performance Analysis of Supervised Learning Classifiers for QoT Estimation in ROADM-Based Networks

Alan A. Díaz-Montiel$^{(\boxtimes)}$ and Marco Ruffini

Connect Centre, Trinity College Dublin, Dublin, Ireland
{adiazmon,marco.ruffini}@tcd.ie

Abstract. Machine learning techniques for optimization purposes in the optical domain have been reviewed extensively in recent years. While several studies are pointing in the right direction towards building enhanced transport network control systems including estimation algorithms, the physical effects encountered in the optical domain raise several challenges that are hard to learn from and mitigate. In this paper, we provide a performance analysis of various supervised learning algorithms when predicting the Quality of Transmission (QoT), in terms of signal to noise ratio (OSNR), of lightpaths when erbium doped fiber amplifier (EDFA) power excursions and fiber nonlinearities are taken into account. The analysis considers F1-scores and computational training times as the main comparison metrics. A customized optical data network simulator was used for the generation of synthetic labeled data samples. Our results depict similar performance among groups of classifiers, and a correlation between the data sample size and the prediction accuracy.

Keywords: Supervised learning · Transport networks

1 Introduction

Transport metro-access networks need fast and dynamic reconfiguration procedures to overcome the challenges imposed by 5G-service driven requirements [1]. While several advancements at the hardware level (e.g., higher capacity transceivers) are being achieved, the disaggregation between such components and their control systems remains a challenge [2]. With the emergence of the software-defined networking (SDN) paradigm a decade ago, multiple consolidated projects have tackled the openness and programmable features of optical network elements (i.e., switches) [3,4]. Due to the heterogeneous and complex nature of equipment at deployment sites today, the development of robust protocols and standards is ongoing but is a lengthy process. In the meantime, the community has been evaluating different control system strategies, which have resulted in a set of recommendations well documented in the ITU-T G.7702 [5]. More recently, the application of artificial intelligence (AI) for multiple use cases in the optical domain has been widely evaluated. The latter has been surveyed

© IFIP International Federation for Information Processing 2020
Published by Springer Nature Switzerland AG 2020
A. Tzanakaki et al. (Eds.): ONDM 2019, LNCS 11616, pp. 598–609, 2020.
https://doi.org/10.1007/978-3-030-38085-4_51

by Mata et al., in [6]. Particular attention is being paid to the utilization of estimation/classification algorithms that could predict the performance of signals traversing networks at various domains and configuration settings (e.g., heterogeneous equipment).

Commercial optical networks are today rather static, and their evolution towards a fully flexible and dynamic system will face control and management challenges. For instance, state-of-the-art wavelength division multiplexed (WDM) networks consider reconfigurable add/drop multiplexers (ROADMs), built up with colorless wavelength selective switches (WSS) and optical crossconnects (OXCs) as the de facto switching and routing networking elements, enhancing higher levels of flexibility. Additionally, in order to reach longer distances with fewer resources, the consideration of automatic gain controlled (AGC)-EDFA systems is the default approach. However optical reconfigurations are still carried out slowly (e.g., in terms of several minutes), mainly due to the effects of power excursions in gain-controlled optical amplifiers [7,8].

Hence, the development of tools capable of handling such impairments at low cost without compromising the current performance is of high interest. Thus, the inclusion of ML-based classification algorithms in the control system of optical networks has been a promising area of research in recent years. For instance, Morais and Pedro [9] reviewed the models of K-nearest neighbors (KNN), logistic regression (LR), support vector machines (SVM), and artificial neural networks (ANN), analysing their performance in terms of predicting the QoT of unestablished lighpaths using simulated data. Their results suggest that ANN outperforms the other models with 99.9% accuracy. On a different study [10], Mata et al., evaluated the models of SVM, LR, classification and regression trees (CART), bagging trees (TREEBAG) and random forests (RF), comparing them in terms of estimation performance and prediction time. In their results, SVM, RF and TREEBAG achieved an accuracy performance up to 99.9%, while keeping their prediction time low. While these studies suggest that the use cases associated with the optical domain may be successfully addressed with ML, we believe further research is required that considers extra physical layer phenomena in the training of the ML-models, including EDFA power excursions and non-linear physical impairments.

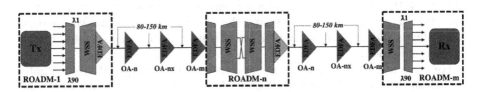

Fig. 1. Linear topology. Deployment may vary in different network settings as per features in Table 1.

In this study, we analyze the performance of various classification algorithms, when considering both topological features (e.g., number of nodes, fibre distance, amplifier span, etc.) and wavelength load [11] (e.g., the active wavelengths in the system before the new test channel is added). Indeed, as shown in [8], the wavelength load configuration is one of the main parameters affecting power excursions in EDFAs. With regard to the comparison of the ML models, two crucial metrics are considered: the accuracy at classifying different classes of traffic (based on OSNR levels), and the computational time required to train (build) the models, together with the size of the data samples. For the execution of the experiments, we used the Scikit-learn: Machine Learning in Python software [12], which provides powerful APIs for ML classification models. Then, for the data generation, we used the Optical-MAN simulator first introduced in [13], which allows for the creation of large scale optical networks deployed with WSS-based ROADMs and EDFA-amplified links, and the simultaneous transmission of 90 channels in the C-band spectrum (1529.6 nm–1565.2 nm).

The remainder of the paper is structured as follows. In Sect. 2, we introduce the system setup and the data generation process with our customized tools. Then, in Sect. 3 we briefly describe the classification algorithms used for the performance analysis. The experiments and results are discussed in Sect. 4. Finally, we present our conclusions in Sect. 5.

2   System Setup and Data Generation

2.1   System Setup

Experimentation procedures with ML-models typically require large data sets in order to achieve good performance when tackling complex systems. In the optical domain, common network-QoT metrics for supervised learning models are the OSNR and bit error rate (BER) of the transmission systems. Hence, in order to collect large amount of samples from a physical testbed, constant monitoring procedures are needed at least at one point of the network. Alas, the collection of physical layer data in the optical domain (e.g., signal power levels) is an expensive task, mainly due to the high costs and complexities of the monitoring equipment. In addition, the deployment of large-scale, topology-variable optical networks is an infeasible task for many of the academic laboratories today. Because of that, the exploration of optical networks via simulation tools has been used in several cases [9, 14–16]. Although these virtual environments enable the low cost, fast generation of physical layer optical data, the experimentation tools (ML-models) would always require further trial with *real* testbed data, which would account for their validation.

For the purposes of this study, we used the customized Optical-MAN simulator first introduced in [13], which allows to deploy WDM network topologies and collect synthetic labeled data to train ML models, as we recently presented in [11] for the analysis of support vector machines (SVM). Our tool simulates WDM networks considering: optical nodes consisting of ROADMs equipped with WSSs, optically-amplified AGC-EDFA links, and also AGC-EDFAs for pre-/post-signal amplification, together with fiber non-linear effects such as stimulated Raman scattering. An abstracted representation of a linear network topology composed of the network elements described is presented in Fig. 1. End-to-end transmission is enabled for up to 90 wavelength channels in the C-band (1529.6 nm–1565.2 nm). For the EDFAs in our system it is assumed gain flattening filtering (GFF) is used for gain equalization. While accounting for GFFs at line-amp sites covers for the smoothing of unequal signal intensities, a residual wavelength-dependent gain (WDG) still remains after the filtering due to imperfect equalization. The latter, may result in the detrimental performance of the transmitted signals. Parting from the models proposed by Junio and Kilper in [8], we take under consideration the power excursions, enabling the analysis of the effects these cause in the system, and how ML-models could learn from these.

For all the simulated network scenarios, we assume optical performance monitoring is implemented at the receiver end, which enables for the tracking of the signal performance in terms of signal power and noise. Then, as first introduced in [13], we compute the OSNR levels of all the individual signals being transmitted.

2.2 Data Generation

Our goal is to analyze the performance of multiple supervised learning classifiers at predicting the QoT of newly established lightpaths in a network with a given topology and wavelength load configuration.

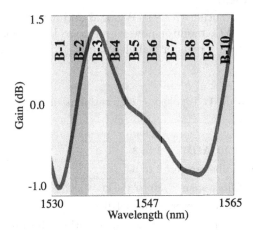

Fig. 2. Segmented spectrum of EDFA wavelength-dependent gain.

Our approach consists in extending the system parameters used to train the ML models, to not only consider network topological settings (i.e., number of nodes, number of links, etc.) as it is the common case, but to also include the number of active wavelength channels (WCs) and their position in the spectrum before installing a new WC. For the latter, we introduce the concept of a 1 × 10 data-array, which represents 10 segments of the transmission spectrum (i.e., the

C-band in our study). In a 90-WC WDM network, each slot (bin) of the 1×10 data-array would correspond to a number of active-WCs in the range 1–10. A graphic representation of this concept is depicted in Fig. 2.

We further exploit the capabilities of the classifiers by attempting to predict the performance of newly established WCs in a network considering WL-scenarios for which we do not train the ML models. That is, in a 90-WC WDM system, for the training data sets we only consider WL-scenarios for n active-WCs so that $\{n|n \in \{1, 5, 10, 15, 20, 25, 30, 35, 40, 45, 50, 55, 60, 65, 70\}\}$. Subsequently, we would register the labeled OSNR levels of the $(n + 1)$-WC to be installed. On the opposite, for the testing data set we consider WL-scenarios where n can take any value so that $\{n|n \in \{1-90\}\}$. Hence, the classifiers would attempt to predict the OSNR levels of the $(n + 1)$-WC, which it may have not been trained for before.

The input labeled data used to train our models consisted in: the wavelength (measure in nm) of the monitored WC, 5 topology configuration settings (depicted in Table 1), and the 1×10 segmented spectrum data-array described above, accounting for 16 parameters in total. The data generation process with the Optical-MAN simulator consist in the following steps:

(i) Set a linear WDM network topology and configuration settings by randomly selecting a combination of values from Table 1.
(ii) Randomly select n-WCs to add to the network as per WL case, and add them to the network.
(iii) Randomly select another $(n + 1)$-WC and add it to the network.
(iv) For the $(n + 1)$-WC, monitor power and noise levels, compute the OSNR levels, and generate a register (labeled sample).

Table 1. Topology configuration parameters.

Feature	Value
Number of ROADMs	2 to 8
Number of fiber spans	2 to 6
Length of fiber span	80 to 150 km
Launch channel power	−10 to 4 dBm
EDFA Preamp gain	Fiber compensation adjustment dB

Through this sequence of steps we can study the effects of the various topological and network configuration settings perceived on the transmitted signals. Also, because the deployed networks may be significantly different from one another, the generated data used to train the ML classifiers enable the performance analysis of such estimation tools in generic use cases. In our case, we attempt for the classifiers to learn about the physical effects resulting of the interaction of the WCs (i.e., power excursions) and the correlation that exists between the number of WCs active in the system, their position in the signal spectrum, and the transmission performance.

Furthermore, we were interested in studying the scalability performance of the ML classifiers. For this we used six sets of independent data samples of different size. In total, we generated 294,343 data samples, which we split as 22.7 K, 42.3 K, 45 K, 51 K, 57.7 K, 75.6 K, for the six sets, respectively. Also, we balanced the input data in order to mitigate misperformance of the classifiers.

3   Classification Algorithms and Optimization Techniques

This section describes the classification algorithms analyzed in this study. Only supervised learning-based algorithms were used for the development of this study. We have reviewed 11 algorithms, which we have split in two classes: normal and ensemble-based. The normal class is composed by K-Near Neighbors (K-NN), Linear-Support Vector Machine (L-SVM), Radial Basis Function SVM (RBF-SVM), Logistic Regression (LR), Decision Tree (DT), Artificial Neural Network (ANN), Naive Bayes (NB), and Linear Discriminant Analysis (LDA). The ensemble-based class is composed by Random Forest, Ada Boost, and Bagging. We have used the Scikit-learn: Machine Learning in Python API [12] for the development of the experiments. We briefly describe the main components of each algorithm and their functionality, for details of the models we redirect to the documentation.

3.1   Normal Classifiers

K-Near Neighbors. This algorithm attempts to classify values in multiple classes by clustering the data and comparing individual values to their K number of immediate neighbours.

Time complexity: $O(kn^2)$, for k nearest neighbors.

Linear-Support Vector Machine. This algorithm attempts to learn from the input data by categorising and building different classes (*hyperplanes*), which are subsequently used for future classification. It relies on regularization parameters C and gamma to avoid misclassification and correlation of individual points, respectively. It also transforms the problem with linear algebra - kernel functions.

Time complexity: $O(n_{features} n_{samples}^2)$, with linear kernel function.

Radial Basis Function SVM. Same as before.

Time complexity: $O(n_{features} n_{samples}^2)$, with radial basis kernel function.

Logistic Regression. This algorithm utilises a logistic function to build a model of dependent variables, more commonly used for binary scenarios. However, by applying optimization algorithms it is possible to use logistic regression for classifying multiple classes. Our implementation considers the Limited-memory BroydenFletcherGoldfarbShanno (L-BFGS) optimization algorithm.

Time complexity: $O(n^2)$, with L-BGFS.

Decision Tree. This algorithm consists in identifying relations between the input parameters and their output values building comparison points (tree branches), to subsequently perform as a binary tree.

Time complexity: $O(n_{features} n_{samples} log(n_{samples}))$.

Artificial Neural Network. This algorithm is based on a multilayer perceptron, which learns correlations between inputs and outputs and generates 'weights' for future inputs that are used for minimizing the error of classification.

Time complexity: $O(nmh^k oi)$, for n training samples, m features, h neurons per layer, k hidden layers, o output neurons, and i number of iterations.

Naive Bayes. This algorithm considers the assumption of conditional independence between the multiple features given the values of the various classes. Our implementation of this algorithm considered the likelihood of the sample features to be Gaussian.

Time complexity: $O(nK)$, for K number of classes.

Linear Discriminant Analysis. This algorithm operates by finding linear correlations of the input features.

Time complexity: $O(n_{features}^2 n_{samples})$.

3.2   Ensemble Classifiers

These types of classifiers are the result of the combination of various classifiers altogether. These can be understood as optimization techniques for algorithms that do not perform well for given use cases, such as overfitting the data or performing weakly due to the lack of data. For the purposes of this study, we reviewed the ensemble classifiers of random forests, boosting and bagging.

Random Forest. This ensemble learning method for classification consists in the combination of multiple decision trees at training time, and operates the classification of various classes by selecting the classification/prediction mode among the decision trees.

Ada Boost. This algorithm, adaptive boosting (AdaBoost), operates by combining multiple "weak" classifiers in order to create a much stronger/accurate tool.

Bagging. This algorithm, bootstrap aggregation (bagging), operates by bootstrapping (random sampling with replacement) multiple models in parallel, and come up with hypothesis of more accurate classifications, making a decision based on the most accurate hypothesis.

4 Experiments and Results

In order to speed up the execution time, our experiments were run in a Linux x86_64 server with 10 Intel(R) Xeon(R) CPU E5-2699 v4 @ 2.20 GHz processors. We used the Scikit-learn: Machine Learning in Python software [12] because it allows for a simplistic and variable implementation of the various classification algorithms. For instance, it enables the declaration of multiple parameters for training the models. Additionally, it enables a dynamic search of the best possible parameters to train specific models for given use cases with the *GridSearchCV* function. Thus, after a wide search of such parameters for our use case, we found those that enhanced a mean tolerable prediction accuracy among the various classifiers, which are depicted in Table 2.

The visual representation of the results of the normal classifiers are depicted in Fig. 3(a) and (b), showing the training computational time and the F1-score against the multiple sample sizes, respectively. We can demonstrate the trade-off between high classification accuracy and high training computational time, which is a well-known feature among these type of classifiers.

However, the novelty of this analysis focuses on the ability for these statistical tools to learn from our selected optical domain features (i.e., active wavelength load) and the topological configurations (i.e., number of nodes and fiber spans) together. Taken these under consideration, the comparison shows that some algorithms perform better than the others, in some cases achieving up to 90% score. While in the literature we can find similar work achieving higher prediction accuracy [9,15,16], our analysis considers EDFA power excursions and nonlinearities (SRS) that introduce power dynamics that are harder to predict. Thus, we believe the results can be further improved in the future by better depicting the physical layer parameters for training the algorithms.

Table 2. Parameters used for training the algorithms.

Algorithm	Model parameters
K-Nearest Neighbours	K:1
Linear SVM	kernel:linear, gamma:100, C:0.0001
RBF SVM	kernel:rbf, gamma:100, C:0.0001
Logistic Regression	solver:lbfgs, multiclass:multinomial, random_state:1
Decision Tree	max depth:5
Artificial Neural Network	alpha:1, max iter:10000
Naive Bayes	default
Random Forest	max depth:5, estimators no.:10, max features:1
AdaBoost	estimators no.:10
Bagging	estimators no.:100, max samples:0.8, max features:0.8

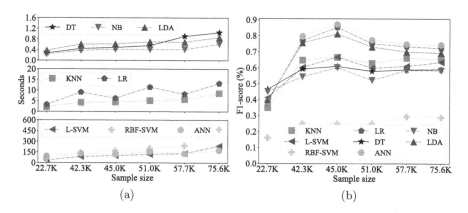

Fig. 3. (a) Training time of each classifier. (b) F1-score of each classifier.

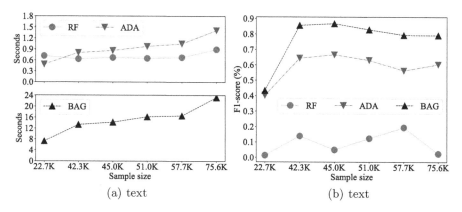

Fig. 4. (a) Training time of each ensemble classifier. (b) F1-score of each ensemble classifier.

In addition, there are two main patterns we can identify in Fig. 3(a). *(i)* Contrary to an expected passive incremental accuracy performance as the volume of the sample size increases, our results show a decreased performance in the classifiers that can achieve the highest accuracy after 45,000 samples, and an increased/convergent performance in the classifiers that achieve a higher accuracy up to 70%. *(ii)* In the figure, we can also perceive a group-like behaviour among some of the classifiers. Neglecting the RBF-SVM model (due to its deficient performance), we can see two groups, one consisting of the classifiers KNN, L-SVM, DT and NB; and the second with LR, ANN and LDA. While the F1-score achieved by the former does not go higher than 70% in our experiments, the latter group show an F1-score performance of almost 90%. By our last sample data (75.6K), all of the classifiers seem to begin convergence. Intrinsically, each of these are mathematically-defined in different forms, however, we require further exploration that could justify a correlation with the manipulation of the

Table 3. Results of the F1-score and training computation time for each classifier against the sample sizes.

[a]SS	KNN		L-SVM		RBF-SVM		LR	
	F1-S (%)	TT	F1-S (%)	TT	F1-S (%)	TT	F1-S (%)	TT
22,723	0.34	2.09 s	0.41	36.03 s	0.16	56.05 s	0.38	3.24 s
42,320	0.64	4.24 s	0.6	1.44 m	0.25	2.32 m	0.76	9.1 s
44,952	0.66	4.45 s	0.66	1.66 m	0.25	2.82 m	0.85	6.31 s
50,984	0.62	5.14 s	0.59	1.96 m	0.25	3.33 m	0.75	11.49 s
57,740	0.66	5.72 s	0.61	2.20 m	0.29	3.99 m	0.73	8.26 s
75,624	0.65	8.6 s	0.63	3.95 m	0.29	7.87 m	0.72	13.27 s

[a]SS	DT		ANN		NB		LDA	
	F1-S (%)	TT	F1-S (%)	TT	F1-S (%)	TT	F1-S (%)	TT
22,723	0.46	0.27 s	0.39	1.55 m	0.45	0.23 s	0.39	0.37 s
42,320	0.59	0.44 s	0.79	2.17 m	0.54	0.37 s	0.75	0.60 s
44,952	0.6	0.48 s	0.87	1.97 m	0.6	0.42 s	0.81	0.61 s
50,984	0.57	0.55 s	0.77	2.62 m	0.52	0.40 s	0.73	0.69 s
57,740	0.58	0.90 s	0.74	2.16 m	0.58	0.41 s	0.7	0.69 s
75,624	0.59	1.04 s	0.74	2.92 m	0.58	0.61 s	0.69	0.86 s

[a] Note: SS: sample size; F1-S: F1-score; TT: training time.

input data to each of them and their performance when attempting to predict unestablished lightpaths as in our use case.

The visual representation of the results of the ensemble classifiers are depicted in Fig. 4(a) and (b). As for the normal classifiers, we can also see a trade-off between training computational time and the classification performance. While the results from the AdaBoost and the Bagging models were expected, the low performance of the Random Forest algorithm was not such. However, these results claim to be implementation-dependent, and due to the (*almost*) reasonable performance of the Decision Tree classifier in the previous analysis, we would further explore the implementation of Random Forest.

We have summarized these results in Table 3. In general, the common trade-off between training computational time and accuracy performance suggests that these algorithms may be suitable for enhancing the speed of metro-access transport networks. Further research is required in the categorization of the physical layer features, so that we could build models performing with higher accuracy. In addition, more complex techniques such as deep-/reinforcement-/transfer-learning, seem promising candidates to tackle the weaknesses of the algorithms presented in this study.

5   Conclusions

In this paper, we have introduced a performance analysis of classification algorithms to address the prediction of OSNR levels of newly established lightpaths in optical networks with different configuration settings and dimensions. Our results suggest that the implementation of such algorithms to complement the decision-making processes of control systems is promising, but requires further analysis of the physical layer features in the optical domain.

Furthermore, we have found an interesting behavioural correlation between some of the classifiers that we will further explore in the future. Also, while in our implementation none of the classifiers achieved a F1-score performance above 90%, we believe that through finer tuning and with the implementation of more complex techniques, such as deep-/reinforcement-/transfer-learning, we could achieve better performance and find a better suitability for the metro-access transport networks scenario.

Acknowledgements. Financial support from Science Foundation Ireland (SFI) 15/US-C2C/I3132 and 13/RC/2077 (CONNECT) are gratefully acknowledged.

References

1. Ruffini, M.: Multidimensional convergence in future 5G networks. J Lightwave Technol. **35**(3), 535–549 (2017). https://doi.org/10.1109/JLT.2016.2617896
2. Ruffini, M., Slyne, F.: Moving the network to the cloud: the cloud central office revolution and its implications for the optical layer. J. Lightwave Technol., 1 (2019). https://doi.org/10.1109/JLT.2019.2891990
3. OpenROADM Project. http://www.openroadm.org/
4. Telecom Infra Project. https://telecominfraproject.com/
5. Recommendation ITU-T G.7702. http://handle.itu.int/11.1002/1000/13540
6. Mata, J., et al.: Artificial intelligence (AI) methods in optical networks: a comprehensive survey. Opt. Switch. Netw. **28**, 43–57 (2018). https://doi.org/10.1016/j.osn.2017.12.006. http://www.sciencedirect.com/science/article/pii/S15734277173 0231X
7. Li, Y., et al.: tSDX: enabling impairment-aware all-optical inter-domain exchange. J. Lightwave Technol. **36**(1), 142–154 (2018)
8. Junio, J., Kilper, D.C., Chan, V.W.S.: Channel power excursions from single-step channel provisioning. J. Opt. Commun. Netw. **4**(9), A1–A7 (2012). https://doi.org/10.1364/JOCN.4.0000A1. http://jocn.osa.org/abstract.cfm?URI=jocn-4-9-A1
9. Morais, R.M., Pedro, J.: Machine learning models for estimating quality of transmission in DWDM networks. IEEE/OSA J. Opt. Commun. Netw. **10**(10), D84–D99 (2018). https://doi.org/10.1364/JOCN.10.000D84
10. Mata, J., et al.: Supervised machine learning techniques for quality of transmission assessment in optical networks. In: 2018 20th International Conference on Transparent Optical Networks (ICTON), pp. 1–4, July 2018. https://doi.org/10.1109/ICTON.2018.8473819
11. Díaz-Montiel, A.A., Aladin, S., Tremblay, C., Ruffini, M.: Active wavelength load as a feature for QoT estimation based on support vector machine. In: 2019 IEEE International Conference on Communications (ICC), May 2019, Accepted
12. Pedregosa, F., et al.: Scikit-learn: machine learning in Python. J. Mach. Learn. Res. **12**, 2825–2830 (2011)

13. Díaz-Montiel, A.A., Yu, J., Mo, W., Li, Y., Kilper, D.C., Ruffini, M.: Performance analysis of QoT estimator in SDN-controlled ROADM networks. In: 2018 International Conference on Optical Network Design and Modeling (ONDM), pp. 142–147, May 2018. https://doi.org/10.23919/ONDM.2018.8396121
14. Sartzetakis, I., Christodoulopoulos, K., Varvarigos, E.: Formulating QoT estimation with machine learning. In: 2018 European Conference on Optical Communication (ECOC), pp. 1–3, September 2018. https://doi.org/10.1109/ECOC.2018.8535429
15. Tremblay, C., Aladin, S.: Machine learning techniques for estimating the quality of transmission of lightpaths. In: 2018 IEEE Photonics Society Summer Topical Meeting Series (SUM), pp. 237–238, July 2018. https://doi.org/10.1109/PHOSST.2018.8456791
16. Barletta, L., Giusti, A., Rottondi, C., Tornatore, M.: QoT estimation for unestablished lighpaths using machine learning. In: 2017 Optical Fiber Communications Conference and Exhibition (OFC), pp. 1–3, March 2017

Programmable Flex-E and X-Ethernet Networks for Traffic Isolation in Multi-tenant Environments

Kostas Katsalis[1](✉) and Rixin Li[2](✉)

[1] Huawei Technologies, Munich, Germany
kostas.katsalis@huawei.com
[2] Huawei Technologies, Chengdu, China
lirixin@huawei.com

Abstract. In this work we investigate the coupling of Flex-E and X-Ethernet technologies as a means to realize interface slicing and fast switching respectively. Flex-E is investigated as a key technology that is able to split a physical interface into isolated sub-channels, decouple MAC rate from PHY rate and achieve *hard* bandwidth isolation. X-Ethernet technology introduces Ethernet PCS switching, eliminates table lookup and buffer queuing and will be investigated as a fast switching mechanism that is exploiting the PCS layer relay. We present evaluation results from implementation activities that showcase the ability of an integrated Flex-E/X-Ethernet solution to enable network slicing features in transport networks. Furthermore we present a technical approach on the way the control plane of Flex-E/X-Ethernet network can be integrated with an orchestration and management solution.

Keywords: Flex-Ethernet · X-Ethernet · Network Slicing · Service differentiation · Throughput guarantees

1 Introduction

In order to couple with the strain raised and satisfy the strict requirements of 5G systems, significant changes have been undergoing in transport networking. Under the umbrella of 3GPP-based mobile cellular networks, transport networks support connectivity services between the various Disaggregated Radio Access Networks (DA-RAN) network components (3GPP TR38.816, TR38.801).

With respect to the terminology used by 3GPP (3GPP TR23.799, TR38.803) as transport network we consider the Fronthaul (FH), Midhaul (MH) and Backhaul (BH) type of communication networks that are used to interconnect Network Functions (NFs). Note that NFs can be either Physical (PNFs) or Virtual Network Functions (VNFs). In the case where the DA-RAN paradigm is adopted, NFs reside in the Radio Unit (RU), Centralized Unit (CU), Distributed Unit (DU) and in the Core Network (CN) [1]. Furthermore, in 3GPP TS23.501 where

© IFIP International Federation for Information Processing 2020
Published by Springer Nature Switzerland AG 2020
A. Tzanakaki et al. (Eds.): ONDM 2019, LNCS 11616, pp. 610–622, 2020.
https://doi.org/10.1007/978-3-030-38085-4_52

the 5G Architecture is described, future network designs also consider network operations in the light of Network Slicing [8].

In this paper we investigate Flex-E and X-Ethernet technologies as a means to realize transport network slicing with the support of fast switching. Flex-E will be investigated as a key technology that is able to split a physical interface into isolated sub-channels, decouple MAC rate from PHY rate and achieve "hard" bandwidth isolation. X-Ethernet technology introduces Ethernet PCS switching, eliminates table lookup and buffer queuing and will be investigated as a fast switching mechanism that is exploiting PCS layer relay.

Traditional deployments where relying on fiber technologies and PDH T1/E1 connections, ATM, SONET/SDH, like also MPLS to support transport network connectivity services. However, the last decade we witness a spiraling adoption of Ethernet technology as a means to implement transport networking for the mobile network. A flat Ethernet solution simplifies provisioning and planning, while also helps to radically reduce OPEX. Solutions like Ethernet over MPLS, Ethernet over SONET/SDH, Packet over SONET (PoS), Ethernet over DWDM Ethernet over OTN and so on, are inexorably driving the Ethernet technology as the de facto standard to support mobile network connectivity. Open Internet working Forum (OIF), a global industry forum for advanced inter-operable optical networking solutions, devised Flex-E in OIF-FLEXE-01.0 – Flex Ethernet Implementation Agreement (IA). The key features of Flex-E are the ability to create larger links out of multiple slower links, multiplex lower speed traffic from different clients in higher speed links, while also utilize a specific portion of some PHY link. As we will analyze in the following Flex-E can serve as an ideal technology to realize the concept of Network Slicing in transport networks and offer guaranteed performance and services per tenant even in scenarios of extreme flow multiplexing.

The main contributions of this paper are the following:

- We present the primitives of operation of Flex-E and X-Ethernet technologies as key enabling technologies towards slicing the transport network.
- We present evaluation results from real testbed experimentation. As we will analyze Flex-E is able to provide strict throughput guarantees, while X-Ethernet is able to bring switching time cost up to level of few nanoseconds.
- Our demonstrator considers the case of channelization where several lower-speed links are created for different ethernet clients.
- We provide insight information on the way a SDN solution could be incorporated in an integrated platform and how an overall orchestration and management solution could be designed.

This paper is organized as follows. In Sect. 2 we present the related work. In Sect. 3, we present the primitives of operation of Flex-E and X-Ethernet technologies. In Sect. 4, we present evaluation results. In Sect. 5 we elaborate on the way programmability can be enabled in Flex-E, X-Ethernet networks and the way they can be integrated with orchestration and management systems. We conclude our study and present future research directions in Sect. 6.

2   Related Work

Flex-E enables Ethernet-based services to be mapped over a next-generation optical transport network with the most efficient utilization of capacity possible. It was originally conceived to meet the challenges of Internet Content Providers (ICPs) for higher capacities and dynamicity, and as a new mechanism for the data center interconnect (DCI). It was originally proposed by OIF in Interoperability Agreement (IA) OIF-FLEXE-01.0 on March 2016. A detailed description of the technology can be found by OIF in IA OIF-FLEXE-02.0 (2018), IA OIF-FLEXE-01.1 (2017), IA OIF-FLEXE-01.0 (2016) and [7]. The forthcoming Flex-E 2.1 project is about prototyping Flex-E over 50 Gbps PHY applications and extending the recently released Flex-E 2.0. Flex-E 2.1 will further specify a new Flex-E frame and multiplexing format and address applications with lower bandwidth needs. Flex-E neighbor discovery is discussed in IA OIF-FLEXE-ND-01.0 (2018). Potential use cases were considered within other organizations such as the Ethernet Alliance and described by certain industrial players like Google in [3]. Proprietary deployments considering an integrated approach of the control and management plane of Flex-E over OTN were also contributed by Huawei [12]. Regarding Flex-E implementation landscape Huawei incorporates Flex-E in PTN990 router series, IXIA presented a demo in OFC 2016 with Altera/Intel, with Flex-E 2x100GbE and Ciena provides the Flex-E Liquid Spectrum solution. A 400 Gbps of Flex-E traffic was sent over four bonded 100 GbE interfaces on network demonstration in OFC 2018 by OIF and Ethernet Alliance.

In [11] a survey on backhaul network technologies is presented with an analysis on the relevant synchronization issues. A detailed analysis on the topic of transport network slicing is presented in [6]. Virtualization techniques for different types of optical networks and technologies where granularities may vary, according to the node and link characteristics. For example, in a wavelength switched network with optical cross connects (OXCs) and Reconfigurable Optical Add-Drop Multiplexing (ROADMs) virtualization approaches are different from networks with sub-wavelength granularity of switching and control [10]. In [5] hardware and spectrum resource virtualization techniques for the optical network are investigated. An adaptive transponder design is analyzed for WXC/WDM, while also multiflow transponder mechanisms for right-sized superchannels with the necessary number of subtransponders. Flex-O is described in ITU-T G.709.1/Y.1331.1 recommendation. Flex-O provides OTN interfaces with comparable functionality as to what was introduced in Flex-E for Ethernet interfaces. It provides an interoperable system interface for OTUCn transport signals; while it enables higher capacity ODUflex and OTUCn, by means of bonding m standard-rate interfaces (see ITU-T G.709.1/Y.1331).

3   Transport Network Slicing with Flex-E and X-Ethernet

3.1   Flex-E Basic Operation and Concepts

In principle, in the OSI stack in the Data Link Layer Logical Link Control (LLC) is performing multiplexing network protocols over the same Media Access

Control Sublayer (MAC), which is used for addressing and channel access control mechanisms. Reconciliation Sublayer (RS) processes PHY local/remote fault messages, while in the PHY Layer Physical Coding Sublayer (PCS) performs auto-negotiation and coding.

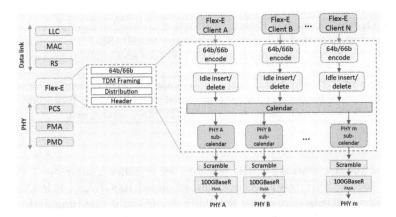

Fig. 1. Flex-E layer between Ethernet MAC and PCS (Physical Coding Sublayer). Additional FlexE Shim distribute/aggregate sub-layer in PCS/PMD

Flex-E technology is introduced as a thin layer, known as Flex-Shim, and being able to support data rates out of the conventional range offered by current Ethernet standards. In more detail, the Flex-E Shim layer (Fig. 1) is responsible for the mapping of Flex-E clients (Ethernet flows) to groups of PHYs. From a layering perspective Flex-E Shim is introduced between the Ethernet MAC and the PCS sublayers. The main idea behind Flex-E is to decouple the actual PHY layer speed from the MAC layer speed of a client. Flex-E is based on a time-division multiplexing mechanism that is able to drive the asynchronous Ethernet flows over a synchronous schedule over multiple PHY layers. The main operational components of Flex-E are depicted in Table 1.

Currently there are three operational scenarios supported by Flex-E, which describe different ways the MAC layer speed is related with the corresponding PHY speed, allowing a distinct manner for multiplexing clients in time:

- *Bonding*: allows a MAC layer speed higher than a single PHY by grouping multiple PHYs to serve a flow (e.g. support a 200G MAC over two bonded 100GBASE-R PHYs).
- *Sub-rating*: MAC layer speed is less than the actual PHY. Allows the MAC layer to use a portion of a PHY to serve a flow (e.g. support 50 Gbps MAC over a 100GBASE-R PHY).
- *Channelization*: enables multiple Flex-E clients over a shared single PHY or bounded PHY via the means of time division multiplexing in the Flex-Shim (e.g. support 150 Gbps and a 50 Gbps MAC over two bonded 100GBASE-R).

Table 1. Flex-E main operational components

Flex-E Client is an Ethernet flow based on a MAC data rate that may or may not correspond to any Ethernet PHY rate. The MAC rates currently supported are 10, 40, and m x 25 Gb/s. FlexE 2.0 augments FlexE 1.0 by providing support for FlexE Groups composed of m x 200 Gb/s Ehernet PHYs and m x 400 Gb/s Ethernet PHYs, and several other features.
Flex-E Group is a group of Ethernet PHYs that are bonded together. OIF supports Flex-E groups composed of one or more bonded 100GBASE-R PHYs. Higher rates like 400GbE are under development in IEEE P802.3bs and will be supported in future Flex-E releases.
Flex-E Shim is the layer that maps or de-maps the Flex-E clients over a Flex-E group. This procedure relies on a calendar-based slot scheduling. Essentially a set of slots are assigned to each client, according to the MAC layer speed.

Hybrids of these scenarios are also possible, for instance a sub-rate of a bonded PHY supporting 250 Gbps MAC over three bonded 100GBASE-R PHYs. These options allow increased resource flexibility for 5G and fine-tuning the offered rate depending on the usage.

3.2   X-Ethernet Technology

X-Ethernet is a Huawei proprietary technology, where X stands for extended distance, expanded granularity and extremely low latency. X-Ethernet introduces Ethernet PCS switching based on the interface offered by Flexible-Ethernet. The basic switching unit is FlexE Client. The switch device will redirect FlexE Clients (64B/66B block streams) from its inbound port to its outbound port without waiting for the arrival of the whole Ethernet frame for FCS checksum and forwarding decision with table lookup. Therefore, all the time consuming procedure, such as encapsulation/decapsulation, queuing and table lookup, can be removed. We give another name to the PCS switching that is PCS Non-Stop Switch (NSS). What's more, the remaining procedure processing time is predictable, which results in deterministic device latency. Idle insertion or deletion according to IEEE 802.3 may be performed to rate-adapt FlexE Client to the Flex Group. Details of the technology can be found in [9].

4   Performance Evaluation

4.1   Flex-E Testbed, Experiment Description and Evaluation Results

We demonstrate and evaluate Flex-E technology, while verifying the theoretical framework proposed by OIF. The system demonstrator under test, is depicted in Fig. 2 where for the implementation of the testbed two Huawei Optix PTN 990 are used. A software patch on VRP V100R008C10, supports the necessary Flex-E functionality. PTN devices are primarily used on bearer networks that carry various services, such as mobile communication and enterprise users' services. It transports packet services on the network and converges them to an IP/MPLS backbone network.

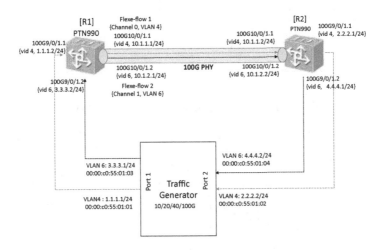

Fig. 2. Flex-E operational scenarios

In principle channelisation enables multiple Flex-E clients over a shared single PHY or bounded PHY via the means of time division multiplexing in the Flex-Shim (e.g. support 150G and a 50 MAC over two bonded 100GBASE-R PHYs). In this demonstrator one 100G link between the two routers is "splitted" using the Flex-E technology. The splitting is made by creating Flex-E channels. The Flex-E clients are identified using VLAN technology and each VLAN is mapped to a specific Flex-E channel.

Fig. 3. Flex-E allocated slots per channel (4 channels supported)

As presented in Fig. 3 for the demonstrator we allocate different time slots for two Flex-E channels, namely *Channel 0* and *Channel 2*. The mapping of channels in Flex-E flows is made on a VLAN basis where for the current implementation the lower two bits of the channel ID and VLAN ID correspond to each other (e.g., VLAN 4 maps to channel 0 and VLAN 5 to channel 1 and VLAN 6 in channel 2 and so on). In Fig. 3 a sample channel configuration is presented for

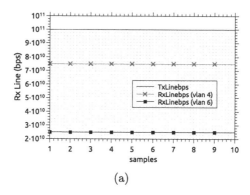

(a)

Fig. 4. Flex-E throughput guarantees per flow

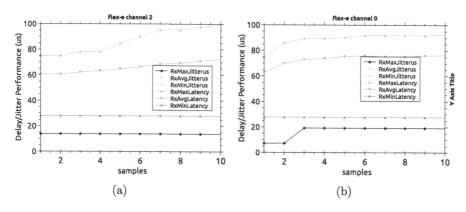

(a)   (b)

Fig. 5. (b) and (c) Delay and jitter results for two different Flex-E channels

router 1 (R1 prompt) while a similar configuration also exists for router 2. In the example depicted, slots 5 to 9 are allocated in channel 2, while all the other slots (1–4 and 6–20) are allocated in channel 0. With this allocation channel 0 receives $15/20 = 3/4$ capacity (translated to scheduling opportunities) from the 100G interface, channel 2 receives 1/4 from the link capacity, while channels 1 and 3 are blocked. Because of the specific flow mapping implementation, channel 0 will support not only VLAN 4 but also all VLAN-ids where the ending bits are 00 (like 0b000, which is VLAN 8) and so on. Different Flex-E client mapping mechanisms are under consideration and development.

To create multiple Ethernet flows with the necessary VLAN identification, traffic has been generated by using a Huawei 100GE traffic generator, which was controlled using Tesegine 2.0 V300R006C10B410 software. Using the Tesegine 2.0 traffic generator software, we were able to generate multiple concurrent flows with different configuration options of all the frames/packets fields (like src/dst MAC address, VLAN-id, src/dst IP address etc.). As a baseline experiment, we created two flows: Flow-1 (VLAN-id 4) that could be critical traffic and Flow-2

(VLAN-id 6) being the background traffic. The goal of the demonstrator was to showcase the ability of Flex-E channelisation to provide precise capacity shares between the two competing channels/flows. Channel statistics were obtained using interface counters that were updated to report per channel reports.

From all the experiments performed, perfect isolation was achieved; not only the capacity ratios were respected but also channels 1 and 3 that could block the traffic are not mapped to "open" Flex-E channels and thus had no effect on performance. Even though we only present here a representative subset of results, our conclusions apply to a wide range of experiments with the adjustment of different network parameters. In Figs. 4 and 5 we present the evaluation results of the experiment described above with two Flex-e channels serving to Ethernet flows that are identified using their VLAN-id. As we can see, the 100G link is precisely sliced exploiting time scheduling on the Flex-Calendar. Flex-E channel 0 throughput is 75 Gb/s on average while channel 2 throughput is 25 Gb/s on average (5 slots out of 25) Fig. 4. An important observation however is that although Flex-e technology is able to provide precise throughput guarantees per flow using very low level slicing, is not able to differentiate delay and jitter per channel for each Flex-E client. This phenomenon was however expected and is depicted in Fig. 5(a) and (b) where, as we can observe, both flows experience similar delay and jitter performance.

4.2 X-Ethernet Testbed, Experiment Description and Evaluation Results

A X-Ethernet testbed was used to carry demonstration activities, where for each X-Ethernet switch the solution is based on a FPGA board, six 100G CFP2 optical module slots, two 10G SFP+ optical module slots, one Ethernet interface slot. The FPGA board is mainly composed by one Virtex UltraScale chip, one ZYNQ chip, two DDR3 SDRAM chips, one DDR4 SODIMM, two Quad-SPI flashes and one Micro SD.

In the following, we provide experimentation results from the execution of three test scenarios that were carried out and showcase the ability of X-Ethernet technology to satisfy challenging switching requirements for a Flex-E network. Three X-Ethernet prototypes are connected to each other and formed a network. A controller (PC) configures each of the devices via the RS232 port on each device. A CPRI tester is used to generate CPRI option 7 traffic. A network performance tester is used to generate Ethernet traffic with 100 Gb/s maximum bit rate. CPRI is injected into the X-Ethernet node device 1 (XE1) and transport to XE2, then loop back to the CPRI tester. The Ethernet traffic pass through three XE devices one by one and loop back to the network performance tester. It should be noted that the connection between XE devices is though 100G links. Particularly, CPRI and Ethernet traffic share the same 100G link between XE No.1 and XE2. Moreover, the connection between Network performance tester and XE devices are also 100G link. Network performance tester generate an Ethernet traffic that has an effective data rate ranges from 0 to 100 Gb/s.

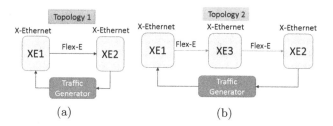

Fig. 6. X-Ethernet experiment topology.

Experiment T1: Setup the test environment as shown in Fig. 6(a). We configured end-to-end Ethernet traffic flow between XE nodes in two scenarios: Flex-E tunnel allocated 2 and 10 slots respectively. The TestCenter generated and send packets of length 128 bytes.

Experiment T2: Setup the test environment as shown in Fig. 6(b). We configured end-to-end Ethernet traffic flows between three XE nodes. The Test-Center generate and send packets of length 128 bytes. In both experiments we modified traffic packet length to 1518 bytes in sequence, and repeated the above operation, while the metric of interest is traffic latency. The experiment results are depicted in the following Fig. 7:

Slot number	Packet length	T1 (µs)	T2 (µs)	Delay of P nodes (µs)
2	128 byte	2.988	3.539	0.551
	1518 byte	4.309	4.903	0.594
10	128 byte	2.116	2.683	0.567
	1518 byte	2.59	3.156	0.566

Fig. 7. X-Ethernet experimentation results.

For the packet streams of different packet length at different rates, X-Ethernet exhibits its ultra-low latency forwarding capability at around 0.5 use. Compared to the classic router/switch performance (30 µs to 200 ms), X-Ethernet has a huge advantage in carrying latency sensitive services. Thanks to its L1.5 Non Stop Switching mechanism, all the time consuming procedures like table lookup, queuing, buffering, etc., are removed. What's more, due to its TDM like mechanism, it provides end-to-end hard isolation pipe, which guarantees a nanosecond level jitter in the transmission.

5   Enabling Programmability on Flex-E, X-Ethernet Networks an Integration with 5G-OS

Software Defined Networking (SDN) is a technology paradigm that drives innovation on the network segment but mainly inside the data center, it has just recently applied also in the wireless access but also in the transport network.

Although there is a proposal to adopt GMPLS as the Flex-E control plane, is not yet standardized [4]. To enable programmability on the Flex-E/X-Ethernet solution a NETCONF protocol-based solution with out-of-band signaling could be also adopted. In the case of NETCONF protocol, a NETCONF server should operate on the switching device to interpret messages send from a remote SDN controller implementing the NETCONF client. NETCONF is connected oriented using TCP while messages are encoded in XML and encrypted by SSH. An SDN controller like ODL or RYU could be used to implement this functionality and be directly connected to an orchestration and management solution like the 5G Operating System (5G-OS) proposed and designed in the context of the 5G-PICTURE project [2]. A 5G-OS instance can be used to manage services and slices on top of the infrastructure provided by multiple Infrastructure Provider(s). A 5G-OS is composed of different orchestration, management and control components that are tightly integrated to control the operational and business aspects of multiple technological and administrative domains. A simplified version of the 5G-OS integrated with a NETCONF based solution for the programmability of the X-Ethernet solution is depicted in Fig. 8. In 5G-OS a controller within a single domain is referred to as a Domain Controller (DC), similarly an orchestrator within a single domain is called a Domain Orchestrator (DO). An orchestrator that spans multiple DOsand is responsible for full service instantiation is called a Multi-Domain Orchestrator (MDO). Depending on the NETCONF approach with the appropriate YANG models RESTCONF API can also be exploited. RESTCONF is a REST like protocol running over HTTP for accessing data defined in YANG using datastores defined in NETCONF.

In both GMPLS and NETCONF cases, new data models need to be devised that expose the Flex-E information and functionalities to the control plane. Although the design of YANG models is possible over RSVP, new YANG models are expected to emerge for Flex-E. As in all control plane models, the design primitives for the Flex-E control plane are security, scalability and fast convergence. To on-board on 5G-OS a possible service descriptor should include:

- Flex-E Group provisioning, configuration and instantiation operations: Routers must advertise the type of Flex-E support that they offer, the current calendar allocation and information like link delay and node delay. Regarding capabilities exposure auto-negotiation procedures also need to be defined.
- Flex-E calendar scheduling: The control plane must be able to provide an efficient mechanism for the optimal assignment of PHYs to a specific group, while also consider for the optimal slot allocation in the group calendar for each Flex-E client.

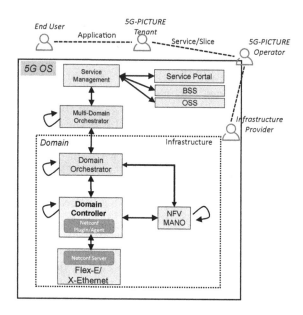

Fig. 8. NETCONF-based programmability of Flex-E/X-Ethernet switches

– Establishment of Flex-E multi-hop paths: Existing solutions consider a pre-configured Command-Line Interface (CLI) based Flex-E group configuration and client assignment. Note that the most important functionality in order to have a functional Flex-E setup is that for each PHY the mux and demux share the same sub-calendar. Otherwise, it would be impossible to decode the slot information to a specific Flex-E client. In a multi-hop setup this information sharing can be challenging.
– Dynamic calendar switching configurations: Control plane must support dynamic switching between calendar configurations (A or B) and allow modifying the configuration of Flex-E clients into calendar slots, based on SLAs and performance criteria.

Regarding X-Ethernet, note that it is a Huawei proprietary experimental solution and the focus in the current development phase is on the dataplane operations. No YANG models are currently available or under development. However, these are planned to be implemented the following period, exploiting NETCONF protocol and enabling integration with the 5G-OS. For an orchestration and management system like 5G-OS a possible X-Ethernet service descriptor should include: VLAN ID, Flex-E client bandwidth, Flex-E group ID, PHY ID, Flex-E calendar slot number, performance monitoring information, system-type. data mode, client signal type.

6   Conclusions and Future Work

In this work we investigated the coupling of Flex-E and X-Ethernet technologies as a means to realize interface slicing and fast switching respectively. Flex-E is a key technology that is able to split a physical interface into isolated sub-channels, decouple MAC rate from PHY rate and achieve "hard" bandwidth isolation. X-Ethernet technology introduces Ethernet PCS switching, eliminates table lookup and buffer queuing and will be investigated as a fast switching mechanism that is exploiting PCS layer relay. We presented evaluation results from implementation activities that showcase the ability of an integrated Flex-E/X-Ethernet solution to enable programmability and network slicing features for future transport networks. As Flex-E is a living standard, we are following all the recent amendments that we are willing to incorporate into our testing infrastructure. Furthermore, we are also investigating solutions where on the top of the end-to-end pipe that Flex-E is able to construct, virtual networks (like VLAN or enhanced VPN solutions based) can be constructed and operate depending on network slice requirements.

Acknowledgements. This work has received funding from the EU H2020 5G-PICTURE project under grant agreement no 762057.

References

1. Chang, C., et al.: Slice orchestration for multi-service disaggregated ultra-dense rans. IEEE Commun. Mag. **56**(8), 70–77 (2018)
2. Dräxler, S., et al.: 5G OS: control and orchestration of services on multi-domain heterogeneous 5G infrastructures. In: 2018 European Conference on Networks and Communications (EuCNC), pp. 1–9, June 2018
3. Hofmeister, T., Vusirikala, V., Koley, B.: How can flexibility on the line side best be exploited on the client side? In: Optical Fiber Communication Conference, p. W4G–4. Optical Society of America (2016)
4. Hussain, I., Valiveti, R., Wang, Q., Andersson, L., Chen, M., Zheng, H.: GMPLS routing and signaling framework for flexible ethernet (FlexE). draft-izh-camp-fiexe-fwk-05. IETF-Draft (2018)
5. Jinno, M., Takara, H., Yonenaga, K., Hirano, A.: Virtualization in optical networks from network level to hardware level. J. Opt. Commun. Netw. **5**(10), A46–A56 (2013)
6. Kaloxylos, A., Mannweiler, C., et al.: Network Slicing. 5G System Design: Architectural and Functional Considerations and Long Term Research, pp. 181–205. Wiley, Hoboken (2018)
7. Katsalis, K., Gatzikis, L., Samdanis, K.: Towards slicing for transport networks: the case of flex-ethernet in 5G. In: 2018 IEEE Conference on Standards for Communications and Networking (CSCN), pp. 1–7, October 2018
8. Katsalis, K., Nikaein, N., Schiller, E., Ksentini, A., Braun, T.: Network slices toward 5G communications: slicing the LTE network. IEEE Commun. Mag. **55**(8), 146–154 (2017)

9. Li, R., Wang, R., et al.: X-Ethemet: enabling integrated fronthaul/backhaul architecture in 5G networks. In: 2017 IEEE Conference on Standards for Communications and Networking (CSCN), pp. 121–125. IEEE (2017)
10. Nejabati, R., Escalona, E., Peng, S., Simeonidou, D.: Optical network virtualization. In: 15th International Conference on Optical Network Design and Modeling-ONDM 2011, pp. 1–5. IEEE (2011)
11. Tipmongkolsilp, O., Zaghloul, S., Jukan, A.: The evolution of cellular backhaul technologies: current issues and future trends. IEEE Commun. Surv. Tutor. **13**(1), 97–113 (2011)
12. Vilalta, R., et al.: Network slicing using dynamic flex ethernet over transport networks. In: ECOC, pp. 1–3, September 2017

Q-Learning Based Joint Allocation of Fronthaul and Radio Resources in Multiwavelength-Enabled C-RAN

Ahmed Mohammed Mikaeil$^{(\boxtimes)}$ (iD) and Weisheng Hu (iD)

State Key Laboratory of Advanced Optical Communication Systems and Networks, Shanghai Jiao Tong University, No. 800, Road Dongchuan, Shanghai 200240, China
ahmed_mikaeil@yahoo.co.uk, wshu@sjtu.edu.cn

Abstract. Multi-wavelengths passive optical networks (PONs) such as wavelength division multiplexing (WDM) and time wavelength division multiplexing (TWDM) PONs are outstanding solutions for providing a sufficient bandwidth for mobile front-haul to support C-RAN architecture in 5G mobile network. In this paper a joint allocation framework for multi-wavelength PONs mobile fronthaul and C-RAN air interface uplink resources is proposed. From the principle that uplink resource allocation in mobile networks (e.g. 4G and 5G) is an NP-hard optimization problem, this paper contributes with a novel method for uplink scheduling based on a reinforcement learning (RL) algorithm known as Q-Learning. The performance of the algorithm is evaluated with numerical simulations and compared with some other relevant work from the literature such as genetic algorithm (GA) and tabu search (TS). The simulation results show that the new algorithm achieves faster convergence, higher throughput, and minimum scheduling time compared to the two other algorithms. The results also show that RL-based dynamic allocation of front-haul transport block capacity based on actual radio resource block size can greatly reduce front-haul capacity requirement and minimize total end to end uplink scheduling latency.

Keywords: 5G · C-RAN · Mobile fronthaul · Reinforcement learning · Resource allocation · WDM-PON · TWDM-PON

1 Introduction

Cloud radio access network (C-RAN) is a leading technology for next generation mobile network 5G. In 5G C-RAN the traditional base station functions are split between three entities known as the central unit (CU) which contains a number of virtualized baseband units (vBBUs) pooled in a central location to facilitate signal processing, transmission scheduling and resource sharing, the remote radio units (RRUs) which are remotely deployed at the cell sites, and the distributed units (DUs) which can be independently deployed together with CUs or DUs [1]. The interface connecting between CU and DU is known as midhaul interface (also known as Fronthaul-II or F1 interface), and the

© IFIP International Federation for Information Processing 2020
Published by Springer Nature Switzerland AG 2020
A. Tzanakaki et al. (Eds.): ONDM 2019, LNCS 11616, pp. 623–634, 2020.
https://doi.org/10.1007/978-3-030-38085-4_53

interface connecting between RRU and DU is known as mobile fronthaul interface (also known as Fronthaul-I or Fx interface) [1].

Passive optical networks (PONs) are promising technologies for supporting front-haul and mid-haul interfaces in next generation mobile network (5G). For example, current commercial PONs such as XGS-PON and 10GEPON are capable of supporting mid-haul interface without any modification as the capacity and latency requirement for such an interface is similar to traditional backhaul network [2]. However, for front-haul interface some modifications regarding the latency and bandwidth efficiency are required because such an interface requires a high capacity and low latency transport network solution.

There are many proposals in literature that studied the latency and bandwidth efficiency issues of PON based mobile front-haul. The existing popular proposals are: 1 - Traffic estimation low-latency PON based mobile front-haul [3], which relies on predictive method to estimate the scheduling grants for the optical network units (ONUs) to minimize mobile front-haul scheduling latency. 2 - Mobile–DBA front-haul [4], which utilizes the mobile uplink scheduling information to compute the scheduling grants for the ONUs in order to eliminate the scheduling delay and the waiting time of ONUs . 3 - Mobile-PON proposal [5] which relies on PHY-2 split option to increase front-haul efficiency and unifies PON and LTE schedulers by dynamically or statically mapping of LTE radio resource blocks (RBs) into the PON front-haul transport blocks (TBs) to eliminate front-haul latency.

The major limitation of these proposals is that all of them consider single wavelength PONs mobile front-haul; whereas, due to the huge data-rate requirement for front-haul interface in 5G mobile network C-RAN architecture, single wavelength PONs are insufficient for supporting 5G C-RAN. Another limitation is that in Ref [5] the authors assume a fixed front-haul TB size to be allocated to every RB independent of actual RB capacity. However, in practical LTE network the actual capacity of the RB depends on many factors such as user equipment UE request size, channel quality status and modulation and coding (MCS) schemes used during uplink transmission [6]. A fixed TB allocation can decrease front-haul efficiency and increase front-haul uplink latency.

Our major contribution in this paper is that we extend the low-latency PONs based mobile front-haul proposal to the multi-wavelength domain (e.g. WDM and TWDM-PON) and try to overcome the latency and the bandwidth efficiency problems we mentioned earlier. To do that, we propose to jointly allocate C-RAN air interface resources and fronthaul uplink resources to the users at the granularity of LTE media access control (MAC) layer sub-frame cycle which known as transmission time interval (TTI) (i.e. one TTI equals 1 ms). We formulate the joint radio and fronthaul resource allocation framework as an optimization problem with the objective of finding an optimum or sub-optimum (RBs/TBs) to UE allocation pattern that minimizes total uplink scheduling latency (as well as fronthaul delay) and improves the total system throughput. Due to the complexity of such an optimization problem, because of the contiguity constraint on single-carrier frequency-division multiple access (SC-FDMA) uplink transmission, we introduce a reinforcement learning algorithm to solve the problem and evaluate its performance against some other heuristic approaches.

The rest of this paper is organized as follows. In Sect. 2, we present the system model for multi-wavelengths enabled C-RAN and formulate the uplink resource allocation optimization problem. In Sect. 3, we introduce a solution to our resource allocation optimization problem based on Q-leaning algorithm. In Sect. 4 we evaluate the performance of our solution, and in Sect. 5 we give the conclusion for our paper.

2 Introduction

2.1 Multi-wavelength Enabled C-RAN Architecture

The system model considers a C-RAN network consists of M RRUs; each RRU is attached to an optical network unit (ONU) (Fig. 1). The ONUs are aggregated over an optical splitter to a TWDM or WDM optical line terminal (OLT) which is connected directly to a DU unit. The DU and CU are co-located together at the central office and connected to each other via a mid-haul network (e.g., TDM-PON or Ethernet). The CU system is virtualized into M vBBUs. Each vBBU is assigned a fixed wavelength channel to connect to its associated RRU. Each vBBU has a bandwidth equal to N RBs, and total C-RAN system is designed to serve K active mobile users.

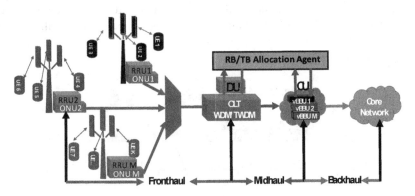

Fig. 1. Multi-wavelength-enabled C-RAN architecture.

We assume that a learning based software agent that coordinates between CU and DU/OLT (assuming a 5G system with dual split as in Fig. 1) is in charge of the scheduling process of uplink air interface and front-haul resources. During the uplink scheduling process, every UEs in the network sends scheduling requests to ONU/RRU. These requests contain UEs buffer status report (BSR) and channel quality indicator (CQI). The ONU/RRU transmits on single wavelength the UE requests to OLT which passes these requests to the CU unit at the C-RAN center. The scheduling agent at CU utilizes BSR and CQI information to compute the scheduling decision for the radio interface and fronthaul resources (i.e.RB/TBs allocation to UEs) every TTI period. The final scheduling decision in form of grant allocations is broadcasted over all wavelength channels of the fronthaul aggregation network to ONUs. Each ONU in the network receives these grant allocations; however, its MAC layer protocol permits only the processing of the allocation associated with the RRU that it is connected to. Finally, the RRU sends the scheduling allocation grants to UEs over the air interface.

2.2 Multi-wavelength Enabled C-RAN Architecture

In C-RAN system described above, we assume that the allocation of air interface resource block (RB) and fronthaul upstream transport block size (TB) to users is done in a slotted scheduling base, with a slot duration equal to one TTI. At each scheduling slot, the RB/TB can be allocated to a one user at most. In order to efficiently utilize RB/TB resources during uplink scheduling while achieving a minimum UE uplink delay in multi-wavelength mobile fronthaul network, we formulate an optimization problem with the objective to minimize the total sum of idle time over the all wavelengths and vBBUs in the network. Figure 2 illustrates the idle time and the UE requests processing time in different wavelength channels during a TTI duration cycle. In this figure A_{ij} denotes the elapsed time from the beginning until the end of the jth request processing on the ith wavelength channel of fronthaul network. $j: j \in \{1, 2, 3 \ldots, J\}$ denotes the index of the request with J as the total number of requests. $i:i \in \{1, 2, 3 \ldots, M\}$ denotes the index of the wavelength channel with M as the total number of the wavelength channels. B_{ij} denotes the off-scheduling time on the ith wavelength channel. λ_i denotes the ith wavelength channel $i \in \{1, 2, 3 \ldots, M\}$. Assuming the above notation and referring to Ref [7] flow-shop scheduling problem, the total sum of ide time as can be written as illustrated in Fig. 2.

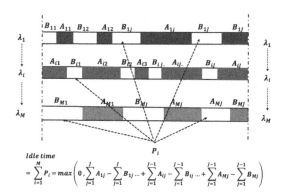

$$\text{Idle time} = \sum_{i=1}^{M} P_i = max\left(0, \sum_{j=1}^{J} A_{1j} - \sum_{j=1}^{J} B_{1j} \cdots + \sum_{j=1}^{i-1} A_{ij} - \sum_{j=1}^{i-1} B_{ij} \cdots + \sum_{j=1}^{i-1} A_{Mj} - \sum_{j=1}^{i-1} B_{Mj}\right)$$

Fig. 2. The of sum of idle time for the wavelengths.

In order to describe our problem define the following notations: $K (k = 1, 3 \ldots, K)$ as the number of active user, $M (i = 1, 3 \ldots M)$ as the number of wavelengths/vBBUs in the C-RAN system, $N (n = 1, 3, \ldots \ldots N)$ as the number of RBs in C-RAN network, P_i as the sum of idle time on wavelength i when assigning TB/RB n to UE requests k and $y_{i,k,n}, y_{i,k,n} \in (0, 1)$ as a selection variable that indicates whether the RB/TB n on wavelength i is allocated to UE k or not ($y_{i,k,n} == 1$ if TB_n is allocated to UE k and 0 otherwise). Given the above notations our optimization's objective function can be written as:

$$\underset{p}{\text{minimize}} \sum_{i=1}^{M} \sum_{k=1}^{K} \sum_{n=1}^{N} P_i * y_{i,k,n}$$

subject to the following five constraints:

$$\sum_{k=1}^{K} y_{i,k,n} \leq 1, \forall n \in \{1, 2 \ldots N\}, \forall i \in \{1, 2 \ldots M\} \qquad (1)$$

$$\sum_{i=1}^{M} \sum_{k=1}^{K} \sum_{n=1}^{N} y_{i,k,n} \leq M * N \qquad (2)$$

$$\sum_{i=1}^{M} \sum_{n=n'}^{N} y_{i,k,n} * B_{i,k,n} \leq B_{i,k,max}, \forall k \in K^* \qquad (3)$$

where $B_{i,k,n}$ is the rate (in bytes) that user k obtains if RB n' is assigned to it, and $B_{i,k,max}$ is the maximum number of bytes requested by user k. K^* is a set contains the UE who has the highest rate over the RB n'.

$$\{n'\} = \underset{n \in N^*}{argmax} \left(\sum_{K=1}^{K} \sum_{n=1}^{N} W_{k,n} y_{k,n} \right) \qquad (4)$$

where $W_{k,n} = \frac{\sum_{i=1}^{M} W_{i,k,n}}{M}$ is the matrix that defines the UE over vBBU gain which is calculated based on proportional fair (PF) metric (Note: proportional fair supports high resource utilization and maintains a good fairness among network flows [6]), $W_{i,k,n} = \frac{R_k(n,t)}{T_k(t)} \forall i$, is the proportional fair metric for the UE k over RB n on sub-frame or TTI index (t), $T_k(t)$ is long-term average throughput of user k computed over TTI index (t), $R_k(n, t) = log(1 + SNR_k(n, t))$ is the achievable rate of user k over RB n and at TTI index t, and N^* is a set contains groups of RBs that maximize total PF metric if they allocated to specific UEs (i.e. $k \in K^*$).

$$y_{i,k,n} - y_{i,k,(n+1)} + y_{i,k,m} \leq 1, m = n + 2, n + 3 \ldots, N \qquad (5)$$

The constraint in Eq. (1) is used to limit the allocation of each RB/TB to one user during a single TTI period to avoid the interference (Note: LTE does not allow the allocation of less than one RB to UE). The constraint in Eq. (2) is used to limit the total number of scheduled RBs over all wavelength not to exceed the total capacity of the system (i.e. system stability constraint). The constraint in Eq. (3) is used to avoid over-allocating of RBs/ TBs to the UEs (i.e. ensure that the agent will not assign transport blocks more what the users have requested). The constraint in Eq. (4) is used to ensure that each RB is allocated to the UE that maximizes the total C-RAN PF metric (i.e. ensure each RB is allocated to UE that achieves highest CQI index or SNR value over that specific RB). The constraint in Eq. (5) is SC-FDMA contiguity constraint which is used to ensure all of the allocated RBs to a single UE are adjacent to each other in frequency domain.

The optimization problem we describe above belongs to the class of NP-hard problems due to the constraint given in Eq. (5) (the proof of the NP-hard can be found in [8]). Therefore, classical optimization methods such as branch and bound methods can only be used to solve the small-scale scheduling problems, for large-scale and complex scheduling problem heuristic approaches or reinforcement learning can be used. Some heuristic approaches such as genetic algorithms [9] and Tabu search [10] have been already evaluated for uplink scheduling problem for disturbed RAN (D-C-RAN case). In this paper a reinforcement learning based solution is presented and its performance is compared with the above-mentioned heuristic methods under C-RAN architecture

3   RL for Resource Scheduling Problem in C-RAN

3.1   Reinforcement Learning (Q-Learning Algorithm)

The resource allocation optimization problem in C-RAN is a complex scheduling problem that fits RL context. reinforcement learning, mainly Q-Learning algorithm [11], has shown positive results in solving some resource allocation problems similar to our problem (e.g. [12], and [13]). QL is an iterative model that can be defined by sets of states, actions and a reward function that produce a reward for each state- action interaction. As shown in Fig. 3, at each iteration the learning agent (TB/RB assignment agent) observes the environment state $s_\tau \in S$, then; applies an action $a_\tau \in A$ to the environment according to the strategy π. The environment transits into a new state $s_{\tau+1} \in S$ producing a reward signal $rw_\tau \in R$ to the agent. The agent updates its strategy based on the new state and the received reward. The basic goal of the agent is to choose the best action for each state that maximizes the cumulative reward as

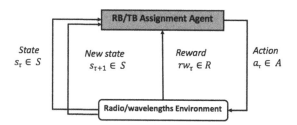

Fig. 3. Reinforcement learning elements

$$Q(s_\tau, a_\tau) := E\left(\sum_{\tau=0}^{\infty} (\gamma^\tau * rw_\tau(s_\tau, \pi_s)) | s_0 = s\right) \qquad (6)$$

where γ is a discount factor that reflects the significance of the upcoming reward relative to the current reward. When the selected action a is the optimal one $\pi^*(s)$, $Q(s_\tau, a_\tau)$ is the maximum of the state. The update formula is given as

$$Q_{\tau+1}(s_\tau, a_\tau) := (1 - \alpha)Q_\tau(s_\tau, a_\tau)$$
$$+ \alpha\left(rw_\tau(s_\tau, a_\tau) + \gamma \max_{a_{\tau+1}\in A} Q_\tau(s_{\tau+1}, a_{\tau+1})\right) \quad (7)$$

where $\alpha \in [0, 1]$ is the learning rate that balances new information against previous knowledge. The Q-learning algorithm does not determine how the actions can be chosen in each state. To determine that, this paper considers $\in$ − greedy policy, in this policy $\in$ is the exploration rate which is used to choose a random action $a_\tau \in A$ with a probability falling between 0 and 1 (i.e. $\in$: $0 < \in < 1$) this known as exploration, in contrast of choosing an action based on previous experience (i.e. selecting action with $1 - \in$ probability), which known as exploitation. The exploration rate decays over the course of the learning until it reaches the minimum value.

3.2 The Uplink Resource Allocation Scheduling Problem in Reinforcement Learning Context

To write the uplink resource scheduling problem we described earlier in reinforcement learning context we can define the states, actions and reward function as follow:

1. **State:** S: $\{s_1, s_2, s_3, \ldots\ldots\ldots, s_\tau\}$: as a combination of the total sum of idle time over the all wavelength channels w_τ and the total C-RAN system PF gain G_τ calculated the state transition (i.e. $s_\tau = (G_\tau, w_\tau)$). G_τ and w_τ can be written as:

$$G_\tau = \sum_{K=1}^{K}\sum_{n=1}^{N} W_{k,n,\tau} y_{k,n,\tau}, \quad (8)$$

and

$$w_\tau = \sum_{i=1}^{M} P_{i,\tau} \quad (9)$$

2. **Action:** A: $\{a_1, a_2, a_3, \ldots\ldots\ldots, a_\tau\}$: as the permutation of RBs allocation strategy to UEs, and the permutation of sequencing order of the allocated RBs over the wavelength channel TBs as well as the permutation of the wavelength channels order.
3. **Reward function:** R: $\left\{rw_{s_1,a_1}, rw_{s_2,a_2}, rw_3, \ldots, rw_{s_\tau,a_\tau}\right\}$ as a function that rewards the unity value if the action has taken by the agent increases the total system PF gain and decreases the total sum of idle time over the past episode, otherwise it rewards the value (-0.1), this function is written as follow

$$rw_{s_\tau,a_\tau} = \begin{cases} 1 & if \quad G_{\tau+1} > G_\tau \, and \, w_{\tau+1} < w_\tau \\ -0.1 & Othewise \end{cases} \quad (10)$$

The optimization objective is to find the optimal/suboptimal RB to UE allocation pattern that maximizes the system PF gain and RB/TB to wavelength scheduling strategy that gives a minimum sum of idle time over the wavelength channels of the fronthaul network. Later on, this allocation pattern and scheduling stagey will be used to update the allocation of RBs to UEs and TBs to ONU/RRUs every TTI scheduling cycle. The complete algorithm for the scheduling is summarized by Algorithm 1.

4 Performance Evaluation Results

We evaluate the performance of our uplink scheduling algorithm in NS-3 simulator [14]. Since NS-3 does not support C-RAN and BBU virtualization, we use eNodeBs to play the role of vBBUs in our simulations. In these simulations, we consider a C-RAN network with 4 RRU connected to over 4 WDM wavelength channels to 4 vBBUs resides in the cloud center. We assume different distances between each RRU/ONU and CU unit at the cloud center as follows: 5, 10, 15 and 20 km. We consider urban propagation environment, where UEs are uniformly distributed in the network, and experience different MCS indexes ranging between 2–28. We assume adaptive modulation schemes for the uplink transmission, in which the C-RAN system senses the UEs channel quality condition and accordingly chooses the modulation scheme and the quantization resolution to be used. In this paper, we adopt three modulation schemes namely; QPSK, 16-QAM and 64-QAM, each with different quantization resolution bits as follow, 8 bit with 64QAM, 6 bit with 16-QAM and 4 bit with QPSK. We consider a random walk mobility model with an average UE movement speed equal 3 km/h. For the traffic model, we assume a full buffer model with UE traffic load equal to 640 kbps. The overall system parameters used during the simulation are summarized in Table 1. For the Q-learning scheduling algorithms, we set the following parameters: $\alpha = 0.5$ and $\gamma = 0.5$. We use ϵ − greedy as action selection policy with $\epsilon = 0.90$ at the beginning and decays until became 0.010 when enough number of the episodes have been explored. The complete parameters and settings used for the scheduling algorithms are given in Table 2. We choose the total system throughput, total scheduling time, and the speed of convergence as performance evaluation metrics. To evaluate these metrics, we run multiple. Figure 4 shows the overall performance comparisons.

Figure 4(a) shows the achieved system throughput by each scheduling algorithm plotted versus the number of the active users during the simulation. From this figure, we can notice that the highest system throughput is achieved by RL algorithm followed by GA whereas TS algorithm achieves the lowest system throughput. We explain RL's superior performance by its ability to produce allocation patterns very close to the optimal as it does not require a long time to simulate the optimization solver as opposed to TS and GA algorithms (see Fig. 4(c)).

Figure 4(b) shows a comparison of the scheduling time consumed by each algorithm. As we can see, the RL algorithm also attains the lowest scheduling time compared to TS and GA algorithms. However, this time TS outperforms GA and achieves lower scheduling time. All of the three algorithms show a total scheduling time of less than 1 ms (TTI period) when the number of active users in the system was less than 150 UEs. However, the scheduling time of GA exceeded 1 ms when the number of users was 200 active UEs.

Algorithm 1

Input: *The initial UE to RB/TB allocation strategy (i.e. G_0, w_0)*
Output: *The optimal allocation strategy.*
Initialize $Q_{(s_0,a_0)} \leftarrow Q_{(s_0=(G_0,w_0),a_0=0)}$, $\tau = 0, \gamma, \alpha$
For *iteration $\leftarrow$ 1 to Max-Iterations* **do**
   Observe current state: $s_\tau \rightarrow (G_\tau, w_\tau)$
   Select an action : $a_\tau \leftarrow$ Select Action

  While $s_\tau \neg$ *terminal episode* **do**

   Perform the action a_τ: $(rw_{(s_\tau,a_\tau)}, s_{\tau+1}) \leftarrow$ Take Action(a_τ)
   Observe new state : $s_{\tau+1} \rightarrow (G_{\tau+1}, w_{\tau+1})$
   Observe reward: rw_{s_τ,a_τ} (Equation 10)
   Decay exploration rate $\varepsilon \leftarrow max (\varepsilon \cdot d, \varepsilon_{min})$
   Sample r ~from uniform distribution (0, 1)
   if $r \leq \varepsilon$ **then**
   Select an action randomly.
   else
   Select an action a_τ such that $a_\tau = argmax\ Q_\tau(s_\tau, a_{\tau+1})$.
                                   $a_{\tau+1}$
   end if
   Update the Q matrix using Equation 8.
   Update $\tau \leftarrow \tau +1$ and the current state $s_\tau \leftarrow s_{\tau+1}$
  End while
End for

Figure 4(c) shows a performance comparison of the three algorithms in term of the speed of convergence considering the objective function given in Eq. 1. As we can see RL algorithm achieves the fastest speed of convergence on the objective function compared to GA and TS algorithms. In other words, RL algorithm converges to the minimum sum of idle time in the first 50 iterations while GA algorithm converges in about 80 iterations and TS algorithm converges in about 60 iterations; however, the convergence of TS is slightly unstable compared to RL and GA.

Figure 4(d) compares the performance of the total uplink delay for static RB to TB mapping, dynamic RB to TB mapping [5] and our new adaptive-TB allocation method. From this figure we can see that our new adaptive-TB allocation method achieves the lowest total uplink scheduling delay in comparison with static and dynamic RB to TB mapping proposals. The reason behind the improved delay performance achieved by adaptive-TB allocation method is the efficient utilization of fronthaul uplink resources (see Fig. 5(a) and (b)). This is due to the fact that adaptive-TB method allocates an adaptive fronthaul TB size equal to the actual RB size calculated by the scheduling algorithm (RL) based on UEs traffic load and channel condition. This method can greatly reduce the capacity required on fronthaul as opposed to static and dynamic RB to TB mapping methods which assume fixed fronthaul TB size for every RB.

Table 1. Simulation parameters

Parameter	Value	Parameter	Value
Simulation length	1000TTI	Channel bandwidth	10 MHz
Link adaptation	QPSK, 16QAM, 64QAM	Number of RB (per TTI)	400 RB
Propagation model	COST 231	Maximum number of users	200
Mobility model	Random-walk	Number wavelength	4 (10 Gbps)
Transmission power	eNB: 30 dBm; UE: 23 dBm	Front-haul capacity per RB	Equal to RB size
TTI	1 ms	UE speed	3 km/h
eNB antenna model	Cosine antenna/3 sectors	eNB number of MIMO	(4×4)
Front-haul distance	5 km, 10 km, 15 km, 20 km	UE traffic model	Full buffer
Propagation environment	Urban	Load	640 kbps

Table 2. Algorithms Settings

Parameter	Value
Number of iteration	200
RL discount factor	0.5
RL learning rate	0.5
RL exploration rate	0.90
RL minimum exploration rate	0.010
RL exploration rate decay	0.99
GA parameters	Same as [9]

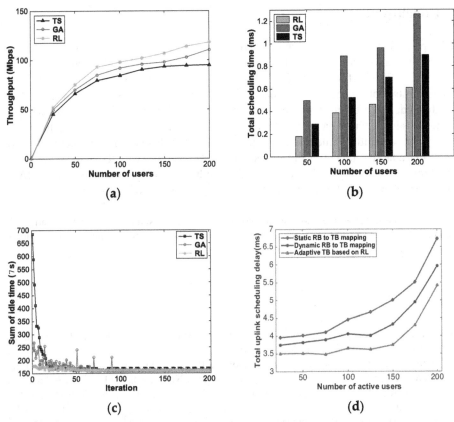

Fig. 4. Performance comparison: (a) The achieved throughput; (b) total scheduling time consumed by each algorithm (The convergence speed); (d) comparison of UE total uplink scheduling delay with static RB to TB mapping, dynamic RB to TB mapping and adaptive TB allocation methods.

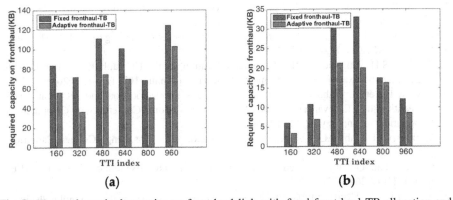

Fig. 5. The total required capacity on front-haul link with fixed front-haul TB allocation and adaptive front-haul TB allocation: (a) 50 active UEs, (b) 200 active UEs.

5 Conclusion

In this paper a reinforcement learning based scheduling algorithm is proposed to address the resource allocation optimization problem for multi-wavelength Enabled-C-RAN architecture. The performance of the algorithm is validated with simulation and compared with two other heuristic approaches. The simulation results have shown that RL based scheduling is the most promising approach, as it outperforms the two other heuristic methods in all performance evaluation metrics, offerings the highest system throughput, lowest scheduling time and total uplink scheduling latency. The results have also shown that adaptive allocation of fronthaul transport resources with RL based scheduling which rely on UE traffic load and actual radio condition can greatly enhance the C-RAN system performance in terms of uplink scheduling delay and fronthaul efficiency.

Acknowledgment. This work was supported by the National Natural Science Foundation of China (NSFC) (61431009, 61371082, and 61521062) and the National Science and Technology Project - China (2015ZX03001021).

References

1. Wey, J.S., Zhang, J.: Passive optical networks for 5G transport: technology and standards. J. Lightwave Technol. **37**, 2830–2837 (2018)
2. Mikaeil, A., et al.: Performance evaluation of XG-PON based mobile front-haul transport in cloud-RAN architecture. IEEE/OSA J. Opt. Commun. Networking **9**(11), 984–994 (2017)
3. Mikaeil, A., et al.: Traffic-estimation-based low-latency XGS-PON mobile front-haul for small-cell C-RAN based on an adaptive learning neural network. Appl. Sci. **8**(7), 1097 (2018)
4. Nomura, H., et al.: First demonstration of optical-mobile cooperation interface for mobile fronthaul with TDM-PON. IEICE Commun. Express **6**(6), 375–380 (2017)
5. Zhou, S., et al.: Low-latency high-efficiency mobile fronthaul with TDM-PON (mobile-PON). J. Opt. Commun. Netw. **10**(1), A20–A26 (2018)
6. Aditya Tiwari, S.S.: LONG TERM EVOLUTION (LTE) PROTOCOL Verification of MAC Scheduling algorithms in NetSim (2014)
7. Stefan, P.: Combined Use of Reinforcement Learning and Simulated Annealing: Algorithms and Applications. VDM Publishing, Saarbrücken (2009)
8. Lee, S.-B., et al.: Proportional fair frequency-domain packet scheduling for 3GPP LTE uplink. In: IEEE INFOCOM 2009. IEEE (2009)
9. da Mata, S.H., Guardieiro, P.R.: Resource allocation for the LTE uplink based on Genetic Algorithms in mixed traffic environments. Comput. Commun. **107**, 125–137 (2017)
10. Khdhir, R., et al.: Tabu approach for adaptive resource allocation and selection carrier aggregation in LTE-advanced network. In: IEEE International Conference on Computer and Information Technology (CIT). IEEE (2016)
11. Watkins, C., Hellaby, J.C.: Learning from Delayed Rewards. Diss. King's College, Cambridge (1989)
12. Gao, Z., et al.: Q-learning-based power control for LTE enterprise femtocell networks. IEEE Syst. J. **11**(4), 2699–2707 (2017)
13. Ye, H., Li, G.Y.: Deep reinforcement learning for resource allocation in V2V communications. In: 2018 IEEE International Conference on Communications (ICC). IEEE (2018)
14. GNU GPLv2: ns-3.25, March 2016. https://www.nsnam.org/ns-3-25

Advanced Interconnect Technologies

Christina (Tanya) Politi[1]([✉]), Dimitris Alexandropoulos[2], and Dimitra Simeonidou[3]

[1] Department of Informatics and Telecommunications, University of Peloponnese, Tripoli,
Greece
tpoliti@uop.gr
[2] Department of Materials Science, University of Patras, Patras, Greece
[3] High Performance Networks Group, University of Bristol, Bristol, UK

Abstract. Advanced interconnect technologies play a prominent role in scaling up the performance of data center networks. Spatial Division Multiplexing (SDM) photonic interconnects have been suggested as means to overcome capacity upgrade requirements and enable disaggregation in future data centers. Here, Holographic Optical Elements (HOE) are proposed for SDM photonic interconnects. The proposed coupling scheme entails the use of holograms as fan out components for coupling light from a source to multicore fibers (MCF). The scheme is versatile and can be adopted to any SDM fiber core arrangement. Appropriate Computer-Generated Holograms (CGHs) are designed for two kind of MCF and the HOE interconnect is evaluated in terms of performance variations against system and fabrication related parameters. Furthermore, the interconnect design is optimized for loss-sensitive applications.

Keywords: Optical interconnects · Holographic optical elements · Spatial division multiplexing

1 Introduction

Information and Communications trends like Internet of Things (IoT) and Cloud Services have been formed to support emerging applications and consequently are driving the dramatic increase of the global Internet traffic. These new and emerging applications collect, store and process massive amounts of data, driving the requirement for large high-performance data centers. Advanced interconnect technologies play a prominent role in scaling up the network performance of data center segments that range from inter data-center links to short-reach rack-to-rack communication, even on-board and chip-to-chip connections [1, 2]. Photonic communication technologies have been long used in global optical networks and proposed to serve on and off-chip interconnects in data centers due to low power consumption and high bandwidth performance. Specifically, for rack-to-rack interconnection, vertical cavity surface emitting laser (VCSEL) based transmitters and multi-mode fiber have been the main candidate for 10 Gb/s throughput server interconnection [2, 3]. As scalability in terms of capacity is vital in data center environments, single mode fibers (SMF) and even MCF have been proposed, where capacity upgrades are guaranteed via various multiplexing techniques like wavelength

© IFIP International Federation for Information Processing 2020
Published by Springer Nature Switzerland AG 2020
A. Tzanakaki et al. (Eds.): ONDM 2019, LNCS 11616, pp. 635–644, 2020.
https://doi.org/10.1007/978-3-030-38085-4_54

and space division multiplexing (WDM) and SDM. SDM systems promise several link capacity upgrades with one fiber-installation while reducing the amount of cable space required in data center networks [1]. Furthermore, the specific architecture is very much in line with the notion of disaggregation.

An important issue in this interconnect evolution is multiplexing of the laser signals to the MCF that will transport signals to several processors. Coupling of MCF to SMF (and vice versa) is technologically challenging and affects the interconnect's overall performance. In the literature, the component that couples light from an SMF to an MCF is termed as fan in/fan out component, coupler or even SDM multiplexer/demultiplexer (mux/demux). Here we use the term coupler as it is used in a broadcasting interconnect architecture. In SDM couplers, an additional degree of complexity is introduced by the fact that while SMF fibers are standardized, MCF are not and there is a plurality of MCF demonstrations that employ various arrangements of cores and number of cores. Hence, a plethora of coupling solutions have been explored and a few have been commercialized [4], while the interest in the field is ongoing. These have been specified for the various SDM fiber technologies namely, MCFs [5], few mode fiber and multimode fibers [6], Vortex Fiber Carrying Orbital Angular Momentum [7] and Hollow-Core Photonic Band Gap Fiber [8]. Coupling schemes can be categorized as fiber/waveguide based in the form of tapers and laser inscribed waveguides in transparent materials (e.g. glass) [9, 10], free space that make use of lenses [11] and integrated methods where mux/demux operation is enabled by grating couplers integrated within a photonic chip [12]. Fiber/waveguide based schemes are compact solutions that offer the possibility for fiber connectors while the fabrication techniques used are fairly mastered. On the downside, the adiabatic transform from single to multicore (and vice versa) can be restrictive in terms minimum size of the device and also require sophisticated splicing technology. On top, in some cases it can be susceptible to crosstalk. Adaptation to any MCF core arrangement is not straightforward fabrication wise. Free space techniques on the other hand, rely on lens systems to image the cores of SMFs to the cores of the MCFs (and vice versa) and are scalable to any number of cores and arrangements. Additionally, losses and crosstalk are minimized. However, this is a bulky solution that does not favor integration.

Evidently it is particularly difficult to establish a universal coupling scheme that accommodates all MCF variations. In the present contribution we address this with fan in/out holographic optical element (HOE) for coupling SMF to MCF. The proposed scheme (illustrated in Fig. 1a) is essentially a free space optics scheme that carries all the pros of a lens system coupling while it relaxes the cons, as it is not as bulky solution as a bare lens system and also there is no requirement for optomechanics and prisms [13]. Relevant to the present work is the work of Calo and co-workers [14] and the more recent of Wilkinson et al. [15] and [16]. In [14] a holographic coupler for coupling SMF to SMF was proposed. Deployment of the scheme was hindered by the technological advances of the rival coupling technology at the time where fiber-based connectivity was preferred. Nowadays this is reversed thanks to developments in fabrication and integration methods. In [15] a hologram is used for the mode coupling of multimode fibers, rather than core coupling in MCF proposed here. Furthermore [16] has proposed the use of microelectromechanical optical mirrors as switchable diffractive elements and the experimental investigation was merely aiming at crosstalk investigation.

Additionally, the implementation involved MEMs rather passive holograms. The latter approach is chosen as it favors small footprint and in addition it is more cost effective as the material assumed is fused silica.

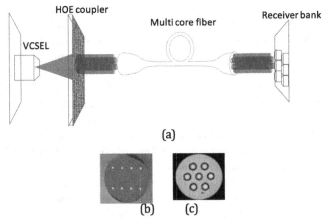

(a)

(b)   (c)

	# of cores	Pitch size (l)	SDM fiber diameter (D)
LA [16]	8	50μm	250 μm
HPCS [17]	7	40μm	250 μm

(d)

Fig. 1. Block diagram of a broadcast short reach interconnect with a directly modulated VCSEL, HOE coupler a MCF and a bank of receivers. The interconnect utilizes either (b) multicore SMF with linear arrays (LA) or (c) hexagonal close packed structure (HPCS) with the multi core fibre characteristics shown in (d).

Here we choose to study binary phased HOEs on fused silica due to the ease of fabrication by standard microfabrication techniques. We perform for the first time to our knowledge, a systematic investigation on how the interconnect performance is affected by possible fabrication and system integration errors. We do this by simulating the performance of the broadcast SDM interconnects when specific parameters are detuned from optimal values.

2   SDM Interconnect Architecture

For the purposes of design and evaluation of the proposed HOE SDM couplers we consider the short reach broadcast interconnect scenario shown in Fig. 1(a). Broadcast interconnects investigation with respect to fanout, to provide multicast communication is one of the crucial demands of interconnects fabric for the future many-core systems [20]. Especially in short reach broadcast interconnect, minimal delay among multicasted signals may be of crucial importance for the operation of a data center. To simulate the operation of a short reach broadcast system: the output of a directly modulated single mode VCSEL is broadcasted to an array of photodetectors (i.e. multiple nodes) by means of a MCF [21]. Coupling to the MCF fiber is achieved with the HOE SDM coupler under study. In short reach optical broadcast interconnects the requirement is that the high speed signal is transmitted to multiple nodes with reduced delay and jitter among the copies. The elaboration of short reach optical interconnects to include MCFs has already been considered [22]. MCFs offer the obvious advantage of massive data transport while for the short reach optical interconnects the requirement for optical amplification is relaxed. HOE SDM coupler is particularly suited for this application as it is inherently bit rate and time delay agnostic. An added bonus comes from the very use of VCSELs, rather than edge emitters with elliptical beam emission. Indeed, the circular characteristics of the VCSEL output simplifies the optical setup as no additional beam shaping optics are required for illuminating the HOE with a circular spot and guarantees the symmetry of the design. The interconnect operates at 850 nm where both VCSEL and fibre cores support one mode. The miniaturization of the interconnect however imposes the incorporation of a lens at the output of HOE. The footprint of the overall setup can be reduced by means of a GRIN lens rather than a typical lens. The light that is broadcasted in all nodes it is then received by a bank of receivers that demodulate and process the signal.

The proposed HOE SDM couplers are specified for two typical examples of MCFs previously considered for use with integrated silicon photonic transceivers namely MCFs with linear arrangement (LA) of core arrays [22] and hexagonal close packed structure (HPCS) [23]. Any type of multi core fibres can be used [14], as shown in Fig. 1b and c.

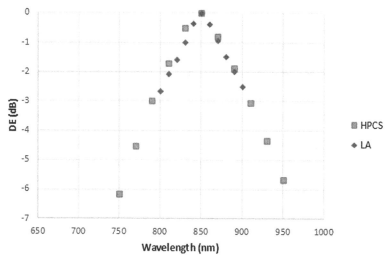

Fig. 2. Relative diffraction efficiency with respect to the source wavelength for two CGH coupler designs. Both LA and HPCS CGH designed at/for 850 nm.

2.1 SDM Coupler Design

In the following we design the Computer-Generated Holograms (CGHs) for the HOEs couplers for LA and HPCS arrangements in context of the short interconnect scenario (Fig. 1a). The evaluation gauge in all cases is the diffraction efficiency (DE) η, a measure of how much optical power is diffracted into designated spots compared to the power incident onto the diffractive element. Here it is calculated as the ratio of the diffracted irradiance integrated in the designated spot areas (intensity) over the beam intensity behind the HOE. Diffraction efficiency η is directly related to the insertion loss of the element and the actual optical power diffracted into one of the targeted N fibre cores (N = 7 or 8 depending on the configuration). Considering loss from the optical system to be approximately 5% and the 1 × N splitting loss the insertion loss of the fan-out is [24]

$$\text{Loss} = 0.05 \ \eta/N \tag{1}$$

Evidently as loss depends on the number of cores N of the multi core fibre, it is avoided as a figure of merit in comparisons between the two HOE coupler that correspond to Fig. 1(b) and (c). For the design of the CGHs and analysis of the HOE optical interconnects we use the commercially available software VirtualLab by LightTrans [25]. For the computation, an advanced iterative Fourier-transform algorithm (IFTA) is used. The iterative Fourier transform algorithm in VirtualLab, enables the HOE design for the targeted beam pattern. The IFTA consists of the following steps, after the generation of an appropriate transmission field. The software creates an optimized output field phase and optimizes the specific merit functions with respect to the specifications. Here DE, uniformity error ε and signal to noise ratio have been used. The HOE is analyzed and light distributions in target plane is calculated. Light distribution is modified in order to fullfill all constraints and element parameters are calculated with light back propagation. The multi step algorithm result is validated and the optimum HOE design is used for the simulation of the short reach optical interconnect.

For the simulation the following are considered: the optical interconnect modelled here assumes one single mode VCSEL source at 850 nm [2]. The VCSEL beam output is a circular Gaussian beam with 600 μm diameter. The required beam size can be modified by means of a collimating lens if necessary. The HOE is placed at the output of the VCSEL. The rectangular HOE is placed in a 2f [14]. At a possible HOE coupler design the lens could be replaced by a GRIN element. For all the calculations presented here f = 10 mm. The HOEs are designed as binary phase CGHs. For each HOEs this translates to an optimal pixel size. This translates into 13.27 μm (LA) and 15.17 μm (HPCS). Judicious HOE design can result to non-trivial savings in fabrication time and costs. It is noted that the proposed design can be readily extended to longer wavelengths e.g. 1525 nm as it will be indeed done here. Given that the CGH pixel size [14, 26] is related to the reconstruction wavelength i.e. the operation wavelength of the interconnect, choice of longer wavelength relaxes pixel size requirements for optimal reconstruction.

2.2 Fabrication Tolerance Simulation

Once the optimal designs have been achieved, a simulation setup in used to evaluate the HOE couplers that were designed. A tolerance analysis is performed in terms of

(a) wavelength (b) MCF position and (c) fabrication errors. The rectangular HOE is assumed to be fabricated on fused silica and comprises 280 pixels for the HPCS and 320 pixels for the LA case. The lens in all cases is considered circular with diameter of 25.4 mm. The DE and uniformity errors are used as figures of merit. Plots are shown in dB, with respect to the highest achieved value, i.e. relative diffraction efficiency. Highest DE is 75.5% for the LA and 76.42% for the HPCS optimal designs. Relative figures are used as different HOE designs yield slightly different values as the scope of the paper is to evaluate and compare the tolerance to changes and not the actual designs.

Figure 2 shows the relative DE versus source wavelength for CGHs that are used in a LA and HPCS couplers. Specifically, the DE is designated with respect to the maximum value (in dB) to evaluate the DE variation when source wavelength is detuned with respect to the wavelength used for the design of the HOE (i.e. 850 nm). Setting the system threshold for maximum tolerable DE deviation to 1 dB, the LA HOE coupler is wavelength agnostic over a span of 50 nm while the HPCS over a span of 60 nm. Thus, both cases are suitable for SDM WDM. Notably the HPCS is more robust to wavelength variations with respect to LA. This however is an artifact of the geometry of the HPCC core arrangement, which includes the 0th order of diffraction in the output reconstruction. As the operation wavelength is detuned with respect to the design wavelength, part of the VCSEL power that illuminates the HOE remains undiffracted. In the case of LA, the undiffracted light, i.e. light that is directed to the zero-order is lost, as the zero order does not coincide with a core. Hence wavelength variation will be translated into increased coupling loss. In the case of HPCS the undiffracted light increases the power that is incident to one of the cores, hence it is translated into uniformity error [24].

The effects of errors in positioning the SDM fiber with respect to the HOE are explored in Fig. 3 for the same cases as in Fig. 2. In interconnects like the one shown in Fig. 1, SDM fibre is assumed to be placed at distance f = 10 mm from the lens in order to achieve the maximum DE. In order to model the effect of misaligning the fibre with respect to its optimal position on the focal point, the fibre position deviates from the optimal position on the z-axis as a percentage of f = 10 mm. Specifically, if the coordinate of the SDM fiber facet is z with respect to the lens facet (where z = 0), then the positioning error is defined as $((z - 10)/10)\%$. Figure 3 shows the relative diffraction efficiency versus positioning error for CGHs that are used in LA and HPCS couplers. The linear features of the LA arrangement yield some tolerance to the integration process. Although it is evident that in both cases the systems require precision with respect to the positioning of the lens, the LA configurations allows more flexibility to possible integration misalignments along the z-axis.

Fabrication tolerances of the CGH for coupling to LA and HPCS fibers are assessed in Fig. 4. Errors in the fabrication process can cause HOE construction with non opti-mal pixel size, or the pixel size that stemmed from the optimisation process cannot be achieved with the accuracy of the fabrication methods. These fabrication errors are sim-ulated by scaling the pixel size of the CGH. In Fig. 5 the relative diffraction efficiency is calculated with respect to pixel scaling. Evidently both designs are highly tolerant to pixel size scaling. The HPCS design seems more tolerant to pixel size deviations with respect to the optimal one. Expectantly the wider pattern of the LA multi core fiber requires finer optimum pixel size (15.17 μm in the case of HPCS and 13.27 μm in the

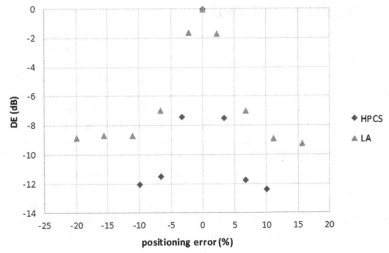

Fig. 3. Relative diffraction efficiency with respect positioning error of the output fibre for two CGH designed for LA and HPCS systems. The positioning error is given as a percentage of the focal length f = 10 mm.

case of LA). The symmetrical HPCS pattern is very relaxed to fabrication errors although even in the case of the LA, a ±10% error in the pixel size does not deteriorate the DE significantly. In the case of HPCS, pixel size scaling of ±10% which corresponds to variation of 1.5 μm can be tolerated before the DE deteriorates further from the 1 dB threshold.

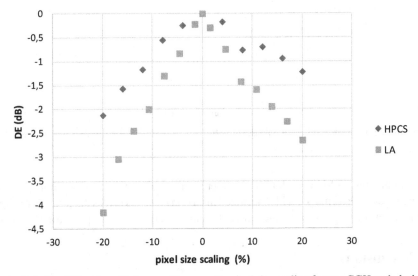

Fig. 4. Relative diffraction efficiency with respect to pixel size scaling for two CGH each designed for the optimal pixel size.

3 Losses in SDM Interconnects

The designs of the previous section have focused on binary CGH structures that can be fabricated with low cost fabrication techniques. Here we elaborate the designs of Sect. 2 to study multi-phase CGHs that can be fabricated with more sophisticated fabricating techniques aiming at the minimization of losses. In this way we investigate the suitability of the proposed cross-connects for loss-sensitive applications like quantum communications [17–19]. To this end we consider the interconnect of in Fig. 1(a) that deploys the MCF of Fig. 1(c) and long wavelength VCSELs operating at 1525 nm. This is a popular wavelength for quantum communication networks. The diffraction efficiency and hence insertion losses can be greatly enhanced if multiphase rather than binary CGHs are used as shown in Fig. 5 [27]. The losses can be optimized further if the design accounts for the cost function of stray light, i.e. light scattered in space rather than contributing to the reconstruction of the desired pattern. The comparative analysis of the optimization process for two lowest possible stray light values (10% and 1% respectively) is shown in Fig. 5, where insertion losses are calculated.

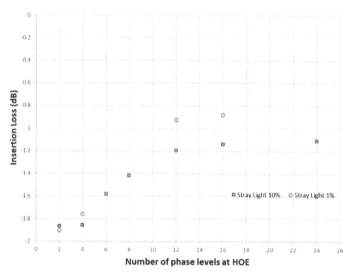

Fig. 5. Insertion loss for various CGH designs for HPCS with varying number of phase levels in the HOE.

Evidently the multiphase HOE based interconnects outperform binary HOEs exhibiting a very good performance with optimized insertion losses as low as 0.8 dB for stray light optimization constraint of 1%, lower than the state-of-art optical couplers for MCFs [4].

4 Conclusions

Holographic elements were explored as a robust solution for high capacity SDM photonic interconnects based on multi core fibers. To this end, appropriate CGHs were designed for SDM multicore fibers with linear and hexagonal core arrangement, two commonly used MCF in literature. The performance analysis of the proposed HOE SDM interconnects in terms of diffraction efficiency variations with wavelength, positioning error and fabrication misfits concluded that both configurations (LA and HPCS) perform well and are tolerant to potential system integration and alignment errors as well as fabrication errors. These results along with the versatility of the proposed scheme suggest the suitability of HOE interconnects for SDM applications. The proposed scheme can be further optimized to address stringent loss requirements in SDM interconnect scenarios.

Acknowledgement. The authors would like to acknowledge EU funded project COSING. Also, they would like to thank Prof Nikos Vainos for helpful discussions.

References

1. Yan, S., et al.: Archon: a function programmable optical interconnect architecture for transparent intra and inter data center SDM/TDM/WDM networking. J. Lightwave Technol. **33**(8), 1586 (2015)
2. Zhang, W., Wang, H., Bergman, K.: Next-generation optically-interconnected high-performance data centers. IEEE/OSA J. Lightwave Technol. **30**(24), 3836 (2012)
3. Yen, J.-L., Chen, X.-N., Chi, K.-L., Chen, J., Shi, J.-W.: 850 nm vertical-cavity surface-emitting laser arrays with enhanced high-speed transmission performance over a standard multimode fiber. J. Lightwave Technol. **35**(15), 3242 (2017)
4. Saridis, G.M., Alexandropoulos, D., Zervas, G., Simeonidou, D.: Survey and evaluation of space division multiplexing: from technologies to optical networks. IEEE Communications Surveys & Tutorials **17**(4), 2136 (2015)
5. Richardson, D.J., Fini, J.M., Nelson, L.E.: Space-division multiplexing in optical fibres. Nat. Photonics **7**, 354–362 (2013)
6. RP Photonics - Fibers. http://www.rpphotonics.com/fibers.html
7. Boffi, P., Martelli, P., Gatto, A., Martinelli, M.: Mode division multiplexing in fibre-optic communications based on orbital angular momentum. J. Opt. **15**(7), 075403 (2013)
8. Cregan, R.F., et al.: Single-mode photonic band gap guidance of light in air. Science **285**(5433), 1537 (1999)
9. Takara, H., et al.: 1000-km 7-core fiber transmission of 10 × 96-Gb/s PDM-16QAM using Raman amplification with 6.5 W per fiber. Opt. Express **20**(9), 10100 (2012)
10. Thomson, R.R., et al.: Ultrafast-laser inscription of a three dimensional fan-out device for multicore fiber coupling applications. Opt. Express **15**(18), 11691 (2007)
11. Klaus, W., et al.: Free-space coupling optics for multicore fibers. IEEE Photonics Technol. Lett. **24**(21), 1902 (2012)
12. Koonen, A.M.J., Chen, H., van den Boom, H.P.A., Raz, O.: Silicon photonic integrated mode multiplexer and demultiplexer. IEEE Photonics Technol. Lett. **24**(21), 1961 (2012)
13. Ruffato, G., Massari, M., Romanato, F.: Diffractive optics for combined spatial- and mode-division demultiplexing of optical vortices: design, fabrication and optical characterization. Sci. Rep. **6**, 24760 (2016)
14. Politi, C., Alexandropoulos, D., Simeonidou, D.: Holographic optical elements for SDM interconnects. In: OSA Advanced Photonics 2018 Congress, Switzerland, 2–5 July 2018 (2018)
15. Calvo, M.L., Pedraza, L.D.: Holographic coupler-optical fiber system: mathematical model for the coupling optimization. Appl. Opt. **28**(11), 2031 (1989)

16. Carpenter, J., Wilkinson, T.D.: All optical mode-multiplexing using holography and multi-mode fiber couplers. J. Lightwave Technol. **30**(12), 2012 (1978)

17. Gadalla, M., François, V., Ung, B.: IEEE Photonics Technol. Lett. **30**(3), 281 (2018)

18. Vest, G., et al.: Design and evaluation of a handheld quantum key distribution sender module. IEEE J. Sel. Top. Quantum Electron. **21**(3), 131–137 (2015)

19. Hwang, W.-Y.: Quantum key distribution with high loss: toward global secure communication. Phys. Rev. Lett. **91**(5), 1–4 (2003)

20. Karkar, A., Mak, T., Tong, K.F., Yakovlev, A.: IEEE Circuits Syst. Mag. **16**(1), 58 (2016)

21. Westbergh, P., Gustavsson, J.S., Kogel, B., et al.: 40 Gbit/s error-free operation of oxide-confined 850 nm VCSEL. Electron. Lett. **46**(14), 1014 (2010)

22. Butler, D.L., et al.: Space division multiplexing in short reach optical interconnects. J. Lightwave Technol. **35**(4), 677 (2017)

23. Takenaga, K., et al.: Reduction of crosstalk by trench-assisted multi-core fiber. In: Optical Fiber Communication Conference, OWJ4, OFC (2011)

24. Trager, F.: Springer Handbook Laser and Optics, 2d edn. Springer, Heidelberg (2012). https://doi.org/10.1007/978-3-642-19409-2

25. https://www.lighttrans.com/

26. Morrison, R.L.: Symmetries that simplify the design of spot array phase gratings. J. Opt. Soc. Am. A **9**, 464–471 (1992)

27. Goebel, B., Wang, L.L., Tschudi, T.: Multilayer technology for diffractive optical elements. Appl. Opt. **35**(22), 4490–4493 (1996)

Supporting Diverse Customers and Prioritized Traffic in Next-Generation Passive Optical Networks

Naureen Hoque$^{(\boxtimes)}$ and Byrav Ramamurthy

Department of Computer Science and Engineering,
University of Nebraska-Lincoln, Lincoln, NE, USA
{nhoque,byrav}@cse.unl.edu

Abstract. A variety of DBA (Dynamic Bandwidth Allocation) and DWBA (Dynamic Wavelength and Bandwidth Allocation) algorithms have been proposed which are based on different PONs (e.g. EPON, GPON, XG-PON, 10G-EPON, etc.). But to our knowledge, no DWBA scheme for NG-PON2 system, with diverse customers and prioritized traffic, has been proposed yet. In this work, this problem is addressed and we focus on the wavelength assignment part, assuming that the system applies conventional DBA method described in the standard ITU-T G.989. Considering this assumption, we propose five different dynamic wavelength and bandwidth allocation (DWBA) schemes. First, mixed integer linear programming (MILP) models are developed to minimize the total delay of the high priority data. Due to the MILP's high computational complexity, heuristic algorithms are developed based on the MILP model insights. The five heuristics algorithms are: No Block-Split Heuristic (NBH), Equal Block-Split Heuristic (EBH), Priority Based No Block-Split Heuristic (P-NBH), Priority Based Equal Block-Split Heuristic (P-EBH), and Priority Based Decider Block-Split Heuristic (P-DBH). Six priority classes of requests are introduced with the goal of minimizing the total delay for the high priority data and to lessen the bandwidth wastage of the system. Finally, experiments for the performance evaluation of the five DWBA schemes are conducted. The results show that P-DBH is the most efficient among the five because this scheme offers the lowest delay for high priority data and the minimum bandwidth wastage for lower priority ones.

Keywords: NG-PON2 · Wavelength allocation · Priority

1 Introduction

The demand for high-speed data services is constantly rising. By 2021, it is estimated that the data requirements of access networks would exceed 3.3 Zettabytes [1], and more than 26 billion networked devices and these connections would produce approximately thrice the traffic generated in 2015 [2]. Due to high

A. Tzanakaki et al. (Eds.): ONDM 2019, LNCS 11616, pp. 645–657, 2020.
https://doi.org/10.1007/978-3-030-38085-4_55

capacity, cost-effectiveness, and coverage potential, Passive Optical Networks (PONs) are becoming a suitable and promising access network option. Recently the deployment of XGS-PON [3] and 10G-EPON [4] have been reported which are capable of providing 10 Gbps in the downstream and 1/2.5/10 Gbps in the upstream direction. NG-PON2 supports a total network throughput of 40 Gbps [5]. According to the latest updates to standard G.989.2, enabling up to a total of 80 Gbps capacity has been approved and a discussion on bit-rate increment from 10 Gbps per channel to 25 Gbps has taken place in the ITU-T [6]. The Full-Service Access Network (FSAN) group has started working on the specification of the future broadband network under NG-PON2 standard. In NG-PON2, the optical line terminal (OLT) allocates bandwidth and specifies the number of the transmission windows (TWs) on the wavelengths to the optical network unit (ONU). After receiving the grant, the ONUs start sending data frames to the OLT. This is termed as dynamic wavelength and bandwidth allocation (DWBA). To achieve maximum bandwidth utilization, an efficient DWBA in the NG-PON2 system is required. Otherwise, improper resource allocation might lead to the degradation in the overall network performance as there would be more delay and increased bandwidth wastage. An efficient DWBA scheme allows the system to support additional customers on the network and to support enhanced services. Thus, DWBA is a method of assigning wavelength and bandwidth to the ONUs based on their traffic contracts and the usage patterns. The standard for NG-PON2 (ITU-T G.989) describes the single wavelength bandwidth allocation, but it leaves the multiple wavelengths allocation issue to the implementers' preferences as long as the base cases, which are discussed in the standard specification, are handled [5]. In this work, the focus is on the wavelength assignment part, assuming that the system applies conventional DBA method described in the standard ITU-T G.989. It is also assumed that the same DBA method is applied for every wavelength. Considering these mentioned assumptions, we propose five DWBA algorithms with the goal of minimizing the total delay of the high priority data and reducing the bandwidth wastage of the system. The experiment results show that the small-sized or low-priority data should be transmitted over a single wavelength to minimize the bandwidth wastage and the high priority ones over multiple wavelengths as parallel transmission reduces the transmission delay.

2 Dynamic Wavelength and Bandwidth Allocation (DWBA) in PONs

Dhaini et al. assumed in [7] that in an EPON, the DWBA scheme grants an ONU request over multiple wavelengths simultaneously. They propose an EPON-based DWBA algorithm with an assumption that the tuning speed of the ONUs are in the microsecond range. Y. Luo et al. propose a DWBA algorithm for the TWDM-based PON where multiple XG-PONs are stacked. Their results show that there are deciding factors such as the load-balance and the tuning cost. With the goal of solving scheduling methods for the transmissions over multiple wavelengths and how to reduce propagation delays in the long reach scenarios, Buttaboni et al. analyze the multi-thread polling in a long-reach PON and propose EFT-partial-VF multi-threaded DWBA algorithm. Their results show improvement in the delays [8]. In [9], the authors proposed a DBA based on Water-Filling or WF algorithm. In this scheme, the grant of an ONU is broken into smaller parts and spread across all the wavelengths. If all the channels have the same finish time for the last bandwidth assignment, this scheme would allocate those grant parts uniformly over all the available wavelengths. This would make all wavelengths busy and unavailable for the other ONUs. This leads to higher packet delays. These smaller parts of grants are not large enough that they can be transmitted over a wavelength. Each frame has to wait for a grant size large enough on each channel to be transmitted to the destination. There is a possibility that the data frames need to wait for several allocation cycles to be transmitted. This situation increases the packet delay. As all the ONUs do the transmission over all the channels in the Water-Filling algorithm, every ONU faces the unordered frames issue. The main goal of the authors of [10] is to ensure fair bandwidth distribution, lower latency, and avoid frame reordering. The proposed algorithm does not equalize all the wavelengths in a single bandwidth allocation; instead, transmission is done by using fewer number of wavelengths. This increases the bandwidth efficiency. Each ONU is assigned to one channel and all ONUs get grants in parallel which confirms the fairness. All the available wavelengths are sorted into ascending order of their start time and the grant is allocated in the wavelength with the earliest start time. Although the results show that the proposed scheme reduces packet drop rate and it does not increase the requirement for a larger buffer, this algorithm does not address the situation when an ONU needs a grant that requires more than one wavelength's bandwidth. M. K. Multani et al. proposed an algorithm, Partially Online Dynamic Bandwidth Allocation Algorithm (PAROND), which is designed for EPON in the hybrid TDM/WDM architecture [11]. This scheme has different ways to deal with the loads (high or low). After receiving REPORT messages from all ONUs, they are sorted based on their arrival times. This DWBA assigns grants to the highly loaded ONUs as soon as they request them. These papers do not consider the priority of the customer or the traffic. Also, the allocation methods are not applicable for NG-PON2. In our work, we propose wavelength allocation methods with diverse customers and prioritized traffic for the NG-PON2 system.

3   Dynamic Wavelength Allocation Problem in NG-PON2

We focus on the wavelength assignment part, assuming that the system applies conventional DBA method described in the standard G.989. It is also assumed that the same DBA is used for every wavelength. Any DWBA is a two-step procedure: the grant size based on the each ONU's request and allocating that over single/multiple wavelengths. The OLT and ONUs exchange messages (Request and Grant). Based on each ONU's Request message, the OLT evaluates the upstream bandwidth allocation. Then it sends the allocated grant information to each ONU through a Grant message. The ONUs start transmission based on the grant. The initial objective of this study is to minimize the total delay of the high priority data. To fulfill the purpose, five methods of wavelength allocation are proposed. They are discussed in the next section.

3.1   Proposed Methods and Priority Classes

No-Split Method: The OLT assigns grants to each request in a single channel if this method is applied in the system. Each grant is assigned in the wavelength which has the earliest available time.

Equal-Split Method: The OLT splits the grants in equal sizes and transmit those parts through all the channels. If a grant size is S and the number of active wavelength is m, then each wavelength would carry $\frac{S}{m}$ amount of the grant.

Priority Classes: The next three methods that are proposed in this work, deal with the priority of both the data and customer type. Two main classes of the priority are introduced in this work: Customer and Traffic. The customer base priority-levels are business customer and residential users. There classes are A and B, respectively. Based on the traffic type, there are three types:

(1) Live: Live telecasting, interactive online game, VoIP calls.
(2) Video: TV shows, other video services (e.g. YouTube, Netflix, etc.).
(3) Data: services such as browsing, email, etc.

Table 1. Priority class combinations

Customer base	Service type	Priority Class	Priority weight
Business	Live	A1	1
Residential	Live	B1	2
Business	Video	A2	3
Residential	Video	B2	4
Business	Data	A3	5
Residential	Data	B3	6

Considering these two types of customer classes, six combinations are possible. Each of these combinations has a weight. The weight range is 1 to 6 whereas 1 represents the highest priority and 6 has the lowest. The business users have higher priority over the residential users. The "live" category service is extremely delay-sensitive. Thus, it has the highest priority than the data service (email, browse, etc.). Table 1 explains all these six combinations with their class and priority weight. The classes A1, B1, A2, B2 include live telecasting, video, tele-conferences, etc. These need parallel data transmission of minimize the delay. On the other hand, A3 and B3 types are delay-tolerant. They do not need to send over multiple wavelengths which lead to bandwidth wastage.

Priority Based No-Split Method: The OLT sorts all the grants based on their priority weights. The grants with priority weight 0 are transmitted first. By this way the grants are sent one-by-one. Each grant is transmitted through one single channel. Each grant is assigned in the wavelength which has the earliest available time.

Priority Based Equal-Split Method: The OLT sorts all the grants based on their priority weights. The grants with priority weight 0 are transmitted first. The rest of the data transferring procedure is same as the Equal Block-Split system: the grants are split equally and send through all the wavelengths.

Priority Based Decider-Split Method: The OLT sorts all the grants based on their priority weights. Unlike the previous two methods, this scheme does not transmit grants only over one or all wavelengths. It transmits the high priority grants (class A1, B1, A2, B2) exactly like the Priority-Based Equal Block-Split methods. Each of the low priority grant (A3 and B3) is sent over one single channel.

4   Mathematical Formulation

To solve the wavelength assignment problem with the goal of minimizing the total transmission delay of high priority data, we construct a Mixed Integer Linear Programming (MILP) model with the integer constraints to obtain the optimal solutions. The formulations can be solved with IBM CPLEX optimization software [12], from which an optimal solution is reached.

4.1   Model Inputs

In the network model, we have OLT and ONUs. Each ONU operates in four or eight wavelengths in an NG-PON2 system. The wavelengths can be defined as: $w_j = (t_s, t_{d_i}, d_r)$. The variable t_s is the available time of the wavelength w_j, t_d is its duration of availability for a grant G_i, d_r is the data rate. We define the set of all requests and denote each element as R_i. Every request has a arrival time A_i, a transmission start time S_{ij} at wavelength w_j. It also has end time E_i and a priority p.

Input Parameters:
N: Total number of requests, R_i: The requested grant for ith request, A_i: The arrival time of the ith request, d_r: The data rate of each wavelength, B_{aT}: The total available bandwidth, B_{aj}: The total available bandwidth in wavelength w_j, p_i: The priority of the ith grant, n: an integer value, K: Large positive value.

Constant Parameters:
M: Total number of wavelengths, W: Set of wavelengths $\{w_1, w_2, .., w_M\}$, t_g: The guard-band between two transmission slots.

Variables:
G_{ij}: The ith grant on w_j, G: The total grant, S_{ij}: Start time of the ith grant on w_j, E_i: End time of the ith grant, E_{ij}: End time of the ith grant's portion at wavelength w_j, x_{ij}: Binary parameter, equals 1 when ith grant uses wavelength w_j, b_{G_i}: Binary parameter, equals 1 if a grant G_i is scheduled for transmission, $\overline{b_{G_i}}$: 1 - b_{G_i}.

4.2   Objective and Constraints

No-split and Equal-Split Methods: The objective is to reduce the total time duration between a request's arrival time to transmission finish time. *Priority Based No-split, Equal-Split, and Decider-Split Methods:* The objective is to reduce the total time duration between the higher priority request's arrival time to the transmission finish time. This means that the higher priority requests should be transmitted before the lower priority ones.

Objective:

$$minimize: \sum_{i=1}^{N}(E_i - A_i) + \sum_{i=1}^{N} K^{p_i} \tag{1}$$

Here, the value of p would always be 0 for the NBH and EBH methods.

Subject to:
We are mentioning some of the most important constraints due to limitation of the space in the paper.

$$\sum_{i=1}^{N}\sum_{j=1}^{M} G_{ij} \leq B_{aT}, \forall i \in N, \forall j \in M \tag{2}$$

$$\sum_{j=1}^{M} B_{aj} \leq B_{aT}, \forall j \in M \tag{3}$$

$$S_{ij} \geq A_i, \forall i \in N \tag{4}$$

$$\sum_{j=1}^{M} E_{ij} \geq E_i, \forall i \in N, \forall j \in M \tag{5}$$

$$\sum_{j=1}^{M}[E_{ij} - S_{ij}] \geq G_i, \forall i \in N, \forall j \in M \tag{6}$$

$$S_{(i+1)j} - S_{ij} \leq x_{ij} * (d_r + t_g), \forall i \in N, \forall j \in M \tag{7}$$

Constraint (2) guarantees that the sum of all assigned grants do not exceed the total available bandwidth of the system. Constraint (3) assures that the available bandwidth remains equal to the sum of all wavelengths' available bandwidth. Constraint (4) ensures that the ith request's transmission start time at wavelength w_j should not be earlier that its arrival time.

Constraint (5) ensures that the sum of the end times of all the portions of a grant is within the limit of the total end time. In NBH and P-NBH systems, only one wavelength would be used to transmit. Thus, end times over the rest of the wavelengths would always be 0. Constraint (6) is used to make sure that the sum of all $E_{ij} - S_{ij}$ is equal to the total grant size of that request. Constraint (7) confirms that two consecutive transmission windows do not overlap.

The priority classes have weights from 1 to 6 respectively. This means the highest priority class A1 has a priority weight of 1 and the lowest priority class B3 has a priority weight of 6. The objective function would obtain a higher value when low priority grants are favored over the high ones because K is raised to a power equal to the weight of the request's priority.

5   Heuristics for Dynamic Wavelength Allocation Problem

The formulations discussed in the previous section can be solved with IBM CPLEX optimization software [12], but the executing time is too long to get allocation results within one scheduling cycle. The wavelength allocation problem is a NP-hard [13] problem. Thus, we propose five heuristic wavelength allocation algorithms of low complexity which are implementable to get near-optimal solutions of the allocation problem. The heuristics have some assumptions: 1. First, the buffer size at the ONUs and the OLT are both infinite. Second, all ONUs are always at a uniform distance from the OLT. Also, all the wavelengths' available times are always set to the same at the beginning of the transmission. Our five time-efficient heuristic algorithms are: No Block-Split Heuristic, Equal Block-Split Heuristic, Priority Based No Block-Split Heuristic, Priority Based Equal Block-Split Heuristic, and Priority Based Decider Block-Split Heuristic. These methods are explained in the following Sections.

Input and Initialization: M = number of total wavelengths, N = total number of ONUs, $W = \{w_1, w_2, ..., w_M\}$ is the set of wavelengths, sorted in ascending manner according to their start time. B_{a_T} = total available bandwidth, B_{a_j} = available bandwidth at wavelength w_j, $maxB_i$ = maximum allowed grant for i^{th} ONU, $R = \{R_1, R_2, ..., R_N\}$ is the set of requests from all ONUs, $G = \{G_1, G_2, ..., G_N\}$ Set of grants for all ONUs, $G_T \leftarrow 0$: total bandwidth grant is initialized to 0. $P_G = \{P_{G_1}, P_{G_2}, ..., P_{G_N}\}$ is the set of sorted grants based on their priority (high-to-low) for all ONUs. $P = \{A1, B1, A2, B2, A3, B3\}$ is the set of sorted priorities from high-to-low and d_{low} is the minimum grant-size that is allowed for multiple wavelength assignment.

5.1   No Block-Split Heuristic (NBH)

The No Block-Split Heuristic (NBH) is a greedy algorithm. The basic idea is to assign each of the grants over one single channel. In addition, it assigns to the wavelength which is earliest available among all four. Based on these ideas, the NBH algorithm comprises of two main steps: after checking if there is enough unoccupied bandwidth in the available wavelength, the allocation takes place.

Algorithm 1. No Block-Split Heuristic (NBH)

1: Update current available resources in the network;
2: OLT collects all the requests from all ONUs;
3: **for all** $R_i \in R$ **do**
4:      $G_i = min\{R_i, maxB_i\}$
5: Sort wavelengths in ascending order (W) according
        to their earliest available time;
6: **for all** $G_i \in G$ **do**
7:      **for all** $w_j \in W$ **do**
8:          **if** $G_i \leq B_{a_j}$: Assign G_i to w_j

As in this scheme a grant is assigned only in one single channel, the NG-PON2 architecture uses the minimum number guard bands compared to EBH. Also, instead using all wavelength for a single grant, this scheme allows the system to keep other channels unoccupied for the next request allocation. The No Block-Split Heuristic (NBH) is shown in Algorithm 1. The total time complexity is $O(N + Mlog(M) + MN)$.

5.2   Equal Block-Split Heuristic (EBH)

The basic idea is to split the grant into equal four parts and then assign those over all the four wavelengths. In addition, it does not care about the earliest available wavelengths. Based on these ideas the EBH algorithm comprises of two main steps: after splitting the grant into equal four parts, the allocation takes place over all the wavelengths. This scheme allows to transmit data in one-fourth time duration than the single wavelength assignment system, but uses four-times more guard-bands. The total time complexity is $O(N+Mlog(M)+N)$ or $O(2N + Mlog(M))$.

Algorithm 2. Equal Block-Split Heuristic (EBH)

1: **for all** $G_i \in G$ **do**
2:      **if** $G_i \leq B_{a_T}$: Assign G_i to all W by equal splitting

---

5.3   Priority Based No Block-Split Heuristic (P-NBH)

It is a greedy algorithm and the basic idea is same as the NBH: to assign each of the grants over one single channel. In addition, before assigning, the grants are sorted according to their priority classes. Based on these ideas, the NBH algorithm comprises of three main steps: the sorting of the grants, then after checking if there is enough unoccupied bandwidth in the available wavelength, the allocation occurs. The high priority grants get the chance to be transmitted before the lower ones. Also, instead using all wavelengths for a single grant, this scheme allows the system to keep other channels unoccupied for the next request allocation. The total time complexity is $O(N + Nlog(N) + Mlog(M) + MN)$.

Algorithm 3. Priority-Based No Block-Split Heuristic (P-NBH)

1: Sort G based on their priorities: from high to low (P_G);

5.4   Priority Based Equal Block-Split Heuristic (P-EBH)

The basic idea is to split the grant into four equal parts and then assign those over all the four wavelengths. In addition, before assigning, the grants are sorted according to their priority classes. Based on these ideas, the P-EBH algorithm comprises of three main steps: the sorting of the grants, then after splitting the grant into four equal parts, the allocation takes place over all the wavelengths. This scheme transmits data in one-fourth time duration than the single wavelength assignment system, but like EBH, it too uses four-times more guard-bands. The total time complexity is $O(N + Nlog(N) + Mlog(M) + N)$ or $O(2N + Nlog(N) + Mlog(M))$.

Algorithm 4. Priority-Based Equal Block-Split Heuristic (P-EBH)

Sort G based on their priorities: from high to low (P_G);

Algorithm 5. Priority-Based Decider Block-Split Heuristic (P-DBH)

1: **for all** $P_{G_i} \in P$ **do**
2:    **if** $P_{G_i} \leq B_{a_T}$
3:        **for all** $w_j \in W$ **do**
4:            **if** $P_{G_i} > B_{a_j}$
5:                Assign P_{G_i} to all W by splitting them equally
6:            **if** $P_{G_i} \leq B_{a_j}$
7:                **if** $P_{G_i} \leq d_{low}$
8:                    Assign P_{G_i} to w_j
9:                **if** $P_{G_i} > d_{low}$
10:                    **if** P_{G_i}'s priority category is A1 or B1
11:                        Assign P_{G_i} to all W by splitting equally
12:                    **else**
13:                        Assign P_{G_i} to w_j

5.5 Priority Based Decider Block-Split Heuristic (P-DBH)

We propose another version of wavelength assignment algorithm, the Priority-Based Decider Block-Split Heuristic (P-DBH), which offers data splitting for faster transmission to the high priority data and single channel assignment to the data with small sizes or with low priority. This algorithm is a combination of P-NBH and P-EBH. The total time complexity is $O(N + Nlog(N) + Mlog(M) + MN)$.

6 Experimental Results and Analysis

The performance evaluation of our proposed schemes are done by examining two cases. First, we compare the static mathematical model with the heuristic cases. Second, we simulate the five proposed heuristic algorithms, and analyze different parameters. In both the cases, we iterate 100 independent instances to confirm that all the values in the plots have a 95% confidence interval.

6.1 MILP Versus Heuristic

The mathematical model discussed in the previous section is converted into AMPL language [14]. The solver that we use is CPLEX [12]. But, this whole process takes a huge amount of time and it increases with the input size. It takes more than two hours to solve the optimal resource allocation for an eight requests experiment in 32-ONU system. Therefore, we only use the proposed heuristic schemes to conduct the experiments for this system. To evaluate the performances of the five proposed heuristic algorithms, a MATLAB simulation system is built. We simulate a NG-PON2 system with 4 wavelengths. Each of these wavelengths support 10 Gbps in both the upstream and downstream transmission. We simulate the system which consist of 32 ONUs and they all are at a distance of 40 km from the OLT. The number of wavelengths available to the OLT is 4 with a line rate of 10 Gbps each. The average data-rate for each ONU is 4 * 10 Gbs/32 or 1.25 Gbps. The guard band is 3 KB. We generated requests with random sizes. For the simulation, we assumed the 35% of the requests belong to A1 & B1 priority classes and the remaining 65% requests belong to the other priority classes. We have some assumptions for the simulations purpose: The buffer size at the ONUs and the OLT are both infinite. All the requests are within the limit of the grant size which means $R_i = G_i \forall i$. All ONUs are at a distance of 40 km from the OLT. The guard band size is 3 KB. All ONUs support four wavelengths. Four of the wavelengths' available time are set to the same at the beginning of the simulation.

In Fig. 1 (top-left), we see that the results of the total delay from MILP and the heuristic shows that the heuristic algorithms perform almost the same as MILP. The heuristics have 7.49% more delay than the MILP on average. Similarly, in Fig. 1 (top-right), the total transmission delay of the A1 class data from MILP and the heuristic shows that the heuristic algorithms perform almost the same as MILP. The heuristics have 8.24% more delay than the MILP on average.

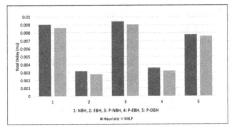
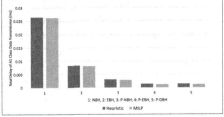

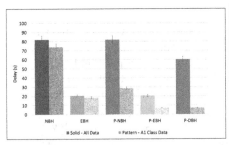
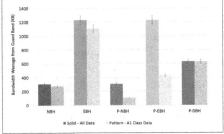

Fig. 1. Top: Comparison among the Five Heuristics: left - Total Delay for all and only A1 Class Data Transmission, right - Total Bandwidth Wastage for all and only A1 Class Data Transmission. **Bottom:** Comparing the Performance between MILP and Heuristics: left - Total delay of five DWBA schemes, right - Total Delay of A1 Class Data Transmission.

6.2 Priority Class Effect in Delay and Bandwidth Wastage

We add priority class in the methods P-NBH, P-EBH, and P-DBH. We compare the system's total delay and also the total delay to transmit A1 class priority requests. In Fig. 1 (bottom-left), the solid bars depict the total delay of the system and patterned bars indicate the A1 class data transmission. Here, the total delay is calculated by as follows: Transmission end time - Request arrival time. The grant requests have different arrival times. The NBH and EBH methods do not care about the priority classes. They process the grant based on the arrival time. For example, if an A1 class grant request arrives after 99 B3 or A3 class requests, these two methods would allow transmitting this A1 class grant after transmitting those 99 requests. Figure 1 (bottom-left) shows that there is not much difference in the total delay of the system and the total A1 data transmission delay in NBH and EBH. Contrarily, the rest of the three proposed methods show significant improvement in terms of the A1 class transmission delay as they allow transmission higher priority data before the lower ones. Among these five methods, P-EBH and P-DBH show almost same and the best performance. In terms of total delay of the system, EBH and P-EBH show the best output as these two methods support parallel transmission. Figure 1 (bottom-left) evaluates the wasted amounts of the bandwidth from the guard bands. According to the above mentioned example, if an A1 class grant request arrives after 99 B3 or A3 class requests, these two methods would allow transmitting this A1 class grant after transmitting those 99 requests. Figure 1 (bottom-right) shows the total bandwidth wastage amount for all requests and for A1 class data transmission. The EBH method has the highest amount of wastage. This is due to the use of four times more guard bands than NBH/P-NBH for parallel transmission. Among these five schemes, P-NBH has the minimum wastage for all and also for A1 class transmission.

7   Conclusion

Our results show that the proposed schemes with priority class consideration show significant improvement in the total delay of the high priority data as those are sent first. P-EBH shows better result as it also provides parallel transmission to the system. Although, P-NBH has higher delay than P-EBH, it results in minimum bandwidth wastage. Finally, P-DBH, the hybrid of P-NBH and P-EBH, supports parallel transmission to the A1, B1, A2, B2 class requests and single wavelength allocation for the rest. This ensures minimum delay for the high priority data and minimum bandwidth wastage for the lower ones. Our future work involves developing DWBA schemes for other TWDM PON and virtualized networks.

Acknowledgement. This work was supported by US National Science Foundation under Grant CNS-1817105.

References

1. Cisco Visual Networking Index (VNI) Forecast and Methodology, 2016–2021, September 2017. http://www.cisco.com/c/en/us/solutions
2. Wang, L., Wang, X., Mukherjee, B., Chung, H.S., Lee, H.H., Park, S.: On the performance of Hybrid-PON scheduling strategies for NG-EPON. In: International Conference on Optical Network Design and Modeling (ONDM), pp. 1–5 (2016)
3. ITU-T G.987 Series Recommendations, 10 Gigabit-Capable Passive Optical Network (XG-PON), June 2012
4. IEEE Standard 802.3av, 10G-EPON, October 2009
5. 40-Gigabit-Capable Passive Optical Networks 2 (NG-PON2), October 2015
6. Nesset, D.: PON roadmap [invited]. IEEE/OSA J. Opt. Commun. Networking **9**(10), A71–A76 (2017)
7. Dhaini, A.R., Assi, C.M., Maier, M., Shami, A.: Dynamic wavelength and bandwidth allocation in hybrid TDM/WDM EPON networks. J. Lightwave Technol. **25**(1), 277–286 (2007)
8. Buttaboni, A., Andrade, M., Tornatore, M.: A multi-threaded dynamic bandwidth and wavelength allocation scheme with void filling for long reach WDM/TDM PONs. J. Lightwave Technol. **31**, 1149–1157 (2013)
9. Wang, L., Wang, X., Mukherjee, B., Chung, H., Lee, H., Park, S.: On the performance of Hybrid-PON scheduling strategies for NG-EPON. In: International Conference on Optical Network Design and Modeling (ONDM), pp. 1–5 (2016)

10. Hussain, S.B., Hu, W., Li, C.: Fair DWBA for WA-PON based NG-EPON (100G-EPON) to mitigate frame resequencing problem. In: 2017 Opto-Electronics and Communications Conference (OECC) and Photonics Global Conference (PGC), pp. 1–2 (2017)
11. Multani, M.K., Rahman, A., Asfandeyar, M.: Partially online dynamic bandwidth allocation algorithm for hybrid TDM/WDM EPON. In: IEEE EUROCON 2017–17th International Conference on Smart Technologies, pp. 902–906 (2017)
12. IBM ILOG CPLEX Optimization Studio. http://www.ibm.com/software/products/en/ibmilogcpleoptistud/
13. Luo, Y., Sui, M., Effenberger, F.: Wavelength management in time and wavelength division multiplexed passive optical networks (TWDM-PONs). In: IEEE Global Communications Conference (GLOBECOM), pp. 2971–2976 (2012)
14. AMPL: A Modeling Language for Mathematical Programming. https://ampl.com/

Correction to: Optical Network Design and Modeling

Anna Tzanakaki, Manos Varvarigos, Raul Muñoz,
Reza Nejabati, Noboru Yoshikane, Markos Anastasopoulos,
and Johann Marquez-Barja

Correction to:
A. Tzanakaki et al. (Eds.): *Optical Network Design*
and Modeling, **LNCS 11616,**
https://doi.org/10.1007/978-3-030-38085-4

In the original version of the book, the affiliation of Johann Marquez-Barja was wrong. The affiliation has been corrected to:

"University of Antwerp - imec".

The updated version of the book can be found at
https://doi.org/10.1007/978-3-030-38085-4

Author Index